# More praise for **A Pickpocket's Tale**

"Informative and fascinating."—Connor Ennis, *San Diego Union Tribune*

"Gilfoyle's excellent biography brings this netherworld into vivid focus."
—Ludovic Hunter-Tilney, *FT Magazine*

"A spectacularly detailed look at the evolution of crime (and especially punishment) in post- Civil War America."
—Whitney Pastorek, *Entertainment Weekly*

"*A Pickpocket's Tale* is an alternative history of nineteenth-century New York, featuring George Appo, pickpocket, victim, and chronicler of crime. It is a Dickensian tale, vivid, heartbreaking, and harrowing, as it reveals the curious plight of the criminal, hounded by prison guards and venal policemen. George Appo is a new kind of hero—forlorn, isolated, with a relentless will to survive in a world that cares so little about him."
—Jerome Charyn, author of *Gangsters and Gold Diggers: Old New York, the Jazz Age, and the Birth of Broadway*

"*A Pickpocket's Tale* is an extraordinary New York tale, a true story more incredible than fiction. Timothy Gilfoyle has done a masterful job in bringing to life a fascinating subject and a colorful era."
—Kevin Baker, author of *Strivers Row*

"*A Pickpocket's Tale* is a fascinating true-crime story. Gilfoyle uses George Appo's unpublished memoirs to re-create the world of the nineteenth-century criminal in astonishing detail. The result is an absorbing book that I could not put down; it's the best study ever of the history of crime in New York." —Tyler Anbinder, author of *Five Points: The 19th Century New York City Neighborhood That Invented Tap Dance, Stole Elections, and Became the World's Most Notorious Slum*

"George Appo was half Irish, half Chinese, and all *goniff*. In this wonderful new book, Timothy Gilfoyle, who knows more than anyone else about American crime a hundred years ago, reveals the scams, takes us inside the prisons, and opens up the Dickensian world of the poor. *A Pickpocket's Tale* brings us to the wellsprings of the American underworld."

—Elliott Gorn, author of *Mother Jones:
The Most Dangerous Woman in America*

"For the first time in our history, a distinguished scholar has opened up the previously undiscovered world of the common criminal in the nineteenth century. What an impressive and unforgettable story by Tim Gilfoyle."

—Kenneth T. Jackson, Jacques Barzun Professor
of History and Social Science, Columbia University

"Authoritative, thoroughly researched, eye-opening and grand, good fun to read."                                                      —*Kirkus Reviews*

"Gilfoyle paints a Hogarthian cityscape . . . colorful, evocative social history."
—*Publishers Weekly*

"In this expertly executed and empathetic study, Gilfoyle shows how Appo's particular type of ingenuity and entrepreneurship produced a variant of success in the cracks of urbanizing and industrializing New York City. . . . Gilfoyle's gripping prose . . . reads like fiction but is meticulously based on facts gleaned from archives."          —*Library Journal*

"Gilfoyle lays out a marvelous narrative of a bright, resourceful, courageous man of his time and his circumstance. . . . It is wonderfully atmospheric, blunt, frightening, enlightening, and thoroughly entertaining."

—Dan Smith, *Blue Ridge Business Journal*

ALSO BY TIMOTHY J. GILFOYLE

*City of Eros: New York City, Prostitution,
and the Commercialization of Sex, 1790–1920*

*Millennium Park: Creating a Chicago Landmark*

# A Pickpocket's Tale

◦§ THE

UNDERWORLD OF

NINETEENTH-CENTURY

NEW YORK ◦§

## Timothy J. Gilfoyle

 W·W·NORTON & COMPANY NEW YORK LONDON

For information about permission to reproduce selections from this book,
write to Permissions, W. W. Norton & Company, Inc.,
500 Fifth Avenue, New York, NY 10110

Manufacturing by RR Donnelley Bloomsburg
Book design by Margaret M. Wagner
Production manager: Amanda Morrison

Library of Congress Cataloging-in-Publication Data

Gilfoyle, Timothy J.
A pickpocket's tale : the underworld of nineteenth-century New York /
Timothy J. Gilfoyle.— 1st ed.
p. cm.
Includes bibliographical references and index.
ISBN-13: 978-0-393-06190-1 (hardcover)

1. Appo, George, b. 1856. 2. Pickpockets—New York (State)—New York—Biography.
3. Juvenile delinquents—New York (State)—New York—Biography. 4. Crime—New York
(State)—New York—History—19th century. 5. New York (N.Y.)—Social conditions—
19th century. I. Title: Underworld of nineteenth-century New York. II. Title.
HV6653.A66G55 2006
364.16'2—dc22

2005036130

ISBN 978-0-393-32989-6 pbk.

W. W. Norton & Company, Inc.
500 Fifth Avenue, New York, N.Y. 10110
www.wwnorton.com

W. W. Norton & Company Ltd.
Castle House, 75/76 Wells Street, London W1T 3QT

# Contents

—

# List of Illustrations

—

# Preface

==

In 1840 NEW YORK CITY had no professional police force, a low murder rate, and no bank robberies. Within decades, however, this changed; serious crime proliferated and modern law enforcement was born. By 1890 Gotham's police budget had grown more than sixteenfold and became New York City's single largest annual expenditure. Detective work was transformed into a public and private specialty. The murder rate had doubled, and larceny comprised one-half to one-third of all prosecuted crime in the state. Newspapers regularly reported that illegal activities were rampant, the courts and police powerless. New York City had become "the evillest [sic] spot in America." For the first time, observers complained about "organized crime."[1]

A new criminal world was born in this period. It was a hidden universe with informal but complex networks of pickpockets, fences, opium addicts, and confidence men who organized their daily lives around shared illegal behaviors. Such activities, one judge observed, embodied an innovative lawlessness based on extravagance, greed, and the pursuit of great riches. A new "class of criminals" now existed. Many of these illicit enterprises were national in scope, facilitated by new technologies like the railroad and the telegraph, economic innovations like uniform paper money, and new havens for intoxication like "dives" and opium dens. For the first time both criminals and police referred to certain lawbreakers as "professionals."[2]

George Appo was one such professional criminal. At first glance Appo hardly seemed a candidate for any criminal activity; his diminutive size and physical appearance evoked little fear. By age eighteen he stood less than five feet five inches in height and weighed a slight 120 pounds. Everything about him seemed small: his narrow forehead, short nose, compact chin, and tiny ears that sat low on his head. Although Appo's face displayed features of his mother's Irish ancestry, his copper-colored skin reminded some of his father's Chinese origins. Appo's brown eyes were less noticeable than his pitch-black hair and eyebrows, the latter meeting over his nose. The tattoos E.D. and J.M. were inscribed on his left and right forearms, respectively.[3]

*George Appo's "rogues' gallery" photograph.*

But Appo was one of New York's most significant nineteenth-century criminals. A pickpocket, confidence man, and opium addict, he lived off his criminal activities during his teenage years and much of his adult life. On successful nights during the 1870s and 1880s, he earned in excess of six hundred dollars pilfering the pockets of those around him, equivalent to the annual salary of a skilled manual laborer. Even more lucrative was the elaborate confidence scheme known as the "green goods game." The most successful operators—"gilt-edged swindlers" according to one—accumulated fortunes in excess of one hundred thousand dollars. By 1884 America's most famous detective, Allan Pinkerton, identified the green goods game as "the most remunerative of all the swindles," "the boss racket of the whole confidence business."[4]

Appo made money, but his life was hardly a Horatio Alger tale of self-taught frugality and upward mobility. The offspring of a racially mixed, immigrant marriage, Appo was separated from his parents as a small child. Effectively orphaned, the young boy grew up in the impoverished Five Points and Chinatown neighborhoods of New York. He never attended school a day in his life. Appo literally raised himself on Gotham's streets, becoming a newsboy and eventually a pickpocket and opium addict. This new child culture of newsboys, bootblacks, and pickpockets, fed by foreign immigration and native-born rural migration, mocked the ascendant Victorian morality of the era. New York needed no Charles Dickens to create Oliver Twist or Victor Hugo to invent Jean Valjean. Gotham had George Appo.

Appo's youthful adventures persisted into adulthood. For more than three decades he survived by exploiting his criminal skills. Appo patronized the first opium dens in New York, participated in the first medical research on opium smoking, and appeared in one of America's first theatrical productions popularizing crime. On at least ten occasions he was tried by judge or jury. As a result he spent more than a decade in prisons and jails. Therein he experienced New York's first experiment in juvenile reform with the school ship *Mercury*, as well as the lockstep, dark cells, and industrial discipline of American penitentiaries. He personally witnessed the lunacy found in the Matteawan State Hospital for the Criminally Insane, the easy escapes from the Blackwell's Island Penitentiary, and the corruption associated with the nation's largest jail: New York's "Tombs." During various incarcerations Appo's teeth were knocked out, and he encountered a wide array of prison tortures. Life outside prison was even bloodier. On the street Appo was physically assaulted at least nine times, shot twice, and stabbed in the throat once. More than a dozen scars decorated his body.

Above all George Appo was a "good fellow," a character type he identified and wrote about. A good fellow engaged in criminal activities while displaying courage and bravery, "a nervy crook," in Appo's words. Good fellows like Appo did not rely on strong-arm tactics to get their way. Instead they avoided violence, employing wit and wile to make a living. Theirs was a world of artifice and deception. When successful, a good fellow lavished his profits on others. He was "a money getter and spender." Such mettle, pluck, and camaraderie implied a level of trustworthiness, mutuality, and dependability. Above all a good fellow was loyal, willing to withstand, in Appo's words, "the consequences and punishment of an arrest for some other fellow's evil doings both inside and outside of prison."[5]

The lives of individuals like Appo—pickpockets, street children, confidence men, opium addicts, counterfeiters, convicts—remain hidden. While historians have explored organized crime and "wise guys" in the twentieth and early twenty-first centuries, nineteenth-century men like Appo are enigmas. Theirs was largely an invisible world, dependent on camouflage and duplicity, organized around an oral culture. Inconsistent arrest records, exaggerated eyewitness accounts, and little participant testimony present difficult interpretive problems in discerning the realities —much less the complexities—of unlawful behavior. The social environments and networks of criminals, specifically the actual workings of the "underground" or "informal" economy, are uncharted territory. Criminal life in nineteenth-century America remains a mystery.[6]

BUT GEORGE APPO was no ordinary criminal: He wrote his own autobiography. He never explained the origin of this document. Most likely, friends and associates convinced the former pickpocket and con man that his was a unique story. Indeed it was. Though fictional accounts and criminal broadsides were centuries old, at the end of the nineteenth century, urban crime narratives were a recent phenomenon. Most of them were designed as moral adventures, evangelical jeremiads warning readers to avoid temptation.

Appo's autobiography represented a new type of criminal memoir. Rather than admonish readers to resist the lure of criminal life, Appo explored its attractions. What motivated children and adults like Appo to resort to crime? How did the new and expanding nineteenth-century penal system treat convicts? How did convicts react to incarceration? When and how did the "drug trade" (in the form of opium dens) appear and flourish in American cities? How did individuals engaged in criminal behavior organize their lives? In what ways did the underground economy shape male subcultures and the emergence of urban gangs? Can contemporary criminal activities be traced back to the late nineteenth century? Appo's saga is a window into this nineteenth-century underworld, a rough but eloquent account of that hidden, clandestine universe. In his own words Appo reveals how nineteenth-century Americans defined good and evil.

George Appo's world was an oral one. Writing was not a common or shared experience for such men. Appo, simply put, wrote the way he spoke. His autobiography is incomplete in certain parts, inarticulate in others. He offers minute details on events that happened three decades earlier, when he was a teenager. At other times he is strangely silent about more recent experiences. The autobiography is full of grammatical mistakes. The typed, ninety-nine-page document contains only thirteen paragraphs. Written in a first-person, stream-of-consciousness mode, the manuscript is plagued by run-on sentences, linked together by plentiful and distracting "ands." George Appo learned to read and write late in life. It shows.

The autobiography serves as the narrative skeleton of this book. In order to allow Appo to speak for himself, I have included extended passages in the following chapters, printed in italics. I have edited Appo's language in minor ways, breaking up run-on sentences, eliminating abbreviations, correcting capitalization and spelling. Any remaining grammatical lapses are Appo's. (The complete and unedited version of the autobiography is available to the public.)[7]

New York, proclaimed the popular writer James D. McCabe, Jr., in 1868, "is a great secret." The ensuing pages expose a furtive world little found in the novels of Edith Wharton and Henry James or the published diaries of elites like George Templeton Strong and Mayor Philip Hone. The major events of the era often associated with New York—the Tweed scandals, the construction of the Brooklyn Bridge, the opening of Central Park, the rise of the "robber barons"—are absent. But clandestine chronicles of pickpockets and green goods steerers, opium addicts and convicts, describe a New York just as important, however forgotten or misunderstood, as those more familiar stories of famous people and events. Here, to paraphrase the British journalist and social reformer William T. Stead, was a strange, inverted world, one that was at once the same, yet not the same, as the world of business and the world of politics.[8]

# A Pickpocket's Tale

◄§

# 1

# The Trials of Quimbo Appo

=

*At two minutes of five in the morning of July 4th, 1856, and in the City of New Haven, Connecticut, at 2 George Street, I was born. My father, a Chinaman, who's right name was Lee Ah Bow, was born in the city of Ningbo, China, and came to this country in the year 1847 and settled down in San Francisco, California in the tea business until 1849, when the gold excitement broke out in that section of the country. He then went to the gold fields and worked out a claim which was panning out successful. . . .[1]*

GEORGE APPO'S LIFE of crime was hardly predestined by his birth. His father, Quimbo Appo, embodied the American dream, an immigrant success story of upward mobility and economic advancement. He arrived in California in the late 1840s, prospected briefly in the goldfields, and then made his way east. Appo initially settled in Boston and worked in a tea store; by 1855 he was running his own enterprise in New York City, living and working on Third Avenue. Shortly thereafter he moved to New Haven, Connecticut, and there his wife gave birth to his son.

At first glance Appo's entrepreneurial success replicated a Horatio Alger tale. Born and raised in or near the Chinese city of Ningbo (some seven hundred miles northeast of Canton [now Guangzhou]), Appo came of age when China was beset by intense conflict: the Opium Wars from 1839 to 1842 (which resulted in the British takeover of Hong Kong), severe population growth, flooding, starvation, and class or family feuds within villages. These events generated a tremendous population movement of Chinese to other parts of Asia and to the Americas. Appo joined the migration, arriving in San Francisco in 1847; he quickly began pursuing his entrepreneurial ambitions.[2]

Most likely Appo resettled without family, as did most Chinese men. But he differed from his fellow Chinese nationals in significant ways.

The overwhelming majority originated in the southern provinces of China, especially those around Canton. Historians believe that most Cantonese immigrants intended to accumulate wealth and return to China. They worked hard, lived cheaply, and saved nearly every cent. In contrast Quimbo Appo came from northern China, spoke a different dialect, quickly learned English, adopted many American practices, and displayed little interest in returning to his native land.[3]

Even after gold was discovered in 1848 and Quimbo joined "the rush" of "Argonauts" and "forty-niners," he remained atypical. Most Chinese miners migrated to the Northern California fields, especially along the Yuba River and its tributaries; Appo went prospecting in the southern fields.[4] By the end of 1852, identified by a California state census enumerator as the twenty-eight-year-old miner "Can Apoo," he was living in Sonora.[5] In contrast to most Chinese miners who lived together in segregated communities such as the nearby so-called Chinese Camp, Appo resided in the immediate vicinity of miners who hailed from England, Australia, Maine, Massachusetts, and Missouri; traders from Italy; a baker from Mexico; and merchants from New York and Maryland. Most Chinese miners resisted Westernizing. Few were fluent in English. Few became Christians. Few instigated contact with white miners or prospectors.[6] Appo was an exception.

Sonora was distinctive among California mining towns. Located on the slope of a hill in the San Joaquin River watershed, the town was established as a mining camp by a group of Mexicans from the state of Sonora. Almost immediately the town attracted considerable numbers of foreign-born miners and a comparatively large female population. Confronting the multiplicity of languages, one miner described Sonora as "the Tower of Babel." Although most of these foreign migrants were Chilean, French, Irish, and Hispanic, at least one Chinese restaurant existed by 1849 and remained popular into the 1850s. By different accounts Sonora's population fluctuated between two thousand and thirteen thousand, and the town remained an "international center" throughout its first decade of existence.[7]

During Appo's residence violence was rife in Sonora and the surrounding region of Tuolumne County. The miner William Perkins lamented that "daily rows" and bloodshed were "so common that I hardly think of putting them down in my Journal." Male residents openly sported guns and other weapons. The historian George Bancroft, in his *Popular*

A gambling saloon in gold-rush California, filled with
Euro-Americans, Chinese, and Mexicans.

*Tribunals*, claimed that at one point there were twenty murders in
twenty-five days in and around Sonora. Violence grew so prevalent that
in 1851 the Vigilance Committee of Sonora was formed by fifty "leading"
American men, explicitly to "take the law into their own hands."[8]

Several factors contributed to the excessive violence. First, local government was virtually nonexistent. Miners and other settlers moved into
the region so rapidly after 1848 that public officials had little time to
establish any kind of effective policing authority. Second, California possessed no formal mining codes when gold was discovered. Miners
quickly adopted a common-law system of "free mining," which required
no surveys, leases, taxes, or royalties imposed by the state. They wanted
no interference in transferring claims from one miner or company to
another. Property rights in mining depended on discovery and development: Discovery gave a miner title to a claim; development allowed him
to keep it. The system's informality and the absence of any strong law
enforcement encouraged the resolution of disputed claims with violence.
Finally, the Foreign Miners' Tax Act of 1850 assessed all non-Americans
a monthly twenty-dollar fee for the privilege of working in the mines.
Although the tax was repealed eleven months after its passage, it generated considerable ethnic tension, particularly in Tuolumne County.[9]

According to his son, George, Quimbo Appo remained undeterred by these obstacles, and soon he had "worked out a claim which was panning out successful." Indeed, the region around Sonora from 1850 to 1858 was among the richest in California. A newspaper in nearby Calaveras County noted that gold was so abundant that storekeepers, landlords, clerks, and teamsters abandoned their jobs to go mining. Later reports concluded that anywhere from $102,000 to $11 million worth of gold was mined in and around Sonora.[10]

Miners working these claims spent most of their time in the fields. If a miner found a rich vein, he immediately pitched a tent and made that his new habitation. One miner admitted that as soon as gold was discovered somewhere, the location was "perfectly crowded with tents sooner than you can say Jack Robinson." These "Canvass Cities" seemed to spring up almost overnight.[11] Appo most likely participated in this rapid migration out of Sonora into the surrounding goldfields, when disaster struck.

> *[O]ne night while asleep in his tent with another Chinaman, [Quimbo Appo] awoke and saw two Mexicans in the tent robbing his partner, the Chinaman, who was killed by them. He shot both the Mexicans dead and left the gold fields and traveled over the mountains, day and night, with a gang of Mexicans trying to run him down. He got safely away and came to New Haven, Connecticut.*[12]

Although violent confrontations between Chinese and Hispanics attracted little attention from the largely Euro-American press and government, Quimbo Appo's did. A story reprinted in several newspapers claimed that three armed Mexicans entered a Chinese tent, assaulted the inhabitants, and proceeded to rob two bags of gold dust valued at sixty and ninety dollars each. "One of the Chinamen, named Akop, refused to give up his money and attempted to defend himself," claimed one newspaper. "One of the ruffians drew his knife and ran the unfortunate celestial through the body, causing almost instant death. The party then escaped with their booty."[13]

While news reports of Appo's (Akop's) demise were indeed exaggerated, such violent encounters were hardly unusual. Chinese miners in particular were driven from their claims, physically attacked, and even murdered. One historian claims that Mexican gangs gave the Chinese "no mercy," attacking and forcing them to disclose the hiding places of their gold dust. In some cases they killed individual Chinese in cold blood. When the governor of California offered a thousand-dollar reward for the capture of the outlaw Joaquin Murieta, Chinese miners reportedly contributed several thousand dollars more.[14]

Fearing either Mexican vengeance or Anglo-American law enforcement, Quimbo Appo fled California. The quickest exit out of the mining district was via the California Trail, by far the most popular route since opening in 1841 and not far from Jackson. By 1851 an estimated fifty thousand people traveled the trail annually. Appo may have made his way north to Sacramento, the trail's western terminus, and proceeded over the Sierra Nevadas, along the Humboldt River Valley, before stopping at Fort Hall along the Snake River in what is today Idaho. From there he would have moved across the high-plateau South Pass along the Oregon-California Trail, the same route followed by the Mormons in their famed trek to Utah. Moving through the Great Plains, Appo paralleled the Platte River and would have passed through Fort Laramie (Wyoming), Fort Kearney (Nebraska), and Fort Leavenworth (Kansas), before terminating at Independence and the Missouri River.[15] At this point Appo could have taken multiple routes to the East Coast, which he probably reached in the spring of 1853.

This 1856 advertisement for Quimbo Appo's New Haven tea business reflected his economic success.

But this travelogue is conjectural. Later reports claimed that Appo sailed to New England as a cook and steward on the *Vandalia*. However he traveled, though, Appo recovered his economic and personal resources on arrival along the East Coast. He first settled in Boston, where he served "as a sort of walking advertisement" for the Robertson & Sons tea store, according to one account.[16] By 1855 Appo was running his own tea business in New York City. Later that year he moved to New Haven, Connecticut, and opened a store on Church Street. Appo's enterprise was successful enough that he advertised in the local directory.[17]

Sometime between spring 1853 and the end of 1855, Appo met and married an Irish immigrant by the name of Catherine Fitzpatrick. In contrast to her husband's, Catherine's lineage remains shrouded in mystery. The best evidence claims that she was born between 1830 and 1833 in Dublin. Later accounts described her as "rather good looking" and "rather free with strange men," the latter characterization a pejorative reference to her interracial marriage. Most likely she was compelled to migrate because of Ireland's Great Famine between 1845 and 1855.[18]

QUIMBO APPO'S MARRIAGE to an Irish immigrant was hardly unusual. Although absolute numbers were small, roughly one in four Chinese men in New York married Irishwomen between 1820 and 1870. Even if Appo wanted to marry a Chinese woman, it would have been difficult. Chinese migration to the United States was heavily male throughout the nineteenth century, and after 1882 Chinese women were all but forbidden to enter the United States.[19]

By the end of 1856 Catherine Appo had given birth to two children. The first reportedly died in infancy, while the second was described as "a handsome, healthy boy, very sprightly, as white as his mother—a Yankee boy to all appearances, with only the Chinaman's breadth between his eyes," according to the *Times*. "The little fellow was born in New Haven on the 4th of July."[20] This was the first description of George Appo in the press. It would not be his last.

Quimbo Appo returned with his family to New York City shortly thereafter, perhaps because of Gotham's increasing dominance in the tea-importing business. George Appo later claimed that his father was hired as a tea tester for the large tea- and coffeehouse firm of Christianson & Wells on Vesey Street.[21] One described him "as a sort of advertising medium, being dressed in Chinese clothes and walking up and down in front of his employer's store." Others believed that he worked as an interpreter for a variety of tea concerns. In any case Appo relied on associations with other Euro-Americans for his employment, not on the Chinese community like most Asian immigrants, and successfully avoided the poverty associated with Chinese and other immigrants in Lower Manhattan. One 1856 report described Quimbo and his family as "comfortably settled." By 1859 Quimbo was running his own tea store on Third Avenue, between Seventh and Eighth Streets.[22]

More significantly, Quimbo Appo made an impression. Although standing only five feet three inches in height and weighing 125 pounds, he attracted the attention of those around him. One reporter indulgently described him as "rather better looking than most of the specimens of his countrymen whom we have seen." Appo almost immediately (probably because of his fluency in English) became a leader and spokesman in the small Chinese community, estimated to number around 150. Although his uptown home on Spring Street was physically and socially removed from the more impoverished surroundings of his fellow Asians in the Fourth Ward, Appo spoke out in defense of Chinese cigar vendors. Indeed, one observer believed Quimbo Appo's fluency in speaking English made him "a great man" among other Chinese immigrants in New York.[23]

But even as he retained important ethnic ties, Quimbo Appo "Americanized." Although he was never naturalized as a United States citizen, Appo and his friends employed in the tea business were described as "dandyish," desirous of learning to read and write English, and becoming American citizens. Appo abandoned his Chinese name (Lee Ah Bow), married a European immigrant, converted to Roman Catholicism, and allowed his son to be baptized in the church, with Irish-immigrant godparents. Appo's religiosity led others to later describe him as "devout." He endorsed efforts to build a church for the Chinese in order "to bring them under civilizing and Christian influence." Appo even inscribed the very symbols of the United States and Christianity onto his body: Tattoos depicting the "Goddess of Liberty" and the crucifixion of Jesus marked his left forearm. But perhaps move revealing was that Quimbo Appo bragged that he named his male offspring after America's first president. The Appos, reported the *Times*, "have given him the name of GEORGE WASHINGTON."[24]

Quimbo Appo had "made it" in America. But in 1859, his hard work and newfound success came to a bitter, violent end.

## THE TRIAL

             *One day, Mrs. Fletcher and my father had a quarrel and Fletcher struck him a blow with a mason's trowel. Both of them clinched together and while in that position, Mrs. Fletcher took up a flatiron and struck him on the back with it, and he stabbed her and she died instantly. He was tried and found guilty and sentenced to be executed.*[25]

"Murder in the Fourth Ward," blared the front page of the Herald. At approximately 8:30 p.m. on a snowy 8 March 1859, in a fit of rage, Quimbo Appo assaulted and killed his landlady, Mary Fletcher. Initial accounts of the incident heaped all the blame on Appo. Newspapers described the immigrant as annoyed at his wife's increasingly frequent bouts of intoxication. Only two or three days prior to the homicide, tenants in the building reported that Appo was so enraged at his spouse that he beat her, compelling her to seek refuge overnight with the landlady.

When Appo returned home on the fateful evening, witnesses reported that he verbally abused his wife so severely that other residents in the house feared for her life. The landlady, Mary Fletcher, and two tenants, Margaret Butler and Mary Gavigan, intervened. Butler and Gavigan later claimed that upon entering the room, they witnessed Appo striking his wife with a stick. Fletcher grabbed Appo, while the other two women joined in defense of Catherine. The women "were getting the best" of Appo, so he pulled out a knife and stabbed Fletcher two times. The second thrust proved fatal, entering just over the heart and causing "almost instant death," according to one report. As Fletcher fell to the floor, she screamed, "My God." Appo thereupon turned on the other women, stabbing Gavigan in the arm and then Butler in the head before retreating out the door.[26]

On learning the circumstances of Fletcher's death, police officials proceeded to a Chinese boardinghouse at the corner of James and Cherry Streets. Everyone present denied knowing anything about Appo's whereabouts. Their behavior, however, aroused the suspicions of one officer, who ordered a search of the building. Within minutes they discovered the suspect hiding under a bed upstairs, his hands covered with blood. The officer told reporters that Appo's first words were, "Yes, I killed her."[27]

Within moments of the incident, word reached Mary's husband, Patrick Fletcher, a mason. He rushed home, and on entering his abode he witnessed a scene of utter chaos. On the floor lay the corpse of his wife. Surrounding her were a half-dozen keening females, venting their grief in heartrending wails and lamentations. Fletcher became enraged. One account claimed that he furiously entered the Appos' apartment intending to assault Catherine Appo before the intervention of others present. Another insisted that he screamed at her for fighting with her husband, whereupon Catherine grabbed a stool and struck Fletcher over the head. In any case an officer placed Catherine and her three-year-old boy under arrest and brought them to the police station for their safety.[28]

By this time Quimbo Appo had allegedly confessed. Newspaper accounts claimed that his wife's constant drinking "made him mad," that he was "determined to whip her for it." Likewise, the female tenants in the house were consistently "making trouble for him," and he "was determined to kill Mrs. Fletcher." For these reasons Appo had purchased the murder weapon. Reporters described Appo as dangerous, one declaring that he "raved like a madman, and expressed his wish to kill someone else."[29]

News of the murder spread quickly. Early the next morning a large crowd gathered, reportedly nearly one thousand strong, ready to lynch Appo the moment he was brought out of the Tombs, New York's infamous jail. Mary Fletcher, known throughout the neighborhood as "the landlady," was reportedly held in high regard by her tenants. Sure enough, when Appo was brought back to 47 Oliver Street as part of the coroner's inquest, the incensed crowd rushed the prisoner, only to be repelled by the police.[30]

News reports and initial testimony portrayed Quimbo Appo as an angry patriarch. By his own admission he claimed that when he moved to Oliver Street, "he wanted no society, and . . . was determined to make his neighbors stay away or he would kill them." Appo resented his wife's Irish acquaintances because they frequently insulted him, calling him a "China nigger" and other racial epithets. Appo even seemed to accept his fate. "I did stab her," he admitted. "Now she is dead, I suppose I must die." When Catherine and Quimbo passed each other in the courtroom, he stared and said: "You see now, don't you, what you have brought me to?"[31]

The trial commenced on 11 April 1859 in City Hall, before Justice Henry E. Davies. Appo seemed to have able counsel in Sidney H. Stuart, a former police court judge and well-connected attorney who was highly regarded for his frequent defense of indigent clients. Stuart's concern for the underdog, however, did not extend to Appo. The day of the trial,

Stuart appeared more than half an hour late and unprepared. At one embarrassing point he requested the assistance of police officer James Youngs, who testified on behalf of the prosecution. Appo also gave Stuart a list of supportive witnesses, including three police officers, to subpoena on his behalf. None appeared.[32]

Worse yet for Appo was the hysteria that dominated New York on the eve of the trial. "Our record of crime to-day is truly appalling," complained the *Herald*. "Scarcely is the excitement attending one murder allayed where a fresh tragedy equally horrible takes place." Almost weekly, New Yorkers were confronted with an array of poisonings, shootings, and stabbings; by the end of 1859, murders and homicides had increased by nearly 50 percent from the previous year, jumping from forty to fifty-nine in number.[33]

The sensationalism had an effect. The trial took less than a day, "a degree of dispatch quite unprecedented of late years in capital trials in this city," noted one editorial. The jury was even quicker than the prosecution. Twelve men reached a verdict of guilty within an hour. Quimbo Appo thus became the first Asian ever convicted of a capital crime in New York City.[34]

Yet the jury must have believed stories about Catherine Appo's intemperance, because they added a recommendation of mercy. Two weeks after Appo's conviction, even the prosecutor, District Attorney Nelson J. Waterbury, signed a petition to commute Appo's sentence to life imprisonment. These pleas for leniency, however, fell on deaf ears. Judge Davies spoke to Appo directly a month later in rendering his sentence. He noted Mary Fletcher's kindness to Appo's family, providing meals, for example, when none were available in the defendant's household. Yet, Davies lectured Appo, "you returned again in the evening and took her life." The judge added that the Chinese immigrant violated the customs of domesticity, excoriating him for taking "the life of a female in the absence of any male protector in the house." Davies acknowledged the pleas for clemency but ignored them; he sentenced Appo to death. The defendant immediately broke down in tears.[35]

Appo's sentence was, to say the least, severe. Execution for murder was rare in nineteenth-century New York: From 1800 to 1874 only 2 percent of all murderers were executed. The very same day that Davies rendered the ultimate punishment to Appo, the judge sentenced five others convicted of murder or manslaughter. None was condemned to death.[36]

Newspaper accounts of the murder and celebratory tales of Appo's economic success camouflaged a more complicated reality. At the time of Mary Fletcher's murder, life was going badly for Quimbo and Catherine. Sometime between December 1858 and February 1859, the Appos moved into 47 Oliver Street, a dilapidated, multifamily brick house. Unlike their previous homes in New Haven and New York, the surrounding neighborhood was densely populated, overcrowded, and frequently disease ravaged. Oliver Street, in particular, was full of boardinghouses and other varieties of transient lodgings. Directly across the street was a brewery.[37]

Compared to the Appos' earlier uptown residence, the Oliver Street neighborhood marked a step down the economic ladder. Indeed, the typical New York housing pattern by the mid-nineteenth century was for the upwardly mobile to move inland and uptown, leaving the dockfront neighborhoods to the poorest and most recent migrants to the city. The Appos were headed in the opposite direction.[38] Oliver Street was part of an international district where a host of impoverished racial and ethnic groups—Chinese, Irish, Haitians, African Americans, and native-born whites—interacted in what the historian John Tchen has described as "a hybrid, creolised New York culture."[39]

Compounding their economic problems, Quimbo and Catherine were experiencing marital difficulties. Fellow residents claimed that the couple argued incessantly, some insisting that on several occasions Appo nearly killed his wife but for the intervention of neighbors. Others asserted that Appo forbade his wife to associate with Fletcher and other Irish female residents because they were "leading her astray." Police officer Charles F. Williams testified that he frequently joined Appo late at night searching stores and saloons for his absent wife. Williams noted that Appo expressed "great anxiety and affection" for his wife, but complained about her frequent and excessive alcohol drinking.[40]

Appo's supporters immediately appealed the death sentence. Stuart was removed as Appo's attorney and replaced by David Dudley Field, one of the richest men in New York, a leading member of the bar, and a national figure. Raised in a Connecticut household with a pedigree dating back to the Pilgrims, Field's brothers included future U.S. Supreme Court Justice Stephen Field and the inventor and developer of the transatlantic cable, Cyrus Field.

At the time of Appo's trial, Field was also immersed in national politics.

A longtime opponent of the extension of slavery into American territories, Field was an influential figure in the new Republican Party. While Appo's case was under appeal, Field joined Abraham Lincoln, Horace Greeley, and William Cullen Bryant onstage at Cooper Union when Lincoln delivered the address that many believed assured his nomination for the presidency.[41]

Field was a maverick in the courtroom, and his readiness to defend underdogs may explain his decision to represent Appo. He argued that Appo deserved a new trial because of numerous irregularities in the proceedings, including indications that the prosecution tampered with witnesses. Field immediately proved more adept than Stuart—New York governor Edwin D. Morgan granted Appo stays of his scheduled execution in July and November. More important, Field produced new evidence. In one affidavit a police officer testified that the day before the start of Appo's trial, he accompanied the district attorney to the scene of the crime. The officer observed that the prosecutor interrogated Mary Fletcher's young daughters, who knew little about the case. On learning that the girls attended Saint James Roman Catholic Church, the prosecutor instructed a servant to take the children to the priest so "that they might be instructed." The district attorney then told one of the girls that when she came into court "she must say so and so, and not to forget it."[42]

At last, on 13 October 1859, Appo was granted an appeal and presented his side of the story for the first time. Field recounted how Appo's attorney botched the trial: First he was absent, then unprepared, and finally failed to call any witnesses on the defendant's behalf. Stuart even accepted the prosecution's claim that his client "was not of a peaceable disposition." Field insisted that Appo was unfamiliar with New York State law and "the niceties of the English language," and therefore unable to judge the implications of his counsel's actions. Moreover, Appo insisted that he killed Fletcher in self-defense. The women interfered when he scolded his wife, calling him a "China nigger." After he ordered them out of his room, Fletcher came after him, joined by the other women, who assaulted him with their fists and a smoothing iron. Appo claimed that another woman was present who could verify his story, but he knew neither her name nor place of residence.[43]

Complicating the matter was new testimony supporting Appo. Frederick Eberhard and George W. Petty, the first police officers at the scene of the crime, claimed that they witnessed two women dragging the victim down the stairs, and then to a back room on the ground floor. Fletcher appeared to be alive at this point. When the officers inquired about what happened, the women simply screamed and hollered at them. Petty concluded that they were "stupid from the effects of liquor." For reasons that remain a mystery, neither officer testified at the coroner's inquest, the grand jury hearing, or the trial.[44]

The key new element was Appo's contention that Mary Fletcher initiated the assault on him, not vice versa. The veracity of Appo's defense was dependent on whether Fletcher had entered Appo's room with a smoothing iron. Both Margaret Butler and the victim's daughter, Theresa Fletcher, denied seeing Fletcher carrying such an object. Other witnesses, however, disagreed. Catherine Appo testified that during the commotion "I saw some of them (I think the servant girl) use a smoothing iron endeavoring to strike my husband." One police officer remembered that on arriving at the crime scene, he found two flatirons on the floor in Appo's room, which was corroborated by two other patrolmen. Whereas this information was ignored during the trial, each one elaborated on it in greater detail in the appeal.[45]

Law enforcement officials even acknowledged that Appo was a victim of racial prejudice. Police officer Charles F. Williams, for example, concurred that Fletcher, Butler, and Gavigan were drunk at the time of the murder. When he attempted to verify that the witnesses were indeed intoxicated, neighbors refused to give testimony. Since all of them were of Irish descent, Williams discovered, they "believed that it would disgrace them if they were to assist in preserving the life of a Chinese."[46]

Now a wide range of individuals came to Appo's defense. Dr. Elwood Irish, a physician who resided near Appo's earlier Third Avenue store, described Appo as "an active and enterprising person—sober and honest, and sociable, quiet, and peaceable in his intercourse with his fellows and his neighbors." While Appo possessed an "excitable and nervous temperament," Irish believed that he would never harm anyone unless threatened. Appo produced letters of support from Protestant clergymen, including Rev. William F. Morgan, the rector of Saint Thomas Episcopal Church on Broadway at Houston Street.[47]

Even law enforcement officials attested to Appo's character. Several police officers described Appo as "a quiet, peaceable, orderly and sober citizen." Two police sergeants testified that Appo bore "an excellent reputation," and a disposition that was "mild and peaceable." By contrast

Mary Fletcher and her friends were drunk "almost daily." The sergeants voiced strong doubts about the veracity of the women's testimony.[48]

Even those who had convicted Appo of murder now came to his defense. One juror acknowledged that he and his fellow jurors rendered a guilty verdict only because they expected a lenient sentence, while another believed that the guilty verdict with a recommendation for mercy was the equivalent of a manslaughter conviction. Both believed Appo to be innocent of premeditated murder, that he committed the homicide while in "a state of ungovernable excitement" resulting from the actions of his wife, "a drunken, bad woman," and the ensuing assault by Fletcher's female friends.[49]

The testimony of these Euro-Americans on behalf of an Asian immigrant was extraordinary. In murder cases involving victims and killers of different races in nineteenth-century New York City, suspects usually marshaled support and alibis from their racial friends and allies. Furthermore, anti-Chinese prejudice was growing in New York. Less than four years later Chinese men suspected of sexual liaisons with white women were attacked on the street during New York's antidraft riots. By 1870 New York mayor Oakey Hall and various city union leaders held rallies denouncing the importation of Chinese "coolies."[50]

On 17 October 1859, Supreme Court Justice James J. Roosevelt, in the Court of Oyer and Terminer, heard Appo's motion to throw out the verdict and seek a new trial. Few defendants could have confronted a judge as different in social background. James John Roosevelt was a sixty-three-year-old descendant of Claes Martenszen Van Roosevelt, the first Roosevelt to arrive in New Amsterdam in 1649. Prominent in the Democratic Party since Andrew Jackson's presidential campaign in 1828, Roosevelt was appointed a judge on the New York Supreme Court in 1851. He remained politically active and identified with the probusiness wing of New York's Democratic Party, and later served as the United States attorney for the Southern District of New York. Supporters claimed that Roosevelt possessed a "stainless" character and an "unimpeachable" integrity.[51]

Perhaps most important for Appo was the fact that Roosevelt was a longtime supporter of David Dudley Field's efforts to reform New York's legal procedures. For whatever reason, Appo's testimony must have been compelling, because a week later Roosevelt ruled that the defendant had been wronged. The judge was convinced that the new evidence would have resulted in a manslaughter conviction, if not an outright acquittal. Roosevelt ordered a new trial. Even the *Herald*, a frequent critic of courtroom leniency, concurred that Roosevelt's decision was fair and humane.[52]

District Attorney Nelson J. Waterbury disagreed. He immediately challenged Roosevelt, contending that Oyer and Terminer had no jurisdiction to set aside a verdict and grant a new trial. In November the New York Supreme Court concurred. Yet Field and his client remained optimistic. A number of recent cases involving the jurisdiction of the court had resulted in new trials for convicted murderers. But on 15 April 1860, their hopes were dashed; the court reaffirmed Appo's conviction and death sentence.[53]

Appo's case, however, was not over. The thick dossier of evidence that Field compiled documenting Appo's innocence, or at least the inadequacy of the prosecution, had an effect. Police officials, courtroom reporters, jurors, and judges at various points agreed that Appo deserved better than death. In the end Field's strategy, if not his moral argument, worked. On 8 May 1860, Governor Morgan commuted Quimbo Appo's death sentence to a ten-year term in a state penitentiary. "The public will approve this merciful act," averred one editorial, "as this is a general feeling of sympathy for the unfortunate prisoner." Appo was immediately sent to Sing Sing.[54]


QUIMBO APPO's initial confrontation with American criminal justice was also his son's. Early in the proceedings, reporters noticed the defendant's young offspring. "The Appos have but one child, a boy of some three years of age," wrote one. The lad "clings to his mother in her cell (where they were taken for safety) and stares with wonder at the crowd of strange inquiring faces outside."[55] For the first time George Appo was behind bars, looking out.

## 2

# Urchins, Arabs, and Gutter-Snipes

═

⏤ᴥ᷾ *Soon after he [Quimbo Appo] received the life sentence, my
mother took passage on board the ship* Golden Gate *bound for California to visit her brother at San Francisco. The ship was wrecked
in a storm on the high seas and both my mother and sister went
down with the other unfortunates who were drowned.*

*I cannot explain how I was saved, only that a sailor brought me
to New York and left me with a very poor family named Allen. The
father of this family was a longshoreman around the docks by occupation and lived in a rear yard which was called by the name of
"Donovan's Lane" at No.14 1/2 Baxter Street. One entrance [was on
Baxter] and the other entrance was on Pearl Street. There lived in
this Donovan's Lane poor people of all nationalities and there were
four old tenement houses and a large horse and wagon stable and
sheds in the Lane. It was a common sight to see every morning
under the wagon sheds at least six to ten drunken men and women
sleeping off the effects of the five cent rum bought at "Black Mike's"
saloon at No.14 Baxter Street. The rear of this place led into the
Lane where all the drunks were dumped out after being relieved of
all their cash. Next door to "Mike's" at No.14 1/2 Baxter St., was a
second-hand clothing store owned by a man named Cohen who was
a "fence" and where all the crooks used to get rid of their stolen
goods. Up over Cohen's store was where all the Chinamen of the
city lived, and on the top floor was the Chinese gambling and meeting rooms. At that time there were only about 60 Chinamen in
all the city and the Lane was then called Chinatown. Such was
Donovan's Lane.[1]*

GEORGE APPO grew up in what was probably America's most impoverished urban neighborhood. Donovan's Lane was but one infamous "rook-

ery" in Gotham's most infamous ghetto—Five Points. Located in the Sixth Ward, a few blocks north of City Hall, the neighborhood took its name from the intersection of four streets at Paradise Square. Popular literature portrayed Five Points as a jumble of slums and sin. After visiting the neighborhood in 1841, for example, the writer and reformer Lydia Maria Child described it as "something worse than Hogarth's Gin Lane." A year later Charles Dickens internationalized Five Points' reputation. "Hideous tenements which take their name from robbery and murder," declared Dickens. "All that is loathsome, drooping and decayed is here!" Over the ensuing two decades, moral contagion, material rot, and frequent death were the repeated metaphors applied to Appo's Five Points.[2]

The sinister imagery derived in part from the vexing problems of disease and poor sanitation. At midcentury Five Points had the highest death rates in New York City. From 1860 to 1863, for example, the Sixth Ward's mortality rate ranged from thirty-six to forty-three per one thousand, almost double the national rate. In 1864 alone, more than seventy-five of Appo's Baxter Street neighbors succumbed to typhus, typhoid, and other contagious diseases; by comparison sixty-nine individuals in the entire city were victims of homicide that year. Throughout Gotham, only Mulberry Street (one block away) exceeded Baxter Street's death rate.[3]

The high rates of sickness and death were products of overcrowding, narrow streets (less than forty feet wide in some places), and atrocious conditions. One reporter described Donovan's Lane as an "Arcadia of garbage," filled with "rambling hovels and Alpine ranges of garbage heaps." Not only did alley residences suffer from few windows and inadequate ventilation, most lacked sewer connections; fluids from toilets and water closets regularly flowed into the street. Tenants lined alleys like Donovan's Lane with stones and boards simply to keep their feet out of the excrement.[4]


THE COMBINED TRAUMA of such poverty and the events surrounding his father's incarceration affected Appo in confusing ways. Most notably he recounted the drowning deaths of his mother and sister while traveling to California. The destruction of the *Golden Gate* was indeed one of the great tragedies of the mid-nineteenth century. As the premier vessel of the Pacific Mail Steamship Company, the palatial, 2,200-ton *Golden Gate* was, according to one account, superior "to any other on the Pacific." But on 27 July 1862, disaster struck. Between 4:45 and 5:05 p.m. the *Golden Gate*'s midsection caught fire, fifteen miles northwest of Manzanillo, Mexico. Some families, in their fear and haste, sought refuge in their cabins, only to be quickly trapped and burned alive. Confronted with the choice of burning or drowning, many jumped while the ship remained several miles from shore; others were crushed under the churning paddle wheels. By the time the ship beached and burned, more than 200 of the 338 on board were lost.[5]

But George Appo, his mother, and his sister were not on board. Newspaper reports revealed that only twenty-two to twenty-nine adult women were among the victims, five of whom traveled in steerage. None included Catherine Appo. George Appo's name never appeared among those of the listed survivors. Furthermore, it is unclear why Appo and his mother would have been on the *Golden Gate* because, in contrast to Appo's memory, the vessel was sailing from California to Panama.[6] More telling was that Appo remembered nothing of this event, even though he was six years old at the time.

In the two years between Quimbo Appo's departure for Sing Sing and the *Golden Gate* disaster, no evidence explains the fate of the young Appo and his mother. Perhaps, like other Irish widows, she joined another household as a boarder or domestic servant. Perhaps she had visited a relative or friend in San Francisco and was returning to New York. Perhaps she had remarried and assumed a new surname.

But most likely Catherine Appo was overwhelmed by the demands of poverty and parenthood. Stricken by the loss of Quimbo Appo's economic support and perhaps suffering from alcoholism, she probably relinquished control of her child to a family friend. George Appo later recounted being raised by the impoverished Allen family, and indeed a number of families with that surname appear in the various censuses of the period. Other sources indicate that in 1874, the eighteen-year-old Appo lived with Mary Ann Allen at 166 Worth Street, directly opposite the Five Points House of Industry. Appo even described Allen as his "sister," indicating that he may have been "adopted" by the Allens, a common working-class-family strategy in times of crisis.[7] One can imagine Appo's adoptive parents telling him that his mother died in a spectacular accident in hopes of alleviating the child's emotional pain.

*Donovan's Lane.*

BY THEN no one remembered how Donovan's Lane earned its nickname. Like other Baxter Street alleys, such as Bandit's Roost and Bottle Alley, the thoroughfare was more accurately a small, unkept courtyard behind the teeming, densely packed tenements. Donovan's Lane shared the block with the more notorious rookeries of Murderer's Alley and Cow Bay, both adjacent to the neighborhood's most disreputable edifice—the Old Brewery. In 1852 Methodist evangelicals purchased and tore down the brewery, replacing it a year later with the Five Points Mission. The new five-story structure included a chapel, schoolroom, and twenty apartments, which—along with the Five Points House of Industry on the other side of Paradise Square—were filled with young boys with whom Appo probably played on the street. From 1855 to 1868 the House of

Industry and the mission served more than eighteen thousand children, educating four hundred to five hundred pupils described as being of "the vagrant class."[8]

But these ameliorative institutions had little, if any, impact on Appo. Rather than submit to the evangelical dictates of the Five Points Mission or the House of Industry, Appo grew up in places like Black Mike's saloon and Cohen's secondhand clothing store. Such enterprises not only operated on the margins of legitimate business but were emblematic of the polyglot community surrounding his childhood residence. African American–operated saloons, Jewish clothing merchants, and the earliest Asian residents of what became "Chinatown" were part of the largest foreign-born population of any New York neighborhood. By Appo's tenth birthday, in 1866, native-born residents comprised less than 5 percent of the community, according to one source. Although the Irish predominated, followed by German Jews and Italians, Donovan's Lane and Baxter Street were singled out as the principal Chinese quarters in the city. By 1880 the Chinese opium den was the "principal attraction" in Donovan's Lane, according to one reporter.[9]

Appo remembered that "crooks used to get rid of their stolen goods" via Cohen's clandestine fencing operation. Most likely this was run by Jacob Cohen, who resided at 14 Baxter Street during the late 1860s. Cohen's shop was hardly unique. During the 1860s, many secondhand clothing and furniture stores lined Baxter Street, unlicensed and operated by Polish and German-Jewish immigrants. But often the real business was fencing; these "junk shops" represented critical components of the neighborhood's informal "underground" economy. In 1876 Jacob Cohen was convicted of receiving stolen goods and sentenced to one year in Sing Sing.[10] George Appo was to follow in his footsteps.

◦§ *[Around the age of nine,] I . . . started out to sell newspapers for a living and remained at this occupation for two years. During the course of that time, I made the acquaintance of two boys my own age who always were well dressed and had plenty of money, earned as I believed, by selling papers. But I soon found out that they were picking pockets on Broadway and used the newspapers as a cover to work their crooked business. After watching them and several other boys, I soon learned the knack, so to speak, of how to pick a pocket. I took one of the boys as a partner. His name was*

*George Dolan and we both worked together for nearly two years and were quite successful.*[11]

The poverty of Five Points transformed George Appo into a street kid. Lacking formal education, adult supervision, and sometimes even a home, youths like Appo were derided as "gamins," "Arabs," "urchins," "gutter-snipes," and "street rats." For more than half a century they were inescapable fixtures of the nineteenth-century industrial city. "Those who have once adopted the semi-savage and wandering mode of life in early youth seldom abandon it," complained *Harper's Weekly* in 1868. Rather, they "continue to the end of their existence Arabs by second nature."[12]

Children like Appo worked at casual, unskilled "street-jobs"—blacking boots, sweeping sidewalks, hauling bags and other goods, scavenging, or selling newspapers. They lived, slept, and ate in streets, alleys, and hallways. Their precise number was always subject to debate, but few doubted that it was substantial. Though some estimates were as high as fifty thousand, such figures were dismissed as exaggerations by the best-informed police officials and reformers. Most likely five to fifteen thousand homeless or unsupervised youths nightly wandered the streets of New York City.[13] Appo typified such children.

Street kids' lives were grounded in the economic realities of the new industrial metropolis, or, as the popular writer George Foster put it, "The Newsboy is a result of the modern civilization." After 1840 apprentices virtually disappeared from artisanal workshops. Factories and sweatshops rapidly replaced craft households and artisanal workplaces. At the very moment that the close supervision of adult craftsmen declined, New York City experienced an unprecedented influx of European immigrants. Between 1840 and 1855, 68 percent of all United States immigrants passed through Gotham. By 1860 half the city was foreign-born. Increasingly certain parts of the working class, especially those trapped in the casual labor market, were pushed into street trades and the informal underground economy. The newspaper editor Horace Greeley estimated that two-thirds of antebellum New Yorkers lived on one dollar per week.[14]

The Connecticut Yankee and social reformer Charles Loring Brace epitomized the contradictory views on street children. On one hand Brace admired their autonomy, describing them as "sharp, ready, light-hearted, quick to understand and quick to act, generous and impulsive, and with an air of being well used 'to steer their own canoe' through whatever rapids and whirlpools." Elsewhere he invoked the horrors of social breakdown. Street children were the "dangerous class," the element most threatening to the property, morals, and political life of civil society.[15] In effect Brace articulated the paradoxical stereotypes of the street child: a cute, fastidious urchin with nascent entrepreneurial values and pragmatic wits, and a corrupted, irredeemable devil full of evil motives and selfish desires, the dangerous class writ small.

Appo's introduction to "professional" street life and pickpocketing was typical. Numerous observers noted that street sellers of all types were introduced to such work before the age of ten. Newsboy and bootblack were the most noticed occupations; indeed they often overlapped.[16] The pickpocket Jim Caulfield believed that young boys were simply too quick and cunning to be captured in their petty plundering. "A boy can get next to a woman in a car or on the street more easily than a man can," he explained. "He is not so apt to arouse her suspicions; and if he is a handsome, innocent-looking boy, and clever, he can go far in this line of graft."[17]

The "newspaper dodge" epitomized the easy transformation from newsboy to pickpocket: Simply wave a newspaper in the face of a potential customer while reaching into the victim's pocket. "I would board a car with a couple of newspapers, would say, 'News, boss?' to some man sitting down, would shove the paper in front of his face as a stall [diversion], and then pick his super [pocketwatch] or even his entire 'front' [watch and chain]," bragged Caulfield. "If you will stand for a newspaper under your chin I can get even your socks."[18]

The rise of child pickpocketing was also rooted in the changing social ecology of the city. For most children the street was a workplace, a social center, a place of amusement. At a time when parks (excepting small squares) were nonexistent and playgrounds almost half a century in the future, streets served multiple functions in a child's life. By the 1860s parts of Park Row and the Bowery—not to mention numerous post offices, hotels, elevated railroad stations, and ferries—were filled with youthful panhandlers. In the vicinity of the Western Union Building on lower Broadway, child pickpockets ranging from ten to sixteen in age preyed on messengers, customers, and company executives. Filled with rivers of people, the most congested pathways of commerce in the metropolis became the workplaces of child pickpockets.

Appropriately lower Broadway was soon identified as a "pickpockets' paradise."[19]

Arrest records confirmed that petty larceny was a boy's crime. One grand jury reported in 1854 that 80 percent of felony indictments and 50 percent of petty offenses in New York were committed by minors under twenty-one years of age. Between 1859 and 1876, the number of pickpockets annually brought to trial by the district attorney nearly quintupled, increasing from 52 to 242. Over 80 percent were between the ages of fourteen and seventeen, native-born, and male. While most worked in the street, only a small percentage involved physical confrontation. Few preyed on the most vulnerable pedestrians—only one out of five victims, for example, was female. The most common purloined object—in two-thirds of all cases—was money. The median value of stolen goods was approximately ten dollars. While this seems like very little money, regular workingmen then averaged only five to ten dollars per week. Newsboys were lucky to make a dollar.[20]

The term "child pickpocket" in some respects was an oxymoron, as such arrested youths rarely considered themselves children. Based on arrest records, the vast majority identified themselves as adult wage earners, not children. Less than 10 percent of those indicted affirmed that they were students. More often they occupied positions of part-time employment or worked in downwardly mobile crafts. Newsboys and bootblacks accounted for 27 percent of all arrested. Those in service jobs such as clerks, errand boys, messengers, and telegraph operators represented another 8 percent. A mere 4 percent labored in factories. The remainder were scattered among a variety of occupations. Particularly striking was the breakdown of the craft system: Only two boys (a cooper and a tailor) claimed to be apprentices.[21]

Most of these youths experienced a swift and sometimes brutal introduction into the market. Older pickpockets—"New York Fagins in the arts of petty pilfering," according to one critic—taught the secrets of the trade to young "apprentices." Larceny had its own division of labor, an everyday apprenticeship system in which youths collaborated in small, intimate groups. Such boys, including Appo and most likely his childhood accomplice George Dolan, never darkened the door of a school. Indeed, throughout the nineteenth century, fewer than half of New York's children regularly attended school. On average males left school at age fourteen. Passage of the Compulsory Education Act of 1875 did little to

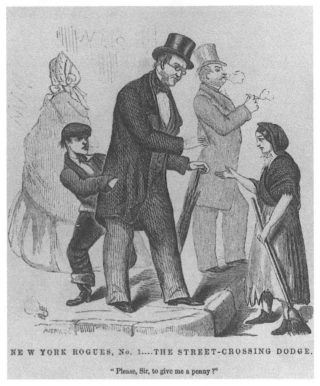

NE W YORK ROGUES, No. 1....THE STREET-CROSSING DODGE.

" Please, Sir, to give me a penny ?"

*The street-crossing dodge.*

increase attendance; in 1894 the journalist and author Jacob Riis complained that compulsory education was "a dead letter."[22]

The Bowery neighborhood served as a surrogate home for street children like Appo. By the 1860s street kids were regular habitués of Bowery theaters, museums, and similar entertainments, "infest[ing] the Bowery at all hours of the day and night," complained one journalist. For a time a group of street children even operated their own theater. The Grand Duke's Opera House, located in a Baxter Street cellar virtually across the street from Donovan's Lane, had its own managers, stagehands, musicians, and actors. The pull of the Bowery and other forms of child nightlife was so great that juveniles often remained away from their real homes for days and even weeks. In 1882 investigator George McDermott was astonished to find an audience in one theater consisting mostly of minors—at least two hundred children between seven and ten years of age, five hundred under fourteen.[23]

The world of the child pickpocket was heavily but not entirely masculine. Newsgirls were to be found, but young females generally enjoyed fewer opportunities within the rough-and-tumble street culture. "Girls can only sell papers, flowers or themselves," wrote attorneys William Howe and Abraham Hummel, "but boys can black boots, sell papers, run errands, carry bundles, sweep out saloons, steal what is left around loose everywhere, and gradually perfect themselves for a more advanced stage

*A night scene on the Bowery.*

and higher grade of crimes." Like their male counterparts, young girls were found in City Hall Park, the Battery, Union Square, and Madison Square.[24]

In most cases child pickpockets and street children were bound together by their social marginalization. Their experiences on city streets broke down common forms of collective identity. "As a rule," concluded social reformer Helen Campbell in 1893, street boys "are known by nicknames and nothing else, and in speaking of one another they generally do so by these names." Rather than identifying each other according to categories based on race, ethnicity, or religion, Campbell noted that "these names indicate some personal peculiarity or characteristic." Commentators and criminals alike rarely discussed the ethnic or immigrant origins of New York's child pickpockets, much less any notion of self-described national identity. More often contemporaries described such youths by their street occupation or activity: newsboys, copper pickers, wood stealers, ragpickers, swill gatherers, bootblacks. The combination of poverty and native-born origins of the majority of Gotham's child pickpockets muted any shared ethnic, racial, or religious bond, for an undoubtedly large percentage of these children had immigrant parents. Street life seemed to neutralize those forms of identity.[25]

In their attitudes toward work, family, life, and property, street children like Appo presented an alternative subculture to pious middle-class ways. The absence of parental authority, the rejection of formal schooling and legitimate employment, and the disregard for personal property, law, and order horrified adults. But it proved functional for children. Asked during one later court interrogation if he knew the difference between right and wrong, Appo replied, "I know that I ain't doing wrong in picking pockets." Queried whether he thought it was right to steal, he acknowledged, "To a certain extent, yes, I do." Within the street milieu, extending into saloons, theaters, museums, and even prisons, youths defended themselves against adult outsiders like the police, truant officers, school authorities, and even parents and their surrogates.[26]

But this alternative subculture, this "criminal underworld," was never oppositional. Political revolution or economic redistribution was not its end; individual gain and personal accumulation were. More often child thieves imitated the middle-class values of consumption and accumulation. Pickpocket crimes were, in part, the result of an expanding market economy with fashionable and expensive consumer goods, evidenced by the diamond-studded stickpins, gold pocketwatches, and wads of green-backs pedestrians conspicuously paraded while traversing the streets. These advertisements of personal prosperity invited their secret removal. George Appo admitted that he admired his teenage pickpocketing peers because they "always were well dressed and had plenty of money." Child pickpockets embodied a new struggle, played out on the streets of America's exploding urban centers, between adults with money, consumer goods, and power and unsupervised children with little of each. Theirs was a different avenue of upward mobility. The goal was not to turn the world upside down but rather inside out.[27]

For children like George Appo, life was organized by their daily strug-gle to survive. These were children who literally slept with rats, who lacked the knee of a supportive adult on which to sit or a shoulder on which to cry. Absent was any family to love them. In Appo's struggle to negotiate a terrain between personal autonomy and adult authority, between self-sufficiency and economic dependence, his childhood iden-tity was framed in the context of everyday street life. Young pickpockets like Appo cultivated their own conception of freedom and independence. But in trying to carve out a place for themselves, they found a world in which few adults cared to understand and many wished they would go away. By avoiding the factory, the school, and the church, child pick-pockets spoke with their feet—and frequently their hands.

# 3

# A House of Refuge at Sea

=

◆; One day in the winter of 1871, I was caught in the act while picking the pocket of a downtown businessman, the name of whom I have forgotten. He gave me in the hands of a policeman and charged me with taking $28 from his vest pocket. I was tried before Judge [Joseph] Dowling and pleaded guilty and sentenced to the school-ship Mercury under the assumed name "George Leonard." I was taken from the boy's prison in the Tombs to Hart's Island, where I was put to work in the grave diggers gang, wheeling a barrow until the ship returned from a cruise from the West Indies, and then I would be transferred aboard of her.

I was about three months on Harts Island, when one day in April the ship Mercury arrived and anchored in the bay and I with twenty-five other boys were transferred aboard of her. On our arrival on board, we were taken and examined by the physician, then given a suit of sailor's clothes and a hammock and a number instead of a name. My number was 182, port watch and stationed as a main top-man. We were then turned over to the "Master of Arms" who took us below and with a rope's end in one hand and a card with the rules and regulations in the other, began to read the rules of the ship to us. After he had finished reading them he gave us a sizing-up look from head to foot, so to speak, and then said: "You understand them now and see that you obey them well. Get up on deck now and learn your ropes."

On reaching the upper deck, the boatswain gave us into the hands of older boys and they teached us all about the ropes and their use and names. Finally about 4 p.m., the boatswain piped "All hands skylark!" meaning all the boys could climb up the rigging and do as they pleased. This was done more to give all the new boys a chance to practice and learn to climb aloft in safety to loosen and *furl sail. In about three weeks, I learned everything that a seaman should know, that is, to "box the compass," to loosen and furl sail, to make all kinds of knots and to splice ropes, and I took a turn at the wheel.*[1]

"**B**OYS," THE WRITER Henry Adams declared, "are wild animals." The easy evolution of street kids like George Appo into street criminals horrified nineteenth-century child reformers. In addition to newsboy lodging houses and harsh punishments, New York witnessed an explosion of new ameliorative institutions to remedy problems associated with homeless, abandoned, orphaned, and criminal youths. Between 1850 and 1870, more than a dozen orphanages and "children's asylums" opened in the city. "The number of vagrant, vicious, and adventurous children around New York is so great," believed the writer and minister J. F. Richmond, "that a new institution for their correction and reformation springs up every few years." By the 1870s, such institutions had the capacity to house more than 5,700 children.[2]

The largest and best-known child-saving institution was New York's House of Refuge. Founded in 1824 by the Society for the Reformation of Juvenile Delinquents, the refuge was considered the nation's first juvenile reformatory and represented a specialized assault on child crime. A new facility opened on Randall's Island in 1854, with a capacity in excess of eight hundred, and marked a transition from a "house of refuge" to a "house of reform." By the 1860s American reformers believed that Gotham's House of Refuge received more "criminal children" than any comparable institution in the United States or Europe.[3]

But to children like George Appo the House of Refuge was more like a prison than a reformatory—to some a veritable "chamber of horrors." The rough punishments—meals of bread and water, confinement in solitary cells, corporal punishment, and fetters, handcuffs, and whippings in extreme cases—only hardened the many incarcerated youths. Appo claimed that the House of Refuge was "feared by the boys who had been there." After one pickpocketing arrest, Appo lied about his age because he was terrified of being sent to what he called the "house of torture."[4]

In 1869, hoping to resolve overcrowding in the House of Refuge, New York's Commissioners of Public Charities and Correction purchased the fourteen-year-old, 1,350-ton packet ship *Mercury*. The vessel was to serve as nautical training school for Gotham's "wild, reckless and semi-criminal lads," according to one commissioner. Hoping to diminish the growing number of unsupervised street boys, the commissioners believed that the ship would provide "a sure and honest means of livelihood suited to their adventurous spirit."[5]

The *Mercury* generated a variety of supporters. Evangelical ministers advocated such a vessel for lawbreaking youths, believing the sea was "the teacher of truths," according to one. The Chamber of Commerce envisioned nautical schools as a vehicle to create a merchant marine comprised of native-born Americans. By the 1860s both prison and naval reformers supported nautical programs to incarcerate vagrants and others guilty of petty offenses. The most innovative was the school ship *Mercury*.[6]

The *Mercury* accepted its first trainees in September 1869. By the year's end, 242 boys were on deck. Initially ship hands were first offenders—teenagers convicted of petty crimes such as vagrancy, truancy, and larceny. Since many, like Appo, had no fixed residences and no visible means of subsistence, the *Mercury* provided a home for "the friendless and refractory waifs," in the words of Capt. Pierre Giraud. Some parents even requested that their unruly children be sentenced to the school ship; a few willingly paid an annual stipend.[7]

Youths like Appo sentenced to the *Mercury* were at first detained at Hart's Island (today Hart Island)—in Long Island Sound, just west of City Island and the Bronx. The island's isolated location made it a favorite spot for illegal boxing matches in the antebellum era. In 1868 the New York City Commissioners of Charities and Corrections purchased most of the island in order to establish an industrial school for delinquent and homeless boys. Most significantly Hart's Island soon became Gotham's massive "potter's field," where New York buried the city's deceased homeless, unknown, and unwanted citizens. By 1885 approximately six thousand anonymous and pauper dead required city burial annually. Most ended up on Hart's Island, interred in mass graves of 150, stacked in three layers on top of one another. In summertime at least twenty-five gravediggers were employed full-time, including George Appo.[8]

On board the *Mercury* corrections officials employed the apprenticeship system of the United States Navy, organizing youths into companies under the charge of twenty-two petty officers, serving as supervisors and teachers. Belowdecks the charges were subjected to a curriculum including reading, writing, arithmetic, and singing, as well as several branches of navigation, seamanship, and military drill. The program impressed one observer, who noted that youths made ropes and "a wonderful variety of mysterious knots, which no one would imagine could be made, but when made once, no human agency can undo."[9]

The daily routine on the *Mercury* was rigid and disciplined. A typical day looked like this:

Reveille at daylight
Hammocks washed and stored, decks and clothes washed
Boys wash
7:30 a.m.: boys muster and line up
8:00: breakfast
8:50: drummer beats "the call," preparation of sails and boats
9:00: boats lowered, sails fall, and booms rigged out
9:30: drummer beats for inspection, allowing boys three minutes to get to stations
9:45: boys of starboard watch march to school-room for study; boys of port watch work on deck
11:30: dinner prepared
11:45: class dismissed
12:00 noon: dinner served
1:00 p.m.: starboard watch boys work on deck, port watch boys attend school
4:00: school dismissed, decks cleared
4:30: supper served
Evening devoted to recreation and relaxation
15 min. before sundown, drum beats for inspection
10 min. before, booms rigged in, boats hoisted, colors hauled down, and boys set up hammocks
7:30: evening exercises of singing and prayer
8:00: "anchor watch" set for the night; boys go to bed
8:30: all loud talking ceases.[10]

Not surprisingly deportment was a key element of the *Mercury*'s curriculum. Boys were required to be neat and clean, to salute officers, and to maintain "an erect carriage." When the ship was in port, religious services were held by both Protestant and Catholic ministers. The "inflexible

*A parade on the deck of the* Mercury.

discipline" on board, claimed the commissioners, was "the most effective mode to reclaim erring boys."[11]

Some observers concluded that the *Mercury*'s training transformed the boys. "One or two cruises are sufficient to quell the most turbulent spirit," wrote one reporter. On one occasion he observed a small boy of thirteen ordering about a gang of eighteen- or twenty year-olds. "Such is the discipline of the ship," he proclaimed. One instructor believed that after the long winter cruises, many boys considered the *Mercury* to be their home.[12]

The school ship was, in essence, an early reform school, strikingly similar to later Progressive Era penal reforms. Boys sentenced to the *Mercury* served indeterminate sentences; in the words of Captain Giraud, the boys "come to us for no stated period." The nautical school abandoned retributive punishments, substituting a program of rehabilitation and instruction. Boys were punished when they failed to follow orders, not simply because they were felons. Ideally boys on the *Mercury* received their first formal educations and legitimate employment when they left the school ship. Like reformers of the early twentieth century, the ship's advocates wanted to transform nightmarish prisons into supportive male communities that prepared inmates for release.[13]

> *During the summer months we made short cruises. When September arrived, the ship would sail to the West Indies to St. Thomas, Barbados, the Canary Islands, Rio de Janeiro and to the coast of Africa. This voyage took us eight months and after many*

hardships, we arrived and dropped anchor in the bay off Hart's Island.

During this long voyage, we came through many severe storms in safety. While anchored in Rio de Janeiro, the "yellow jack fever" was raging there and six boys died out of thirty cases we had on board. To make matters still more worse, while the ship was crossing the

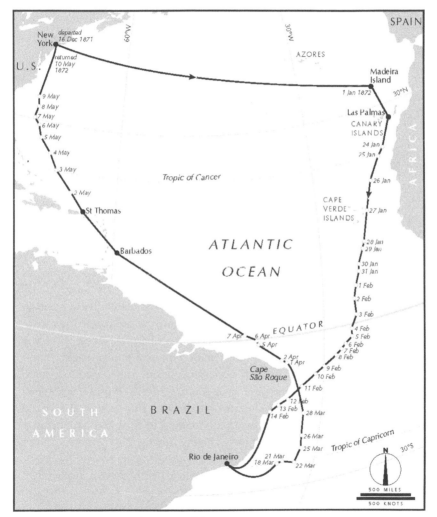

The cruise of the Mercury, 1871–72.

*equator, we got caught in a calm and we were out for 65 days with-
out a sight of land. We had to live on hard tack full of maggots and
had to put lime and charcoal in our water tanks. We were allowed
one half of a condensed milk can of this filthy water three times a
day to drink. Captain Giraud was greatly worried on account of the
fever aboard, and the doctor kept us busy burning pitch to fumigate
the ship between decks and aft. Finally, a severe storm came along
with plenty of rain and we spread the awnings in order to catch all
the rain possible for drinking and managed to fill several large casks
which was a great relief. After the storm we had good wind for many
days which brought the ship across the line and soon into a colder
latitude where the fever left us.*[14]

In December 1871 Appo joined 253 boys, twelve seamen, and a full
complement of officers under Captain Giraud on the second winter voyage of the *Mercury*. They remained at sea until the following May, sailing
more than fifteen thousand miles.[15] Newspapers sent correspondents
onto the *Mercury* to provide firsthand accounts of these early voyages,
making it possible to reconstruct Appo's journey across the Atlantic.
Undoubtedly Appo and his fellow sailors witnessed sights most never saw
again. Islands like Madeira and the Canarys offered views of snowcapped
mountains, volcanic terrain, and tropical rain forests, "beautiful to the
extreme," in the words of one reporter. When the young shipmates
behaved, Giraud allowed them to go ashore in such exotic ports.[16]

In his official reports Giraud gushed with enthusiasm: "The advantage
to the boys of cruising [the high seas] can hardly be estimated; their associations with shore influences of a pernicious character are severed, the
monotony of confinement is relieved by new and strange sights, their
duties become a necessity." By working alongside experienced seamen,
he believed the youths adopted their positive spirit and pride, evidenced
by their prompt and even cheerful obedience. The captain also noted
that numerous boys for the first time learned to read and write. Above
all they experienced a masculine transformation. "The patrons of the
institution will be surprised to see the manly set of boys we bring back,"
bragged Giraud, "when we contrast them with those that were taken
away." Reporters on board concurred.[17]

The reality of life on the *Mercury*, however, bore little resemblance to
these buoyant evaluations. In addition to poor food, filthy water, and con-

tagious disease, George Appo insisted that discipline on the *Mercury* was anything but benevolent. "The punishment inflicted for disobedience was severe—flogging and the stocks," he remembered. Appo insisted that the latter was especially painful when the ship rolled about on the high seas. "Many boys have broken their wrists and ankles while in the stocks for punishment in the back hold of the vessel."[18]

Indeed, critics questioned the reformative impact of the *Mercury*. Some believed that the socially disruptive street culture that reformers strived so hard to destroy was only replicated on board. Commissioner William Laimbeer observed boys on the school ship and conceded that the vessel was "simply a plaything in the hands of the boys." When asked to elaborate, he remarked that most boys simply learned new forms of crime because "their time, I think, is spent in studying rascality." Rather then prepare for careers as seamen, Laimbeer concluded that the majority devoted their time to learning "some deviltry [for] after they get out."[19]

Others complained that the *Mercury* had too many charges. At one point in 1870 222 boys were on board at one time, forcing a halt to instruction for two months. A year later 667 pupils passed through the *Mercury*. Too often, admitted Giraud, shipmates were discharged before they even learned the parts of the ship, much less seamanship. Some instructors complained that, for the boys, "nothing seems to them an object of more aversion than a *hook*."[20]

By 1875 public officials acknowledged the validity of some of these charges. Representatives from the Board of Public Charities and Correction complained that the rehabilitation of the youths failed to meet the board's expectations. Furthermore employment opportunities after service on the *Mercury* were less than glowing. One conceded that the ship's graduates had less than a 50–50 chance of future employment as sailors. A sympathetic *New York Times* reporter reluctantly admitted that economic conditions created little demand for sailors. Disease and occupational hazards also proved troubling. At various times boys fell to their deaths while aloft on the sails; still others contracted serious illnesses like typhus.[21]

Sex was also a problem. Critics of mariner life had long complained that ships in port were little more than "floating Sodoms," allowing prostitutes to board ships with little regulation. While *Mercury* officers succeeded in keeping prostitutes off the vessel, they were less successful in controlling the open homosexual behavior belowdecks. In an unusually frank report in 1876, instructor John C. Johnson complained that the hammocks were in such close proximity that the boys virtually shared their sleeping spaces and engaged in various forms of sexual play. Such behavior was "very prevalent" during the long cruise. Johnson described one boy who "committed sodomy six times since I have been on the ship, and how often before I came, I know not." The youth not only served on the ship for six years but was promoted to petty officer and later captain.[22]

In the world of the sailor, this was "chickenship." In his diary written in the 1850s, the sailor Philip Van Buskirk bluntly proclaimed that "no boy can ever remain a year on board of an American man-of-war without being led or forced to commit this crime [sodomy]." But many of the apprentice sailors never considered such sexual activity to be criminal. Boys frequently sought secret physical and sexual relationships with other boys under the boom cover, leading one observer to label the practice the "boom cover trade." At times formalized sexual relationships between either men and boys or older and younger boys flourished. The junior partners were called "chickens," the arrangement "chickenship." Of all the boys Van Buskirk met during his naval career, he remembered only one who avoided such homosexual liaisons with shipmates.[23] Such relationships were part of the fluid, informal, homosocial world of the mariner.

Officials also worried about another commonplace sexual behavior in most adolescent, all-male environments: masturbation. Supporters of the House of Refuge, for example, acknowledged in 1860 that the "solitary vice" was "fearfully prevalent" among inmates. A decade later a contractor at the House of Refuge conceded that youths, some "so young that they could hardly speak plain," were taught how to masturbate, chew tobacco, and other things by older youths. In his diary Van Buskirk described teenage seamen as "practicing onanists," many never bothering "to hide their mutual masturbation from their peers." They talked of it, joked about it, watched others do it, and sometimes even assisted (called "going chaw for chaw"), almost always without any sense of scandal. Masturbation was a convenient activity for passing idle time.[24] Most likely the same occurred on the *Mercury*.

The all-male environment, the youthful resistance to authority, and the disdain for discipline induced some *Mercury* youths to escape at the first opportunity. Captain Giraud later admitted that boys sentenced to the *Mercury* for an indeterminate period concentrated primarily "on the probable time of their discharge." By 1874 and 1875 newspaper accounts claimed that a great number of the boys abandoned ship at the first opportunity, and that there was "an occasional mutiny" among the young sailors. Worse yet, one discouraged instructor concluded that many boys after leaving the *Mercury* ended up in jail or prison.[25]

The *Mercury* experiment was abandoned after 1875, ostensibly for reasons of expense. Over five years the budget for the *Mercury* was slashed from $52,000 to $24,000. Budget cutting contributed to increasingly squalid conditions on board. One observer claimed that the *Mercury* was so infested with rats that they "kill one another." In 1875 a new school ship opened at Twenty-third Street on the East River. Operated by the Board of Education, SS *St. Mary's* trained only apprentice sailors, not convicted criminal youths. Critics claimed that New York did not need two school ships. The *Mercury* soon returned to commercial service.[26]

Appo's graphic and detailed ruminations on his *Mercury* sojourn reflected the intensity, indeed the excitement, of his education at sea. Climbing the rigging, enduring disease, boxing the compass (that is, naming all thirty-two principal points of the compass in clockwise order), and surviving Atlantic storms became indelible childhood memories. Life on the *Mercury* was an adventure.

But it was also an ordeal. He hated the doldrums and despised the discipline. He never learned to read or write. Official rules may have prohibited corporal punishment, but Appo remembered flogging and stocks.[27] Despite his embryonic "pride in craft" and adventures at sea, Appo described the world of the *Mercury* as less of a reformatory and more like a prison.

Appo's captain, Pierre Giraud, rarely talked with his young charges. He believed that even if youths on the *Mercury* never sailed again, the boys "will at least have had their heads turned the right way. . . . They will have learned to recognize the necessity of law and order."[28] Not George Appo.

    *The ship arrived and dropped anchor in Barbados where we lay for one week and one day, the order given to "Up Anchor for the United States!" [In May 1872] the ship arrived at Hart's Island, where we anchored in the bay. I was one of the third cutter's crew and this boat was always used to carry passengers and provisions* from shore to ship or on any special occasion. The crew were all boy prisoners and whenever the cutter was called away for service, a paid sailor, like a keeper, would sit in the stern of the boat and watch us.

One day the cutter was called away and a new German sailor was assigned to guard us. He got into the cutter and ordered us to pull for City Island. When the boat reached there, a man on the dock handed the paid sailor a paper and said: "The goods are down the dock, that's the bill." The sailor jumped on the dock from the cutter to get the goods.

In an instant, one of the boys said, "Give way, let us go home." We all dropped our oars and pulled with might and main, so to speak, for the other end of City Island, where we jumped ashore. We all scattered and left the boat on the beach. I managed to get hold of an old jacket and cap and discarded the sailor's shirt and hat and reached Donovan's Lane where I soon got clothes. After laying quietly under cover for a week, I was out stealing again in the same business.[29]

# Violence

◆§ *Now as I look back on the past, I wonder how I ever lived through it all and escaped the many close calls of death from the knife, blackjacks and pistol shots I received.*

*The first time I received a bullet wound was in the stomach when I was about 18 years of age. The shot was fired from a pistol in the hands of a detective down in Wall Street, who with a large crowd of excited men were in hot pursuit after me and shouting, "Stop Thief." The fact is, I had picked the pocket of a man who had a bankbook full of greenbacks conspicuously sticking up from his coat pocket and the detective must have seen me do it, but I seen him before he could grab me, and I dodged through an office building into Nassau Street. Then, seeing the crowd was closing in on me, I threw the bankbook and the bills which scattered in all directions among them and they fell over one another trying to secure the money. On reaching the street, I ran down Wall Street to Pearl Street.*

*As I was turning the corner I heard the report of the gun and immediately felt a burning feeling in my stomach. I ran into the building 300 Pearl Street, where over a cork store lived a family named Maher, with whom I was acquainted. The good woman, Mrs. Maher, hid me between the mattress of the bed where I remained until her son went out, looked around and returned, saying everything was all right. After having the wound attended to by a doctor to whom we told I was accidently shot, I then got skillful medical treatment at St. Luke's Hospital through the kindness of a gentleman who had some influence there. I believe whoever fired that shot did not know I was hit by the bullet that lodged in a muscle of the stomach and [was] removed.*

*I soon got well and strong enough to leave the hospital and through necessity was compelled to take up my dishonest life once more and was soon again behind the bars and serving a term of two years and six months.*[1]

# 4

# Factories for Turning Out Criminals

=

∞ß   *On April 3rd, 1874, I pleaded guilty before Recorder [John K.]
Hackett, who sentenced me to state prison for a term of two years
and six months. I was not yet sixteen years of age at the time, but
through fear of being sent to the House of Refuge, which place at
that time was a house of torture, and feared by the boys who had
been there, I gave the name of George Dixon, age 18. As the detective had told the judge I was anything but good, he sent me to State's
Prison instead of the Penitentiary.[1]*

*On my arrival there at Sing Sing, my unfortunate father, who
was there at the time, learned from someone of my being sent there,
and instead of being quiet about it, got permission from the warden
to see and speak with me at his office. The result was: "The son of
Quimbo Appo, the notorious murderer is now at Sing Sing, etc.,"
got into the newspapers and made things in general very unpleasant
for me, and I was stamped a bad man and put to work in the laundry contract, ironing new shirts.*

*I was at work only three days when the paid instructor of the con-
tract put a dozen shirts on my table, saying, "You will have to do
these shirts today and see that you do them perfect or I'll know the
reason why, if you don't." I told him I would do my best, so I started
to do so and finished two shirts, but unfortunately while on the
third shirt, I had to go and get a hot iron and before I used it, I had
dipped it in water to cool off. Then I started to iron the sleeve of the
shirt and accidently scorched it. The result was I reported the accident to the citizen instructor (Spencer by name) and he went to the
keeper (Harris by name) and told him that I wilfully burned the
shirt. The keeper said to me: "Go and get your hat and coat."*

*I did so, and he with the instructor, took me to the guard room,
where the Principal Keeper was and reported me to him as wilfully*

and deliberately burning shirts. "What have you to say about that?" said the P.K. [Principal Keeper]

"It was an accident and I could not help it," said I.

"Accident, hey! Couldn't, hey! Well, we'll make you be more careful after this. Take off your clothes," said he.

"Why, Principal, it was an accident, I could not help it," said I.

"Take off your clothes," he again demanded. As I did not respond quick enough, he shouted: "Seize him" and a big, six-foot keeper and another grasped me by the throat, tore off my coat and pants, knocked out my front teeth by shoving me violently over the paddle board, pulled my hands behind my back, handcuffed me and pulled them up behind my back as I lay across the paddle board, by a small tackle attached to a frame work on [the] sides of [the] paddle board. After securing me, the six-foot keeper took a board shaped just like a canoe paddle with small holes in the blade and swung it over his shoulders and brought it down with all his might on my bare back and spine. I counted nine blows and became insensible thereafter.

When I came to, I was lying on the floor and the doctor said, "He's all right now."

The ironing department in the Sing Sing laundry.

*The Principal Keeper said to me: "Do you think you can go back and do your work all right now? If you don't, we have a way to make you."*

*I replied, "You punished me for nothing and the next time I am brought here, you will punish me for something."*

*"No insolence, take him back to the shop." When I got back to the shop with my teeth knocked out and my body black and bruised from the paddle, I took the shirts that were on my table to iron across the shop to the stove, kicked open the stove door and put the shirts into the fire and slammed the door shut again. I was again brought over to the guard room and asked why I did it and I would not answer, and he said: "Put him in again" but the Doctor said: "No, lock him up in the dungeon."[2]*

*So they took me to the "dark cells" and I lay there for 14 days on two ounces of bread and a gill of water every 24 hours, and when I was taken from the dark cells, I was carried to the hospital injured for life.[3]*

W ITHIN DAYS of entering Sing Sing, Appo bore witness to the three fundamental realities of nineteenth-century prison life: work, profit, and torture. Appo's daily prison regimen reflected how prison and state officials sought to transform the penitentiary into a profitable, self-sustaining factory. In order to achieve that goal, state officials demanded inmates work, imposing a rigid and intensive physical regimen on the incarcerated. During his multiple incarcerations, Appo ironed clothes in the laundry, "wheeled" sand and lime dust, served as an assistant tier boy (cleaning the different floors or tiers of the prison hall), chopped wood, and manufactured stoves and hats.[4] Those prisoners who refused to comply were punished through formal and informal mechanisms of physical abuse and torture.

By the second half of the nineteenth century Sing Sing was America's most famous prison. Originally called "Mount Pleasant Prison," the complex was located thirty-two miles north of New York City in the village of Ossining, New York. The name originated from several Indian names for the location—*Sint Sinks* and *Ossine Ossine*—meaning "stone upon stone." The name was apropos: The penitentiary was literally carved into the steep slopes on the eastern bank of the Hudson River, overlooking Tappan Bay. State officials originally believed that the adjacent stratum of white marble was inexhaustible. Convict labor, predicted one defender of the location, would soon transform New York City into a "vast expanse of marble palaces." Indeed the New York Customs House (now Federal Hall) and Grace Church on Broadway in New York City were constructed of stone hewn by Sing Sing's so-called "quarry slaves."[5]

On entering Sing Sing prisoners like Appo confronted the main prison hall—a grim, 484-foot-long structure only 42 feet wide and 50 feet high—containing 1,191 prison cells. Inside, the stone walls, floors, and ceilings gave the impression that the building was literally cut out of solid rock. Harshness seemed "to reach out and grip one with ghastly hands," wrote a later warden, "a coldness that hovers like a pall, and a heaviness that presses down upon the spirit like a huge millstone."[6]

Sing Sing cells were indeed forbidding. Stacked atop one another in six tiers, and secured by heavy iron doors (not bars), walls, floors, and ceilings, were each eighteen inches thick. The cells were, to say the least, tiny: eight feet long, three and a half feet wide, and seven feet high. The sole physical comfort was provided by a two-foot-wide iron cot suspended from the wall by a rope, on which lay a straw mattress and three blankets. Beside the bed were a kerosene lamp, a quart drinking pail, a wash kit, a slop bucket for human waste, and a Bible. Prisoners received soap twice a month, a ration of oil and two ounces of tobacco once each week.[7]

Not surprisingly Sing Sing suffered from inadequate sanitation. Before 1883 the prison lacked any bathing facilities whatsoever. While some prisoners cleaned themselves in the wash basins of the shops (some of which were also used as toilets), most inmates were compelled to bathe in a nearby pond. Consequently most prisoners never bathed in the fall and the winter. Appo claimed that during his incarcerations in Sing Sing he "never saw or knew of a place to bathe after a hard day's work."[8]

The main hall of Sing Sing also suffered from inadequate ventilation. The proximity of the main cellblock to the river, the elevation barely above the tidewater mark, and the heavy stone construction transformed the continually damp cells "into a vast refrigerator," claimed one observer. In winter months inmates could see their breath. "Night buckets," saturated with urine and feces, were a common source of disease and filled the air with an awful stench. Overcrowding made the pungent odors even more "offensive and sickening," wrote one visitor. Within six months of its opening in 1825, the prison surpassed capacity, and officials promptly doubled up inmates. The practice never stopped for the rest of the century. At peak years, 1877 to 1878, the population exceeded sixteen hundred, a circumstance that one Sing Sing physician admitted was "unwholesome and demoralizing." The combination of overcrowding and small cells convinced more than one warden that Sing Sing was "altogether unfit for human habitation."[9]

By the time of Appo's first incarceration in 1874, Sing Sing was a sprawling, seventy-seven-acre industrial complex, simultaneously a "great human cage" and "a leviathan" factory complex. When in full operation, the prison's tall, redbrick chimneys emitted thick volumes of black smoke. Steam-pipes sent white, billowing clouds into the sky. Passersby could not avoid hearing the great roar of whirling machinery. Inside, horses and wagons moved hither and thither, ship masts towered above the quay walls, and freight trains thundered through the prison grounds. In the age of industry, wrote another observer, Sing Sing was a "vast creative emporium." It was arguably the largest manufacturing complex in the country, if not the world.[10]

Sing Sing's multiple workshops were adjacent to the main prison hall. They included three for cabinetmaking, two for iron or stove forging, two for shoemaking, two for saddlery hardware, and one for chain making.

*Sing Sing in 1869.*

During the 1870s and 1880s, more than nine hundred men daily labored in the stove shop manufacturing between two hundred and three hundred stoves, while another three hundred in the shoe shop produced between 1,500 and 2,300 pairs of boots and shoes. New inmates to Sing Sing, like George Appo, were initially assigned to the laundry, considered to be the severest assignment because temperatures in the drying room often reached 150 degrees. Anywhere between 130 and 160 men washed, dried, starched, and ironed 2,400 shirts daily.[11]

East of the main hall and the railroad tracks, inmates "broke stones" in five marble quarries. Employing as many as 225 convicts in 1870, the "inexhaustible" supply of marble and limestone required an extensive quarry railroad to move materials about, as well as a marble dust mill, a lime storehouse, and five limekilns. To service this industrial compound, Sing Sing included stables, a barn with more than one hundred hogs that were annually slaughtered on the grounds, a clothing shop, laundry room, kitchen, dining hall, chapel, and hospital.[12]

The size of Sing Sing's labor force dwarfed those of most American factories. In 1880, for example, cotton mills in the United States averaged 228 employees. Although at least five American iron and steel mills employed more than 1,000 workers, the majority were considerably smaller, averaging 140 employees per factory. Even the thirty-six Bessemer and open-hearth steelworks in the United States employed only 302 workers on average.[13] Prior to Emancipation and the elimination of African slavery in the United States, plantations with more than fifty slaves were considered large; the largest, along the Mississippi River, counted more than two hundred slaves. With the passage of the Thirteenth Amendment and termination of legal slavery, Sing Sing's more than twelve hundred inmates represented perhaps the largest coerced labor population in one location in the United States. Appo had Sing Sing in mind when he wrote that prisons were "nothing more than factories for turning out criminals."[14]

But Sing Sing was better understood as a haphazardly organized industrial plantation than an efficient, modern prison. The outside world, for example, regularly penetrated the facility. One public highway bordered its eastern edge, while two others passed through the entire length of the prison complex. The Hudson River Railroad tracks also ran through the grounds, literally within forty feet of the main prison hall. With scores of

*The Hudson River Railroad line running through the Sing Sing grounds generated numerous escape attempts by inmates.*

trains rushing through the compound daily, desperate convicts some-times jumped aboard passing locomotives and escaped.[15]

Most unusual was the absence of any wall. In 1864 state prison inspec-tors admitted that visitors were surprised to find the prison "wholly unprotected." On the western edge, by the Hudson River, one visitor complained that Sing Sing lacked any fence to keep the public out or the convicts in. Inmates, reported Sing Sing officials, enjoyed unobstructed and monumental vistas of the Tappan Zee and the majestic hills towering above the Hudson River. The only safety against inmates taking flight was the small guard force of approximately thirty men. In 1876 the prison reformer Sinclair Tousey bluntly wondered why more did not escape.[16]

Outsiders also enjoyed unusual access to the prison property. Local residents routinely used prison wharves "for their own purposes," com-plained one state investigatory committee. Grocers and peddlers entered the grounds daily, selling food and other items to prison officials and inmates alike. Nearby villagers even stored their private gunpowder on the Sing Sing premises. Since ordinary citizens enjoyed access to the prison grounds from the railroad tracks, visitors frequently introduced contraband materials—alcohol, clothing, newspapers, tobacco—by secreting them in holes and other hidden places. Other commodities were less hidden: Sing Sing officials admitted that "lewd" and "disreputable" women regularly entered the prison yard and offered their sexual services.[17]

Only in 1876 did the state authorize funds for the construction of a permanent fence. On completion, along with guard towers, in 1878, the twenty-two-foot-high wall was the coup de grace for any unauthorized departure. Reporters claimed that thereafter any escape attempt by even the most daring convict would be considered utterly hopeless. An iron fence along the waterfront completed the prison enclosure in 1879.[18]

## "THE CONTRACT SLAVE SYSTEM"

Work and torture disciplined the daily lives of inmates like Appo. All labor was organized under a contract system: New York State prison officials leased convicts to outside contractors for a fixed daily sum. Private entrepreneurs then brought raw materials to the prison, paid for the employment of inmates, and marketed the finished products at their own risk. In return the contractors employed convicts and helped maintain the prison. Theoretically the system allowed prisons to meet two fundamental ideals of the state prison system—self-support and inmate employment. Contractors thereby enjoyed cheap and compliant labor.[19]

As early as 1824, prison reformers and state officials believed that healthy prisoners should be compelled to work and defray their prison expenses. In 1866 New York State dropped all restrictions on prison labor and empowered state prisons to employ convicts at whatever financially advantageous labor. In 1895 the reformer Frederick Howard Wines admitted that the primary purpose of prison labor was financial profit. The ideal warden, he conceded, "was the man who could show the best balance-sheet at the end of the year."[20]

But few could. From 1870 to 1900 all three state prisons annually spent more than one hundred dollars per inmate—an extravagant sum, many believed. In fact the 1870s, the decade of Appo's first two admissions to Sing Sing, were the most expensive of the century. Between 1870 and 1876, for example, Sing Sing never spent less than $169 per convict per year, reaching a high of $316 in 1872. Before 1878 contract labor rarely made a profit in any of New York's three state penitentiaries. Observers complained that the sum total of New York's three state prisons, with only three thousand inmates and one thousand "graduates," annually cost more than New York's 210 high schools, with more than thirty thousand students and ten thousand graduates.[21]

By 1877, just when Appo began his second Sing Sing incarceration, New York's penal contract labor system was under attack. State investigations revealed that favoritism and fraud were commonplace in awarding contracts. Oral agreements, false damage claims by contractors, and contractors reneging on their debts to the prisons resulted in annual financial deficits. If state officials were dissatisfied with a contract, their only recourse was to buy out the interest of the contractor, who in turn set his price extremely high. Some Sing Sing contractors made profits of 75 percent above their capital investment. Another, one Alfred Walker, not only had a five-year contract to run the Sing Sing marble and limeworks but served as the Sing Sing warden from 1874 to 1876. Prison management, charged one critic, was better described as "prison mismanagement."[22]

Critics called for reform. Former Sing Sing warden Gaylord B. Hubbell recommended abolishing contract labor and substituting state-run prison industries. Reformers associated with the Prison Association, believing that contract labor corrupted prison officials and guards, advocated permanent tenure for all wardens, along with the appointment and removal power over all keepers and guards. Others believed that political influences could be eliminated by adopting a single superintendent overseeing all prisons.[23]

In 1877 the New York legislature did just that. A centralized state department of prisons was created, and Louis D. Pilsbury became the first superintendent. For some Pilsbury was the ideal candidate to transform New York's prisons, representing the third generation of a family intimately involved in nineteenth-century penal reform. Louis and his father, Amos Pilsbury, supervised the Albany Penitentiary for nearly half a century. As one of the first profitable, self-supporting prisons in America, Albany was called by one penal reformer "the model penal institution of the state."[24]

Inmates, however, detested Pilsbury. To Appo he was little more than "a petty tyrant," a sham reformer who awarded positions only to his political allies in Troy and Albany.[25] Pilsbury saw his superintendency as an opportunity to make New York's prisons profitable and had no interest in eliminating contract labor. Pilsbury's administration necessitated a new disciplinary regime for inmates, meting out more punishments, forbidding inmates from roaming around the grounds, and forcing all healthy convicts to labor from sunup to sunset.

Above all there was silence. Sing Sing had officially operated under the silent system since opening, but the method had fallen into disuse. Under Pilsbury it returned with a vengeance. "Every convict went through his task of daily work must fold his arms, look down on the floor, not to talk even to a keeper," recounted Appo. "Should you need anything, [you] raise your hand and point out to the keeper what you wanted." Prisoners now worked, ate, and prayed in strict silence; in their few moments of idleness, inmates were expected to cross their arms and look at the ground.[26]

The lockstep was the most conspicuous aspect of Sing Sing life. Outside their cells inmates marched in group formations of fifty or sixty to meals and workshops. The first individual stepped in advance and marked time, followed by a line of fellow inmates, each of whom placed his right hand on the right shoulder of the prisoner in front of him, his left hand on the same inmate's hip. After lining up they moved in unison in military step, as "close as sardines in a box," wrote one observer. The striped dress, the uniform motion, and the slow-moving mass gave them, wrote another, "the appearance of a gigantic reptile." The physically tight, marching formation enabled guards to monitor more than fifty inmates at once and prevent them

*The lockstep.*

from sneaking away. The lockstep remained a part of New York prison life until 1900.[27]

Pilsbury's rediscovered emphasis on discipline and control was not lost on potential contractors, who quickly came forth to bid on the now-disciplined convict labor. By the end of his first year he bragged that every Sing Sing inmate was employed, making the prison self-supporting. Whereas only 558 of Sing Sing's 1,139 convicts were employed on contract labor in 1872, at least 87 percent of them were so employed by the end of 1877. As Appo noted, Pilsbury expanded stove foundry production so significantly that by 1879 about 80 percent of Sing Sing's 1,253 inmates labored in that shop. By the end of 1878 Sing Sing's budget showed a surplus of $43,000, a vast turnaround from the $258,000 deficit two years previous.[28]

PILSBURY'S REFORMS marked a sea change in American incarceration. Sing Sing inmates were like machines, declared one former warden, "wound up in the morning to work so many hours, and at night laid away to remain silent and motionless until the morning came again." Another concurred, noting the absence of talking, idling, and smoking in the prison workshops: "As the machinery, so the prisoners." New York penitentiaries were little more than large factories where profit determined most things, with convict bodies sold to the highest bidder.[29]

More important for inmates like Appo, the Pilsbury reforms reinforced the shift in power and control over inmates from wardens and guards to private, outside contractors. Inmates were placed in various shops based on the interests of contractors. Even inmates' cell assignments were determined by outside employers. Contractor favoritism and the offering of "overwork rewards" to certain inmates enabled, wrote one critic, "the worst and most degraded fellows to secure the greatest advantage in prison." Favored inmates thus imposed "a system of terrorism" on other prisoners, admitted one contract superintendent.[30]

In reality such rewards corrupted not only the contract labor system but the very purpose of the penitentiary. In 1871 one Sing Sing contractor admitted that he and other contractors did "things which we knew were contrary to good discipline." Usually this meant paying convicts and keepers an additional six to ten dollars monthly. He insisted that all contractors did this. Another claimed that keepers earned more money from contractors than as state employees. Contractors, shop superintendents, keepers, and guards admitted to introducing contraband articles to motivate convicts in return for extra work. In time a combination of bartering and monetary exchange emerged, enabling guards, contractors, and civilian employees to ignore formal prison rules and give small "benefits"— liquor, mail, newspapers, coffee, sugar, food, extra tobacco—to select prisoners.[31]

Pilsbury's regime represented an open and public rejection of the rehabilitative ideal. Penitentiaries existed not to transform the character or temperament of inmates, as reformers half a century earlier had argued. Pilsbury, like many critics of prison reform, believed that the purpose of prison was retributive. Once convicts were released, few returned to "honest work," he believed. Not surprisingly Pilsbury was a staunch opponent of such reforms as indeterminate sentencing and parole. Prisons were for punishment: Rehabilitation was a "senseless notion" propagated by "morbid sentimentalists." Military order and coerced labor transformed New York's prisons into profit-making ventures.[32]

## PUNISHMENT AND INMATE LIFE

Crucial to the maintenance of Sing Sing's internal social and economic order were torture and punishment. Torture—sometimes called "third-degree methods" and "hard-boiled discipline"—was such a common part of Sing Sing life that future warden Lewis Lawes claimed that in the 1870s, "repression and physical suppression were the last words in penal administration."[33]

According to official pronouncements Sing Sing punishments during the 1870s were not severe compared with earlier years. Before they were outlawed in 1847, flogging and whipping with the cat-o'-nine-tails were the most often-used punishments. But these were soon replaced with equally terrifying mechanisms of pain: the yoke, the buck, and the shower bath. The yoke—sometimes called the crucifix—entailed strapping prisoners by their outstretched arms and neck to a thirty- to fifty-pound iron bar. The weight of the bar forced inmates to bend forward, imposing the bar's total weight on the lower vertebrae. Soon the arms numbed, hands swelled, and fingers turned purple. As an instrument "of torture and death," some argued that the yoke was worse than the lash.

In the buck an inmate's wrists were tied together in front of his knees. A stick was then passed between the legs and arms, thereby doubling up and binding the body. The stick was then raised onto chairs, forcing the body to swing down. The inmate then had a "choice": allow his head to hang down and let the blood rush to it, or hold up his head by the muscles of his neck. Finally, a convict subjected to the shower bath was stripped naked, held in stocks with his head encased in a troughlike collar tightly secured around his neck. Near-freezing water was then poured over the convict's head. After reaching "high tide," the inmate was threatened with drowning.[34]

Sing Sing administrators emphasized in their official reports that most punishments did not involve the physical assault of convicts. As in Appo's case, officials resorted to the dark cell, also called the "dungeon" and "the cooler," and an early version of solitary confinement. Sing Sing authorities used ordinary cells three and one half feet wide, seven feet long, and six and one half feet high; covered up all sources of light; and removed all furnishings except for the slop bucket. In some cases inmates were shackled to the floor. Convicts were thus forced to live on three slices of bread and water in cold darkness for days if not weeks at a time. By 1875 and 1876 more than a thousand of the more than thirteen hundred annual punishments were in the dark cell. The practice continued into the twentieth century.[35]

Appo's experience, however, reflected a hidden world of prison discipline. Specifically, prison officials ignored the ban on corporal punishment after 1869. Most often the principal keeper or his designated assistants were responsible for administering such penalties, the most common of which was the paddle, vividly described by Appo above, literally a twenty-five-by-four-inch perforated board. Upon striking the victim, by one account, "the apertures acted as suckers which raised blisters on the flesh and sometimes brought parts of it away." One principal keeper admitted that some convicts received from one hundred to two hundred blows. An inmate working just outside the principal keeper's office claimed that he counted three hundred blows on several occasions. Most, however, submitted after less than a dozen. The punishment remained in effect until at least 1882.[36]

Guards and inmates alike considered the paddle a form of torture. Inmate Joseph Morgan testified that a paddled inmate once pulled down his pants in front of him, "and his bottom was like a piece of raw liver."

Dominick J. Killoran testified that not only was one African American teenage inmate unable to sit down for four days after a paddling, but his buttock was so discolored that it "looked as though it had been dyed." Three other inmates' posteriors, he observed, "were all the colors of the rainbow." Guard Norman Blodgett testified that he quit Sing Sing because he could not bear to hear "the moaning and groaning of those fellows" who were paddled. At dinner he passed men silently crying, "Catholics particularly, praying to the Virgin." On learning that they were about to be paddled, some terrified inmates attempted suicide by jumping off the third- and fourth-floor galleries.[37]

More invidious to inmates was the arbitrary imposition of many physical punishments. Sing Sing guards and agents, for example, were permitted to strike inmates with any object that came to hand. "We have no rule any more than judgment," testified one Sing Sing keeper. Guards, keepers, and contractors admitted that many punishments occurred hastily and went unreported to the principal keeper, who was responsible for keeping a log of all punishments. Shop foremen, for example, punished inmates on the shop floor for refusing to work or performing poor work. Keepers regularly sent convicts to the dark cell without informing the principal keeper.[38]

Official statistics indicate that these penal practices were commonplace in Sing Sing. In 1864 Sing Sing officials issued 1,403 punishments to 796 inmates, including one who was punished twenty-two times. Public opposition convinced the legislature to abolish all kinds of corporal punishment, except "the dark cell to curb the insubordinate" in 1869. Over the next five years only 350 to 400 punishments were officially recorded in Sing Sing. But beginning in 1874, the year of Appo's first admission to the prison, officials gave out 682 punishments, including 390 in dark cells. During the ensuing two years, things grew worse. Guards issued more than 1,350 official punishments in 1875 and 1,433 in 1876, virtually one per prisoner. In each year more than 1,000 of the punishments were the dark cell.[39]

The impact of such arbitrary, informal, and publicly hidden forms of punishment was profound. Originally, harsh discipline—however severe or cruel—was justified as a tool of rehabilitation. But with the growing emphasis on profits, physical coercion was increasingly employed to extract more labor from convicts. Contractors enjoyed considerable leeway in the punishment of prisoners, reporting unproductive or rebellious inmates to keepers who then inflicted punishments. While Pilsbury claimed that the financial success of New York prisons was accomplished "without resort to cruel and unnecessary punishments," official records indicate otherwise. By the 1870s more than half of all prison punishments were related to the contract labor system. Solitary confinement was one means of punishing poor work; inflicting physical pain and torture was another. One former Sing Sing convict charged that men were "butchered to death because they couldn't do the task assigned them." *Harper's Weekly* claimed that Sing Sing inmates were "condemned to work when they are on the verge of death."[40]

Punishments designed to torture and terrorize affected inmate life in two fundamental ways. The first came in the form of resistance, specifically attempted escapes. Before the completion of the surrounding wall and fence in 1879, escapes from Sing Sing were commonplace. From 1870 to 1876 Sing Sing official reports reveal an average of more than ten escapes annually. Even after 1880 officials admitted that escapes from Sing Sing were "frequent," although they diminished after 1884.[41]

In the year prior to Appo's first admission, twenty-seven different individuals escaped from Sing Sing. In 1874 Sing Sing officials conceded that convict escapes were frequent and easy because a network of former keepers and burglars systematically assisted convicts.[42] But most inmates never conspired with Sing Sing guards. Some simply sneaked out of the quarry. A few tried to leave via the river (a route most avoided because they could not swim). Others hijacked passing Hudson River Railroad trains. Some were quite creative. In 1872 friends of convicted bank robber Ned Lyons sent bogus invitations to the funeral of newspaper editor and presidential candidate Horace Greeley to the warden, agent, and clerk of Sing Sing. While the officials were away, Lyons donned civilian clothes and jumped into a waiting carriage just outside the prison.[43]

A second impact of torturous punishment was the successful suppression of organized inmate resistance. Convicts occasionaly protested against the inhumane living conditions. In 1874, for example, convicts led by "Black Jim" refused to work on the grounds claiming that they were maltreated by several keepers. In 1883 more than four hundred inmates refused to work and expressed their discontent with the contract system. Reportedly fourteen fights broke out between inmates and guards, convincing Warden Augustus A. Brush that the prison population was on the verge of revolt.[44] But such incidents were noteworthy, in part, because of their infrequency.

More striking was the virtual absence of gangs in Sing Sing. On the surface, conditions were ripe for communal feelings among teenage and young adult males to blossom. Just prior to Appo's admittance to Sing Sing in 1874, the Prison Association complained about "the appalling percentage of minors immured in our State prisons." During Appo's first term in Sing Sing, 16 percent (307 in number) of the 1,877 new inmates were nineteen years old or less. Since teenagers intermingled, worked, and socialized with older inmates, "there is little chance for reformation," conceded one report.[45]

More significantly not only were the majority of Sing Sing's inmates residents of New York City, but many were Appo's teenage neighbors. The youthful, teenage subculture of Donovan's Lane and Five Points literally followed him into Sing Sing. During Appo's first Sing Sing incarceration at least fifteen newly admitted teenage inmates resided within a few blocks of Appo's Donovan's Lane home; by his second incarceration at least twenty-three teenagers were fellow Five Pointers.[46]

Despite these mutual geographic and generational associations, however, organized or collective action by convicts was rare. Appo found none of the oppositional prison subculture that would typify twentieth-century incarceration. Absent was even a communal identity among fellow larcenists. At least a dozen of the nation's leading pickpockets identified in Thomas Byrnes's *Professional Criminals of America* (1886) served time simultaneously with Appo between 1874 and 1876.[47] Appo never mentioned any interaction with them.

The coercive regime of Sing Sing stifled gang recruitment several ways. Guards—"inhuman brutes," in Appo's words—exercised arbitrary power and punishment. Inmates were granted only one personal visitor every two months, and newspapers were prohibited. Inmates were cut off from their immediate families, while experiencing a physically coercive internment with the lockstep, corporal punishment, hard manual labor, and poor sanitary conditions. Courts treated inmates as "slaves of the state," offering them no access to the legal system.[48] In Sing Sing privileges and punishments alike were random, based on personal circumstances, and ultimately subject to the individual whims of guards, contractors, and prison officials.

This carceral regime was dramatically different from that of the late-twentieth-century penitentiary. Most prisons after 1960 were dominated by prison gangs, sometimes with memberships exceeding one hundred. Many gang members were motivated by militant political ideologies; invoked rhetoric and language associated with various movements based on race, religion, or gender; benefited from greater internal freedom (access to television, physical exercise, college extension courses, libraries); and displayed a limited interest in social change within their communities. Such inmates considered the gang a surrogate family and a source of personal identity. Many admitted that the gang provided a sense of belonging and made them "feel like a man."[49]

In Appo's Sing Sing, punishment no longer served merely to discipline or "morally improve" inmates' character. Nor were punishments intended simply to increase production. Corporal punishment in the form of torture enabled prison officials to humiliate and psychologically emasculate inmates. The irregular, unpredictable, and capricious implementation by guards, keepers, and private contractors transformed punishment into an indiscriminate form of terror. Secreted from public knowledge and impulsive in implementation, these punishments gave inmates no recourse of protest, mortified both body and mind, and attacked the very manhood of inmates. A carceral ideal intended to rehabilitate and reform thus evolved into a system of cruelty and contempt. Just as the whip epitomized the violence indigenous to American slavery, so the paddle evoked the hidden terror inherent in Sing Sing.

Sing Sing's torturous industrial discipline humiliated and broke the spirit of many an inmate. But it did little to change their behavior on leaving the penitentiary. Depressed, dispirited, and in his words "injured for life," Appo was released on 2 April 1876.[50] He quickly returned to pickpocketing.

# 5

# The "Guns" of Gotham

=

*◦ When I was released from Sing Sing Prison [on 2 April 1876], I had to go to St. Luke's Hospital to be operated on by Professors Otis and Peters. After nearly three months under good medical treatment, I left the hospital. As I had no means or way to obtain the necessities of life, I naturally went back to stealing for a living. But the two years in state prison made me wiser than before so I left New York and went to Philadelphia, where I remained about four months and then returned to New York looking very prosperous.*

*The year was the Centennial Year, 1876, and near to a close, the time being November. New York City was full of strangers from all parts of the world, and the crooks were all doing well, in general, at their business. In fact, New York was overrun with crooks from the West. . . . I soon became intimately acquainted with the crooks and learned many ways and means to earn money dishonestly with not so much risk as picking pockets, but I could not read nor write and my mode of talking was too slangy. Therefore, I could not operate with safety and success as my general appearance was against me, so I had to continue picking pockets.[1]*

THE SECOND HALF of the nineteenth century was the era of the "gun"—the pickpocket—in American cities. "Of all the departments of crime as now practiced," admitted America's most famous private detective, Allan Pinkerton, in 1884, "there is not one which contains a larger number of adept operators than that of pickpockets." As regards New York, Pinkerton was right. From 1861 to 1863 the municipality successfully convicted only 74 individuals for larceny. But a decade later, from 1873 to 1875, 519 felons landed in the state penitentiary for the same offense. The period from 1866 to 1887 might better be described as the age of larceny. During those two decades larceny comprised between one-third and one-half of all crimes in New York State. In the words of one pickpocket, the decades following the Civil War were "the halcyon days for us."[2]

Yet pickpocketing was a poorly defined crime. Although the act was among the most common and frequently mentioned transgressions in the nineteenth-century city, it never appeared in any criminal code. Picking a pocket or snatching a purse was larceny, "one of the primordial crimes of Western culture," according to the legal historian George Fletcher. Larceny, however, was never authoritatively defined until the twentieth century. Judges punished such acts on the simple assumption that they knew what it was—taking the goods of another. Hence no clear boundaries separated larceny from burglary and robbery.[3]

Similarly the precise dimensions of the pickpocket's world remain impossible to measure. Purloined goods were rarely recovered, and even smaller proportions of pickpockets were ever prosecuted. In the seventeen known years in which George Appo worked as a pickpocket, for example, he was arrested for and convicted of larceny four times. To the average law-abiding citizen, four convictions were considerable. But Appo picked hundreds—quite possibly thousands—of pockets *without* being apprehended. Once, while working a county fair outside Toronto, Appo pickpocketed approximately twenty-five different individuals.[4] His four arrests for pickpocketing quite likely account for less—maybe much less—than 1 percent of all his thefts.

Pickpockets like Appo were part of a distinctive criminal order. Numerous observers described pickpockets as "professional thieves" and "artists," part of a social underground fraternity with hidden rules and practices. Allan Pinkerton believed that criminal subcultures replicated the American middle class by dividing into specialized professions, each concerned with their own particular status and reputation. Petty crooks operated in social isolation, noted writer James D. McCabe, Jr., but pickpockets were different: They "have certain habits, attitudes, haunts; they act in certain ways when placed in certain positions." For George Appo such people were "good fellows," individuals who refused to cooperate with law enforcement authorities, who eschewed testifying against enemies. "What constitutes a Good Fellow in the eyes and estimation of the underworld is a nervy crook, a money getter and spender," wrote Appo. A good fellow valiantly accepted the consequences and punishment of an arrest, even if the crime was committed by another.[5] A good fellow was a member of a fraternity of thieves.

This fraternity shared a distinctive, arcane language. One reporter confessed that he found pickpockets impossible to comprehend, sounding as if they spoke a foreign tongue. Pickpockets referred to their accomplices (numbering two to six) as "mobs." The streets, parks, or trolleys where they worked were "beats." Pocketbooks were "leathers," and money was a "roll." The actual larceny was a "touch," which was performed by a "wire," a "pick," a "bugger," or a "tool," while "stalls" distracted or jostled the victim. The "cover" made sure the theft took place unobserved. The novelist Herman Melville described the underworld vocabulary as "the foulest of all human lingoes, that dialect of sin and death, known as the Cant language, or the Flash."[6]

This specialized argot even delineated the geography of the illicit trade. "Kirkbuzzers" worked in churches. "Reader merchants" operated around banks. "Carbuzzers" rode streetcars, omnibuses, and other forms of public transport. "Groaners" attended charity sermons. Some pickpockets specialized by working certain kinds of crowds, be they in railroad stations, streetcars, steamboat landings, theaters, racetracks, churches, markets, or busy street corners. Certain pickpockets assumed labels according to *whom* they robbed. Those who preyed entirely on women were "Moll-buzzers" or "flies" that "buzz" around women.[7]

When necessary pickpockets went on a "jump-out," traveling to fairs, circuses, racetracks, sporting events—in essence, any large assembly or festivity in a nearby town. Swarms of pickpockets followed traveling circus shows as they moved about the country. Some concentrated on certain types of public gatherings, such as funerals, weddings, and parades. Such "rovers" literally roamed the United States in search of such gatherings, forcing police officials to take special precautions. For example, before the ceremonies surrounding Ulysses S. Grant's funeral, the opening of the Statue of Liberty, and the Centennial of the Constitution, New York's chief detective, Thomas Byrnes, ordered the summary arrest of all known pickpockets, including Appo. The practice—known as "caging"— was "truly a bold one," admitted Byrnes, "but the ends certainly justified the means." Detectives literally waited at the city's railway stations and arrested suspects on their arrival. The policy continued into the twentieth century.[8]

Pickpocket mobs working in specialized locations were probably the most successful in the fraternity. Arrest records indicate that individuals working alone—like Appo—were more likely to get caught. More than three-quarters of those prosecuted labored by themselves, and most were simply "working the street." Quite likely arrested pickpockets like Appo enjoyed no relationship with a "percentage copper"—a police officer who tolerated their pilferings for a bribe or "percentage" of their haul. Still, many ignored the danger. "If I needed a dollar quick I'd take any risk," admitted one pickpocket. "I'd jump on a car, and tackle the first sucker I saw."[9]

Streetcars—with more than 90 million annual riders nationwide by the 1880s—were among the most favored workplaces for pickpockets. Riders complained that the cars were so bumpy and crowded that it was impossible to feel the arms or hands of adjacent passengers. By the 1860s, New York streetcars conspicuously posted signs warning BEWARE OF PICKPOCKETS! Many passengers felt their pockets immediately on reading the warning, allowing conscientious thieves to determine which ones to pick. Nearly a decade later, a state assembly report admitted that well-known pickpockets routinely boarded streetcars, "hustled" passengers with ease, and made "scarcely any concealment of the matter." If a conductor resisted or warned passengers, pickpockets simply took "the first opportunity to knock him on the head."

Harper's Weekly *satirized streetcars as "Pickpocket's Paradise."*

Conversely, sympathetic drivers frequently worked in league with pickpockets.[10]

Pickpockets did not often knock people on the head, however. The craft attracted individuals who avoided violence. "Knockdown pickpockets"—individuals who physically assaulted pedestrians, snatched the object, and immediately ran away—were rare. "The pickpocket never commits violence, as the footpad, the burglar or the garroter does," concluded one detective. "He performs his work unostentatiously, unobtrusively—I might say delicately." Pickpocket dress and fashion placed a premium on blending into the general populace. Law enforcement officials like George Washington Walling argued that leading pickpockets were "stylishly dressed, easy in their manners and correct in speech." Pickpockets like Jim Caulfield confirmed as much, emphasizing that they always tried to be neat, clean, and as fashionable as possible. An attractive personal appearance, he admitted, was part of "the capital of a grafter."[11]

Pickpockets may have differed over precisely where and how they worked, but they shared certain demographic characteristics. First, picking pockets was a young man's game. More than three-quarters (80 percent) of those arrested were male, more than half (56 percent) being fifteen to twenty-four years of age. Like Appo, however, many pickpockets continued working well into adulthood. (Appo's final conviction occurred when he was twenty-six.) Fully a quarter of all arrested pickpockets during these years were twenty-five to twenty-nine years old, and another 17 percent continued their stealthful ways throughout their thirties. Less than 4 percent were forty or over. Finally pickpockets were striking in their affluence. Among the more than 150 different occupations claimed by arrested pickpockets, 60 percent identified themselves as skilled craftsmen or higher-status professionals—49 percent claimed that they labored in occupations such as blacksmithing, cabinetmaking, and machine making, while another 11 percent were clerks, bookkeepers, and shopkeepers. A few even described themselves as "gentlemen" and "entrepreneurs."[12]

Females were part of this criminal fraternity. Detective Allan Pinkerton, for example, believed that female thieves were as successful as their male competitors. His counterpart and rival detective, Thomas Byrnes, even considered female pickpockets to be more dangerous. Like their male counterparts, many women worked in "mobs" and directed their pirating toward men. Most significantly female pickpockets tended to be poorer than men, the majority occupying the lowliest wage-labor positions, such as servants and prostitutes; more than half were associated with a brothel, concert saloon, barroom, or boardinghouse. Sex was the lure.[13] Michael Springer, for example, agreed to treat several females in an East Tenth Street restaurant. After ordering wine and sitting down beside one young woman, Springer suddenly felt her hand in his pants. "What are you doing with your hand in my pocket?" he asked. Sexual stimulation was not her purpose—Springer was missing $273.[14]

Pickpockets prospered in nineteenth-century New York and other urban centers for many reasons. First, the forced, physical intimacy of the new, densely packed industrial city made picking pockets easy. "It's only a big city that can furnish one of this craft with his daily supply of purses and pocketbooks, jewelry and small wares," declared one observer. Moreover, fashion encouraged pickpocketing. For most of the nineteenth century, men tended to carry valuables in their coats, not their pants.

Before the Civil War frock coats tended to be long, extending to the midthigh, if not the knee, and providing a protective cover for the front pants pocket. But after 1860 the shortened length of frock coats facilitated pickpocketing. Although overcoats were longer, they included external pockets with no flaps. By midcentury many New Yorkers argued that a majority of the city's pickpockets were newsboys and bootblacks who learned the technique during cold weather when pedestrians wore overcoats with external change pockets.[15]

During the final decades of the century, frock coats were replaced by the popular sack coat. "Every man in America, multi-millionaire as well as laborer, wears a sack coat," wrote one designer. "It is the great American business coat,

*A sack coat.*

*Frock coats did not discourage pickpockets.*

and in other countries is recognized as the badge of the American." Sack coats were short, extended to the waist, included a small collar, and offered comfort and easy movement. Most important, with a plentiful number of pockets, the sack was a coat waiting for a pickpocket.[16]

Most men on the street did not guard their valuables with proper care. Gentlemen routinely kept their watches in the lower vest pockets, making them easy objects to steal without detection. Allan Pinkerton complained that people were naive, putting bankbooks and money in outside pockets, thinking that a robbery was impossible if they kept their hand on their pocket. Pickpockets simply distracted such people and removed their wallets. After one arrest George Appo recounted how the judge gave his victim "a lecture on his carelessness with his valuables, as such was the cause of leading boys into temptation to steal."[17]

Female clothing was even easier to pilfer. Nineteenth-century women generally wore layers of clothing, some with long skirts and hoops underneath, making it difficult to detect the touch of a pickpocket. On street-cars and other forms of public transit, the dresses of seated women frequently fell over the legs of passengers sitting beside them. Pickpockets then simply slid a hand underneath the dress and cut out the pocket.[18]

A third contributing factor to the rise of pickpocketing was tolerance by law enforcement officials. "The old system," wrote journalist Lincoln Steffens, "was built upon the understood relations of the crooks and the detective bureau." "Professional" criminals were allowed to operate "within reason." For pickpockets specific blocks or streetcars were divided among themselves, each of whom had a "monopoly." In return for such privileges, pickpockets reported on others who violated such agreements, and were expected to return stolen goods on police request.[19]

When larceny on streetcars grew excessive, "the riot act was read to the dips," claimed one pickpocket. Some pickpockets were "shaken down" by police, forced to pay a bribe or risk arrest.[20] Other cops resorted to "four-flushing"—arrest an old crook or "doormat thief," portray it as a big arrest, and ignore the more important criminals. During the 1860s well-known burglars and pickpockets like William Vosburg and Dan Noble reportedly bribed police officials in central headquarters on a weekly basis. Some police detectives were so familiar with certain pickpockets that they could identify them from a simple description of when and how a victim lost his or her possessions. Even when the police hauled pickpockets into court, they hired clever attorneys who fought these arrests with writs of habeas corpus.[21]

But the greatest incentive for pickpockets was the exorbitant amount of cash in people's pockets. Nineteenth-century businessmen, bank messengers, and ordinary pedestrians routinely carried large quantities of money and other valuables on their persons. This was especially true in the Wall Street area before 1880. "It is remarkable," concluded another detective, "how careless business men are about their watches, however valuable they may be." Some cases involved extraordinary sums. In 1866 a Williamsburg Bank messenger was picked clean on his way to the Park National Bank of New York with a satchel containing fourteen thousand dollars in cash and checks. The carpet manufacturer J. H. Higgins was separated from the sixteen thousand dollars he was carrying to pay his workers' wages. A federal judge was pickpocketed at an apple stand at

Nassau and Liberty Streets in the 1870s while carrying seventy-five thousand dollars' worth of bonds in his wallet.[22]

Appo himself admitted that it was easy to get rich quick. After a few days of pickpocketing, he usually accumulated six to eight hundred dollars. Once while traveling through Toronto, Canada, he went on a "jump out." "There was a big county fair going on," he recalled, "and I left the fair grounds with $600 and 22 watches." Court cases confirm that Appo's success was not unusual. For victims who prosecuted their pocket pickers between 1859 and 1876, the median cash value of all purloined money was thirty dollars (roughly four hundred dollars in early-twenty-first-century dollars). One-quarter lost more than one hundred dollars (equivalent to nearly fifteen hundred dollars today). Examples abound of individuals losing astonishing amounts. Leonard Haskin unknowingly surrendered $1,478 to a pickpocket in the Hudson River Railroad Depot. James McKenna lost $977 while walking the street. Frank Linton absconded with $2,767 from an unidentified woman on the street. The $4,440 in Harvey Nevins's pocket disappeared after he sauntered down Nassau Street. George Boyden lost $6,252 to a pickpocket on a Brooklyn streetcar. Charles Gibbons, a self-described "gentleman," proved less gentlemanly when he pilfered $900 from detective George McWaters's pocket.[23]

Necessity demanded that pedestrians carry significant sums of money. (Credit cards did not become a financial instrument until the twentieth century.) Only a minority of Americans entrusted their money to banks, so few people rendered payments with personal checks. Even then, many merchants refused such forms of payment, especially from strangers. Hence to purchase most goods—expensive or cheap—shoppers had to carry cash. This reality made the streets of New York and other American cities pickpocket heaven.

The perception that pickpocketing was an increasingly common urban experience produced a hostile public reaction. Prior to the Civil War, pickpockets evoked little public fear. Novelists like George Thompson treated such thievery as a unique urban adventure, while George Foster portrayed the best pickpockets as "genteel." Even the detective Thomas Byrnes described pickpockets as "an interesting class of thieves." One newspaper openly acknowledged that "a tinge of romance [was] connected with the profession of picking pockets."[24]

The romance disappeared after 1870. In that decade, New Yorkers were besieged with numerous publications warning residents of the dangers presented by pickpockets and other criminals. Charles Loring Brace's *The Dangerous Classes of New York and Twenty Years Among Them* (1872) and Edward Crapsey's *The Nether Side of New York; or, the Vice, Crime and Poverty of the Great Metropolis* (1872) were but two examples reflecting a new consciousness of the city's criminal dangers. The New York State Assembly even created a special select committee in 1875 to investigate and address Gotham's growing crime rate.

Critics of crime frequently singled out pickpockets for attack. In 1883 the newspaper *Truth* declared that the pickpocket was "the meanest of criminals . . . , the sneaking weasel of society." Trials should be quick, sentences extreme (two to five years of hard labor), and justice summary. Pickpockets and similar thieves should be "showed no mercy." Nearly a decade later the *Times* classified the thieves and pickpockets who loitered around Chatham Square and the Bowery as Gotham's worst criminals. For detective Thomas Byrnes, the pickpocket was a contagion, like a case of smallpox in a tenement: "He is a menace to all about him, and should be put where he could do no damage."[25]

Criminal prosecutions of pickpockets reflected this growing fear. Between 1859 and 1876 the number of pickpockets brought to trial by the district attorney nearly quintupled, increasing from 52 to 242. Since no systematic sentencing policy existed in New York's criminal courts, judges enjoyed wide discretion to crack down whenever and on whomever they wanted. Examples abound reflecting the judicial intolerance of street crime. One thirty-four-year-old pickpocket received a five-year sentence for picking $210. A twenty-two-year-old stole ten cents; the judge sentenced him to two and a half years in the penitentiary. Upon learning that a thirty-five-year-old female was an experienced pickpocket, the judge sentenced her to five years in prison, specifically "to protect the community from pickpockets." Even pleas of poverty and contrition fell upon deaf ears. Young, unemployed men begged judges for mercy, only to be sent to Sing Sing for terms ranging from two to five years.[26]

Youthful mischief likewise engendered little judicial sympathy. One fourteen-year-old Irish immigrant was convicted of stealing one dollar; for that he was sent to the House of Refuge for a year. When two teenagers, in separate cases, were convicted of pilfering fifty cents, they each received three-year sentences. Similarly one nineteen-year-old was sent to Sing Sing for five years for stealing eighty cents; another was given four years for absconding with five cents.[27]

These harsh punishments reflected a new conception of larceny. During the second half of the nineteenth century, Anglo-American courts expanded the law of larceny to encompass a broader range of cases and common law. Whereas earlier larceny law was based on "stealthful or forcible conduct," new interpretations of such criminal behavior encompassed taking that was outwardly innocent. As criminal law increasingly protected social interests, police and courts intervened prior to the occurrence of harm. Hence larceny came to be defined as a crime against property, and police began arresting suspects as soon as they simply touched another with the intent to steal.[28]

In fact larceny (and hence pickpocketing) was treated more severely in New York City than in the rest of New York State. In 1860 the legislature passed a law applicable only to the city whereby any "stealing, taking and carrying away" of property from a person was to be treated as grand larceny, even if the property was less than twenty-five dollars in value. Simply touching a potential victim, or even his or her clothing, now constituted an assault with intent to steal, irrespective of whether any violence was inflicted. One judge later remarked that these statutes deliberately addressed a defect in criminal law that previously rendered pickpocket convictions difficult if not impossible.[29]

In reality "degrees" of grand larceny now meant little. Any intent to take something was a felony, irrespective of the amount or value of the article. Stealing $499 from a safe in the daytime was grand larceny in the second degree with a maximum sentence of five years. By contrast picking a man's pocket of a train ticket after sunset was grand larceny in the first degree with a maximum sentence of ten years. In fact picking pockets was more severely punished than stealing trademarks, counterfeiting labels, adulterating food or drugs, declaring an unearned dividend on stock, or committing corporate fraud. Those crimes were simple misdemeanors. Nineteenth-century law, concluded the attorney Arthur Train, distinguished the grafter from the professional thief, the bribed politician from the bank robber.[30]

In general the New York ninteenth-century judiciary was extraordinarily lenient in meting out punishments from 1830 to 1880. Violent crimes like assault and battery were punished with fines, probation, and indeterminate sentences 25 percent of the time. Serious offenses like rape and manslaughter were rarely penalized with prison terms approaching the available statutory maximum. In the most comprehensive examination of New York City's 1,560 murders from 1800 to 1875, the historian Eric Monkkonen found that only 10.7 percent of all murderers were caught, tried, and convicted. Of those convicted 75 percent were sentenced to seven or fewer years in prison; only 2 percent (thirty-one total) were executed.[31]

Not so with pickpockets. After 1870 New York's judges punished such convicts not only with increasing severity but with more rigor than murderers. Of the twenty-one convicted pickpockets sentenced in the Court of General Sessions in 1859 and 1864 for stealing one hundred dollars or more, only two, or 10 percent, received sentences of three years or more. By contrast after 1871 54 percent of pickpockets convicted of stealing one hundred dollars or more received such stern sentences. Meanwhile, two-thirds of those convicted of stealing one dollar or less were sentenced to one or more years, and nearly half drew sentences in excess of two years. Perhaps most significant was that sentences longer than four years were rare before 1870, but thereafter 12 percent were given such punishments.[32]

Appo confronted this changing judicial reality on multiple occasions. Recorder John K. Hackett, for example, was well known for his unremitting hatred of pickpockets. Once, while sitting on the bench, he proclaimed "that the law ought to condemn them to be shot." On another occasion Hackett instructed a jury that simply because a purloined watch was not found in the possession of a pickpocket was no reason to acquit, because "pickpockets generally went in couples." The jury rendered a verdict of guilty; Hackett happily sentenced him to five years in Sing Sing.[33]

This was not unusual. Between 1871 and 1874 Hackett issued harsh sentences to a variety of pickpockets. One Civil War widow and former inmate in a lunatic asylum received a five-year sentence from Hackett. He sentenced another man to five years in Sing Sing for stealing a sixty-dollar watch. One boy caught robbing his mother of eight dollars was sentenced to twenty-five years in prison. And on 3 April 1874, Hackett sentenced seventeen-year-old George Dixon, better known as George Appo, to two and a half years in Sing Sing.[34]

Another judicial adversary of pickpockets was Henry A. Gildersleeve. "Dear old Gildy," as his friends called him, was a Civil War veteran who ultimately captained the American rifle team to a world championship. Elected judge of the Court of General Sessions in 1875, he served until 1889, when he failed to be reelected because of opposition from the city's liquor dealers. For a short time he returned to the private practice of law. By 1891, however, he was back on the bench, serving first as a justice of the New York Superior Court from 1891 to 1896 and then on the New York Supreme Court until 1911. During his judicial career Gildersleeve disposed of more than fifteen thousand criminal cases, decisions that were reportedly reversed in only two instances. The writer Francis Wellman described him as a "gentler, milder mannered judge" who never issued a death sentence.[35]

*Judge Henry A. Gildersleeve.*

Gildersleeve's mild manner, however, rarely extended to pickpockets. In 1876, for example, a seventeen-year-old Five Points clerk was accused of pilfering a watch. Authorities never found the purloined item on the young man. The owner admitted that the watch was relatively inexpensive, worth only eighteen dollars. The defendant consistently denied the charge. And even on convicting, the jury recommended leniency. Gildersleeve ignored all this; he sentenced the accused to three years in prison. Such property crimes, he believed, reflected "a spirit of lawlessness, bred of extravagance or greed of great riches," which was "spreading throughout our community." Gildersleeve concluded that a new "class of criminals" now existed.[36]

Six months later Appo came before Judge Gildersleeve:

❧ *In the month of December, 1876, I was again arrested for picking the pockets of Arad Gilbert, of a gold watch. I pleaded guilty on January 9th, 1877, and was sentenced by Judge Gildersleeve to State Prison for a term of two years and six months at hard labor.*[37]

# 6

# Drafted

=

*On my arrival at the Sing Sing Prison, I was assigned to work by the doctor out in the open air, wheeling sand. I worked outdoors for about six months and during the course of that time, I learned to read and write pretty good through the kind and patient teaching of an old German scholar with whom I had the good fortune to be doubled up in the same cell. This man was 70 years old and pleaded guilty to forgery and was sentenced to two years and six months. His name was Louis Stein. I was then transferred from outdoor work to the jail hall as an assistant tier boy. The work was very hard and the confinement and dampness of the place made me very sick after four months work.*

*I was then taken and sent away in a "draft" with fifty other convicts to the Clinton State Prison at Dannemora, where I was put to work chopping and sawing wood. In those days there was no coal used at the prison. All fires were burning log woods and there were no railroads running from Plattsburg to the prison, about 17 miles. It was very tough to be shackled hand and feet, put into an open cart with no springs, and in the coldest part of the winter with no covering and carried from Plattsburg Railroad Station to the prison over the rough mountain road, those 17 miles and with nothing to eat or drink save the water on the train from Sing Sing to Dannemora.[1]*

On 13 October 1877 George Appo was drafted. Reflecting the emphasis on contract labor and industrial production, New York's three major prisons borrowed, or "drafted," convicts from one another whenever they suffered a labor shortage. Equally important, Sing Sing relied on drafts to relieve overcrowding, and the years of Appo's second Sing Sing incarceration were among the most overcrowded in the prison's history. Official

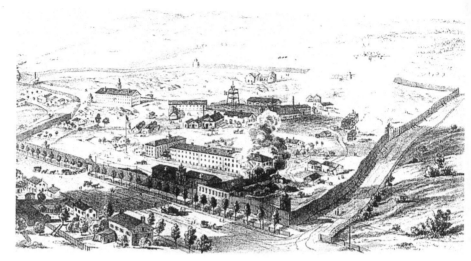

*Clinton State Prison in 1869.*

reports listed the year-end populations in both 1877 and 1878 in excess of sixteen hundred souls. By contrast Clinton penitentiary's population hovered around six hundred.[2]

Established in 1845, Clinton State Prison was nestled at the base of the Adirondack Mountains in Dannemora, New York, seventeen miles west of Plattsburgh and twenty miles from the Canadian border. Because the town was located on top of a supposedly inexhaustible vein of iron ore, the community was christened "Dannemora," after a well-known Swedish mining center. Clinton, however, suffered from isolation, epitomized by poor roads, no nearby railroad station, and an elevation exceeding that of nearby Plattsburgh by seventeen hundred feet. The harsh environs led some prison officials to label the region "the Siberia of America."

State officials admitted that the prison was built in an isolated location to avoid competition "with the honest mechanical classes." They hoped inmates would mine the iron and thereby provide for their keep. But by the 1870s, 70 percent of the surrounding ten-thousand-acre forest was gone, cut down for wood and coal. A treeless six-mile landscape now surrounded the prison. Furthermore, the plentiful vein of ore proved to be so deep that it extended under private real estate, forcing New York

State to pay a royalty of one dollar per ton of mined ore to the neighboring property owners.[3]

Nevertheless, by the 1870s, from fifty to one hundred Clinton inmates annually mined iron ore. Two privately owned mines, nine hundred to one thousand feet in length, were located on the western edge of the prison complex. The ore was then forged into iron bars, metal plates, and nails in the prison's rolling mills. Clinton also burned forty thousand cords of wood annually to manufacture charcoal, much of which was then consumed in the prison forges.[4]

Appo's selection for the draft probably indicated that he suffered a poor relationship or a bad reputation with Sing Sing officials. Principal keeper Archibald Biglin himself acknowledged that no rules governed the process. Keepers generally informed the principal keeper of troublemaking inmates, who were then punished by drafting. Those drafted, whom Biglin described as "the hardest men," usually had the longest sentences and most punishments.[5]

Superintendent Louis Pilsbury claimed that drafts were beneficial to the health of inmates. The elevated location, clean air, generous diet, and plentiful employment at Clinton "arrested the progress of chronic diseases," believed Pilsbury. The healthy environs even justified transferring sick prisoners to Clinton.[6]

By the 1880s, however, prison officials increasingly acknowledged the drawbacks of drafting. Sing Sing warden Augustus Brush complained that many prisoners were poor, and their families and friends simply could not afford visits so far upstate. Clinton officials also believed that drafting was a way for Sing Sing and other prisons to get rid of undesirable inmates. In 1872 Warden John Parkhurst of Clinton complained that his prison ended up with "the sick, the lame, the imbecile and the decrepit." Worse yet, Sing Sing officials often sent prisoners during the severest part of the winter, further hastening their physical decline.[7]

In his fifteen months at Clinton, Appo managed to avoid the mines. At first he was assigned to work the furnaces that transformed wood into charcoal. But the contracted employer, after receiving payment from the state, left the wood exposed to the elements, rendering it worthless. Appo then moved to the hat-making operation, which employed more than two hundred inmates when he began in June 1878. The prison's contract labor force grew steadily during Appo's term in Clinton, accounting for 60 percent of the inmates by the end of the 1870s.[8]

Despite the severe climate, some believed that prison life was less harsh in Clinton than Sing Sing and Auburn. Although Clinton's cells were only slightly larger than those in the other prisons, the main hall was newer and less crowded than Sing Sing's, containing but 544 cells (compared to the nearly 1,200 in Sing Sing). Although doubling up of inmates took place during Appo's term in Clinton, the overcrowding was never as severe as in Sing Sing. Since Clinton lacked a common mess hall, inmates ate meals in their cells, offering a level of personal privacy absent in Sing Sing.[9]

More important, the extensive prison grounds at Clinton provided inmates with considerable space to roam about. Even more than Sing Sing, the Clinton complex was dotted with small houses and shanties for convicts to warm themselves during the winter months. Officials complained that these structures served as hiding places for convicts, enabling them to "cook, traffic and plot." Like Sing Sing, Clinton lacked extensive bathing facilities. There was one bathtub in the barbershop and a slightly larger facility in the hospital. During warm weather inmates bathed at the mines once a week. In wintertime they rarely even washed.[10]

Like their Sing Sing counterparts, numerous Clinton inmates enjoyed informal privileges that dramatically affected the quality of prison life. For example, convicts were given a weekly ration of tobacco, which many promptly exchanged with the prison employees and guards in return for a newspaper. Other prisoners claimed that alcohol was available for fifty cents a pint. And, as at Sing Sing, outside contractors introduced contraband articles to encourage convicts to do extra work.[11]

More often than not, prisoners with money simply bought privileges. One guard, for example, allowed a convict to cook and eat steak in his cell every Sunday night. Other officials permitted certain convicts to keep and maintain chickens and other fowl on the prison grounds. The most trustworthy inmates guarded entrances and ran outside errands for prison officials. During the 1890s Plattsburg residents testified that convicts were regularly seen visiting local hotels and saloons with female friends.[12] Appo, however, received no such benefits.

     *I had a tough deal from being hounded and punished by a keeper named Haggerty, who had charge of the jail hall. This keeper in 1878 and I had trouble with each other. In fact, he was the most inhuman brute that ever existed in my estimation and many a poor, unfortunate convict was driven insane and made sick unto death from this brute's inhuman treatment. He had charge of the dark cells and did most of the paddling of convicts under punishment at that time.*[13]

I had been reported for having a piece of a New York newspaper (The Herald) and reading it in my cell on a Sunday. The guard who caught me reading it unlocked my door and took me and the piece of newspaper to the guard room and the deputy warden asked me where I got it. I told him the truth, that I found it in the officers toilet. He demanded to know which one. I refused to tell him, not wishing to get my shop keeper or the contract foreman into trouble. Consequently, he ordered me locked up in the dark cell and kept there until I told where I got the newspaper. I was then taken and put in the "cooler," as the dark cells were called. As it was on a Sunday, keeper Haggerty was off duty for that day, but on Monday morning he came to the dark cells to feed the men in the coolers on two ounces of bread and a gill of water.

When he came to my door, he swung it violently open and shouted at me. "D—— you! Get up here and take your ration."

"I don't want it," I replied.

"You don't, hey? I'll bet you will before I get through with you," and he threw the little piece of bread at me and the gill of water on the cell floor, and then slammed the door and locked it.

In about an hour the deputy came with Haggerty, opened my door and said to me: "Have you made up your mind to tell me where you put that paper?"

"I have told you all that is necessary and I have nothing more to say," said I.

"We will see about that," said Deputy Warden [James] Moon.

Keeper Haggerty said to him: "You see he has thrown his ration of bread and water on the floor."

"What did you do that for?" asked Moon.

"I did not throw it there. The keeper did and threatened me because I told him I did not want it."

"You lie!" said Haggerty and violently pushed me back from the door into the cell and slammed the door. Haggerty every morning came. When I refused to accept the punishment rations, he would swear at me and throw the bread and water on the floor, where he

*would find the bread still lying there each morning on the floor
where he threw it. For 14 days, I never even drank a drop of water
or ate a crumb of bread.*

*Finally, on the 15th day, he came and found me lying on the floor
weak and sick. He came in the cell, gave me a kick and said: "Get
up on your feet." I got up and as he stepped out from the cell, I
picked up the wooden pail and threw it and all its contents at his
head, and I fell helpless on the floor. The doctor, Ferguson by name,
came and gave orders to remove me to the screen cell.*[14]

*These cells are not so bad as the coolers as there is a cot and one
gets two meals a day. In these screen cells at that time, there were
three other poor fellows gone insane from brutal treatment. One
poor fellow, named Mike Hicks, was chained down to a ring bolt on
the floor where he died. I used to hear keeper Haggerty cursing and
kicking this poor fellow every day. I reported it to the doctor who
told me to "shut up."*

*One day the doctor came and took Mike Hicks up to a room in
the hospital, a dead man, and put me in confinement to a light cell.
This all happened in 1878.*[15]

Clinton was a troubled facility. With only a small staff of poorly trained
guards—roughly one for every forty to fifty inmates—it employed harsh
punishments to maintain discipline. Just prior to Appo's arrival at Clinton, at least three guards were suspended and six prisoners attempted to
escape. On 5 June 1877, four inmates attacked a guard and were later
severely punished. While Appo served his Clinton term, he must have
heard of, if not witnessed, several escape attempts. On separate occasions two convicts "stowed away" at night to elude authorities, only to be
discovered in a snowbank. Another escaped from the meadow while
raking oats but was captured five days later. The most serious attempt
came in April 1878, when five members of a work detail seized the officer
in charge, forced him against the fence surrounding the prison, and used
him as a shield while the inmates hacked at the planking of the stockade.
Only the marksmanship of several guards forced the inmates to
surrender.[16]

A few months later convict Michael Feeney attempted "to raise a riot
among the men working in different shops," according to principal
keeper James Moon. Feeney first attacked and knocked keeper D. E. Gay

unconscious with an iron pipe. When Feeney grabbed and cocked Gay's revolver to shoot him, another prisoner intervened, seized Feeney, and struggled to remove the weapon. Feeney, however, broke away and fired one shot at a guard. The prisoner then dashed through the shop, yelling to his fellow inmates to join him. When Feeney ran into the next shop, he fired at still another guard and repeated "his invitation to convicts to join him in a rush for the front gate," according to Moon. Two keepers returned fire, including Haggerty, who hit Feeney in the leg. For his trouble Feeney was tried and convicted, the judge adding an additional ten years to his previous twenty-year sentence.[17]

Outsiders corroborated Appo's charges that Clinton was a violent place. In 1891, for example, a newspaper reporter who had posed as a guard described Clinton as "a den of brutality of the vilest description." Most keepers and guards were little more than "creatures without souls or hearts, utterly devoid of intelligence." He specifically cited the very individuals Appo accused—James Moon and hall keeper Michael Haggerty. Both were described as "reckless," operating with impunity and virtually no supervision from the warden. A critic characterized Moon as "the worst product of a lumber camp—intemperate, profane, swaggering, and ignorant of any of the amenities of civilization." Haggerty was hated for shackling inmates to a long steam pipe by the wrists with their feet barely touching the floor, and then beating them. Some remained suspended for periods of twelve, twenty-four, and thirty consecutive hours, their only relief coming with unconsciousness. Inmates labeled this "Haggerty's Christmas Tree." On other occasions Moon and Haggerty resorted to less sophisticated methods of punishment: roasting convicts against a laundry heater, forcing them to work "almost naked" in the prison yard in the winter, depriving them of food and water for four to six consecutive days.[18]

    *I worked in the hat contract up until six weeks before the expiration of my term. Then I was taken very sick from the bad food and the inhaling of the fur dust of the shop and was admitted to the prison hospital where I remained for three weeks. From there I was put to work chopping wood outdoors until my time expired.*

    *On the day I was discharged, I was taken to the State Shop and given a cheap suit of clothes made out of stuff resembling saltbagging and dyed black and then taken to the warden's office where* the clerk handed me a ticket to New York and five dollars and I left the prison. The date was January 8th, 1879 and it was snowing very hard and I was very cold as the clothes they gave me was of no use in such weather. In fact, the dye was running down the cloth from the wet of the snow melting while on the train to New York.

On my arrival in New York, I went to the editor of the New York World in company of a reporter and exposed the brutality and graft that was inflicted on unfortunate men and going on in the state prisons, and made particular mention that the prisons should be investigated by a regular live committee formed outside of politicians. The result was [that] the press got after the prison authorities and stopped the paddle and other brutal punishments that has killed and driven many young men insane. I can name unfortunates who were killed and others who were driven insane by brutal keepers in those years of 1874 and 1879.[19]

The first week after I left Clinton Prison, I started looking for work in a hat factory. I went to Garden & Company, 82 Greene Street, and applied for a job. He asked me where I worked last. I told him, in state prison. He got up from his chair, looked at me and said: "We have no vacancy. Our mill room is full."

So I left his office knowing that he told a fib as I had got a "tip" that he needed a young man to run his coning machine. From there I called at the Carroll Hat Company, but failed to obtain work of any kind. I then went to Newark, New Jersey, and applied at two different hat factories, but met with no success. As my money was all spent but about forty cents, I returned to New York and went direct into an opium joint at 4 Mott Street, where I knew I could meet some of my former associates and get financial aid from them.[20]

# 7

# Opium Dens and Bohemia

＝

◀§ *On entering the place [4 Mott Street], I was surprised to see so many new smokers. In fact, the joint was crowded with young men and girls. Most of them were strangers to me. I was unable to order an opium layout, still having the prison clothes on. I felt out of place and was about to go out, when a young man called out: "Hello, George! Come over here." As I approached, he got up from the bunk. He shook hands with me, and said: "When did you come down from 'above' (Sing Sing Prison)." I told him and showed him the clothes they gave me coming out. He laughed and said: "I'll fix you up in the morning with a front (clothes) so that you can get out and make some coin. So lay down here and roll up some pills for me and have a talk." So I lay down, cooked up the card of opium and we both fell asleep. The next morning he bought me a complete outfit of wearing apparel and loaned me five dollars besides. This man was a crook and his business was a confidence swindler, or better known as a "handshaker." His name was Burt Fitzgerald.*

*Every night I would go to the opium joint and I soon got acquainted with all the* habitués *of the place and their line of business. Every one of them with the exception of a few were crooks in every line of graft. As I learned the different systems by which one could earn money easy and with less risk than picking pockets and other rough ways, I started in for myself and was quite successful in making money in "sure thing graft" as it is called by crooks. I had a run of good luck for nearly five months. . . .*[1]

*Mott Street was being deserted by the good American people on account of the Chinese tenants drifting into the neighborhood rapidly. With the Chinamen came many American opium* habitués *from the West, most of them from San Francisco, and all crooks in every line of stealing brought on to the East by the Centennial*

Exhibition at Philadelphia. They worked their different lines of graft, and then drifted into New York and made the opium joint in the basement of 4 Mott Street their hang-out. This place was the first public opium joint opened for the American habitués and was managed by a Chinaman called "Poppy." The place was crowded day and night by opium habitués from all stations in life, both men and women, some of good social and financial standing. Most of the rest were crooks in every line of dishonest business, from the bank burglar down to the petty thief.[2]

GEORGE APPO'S EXPERIENCES in Gotham's earliest opium dens marked the emergence of a new kind of criminal—the drug addict. Opium dens represented a unique place of criminal assembly, an underworld collectivity devoted to the pleasures of the pipe. Like the street and prison, the opium den served as a school for Appo, providing the means to learn alternative and safer forms of illicit enterprise. "Sure thing graft"—confidence games or swindling operations with very high rates of success like bunco, flimflam, fake jewelry, and green goods—supplanted pickpocketing. The opium den proffered a new criminal career for Appo.[3]

Opium was a commonplace drug in the nineteenth-century United States. While its precise use prior to 1920 remains uncertain, contemporaries and later historians acknowledged a dramatic increase after the Civil War. By 1870 opiate use in the United States was not only widespread but virtually unregulated; it was more popular and widespread than tobacco would be a century later. Physicians and pharmacists, for example, prescribed laudanum, morphine, and other addictive opiates as painkillers. Since opium did little damage to the kidneys and liver, some doctors assumed the drug was less detrimental than alcohol. Others falsely believed that opium cured alcoholism. For these and other reasons, the United States never prohibited the use of opium for nonmedical purposes until the twentieth century.[4]

Like his contemporaries Appo attributed the rise of opium smoking to Chinese immigrants. The missionary E. W. Syle reported finding extensive opium smoking among the few Chinese immigrants in New York in 1854. "There is no question that the Chinese imported the opium habit into America," complained one newspaper in 1883. While racial stereotyping—if not outright racism—characterized most analyses, probably a minimum of 20 percent of Chinese immigrants used opium.[5]

The growth of opium smoking, however, was more than a product of Chinese immigration. Indeed, the emergence of opium dens—commonly called "opium joints" or simply "joints"—was stimulated by their popularity within the non-Asian population. During the 1840s and 1850s, the increasing Chinese population generated little, if any, discussion of the drug. Opium smoking, for example, was never mentioned during Quimbo Appo's trials for murder in 1859 and 1860. Only as opium grew popular in underworld, entertainment, and leisure venues after 1865 did contemporaries take notice.[6]

Opium smoking differed from other forms of drug use. In contrast to orally ingesting the narcotic, smoking required a lengthy preparation process and an expensive "layout." Smokers needed a special eighteen-inch pipe, bowl, sponge, chisel, and tray. The "cooking" was usually performed by a resident "chef," who shredded and then boiled raw opium, allowing him to separate the "essence" or "purified" opium. The residue was then kneaded in a pan and fermented into a gooey, thick black paste, which smokers called "dope." Unlike "opium eaters," who usually became addicted because of a medical condition, opium smokers used the drug for pleasure.[7]

Opium smoking attracted increasing attention after the Civil War. In 1871 one writer noted that opium shops were found in cities "where the *hoi polloi,* the 'filth and scum' are prone to live." By 1873 Donovan's Lane, where Appo lived as a child, had at least one reported Chinese "opium saloon," later documented in a lithograph by the artist Winslow Homer. Manhattan pharmacists claimed that numerous poor, "half-stupid" men and women came in and purchased opium to get high. By the early 1880s numerous observers claimed that scores of overcrowded joints operated in Pell, Mott, and Doyers Streets and on the lower Bowery.[8]

Despite the growing visibility of opium smoking, legal authorities were slow to respond for several reasons. First, the practice was considered an "imported vice" identified with Chinese immigrants. In the 1880s, when various officials expressed outrage regarding opium use, their concern focused on non-Chinese users.[9] Second, opium smoking was hidden and confined to Chinese boardinghouses, groceries, laundries, and gambling dens, some of which secretly supplied opium to select customers. By the 1880s Chinese laundries in different parts of New York functioned as opium dens for American customers, part of an informal network of dens extending throughout the United States. Appo testified that "Poppy" on

*Winslow Homer's depiction of a New York opium den.*

Mott Street provided friends with addresses and "tickets" to laundries with opium dens in Syracuse, Chicago, Buffalo, and Cleveland. "It's a poor town now a-days that has not a Chinese laundry," wrote one critic in 1883, "and nearly every one has its opium lay-out." Finally opium dens were frequently hidden or overshadowed by other underground enterprises on the same premises. Appo remembered that 4 and 17 Mott Street, for instance, were also gambling dens and houses of prostitution.[10]

The den at 4 Mott Street was one of the best known, but not the first opium den in New York City, as Appo believed. More accurately, it was the first well-known opium joint that allowed Euro-American visitors to indulge in opium smoking. In 1882, an *Evening Post* reporter described a visit to 4 Mott Street as "an extraordinary experience." The den was situated in a four-story tenement just off the Bowery, only a few steps from several prominent concert saloons. Inside, smokers reclined on low platforms extending the length of the small, dimly lit room, their heads supported by small wooden stools. The Chinese proprietor, Poppy, weighed and served opium in little seashells. Fumes from the pipes filled the room with such a thick, bluish cloud that one visitor claimed it was impossible to see his hands held at his waist. When the smoke cleared, he observed a dozen small peanut-oil lamps glowing "like the fire flies in a fog," and a room packed with smokers, all of whom were Euro-Americans. Poppy busily moved from patron to patron supplying opium, many crying out, "Poppy, gimme a quarter's worth."[11]

The proliferation of Chinese-operated opium dens evidenced a more significant phenomenon: the emergence of an American bohemian subculture. An ill-defined intellectual proletariat of penniless and carefree writers, journalists, poets, actors, and artists, bohemians challenged a host of Victorian social norms. For a variety of people, the bohemian milieu of opium smoking was accessible to almost anyone, allowing not only men and women to intermingle but also individuals of different class, ethnic, and racial backgrounds. The opium dens frequented by Appo in Lower Manhattan embodied the popularization of bohemian life in the United States. After visiting one Pell Street den, one reporter wrote that "in five minutes [we] found ourselves in busy Printing-house Square, mingling again with that civilized half of the world which knows not, nor could ever dream, how the other half lives." Another claimed that by the 1870s, the opium dens in Chinatown competed with the city's most popular concert saloons, attracting patrons from uptown spots like the Bijou and the Haymarket.[12]

Elements of a bohemian subculture with alternative views on sexuality appeared before the Civil War. The most notable was Henry Clapp's group of writers, actors, and intellectuals that gathered at Pfaff's Broadway saloon just north of Bleecker Street. Clapp fostered a reputation as "king of the bohemians," and attracted the patronage of writer Fitz-James O'Brien, poets Walt Whitman and Ada Clare, actress Ada Menken, and journalist and future French prime minister Georges Clemenceau.[13] Other, less ideological males ascribed to an ethic of pleasure, even hedonism. "Sporting men," "fancy men," dandies, and nabobs challenged "respectable" definitions of urban masculinity and male sexuality. A heterogeneous mix of wealthy and poor, educated and ignorant, fashionable and ragged, sporting male culture valorized a sexual ethic based upon male aggressiveness and licentiousness. Some even attributed the growing popularity of opium smoking to sporting men.[14]

American writers like Edgar Allan Poe and Fitz-Hugh Ludlow were the first to describe in detail the world of opium users and abusers. While their examinations emphasized orally ingested opium, Poe introduced some of the earliest opium-addicted characters in American literature, in some quarters becoming "the prophet of organized Bohemianism." Fitz-Hugh Ludlow went one step further: He became addicted to hashish as a teenager. After he published *The Hasheesh Eater* in 1857, Ludlow became a regular at Pfaff's and went on to a writing and editorial career, during which time he remained addicted to the narcotic. He published *The Opium Habit* (1868) before his premature death in 1870.[15]

The opium use and bohemianism popularized by Poe, Ludlow, and the Pfaffians was limited to a small, elite group of intellectuals and artists. "Opium eating," in particular, tended to be a solitary activity. This changed by the 1870s. As opium use shifted from eaters to smokers, the drug became more accessible and communal. In fact smoking was a social experience. In places like Poppy's Mott Street den, smokers organized themselves into small groups of two to six persons, all sharing a pipe and smoking equipment. One individual cooked the drug and prepared the pipe, which was then shared and smoked in turn by the others. Opium den patrons told stories, cracked jokes, sang in low voices, and drank beer. In contrast to the raucous and sometimes violent atmosphere of the saloon, the opium den was a place of relaxation and quiet contemplation. Numerous smokers maintained they enjoyed a kinship with fellow habitués. Opium smoking "loosens the tongue and develops social qualities," observed one writer, "rather than the fighting spirit engendered by whiskey."[16]

Opium smokers saw the drug as the raw substance of dreams. Smoking opium put the user in a deep but refreshing sleep, lasting anywhere from fifteen minutes to several hours. Upon waking, the smoker felt no aftereffects like a hangover. Opium induced a subdued tranquillity, "an indescribable sense of complete satisfaction," "dreamy wakefulness," and "paradise," according to various smokers.[17]

A new language emerged in this paradise. Habitual opium smokers were labeled "hop fiends" or just "fiends." Novices and infrequent users were simply "pleasure smokers." By the 1890s the drug was called a variety of names: "victor medicine," "Spanish cigarettes," and "dope." As opium dens spread throughout cities in the United States, they became part of an underworld social network with a common argot, shared rules, and peer reinforcement, anticipating the pattern of twentieth-century drug subcultures.[18]

The opium den promoted a certain egalitarian ethos. One former addict and otherwise critical observer noted that "the old saying, 'There is honor among thieves,' applies equally well to opium fiends. They never steal from each other while in the joint." He was most impressed by witnessing intoxicated men and women enter opium dens, lie down, and go to sleep with jewelry exposed and money in their pockets. Fighting, he and others noted, rarely occurred. Similarly a reporter was impressed with the loyalty and camaraderie among opium smokers, in which social position accounted for little.

Opium dens also promoted an exotic, "Oriental" ambience of Asian mystery. Typical was one Pell Street den with a narrow room decorated with vases, color prints, mirrors, and Chinese inscriptions. Two broad shelves or divans extended along a wall, the upper about six feet above the floor, the other less than two feet high. Each was covered with bamboo mats and pillows, turning them into "bunks" on which opium smokers reclined. "The mysterious gloom, the flickering opium-lamps, the barbaric colors on the walls, the trance-like appearance of the smokers, and the deathly stillness," wrote one visitor, "contributed to make the scene a weird and impressive one."[19]

Although opium smoking induced sleep and lethargy, opium dens were identified with "licentiousness." The physician and opium researcher Henry H. Kane believed that opium smoking produced "satyriasis" in men and nymphomania in women. Opium dens were consequently perceived as sites of seduction. Repeated observations noted that opium dens were filled with scantily clad women who disrobed on entering in order to make themselves comfortable.[20] At the very least the atmosphere was erotic.

The presence of prostitutes further sexualized the opium den. By 1887 certain businessmen and property owners complained that prostitutes worked out of most of the buildings along Mott Street and north of Chatham Square. Opium dens on adjoining streets displayed a similar mixture of drug use and commercial sex. When the police raided establishments on Pell and Mott Streets for prostitution violations, they found the inmates "hitting the pipe." By 1890 at least six tenements on Doyers Street were noted for their mixture of prostitution and opium.[21]

The link of opium with prostitution and various illicit activities convinced some that the milieu of the hop was filled with social outcasts. "The people who frequent these places are, with very few exceptions, thieves, sharpers and sporting men, and a few bad actors; the women, without exception, are immoral," wrote one. The writer James L. Ford admitted that "the criminal classes of New York"—gamblers, prostitutes, confidence men, and thieves—took up opium smoking early on.[22]

Numerous other commentators, however, noted the diverse clientele of the joints. Entertainers associated with the theater were among the most frequently cited opium smokers. "Together with a few brilliant Bohemians," surmised writer Allen Williams, theatrical people "compose the aristocracy of the joints." Some, like the den under Paddy Martin's Wine Room at 9 Bowery, were known for their patronage by well-known actors. Others, like Bessinger's Fourteenth Street opium joint, attracted so many thespian addicts in the 1880s that the proprietor admitted patrons simply to observe famous stage performers getting high. One police reporter concluded that the "lower order" of theatrical people— variety actors and dancers—represented "the greater part of the white devotees of the pipe in New York."[23]

Yet Euro-American opium smokers also came from affluent backgrounds, in part because opium was expensive. One Chinese writer claimed in 1888 that some addicts needed to smoke three dollars' worth of opium daily in order "to keep straight," a habit costing approximately one thousand dollars a year, roughly the entire annual wage of most American workers. Reports describing dens full of "society women," "richly-dressed ladies," "respectable people," and "the best class of customers" multiplied in the final quarter of the nineteenth century. Opium smoking, concluded one writer, was an indulgence for primarily "the indolent and rich."[24]

For many opponents of opium use, however, the most controversial element of the den was the random, unregulated intermingling of classes, races, and sexes. The societal markers of the "outside" world broke down under an ethic of individual hedonism and narcotic license. In contrast to opium dens in London, the joints Appo frequented, like 4 Mott Street, were filled with "men and boys of respectable conditions, girls and hardened women, thieves and sporting men, actors and actresses, drunken carousers and Chinamen," according to one reporter. One detective noted that all "castes" were set aside in opium dens. Homeless beggars lay down beside offspring of the wealthy; whites, blacks, and Asians shared the same physical space. A reporter concurred, noting how in certain dens a "Union League Club man will lie with the head of a City Hall Park bunco steerer upon his chest, laughing and joking with him as if they had been 'comrades, comrades, ever since we were boys.' " Periodic police raids, random arrests, and prosecutorial indictments confirmed many such charges.[25]

These behaviors alarmed critics, but to little avail. New York's Koch Law of 1882 made buying, selling, giving away, or using opium for the purpose of smoking a misdemeanor, but most arrests resulted in little more than suspended or dismissed cases. More often than not law enforcement officials tolerated opium dens. Numerous reporters and observers claimed that police officers stationed in Chinatown routinely brought "slumming parties" of outsiders, curious about the goings-on in opium dens. One addict remembered policemen entering a Pell Street opium den, arresting several suspects, and walking out without bothering the smokers. Reportedly the ward man was a close associate of the proprietors.[26]

In the final decades of the nineteenth century, the opium dens of Chinatown facilitated and represented an ill-defined, inarticulate bohemian world. While this intercultural milieu fostered little intellectual debate, displayed less middle-class self-consciousness, and attracted fewer females compared with Greenwich Village bohemia after 1900, it nevertheless embodied a liminal space fostering an ethic of mutuality, hedonism, and fantasy.[27] The bohemia George Appo confronted in these early opium dens at once conveyed an exotic and erotic "Orientalism" alongside a "rough," male underworld. In Gotham's opium dens pickpockets like Appo met their "genteel" Victorian counterparts. Respectable actors, actresses, artists, and "clubmen" fraternized with sneak thieves, confidence men, and prostitutes. Evoking an ambiance of Asian mystery, this hidden subculture was devoted to the pleasures of the pipe and the body. Opium smoking then gave birth to a distinct American bohemia.

⊷  *[In 1880] I started in the express business. I bought a horse and wagon with the aid of Tom Lee, the then "Mayor of Chinatown." I got all the Chinamen's expressage work and worked steadily for about four months. During the course of that time, I built up a good trade with the laundry supply and foolishly took in a Chinaman, Wong I. Gong, as a partner through the advice of Tom Lee. After I introduced Gong to the wholesale dealers in soap, starch, etc., he got the run of the business and followed my advice and instructions. [Then] Tom Lee sold out the business to Gong for $300.00 and I was told since he had put up the $300.00 to start the business, he kept the money. I was again soon in need and destitute and naturally drifted back to the "hang-outs" of my former associates, and through dire necessity started on the crooked path once more.*[28]

*Tom Lee.*

Tom Lee was the organizational force behind Chinatown's early underground economy. By the late 1870s Lee's cigar store at 4 Mott Street, above Poppy's opium den, was the headquarters of both his legitimate and illegitmate operations. In certain respects Lee personified how the legal and illegal worlds of commerce permeated each other. From 1879 into the 1890s, literally the formative years of New York's Chinatown, Lee officially served as a deputy sheriff, unofficially as "the Mayor of Chinatown." He allegedly owned several restaurants and cigar stores in Chinatown, as well as an insurance company. By 1883 one reporter described him as "the great Mongolian magnate of Mott Street."[29]

Appo's frequent visits to the opium den at 4 Mott Street probably introduced him to Lee. Some even believed that Lee was Appo's uncle. In his autobiography, however, Appo never mentioned any such relationship, and given the pattern of Quimbo Appo's immigration to New York and his later incarcerations, no evidence supports such a conclusion.

Lee's personal background remains mysterious. Conflicting accounts dated his birth between 1828 and 1842 in Canton. After immigrating to the United States, he reportedly lived in St. Louis (where he was naturalized in 1876) and Philadelphia, married a German American woman, and eventually settled in New York. Like Quimbo Appo a generation earlier, Lee displayed an ability to function within both the Chinese and Euro-American communities. One reporter described him as a "good-looking, smooth-talking Celestial." Like Quimbo Appo, Lee also converted to Christianity and married a European immigrant. Most important, Lee ingratiated himself with the New York political establishment, specifically district leader Tom Foley of Tammany Hall.[30]

Lee himself embodied the three forms of association which emerged in Chinese neighborhoods across the United States. The Lee family or "clan" (*kung saw* in Chinese) initially served as a governing agency within the Chinese community by providing hostelries, immigrant aid, food, and employment, while establishing a monopoly in certain trades like laundry services. Such societies protected the welfare of extended family members, offered relief in times of distress, and supplied material resources when necessary.

Lee's clan grew so large that at times it more accurately represented a *hui-kuan*—an organization including Chinese immigrants who spoke a common dialect, came from the same district, or belonged to the same regional group. In some respects, the *hui-kuan* mirrored European immigrant aid societies such as the *landsmannshaften* among Jewish immigrants. The *hui-kuan* represented their constituencies in relations with other Chinese and Euro-American officials by adjudicating disputes and conducting arbitration and mediation hearings between individuals and groups.[31]

Finally Lee was one of the founders of what became Chinatown's leading secret society, or tong. In 1880 Lee and four other Chinese men established the On Leong Tong, self-described as a lodge of Freemasons promoting "friendship, brotherly love and service to the Supreme Being" and offering aid to members in distress. Some identified the organization as the "rebellion party" because of its alleged origin in China during the Taiping Rebellion. From 1883 to 1898 Lee led the four-thousand-member On Leong, New York's dominant tong.[32]

Appo's relationship to Lee revealed how the activities of Chinese social organizations like the family, immigrant organizations, and tongs overlapped in confusing or indiscernible ways. Like many Chinese immigrants and their offspring, Appo looked to a prominent Chinese official in seeking employment, a function historically associated with *hui-kuan* leaders who frequently provided jobs to their members and families. In Appo's case, Lee invested or "loaned" Appo three hundred dollars, enough money to purchase a horse and wagon, and then encouraged other merchants to employ Appo whenever they needed to transport goods and supplies.

But *hui-kuans* also attracted merchants as members, like Appo's brief partner Wong I. Gong. Like Lee and more than 90 percent of the Chinese immigrants to the United States, Gong was born in the Guangdong Province, around Canton. In 1873, at age fourteen, he moved to Hong Kong with his father, who ran a quilt factory. Shortly thereafter he immigrated to California. By 1876 he was employed as a railroad construction foreman in the western United States. He apparently exploited both that experience and his familial ties in Asia, because soon after he became a labor contractor. In 1879 he moved to New York City. Later records indicate that he worked as an expressman from 1879 to 1885, precisely the time when George Appo came into contact with him. In 1885, for unknown reasons, Gong moved to Massachusetts and ran a tea store for two years before returning to New York in 1887 to operate a laundry supply business on Doyers Street for the ensuing thirty years.[33]

Appo's experience with Lee and Gong also demonstrated how Chinese employment and entrepreneurial opportunity in New York were tightly controlled by small groups of merchants by the 1870s. Quite likely, Gong's previous work as a labor contractor, his family connections in Hong Kong, and his origins from Guangdong ingratiated him with the ever-ambitious Lee. By contrast, Appo enjoyed none of these advantages—he had no family, no business experience, and his father originated from northern China, not Guangdong. Forces advantageous to Gong were nonexistent for Appo; indeed, they reflected larger divisions within the Chinese community. In the end Lee probably saw greater potential profits with Gong. Appo's entrepreneurial venture proved a short-lived failure.

More significantly, Tom Lee's activities revealed how Chinese social organizations—the family, the *hui-kuan*, the tong—further blurred the lines between the legal business world and Chinatown's informal underground economy. Indeed, 4 Mott Street illustrated the mixture of legitimate and illegitimate enterprise. By the 1880s a restaurant was located at the address. In the rear a small passageway led to a large, windowless but well-lit gambling den, usually filled with Chinese males.[34] Elsewhere other members of Lee's family joined him in operating certain illicit enterprises. Ah Lee, for example, was the proprietor of the gambling and opium dens at 13 and 17 Mott Street, the latter being one of the largest such operations in the city. Others charged that it was a house of prostitution. In fact it was all of them. Later in the decade, Ah Lee was arrested for running Tom Lee's gambling and opium den at 41 Bowery, while Charles Lee ran a Pell Street brothel. Ah Toy, one of Lee's rivals, claimed in 1883 that "Lee had many cousins and much money," enabling him to avoid prosecution for his crimes.[35]

Most important, by boldly organizing Chinatown's opium trade, Lee effectively created and promoted Gotham's first narcotics economy. As deputy sheriff Lee reportedly approached immigrant merchants, showed them his badge of office, and advised them to open a gambling den in return for a weekly payment of five dollars, or an opium den for ten dollars per month. Lee told Chinese storekeepers that he knew American law and enjoyed the right to permit gambling. Many Chinese thus assumed that such activities were sanctioned by the municipality. When proprietors were arrested, Lee provided bail. By 1884 various reports claimed that Lee owned or controlled between sixteen and thirty-seven gambling dens along Mott Street, generating annual profits of twelve to twenty thousand dollars.[36]

But Lee's heavy-handed methods made him unpopular with many of his fellow Asian immigrants, especially those affiliated with a rival Cantonese group in New York. Their opposition to Lee led to his indictment in 1883 and a neighborhood rebellion that Lee successfully suppressed. Newspaper accounts implied that Lee, with the prominent criminal attorney Edmund E. Price and a former judge as counsel, employed bribery and physical intimidation, resulting in dismissal of the cases.[37] Tom Lee, noted one newspaper, "is very unpopular, but yet his country-men patronize his places, knowing full well that they have but a poor chance of coming out ahead."[38]

Other Chinese groups thereafter periodically challenged Lee's control over the Chinatown underground economy. The Chu and Moy families, numbering more than six hundred each, were frequently identified as rivals to Lee's clan of five hundred to three thousand members, especially in controlling the small Chinese theater business. By the 1890s Lee's On Leong Tong competed with the 450-member Hip Sing Tong. When Lee accused the rival tong of blackmailing various Chinatown opium dens and fan-tan gambling shops, tong leaders allegedly placed a five-thousand-dollar bounty on Lee's life. He survived four murder attempts, but others estimated that the conflict between the rival tongs resulted in more than fifty deaths.[39]

The On Leong and Hip Sing Tongs provided a veil of legitimacy for their members. During the 1890s, for example, Lee convinced many out-side observers that he was a reformer interested in encouraging law and order in Chinatown. The journalist Thomas Knox described Lee as "a prosperous merchant" in 1891. The writer Louis Beck believed that the On Leong was a social organization of upper-class Chinese seeking to encourage good order and respect for city laws. Conversely, the Hip Sings formed an alliance with the Reverend Charles Parkhurst of the Society for the Prevention of Crime in their attacks on Lee and the On Leong Tong. Eventually a municipal judge brought the rival factions together and a formal peace agreement was signed in 1906.[40]

George Appo remained largely unaffected by these developments. Like the polyglot world of Baxter Street where he grew up, Appo never labeled himself by a single ethnic category. His brief and unsuccessful entrepreneurial venture as an expressman originated with the support of Tom Lee; yet Appo never identified himself as Chinese. The ethnic bonds he exploited to attract Lee's attention proved short-lived and inef-fectual. He remained aloof from the Asian world of Chinatown, as well as from the violent turbulence associated with Lee and the tongs. Instead he sought solace in the opium den and from his fraternity of good fellows.

So one cold winter's night, I drifted into a Mott Street opium joint at No.17 (basement at the time) where a man named Barney Maguire and his "green goods" employers were smoking opium and drinking wine at Maguire's expense. In the place at the time I noticed a young man lying on the bunk all alone smoking opium. As he was an entire stranger and I had never seen him around before, I sat down on the foot of the bunk near him and without a word between us, he handed me the opium pipe with a pill on it to smoke. I took it and lay down and we soon became acquainted. I asked him where he was from and he said from the West. Every evening I would meet him at the joint and soon learned that he was a traveling house thief and robbed wealthy people's homes at supper or dinner hours in the fall and winter.

One evening I went out with him to see how he worked, but he made a failure that evening. He then told me he was going West. I told him I would join him and we would work both ways, that is, I would help him at his work and he would help me at mine. He agreed and the next day we both went to Philadelphia, where we stayed three days. He made no money there, but I was successful and we went to Scranton, Pennsylvania.

On arriving there, I said to him: "Should you ever get arrested, what name would you give in?"

He replied: "Fred Crage."

"Is that your right name?" I asked.

"No, my right name is Fred Young."

I told him I would give the name of George Leonard, so we worked Scranton and many other cities until we reached the city of Chicago, where we made a long stay, about 3 months, and all the money he made from New York to Chicago was $17. I paid railroad fare and all other expenses from the results of my stealing from New York to Chicago.

So one day, just the beginning of winter time, Fred said to me: "We will go to St. Paul, Minnesota. I have a good 'thing' up that way and if I am lucky we will be 'away up in G.' "

"Well, all right, any place suits me." So we went to St. Paul. In two weeks, he made eight dollars. Finally, one afternoon we took a train for Minneapolis, only a short ride from St. Paul. That night he took me up to a place called the "Five Corners."[41] Above this section all the rich people live. He went to a house, climbed the porch and opened a window and got in while I was on the lookout for him. He soon came out and when a safe distance away we met and he showed me a silver watch and a cheap stickpin. I told him that was very poor graft and too risky and that he had better give it up.

He replied: "You just wait, I'll get there, good and fat."

"I hope so," said I, so we went back to St. Paul to our room. On the next evening at 5:45 p.m., I was at the St. Charles Hotel in Minneapolis by appointment with Fred, who told me to be sure to be there. I waited for him until 10 p.m. at the hotel, but he did not show up himself, so I went back to St. Paul to my room and waited there all night. As he did not appear, I went and got the morning paper and therein was an article about the house being robbed of jewelry and money to the amount of $37,000 while the family were at dinner. The fact that Fred had tried the night before to rob the house and failed and he disappointed me at the hotel by not showing up to [meet] me, led me to believe that he robbed the house alone and left me out.

I then made up my mind to hunt him up and bring him to account for his mean act, or as the "crook" says—"Putting me in the hole for my share of the coin." I knew that he was deeply attached to a young girl about 17 years of age who was an inmate of a parlor house in St. Louis on Elm Street. In fact, he was all the time talking about her to me, so I got a move on myself, made some money picking pockets that day and then bought a ticket to St. Louis and left St. Paul that night.

On reaching St. Louis, I went direct to the fast house where his girl lived. I saw and talked with her and she said to me: "Fred was here and left about an hour ago for New York. See what nice presents he made me," showing me a pair of diamond earrings, a diamond ring and a sealskin sacque. "Fred is going to send for me and take me to New York in a few days," said she. I commented upon his generosity and bid her goodbye.[42]

After one day's graft in St. Louis, I left for Louisville, and from there to Cincinnati, and kept on going from town to town until I arrived in New York. Then began a search for Fred in the opium joints. After visiting three of them and not meeting him, I finally *learned that Barney Maguire, the green goods financial backer, had opened a swell opium joint on Crosby Street, opposite Niblo's Garden Theatre. I called there and was informed that Fred had been smoking there and that he had taken a ship and sailed for Paris, France. This information I found to be true, so I gave up the chase and soon forgot about Fred's meanness until one day about five months after he sailed for Europe, I heard from a friend of Fred's, who got a letter from him, stating that he was sentenced to fifteen years imprisonment in Paris, France for burglary. Then I forgot him entirely.[43]*

# 8

# The Old Homestead

$=$

*⮞ In the early part of June 1879, I was arrested on Broadway near Pine Street on suspicion, or rather for being on the Dead Line by Detective [Joseph] Woolsey. As he punched me in the face for demanding why I was arrested, I punched him back. He told the judge I assaulted him and I was sent to the Workhouse [on Blackwell's Island] for six months.[1]*

**B**LACKWELL'S ISLAND (now Roosevelt Island) embodied the confusion of the poor and criminal classes. There municipal officials sought to remedy what many considered the most perplexing problem of the modern metropolis: where to isolate and control what nineteenth-century Americans considered human contagion: criminals, vagrants, prostitutes, the insane, chronically ill, homeless, and impoverished elderly. Located in the middle of the East River between Manhattan and Queens, Blackwell's Island was Gotham's living nightmare: "a vast mass of . . . decaying bodies," wrote one; little more than "a festering ulcer" on the body politic, opined another. The State Charities Aid Association described Blackwell's Island as virtually a city unto itself, as a "municipality of misery."[2]

Owned by the Blackwell family for more than a century, the island was purchased by the city in 1828. As late as 1842 Lydia Maria Child described Blackwell's Island as "unusually beautiful," a place "unsurpassed by anything I have ever witnessed." The island was full of open wells, shady retreats, weeping willows, natural gardens, and arbors running down to the river's edge. But municipal officials eventually concluded that the island's isolation in the middle of the East River made it an ideal place on which to segregate the unwanted, the incurable, the criminal, and the deviant. By 1850 the nation's first municipal insane asylum, the city's almshouse, and a new workhouse were located on the island.[3]

By the time of Appo's incarceration, Blackwell's Island was also the nation's largest medical center. Hospitals and wards devoted to specialized physical and mental infirmities dotted the island: smallpox, epilepsy, conjunctivitis, paralysis, and other "incurable diseases." The most imposing was the Charity Hospital, which replaced the Penitentiary Hospital when it burned down in 1858. Constructed of stone quarried from the island by convicts and designed to treat twelve hundred patients, the new ornamental edifice was the largest such facility in the United States. It was also the city's primary venereal facility.[4] Blackwell's Island—inhabited by Gotham's most undesirable population—was perhaps the most functionally segregated residential community in the world.

By the 1870s the penitentiary, charity hospital, almshouse, and workhouse were the island's most prominent and largest institutions. Technically each served a distinctive purpose. The penitentiary served as the county jail, housing those convicted of misdemeanors and felons sentenced to one year or less. The workhouse was intended to house the poor and jobless, as well as individuals convicted of minor offenses with terms stretching from ten days to one year. In both, healthy inmates were expected to work and help pay for the costs of their incarceration. Those suffering from chronic illness or unable to afford adequate care ended up in the almshouse.[5] Reformers and city officials hoped that these distinct institutions would separate the young from the old, men from women, hardened felons from simple misdemeanants, the indicted from the convicted.

Such hopes proved futile. In reality the four institutions shared overlapping constituencies. As early as the 1850s the almshouse governors complained that courts and magistrates treated the penitentiary as a "general receptacle for the sweepings of the city." Inside were prostitutes suffering from venereal disease; paupers, alcoholics, and vagrants of all sorts; the lame, the maimed, and the blind; the "half idiot" and the insane; thieves, rowdies, and ruffians; and even homeless children. So many prostitutes were sentenced to the penitentiary that officials described the facility as a "lazar house for the poor diseased and worn out victim." The charity hospital treated vagrants and women afflicted with venereal disease, all of whom were found in the almshouse, workhouse, and penitentiary. One grand jury chided that the term "workhouse" was a misnomer, since the majority committed were unable to work and better placed in a hospital or almshouse. At the same time the almshouse, not the charity hospital, became the acknowledged dumping ground for the chronically and incurably ill. More significantly, complained another, the almshouse mixed "the wicked and the hardened" with "the innocent and unfortunate." At various times children under fifteen years of age were found in all four institutions.[6]

Distinctions of gender and age mattered little. In 1876 one government report charged that male and female prisoners intermingled in the penitentiary. Men were found in all three wings, including the one intended for women. More common was the mixing of young misdemeanants and older felons. Prisoners were never separated by age or crime, even though approximately one-half the penitentiary inmates were under twenty-five years of age, one-third of whom were teenagers. "No more hopeful means of turning the innocent youth into hardened criminals could possible be devised," concluded one assembly report in 1875.[7]

Major reasons for so much institutional overlap and inmate intermixing were overcrowding and inadequate funding. By 1870 the penitentiary had more than 750 cells for a daily population fluctuating between 950 and 1,100. For the remainder of the nineteenth century, nearly half or more of the penitentiary's cells contained two inmates each. In fact, until the introduction of bunk beds late in the century, penitentiary inmates shared the same bed.[8]

The workhouse was even worse. After 1870 the daily population usually exceeded 1,500, while anywhere from 15,000 to 29,000 individuals were admitted annually. At times the workhouse was so overcrowded that cells housed four inmates apiece. By the 1870s the total daily inmate population of all Blackwell's Island institutions fluctuated between 6,000 and 8,000.[9] During the final three decades of the nineteenth century, numerous investigations, reports, and public officials concluded that all the carceral institutions of Blackwell's Island were ill equipped for such a large population.[10]

Blackwell's Island was overcrowded even by prison standards, especially compared to New York's penitentiary population. Between 1870 and 1900, the state's daily prison population—the nation's largest—fluctuated between 2,526 and 3,614. During any year roughly 3,500 to 4,000 passed through New York's state prisons. The asylums of Blackwell's Island accommodated four to eight times that number. More sobering was that New York State's prison population represented *three* carceral institutions scattered in different parts of the state.[11] Compared to Sing Sing and other state prisons, the facilities on Blackwell's Island treated far more people, more directly touching the lives of the rough, the tough, and the poor.

Overcrowding on Blackwell's Island was magnified by the abysmal living conditions. In winter the coal supply frequently ran out, leaving the facilities with no heating and dropping indoor temperatures below fifty degrees. One hospital visitor noted seeing the breath of the female and child inmates. When coal was available, only the corridors were heated, leaving the cells—deemed "caverns" by the inmates—cold. The flagstone floors made them as chilly as ice even in the summer.[12]

Hygiene was mostly an abstract ideal. Every morning inmates were allowed to wash for two minutes, sixty to seventy men at a time. Prisoners received small pieces of soap every two months, while six towels were shared by nine hundred men. Flush toilets and individual sinks were nonexistent. In the male wing of the charity hospital, the water closet was an exposed iron trough covered by two wooden seats. Running water was frequently cut off for months at a time, forcing residents to flush the trough with ordinary bucket water. The large iron sink used by doctors for postsurgical washing was simultaneously employed for cleaning food and dishes. Medicine and drugs were stored in empty pickle jars. Some wards in the hospital had only sinkholes in a corner to provide drainage. During a grand jury inspection, a cat captured a large dock rat before the very eyes of jury members.[13]

Not surprisingly Blackwell's Island residents suffered from poor health. One worker claimed that large numbers of workhouse inmates contracted scurvy, evidence of their inadequate diets. The overcrowding and poor food resulted in numerous cases of diarrhea and dehydration. Some inmates joked "that one must carry his certificate of death . . . before he can expect to be transferred to the hospital."[14]

By the mid-nineteenth century, the penitentiary was deemed "one of the worst governed prisons in Christendom," in one report. Half a century later another critic described it as a "correctional dunghill." Several developments contributed to this state of affairs. First, civil service among island workers was nonexistent; appointments were based on politics. As in state prisons, Blackwell's Island occupations, from superintendents to cooks, were political positions. Since island workers received their appointments from other public officials, they routinely ignored the warden's orders and wishes. Second, inmates and patients far outnumbered administrative personnel, including guards and keepers. The penitentiary, for example, had three types of correction officers: coxswains who operated the boats, guards to watch and prevent prisoners from escaping, and keepers to "work" the men. At best they totaled fifty, of which less than half were on duty at any one time. Consequently one guard or keeper was responsible for forty to fifty inmates.[15]

Inadequate numbers of guards and overcrowding made control of the inmate population difficult. While officials claimed that only a dark cell was used to punish incorrigibles, prison reformers like Sinclair Tousey testified that keepers routinely and illegally beat prisoners. During the 1880s Deputy Warden Charles Osborn was repeatedly singled out for his cruelty. One prison commissioner bluntly described the keepers as the "damnedest scoundrels that ever lived." Sexual improprieties were frequent in the workhouse, some "so shocking," claimed one newspaper, that they were unprintable.[16]

More often keepers and guards were just plain incompetent. Some, upon arriving for work, proceeded directly to the infirmary, declared themselves sick, and spent the day recovering from a hangover. Others were so inebriated that they simply fell asleep on the boat. Fraternization between inmates and guards was a frequent problem, as evidenced by the warden caught "in criminal connection" with several incarcerated prostitutes. Another charged in 1860 that every institution on Blackwell's Island had a "rumshop" that dispensed liquor and cigars. In 1876 one keeper permitted two inmates to take an "outing," allowing them to row across the East River and visit the nearby saloons. When it was time to return, one refused while the other fought with the keeper, fell into the river, and drowned. At times the employees were worse than the convict population, as when two resident physicians were charged with raping two nurses in the asylum. The only difference between guards and prisoners, believed one workhouse superintendent, was that "the latter are locked up, while the guards are not."[17]

Some convicts even assumed the responsibilities of guards. At certain times penitentiary inmates were employed as keepers in the insane asylum. In the charity hospital, convicts assisted doctors in dispensing various medicines and drugs, while convicted prostitutes worked as nurses. Even though many employees in the insane asylum were inmates from the workhouse, charges of official neglect and corruption were often dismissed as the rantings and ravings of the drunken and dissipated.[18]

The leisurely social intercourse Blackwell's Island inmates enjoyed was even reflected in the physical landscape. Like Sing Sing before 1878, no wall surrounded the penitentiary. In fact no large barrier enclosed any Blackwell's Island facility. During the 1850s a wooden fence surrounded the prison, but by 1871 it was gone.[19] Consequently inmates from the multiple facilities easily and frequently interacted as they moved about the island.

In the absence of the harsh punishments and tortures associated with prisons like Sing Sing, many clamored to get in. State investigators discovered that men and women frequently left the workhouse one day and returned to the almshouse a few days hence as "voluntary" inmates. Judges sentencing individuals to the workhouse, almshouse, and even the penitentiary had little knowledge if a prisoner was a recidivist offender—a "repeater," "rounder," or "revolver" in the parlance of the time. Consequently such inmates served ten to twenty sentences annually. One convict, for instance, bragged that he received more than fifty-five sentences during the 1880s.[20]

Revolvers and rounders multiplied during economic depressions and harsh winters. Thousands of unskilled laborers who found themselves

*As late as 1908 the penitentiary* (foreground) *and charity hospital* (top) *on Blackwell's Island still did not have a wall.*

unemployed in the winter requested incarceration in the workhouse as vagrants. Homeless children also initiated proceedings before police court justices to get themselves off the street. Others, admitted one workhouse superintendent, were repeatedly committed on thirty-day charges for drunkenness. When their term expired, he related, "they return to the city, immediately proceed to drink again to intoxication, and are recommitted on the day following." Police court judges believed that they sentenced some individuals to Blackwell's Island more than one hundred times for intoxication.[21]

Rounders and revolvers were hardly unique to the workhouse; they were found in the penitentiary as well. As early as 1851 Warden Joseph Keen claimed that a majority of inmates did not consider the prison a punishment; rather, many sought incarceration because it was "a pleasant and comfortable residence." Two years later he added that the penitentiary was the chosen abode for prostitutes and vagrants, making it "the convenient, occasional resort of the scum of our city." Convicts admitted that they lied about their age in order to be sentenced to Blackwell's Island because of the easier conditions. One guard remarked that some offenders returned so often "that we hardly miss them." For these reasons, revolvers and reformers alike sarcastically referred to the Blackwell's Island penitentiary as the "Old Homestead."[22]

The most controversial revolvers were prostitutes. By the 1850s officials described the penitentiary hospital as "the great venereal hospital of the city." So many young women moved back and forth between the city and the penitentiary hospital that one report concluded that many effectively made Blackwell's Island their home. Prostitutes suffering from sexually transmitted diseases, as well as their brothel keepers, routinely chose to be committed for medical treatment. At the hospital prostitutes enjoyed medical advice, good nursing, decent food, and a comfortable bed. When they were cured, their lawyers secured a writ of habeas corpus and a quick discharge.[23]

Judges, too, were part of the problem. Some were not simply lenient; they were corrupt. In 1842, for example, the judge and future police superintendent George Matsell and two other magistrates were charged with releasing 70 prisoners from Blackwell's Island for the purpose of voting. In other cases convicted felons with political influence were sent to Blackwell's Island instead of state prisons. In September 1889 police justices released more than 137 prisoners within only two days of their incarceration on the island.[24]

The number of revolvers was difficult to measure; most figures were guesses at best. In 1870 penitentiary warden John Fitch estimated that 50 percent of all inmates were repeaters. In 1878 the workhouse superintendent believed that the approximately twenty thousand inmates who entered the establishment annually represented only five thousand individuals. A former Tombs warden claimed that some revolvers left from and returned to the workhouse twenty to forty times annually. While revolvers were highly visible and numerous, most of these tallies were most likely exaggerations. In 1886 one unpublished report by the Department of Charities and Corrections calculated that only 11 percent of those admitted to the workhouse were in fact self-committed.[25]

Once on the island the more astute revolvers and criminals like George Appo exploited the lax security. Appo recounted during a later incarceration that upon reaching Blackwell's Island he was required to state his trade. "Carpenter," he lied, knowing from other "old-time crooks" that the carpentry shop was the eas-
iest place to work. He was assigned to the coffin bench beside Ike Vail, a well-known confidence man and frequent inmate on Blackwell's Island.[26] Vail quickly realized that Appo knew nothing about carpentry but promised to turn him into a "boss carpenter" and "square him up" if a keeper grew suspicious. "In about two weeks," Appo bragged, "I was an expert coffin maker."

Lax discipline, inadequate security, abandonment of any rehabilitative goals, and overcrowding made escape from the island easy. Warden John Fox admitted that getting off Blackwell's Island was so simple that friends of inmates arrived in boats daily to facilitate their early and illegal departures. Workhouse customs assigned soon-to-be released prisoners to general work around the island, while both the penitentiary and

*Ike Vail.*

*This 1879 Leslie's cartoon satirized convict escapes from Blackwell's Island.*

the workhouse employed inmates as "runners" with considerable freedom of movement throughout the island. In 1875 alone workhouse officials admitted that 488 inmates escaped or "eloped." Escape from Blackwell's Island was virtually a daily event.[27]

Resourceful inmates mocked the discipline on Blackwell's Island. One teenage prisoner argued that "nobody that had any 'nerve' in them" stayed on the island, while another proclaimed that he could "escape at almost any time." In 1888 officials discovered that workhouse inmates were frequently liberated by purchasing blank discharge forms from prison keepers and then forging the signatures of police magistrates. Some escapes were ingenious. Prisoners supplied the coxswain with so much liquor that they were able to run off on reaching Manhattan. A former inmate knew of at least three men who unhinged doors, converted them to rafts, and paddled to freedom. Still others literally played dead. Inmates assigned to the penitentiary carpenter shop manufactured coffins for the Hart's Island potter's field. After poking airholes on the side for breathing, escaping prisoners hid themselves in the coffins. One inmate gloated that he had escaped during two of his three previous incarcerations. During one he dived into the river and swam. The guard fired but missed because, declared the convict, he "was more loaded than the gun."[28]

At times the ease of escape from Blackwell's Island bordered on the absurd. In April 1874, for instance, police justice Butler Bixby sentenced Kitty Devine to the penitentiary for three months for drunken and disorderly conduct. A week later Devine reappeared before Bixby on the same charge. She confessed that her friends had removed her from the island in a boat. Bixby immediately resentenced her, only to find her before him again several weeks later. Enough was enough, thought Bixby. On 8 June 1874, he sentenced Devine to one year for her multiple escapes. Alas, less than two months later, Devine was arrested on Bayard Street and brought before Bixby. Again she testified that she had escaped in a boat. Bixby was at a loss what to do, openly wondering "whether a commitment to the island means incarceration or not."[29]

DURING APPO'S SECOND TERM on Blackwell's in 1895, he encountered an old nemesis: Louis D. Pilsbury. After his dismissal as superintendent of state prisons in 1882, Pilsbury resurfaced four years later when he was named warden of the Blackwell's Island penitentiary. His nearly twelve-year tenure proved to be one of the longest of any high official there.[30]

Pilsbury immediately imposed more discipline. He required prisoners to say "Yes, sir" and "No, sir" when addressing guards and other officials. For a time he instituted the lockstep when inmates walked between their cells and the dining hall. He eliminated most visiting privileges, limiting inmates to one monthly visit on a designated day. To frustrate escapes he adopted a stricter monitoring system, counting inmates as frequently as ten times daily. Finally he restricted boat traffic to and from the island.[31]

Pilsbury was among the earliest proponents of breaking up the institutions of Blackwell's Island. In 1884 the commissioners of Charities and Correction purchased Riker's Island specifically for constructing a new penitentiary and thereby physically separating facilities for relief of the distressed and those for punishment. Pilsbury recommended moving the penitentiary to Riker's Island for just that reason. By the 1890s several grand juries concurred, condemning the deteriorated condition of the buildings on the island. Municipal officials, however, were slow to respond: Only in 1936 did the penitentiary finally move to Riker's Island.[32]

IN 1842 a Blackwell's Island superintendent confessed that the prison system only encouraged inmates to engage in more crime. "It is as regular a succession as the classes in a college, from the house of refuge to the penitentiary, and from the penitentiary to the State prison," he concluded. More than a generation later little had changed. Inmates like Appo not only learned the ways of the underworld; they frequently determined the conditions of their incarceration. The failure to enforce rules of silence found in other penitentiaries, the inadequate number of guards, the ability of inmates to control their work assignments, the easy physical movement about the island, and the frequency of escape reflected a degree of internal inmate control found in few other carceral institutions. Such conditions convinced many inmates that life was little more than a game of fortune. The experience of Blackwell's Island did little to humiliate or discipline convicts as did Sing Sing or Clinton penitentiaries. "The prevailing feeling of criminals, of all grades, is that they are *wronged*," noted Lydia Maria Child. "What we call *justice*, they regard as an unlucky *chance*."[33]

> ⌁  *I was about three weeks in the Workhouse [in 1879], when I made up my mind to try and escape from there. I managed to get a little steel saw brought over to another prisoner by a visitor. The night guard made his rounds every half hour and after 9 p.m., and he would never count the men in the big cells. I cut the bar of the window and one stormy, rainy night about 1:35 a.m., pulled the bar out and lowered myself from the top window to the ground by strips of my blanket. The other fellow did not come down and I saw him pull the rope blanket up.*
>
> *I went to the river and tried to swim across to New York, but the tide was too strong for me to swim against, so I swam under the boathouse. As the big sweep boat pulled up on the davits, I had to climb up to get into the boat as quietly as possible as the crew slept inside the boathouse. I unhitched one pulley at a time, first lowering the bow a little, then belay [sic] the rope and go to the stern, lowered that end down and so on, until I got the big boat on the water. Then to make matters worse, I found that the boat had a double bow and no place to scull it. I had to pull on one oar and then climb over the seat and pull on the other oar. In all events, I got the big boat safely across, although I came nearly being run down by a passing steamer.*
>
> *On reaching New York, I tied the oars to the seat and pulled out the plug from the bottom of the boat and sunk her at the dock. Then*

*I walked in my underclothes to a tenement house and by good luck,
I saw a pair of overalls lying on the bedroom window. I took them,
put them on, and rolled up the bottoms about ten inches. I then
took a Third Avenue car and rode downtown to Mulberry Street
where I got some clothes. The next day I left New York for
Philadelphia.*[34]

# 9

# The Dives

=

AFTER A SHORT STAY in Philadelphia, Appo returned to New York.

> ◄§   *I then lay around the opium joints and dives of the city, such places as Owney Geoghegan's, Billy McGlory's and the Haymarket. I would pass the nights in these dance halls making a good fellow out of myself, spending the dishonest money I made grafting during the day.[1]*

In ways that George Appo little understood, the "dives" of New York organized the lives of pickpockets and con men. Concert halls like Geoghegan's, McGlory's, and the Haymarket, as well as opium dens and certain saloons, promoted an unstated but distinct subculture and code of behavior. Here Appo went on release from prison. Here he spent the hundreds, if not thousands, of dollars he earned every month. Here he met and socialized with former associates and future accomplices. Here he endeavored to make himself into a good fellow.[2]

Origins of the term "dive" are difficult to pinpoint. Mid-nineteenth-century New Yorkers apparently employed the word to describe disreputable drinking establishments located in basements, thereby requiring patrons to figuratively "dive" into them to escape public view. One reporter defined a dive as "a place that is low down, beneath the street level, and is devoted to drinking or dancing." By the 1880s, however, many accepted police detective Thomas Byrnes's assumption that a dive was any unlicensed leisure establishment: a house of prostitution, gambling den, policy office, or opium den.[3]

In reality such places were more than low-down cellars. Geoghegan's, McGlory's, the Haymarket, and other concert saloons generated controversy and public outrage for a host of reasons. First, they openly promoted illicit forms of sexuality, allowing prostitutes to work as waitresses or "waiter girls," and to solicit customers as they worked. The fact that a state statute regulating concert halls outlawed female waitresses in 1862 hardly discouraged establishments from finding loopholes to escape the restriction. Second, concert saloons routinely violated excise laws regulating the sale of alcohol. Police officials received monthly payments from concert saloon proprietors in return for ignoring excise regulations. Third, dives were the physical spaces that fostered an unlicensed leisure underworld, an institutional rendezvous for Gotham's criminal universe. Bob Crumley, a former actor and associate of the popular tragedian Edwin Forrest, admitted he entered the green goods business as a steerer like Appo after hanging out at Harry Hill's concert saloon and other prominent dives. Not only did proprietors tolerate convicted felons like Appo, they were frequently ex-convicts themselves. "The dives of New York," summarized former police chief George Walling, "are the hot-bed of its crime."[4]

Finally concert saloons combined these illicit activities with stage shows and other forms of popular entertainment, making such places the most celebrated nighttime venues in the metropolis. Dives not only connected elements of working-class and plebeian culture with the underworld, but, as the historian Daniel Czitrom has written, confused the line between entertainments that were licensed and those that were licentious. Dives "were the centers of 'high life,'" remembered police officer Cornelius Willemse, "and people flocked to see them from all parts of the world."[5] They were the first nightclubs.

The most notorious dives were on the Bowery. By the 1870s Geoghegan's was the best known and the first to enjoy a national reputation. Inside, the establishment was full of "flash pictures," gaudy decorations, and cheap furniture. Images of noted English and American prizefighters adorned the walls, giving the establishment an atmosphere of pugilism and muscle.[6]

Owen "Owney" Geoghegan personified the rough-and-tumble underworld of mid-nineteenth-century New York. Born in Ireland in 1841, on the eve of the Great Famine, Geoghegan arrived in New York at the age of eight and grew up in the "gashouse" district on the East Side. He eventually developed a reputation as a courageous street fighter and hard hitter despite his five-foot-four-inch height and 140-pound weight. Geoghegan was noted for spitting in the faces of opponents when they faced off in the ring. In 1861 the "Irish Terror," as his admirers called him, defeated

Ed Touhey in a prizefight at Kit Burns's Sportsman's Hall on Water Street, making him a favorite among "the short-haired fraternity." The *Times* described him as "bold, intrepid, and fearless," adding that Geoghegan "could take any amount of punishment without feeling it."[7]

Violence followed Geoghegan outside the ring. In 1872 he joined William Hennessy in physically attacking Michael J. McNally on the front steps of Tammany Hall, the headquarters of New York's Democratic political machine. Geoghegan was charged with assault and battery with intent to kill, but the jury acquitted him without ever leaving the jury box. Three years later he was accused of murdering his associate Jimmy Rose, but was released when officials declared the death a suicide.[8]

Geoghegan avoided criminal conviction in part because he parlayed his pugilism into politics. A rival of future Tammany leader Richard Croker as a youth, Geoghegan nevertheless became an influential member of Tammany Hall. In 1864 Geoghegan and a group of friends confronted an opponent, James Irving, in Tammany Hall with pistols and knives, openly threatening to kill him. Two years later Geoghegan and Irving briefly resolved their differences and agreed to support each other's bid for elective office. But when Geoghegan later learned that Irving double-crossed him, he found him along Second Avenue and belted him into the gutter. By the 1870s Geoghegan was a master at illegally registering thousands of people to vote at his Bowery establishment. These "repeaters" or "colonizers," as they were called, were known for voting early and often.[9]

Geoghegan exploited his political connections and fisticuff fame in the liquor business. Although he proclaimed himself a "tea-totaler," he opened the first of several sporting houses in 1862. Geoghegan's dives might best be described as palaces of pugilism, openly promoting a rowdy and rugged ambience. He required, for example, that any boxer performing in his place had to fight like a demon. "I don't want any fancy light sparring," Geoghegan allegedly warned all fighters. "I want you mugs to fight like hell or yer don't get a damned cent." Hence many poor, punch-drunk, battered patrons slugged, scuffled, and smashed away at each other until they were blood soaked and exhausted, all for the reward of $2.50. By contrast Geoghegan reportedly accumulated a fortune of $75,000.[10]

By 1877 Geoghegan was running "the Old House at Home" on the Bowery, better known as "the Bastille of the Bowery." The inconspicuous two-story building had small stages on each floor on which performers danced, belted out bawdy songs, and even belted each other when the stage was converted into a prize ring. One reporter described Geoghegan's patrons as "the toughest and most disreputable element in the city." Not to be outmuscled, Geoghegan hired former convicts and men of "unexampled ferocity" as waiters and bouncers. Even professional con artists were loath to ply their trade in Geoghegan's. "Once within its walls," wrote one, "the blind man saw that he got the right change, the cripple laid aside his crutches and the victim of starvation paid for his drinks from a full purse."[11]

Geoghegan was even controversial with police officials. He had numerous conflicts with the local police captains Foley and Anthony J. Allaire, accumulating more than one hundred indictments. But Geoghegan's political pull eventually secured Foley's dismissal, an event he celebrated with a mock wake over the captain's effigy. In 1883 the Society for the Prevention of Cruelty to Children (SPCC) prosecuted Geoghegan for admitting underage youths. When Geoghegan accused SPCC agents of accepting bribes, the organization made the prosecution of Geoghegan a test case. He was convicted of excise violations, fined five hundred dollars, and sentenced to three months in prison.[12]

Owney Geoghegan.

The conviction stunned Geoghegan's admirers and marked the onset of his decline. The concert saloon proprietor contracted rheumatism while in prison, left Blackwell's Island in shattered health, sold his business, and reportedly moved to San Francisco, Hawaii, and finally Hot Springs, Arkansas. There Geoghegan died in 1885 at the age of forty-three.[13]

The chief beneficiary of Geoghegan's downfall was his next-door competitor Billy McGlory. Whenever Geoghegan offered variety performances in the rear of his place, McGlory hired bands, stationed them near an adjoining window, and instructed them to play whenever a performer

*Billy McGlory.*

at Geoghegan's opened his or her mouth. Geoghegan eventually abandoned vocal entertainment. On other occasions, when patrons of Geoghegan's entered the wrong establishment, McGlory's men pretended they were in the right place, encouraging them to purchase many drinks. Not surprisingly Geoghegan's employees returned the favor to McGlory.[14]

McGlory, however, was no angel. William H. "Billy" McGlory, alias William McGrory and Henry Thompson, was born in the Sixth Ward to Irish immigrant parents. One newspaper claimed that "Five Points was his school and the Bowery his college." Little is known of his childhood, although some alleged that he was the half brother of John Thompson, the eminent tragedian. As an adult McGlory stood five feet nine inches in height and weighed approximately 135 pounds. He carried an air of bravado, dressed in loud attire, wore large diamond stickpins, and sported a shiny silk hat. Some described McGlory as the perfect representation of a Bowery boy. For a brief time in the 1880s, McGlory personified the underworld. He was dubbed the "high priest of vice" and the "wickedest man in New York." By 1888 McGlory owned an eleven-acre estate on Long Island.[15]

The earliest record of McGlory appeared in 1866 when he was convicted of first-degree robbery and sentenced to five years in Sing Sing. Somehow he secured an early release and eventually opened two of the leading nighttime resorts in New York: the Windsor Palace on the Bowery near Canal Street, and the Armory Hall concert saloon, a short block west of the Bowery. His proprietorships generated numerous arrests. Between 1878 and 1882 McGlory was arrested at least eighteen times on charges ranging from violating excise laws to assault and battery. In each instance the charges were dropped. By the early 1880s McGlory's joined

Harry Hill's, "The" Allen's, and Tom Gould's as one of Gotham's four leading concert saloons.[16]

McGlory was best known and remembered as the proprietor of Armory Hall, reportedly a former military facility with an imposing yellow facade marked by Corinthian columns and flashing lights from its many windows. Inside, patrons were first met by a long bar, beside which was reputedly the largest dance hall in the city, surrounded by tables. Above was a three-sided gallery holding an orchestra, wine rooms, and private booths where patrons, for the right price, indulged in more sexually intimate exchanges.[17]

The journalist Herbert Asbury later described McGlory's as "probably the most vicious resort New York has ever seen." While Asbury was frequently guilty of hyperbole, contemporaries acknowledged that the establishment was populated by underworld figures and promoted an environment of promiscuous sexuality, interracial mixing, and physical violence. A typical McGlory event was the Grand Scarlet Ball of 1883. With more than two thousand masked patrons in attendance, the Armory Hall program included a grand cakewalk with fifty African American men and women, several boxing matches between men *and* women, a beauty contest, a heavyweight boxing championship, a drill contest between "Billy McGlory's Light Zouaves" and Dan McSorley's "Brigade," concluding with a spectacular masquerade and fandango. At other times McGlory's was filled with numerous teenage girls, dancing the cancan and various erotic dances in which they pulled up their dresses. Such behavior stereotyped them, rightly or wrongly, as prostitutes. McGlory charged a fifteen-cent admission price because, in his words, "It keeps the lovers out and brings the suckers in." Whenever fights broke out between women, McGlory's response was to let them fight it out.[18]

McGlory's establishments housed an openly underworld element. McGlory's henchmen included Henry Snyder, Philip Marks, and John Flynn, all of whom were serving long prison terms by 1883. Waiters included fighters like Joe Morris, a professional boxer and flimflam man. Another, "Sheeny Joe," was a former inmate of Sing Sing. John Craig (alias John Corkey) was reputed for his "tough character" and dexterity in handling a knife. Other McGlory associates were reputed opium smokers. When the detective Charles Rillings investigated Armory Hall in 1883, he wrote that McGlory approached him and recommended he leave because several patrons were out to kill him.[19]

McGlory countered these unsavory charges in a variety of ways. He proclaimed his Bowery establishment "respectable," himself a teetotaler. He ran an informal community assistance program, giving money to impoverished local residents to pay their rent and meet other daily needs. He sponsored Jerry McAuley's evangelist revival meetings in Armory Hall as proof of his sincerity. And he remained active in Republican Party politics.[20]

Late in 1883 J. B. Gibbs of the Manhattan Temperance Association and the *New York Press* made McGlory and Armory Hall a cause célèbre. After Gibbs had McGlory arrested for selling liquor without a license, he posted daily bulletins in front of his Nassau Street restaurant describing the progress of the case. Reporters from the *Press* and *Star* testified during McGlory's trial that waiters served alcohol and introduced them to women who described themselves as "good bedfellows." In the end Gibbs prevailed. McGlory was convicted and sentenced to six months on Blackwell's Island.[21]

Such prosecutions proved to be show trials for McGlory, however, enhancing his popularity with Gotham's working poor. His defiant attitude and flamboyant style generated packed courtrooms. When Gibbs left his Nassau Street restaurant after McGlory's conviction, he was greeted, according to one reporter, by "a score of tattered and bedraggled bootblacks," who serenaded him with sarcasm: "Ows Billy, Gibbsey? Eh, ows Billy?" Upon McGlory's release his supporters threw a wild celebration, marching in to the tune of "When [Billy] comes marching home again, hurrah, hurrah." On another occasion when McGlory was brought to court in the Black Maria, he was handcuffed to a young suspect, "who looked upon him in awestruck admiration," noted one observer. "The boy seemed to think the contact a glorious event in his life."[22]

Armory Hall was not just a locus of criminality. McGlory's dive was among the most racially integrated venues in the city. African American men, for example, worked as waiters in the private booths and wine rooms, while others performed onstage. Peter Patience was known for his success at removing change from customers while telling them humorous stories, a talent that earned him the nickname "Conversation Pete." Indeed, McGlory's clientele was often socially mixed, one observer noting that patrons included girls "in torn dresses and bare hands" as well as "women in silk."[23]

When police and municipal officials cracked down on unlicensed concert saloons in 1886 and 1887, McGlory kept a low profile by advertising that he served "temperance drinks" and claiming that his theatrical license was for sponsoring Jewish and other ethnic plays. The music and dancing inside was "no different from what could be found in any dancing academy," argued McGlory. Eventually, according to some reports, McGlory was forced by police officials to close. In 1891 he sold Armory Hall for a reported eighty-seven thousand dollars.[24]

Shortly thereafter, however, McGlory was back in business. In 1891 he joined his nephew, Edward Corey, and a local ward detective in opening the Hotel Irving on East Fourteenth Street, opposite the Academy of Music. Because of his now-infamous reputation, McGlory needed a front man, so businessman Frederick Krause served as the legal owner. Through physical violence and legal chicanery, McGlory took control of the hotel from Krause, introducing numerous prostitutes into the establishment. When Krause objected, McGlory beat him so badly that Krause was bedridden for seven weeks.[25]

McGlory was soon hauled into court. This time he was represented by Congressman John R. Fellows. Years earlier, as a prosecutor, Fellows had sent McGlory to the penitentiary for a six-month sentence. Even a former district attorney, however, could not save McGlory this time. After two days of testimony, the jury convicted McGlory in three minutes. More significant, on 8 January 1892, Recorder Frederick Smyth concluded that McGlory was "utterly bad," sentencing the defendant to one year of hard labor on Blackwell's Island and a three-hundred-dollar fine.[26]

A year later, on his release from prison, McGlory was reportedly a broken man. He tried unsuccessfully to open several establishments over the ensuing six years, but creditors chased and judges fined him, in one case to the tune of twelve hundred dollars. On skipping bail and contracting consumption, McGlory traveled with his wife throughout the West under an assumed name. When he returned to New York in July, he was incarcerated in Ludlow Street jail. In 1899 he opened a combined saloon, music hall, and ballroom on West Fifty-ninth Street. Public opposition led to its closing within the year. "We can't all be Sunday school teachers and bank presidents," complained McGlory. He was never heard from again.[27]

## THE HAYMARKET

The Haymarket was among the most notorious underworld establishments of Gilded Age New York. Located on Sixth Avenue between Twenty-ninth and Thirtieth Streets, the concert hall was described as "a marketplace for wholesale prostitution." Originally a playhouse called the Argyle Rooms in the 1870s, the Haymarket was converted into a dance hall in 1878 and remained in business until 1913. Critics remarked that its nighttime facade was as brightly lit as a Broadway theater and reflected "the licentious life of the avenue." On and around the dance floor, women smoked, drank, and accosted patrons to "treat" them. In 1907, the Ashcan school artist John Sloan immortalized the establishment in one of his paintings.[28]

Both geographically and symbolically the Haymarket was in the heart of Gotham's nightlife district. One block east, along Broadway, were New York's leading theaters, hotels, and restaurants, catering to the city's

*John Sloan's* The Haymarket *(1907).*

upper-class residents and tourist trade. A block west was Seventh Avenue, described by one observer to be "as 'tough' and certainly more rough, than the Bowery." In between was Sixth Avenue, populated by concert saloons like the Haymarket, as well as department stores, restaurants, theaters, gambling dens, and unlicensed taverns. Better known as the "Tenderloin," this section of the city provided entertainments of all kinds. The "Tenderloin is more than a place," concluded the writer Stephen Crane. "It is an emotion."[29]

The Haymarket was populated by a cross-section of the underworld. In addition to the many prostitutes, other women routinely robbed customers inside. One reporter claimed its male clientele consisted of gamblers, confidence men, thieves, pimps, and other "fancy men." Indeed, the Haymarket was where Appo met pimps and opium smokers like Harry Hilton and Dolph Saunders, who later hired him as a con man. Abutting the back entrance to the Haymarket was the Artistic Club, best known for accommodating male homosexual prostitutes and their customers. When public opposition and police harassment forced the closing of the Haymarket, proprietors simply changed the name and reopened it. In 1897 and 1898 the Haymarket assumed a variety of new names, becoming at various points the Newmarket, the Gramercy Club, the Belden Club, and the Metropole Club.[30]

By the 1890s the Haymarket's proprietor was Edward W. Corey, the nephew or stepson of Billy McGlory. Corey practiced the same public relations techniques as did Harry Hill, another leading concert saloon proprietor, insisting that "everything was aboveboard" and no pickpocketing was tolerated. One police captain in 1899 claimed that homosexuals (referred to as "French people" and "degenerates") were not permitted. By 1902 Haymarket proprietors demanded "outward decency" from every patron. Prostitutes arrested for robbing clients were barred. Couples who danced the foxtrot or "cheek to cheek" were thrown out. "An innocent man and his wife could have wandered into the Haymarket," wrote one police captain, "and been entirely unconscious of what was going on around them."[31]

While the Haymarket was the best-known dive for much of the final quarter of the nineteenth century, a plethora of similar institutions populated the area. Other nearby resorts included the White Elephant, the Cremorne, Buckingham Palace, the Tivoli, the Chelsea, the Bohemia, and the Columbia. Some, like the Cairo at 36 West Thirty-ninth Street, were decorated in exotic "Turkish" styles; sexual solicitation was so open that one patron referred to it as "an exchange for prostitutes."[32]

The Haymarket's leading competitor, however, was the Sans Souci. Some even considered it to be "the most noted resort in the Tenderloin." Many knew the Sans Souci by simply the name of its proprietor— Gould's. Born in New York City between 1845 and 1852, Thomas Edmund "Tom" Gould joined a volunteer fire company as a youth. He soon devel-

oped a heroic reputation, allegedly for saving as many as fifteen lives. Standing five feet seven inches in height and sporting a long blond mustache, Gould was described as "big chested," "lithe limbed," and "handsome." After briefly working as a railroad employee and detective, Gould attracted the attention of various Tammany Hall officials. Although he was too young to serve, Gould was nominated for Congress in the Fifth Congressional District of New York when he was only twenty-two years old.[33]

Politics was not Gould's great ambition, however. Entertainment was. By 1875 he ran a Broadway saloon. Several years later he was identified as the proprietor of the Burnt Rag on Bleecker Street, indicating that he enjoyed some relationship with Billy McGlory. By 1881 Gould was running the

*Tom Gould.*

Sans Souci, conveniently located on West Thirty-first Street between the elite theaters to the east on Broadway and prostitute-populated concert halls along Sixth Avenue to the west.[34]

While the Sans Souci most likely tolerated, if not encouraged, prostitution and gambling, the establishment was noted for sponsoring performances by African American musicians and singers. Critics like J. W. Keller of the evangelical publication *Truth* admitted that "Gould generally managed to keep the place in pretty good order." Yet, from 1885 to 1887, Gould was cited for violating excise or theatrical statutes at least thirteen times, but was never successfully prosecuted.[35]

In 1887, in the wake of Mayor Abram Hewitt's antiprostitution campaign, Gould's Sans Souci was forced to close. When he was brought to court to answer seven "pigeon-holed" or unprosecuted indictments, Gould fled to Toronto and Montreal. There he quickly parlayed his fame, becoming "the king pin of all select social circles," according to one report. Eventually, Gould's attorney, Abraham Hummel (who also represented Harry Hill and George Appo), negotiated a settlement in which Gould paid one thousand dollars in fines and received a thirty-day sentence.[36]

Despite these prosecutions the Sans Souci remained in business for at least another year, usually under the name of Thomas or John J. Wogan, allegedly a twenty-one-year-old cousin of Gould's. In 1889 Gould opened a basement restaurant on Sixth Avenue. A huge picture of Gould dominated the establishment, which was reportedly filled with enough ex-convicts "to make a fair-sized rogues' gallery," joked one reporter. Gould denied any direct involvement, insisting that Wogan hired him as a "drawing card." By 1891 the establishment did a brisk business, reportedly surpassing McGlory's.[37]

Like many dive keepers, Gould was a violent man. In 1880 Millie Freeman charged that after she refused Gould's request that they cohabitate, Gould promised to "blow her brains out." Instead he simply shot her. Moreover, plentiful cases of assault, battery, robbery, and excise violations were filed against Gould and his establishments. In 1890 Wogan and Gould allegedly belted several drunk patrons and stole more than one hundred dollars from their persons. On Christmas evening 1891 Wogan was shot and killed when he attempted to remove a patron from the premises. Two years later, while running an "all-night joint" on West Twenty-fourth Street, Gould assaulted one of his barkeepers, reducing the barkeeper's head "to a bloody pulp." Soon after, Gould's creditors and police officials forced him to retire.[38]

Despite his many run-ins with the law, Gould remained active in New York politics, thus illustrating the fluidity of the line separating Gotham's political establishment from the institutional supports of the city's underworld. In 1890 reports circulated that Gould had approached the People's Municipal League, a reform group, asking for the nomination to be alderman in the Thirteenth Assembly District. A year later he was nominated by the Brewer and Liquor Dealers' Association for a judgeship.[39]

Although Gould had a short-lived acting career in 1894, he never reclaimed his success. He was unsuccessful in opening a new establishment after 1895, even serving time in the Ludlow Street jail on a civil action. He briefly worked on Coney Island and as a watchman for a contracting firm. After being diagnosed with consumption, he allegedly experienced a spiritual conversion and joined the Salvation Army. His health worsened during 1899, and he suffered several strokes, the final one proving fatal on 18 February 1900. Gould was forty-seven years old and, reported the *Times*, "forgotten by all of his old associates." Like Owney Geoghegan, he was buried in Calvary Cemetery in Queens.[40]

WHY DID DIVES, despite their illegality and repeated affronts to propriety, thrive? The most obvious answer was the intimate relationships they fostered with municipal officials. Owney Geoghegan and Tom Gould were longtime members of Tammany Hall, even running for elective office. Billy McGlory was allied to the Republican Party. Politically active dive keepers were important sources of revenue for both elected and appointed municipal officials. At election time dives contributed handsomely to politicians who allowed them to operate. In other instances, they enabled other officials to move up the municipal ladder. When captain positions were available in the Police Department, for example, they were often "sold" for considerable sums of money. In 1891 Timothy J. Creeden learned that in order to be promoted to captain, he needed to pay fifteen thousand dollars to one of the police commissioners. A coalition of dive keepers established a fund and provided loans or promissory notes to support Creeden's candidacy. To the aspiring public official, lamented the editor E. L. Godkin, "the liquor-dealer is their guide, philosopher, and creditor."[41]

Under such conditions proprietors developed close and personal relationships with local police officials. Some, like Owney Geoghegan, had family members on the police force. Edward Corey, Billy McGlory's partner, relative, and later Haymarket proprietor, had a stepfather who was a ward detective and reportedly introduced him to the business. In 1879 the Society for the Prevention of Crime complained that one of the greatest drawbacks to law enforcement was the familiarity of police officers with saloonkeepers.[42]

A third factor was ineffective law enforcement. Excise violators were so numerous and court calendars so crowded that district attorneys admitted that dive cases were infrequently, if ever, prosecuted. Thus, in 1886, Tom Gould and his bartenders were arrested twenty-three times.

The pattern was the same for McGlory's, the Haymarket, and other popular dives. Concert saloon owner Theodore "The" Allen alone was arrested more than thirty times for bookmaking, pool selling, and assault and battery, but was never convicted of any charge. Even when convicted, excise violators paid the fine, had their license revoked, and then reopened under another name. At worst dives ran without a license. When waiters working in Tom Gould's Sans Souci were sentenced to six months in prison for excise violations, their lawyer appealed, obtained a writ of habeas corpus, and posted their bail. They never served any time.[43]

Bewildering laws did little to facilitate prosecution. Tom Gould complained that licenses were often issued under the old 1857 statute, not in accordance with amendments passed in 1873. Since almost anyplace selling liquor was in technical violation of the law, enforcement was "confused and contradictory." Others noted that upscale hotels fell under different rules regarding the sale of liquor. More important, unlicensed establishments that did not sell alcoholic beverages were not required to follow excise regulations; thus they never had to close. Proprietors of dives often lied and claimed that they sold no alcohol. Some, like Geoghegan and McGlory, pretended to be teetotalers. In this fashion unlicensed dive keepers were better off than their licensed competitors.[44]

Finally the success of Geoghegan's, McGlory's, and Gould's rested on their popularity. These were among the earliest "bohemian" enclaves in the United States. Here pickpockets and prostitutes socialized with millionaires and society matrons. Wall Street magnates interacted with Broadway sharpshooters. Such places even inspired the literary realism of American writers like Stephen Crane and William Sidney Porter (better known as O. Henry). Future Nobel laureate Eugene O'Neill's sonnet "The Haymarket" immortalized that establishment.

> The music blares into a rag-time tune—
> The dancers whirl around the polished floor;
> Each powdered face a set expression wore
> Of dull satiety, and wan smiles swoon
> On rouged lips at sallies opportune
> Of maudlin youth whose sodden spirits soar
> On drunken wings; while through the opening door
> A chilly blast sweeps like the breath of doom.[45]

Geoghegan, McGlory, and Gould were, in the words of one pick-pocket, "celebrities in the saloon." When Appo wrote retrospectively of passing the nights in these establishments, transforming himself into a good fellow, he assumed that readers knew these places and their propri-etors. Most likely they did. In Gilded Age Gotham, Geoghegan, Gould, and others like them were luminaries in no need of explanation. Like P. T. Barnum and nineteenth-century theatrical boosters, dive keepers recognized the entertainment value of their personal appeal, the com-mercial worth of their fame. Before an age when entertainment impresa-rios advertised the stardom of their patrons, the entrepreneurs of concert saloons were celebrities and self-promoters.[46]

Dive keepers understood the affinity they shared with male, and often working-class, customers. If dives were just abodes of spontaneous and unregulated violence, pickpockets and con men like George Appo would never have patronized them. But by emphasizing their own rugged mas-culinity and criminal records, dive keepers attracted a male audience seeking to connect with or reaffirm elements of the "forbidden." Drink-ing, gambling, and relaxing in the dens of Geoghegan, McGlory, or Gould made one more of a man.

The public popularity and celebrity status of dive keepers made them controversial figures in their time, confusing ones in ours. Each one of them generated contradictory images. McGlory promoted an atmosphere of rough masculinity while tolerating male homosexual liaisons. They consorted with thieves and spent time in prison; yet some described them as personally honest as they allied themselves to the political estab-lishment of national parties and Tammany Hall. They were idols to some, tyrants to others. The dive keeper, concluded one, was "a strange man in a strange community."[47]

## JACK COLLINS

&#8667;  *On my arrival in New York, I left the depot and went downtown to a saloon called Speigle's at 45 Bayard Street, where I know many of my acquaintances could be found. On entering this saloon I saw six of them seated at a table playing cards. Two of them got up and greeted me with "Hello, George! Where have you been?"*

*"I just got in town," I replied. "Let us have a drink."*

*The six men came up to the bar and the proprietor waited on us. I handed the proprietor a ten dollar bill to take out the cost of the drinks, and in giving me the change, he laid a five dollar bill on the bar. As he did so, one of the six men, a bully and a fighter named Jack Collins, picked up the money, put it in his pocket and said: "I'll take care of this."*

*"Oh, no, you won't, give me that back, you are too funny." At the same time I took hold of his coat collar. He then struck me a violent blow on my neck. I held onto him and had him bent over the bar counter. He reached for a beer glass to hit me and I knew he would do it if I gave him the chance. So I took out my pen knife, broke loose from him, got the blade open and as he rushed in at me with the beer glass, I cut him. He fell in a heap on the floor with the glass still in his hand.*

*I walked out quietly from the place, saw the officer running over to the saloon, went up to him and said: "There's a fellow hurt inside."*

*The proprietor said to the officer, pointing at me: "This young man must have cut him, I'm not sure, but he is badly hurt and deserves it."*

*"Did you cut him? Where's the knife?" asked the officer (Gleason by name). He began to search me, blew his whistle and another officer came and got the ambulance from St. Vincent's Hospital, took me to the station house, and the next morning, to the bed side of Collins at the Hospital, and asked him: "Is this the man who stabbed you?"*

*He would not answer yes or no but said "Never mind, I'll fix the ———— when I get up out of here." Finally, on going out of the hospital ward, he called the officer back and said: "Hold him anyhow, don't let him get out. I'll see about him later on."*

*"Did he stab you? Answer that question, yes or no," demanded
the officer. He would not answer. I was then brought to court and
held to await the results of his injuries anyway. Collins got better
and I was indicted and charged with felonious assault with attempt
to kill and the newspapers were calling me all sorts of names and
bringing up the father's misfortunes.*

*Finally, I employed [the] lawyer Edmund E. Price, and he advised
me to stand trial. I did so and was surprised to see all the witnesses
of good standing take the stand in my behalf. Even the good hospital
Doctor Walsh told the judge that Collins was the meanest foul
mouthed loafer that ever came under his medical care and how he
would insult the good Sisters of Mercy[1] who nursed him back to life.
Even the unfortunate girl off whom he lived told the judge and jury
of his mean brutality he inflicted upon her if she failed to bring him
money. The judge, in charging the jury, told them "That he considered a glass in the hands of an enraged man as deadly a weapon as
a knife." The result was the jury went out and returned in a few
minutes with the verdict* "Not Guilty."[2]

# 10

# Tombs Justice

=

GEORGE APPO'S INCARCERATION and indictment for his fracas with Jack Collins took place in New York's Halls of Justice, better known as "the Tombs." Here, under one roof in the heart of New York City, was the physical representation of criminal justice in New York. Inside was the entire corpus of criminal law: judges, juries, magistrates, attorneys, courtrooms, and jail cells. Considered by many to be the most famous prison on the continent, the Tombs was "America's greatest criminal barracks." Appo would be incarcerated there on at least eight occasions.[1]

Gotham's jail was commonly described as a terrifying place. "Vast, lofty and forbidding," according to one writer, "an echoless quarry of cold, unpitying stone." The writer George Foster referred to the Tombs as a "grim mausoleum," a "foul lazar-house of polluted and festering humanity." The very name of the Tombs was suggestive of death. The Tombs appropriately served as the final setting for the demise and death of the main characters in Herman Melville's "Bartleby the Scrivener" and *Pierre*.[2]

New York's Halls of Justice faced Centre Street and occupied the entire block bounded by Elm, Leonard, and Franklin Streets. Designed by the architect John Haviland and constructed between 1835 and 1838, the structure was long considered the finest example of Egyptian revival style in the United States. Almost immediately nicknamed "the Tombs," the building remained the nation's largest jail until its destruction in 1897.[3]

The original Tombs housed 173 individual cells and two police court cells for males and females, each capable of holding up to two hundred prisoners. In addition the Courts of General and Special Sessions, the First District Police Court, the House of Detention, and the offices of the district attorney, sheriff, and clerk were located in the Tombs. Most of these courts and officials' offices later moved to the new courthouse building (better known as the "Tweed Courthouse" because of its con-

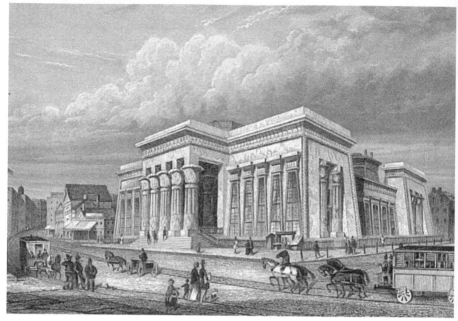

The Tombs (1850), W. Heine.

struction during the political reign of William M. Tweed) in 1872. And by 1880 the constant overcrowding of inmates led to the construction of two more buildings in the courtyard, increasing the number of cells to 303.[4]

Inside, the main hall was divided into four tiers of cells, connected by narrow stairways and heated by two large stoves. Cells were eight feet long, six feet wide, and eleven feet in height. Each contained a single bed thirty inches wide and a twelve- by three-inch window. Tiers were allegedly divided by class of criminal. The bottom tier was reserved for lunatics, delirium tremens cases, and convicted felons prior to their removal to state prison, Blackwell's Island, or the gallows—hence the name "Murderer's Row." The second tier was occupied by those charged with murder, robbery, and other serious crimes, while "lower grade" criminals such as burglars and larcenists were relegated to the third tier. The uppermost level was filled with misdemeanants and petty criminals.[5]

Almost upon opening the Tombs suffered from physical decay. The edifice was constructed on the sinking, marshy landfill of the old Collect

Pond, so dampness pervaded the entire structure. The unstable foundation quickly produced four-inch cracks in some walls. Sewage regularly backed up through the drains into lower-level cells, while cesspools and piped water underneath the police court sometimes overflowed into the courtroom. By the 1880s sewer gas permeated the Tombs ventilation system and individual cells, nearly suffocating the men confined there. One reporter compared living conditions in the Tombs to steerage on a ship. "The difference," he wrote, "is that there is more fresh air in steerage quarters."[6]

Overcrowding made these physical circumstances worse. City officials admitted as early as 1850 that doubling and tripling up was a necessity. By 1860, with fewer than three hundred cells, the Tombs regularly incarcerated between four hundred and six hundred persons. Consequently nearly every cell contained two prisoners, sometimes three. "Doubled-up" inmates usually slept on the same narrow berth, each one sharing his pillow with the other's feet. In August 1895, when Appo was incarcerated in the Tombs, 428 prisoners were held in 298 cells—that was an improvement: In January 1894, only 280 cells were available for the 581 inmates. In periods of severe overcrowding, Tombs officials sometimes strung up hammocks for a third or even fourth prisoner per cell.[7]

Some never even had the floor. Five- to ten-day prisoners—vagrants, drunks, and minor offenders—were confined to large, converted office rooms. Nicknamed the "bummers' cell," "bummer's hall," or the "ten-day house," the cell was as small as twelve by thirty feet and held up to two hundred individuals. Inmates were forced to stand or sit until they were moved. These conditions were magnified in the summer, when the criminal justice system literally shut down as judges, court officials, and staff avoided the stifling, unbearably hot conditions by going on monthlong vacations.[8]

Yet the Tombs was more than just an unsanitary, overcrowded jail; it was Gotham writ small, a gathering place of nineteenth-century urban society. While sensationalized accounts focused on murder, passion, and deviance, most Tombs prisoners were not convicts. More often those incarcerated were individuals awaiting trial and too poor to afford bail.[9] The overwhelming majority (95 percent by 1895) of Tombs and other police court defendants were arrested summarily and "without process"; that is, without a warrant. By the mid-1870s New York's police courts annually disposed of more than eighty-four thousand cases, equivalent to one of every nine male residents. Indeed, during the last quarter of the nineteenth century, the total number of men arrested every five years roughly equaled New York City's entire adult male population. Tombs justice was a commonly shared experience not only for the law breaker but for the transient working-class male.[10]

## PRISON CASES

Appo, like the overwhelming majority of Tombs inmates, was a "prison case." Defendants unable to procure or afford bail languished in the Tombs for weeks, if not months. At some point private attorneys urged them to plead guilty and accept a sentence. A state assembly report in 1875 described the injustice of such practices as "too apparent to need comment." Others noted the fundamental hypocrisy involving prison cases. "The offender with money goes unmolested," complained the *World*, "while his poorer fellow-criminal goes to trial."[11]

For prison case defendants, incarceration in the Tombs was a bewildering experience. Once inside a Tombs cell, prisoners encountered a corrupt and confusing array of "runners," "steerers," "drummers," "shyster lawyers," and "straw bondsmen"—"Tombs vermin" in the words of Congressman Mike Walsh. Criminal attorneys routinely hired Tombs guards and other court officers as "runners" who were always searching for a "prize," namely an arrested individual with money. In return for being "touted," some lawyers paid keepers for the referral (usually half the fee), thereby doubling their salaries. Other keepers allowed outside agents working on behalf of certain criminal attorneys to interview various prisoners, determine who had money or friends, and then intimidate them into choosing their lawyer for legal representation. Defense attorneys complained that representing clients in criminal cases was impossible without bribing the keepers, who acted like "petty tyrants" and "absolute monarchs." One German visitor concluded that the jailers were such a shoddy-looking bunch that they "looked as if they ought to have been among the prisoners."[12]

While awaiting trial Tombs prison cases were treated according to their social and economic status, not the prescriptions of law. Up for sale were extended visiting hours, longer periods of exercise, free movement within the prison, better food, and clean sheets. For a price inmates were allowed to walk from their cells to court without handcuffs. Some visited friends and saloons on the way. Since a single cell was among the most desirable privilege, keepers routinely reserved six to ten cells located over the main entrance for wealthy criminals. Bribed guards even sold sexual favors. If a prisoner was rich or had political influence, the *Tribune* alleged, he lived "like a gentleman, surrounded with every comfort."[13]

Such "fancy prisoners" or "stars," as they were called, attracted attention because of their special status. When Alderman Henry J. Jaehne was incarcerated for bribery, the *World* reported that despite being confined to a ten- by six-foot cell, Jaehne lived in comfort, ate in the warden's kitchen, and was fully supplied with cigars. Charles Sutton, a former Tombs warden, admitted that the wealthy inmate Edward S. Stokes retained a personal servant who waited on him and brought food from a nearby restaurant. To avoid sitting with other prisoners in the Black Maria, he paid for his own carriage to transport him to court every day. At times guards even allowed him to leave the prison for short intervals.[14]

Such disparities in treatment were nominally "legal." Tombs keepers were among a host of municipal officeholders who derived considerable legitimate income from fees. In 1890 a grand jury concluded that it was impossible to indict participants engaged in such corruption. Thus jailers, clerks, deputies, and others legally accepted fees—later called bribes—with impunity on behalf of prisoners. "Here money governs everything," summarized one attorney.[15]

Tombs inmates also enjoyed a level of internal freedom unknown by their twentieth-century counterparts. Daily visitors numbered more than three hundred and frequently came and went with little supervision. Entering on a side street, callers met two guards, one standing by a desk and the other by a narrow gateway. The guards recorded the name of each one, whom he or she wished to see, and then issued an admittance ticket. Once inside, guests witnessed a scene of confusion, with people constantly moving about. One reporter noted that the balconies of each tier were "alive with visitors" meeting prisoners in their cells or on the tiers, at least until the famous escape by William J. Sharkey in 1873. But even thereafter unsupervised prisoners were found walking, talking, and smoking cigars throughout the Tombs. Others met privately with their wives in the counsel room at night.[16]

Tombs administrators had little choice but to allow unusual levels of internal movement. Feeding large numbers of prisoners in the Tombs, for

*The crowded tiers of the Tombs.*

example, was simply impossible. With a small, inadequate kitchen and no dining room, prisoners had to eat in their cells. Food—consisting of meat (or fish on Fridays), vegetables, and potatoes—was served as a stew, eliminating the need for knives and forks. For the wretched fare, inmates were charged between twelve and twenty-five dollars per week.[17]

The inadequate kitchen facilities compelled Tombs officials to permit family members and friends to bring in food for inmates. In time an informal, privatized system of feeding emerged whereby prisoners purchased their meals from neighboring restaurants. Eventually outside vendors selling food, cigars, and other items moved freely from tier to tier, bellowing out what was for sale. Visitors smuggled in food, supplies, and other contraband for their incarcerated friends. Keepers reported finding whole chickens concealing flasks of whiskey. One murder suspect was reportedly so drunk at his trial that he was unable even to respond to his name.[18]

This free flow of contraband enabled Appo and others to support their addictions while in the Tombs. After his arrest in April 1882, for example, Appo maintained his opium habit for a short time with opium pills. When the pills ran out Appo reportedly "howled until he had all the officers and inmates of the Tombs nearly as crazy as himself." Shortly thereafter a vial of opium was smuggled into his cell. Such stories induced Warden Thomas P. "Fatty" Walsh briefly to suspend the private supply of meals in 1888. Some charged that Walsh's action smacked of hypocrisy, since he reportedly earned a handsome profit by confiscating contraband from visitors and then selling it to prisoners.[19]

The free flow of contraband and people in and about the Tombs made for easy escapes, which some commentators described as quite common. For example, while roaming the halls, pickpockets often heisted visitors' pass tickets, and then used them to walk out of the Tombs; they were long gone before anyone noticed. Sloppy record keeping, however, made it impossible to know with any certainty the frequency of such breakouts.[20]

Lax disciplinary procedures in the Tombs gave some the impression that the inmates ran the asylum. In some respects they did. "Ten-day prisoners"—convicts with comparatively light offenses and numbering between twenty-five and thirty—did most of the cleaning, repair, and kitchen work. Such inmates expressed little desire to run away because their terms were short and the penalty for a failed escape severe. In extreme cases some became "voluntary inmates," residing in the Tombs for decades, performing unpleasant tasks like cleaning drains and sewers.[21]

The combination of overcrowding, lax security, and inmate maintenance allowed for considerable interaction among the incarcerated. Unlike the enforced isolation at Eastern State Penitentiary or hard labor and the lockstep at Sing Sing, Tombs inmates constantly socialized with one another, much to the chagrin of many observers and prison reformers. Life in the Tombs was more reminiscent of older, preindustrial forms of punishment—the absence of penal routine and labor; the lack of special diets or separate cells; and access to family, friends, games, and recreation.[22]

This intermingling facilitated and reinforced various male underworld subcultures. Several former inmates claimed that their initial Tombs incarcerations introduced them to other criminals—"de mob," in the words of one. Others learned new methods of crime, such as how to "bang a super"—steal a watch by detaching it from the chain with a thumb and forefinger. They were not alone: More than twenty-five hundred youths aged fifteen to twenty served time each year in Gotham's jails during the 1860s, while more than eighteen hundred males under fifteen years passed through them. The creation of a special boys' prison, established in the Tombs during the 1880s, did little to remedy the problem. So many disorderly or truant youths sent to the Tombs departed as thieves or burglars that numerous critics described the jail as little more than a school of crime.[23]

Teenage boys like Appo gloried in their Tombs experience. Youths became heroes in the wake of their new associations with older, experienced criminals. The young thief who "has 'done his bit' [served a sentence for some crime], is regarded with a reverence almost amounting to awe by his companions," complained one observer. The Tombs, admitted one teenage pickpocket, was "the turning point of my life."[24]

Such tales of carceral laxity and criminal association may strike contemporary readers as sensational exaggerations. But nineteenth-century law never specified how to structure jails; no guidelines existed for the management of such institutions. Instead jails were dependent on "common sense" and the "enlightenment" of a constantly changing board of supervisors, most of whom never saw another penal institution, or knew little about running a prison. Wardens and keepers alike were selected not for merit or qualifications, but because of their relationships to local politicians.[25]

## POLICE COURT

For some the Tombs was pure drama. In 1881 the *Times* summarized:

> There is a theatre in this City that is not usually included in the list of places of entertainment, though it is one of the most entertaining places in the City. It has no bill-boards, no advertisements, no ticket agencies in the hotels. It is too far downtown to be fashionable; indeed, it is not only unfashionable, but decidedly unpopular, yet it is well patronized. Its seats are never empty; its boxes always have occupants, and its manager, unlike most theatrical managers, is sure of making a successful season. In this theatre, unfashionable as it is, some of the most realistic tragedies are produced. And as tragedy long-continued palls upon the appetite, the programme is varied with dramas, farces, and comic operas. This theatre has a large, substantial building, well designed for the purpose, and well suited to its patrons. It is . . . called the Tombs.[26]

In nineteenth-century criminal law, stage presence and theatrical talent determined courtroom success. Police and other criminal courts required defendants to present evidence, organize testimony, and influence a judge or jury in the space of a courtroom of spectators. Those with superior oral and performance skills enjoyed distinct advantages. More often than not the successful courtroom attorney was one who dramatized the majesty, impartiality, and mercy of criminal law; that is, he "played to the gallery." Judicial critics and reformers like Frank Moss admitted that a major requirement for a successful prosecutor was "the ability to manufacture a convicting atmosphere." Justice was thus transformed into theater.[27]

Prison cases like Appo's, however, rarely enjoyed such days in court. Defendants charged with misdemeanors and other minor crimes were brought to the police court and placed before the judge. The magistrate sat on "the bridge," a raised platform where he examined prisoners, received complaints, issued warrants, took bail, and discharged the business of the day. To one side stood the complainant, usually a police officer; on the other, clerks collected fines and recorded complaints.

Below the bridge and separated from it by a railing was the defendant, surrounded by a noisy scene often characterized as bedlam. Cases were

*The Tombs police court.*

heard quickly with little deliberation or orderly presentation of evidence. Attorneys screamed epithets at one another and at witnesses, who often responded in kind. Magistrates pounded the podium futilely, trying to preserve order. Prisoners barely understood what was happening. One observer described the proceedings as a "hearing only in name."[28]

Police court justices generally assumed that defendants—especially ones like Appo—were guilty until proved innocent. One critic claimed that judges fired "sharp and decisive justice at the prisoners, as out of a Gatling gun." Some did little to camouflage their prejudice and bias. Justice Joseph Dowling, for example, was described as "the terror of the criminals," so much so that they considered an arraignment before him equivalent to a conviction. Justice P. G. Duffy was openly hostile to defendants unable to speak English. Magistrate Henry Brann bluntly told one robbery suspect: "Men of your stamp should not have a trial. You ought to be taken out and shot."[29]

Police court judges retained enormous power because their courts required no prosecuting officer and lacked a chief magistrate. In theory cases involving doubt, argument, or proof were remanded to the Court of

General Sessions for a jury trial, a right all convicted police court defendants enjoyed. Few, however, were advised of such rights. By the 1890s, 79 percent of all police court cases went without appeal. Since police court judges enjoyed summary jurisdiction over all disorderly conduct and other minor offenses, magistrates not only acted as both judge and jury, but as prosecuting attorneys and counsel for the prisoners. These powers convinced Mayor Abram Hewitt that police courts were "the great clearing house of crime, 'the Poor Man's Court of Appeals.' "[30]

Elected to uphold the law, police court judges repeatedly broke it. Some, like Maurice J. Power, openly refused to prosecute certain gambling offenses. "I am not opposed to gambling houses," he argued, "if they are conducted honestly." Numerous magistrates never bothered to learn the rules of criminal or courtroom procedures. Rare was the judge who privately met defendants with counsel to discuss the circumstances of the case, as required by law. Instead most encouraged defendants to waive the examination, which in itself was a violation.[31]

## BAIL CASES

Bail was the great divide in the distribution of justice in the Tombs. Defendants charged with misdemeanors and certain felonies were routinely granted bail if they pledged money or property to guarantee their future appearance in court. In theory the process assumed that defendants were innocent and ensured that they showed up for trial. Most defendants, however, could not afford bail; their resort was a private bail bondsman who held their capital or property as bond while charging the defendant a fee (usually 10 percent of the bond).[32]

By the mid-nineteenth century, bail in New York was an unregulated commercial enterprise riddled with abuse. Prisoners with little or no property employed "professional," "bogus," or "straw" bondsmen, sometimes for as little as five or ten dollars. Such bondsmen routinely offered real estate for bail, and shortly thereafter secretly transferred title to that property to another individual. If the defendant failed to appear for trial and forfeited the bail, there was no property or collateral to confiscate. One reporter described the straw bondsman as an "individual who can own real estate at a moment's notice." Bondsmen, like shyster lawyers, were "touted" and notified by court officers and jail attendants in return for sharing their profits. By the 1860s critics derided New York's bail system as a sham and a mockery.[33]

More significant, securing bail was tantamount to acquittal. An 1876 state investigation concluded that bailed defendants were effectively released from further prosecution. Numerous elected officials concurred. The district attorney's office was so badly managed that important criminals were discharged with no good reason and without the knowledge of the chief prosecutor. Not only was the trial of a bail case a rare occurrence, complained the *World*, but "almost any criminal who has money and influence can escape punishment."[34]

In some instances even conviction did not mean punishment. In 1867 police court justices Richard Kelly and Joseph Dowling admitted that convicted parties were often discharged on bail, allegedly to allow for review of their cases. In no instance, however, was the writ served on either the justices or the clerk. At least thirty-seven individuals, some of whom were described as "the worst of their class," escaped punishment altogether by employing such tactics. Even for those convicted and sentenced to prison, lawyers often successfully appealed their cases, obtained a writ of habeas corpus, and posted bail. " 'Out on bail' nowadays is practically out for good," concluded one critic in 1887.[35]

Those with the right political connections secured more than just bail. Indictments were often "pigeon-holed"—literally put in pigeonhole-shaped filing cases and never removed, and thus never prosecuted by the city. In 1875 District Attorney Benjamin Phelps defended the practice, insisting that disorderly house, gambling, and excise indictments were simply too numerous to bring to trial. Excise violations—"dive cases," in the vernacular of the period—enjoyed a two-year statute of limitations, encouraging bailed defendants to seek court delays and additional appeals. Even when convicted, most simply paid the fine and reopened under a new name. In 1887 former police superintendent George Walling claimed that the district attorney routinely failed to prosecute thousands of cases, which accumulated in the pigeonholes for years.[36]

The most astute criminal lawyers understood that prosecution was more a process of negotiation than justice. By midcentury a distinct criminal attorney subculture had emerged—"shyster lawyers," in the language of their critics. Such counselors were described with a variety of slurs that identified them as little more than moneygrubbing entrepreneurs on the margins of the legal profession. Tombs warden Thomas Walsh remembered one attorney who asked to consult with a client. "Before I had got through asking him for credentials a second one came to see the same prisoner," claimed Walsh, "then a third and presently a fourth put in an appearance—all claiming that they were engaged, or would be, as the felon's counsel." For the newspaper editor George Wilkes, such attorneys were simply "bloodsucking lawyers."[37]

Some shyster attorneys, however, were highly effective. The good ones sued for writs of habeas corpus, claiming that their clients were illegally deprived of their liberty. This often took the case out of the control of the police courts. Most were successful, as procuring a writ was easy if the proper complaint was filed, and refusal to grant such a writ was a misdemeanor for a State Supreme Court justice. When a case came before a New York court, insufficient evidence usually led to the prisoner's discharge. Although procuring a writ cost only twenty-five cents, lawyers charged fees between ten and twenty-five dollars, which defendants viewed as preferable to three months on Blackwell's Island.[38]

Some criminals were so familiar with this system—pickpockets and burglars, in particular—that they left sums of "fall money" with friends, lawyers, or bondsmen in the event of an arrest. The money was then used as collateral for bail, bribery, and attorney fees. The renowned "fence" Fredericka Mandelbaum allegedly did this so often that cynics described her as "the head of the District-Attorney's office in this city."[39]

The precise number of pigeonholed indictments remains impossible to guess. Former police superintendent George Walling claimed that twenty thousand existed by 1887. Later estimates were much more cautious. In 1892 the *Telegram* counted six thousand such indictments in the district attorney's office, thirty-two of which were for murder. In 1895 the *Sunday Advertiser* reported that fifteen hundred forgotten indictments were discovered, covering the years 1863 to 1883. The indicted included dive keeper Theodore Allen, State Senator Michael Norton, theater owner Jacob Aberle, and several prominent gamblers. By the early twentieth century, prosecutor Arthur Train estimated that 75 percent of all cases were disposed of by court recommendation because of the difficulty of obtaining convictions.[40]

Even when prosecutors intended to bring a case to trial, bailed defendants successfully intimidated or bribed witnesses and eliminated the chance of conviction. As early as 1845 the politician Mike Walsh complained that criminal trials were farcical and that defendants and wit-

nesses routinely lied in court. The result was not just convictions of innocent men but the acquittal of "the most lawless and besotted knaves."
Thirty years later police court judges concurred. Perjury was a pervasive
daily experience in Gotham's criminal courts, concluded one state investigation in 1876. Well into the twentieth century, prosecutors estimated
than between 25 and 75 percent of defense testimony was perjured.[41]

To counteract such practices prosecutors frequently held witnesses in
the House of Detention. Court officials lamented that such individuals
were sometimes treated more severely than indicted defendants. Overcrowding even forced Tombs officials to mix previously convicted felons
with detained witnesses, a practice city officials described as "cruel and
unjust." Here was the ultimate paradox of Gotham's criminal justice:
Rich criminals were released on bail while less affluent witnesses against
them were held for months in the Tombs.[42]

This system of "Tombs justice"—straw bondsmen, phony bail, unprosecuted indictments, perjured testimony—flourished for multiple reasons. First, city courts were poorly administered and suffered from
systematic political malfeasance. Examples abound of defective and fal-
sified record keeping: Sheriffs and other officials failed to keep jail registers; county clerks neglected filing monthly records with the secretary of
state, as required by law; police court clerks "forgot" to document the
fines collected, simply depositing such proceeds in their personal bank
accounts. In other cases clerks willingly altered, mutilated, or destroyed
public documents in return for bribes. The absence of any index made
identification of repeat offenders impossible. When bonds were issued
by different police court judges, they were mixed indiscriminately before
being sent to the Court of Special Sessions in the Tombs. Others were
simply wrapped in a bundle and marked by month; locating a specific
bond thereafter was nearly impossible. Bondsmen thus knew that failure
to repay would not result in their prosecution. Prisoners were released on
bonds for good behavior, later arrested on another charge, and released
again on a similar bond. "A policeman takes a disorderly character to
court, and hears him put under bonds," wrote one observer. "When he
returns to his post his late prisoner is there before him, with his finger at
his nose."[43]

Furthermore, a veil of secrecy covered the criminal justice process.
The docket of cases was closed to the public, making it impossible to
learn the schedule and disposition of individual cases. Bondsmen were

never regulated or adequately monitored, allowing defendants and bondsmen alike to play fast and loose with their obligations. On other occasions the district attorney's office simply failed to verify the collateral of bondsmen. Finally courts were hindered by an overload of cases, so expeditious judges routinely lumped disparate cases together—especially those of prostitutes—even if they occurred at different times and places.[44]

Ultimately the bail business was driven by politics. Many observers charged that defendants with political influence or money readily procured bail. Typical examples were Tammany Hall members William R. "Bob" Nelson, Max Hochstim, and Gustave Blumenthal. Nelson owned an interracial black-and-tan saloon on Seventh Avenue and regularly posted bail for numerous prostitutes (sometimes as many as twenty to twenty-five per night), pickpockets, and other patrons of his saloon. He usually charged five dollars per bond for his services, thereby earning fifty to one hundred dollars nightly for his services. Similarly, Hochstim in the Essex Market Court and Blumenthal in the Jefferson Market Court posted bond for arrested prostitutes (usually ten dollars) for a fee they then reportedly split with police officials. One newspaper editorialized in 1885 that if judges prosecuted bondsmen when prisoners reappeared, the result would be "a panic among the politicians and professional bondsmen."[45]

SAINT AUGUSTINE of Hippo once wrote: "When there is no justice, what is the state but a robber band enlarged?" For inmates like Appo, the Tombs represented such a robber band. A host of judicial practices and actors did little to instill faith in New York City's criminal courts. Shyster lawyers, pigeonholed indictments, ignorant judges, shoddy record keeping, perjured testimony, corrupt clerks, phony bail, bribed guards, fancy prisoners, bogus bondsmen, and chaotic courtrooms convinced defendants that Gotham's system of justice was anything but. In his examination of urban police courts, the nineteenth-century sociologist A. G. Warner concluded that local and lower-level representatives of the state—policemen, police justices, sheriffs, jail keepers—were little better than the criminals themselves. Warner echoed Augustine more than a millennium later, concluding that "the classes that tend to criminality cannot but infer that the state is fundamentally as criminal as themselves."[46] George Appo would have agreed.

GOOD FELLOWS

∽ *I then went directly down to the opium joint at 4 Mott Street, and was agreeably surprised to meet my former partner in grafting, Thomas Wilson, smoking opium.[1] I told him I had just got out of prison after serving a year. He said: "I heard you 'settled' but did not know where you were or what name you were under or I would have looked after your small wants. I myself only got in from the road only a few weeks ago and will start away West again in a short while. What are you going to do George?"*

*"What else can I do but get out and get the necessities of life as soon as possible. Why, I'm hungry now!"*

*Wilson got up from the bunk and we both went to lunch at his expense, and then back to the opium joint where I sat watching him and ten other girls and men smoking the drug and listening to the plans of Wilson's intentions about leaving New York. Finally, I agreed to go away with him on the road stealing again. We left the opium joint about 2:00 a.m. and slept in Wilson's until after 9:00 a.m. We both went to have breakfast, and afterwards Wilson had to go to the joint for relief. I told him I would meet him down there, after awhile, as I was going downtown to try and get some money. We separated and I walked down to Broadway and Fulton Street.*

*The first thing I saw was a young man with a wad of bills almost falling out of his vest pocket as he passed me near the crossing. I reached and got the money, walked through Fulton Street to Nassau Street and counted the money in an entrance hall and found I had $48. I then bought a suitcase and some clothes. I rented a room just to put my grip[2] and things for safekeeping and then went to the opium joint on Mott Street and found the place full of* habitués, *all lying down beside the opium layouts, both men and women smoking opium. I then went to where Wilson was smoking and lay down beside the "layout," and began to smoke opium once more with Wilson. I told him I was going to leave New York for Philadelphia in the morning. He said he would go with me and we became partners again. The next morning we both got our grips and started on the road to graft together once more.*

*We remained about two weeks in Philadelphia. From there we* traveled from town to city until we arrived at Kansas City, where my partner, Wilson, was taken very sick with a hemorrhage of the lungs.³ Consequently, he wanted to reach Denver, where he believed he would recover by the good effects of the climate there. So I hustled about to get the money for necessary expenses and we left Kansas City for Omaha, Nebraska.

That night on the train Wilson took a severe hemorrhage and fell unconscious. The conductor brought a doctor from the "sleeper" who stopped the hemorrhage and told me I had better take him off at the next stop and bring him to a hospital, as he would probably not live if he got another attack. I then said to Wilson: "Now, Tommy, the doctor says you are in a bad condition. We have been together for some time. You are a well-educated man and you must come from good people. Tell me your right name and where your folks are and home is, and I will bring you safely there if I have to carry you there myself."

He replied: "My name is Thomas Woods and my home is in Lindsay, Canada."

The morning brought us to Omaha, where I put him in a room, as he would not go to a hospital. To make matters worse, we both had an opium habit. As he could not leave the room, I had to get an opium outfit and smoke the drug in the room with him, instead of going to a joint (a Chinese laundry). At all events, he seemed to improve and gained strength. After a two week stay, we left Omaha for Kansas City and kept on going from town to city without any mishaps, until we reached the town of Lafayette, Indiana, where there was no opium to be obtained at any price. Consequently, we had to leave that town, and when I got to the railroad depot at 7:30 p.m. in wintertime, I found I had but enough money for one fare to Logansport, Indiana. So I had to use my wits, so to speak, and get us both there on one fare. I went to the telegrapher in the station and asked him in a railroad employers way for the conductor's name. I said: "Who goes out on the 7:45 this evening?"

He replied: "Edmonds."

"Johnny Edmonds?" asked I.

"No, Eddie Edmonds," said the telegrapher.

So I got the full name of the conductor and went out on the

platform of the station where I saw the conductor standing with a lantern in his hand by his train. I approached him and said: "Mr. Edmonds can I speak to you?"

"Yes, what is it?"

I replied: "I'm taking a very sick friend home and unfortunately I am run short of money, so if you will kindly take us over your division with one fare, you will do me a favor and when I see you at Logansport sometime, I will make good the balance. Eddie, there's my sick friend sitting on the window sill."

He looked at Tommy, and said: "I don't like to do it, but under the circumstances, board the train and meet me on the platform of the smoker, when the train starts." I thanked him, and Wilson (Woods) and I took our grips, boarded the train and took a seat in the smoker car. When the train got in motion and some distance from the station and the conductor came to punch and collect the tickets, I met him on the platform, as instructed, and handed him the money, $8. He checked my hat with two slips and I gave one to Woods. The next morning we arrived in Logansport, where we stopped at the St. Charles Hotel and got a supply of opium at a Chinese laundry and remained four days in the city, and I was financially successful during the course of that time.

We left Logansport and kept on going from town to town until we reached Buffalo, New York, where we stayed two days only. From there we went to St. Catherine, Canada, then to Hamilton and then to Toronto, Canada, where I was very successful, as there was a big county fair going on. I left the fair grounds with $600.00 and 22 watches.

When we got back to Toronto, Woods and I bought new clothes. I said to him: "Tommy, you and I had better leave here tonight for your home in Lindsay, Canada, and I won't do any more grafting until I land you there safe. You ought to telegraph your people you are coming home," said I.

He replied, "No, it is best not to." That night we took the train for Lindsay and when we arrived there we went to the only hotel in the place—the Gibson House.[4] After Woods got rested, we both started to go out to the farm where his folks were. When Woods entered the dairy where he knew his mother and sisters were, I remained down the road. The meeting between Woods and his mother was both sad and joyful. I remained in Lindsay five days and had a very good time there with Tommy Woods's two brothers, who drove me all about the country, and on Sunday, took me to church where their sister belonged to the choir and was an excellent singer.[5]

I then bid them all goodbye, and left Lindsay for Toronto, where I stayed three days and then went to Montreal and stopped three weeks at the Rosin House. I was very successful during the course of my line of grafting. I then came to New York City by way of Buffalo, and on my arrival in New York, I went directly from the depot to an opium joint and found the place crowded with American men and women of all professions in life—high, low and degraded—all smoking opium in the Crosby Street joint. The proprietor of this place was Barney Maguire, the green goods financial backer at that time. Maguire merely opened this place more for his own whims than to profit financially by it. The place was located just across the street from the rear of Niblo's Garden Theatre on Crosby Street, and . . . was soon advertised throughout the country as Maguire's Hop Joint.[6]

Maguire's Hop Joint was behind Niblo's Garden Theater on Crosby Street in 1870.

# 1 1

# Fences

=

◆§ *Soon after I arrived in New York, I started to pick pockets again.
One day [1 April 1882] I was standing at St. Paul's Church on
Broadway and Fulton Street, when I noticed a very refined looking
man, wearing plenty of diamonds and a heavy gold chain, come
along and stop on the curb of the crossing. I stepped beside him and
took his watch and chain without him knowing his loss. Then I
went to the Crosby Street opium joint and examined the watch and
concluded I ought to get at least $30 for the watch alone. I went to
[Barney] Maguire who was smoking opium on an opposite bunk
and offered to sell the watch to him. He took and examined the
watch and said, "No, I got too many of them."*

*I then left him and the joint and went to a "fence" and sold both
[the] watch and chain for $50. The very next night, I was in the
Crosby Street joint smoking with a girl acquaintance, when I was
tapped on the foot. On sitting up, I found two detectives, [James]
Mulvey and [Patrick] Feeney, who told me to get up, as I was
wanted at police headquarters. I got off the bunk, put on my hat
and coat and asked them what I was wanted for. "You will find out
when you get there," said they.*

*I was brought before Chief [Thomas] Byrnes, who said to me,
"What did you do with that watch and chain you got away with on
Broadway and Fulton Street the other day?" I denied all knowledge
of the charge and after a lot of questions, I was locked in a cell. The
next morning, [I was] brought to the police court, where the owner
of the jewelry and a witness for him were on hand to prosecute. I
sent for lawyer [Abraham] Hummel [and] engaged him as [my]
counselor. When my case was called for a hearing, I learned that the
complainant's name was Pedro Del Valle. He was the Ambassador
for Mexico and he valued his lost property at $360. The witness*

*merely identified me as being on the corner at the time the crime was committed, and suspected me as the one who picked the pockets of the Ambassador.*

*Now the only person who knew I had that watch and chain, outside of the fence who bought them from me, was Barney Maguire, from whose opium joint I was arrested. I am certain the fence would not dare to take a chance to give me up to the police, for I knew too much about his business for him to do so.[1]*

IN THE THREE YEARS following his release from Clinton prison in 1879, Appo emerged as one of Gotham's leading pickpockets. A frequent habitué of Barney Maguire's opium den, he was briefly an underworld celebrity. According to the writer Allen Williams, Appo was a favorite of Maguire's white patrons "because he was cultured, gentlemanly, and notably neat about his person." Appo was so well known that police detectives knew exactly where to find him when he came under suspicion. And hiring Abraham H. Hummel as his attorney further betrayed his economic success. Hummel was not cheap; he partnered with William Howe in what many considered to be the leading criminal defense firm in nineteenth-century America. Hummel specialized in entertainment law, representing numerous actors and dive keepers—Tom Gould, Billy McGlory, Harry Hill, and Theodore "The" Allen. He was now George Appo's "fall guy."[2]

Appo's suspicions also proved accurate—Barney Maguire was an informant. After his arrest by the U.S. Secret Service in 1878, Maguire began secretly meeting with agent Andrew L. Drummond. Over the next six years Maguire provided critical evidence in the prosecution of numerous counterfeit operations in New York. In return for that cooperation federal charges against Maguire were dropped. Furthermore, in 1885, when an accused counterfeiter sued Maguire for causing his false imprisonment, Drummond intervened; the suit was dropped by the U.S. attorney.[3] Appo was betrayed by one of the leading informants in Gotham's underworld.

For law enforcement agents, Maguire was an ideal snitch. Few people functioned and thrived in so many underworld enterprises. As Appo described, Maguire operated several opium dens. "Maguire's Hop Joint," located over Matt Grace's saloon at 126 Crosby Street and noted for its "lavish hospitality," was one of the first uptown dens. Maguire fenced goods for pickpockets like Appo. And he was a leading confidence man. For a time Maguire was the reputed "king of the green-goods men" and the "Prince of the Joints."[4]

FENCES LIKE MAGUIRE were critical components of the nineteenth-century pickpocket economy, middlemen in the success or failure of pickpockets to avoid arrest and prosecution. With one foot in the criminal universe of pickpockets, burglars, and thieves, and another in the legitimate world of business and trade, fences served as the commercial conduit for the movement of illicitly obtained goods. Every city had "backers" of thieves—individuals who took stolen goods off their hands, found hiding places for criminals, advanced money to those who ran out of funds, and even paid family expenses when they were imprisoned. Fences concealed their more lucrative business activities by running clothing, fancy goods, or jewelry stores. Some specialized in moving specific commodities: bonds, securities, diamonds, or watches. The writer Edward Crapsey concluded that dealing in stolen goods was "one of the leading industries of the metropolis."[5]

Such high-end fences, as well as those like Barney Maguire who ran opium dens, were atypical. More often fences were retailers running junk shops, secondhand stores, and pawnbroking establishments. Some observers insisted that such outlets in New York City bought almost any article offered under suspicious circumstances. Retailers functioning as fences were so well known, according to one reporter, that police officials investigating a property crime regularly went right to where the stolen goods were taken and negotiated for their recovery. Detectives, pawnbrokers, and thieves thus colluded for their shared enrichment.[6]

Pawnbrokers who doubled as fences enjoyed considerable advantages in the underground economy. They always negotiated low prices from pickpockets, as seen in Appo's experience, because they automatically suspected that pawned watches and jewelry were stolen. In order to avoid detection, pickpockets never demanded tickets for their pawned objects. In some cases pawnbrokers quickly moved goods to other cities for sale. One *Harper's* reporter even believed that fences offered such insignificant returns that thieves were hardly paid for the trouble and risk. The pickpocket and underworld doyenne Sophie Lyons described receivers of stolen goods as "the greediest, tightest-fisted individual[s] who ever squeezed a dollar." As late as 1927 law enforcement officials not only considered fences to be influential factors in the movement of stolen property but also often to be the instigators of many crimes.[7]

Fences flourished for several reasons. First, the legal onus of proof was on the victim. Even if a victim identified stolen property, pawnbrokers were not required to surrender the goods until the individual proved ownership. Second, evidence was hard to obtain because purloined property was frequently altered and unrecognizable. Most important, nineteenth-century law did little to punish the practice, giving fences considerable legal protection. Receivers of stolen goods were safeguarded by the doctrine of "manifest criminal behavior"—pawnbrokers and other shopkeepers had to "manifestly know" that various items were illicitly obtained in order to be convicted. Fences were not even legally obligated to determine that goods sold to them were indeed stolen. Throughout the nineteenth century New York courts treated larceny and receiving stolen goods as separate, distinct offenses. Judges ruled that fences could not be convicted on the uncorroborated testimony of an accomplice, including the person who sold the goods to the fence. Hence, receiving stolen property usually went unpunished. Only in the twentieth century did courts finally recognize subjective criminal behavior as grounds for conviction, thereby removing the longtime freedom fences enjoyed.[8]

The law proved so inadequate for property owners that they resorted to private protection. Indeed the emergence of the private detective was in part a reaction to the failure of American law enforcement adequately to prosecute certain forms of property crime. In 1858, for example, the Merchants' Independent Detective Police was founded to protect the property of members. Twenty years later, urban-based jewelers established the Jewelers' Protective Union specifically to protect traveling salesmen. In 1883 the Jewelers' Security Alliance was formed to provide specialized detective services, doing for jewelers what the Pinkerton Agency did for railroads. Finally the American Bankers' Association established a similar protective agency in 1894 and simply hired the Pinkertons.[9]

Together these factors discouraged courtroom confrontation when stolen property was discovered. Owners wanted their property, policemen their reward, and the fence immunity from any prosecution. Consequently, when police located stolen goods in a pawnbroker's possession, former owners were compelled to pay the pawnbroker for the return of their property. Police officials justified the practice by arguing that owners willingly made such payments; critics referred to it as blackmail. By the 1860s an understanding existed among police detectives: Pawnbrokers and thieves promptly returned purloined property provided owners repaid pawnbrokers for the amount advanced on the stolen property. Pawnbrokers and fences were thus transformed into clandestine accomplices with police in returning stolen goods.[10]

The most famous nineteenth-century fence was Fredericka Mandelbaum. Known as the "Old Woman," "Marm Baum," "Mother Baum," the "Queen of Fences," the "Mother of Crooks," and most often as just plain "Mother," Mandelbaum kept a small, inconspicuous dry-goods store on the corner of Clinton and Rivington Streets. The *Times* identified the establishment as "the most notorious depot for the reception of stolen goods on this continent." The pickpocket Sophie Lyons considered Mandelbaum to be "the greatest crime promoter of modern times." Later historians even described Mandelbaum as the most influential American criminal after the Civil War.[11]

*Mandelbaum's fake chimney.*

Considerable mystery surrounded Mandelbaum's personal history. Some claimed that she immigrated to the United States with her "rather meek husband," Wolfe Mandelbaum. They soon established a home and opened a dry-goods store on Clinton Street in 1854. Others, notably Sophie Lyons, claimed that she married Mandelbaum in order to take over his pawnbroker business, after which she developed close relationships with young pickpockets. The most reliable evidence indicates that she was born in Germany between 1818 and 1832 and migrated to New York with her husband sometime between 1849 and

1860. Wolfe Mandelbaum appears to have preceded in and introduced his wife to the fencing business. As early as 1860 he ran a saloon reputed for its criminal patronage. Friday-night gatherings were described as the "pickpockets' ball."

By 1861 Wolfe Mandelbaum appeared in the city directory, living on the Lower East Side and identified as a cigar salesman and peddler. By 1866, however, he had accumulated enough savings to open his own dry-goods enterprise at 163 Rivington Street. Fredericka's work as a lace peddler gave her an expertise in fine dry goods and an advantage over competing fences. The Mandelbaums ultimately sired two sons and two daughters, all of whom were educated abroad. One son later worked with his mother. Another was a Centre Street attorney, and a daughter married a prominent Tammany politician. When her husband died in 1874 or 1875, Mandelbaum took over the business, accumulated more wealth, and invested in New York real estate. She eventually established secret storerooms in Brooklyn and New Jersey. One newspaper estimated her worth to be $1 million in 1884.[12]

Mandelbaum's considerable wealth gave her distinct advantages, since most other fences had little savings. When wealthy larcenists and burglars were arrested, for example, she provided "fall money" and helped them fight prosecution. Mandelbaum negotiated with lawyers, bondsmen, police, and prosecutors—"the squarers of squealers," according to Sophie Lyons. As she grew more successful, Mandelbaum conducted business through messengers. Her Clinton Street dry-goods or haberdashery shop became a veritable clearing house for crimes of larceny, an underworld haven attracting the nation's most famous criminals. Police superintendent George Walling sarcastically dubbed Mandelbaum's establishment the "Bureau for the Prevention of Conviction." Indeed, Mandlebaum enjoyed close relationships with leading underworld figures, including George Howard (alias George Leonidas Leslie), the mastermind of the $1.5 million Northampton Bank robbery of 1876 and the Manhattan Bank robbery of 1878, which totaled $2.7 million.[13]

Mandelbaum's criminal success originated not only in her underworld connections, but also through her relationships with legitimate enterprises. Detective Robert Pinkerton noted that both large and small dealers purchased wholesale goods from Mandelbaum because they were cheap. She usually secured various goods for one-fifth or one-tenth their wholesale price, which allowed her to resell them to merchants at half or two-thirds the regular wholesale price. Pinkerton added that Mandelbaum's agents sold her merchandise to dealers and dressmakers in Trenton, Albany, Buffalo, and Cincinnati. Another reported that she enjoyed regular dealings with the prominent wholesale dry-goods houses because her credit was good and she met her obligations on time. Indeed, when Mandelbaum was finally prosecuted, the participating stores were among Gotham's largest and most profitable: Simpson, Crawford & Simpson on Sixth Avenue and Hearn's on Fourteenth Street.[14]

Mandelbaum reportedly enjoyed good connections to New York's political establishment. By one account she worked in concert with Henry Jaehne, the vice president of the Board of Alderman who was later convicted of bribery. Jaehne was a diamond setter with a melting works. Whenever Mandelbaum needed to remove precious stones and melt rings, she called on Jaehne. Business relations between the two were described as "very intimate." Mandelbaum eventually recognized that diamonds were easy to alter and disguise, hiring engravers and silversmiths for that purpose and exhorting her pickpocket clientele to specialize in stickpins. Furthermore Mandelbaum cooperated with the police throughout her career, giving evidence against small-time crooks like Appo in return for the police ignoring her larger operations.[15]

Mandelbaum's downfall only came when law enforcement officials resorted to extraordinary measures. In 1884 District Attorney Peter B. Olney, considered one of the few honest law enforcement officials in nineteenth-century New York, secretly enlisted the help of detective Robert Pinkerton. Unbeknownst to police officials, the Pinkertons infiltrated Mandelbaum's network and entrapped her. On 22 July 1884 four Pinkerton operatives raided Mandelbaum's establishment and arrested her and her son Julius for receiving stolen property, specifically sixteen pieces of silk and satin worth $633.[16]

Olney also benefited from the testimony and cooperation of Mary Hoey, an associate of Mandelbaum and, according to detective Thomas Byrnes, "the most notorious and successful female thief in America." After receiving a five-year sentence for larceny in 1884, Hoey began cooperating with prosecutors. Officials later admitted that she provided key evidence and information leading to the indictments against Mandelbaum. For her assistance Hoey was pardoned by the New York governor Grover Cleveland in 1885.[17]

Although Mandelbaum's attorney, William Howe, managed to delay the trial, he grew increasingly pessimistic about her chances. Consequently, just after the Thanksgiving holiday, Mandelbaum fled the city for Canada reportedly with $1 million and settled on affluent Victoria Street in Hamilton, Ontario. Appropriately the fourteen thousand dollars in bail bonds proved to be based on backdated property that New York never recovered.[18]

## THE "SWELL JOINTS" UPTOWN

Daily contact with Gotham's multiple criminal subcultures gave fences like Mandelbaum and Barney Maguire ever-new opportunities. Maguire's foray into opium was one such example. While opium smoking was introduced to the United States by Chinese immigrants, Euro-Americans like Maguire quickly recognized its potential profitability. By 1880 Maguire was not only operating a den on Mott Street that reportedly attracted well-to-do patrons, but was also running "swell joints" uptown noted for their luxury, opulence, and elite clientele. Maguire's Hop Joint on Crosby Street attracted prostitutes and sporting men from nearby concert saloons like Harry Hill's, "The" Allen's, and the Brighton.[19]

Opium's link with the bohemian and theatrical worlds was evidenced by Niblo's Theater, whose rear entrance was directly across from Maguire's. Niblo's history dated back to 1829, when the Irish immigrant William Niblo opened a "garden theater" at Broadway and Prince Street, opposite the residence of John Jacob Astor. When the large "monster" hotels were constructed along Broadway in the 1850s, the theater was incorporated into the Metropolitan Hotel, and by 1860 Niblo's was New York's largest theater. By the 1870s, however, the establishment had abandoned "legitimate" drama for ballet and "spectacle." As the theater district moved uptown, critics complained that the theater had more in common with the Bowery than Broadway, periodically reviving *The Black Crook*, staging Jack Sheppard plays, and sponsoring acrobatic dog shows. One theater critic in the 1890s described Niblo's as "a corpse that did not know it was dead."[20]

Appo's unlucky encounter with Barney Maguire also reflected a little-recognized transformation in New York's drug subculture: The joints were moving uptown. "It is a mistake to assume that Chinatown is honeycombed with opium 'joints,'" the photojournalist Jacob Riis admitted in 1890. "There are a good many more outside of it than in it." By then dens in Lower Manhattan tended to be inexpensive and sparsely furnished with open, public bunks. Uptown competitors offered a more exclusive setting: private, sumptuous apartments, large beds decorated with lace or silk canopies, and the exclusion of Chinese patrons. In 1896 the writer Stephen Crane asserted that whole streets in the Tenderloin were lined with "splendid joints." He estimated that New York's regular opium-smoking population numbered twenty-five thousand. Opium smoking was, in the words of one undercover investigator, "one of the features of New York life."[21]

Tenderloin opium dens enjoyed a symbiotic relationship with the neighborhood's concert saloons and brothels. Prostitutes from the Haymarket, Tom Gould's, and other similar establishments were frequent patrons of nearby opium dens, according to detective Thomas Byrnes. The pioneer in the Tenderloin opium den business was Frederick D. Hughes, who maintained dens in apartments adjoining the Cremorne Garden, a West Thirty-second Street concert saloon. The extravagant interior was filled with beautiful paintings, curtains, carpets, and chandeliers, and nightly attracted ten to thirty habitués. Numerous Wall Street brokers seeking anonymity reportedly secured private rooms to maintain secrecy. By the end of the century, in the elite brothels along West Thirty-ninth Street adjacent to the Metropolitan Opera House, known as "Soubrette Row," one could purchase opium along with sex.[22]

West Thirty-third Street between Sixth and Seventh Avenues attracted the greatest density of swell opium joints. Half of the apartments on the block were allegedly occupied by opium dens. Some, in addition to the opulent furnishings, possessed over 150 smoking bowls. The city's most selective was at 138 West Thirty-third Street and run by Siegfried Hess, alias Sydney Herman. In addition to pipes valued at seventy-five dollars apiece, the den had expensive bowls, trays, and an elaborate sandalwood case with inlaid pearl for storing the opium implements. In Hess's dens "dainty women from Fifth avenue," "queens of the demi-monde," and "swell members of Knickerbocker families" fraternized and smoked, wrote one visitor.[23]

Like dives and concert saloons, opium dens were central locales in the social networks of criminals like Appo. All large cities, wrote police officer Cornelius Willemse, had "resorts which are rendezvous for criminals fleeing from arrest elsewhere."[24] Indeed, Appo's eventual introduction to other, less risky forms of larceny originated with his frequent attendance in Barney Maguire's opium den. These informal associations worked to Appo's advantage, particularly when it came to disposing of purloined property. Yet, as his relationship with Maguire revealed, such liaisons were treacherous, as fences snitched on pickpockets when threatened.

Opium dens even injected Appo into the world of medical research. When Dr. Henry Kane began examining the addictive effects of opium smoking in 1880, Appo was introduced to Kane by another habitué. Over the next two years, Appo worked as Kane's tour guide through New York's labyrinthian world of opium. Kane became the first medically trained physician to study opium use in an underworld setting, at times even engaging in the practice himself.[25]

Kane personally transformed the medical debate regarding opium. In 1881 he published *Drugs That Enslave: The Opium, Morphine, Chloral and Hashisch Habits*, more than ten scholarly essays in medical journals, and a series of sensationalized articles in *Harper's Weekly*. Kane was among the earliest to recognize that opium was as detrimental as other addictive substances like cocaine, alcohol, caffeine, and nicotine. He generated considerable controversy when he attributed the rising addiction rate to physicians and pharmacists for relying on chloral hydrate as a "cure-all for every known disease." A year later Kane founded and edited the *American Journal of Stimulants and Narcotics*, while popularizing his research in articles in the *Truth*, *Sun*, and *Graphic*. By 1882 Kane was not only the nation's leading medical authority on opium smoking, but had established one of the earliest drug-treatment programs in the United States. His publications contributed to passage of the Koch Law of 1882 outlawing opium smoking in New York State.[26]

Criminalization had minimal impact, however. In the final decades of the century, opium dens were not only habitats of the underworld; they were components of Gotham's popular cultural landscape. By the 1890s numerous dime museums and theaters offered short vaudeville acts with titles like "E. W. Moore's Opium Joint" and "Wood's Opium Joint." Ironically the growing visibility of opium dens in popular culture appeared just at the moment of their decline. In 1891 newspapers reported that morphine use was on the increase and associated with opium smoking, since most opium smokers took morphine in some form. After 1893, when heroin was produced for the first time, injectable derivatives of the opium poppy grew ever more popular. Addictive substances like absinthe, cocaine, heroin, and morphine grew widespread, in part because they were cheaper, more convenient, and easier to conceal. National legislation such as the Smoking Opium Exclusion Act of 1909 banned the importation of opium for smoking and criminalized possession. Five years later the Harrison Act added still more restrictions.[27]

But for George Appo, these events lay far in the future. Throughout the 1870s and 1880s, opium was a fixture of his daily life, the swell joint and the dive his nightly rendezvous. One such place was run by Robert Howe. After his Thirty-ninth Street establishment adjacent to the Metropolitan Opera House was shuttered in 1886, Howe opened another opulent opium den under the alias of Harry A. Hamberger on West Forty-sixth Street. His partner was James McNally, a leading green goods "capitalist" and soon to be Appo's employer. The den was the most luxurious in the United States, and Howe "the McAllister of opium society," a reference to socialite Ward McAllister's role in identifying the most important four hundred families of Gotham's elite. According to the writer Louis Beck, smokers included "high-class crooks," as well as actors, clerks, bookmakers, theatrical men, lawyers, and journalists. Howe adopted a "color line," admitting only white patrons and excluding Chinese ones. The proprietors provided elegant rooms on the second floor of the house for smokers seeking privacy. Many of the patrons, observed Beck, included some "whose faces were well known to the public."[28] Beck was wrong, however, about the Chinese exclusion, for among those faces was George Appo.

> ◦§ At all events, I learned that Del Valle had offered a $500 reward for the return of his watch and chain, and that the police were searching high and low for the property. I got a word of warning to the fence to whom I sold the articles and by the advice of my counselor, when I was called to plead to my indictment, I pleaded guilty to grand larceny. Judge Smyth sentenced me to three years and six months in state prison.[29]

# 1 2

# "That Galling Yoke of Servitude"

=

◦⟩  On my arrival at Sing Sing Prison, I found a new warden in charge, but the discipline just as severe and brutal. The food and everything in general [was] unfit for the lowest animal life. In fact, there was a general epidemic among the prisoners caused by the rotten and filthy meat and other foodstuffs they had to eat.[1] During the whole course of my other two terms, I never saw or knew of a place to bathe after a hard day's work in the stove foundry.

As soon as I had my convict clothes on and [was] examined by the prison doctor, I was locked in a cell until the next morning. When the hall keeper came, [he] unlocked my door and told his convict runner to take me over to section E, south foundry, to Keeper [Patrick] Mackin as his runner for the shop. I realized I was getting a fine job, as a runner in prisons was a graft job. I was surprised and could not understand my good fortune. When the hall runner presented me to keeper Mackin, who was seated at his desk on a raised platform, he said: "This man is sent to be your runner for the shop by the principal keeper, Mr. Biglin."

"All right," said Mackin, "sit down on the platform and fold your arms."

I did so and in about ten minutes, he called me up to the desk, my arm folded and asked me: "What is your name?"

I replied, "George Appo."

"Oh! Oh! I hear you are a bad man."

"You must not believe what you hear, but judge a man as you find him," said I.

"Well, how much time have you got?" I told him three years and six months. "Do you know what you have to do here?"

"I await your orders, sir."

"Now you go to every man in the shop on each floor and take up all the dirty clothes. See that every piece is checked up, count them, put them on a barrow and take them down to the laundry. Be sure you make no mistake in your count and that you get every piece back again. You understand me now?"

"Yes sir." I gathered up all the dirty clothes, counted them, 148 pieces, gave Mackin the account slips, and was surprised to see that he could barely read or write. I brought the wash to the laundry, came back to the shop, sat down on the platform, [and] folded my arms.

Finally, Mackin, who was at the far end of the shop, at the door, signaled me to come there to him, and said: "Take all them buckets down to the water, clean everyone of them, bring them back, set them in line as you found them with the lids off and then report to me when you are through." Such was the daily work of a runner. . . .

One day, a man named [Martin] Moran who had a ten year sentence, and [was] one of the best stove molders in the shop, accidently spoiled one flask. He was reported and punished. When he returned to the shop, he took a ladle of red hot iron and burned half of his foot off, and the contractors, Perry & Co. lost a skilled molder as a result.

This incident put me on intimate speaking terms with Mackin. He said to me: "What a d—— crazy fool that fellow was to burn his foot off."

"Well, Mr. Mackin," said I, "the young man has a long term of ten years to serve and he is the best molder you had in the shop. Had you instead of bringing him over to the guard room to be punished, taken him aside and said: 'You had been reported for bad work. I don't want to punish you this time, try and not do it again,' you would then see the good results of your kind words."

I told him that the citizen foreman, Trip by name, was for the financial benefit for the contractors and would sacrifice a human life everyday to get the labor for them. "As keeper, Mr. Mackin, you are in charge of the convicts to look after their interest and welfare and not as a slave driver for the contractors." After many such talks with Mackin, he turned out to be one of the best hearted keepers in the prison and the men under him turned out the finest of work in appreciation.

When I had about 18 months of my term served, I was allowed

*much freedom out of the shop after my work was done and was in a position where I could go into the ladle shanty where the waste hot iron was thrown and cook coffee there for the convict bookkeeper of the stove contract whose office was next door to my shop. This bookkeeper's name was Greenfield and had a five year sentence.*

*One day, I had written him a note asking him if he could pay me some coffee if I gave him the money. To my surprise, he stopped me in the yard the next day and asked me if I had written that note myself. "Of course, I did," said I. Why?"*

*"Well, tomorrow afternoon, about 3 p.m., meet me in the storage rooms over my office. I'll give you some papers and I want you to copy the writing on them on the blanks I give you as near as you possibly can and return all of them to me in the morning. I'll see you up in the storage [room], when you go for a relief for your keeper. You can copy them in your cell at night," said he.*

*"All right." The next day he handed me three different bills for stoves that were to be shipped and five blank bills to copy on. I took them to my cell and copied them perfectly. The next morning I handed them to Greenfield, the bookkeeper, and he was extremely pleased. Every night I would copy at least six bills for different kinds of stoves that were to be shipped by rail to the Dakotas and other northwestern towns. Every week I would be paid a pound of coffee for my work.*

*I [later] found out that this bookkeeper and two keepers, Tierney and Nixon, were robbing Perry & Co., the stove contractors, by shipping stoves to buyers and that my handwriting was exactly like the citizen's shipping clerk for the stove contract. I was used to forge the bills for them unknowingly.*[2]

APPO'S PENITENTIARY ORDEALS marked him for the remainder of his life. His original response to Sing Sing's disciplinary regime of physical torture and psychological humiliation was aggressive resistance and confrontation. By 1882, however, the severity of punishment—the paddle, solitary confinement, near-starvation, constant illness—convinced Appo that insubordination was futile, defiance self-destructive. Rather than rebel Appo now cooperated.

Appo recognized the tangible benefits of compliance, a commuted sentence prime among them. Although Appo received two-and-a-half-year terms in 1874 and 1877, in both instances he served only two years. This was hardly unusual. New York was a pioneer in commutation laws, and by the 1860s the majority of state inmates had their sentences short-ened for good behavior. In 1868, for example, only 68 of 1,128 prisoners released fulfilled their complete term. By 1880 of all Sing Sing inmates discharged during the year, only one had served his full sentence. The vast majority (666 of 703) were set free by commutation. In 1884 Appo earned ten months' commutation from his three-and-one-half-year sentence.[3]

By his third entry to Sing Sing, Appo was also cognizant of the prison aristocracy of "privileged convicts," the foundation of an informal but well-organized convict economy. Inmates with money procured easy posi-tions and special privileges. Upon arrival, for example, prisoners were directly questioned about their ability to "put up"—to bribe guards and keepers for various privileges. Those who could were granted easy tasks. Hospital jobs, chapel duty, and other tasks were less taxing than positions in the various industrial shops. Better-educated inmates not only worked as bookkeepers, according to one prisoner, but were "allowed to do pretty much as they pleased." Others received comfortable rooms, luxuries such as food and drink, special visiting permits, sleeping in the hospital, eating in the warden's kitchen, fishing along the docks, roaming around the prison grounds "at pleasure," and even taking part in theatrical perform-ances. Walking about Sing Sing, visitors and wardens observed convicts relaxing, gambling, and lying about under trees and in shanties scattered around the grounds. In the words of convict John Connelly: "Any man in the prison can get anything he wants if he has the money to buy it."[4]

Perhaps the most extreme example was inmate Solomon Kohnstamm. In 1868 former keeper Alfred Locke claimed that Kohnstamm operated a grocery within Sing Sing, supplying inmates with liquor, cigars, sugars, tea, coffee, and fruit. Furthermore his wife boarded in the adjoining vil-lage of Sing Sing and was permitted frequent, private three-hour visits. Kohnstamm's wife reportedly gave birth to two of the convict's children during her husband's incarceration.[5]

The easy availability of contraband, the prominence of an internal inmate economy controlled by private contractors and privileged inmates, and the absence of any prison wall around Sing Sing before 1876 contrast sharply with recent claims by historians that the nineteenth-century penitentiary was a distinctive "sealed-off" space, isolated from the larger world outside its walls. Most recently David Rothman has argued that nineteenth-century prisons were impervious institutions that successfully separated inmates from outsiders. The high walls and rigidly organized daily routines ensured that "nothing casual or random" affected the daily activities of inmates.[6] The prominence of Sing Sing's informal convict economy and the prevalence of special privileges among the richest and politically connected inmates present a far different carceral reality.

The system of special privileges thrived in part because of the corruption of the Sing Sing staff—"the gross unfitness of many of the keepers," according to the *Herald*. In contrast to European prison guards, who were increasingly recruited from the middle class and supervised by "gentlemen officers," Sing Sing keepers were described as originating from "the lowest walks of life." In 1868 a former keeper claimed that two-thirds of his coworkers drank while on duty. Another complained of a hospital keeper who was drunk every day, "frequently to such a degree that if he undertook to sit down he would be as likely to come to the floor as to a seat."[7]

Furthermore guards and keepers were poorly trained. For example, they received no written instructions on assuming their positions. Keeper Zalmon Smith admitted that his training was so inadequate that the most informative instructions originated with the convicts. Keepers and guards wore no identifying garb because they considered uniforms degrading. Most were not only inexperienced and ill prepared for prison work, they were poorly paid. Keepers only earned between $480 and $780 annually, although they often worked fourteen-hour days.[8]

Wardens were powerless to change these conditions. Prior to 1877 guards and keepers were appointed by one of the three state prison inspectors—elected statewide officials who generally regarded their positions as patronage plums. From the highest warden to the lowest guard, political connections dictated who received the approximately two hundred Sing Sing appointments. From 1870 to 1880 eight different men served as warden of Sing Sing. Appo's first warden, Gaylord Hubbell, believed that nearly the entire corps of guards turned over with each administrative change. Indeed 85 percent of all prison employees changed with the election of new inspectors in 1876 alone. In general guards with more than two years of experience were unusual. Only with the introduction of civil service in 1883 did this change.[9]

Constant turnover of guards and keepers made it impossible for wardens to discipline their force and, in turn, for guards to control inmates. In some cases politically connected guards and keepers avoided discipline by threatening the *warden* with removal. The absence of cooperation among prison officials meant that the warden had his special stool pigeons, the principal keeper his favorite informers, and his assistant his own spies. Gaylord Hubbell noted how "saucy and lazy" convicts mingled with officers "on a complete social basis." Life in Sing Sing was, he concluded, "rotten to the core."[10]

Guards and keepers felt further compelled to dispense privileges to select inmates because they were so badly outnumbered. At any given time from 1868 to 1885, Sing Sing employed a combined total of between fifty-nine and ninety-five guards and keepers. Since less than half the guards and keepers were on duty at any one time, each prison officer oversaw between twenty-four and forty-six inmates. By contrast late-twentieth-century prisons employed an average of four to five guards for every inmate.[11]

The power guards wielded over inmates was best exemplified in its most unspoken and often hidden form—sexual coercion.

> ❧ *The principal keeper of Sing Sing Prison, by name Archibald Biglin, was an immoral scamp whose immorality which he practiced on convicts, was unspeakable. Biglin was of an effeminate nature and practiced unspeakable crimes on the convict runner he had at his office whose name was Ward and known by the name of Hunt. I accidently caught Biglin in the act one day, that my keeper sent me to get a relief ticket signed by Biglin. I pretended not to have seen him.*[12]

Information on Biglin, like other keepers and guards in New York prisons, is hard to find, confirmation of sexual predation nearly impossible. Biglin began his career as a keeper in Clinton prison in 1869, eventually rising to the position of hall keeper in 1876. Later that year, in the wake of several successful escape attempts from Sing Sing, Biglin was promoted to principal keeper of Sing Sing, responsible for prison discipline, assigning keepers, and supervising the shops. Over the next several years Biglin attracted considerable praise from Sing Sing wardens and visitors.[13]

Homosexuality remained a pariah topic among prison officials and inmates alike well into the twentieth century. Those who addressed the issue, like Appo, commonly displayed a certain homophobic outrage, most likely because of the sexual exploitation of inmates by guards. Reformers in the Prison Association sometimes described keepers as "vicious and immoral persons," their conduct having "a most deleterious influence" on inmates. Among inmates, however, such behavior was quite likely common and encouraged at times. By the early twentieth century, the famed sex researcher Havelock Ellis estimated that 20 percent of Sing Sing inmates were active homosexuals.[14]

Some believed that doubling up and the lockstep encouraged homosexual behaviors. As early as 1871 former warden Gaylord B. Hubbell complained that the policy resulted in "great abuses." Some reports admitted that frequent overcrowding in Sing Sing and Clinton not only created discipline problems but afforded inmates opportunities "for indulging in degrading practices." Doubled-up convicts complained that cellmates engaged in a "species of immorality." While terms like "immoral practices," "great abuses," and "degrading practices" may have referred to masturbation as well as homosexuality, later corrections officials were more direct. One keeper insisted that double cells induced sexual behaviors "so loathsome and disgusting" that they were unprintable, adding that the "friends of Hell [will] clap their hands and dance for joy."[15]

By the early twentieth century, prison officials and other observers acknowledged the existence of a visible homosexual subculture in Sing Sing. Warden Thomas Mott Osborne conceded that in any all-male community like a prison, "certain unnatural immoral acts" were inevitable due to "the unnatural social conditions." In Osborne's opinion such behaviors were simply impossible to eradicate. Former Sing Sing physician Louis Berg admitted the prison had "a group of men like women" referred to as "fags," "punks," "gonsils," and "ladies," with "rouged faces, mincing gait and coquetting manner." Another Sing Sing physician claimed that doubling up was discontinued in 1912 in order to eliminate homosexual liaisons. Warden Lewis Lawes later conceded that 75 percent of all Sing Sing cases of "sex perversion" were attributable to doubling and tripling up in cells. He believed that prison officials were well aware that inmate homosexuality and "sex emotionalism" were commonplace, but were difficult to detect and control. Most simply ignored such sexual behavior.[16]

Inmates concurred. Prisoner Joseph Morgan based his complaint on experience. The day after he was placed in a cell with another man, Morgan recounted, "I woke up and I found that man with my penis in his mouth, and I gave him quite a crack with my knee." He later complained to the keeper, who acknowledged his predicament and admitted that Morgan's cellmate was not "fit for any one to be with." Morgan further added that numerous individuals convicted of sodomy were consciously "put in with other men." Yet complaints of homosexuality were never universally shared among inmates. In fact warden A. A. Brush claimed that more inmates applied to be doubled up than to remain in single cells. "Men, even prisoners, are social beings." More often than not, he admitted, "they like to be together rather than separate."[17]

Other inmates simply resorted to masturbation. Sing Sing physician Hiram Barber, for example, believed certain convicts masturbated so much that it killed them. Prisoner George Henry, according to Barber, "was addicted to self-abuse." After placing a guard to observe Henry while in the prison hospital, Barber was stunned to discover the patient masturbated two or three times a day. When Henry later died, Barber's prognosis was "nervous exhaustion, . . . brought on entirely by masturbation." Similarly James Makinson regularly masturbated up to the day of his death. "I examined him afterward," testified Barber, "and found the bloody semen was running out of his organs."[18] Such was the state of nineteenth-century medical expertise.

Beyond consensual sex, certain inmates must have been easy prey for guards or other prisoners. "The prison body always contains boys at that uncertain age where they have a good deal of the feminine in them or ones who are potential homosexuals," wrote a future Sing Sing physician. With 15 to 20 percent of Sing Sing's population under the age of twenty, there were hundreds of teenagers in Sing Sing during Appo's incarcerations. Many, with their fragile size and childlike stature, were susceptible prey for "wolves" in both the inmate and guard populations.[19]

Prisons throughout the century were considered sites of deviance, as defined by middle-class heterosexual standards. One of the few surveys of nineteenth-century inmate sexuality originated in Philadelphia's Eastern State Penitentiary between 1886 and 1888. For three years prison officials questioned newly admitted convicts about their sex lives. Well over half claimed that they were experienced with prostitutes, including 14 percent who described themselves as either friends of or intimately involved with prostitutes. Another 19 percent admitted to premarital sexual intercourse, while less than 2 percent were identified as "sodomites." A mere 10 percent claimed to follow "lives of sexual purity."[20]

George Appo's muted description of Biglin's sexual predation underscored the relationship between sex and violence in prison. Sexual violence and male rape by corrections officials reinforced the arbitrary power of Sing Sing's guards and keepers. Given what we know of prison life, most likely Appo's observations reveal that certain inmates were raped and "effeminized" by prison guards, effectively transforming those inmates into a kind of personal property of the guards. Such relations became, over time, a hidden but integral part of prison social life. Homosexual practices emerged within prisons as a way for keepers to control inmates by treating them as female, much the same way defeated parties were treated on a military battlefield. These practices soon became the basis of the social order of the penal system, a coercive collectivity of male power.[21]

APPO ENJOYED a new advantage during this third stint in Sing Sing: literacy. His role in "fixing" the account books for the stove foundry was hardly unique. For decades the lack of sufficient personnel encouraged prison officials to assign clerical and other administrative tasks to trustworthy inmates, hence the label "trusties." In 1888, for example, inmate Edward Meredith claimed that Sing Sing warden Brush demanded that he fix the account ledgers on one Sing Sing contract. Meredith quickly realized that eighty to one hundred thousand dollars of property listed simply did not exist. Most citizen foremen and superintendents in the various Sing Sing shops, Meredith concluded, depended entirely on cooperative convict bookkeepers. When he went public with these charges of corruption, Brush and Sing Sing officials declared the accusations a "delusion." They transferred Meredith to the asylum for insane criminals.[22]

Other investigations discovered convict clerks with easy access to prison books who altered commitment papers and discharged convicts before the completion of their terms. Trusties were commonly threatened and pressured by other convicts to obtain and give information to other inmates. Later inquiries claimed that a prison code among convicts required inmates never to inform authorities regarding other prisoners. Those who did, claimed one, were sometimes killed while incarcerated or after their release. Only in 1928 did state officials finally prohibit inmates from performing clerical duties.[23]

This system of inmates running the prison, however, was not unique to clerical duties. Convicts who were skilled locksmiths repaired the extensive system of locks, keys, and bolts throughout the complex. Those who were apothecaries prescribed drugs to sick inmates. In some instances convicts even guarded the gates to the prison. When Sgt. Joseph Gill assumed his office in 1876, he was stunned to find a convict at every guard post.[24]

The special privileges enjoyed by Sing Sing's elite reached their apogee in the 1880s. Ferdinand Ward, Henry J. Jaehne, and Johnny Hope were three prominent examples. Ward attracted national attention when he established the Wall Street brokerage firm of Grant & Ward in 1881 in partnership with Ulysses S. Grant, Jr. Three years later, however, after the former United States president had invested one hundred thousand dollars in his son's business, the firm went bankrupt. Investigations immediately revealed that Ward had engaged in a confidence scheme, illegally pledging the same stocks to support different and multiple bank loans. By contrast, Henry Jaehne was a diamond setter who entered politics and eventually became the vice president of New York's Board of Aldermen. He became the infamous "boodle alderman" upon his conviction for bribery in the awarding of streetcar contracts by the city. By the late 1880s both Ward and Jaehne were Sing Sing inmates.

"Sing Sing's Upper Crust."

In prison both men enjoyed easy work assignments, carpeted cells with lamps, and reading materials. Jaehne allegedly paraded around the prison yard with two pet dogs. By one account Ward "had the run of the prison," and worked fewer than three hours daily. Jaehne only had to pack tobacco in small packages for four hours a week instead of the usual sixty for other prisoners. Both had access to liquor and private poker games with inmates and keepers of their choice.[25]

During the 1880s the famed Manhattan Bank burglar Johnny Hope allegedly served as principal keeper James Connaughton's "henchman and go between." He strolled carelessly throughout the prison, frequently puffing on a cigar. After a new prisoner complained of the harsh discipline, Hope offered—for a price—to bribe prison officials for an easier assignment. By 1889 nearly every easy position in Sing Sing was reportedly filled by associates of Jaehne, Hope, or Warden Brush.[26]

The treatment of Ward, Jaehne, and Hope illustrates how special privileges and inmate autonomy were never equally shared among inmates. Critics recognized that these entitlements replicated in crude fashion the class divisions of the external world. In the quarry, prisoners who bribed keepers were allowed to "loaf," while poorer ones –the "small fry convicts"—suffered from overwork and the paddle. In most instances only a few enjoyed these privileges. "Moneyed men," lamented another inmate, "have sinecures, while the poorer convicts must work like slaves."[27]

Appo recognized this reality, describing Sing Sing's discipline as "just as severe and brutal" as in his earlier sentences. Torture remained the order of the day. By then the preferred method of torture was the "pulley" or "weighing machine," reminiscent of the weighing machines employed by butchers. Inmates were tied to a panel by their thumbs or wrists and then suspended with their toes barely touching the floor. In this position prisoners were unable to clasp the fingers of their hands together, causing the rope to cut their flesh and numb their hands and arms. Men were elevated so long that they bled from the mouth, claimed one investigatory commission in 1877. Prison officials justified the method because the punishment evoked such fear from convicts that they did anything to avoid it. Without the weighing machine, argued one, "life in the prison would be unbearable to the keepers."[28]

From the day of his appointment as Sing Sing warden in 1880, Augustus Brush insisted that the weighing machine was "the safest, the quickest and the most humane method of punishment ever devised." Other prison officials extolled the weighing machine because the punishment was short and effective. Superintendent Isaac V. Baker, Jr., even demonstrated the punishment to New York governor and future United States president Grover Cleveland. After the loops were placed and tightened around Cleveland's wrists, he reportedly approved the method. The governor, however, never experienced what made the weighing machine unbearable, namely the paddling while suspended in the air.[29]

Sing Sing's principal keeper, James Connaughton, allegedly employed the weighing machine so frequently that he was personally identified with the contraption by the mid-1880s. Others claimed that Connaughton "hung up" as many as sixteen inmates daily. In time he was even credited as the inventor of a "stretcher" used in torturing prisoners. One critic claimed that convicts were scarred for life, carrying the physical "marks of torture . . . to their grave."[30]

Among the most detailed accusations originated with Charles Wilson, a Sing Sing inmate from 1884 to 1886, when he was eighteen to twenty-one years of age. After Wilson entered Sing Sing with an infected lung, prison physician Hiram Barber prescribed medication, which Wilson vomited. Barber then sent Wilson to Connaughton, who immediately handcuffed and tied him up on the weighing machine, his toes suspended above the floor. Released after two minutes, he fell unconscious. Over the course of the next two and a half years, Wilson was subjected to the weighing machine at least seventeen times, sometimes as long as fifteen minutes, usually for failing to meet the requirements of the stove-manufacturing shop. Wilson charged that men were often "weighed" for ten to fifteen minutes, but only one minute was recorded in the official prison records. While prison officials claimed that inmates were kept in the dark cell only 24 hours, he recounted five examples of men confined for more than 120 hours. Others were maimed or died from the tortures. Those who complained to inspectors were "tied up daily" and placed in the dark cell. Some feared that Connaughton would kill them.[31]

Such sadistic punishment explains why some inmates resorted to self-mutilation. Appo's memory of Martin Moran intentionally incinerating his foot to avoid punishment was hardly unusual. The prison critic Irving Ward, for example, recounted in 1886 how one stove shop prisoner stuck his hand into molten metal, thereby burning off his fingers, in order to avoid working. Another gouged out his eye with a file; one self-amputated four of his fingers. When a prisoner named Gallagher failed to meet his daily assignment in the foundry, he deliberately put his hand into a vat of molten iron. "The flesh fell off the member, the bones shriveled and twisted together, and the man fainted away," described one report. A month later William Whalen did much the same, sticking in his arm up to his elbow before falling unconscious. One Sing Sing inmate remembered two men self-amputating their fingers in order to escape prison work. To get into the hospital, he added, foundry convicts dropped molten iron on their feet. Prison officials responded by denying that these events ever happened. Yet, years earlier, in a moment of honesty, Brush admitted that such cases were common in Sing Sing. "If they can maim themselves in some way," he concluded, "they will do it."[32]

•§   *The former keeper Tierney,[33] before he became keeper of the stove shipping office, was the keeper of the jobbing shop where convicts, who were skilled mechanics, were employed by the State to do all the plumbing and other mechanical jobbing work about the prison. In this shop a convict known by the nickname of "Ginger" [who] I believe was there under the name of Thompson with a five year sentence to serve, had occasion to speak to the convict who worked next to him on the work bench instructing him how to finish a piece of work. The keeper Tierney saw him talking to the man and rushed over with his big stick and poked Ginger in the neck.*

*"Stop your talking, Ginger!"*

*Being taken by surprise, Ginger jumped from his bench with a hammer in his hand and tried to explain that he had to instruct the other man. But Tierney, with another jab of his stick, told Ginger to shut up, put his hammer down and not give him any back talk. Ginger tried to explain and the keeper raised his stick to strike him, [and] he jumped back. Tierney pulled out his gun and shot him dead and claimed that he shot poor Thompson in self-defense.*

*Nothing was said or done to Tierney, for Thompson had no relatives or even a good friend in the outside world to take an interest in the case. He was only 27 years of age at the time and was raised up from boyhood in the Fourth Ward. The prison authorities nailed his body in a pine box and buried him up on the hill, or as the graveyard is called by convicts, the "25 Gallery," without even a prayer from the so-called chaplain.[34]*

*Keeper Tierney was rewarded by being promoted as keeper in the stove shipping office for Perry & Company for shooting dead a young man whom I and many others of his outside associates knew would not use a weapon on his worst enemy, let alone a keeper. Such was the kind of officials placed over men to reform them under the Louis D. Pilsbury administration.[35]*

Throughout his memoir Appo repeatedly charged that prison life and the cruelty of guards in Sing Sing drove many to insanity, death, and suicide. He was not alone. As early as 1868 the Prison Association concluded that punishments frequently "resulted in death, insanity, incurable imbecility, and life-long decrepitude." Five years later Auburn physician Theodore Dimon completed a study of 227 Auburn inmates with life sentences. Dimon discovered strikingly higher death and insanity rates among "lifers" than among the larger inmate population. The average percentage of deaths in the whole prison over a five-year period was 9.3 percent, for "life men" it was more than double, at 19 percent. Their insanity rate was sixteen times higher.[36]

By the 1880s stories of attempted inmate suicide were commonplace. Before a state assembly committee in 1882, convicts described fellow prisoners choosing deliberately to jump off the third- and fourth-floor galleries on learning that they were to be punished. Inmate Edward Smith failed in two such attempts. "The second time I was tired of my life," he testified. "I didn't care whether I killed myself or not." Another assembly committee in 1883 found that the fear of punishment induced some convicts to take their lives. Four years later another inmate committed suicide and left a note: "I cannot endure the intense agony when forced in a cell with one slice of bread each day from Thursday to Sunday," of being forced to sleep on stone "for the crime of not being able to iron a shirt."[37]

Prison officials dismissed such stories as outright lies. Warden Brush insisted that only "dead-beats" received punishments. Sing Sing physician Hiram Barber concurred, claiming that the majority of men who visited the doctor were engaging in subterfuges. "They lie and in every other way try to get excused from work," argued Barber. The *Times* defended such views—prisons were filled with "brutal ruffians" who could "only be controlled by fear." Indeed it was a rare day in Sing Sing when an inmate was *not* punished. On 27 August 1880, for example, Sing Sing officials proudly proclaimed that no inmate was punished, allegedly an unprecedented event in Sing Sing history.[38]

At first glance the Sing Sing death rate did not appear unusual. Physician Barber—nicknamed "the Butcher" according to Appo—even argued that the prison's death rate was lower than that of the nearby village of Sing Sing. Statistics supported Barber's argument. Compared to the mortality rate of New York State, which was between twelve and eighteen persons per thousand from 1850 to 1890, Sing Sing's rate was roughly equal, if not lower, most years. Based on broad, aggregate data, prison inmates died at a lower rate than even the residents of the largest cities. In 1883 Brush described the Sing Sing death rate as "wonderful," bragging "that no country town has as low a death rate as this prison."[39]

A closer examination, however, reveals a more sobering picture. Mortality statistics usually encompassed entire populations, including infants and young children who accounted for a disproportionate share of deaths in nineteenth-century America. In 1880, for example, approximately 44 percent of all male deaths in New York State were children ten years of age or less. Indeed, two-thirds of all male deaths in the United States that year were under the age of five.[40] If the deaths of boys age ten or less were ignored, the statewide mortality rate was almost halved. With *no* inmates under the age of thirteen, Sing Sing's annual death rates should have been 40 to 66 percent less than state and national figures. In fact, however, they were similar.

Most illuminating was the young age at which most Sing Sing prisoners died. From 1870 to 1900 more than 77 percent of all deaths in Sing Sing were inmates between the ages of fourteen and thirty-nine. By contrast only 68 and 55 percent of the inmates at Auburn and Clinton, respectively, fell into that age category. Few Sing Sing convicts died of old age.

More telling was Sing Sing's "insanity rate." Admittedly such statistics were highly subjective and manipulated by authorities. Nevertheless a rough comparison can be made between New York's prisons and the state's institutionalized mentally ill population, as well as that of the United States as a whole from 1880 to 1903. For every 1,000 Americans during those years, fewer than 2 were classified as insane. In New York State the figure was higher—from 2.76 to 3.39.[41] By contrast, from 1870 to 1900 Sing Sing's annual insanity rate usually exceeded 4, exploding to approximate highs of 19 in 1892 and 1893.

Appo was right: Sing Sing drove many an inmate insane or to an early death. From 1870 to 1895 the annual Sing Sing death rate dropped below 10 per 1,000 only seven times. Indeed, when the Sing Sing population declined after 1885, the death rate increased and exceeded 20 from 1890 to 1892, with a high of 33.3 in 1891. In some years the number of inmates declared insane actually *exceeded* those who died. In most years the combined death and insanity almost always exceeded 15 (and in many years 25) per 1,000 of the Sing Sing population.[42]

Officials from other prisons confirmed that Sing Sing's death rate was artificially low. Auburn prison physician B. K. Hoxsie charged that Auburn's higher death rate originated from Sing Sing and other penal institutions which sent "their invalids here to die." In 1887, for example, thirteen of thirty-two deaths in Auburn were transfers from Sing Sing. By 1893 Clinton physician J. B. Ransom repeated the same charge, arguing that most of the 200 Clinton inmates suffering from tuberculosis were drafted from Sing Sing. Even Sing Sing officials acknowledged their records were untrustworthy. When Dr. William Manlius Smith assumed office as Sing Sing physician in 1874, he discovered that all the hospital records from the previous year were missing. While inmate names and dates were available, the causes of death remained a mystery.[43]

Only after 1885 did Sing Sing officials finally acknowledge the exorbitant levels of mortality and insanity. Sing Sing physician Hiram Barber and others recognized that doubling up inmates contributed to the noticeable rise, but Barber also placed blame outside Sing Sing. The termination of contract labor, for example, resulted in more pulmonary illnesses since inmates spent more times in their cells. In other cases Barber blamed conditions in the Tombs, where men who awaited trial came down with consumption, scrofula, syphilis, and other diseases.[44]

The exorbitant number of inmates who applied for medical treatment revealed the harshness of Sing Sing life. In 1875 an average of 1,718 male prisoners petitioned for medical assistance each month, a figure exceeding the entire prison population (1,487). During the summer the number surpassed 2,000 every month. This pattern continued well into the 1880s. Even prison officials acknowledged the poor health conditions in Sing Sing—more than 90 percent of all inmates required some form of medical treatment every four weeks.[45]

Torture, disease, injury, insanity, and death: These were the daily realities of Sing Sing life. Indeed they were persistent features in all three of New York's major penitentiaries. "Sing Sing Prison, as a penal institution, does not need to be reconstructed," editorialized the *Tribune* in 1894, "it needs complete destruction." Nineteenth-century Sing Sing, declared Frederick Howard Wines, "represented all that was vile in American penology."[46]

HALF A CENTURY before George Appo ever set foot in Sing Sing, American reformers "invented" the penitentiary. Generations of historians since have argued that nineteenth-century ideas of penal reform were an emblematic element of American—indeed Western—society.[47] Appo's years in and descriptions of Sing Sing, however, reveal a more complicated, even paradoxical carceral system. On one hand, systematic violence and state-sanctioned torture were imposed on certain inmates. Sadistic punishments in the hands of keepers, guards, contractors, and prison officials were sometimes incidental, random, and personal, hidden from the public gaze. But after 1875, they were increasingly implemented to improve industrial productivity and reinforce inmate discipline.

By contrast a competing system of informal, often illegal entitlements bestowed on other so-called privileged inmates thrived alongside these mechanisms of torture. The networks of special privileges described by Appo not only fertilized the criminal subcultures the penitentiary was designed to eliminate but enabled select inmates to create spaces of personal autonomy and independence. Ironically convicts who enjoyed such benefits undermined the internal penitentiary discipline reinforced by torture. The tension and conflict between these two extremes of inmate life defined the paradoxical interior world of nineteenth-century Sing Sing.

Most inmates never enjoyed the privileges accorded the Sing Sing elite. Most were subjected to a variety of violent practices authorities deemed to be a necessary part of criminal justice. In Sing Sing, torture did not simply decline or vanish as a public spectacle over the course of the nineteenth century; rather it assumed a new, more invidious form.[48] Dark cells, weighing machines, and paddles represented new, irregular, unpredictable, and capricious forms of bodily mortification implemented by guards, keepers, and private contractors. Contempt replaced rehabilitation, even retribution, as the purpose of inflicting such pain.

But physical torture more than mortified the body. By shaming inmates before their peers, regularizing such practices into daily rituals, torture also terrorized the mind. Stripping inmates of their clothing and paddling their naked posteriors humiliated, degraded, and challenged their very manhood. Punishment was thus transformed into indiscriminate terror, a form of psychological emasculation. Sanctioned by prison officials, endorsed by private contractors, and impulsive in implementation, such discipline offered inmates little recourse of protest.

In some respects this carceral system was even more oppressive than its preindustrial predecessor. Earlier forms of punishment were immediate and short, whether they were flogging, death, or banishment. Public torture was acceptable because many believed that such methods revealed truth and the operation of power.[49] By contrast Appo's punishments in Sing Sing and Clinton employed torture in demeaning, secretive, and arbitrary ways, at the personal, mercurial, and sadistic whims of individual guards. Many punishments took place with minimal supervision by agencies of the state. Whereas twentieth-century inmates lived in terror of physical reprisals from fellow prisoners, George Appo feared guards and keepers. Furthermore such degrading discipline was no longer a singular, onetime event. With the reality of long periods of detention, penitentiary punishments were repeated, continual, and privately removed from the public eye.

Sing Sing actually had more in common with a Soviet gulag than with any reformatory. The common resort to torture, the high levels of hospitalization and illness, the excessive rate of death, the callousness of guards, the privatization of profit, the emphasis on cheap labor—all marked a sharp departure from the penitentiary ideals of nineteenth-century reformers. Some convicts considered Sing Sing worse than war. "I have known the agony of soul that comes to a man in the trenches when his buddies are being slaughtered all around him and with the brains of his best pal spattered all over his face," wrote a veteran of World War I. "I have known the misery of a German prison camp where, half starved, I sweated by day and froze by night. But all of this put together and then doubled I would endure in preference to [Sing Sing] which is just plain hell."[50]

Nor was the consolation of religion offered at this gate of Hades. "I never had a chaplain of a prison come to my cell and talk to me or to any other convict," complained Appo regarding his entire prison experience, "not even at the deathbed in the prison hospital." From the lowest guards to high-ranking chaplains, convicts died "without any religious consolation just like an animal," charged Appo.[51] He was right. Officials openly denied funerals to deceased convicts who remained unclaimed by their families. Prison authorities simply deposited the bodies in unmarked graves.

Appo singled out Sing Sing chaplain Silas W. Edgarton for his callous disregard of inmates, noting his "sarcastic remarks" whenever "an unfortunate creature is being punished and tortured by a brutal official."[52] Others concurred. One convict charged that Edgarton was frequently drunk, profane in his language, and present when prisoners were punished. Other inmates accused the chaplain of displaying more interest in baseball and yachting than dying prisoners requesting his services. On numerous occasions Edgarton provided not even a prayer for deceased inmates. Instead their corpses were hurried to the graves with no farewell religious rite.[53]

The heartless treatment of Sing Sing's dead moved Appo to poetry. An undated verse entitled "A Convict's Grave" evoked the alienation undoubtedly shared by fellow inmates:

I remember the day, 'twas wild and drear
    And nigh to the Hudson waves.
Our parson bore a corpse on a bier
    To lie in a convict's grave.

I remember too no prayers were said
    Nor anthems chanted o'er the dead.
But the wild birds cried as they flew bye,
    O'er the convict's silent grave.

I remember too 'twas the road by the hill,
    And nigh to a rocky cave
Where they rested their load in its last abode,
    And gazed on a convict's grave.

Friends he had none, no brother dear,
    No sister to weep or wail,
No sweetheart to shed a friendly tear,
    O'er his lonely silent grave.

No mother weeps o'er the place he sleeps,
    No stone marks the place where he lies.
But the violets bloom on the hillside steep,
    O'er the convict's lonely grave.[54]

Convicts like Appo acknowledged death's omnipresence by treating the steep hillside and the silent, lonely graves as a physical extension of their daily residence. Inside the main hall, cells were arranged in twenty-four tiers or "galleries." Outside, situated on the crest of a hill overlooking the vast, seventy-seven-acre Sing Sing complex, inmates nicknamed the burial ground the "twenty-fifth gallery." The cemetery was, noted one observer, "considered by them one tier higher."[55]

> ◦ç   *Now I look back to the scenes of inhuman treatment and cruelty inflicted on prisoners I have witnessed and experienced myself at the hands of brutal keepers who are placed in such positions and power through political influence. Many [were] the pickings from the bar rooms of the saloons of the country towns and villages along the Hudson, particularly Albany and Troy, where I have met several of them who were under the influence of liquor and in the company of fast women, having a jolly good time as they called it. One night, two Sing Sing keepers had the nerve to make a night of it on the Bowery in New York and were seen by three ex-convicts who gave them a terrible beating up and never was caught for doing so. The*

*The main cellblock of Sing Sing with the workshops and Hudson River in the background.*

names of both these keepers were Mr. Mulligan and Mr. McCormick. This fact goes to show that fear of the then brutal system never reformed any man whom I knew of during all my prison experience. Instead, the brutal discipline made them worse criminals after their release from that galling yoke of servitude.[56]

# 1 3

# Danny Driscoll and the Whyos

=

> ❧  *A few of them [prison inmates and criminals] with whom I was intimately acquainted from boyhood ended their careers on the gallows and the electric chair. The names of three of these unfortunates were Danny Driscoll, Danny Lyons and Tommy Tobin. All three [were] born and raised in the then-known "bloody Sixth Ward" which environment at that time was a nest of crime, so to speak, and turned out many clever crooks of the youth of the neighborhood. Most of them are now dead or in the insane asylum.[1]*

AT THE MOMENT OF Appo's release from Sing Sing in 1884, a childhood associate had become "the terror of the wicked Sixth Ward," according to one reporter. Forgotten in the twentieth century, unknown in the twenty-first, Danny Driscoll was the most infamous gang leader of nineteenth-century New York. For many contemporaries Driscoll was the personification of violence, the "dangerous class" in flesh and blood.

One reporter's description was typical. Driscoll was the "leader of the 'Whyo' gang, the toughest of the tough, the readiest with knife or revolver, the most reckless in threats against all who thwarted him, the steadiest in drink, the most industrious in thievery, the most learned in the science of picking pockets, the bravest and most skillful in slipping steel into an adversary's back without exposing himself to danger, the most venomous, worthless, sneaking, drunken, quarrelsome and murderous reprobate known in the city."[2]

Newspaper accounts described Driscoll as medium-size and muscular in stature, sporting wavy brown hair and sometimes a moustache on his square-shaped face. To friend and foe alike, he had a determined look and walked with a swagger. His gray felt alpine hat, cocked over one ear, became the insignia of the Whyo gang. Driscoll's face, wrote one, was "coarse, sensual, vicious, with every evil passion stamped upon it, and not a redeeming feature." He was George Appo's childhood friend.[3]

Driscoll's early years are shrouded in mystery, primarily because most biographical information originated after his twentieth birthday. Nevertheless considerable circumstantial evidence indicates that Appo was indeed acquainted with Driscoll as a youth. They grew up in close proximity to each other in the tenements of Five Points and the nearby Fourth Ward along the East River. Driscoll appears to have been born to Irish immigrants living in England in 1858, making him two years Appo's junior. Little is known of how and when he immigrated to the United States, but later reports claimed his mother, known as "Apple Mary" or "Apple Mag," kept a fruit stand in front of the Tombs as early as 1861.[4]

*A rogues' gallery photograph of Danny Driscoll.*

Driscoll's childhood mirrored Appo's in other respects: Both were poor, became newsboys, and soon after, child pickpockets. Most likely Appo and Driscoll befriended each other while working in these youthful occupations. Some evidence even indicates that Driscoll was convicted of pickpocketing at the age of twelve in 1870. For that he was sentenced to six months in the Blackwell's Island Penitentiary. As with Appo, prison did little to discourage Driscoll's criminal activity. Between 1873 and 1877 Driscoll had numerous run-ins with the law. He was convicted of several larceny charges, as well as operating an unlicensed saloon. In 1876 he was shot in a gun battle in a Five Points saloon. Driscoll soon recovered, and charges were later dropped. Shortly thereafter he was convicted of pickpocketing and sentenced to three years in Sing Sing.[5]

Driscoll's criminal path, however, departed from Appo's in three important ways. First was Driscoll's ability to form alliances with local political figures and law enforcement officers. More significant, since these relationships kept Driscoll out of prison, later observers believed that Driscoll grew more daring over time. A bolder Driscoll was a violent Driscoll, another departure from George Appo. Whereas Appo was victimized by violence and resorted to physical assault only in self-defense, Danny Driscoll defined himself by such behavior. His body was reportedly covered with a plethora of scars obtained in forty to fifty violent confrontations, best evidenced by the disfiguring laceration on his chin from a gun battle. One friend later reported that Driscoll endured four surgeries without anesthesia. Driscoll gloried in his bloodiness, openly bragging that he had five to seven bullets in his body.[6] Such remnants of battle were badges of honor for Driscoll.

Driscoll's many confrontations reflected this simultaneous pattern of political influence and violence. For example, in 1881 Driscoll assaulted James Lemon on Baxter Street. Three days later, Driscoll attacked police officer John Dunn in order to rescue a friend from arrest. Records indicate that he was never convicted of either assault. One evening in 1883 Driscoll and a friend passed a Cherry Street tenement, where they stopped and engaged a group of Italian immigrants in a verbal confrontation. The exchange grew heated, and within seconds Driscoll shot both a nearby resident and his own accomplice. Neither of the wounds proved serious, and Driscoll was convicted of assault in the third degree. He was sentenced to one year in the penitentiary.[7]

Apparently Driscoll never served this sentence, because a few months later he shot lodging house keeper Patrick "Paddy" Green in his Pell Street saloon. Driscoll was out of jail only a few months in 1884 when he shot John Ohm and his wife in a Chrystie Street saloon. The first concrete evidence of Driscoll's political alliances appeared in this case when the Sixth Ward political leader Fatty Walsh interceded and had the case discharged.[8]

Driscoll's ability to escape punishment for his violent, criminal activity became the stuff of legend. By his own account in 1886, Driscoll admitted being arrested six times, serving four prison terms for a total of seven years. Newspaper accounts argued Driscoll was too modest, claiming that he was arrested at least twenty-seven times, twelve times in 1884 alone. Like Appo, Driscoll also moved beyond simple pickpocketing into more exclusive forms of criminal activity. In 1885, for example, Secret Service agents believed that Driscoll and two accomplices were engaged in counterfeit activity in both New York and New Orleans. Some even claimed that he briefly moved to San Antonio, Texas, opening a successful saloon, "until somebody carved him with a sword," according to one reporter.[9]

Finally Driscoll differed from Appo in the former's association with the "Whyo" or "Why oh" gang. The origins of the Whyos are imprecise. Some believed that they first appeared in 1880 or 1881, their name allegedly derived from a peculiar cry—"Oh! Why! Oh! Why! Oh!"—members yelled to each other at the approach of a policeman or some other danger. Early on, they typified most street gangs, numbering only a dozen, but eventually grew to be the largest gang in the city. By 1884 police officials reported that the gang claimed more than one hundred members, most residing in the Sixth Ward, with others scattered in other parts of Manhattan and Brooklyn. "Of all the gangs that have dominated this city, this one has been the largest and the most desperate," claimed one reporter.[10] Danny Driscoll was their leader.

George Appo's acquaintance with Driscoll as a youth was probably facilitated by the racially mixed and integrated neighborhood of their youth. The principal thoroughfare of the Whyos was Baxter Street, where Appo grew up, an area derided for its racial "amalgamation" and "mongrel population." Not only was Baxter Street's population "strikingly polyglot," wrote one reporter, "but the color line is not drawn." Driscoll's Pell Street residence was not only described as the home of the Whyos, but also as the "great barracks" of Chinese immigrants. One gang member remarked that female members of the Whyos (who engaged in shoplifting and pickpocketing) were frequently married to Chinese males. Driscoll even developed a close friendship and political alliance with Charles Simmons. Known as "Black Charlie" and "Captain Charlie," Simmons was described as the leader of the "Sixth Ward colored gentry" and ran a Baxter Street saloon frequented by Driscoll and his wife. When Driscoll was later arrested and tried in 1886, Simmons paid his legal expenses.[11]

Driscoll would have remained one of the thousands of faceless and forgotten teenagers and young men associated with gangs in nineteenth-century New York but for a series of events in June 1886. Early in the month Driscoll was in John McCarty's Hester Street boardinghouse, a so-called bilking house (where patrons of prostitutes were regularly robbed) and brothel across the street from Billy McGlory's Armory Hall. According to later reports, Driscoll became violent and McCarty evicted him. His manhood insulted, Driscoll returned a week later and fired an errant shot at his nemesis.[12]

McCarty was a formidable opponent. Reportedly a former member of the Whyo gang, he had served prison terms in Sing Sing, Blackwell's Island, and Philadelphia's Eastern State Penitentiary. A later conviction for counterfeiting would land him in Auburn prison. Around four o'clock in the morning of 26 June 1886, Driscoll sought his vengeance. Accompanied by Beezy Garrity, Owen "Owney" Bruen, and Katie Courtney, Driscoll went to McCarty's place. What happened next remains a subject of dispute. Several shots were fired, and Garrity fell to floor, mortally wounded in the stomach. Driscoll, McCarty, Bruen, and Courtney quickly fled the scene. Driscoll ran to 128 Baxter Street, allegedly with detectives in pursuit. The suspect was quickly discovered in an empty room feigning sleep. In the meantime McCarty was arrested as he left the house and returned to the room where Garrity lay moaning on the floor. When asked who shot her, Garrity pointed to McCarty. Confused about what had happened, police officials arrested both McCarty and Driscoll. In the meantime Garrity was taken to St. Vincent's Hospital and continued to implicate McCarty when questioned. Later that afternoon she died.[13]

Handing his weapon to the investigators, McCarty immediately denied the allegation. Police officer Peter Monahan concluded that the revolver was "clean" and every barrel loaded. Several witnesses testified that they were asleep or playing cards in McCarty's place when they were startled by a shot. Peering out their doors, they saw McCarty jumping out a window while Garrity moved across the room to the rear door. As she swung open the door, another shot rang out. Garrity fell to the floor, yelling, "I'm shot."[14]

Police officials surmised that Driscoll and Garrity intended to attack McCarty. Garrity, described by some as "a habitué" of McCarty's place, was to go in, hold open the door, and allow Driscoll to shoot McCarty. But McCarty was street smart. The instant Garrity entered, his suspicions were aroused. He jumped up, slammed the door in Driscoll's face, and held it closed with his foot. Driscoll responded with a shot but missed McCarty. Driscoll ran around to the rear, only to find that door bolted. In the meantime McCarty escaped out a window, while Garrity ran to unlock the rear entrance. Thinking McCarty was at the door, Driscoll shot the moment the rear door moved. The bullet hit Garrity.[15]

Driscoll and Garrity were lovers, a fact that added to the sensational coverage of the event. Newspapers described Garrity as an "attractive brunette," a "woman of the town," "dissolute," and "a fast woman," all implying that she was a prostitute. Others simply identified her as Driscoll's "worshipper" and his "latest love." Some claimed that she came from a respectable family living on Leonard Street. Further complicating matters were reports that Garrity not only resided with Driscoll's legal wife, Mary, on Pell Street, but lived with Driscoll "as his wife."[16]

Driscoll's trial began 27 September 1886 in the courtroom of Recorder Frederick Smyth. William Howe, New York's best-known criminal attorney, defended Driscoll. While the prosecution's version of the events indicated that Driscoll's shooting of Garrity was accidental, New York law determined that because Driscoll contemplated a felony, he could be executed for murder regardless of the identity of his victim. Consequently Driscoll was on trial for his life. Everyone knew this, especially courtroom officials who, fearing Whyo intervention, doubled the number of guards.[17]

Various witnesses implicated Driscoll in the crime.[18] Nevertheless the evidence against Driscoll was largely circumstantial and based on McCarty's testimony. Then, on the third day of the trial, Margaret Sullivan, mother of Bezzy Garrity, took the stand. In a statement that Driscoll's lawyer sought to suppress, Sullivan claimed that her daughter gave a dying declaration in St. Vincent's Hospital. "Danny Driscoll shot me, mother," testified Sullivan.[19]

Garrity's dying declaration compelled Howe to put Driscoll on the stand. Under oath Driscoll changed his story, now claiming that he had rendezvoused with Garrity and friends in a nearby Chatham Square saloon on the evening in question. After an evening of intoxication, they headed off to a lodging house to rent bedrooms for the remainder of the night. Driscoll testified that he was too drunk to know their destination. When Garrity entered 163 Hester Street, McCarty greeted them with a pistol. He shot at Driscoll but missed and hit Garrity. Only at this point, Driscoll claimed, did he realize that he was in McCarty's establishment. He quickly turned to his friend Owen Bruen: "Come, let's get out of here or we'll be shot."

Driscoll's testimony implied that the prosecution's witnesses were lying. He had many enemies, and McCarty had many friends. Sitting in the Tombs on the morning of 27 June as the police completed their preliminary investigation, Driscoll insisted that McCarty leaned over to him and whispered, "You better get me out of here. If you don't I'll fetch witnesses to better you."[20]

The police and prosecution, of course, charged that Driscoll was the liar, generating false witnesses and perjuring himself. Under an intense face-to-face interrogation by assistant district attorney John R. Fellows, Driscoll reportedly grew "pale with rage." Moving within two feet of Driscoll's face, Fellows challenged Driscoll to tell the truth. "Your impudence will avail you little here." Driscoll yelled back, displaying, according to one courtroom reporter, "a fierceness which caused the court officers to move a little nearer the witness stand." Smyth pounded his gavel for order. Fellows confronted Driscoll, repeatedly asking how many times he had been arrested. The defendant refused to answer. Driscoll left the stand, his face flushed with anger.[21]

On 30 September, after a three-day trial, the jury reached a verdict—guilty. The decision took only twenty-nine minutes, what some believed was the quickest conviction ever in a capital case. The news "spread like wildfire in the Fourth and Sixth wards," reported one newspaper. "Every corner in the vicinity was crowded with short-haired young men who discussed the case with bated breath." A week later Driscoll's greatest fear was realized. On 8 October 1886 Smyth sentenced Driscoll to death.[22]

## GANGS

Gangs like the Whyos and their leaders, such as Danny Driscoll, were the inspiration for the sometimes sensational and melodramatic writings of the journalists Jacob Riis and Herbert Asbury, key figures in constructing the historical image of nineteenth-century gangs. "By day they loaf in the corner-groggeries on their beat, at night they plunder the stores along the avenues, or lie in wait at the river for unsteady feet straying their way," wrote Riis in his classic *How the Other Half Lives* (1890). Asbury viewed Gilded Age gangs as little more than juvenile terrorists defined by their violence. Living on the docks—in alleys, cellars, and tenements—the nineteenth-century gang member lacked both a moral bearing and work ethic. The only outlet for his turbulent spirit was sex and fighting. A "stupid roughneck born in filth and squalor and reared amid vice and corruption," concluded Asbury, the gang member "fulfilled his natural destiny."[23]

Both writers singled out the Whyos. For Riis the Whyos represented "the worst depravity" in Five Points. Bottle Alley off Baxter Street, the site of twenty murders and the home of the Whyo Gang, was "the wickedest" and "foulest spot in all the city." Asbury echoed Riis, describing the Whyos as the "greatest of the gangs which came into existence in New York after the Civil War." Writing in the age of Al Capone, Asbury concluded that the Whyos were "the most ferocious criminals who ever stalked the streets of an American city."[24]

Sources that allow historians to recreate and interpret Gotham's nineteenth-century gangs are few and poor. Contemporaries offered confused, conflicting, and contradictory definitions of gangs, often equating informal, street-corner groups with organized bands of extortionists and murderers. For male youths with little education and adult supervision, gangs were more than crazed terrorists. These informal bodies addressed the psychological needs of outcast teenage males, offering companionship, protection, and respect. Some neighborhoods, like the Lower East Side and the West Side north of Fourteenth Street reportedly had gangs on almost every block. The area between West Thirtieth and West Fiftieth Streets was the most notorious, with gang-controlled blocks and alleys dubbed "Hell's Kitchen," "Battle Row," "Little Hell," "Sebastopol," and "Tub of Blood."[25]

In most cases contemporaries rarely knew the names of individual gang members, often identifying them by the name of their alleged leader, like the Armstrong Gang, the Hardigan Gang, or the McGloin Gang. Some were little more than homeless youths with no place to go, illustrated by the numerous so-called shanty gangs. Consequently we know virtually nothing about their memberships.

Nevertheless Gotham's gangs were the by-product of distinctive nineteenth-century forces. First was the absence of formal education. Schooling had little impact on youths like Driscoll, and many never attended school. Most who did stopped at age fourteen; rare was the boy educated beyond the sixth grade. Throughout most of the nineteenth century, the majority of New York's school-age children were truant, hanging out on neighborhood streets.[26]

If formal education failed to organize the daily lives of teenage males in New York, neither did the city's economy. While New York witnessed unprecedented economic expansion during the nineteenth century, that growth was uneven and punctuated by major depressions in 1837, 1857, 1873, and 1893, each lasting several years. In the winter of 1873–74 alone, an estimated 25 percent of Gotham's workforce lost their jobs.[27] Under such conditions, employment prospects were few for the city's immigrant, poorly educated, low-income youths. Teenage males almost naturally gravitated toward gang activities.

Finally gangs flourished because of inadequate and minimal law enforcement. Nineteenth-century New York had few police officers for its growing population. For most years between 1855 and 1900, New York had one police officer for every 400 residents; some years the figure exceeded 500 residents. By contrast, in 1975 the city employed one officer for every 177 residents. The *Tribune* complained that gangs were too powerful for solitary patrolmen on the beat. Some police admitted that they were afraid of gangs and left them alone. The inadequate number of officers, poor funding, state control of punishment systems, and the inability of local courts to mete out justice did little to discourage teenage boys from joining gangs.[28]

By the 1880s Gotham's gangs had three distinctive characteristics. First, an overwhelming number of gangs were identified, even named, by geography. For most their neighborhood or thoroughfare of residence served as their *nom de guerre* in street battles. From the Eighteenth Street and Kips Bay Gangs uptown to the Bottle Alley Gang at 43 Baxter Street and the "Big Flat" Gang in Lower Manhattan, "territory" defined most memberships.[29] Second, the more organized, like the Whyos, generated some level of community support, reflected in the ability of individuals like Driscoll to foster alliances with local political officials and community leaders. Finally gangs fostered a distinct sense of manhood and honor, structured around notions of toughness, hardness, fighting, and rough masculinity. Being a gang member meant being violent.

Despite these characteristics, gang identities were nevertheless fluid, amorphous, and ill defined. "Growler gangs," for example, were unorganized, informal, and casual in their violence and criminal activity. In many working-class households, "rushing the growler"—nineteenth-century parlance for bringing ("rushing") a bucket ("the growler") to a saloon to fill with alcohol for home consumption—was a responsibility of women and children. Growler gangs accosted women, children, and "lushers" (drunks) in the street, compelling them to relinquish their money and property. "Growler gangs," complained one citizen, are "the curse of the whole city."[30]

The geographical identity of most gangs masked how economic forces structured gang formation. After 1860 gangs were increasingly associated with New York's maritime economy. Neighborhoods in the center of Manhattan, claimed one observer, were "unfavorably situated" for gangs because they had no waterfront. The proliferation of "wharf-rats," "river pirates," and "slaughterhouse gangs" reflected this little-recognized transformation. "Besides regularly organized gangs," wrote one, "there are bands on almost every pier along the river, whose members have never formally organized and who lead a miserable existence." Former police superintendent George W. Walling considered waterfront gangs to be the roughest and most violent of criminals.[31]

Ironically the so-called river rats and slaughterhouse gangs were an unanticipated by-product of Gotham's economic success. Much of New York's nineteenth-century economy was organized around the importing, processing, and manufacturing of commodities such as cotton, flour, sugar, and clothing. The sheer volume of both unprocessed and manufactured commodities passing through the port and streets of Manhattan proved to be tempting targets for gangs interested in extortion and robbery. Public and private officials acknowledged their failure to control such behavior. Police captain E. O. Smith, a former captain of the harbor patrol, admitted that nearly every vessel entering the port had a portion of its cargo stolen. By the 1870s Cotton Exchange officials estimated that at least one percent of the annual raw, unprocessed cotton passing through New York Harbor was stolen by gangs. Along the Harlem waterfront, a brickyard proprietor gave up fighting nearby gangs. "We are in mortal terror of these men and try not to give them offence."[32]

The most organized gangs even specialized in certain kinds of crime. The Eighteenth Street Gang along the East River stole from the coal barges. Farther up the river, the Shanty Gang, named for their temporary houses from Seventieth to Seventy-third Streets, helped inmates escape from Blackwell's Island. The Fourth Avenue Gang in Harlem focused on the railyards of the neighborhood. Nearby, the Brickyard Gang was named after the object of their criminal activity. The Forty-Sixth Street Gang, off Eleventh Avenue, was noted for stealing rope from riverboats.[33]

Finally gangs flourished because of familial and local community support. Waterfront gangs, in particular, worked in league with a host of dockfront workers: watchmen, junkmen, stevedores, longshoremen, draymen, pursers, warehousemen, weighers, and samplers. The movement of cotton again proved illustrative. On the dock the staple was "roughly handled" by stevedores, complained one observer, creating "as much sweepings as possible, as the gang at night collect this, sell it to the junkmen and divide the proceeds." Others permitted women and children, some of whom were related to the stevedores and draymen, to pull handfuls of cotton from the bales, filling their aprons and bags.[34]

Community support was evidenced in the political connections gangs exploited. For decades local elected officials relied on certain gangs to provide protection and "muscle" in their political campaigns. In return such gangs received lenient treatment in court. "The influence of the pothouse politician seems to be omnipotent," complained the *Sun* in 1884. "It is the secret of the power of the gangs." According to that account, twenty recent assaults on police officers resulted in only six convictions with punishment, and the worst was six months on Blackwell's Island. Police captains and officers consistently complained of this practice to no avail.[35]

Driscoll and the Whyos thrived for just this reason. Their political pull was reflected in the personage of Thomas "Fatty" Walsh. At various times a Mulberry Street saloonkeeper, street inspector, superintendent of markets, state assemblyman, and city alderman, Walsh was a popular Sixth Ward figure and an ally of concert saloon proprietor Owney Geoghegan. On numerous occasions, according to newspaper reports, Walsh secured the release of different members of the Whyo gang members from prison, even when they were incarcerated for assaulting police officers. In return Driscoll reportedly helped Walsh in his electoral contests, "colonizing" the Mechanics' Lodging-House near Five Points with homeless men on election day and breaking up rival political meetings. "Whenever the Whyo was in a specially close corner it was usually Walsh's influence and intercession that saved him," claimed the *World*.[36]

Community sympathy for gang leaders like Driscoll revealed itself in court proceedings. During Driscoll's trial he attracted an audience of young male admirers, noted for the cowlicks pasted onto their foreheads and for their collarless shirts. They gazed in awe at Driscoll when he entered the courtroom. A reporter remarked, "All toughdom seemed to have turned out to do him honor." District Attorney John R. Fellows admitted that many in the courtroom considered Driscoll a hero.[37]

Bandits depended on community protection, and the same was true for gangs like the Whyos. One reporter expressed outrage that the parents of Whyos living in Five Points rejoiced when their children performed a successful heist. Similarly, neighborhood youths held gang leaders in high regard. "Who proves the successful thief becomes great at once among his fellows," complained one observer. Those who employed pistols or knives were profoundly respected and deemed "tough" by other youths.[38] Incarceration was a badge of honor. Applause and honor greeted gang members on release from prison, according to police official Thomas Knox. A reporter concurred, concluding that jail time transformed a gang member not only into a hero but a recognized leader.[39]

The gangster's search for respect and honor generated direct confrontations with law enforcement. Several observers described the relationship between police and gang members as akin to war. One popular pastime was dropping bricks from tenement roofs onto passing policemen. Assaults on police came not only from above but literally from below. Police officer Cornelius Willemse remembered that a common trick by gang members was to extinguish gaslights on a street and then yell for the police after opening coal chutes and sewer covers on the sidewalk and street, or stretching a rope across the sidewalk. If successful, the ploy broke the legs of policemen who fell into the open holes. Such incidents even generated sympathy from police critics like the reformer Frank Moss. "The life of the policeman in the Five Points was always hard and uncomfortable," he admitted.[40]

Here was a key element of the gang mentality. One reporter noted that "the love of money" was not the primary motivation for young gang members. They sought respect, honor, and adulation from other neighborhood youths for performing deeds others feared. Unlike with pickpocketing and other forms of high-level crime, such respect was not grounded in trickery, deceit, or chicanery. Rather, physical confrontation and violent intimidation were the governing behaviors for a gang member. "These rowdies would rather break a policeman's head," wrote another, "than make an easy capture of somebody's money."[41]

This ethic of violence differentiated gang youths from the "civilizing" trends of nineteenth-century society. New York is "terrorized by gangs," wrote one. A gang's success, wrote another, relied on "a system of terrorism." The reputations of men like Driscoll were enhanced not only by dishing out violence. Their ability to withstand violence raised their status among their fellows; thus Driscoll bragged about the bullets in his body.[42] For gangsters violence was an accepted element of their social order, the defining element of their self-worth and honor.

Such glorification of violence persuaded law enforcement officials to do the same. Police superintendent George Walling defended police brutality on the grounds that policemen were like armed soldiers in the midst of a hostile camp. The failure of prosecutors and judges to enforce the law compelled many officers to mete out their own punishments. When asked what was the best way to discourage gangs, police captain John McCullagh was candid: "Give them the stick." McCullagh offered a simple philosophy: The police officer "must terrorize them or they'll terrorize him."[43]

The valorization of violence distinguished gang culture from other forms of criminal association. For pickpockets like George Appo, manhood was defined by being a "good fellow," a "nervy crook," someone who took risks, employed his wits, and *avoided* violence. Honor, status, and success were based not on physical assault but rather deception. Gangs were despised by so-called professional criminals, believed one reporter, because they relied on brute strength. Their predisposition to violence made them outcasts not only to law-abiding citizenry but to other underworld elements. Another noted that "plunder" was the objective of professional criminals who resorted to violence only in self-defense. To them gangs were simply "cowardly bullies."[44]

Significantly the Whyos displayed some of the earliest structural elements emblematic of twentieth-century organized crime. The older age of members like Driscoll indicated that the group was less like a youth gang and more like a criminal association. The random violence and spontaneous mischief emblematic of youth gangs were replaced by more structured forms of illegal activity. As criminal conspirators living off the work of others and maintaining their power by intimidation, terror, and political favoritism, the Whyos were early racketeers.

Observers frequently noted the variety of Whyo criminal activity. Members not only engaged in "traditional" forms of crime like pickpocketing, pimping, and prostitution but experimented with new opportunities like counterfeiting. Gang members were recruited not only from nearby blocks or wards but from other parts of Manhattan and Brooklyn. Driscoll's criminal activity extended beyond New York, reaching as far as New Orleans and San Antonio. Like members of the Mafia in the twentieth century, Driscoll and his supporters denied that they were members of the Whyos, some even insisting that no such band existed. The Whyos, they charged, were the myopic creations of corrupt police officers, overzealous prosecutors, and sensationalistic newspapers.[45] Driscoll embodied the transition from juvenile delinquency to organized crime, from a boy pickpocket to convicted felon to gang mastermind, the Whyos from a youth gang to a criminal organization. "By his prowess as a thief and his deftness with knife and pistol," observed the *World*, "he had risen to the summit of his ambition as a leader among his fellows."[46]

## DRISCOLL'S LAST BATTLE

Even with a death sentence hanging over his head, Danny Driscoll was not easily beaten. His attorney, William Howe, immediately appealed the verdict, while Driscoll went to the press. Many of the stories were scurrilous exaggerations, if not falsehoods, charged Driscoll. "I'm not as black as I'm painted," he told one reporter. "I am a human being with human feelings and human sympathies in me." Driscoll admitted that he suffered from a "bad name," but reminded critics that only two weeks before the fatal night McCarty had fired a shot at him.[47]

More significant, Driscoll screamed that justice in New York was for sale. Driscoll and his wife, Mary, testified that the incriminating testimony of the prostitute and witness Carrie Wilson was false. "Why, she has come here to the door of my cell and, with tears streaming down her face, has confessed to me that she perjured herself," claimed Driscoll. Other witnesses like Tombs keeper Patrick Foster supported Driscoll's version of the events. "I am the victim of a conspiracy hatched by a pot-house politician," charged Driscoll.[48]

The "pot-house politician" was Driscoll's former ally Fatty Walsh, who by this time had been appointed Tombs warden by Mayor Abram S. Hewitt. Walsh's success in frustrating Driscoll's escape attempts earned the warden the inmate's enmity. Driscoll attacked Walsh as little more than a "licensed ruffian." Walsh, Driscoll accused, withheld meals and tried to starve him, maltreated elderly and teenage prisoners, and extorted rich ones. In a bit of hyperbole Driscoll added that "the public can believe me when I say I welcome death as a sweet relief to escape from the cowardly brutality of this man."[49]

But Driscoll's appeal fell on unsympathetic ears. On 29 November 1887, Driscoll's argument was rejected by the New York Court of Appeals. Writing for the majority, Judge C. J. Ruger concluded that the newfound testimony was simply not to be believed. Ruger openly wished for testimony from "reputable witnesses" but believed that "crimes committed in the haunts of vice and dissipation" made that unlikely. Imperfect evidence, wrote Ruger, "should not shield a criminal from the just consequences of his crime."[50]

In New York, as well as elsewhere, murderers awaiting execution attracted considerable attention, emblematic of what the *Police Gazette* described as "the strange passion for hero-worship." Executions traditionally occurred on Friday, giving it the names "Hangman's Day" and "Black Friday." Officials feared a riot or rescue attempt on the day of Driscoll's execution, leading the police to station 150 officers around the Tombs. According to newspaper accounts Whyo gang members believed that Walsh sacrificed Driscoll and promised revenge. Walsh himself received several death threats signed by "Whyo."[51]

Media coverage of Driscoll, his trial, and his family was transformed into a form of theater, a real-life drama with the criminal at center stage. Newspapers offered daily detailed descriptions of the events leading to the penultimate moment: the erection of the gallows in the Tombs courtyard, the names of daily visitors, Driscoll's diet, notes between the defendant and his lawyers, the condemned's reaction to certain messages, his final letter to his wife, interviews with guards on the death watch, an hour-by-hour account of his final day alive, his last mass in the Tombs chapel.[52]

While condemning Driscoll in the most sensational terms, however, many news accounts transformed him into a heroic figure, especially for working-class Roman Catholics. The intense coverage described how Driscoll gave away personal mementos to guards before his death, many chock-full of religious meaning: a cross, a scapular, a prayerful note. Driscoll acknowledged the loyalty of his supporters. In a letter to Owen Bruen, Driscoll expressed his gratitude for Bruen's "many acts of kindness," promising, "I will never forget you. God bless you, my boy. Be a good man and pray for me now and again." Approaching the gallows, he reportedly whispered into a priest's ear: "Please ask Warden Walsh to forgive me for what I have said and done to him."[53] Like Jesus Christ on the cross, Driscoll on the scaffold forgave his enemies.

Driscoll, previously described as "thief, brawler, and assassin," "a stunted, miserable wretch," "the most desperate criminal ever caught in the United States," was even transformed into a bard. On the eve of his execution, he composed a poem to the Sisters of Charity:

God bless you, Sister Mary,
For you are good and brave,
May we meet, my dearest sister,
In the land beyond the grave,

Where the wicked cease from troubling,
And the weary are at rest,
There I hope to meet you, sister,
In that dear land of the blest,

Where the body will be free from suffering
And the soul be free from care;
There I hope to meet you, sister—
This is my heartfelt prayer.[54]

When the moment of his execution came, Driscoll kissed a small crucifix, looked to the sky, and muttered a prayer. Another witness reported that as the black cap was pulled over Driscoll's face, he uttered his last words: "Jesus, have mercy upon me!" At that moment the priests stepped back, and the hangman gave the signal. "The sound wounded the awful stillness like a knife thrust," wrote one reporter. At 7:24 a.m., the ax cut the cord, Driscoll's body shot into the air, then dropped back with a jerk, motionless.[55]

Driscoll's execution briefly transformed him into a martyr. His family chose not to hold a wake, forsaking a long-held Irish tradition, and refused to publicize the time of the funeral, allegedly to prevent a crowd from following the funeral precession. The tactic failed. The day of his burial hundreds, if not thousands, of onlookers appeared at his mother's Baxter Street home. Described as "the ones who had slept behind coal bins and down cellarways and on the trucks," the throng made Baxter Street impassable and forced the impromptu funeral procession to begin an hour early. Driscoll, now a heroic outlaw, was laid to rest in Calvary

Cemetery in faraway Queens, not far from the grave of Owney Geoghegan.[56]

DANNY DRISCOLL'S popularity with those who slept in coal bins, cellarways, and trucks convinced some contemporaries that Driscoll's gang activity was an embryonic form of urban banditry. Driscoll, wrote one reporter, "was as near in nature to a bandit chieftain as any ruffian in the Sixth Ward and in modern times could be expected to be." According to Eric Hobsbawm and other historians, social bandits were complex and contradictory characters, products of rural, peasant life, and reflective of the transition from traditional, kinship forms of social organization to modern, capitalist industrial society. So-called bandits were heroes, champions, avengers, and liberators in the peasant mind.[57]

Gang leaders like Danny Driscoll were transitional figures. Driscoll displayed many of the characteristics associated with bandits: a confrontational personality, a demand for respect, a sense of individual rebellion. Driscoll was an avenger, not an agent of justice. He refused to accept poverty and resorted to the only mechanisms available: strength, cunning, determination. He relied on cruelty and terror to exert his will; he thrived on revenge and vendetta. He lacked a social consciousness that evolved into organized revolt or revolution. Five Points, filled with unmarried, unemployed, and uneducated young men, offered fertile ground for gangs. Their large numbers combined with a weak and unpopular municipal government drove political leaders to accommodate gangs. Forming tacit alliances with parts of the impoverished working-class community of Five Points, Driscoll compelled local leaders like Fatty Walsh to tolerate such gangs, allowing them to multiply and become part of the political landscape.

Driscoll's popularity rested on the shared belief that the criminal justice and legal systems were riddled with corruption. "Law" and "justice" were two separate things. Driscoll believed, rightly or wrongly, that he was convicted not because he did wrong, but rather because McCarty had paid off the cops. "The reason my liberty was sworn away was because I had no money to put up," charged Driscoll. "That other man could easily out bid me, and he did."[58]

But Driscoll was a victim of circumstances. By the mid-1880s, some contended that the power of gangs was on the wane. According to Justice Solon B. Smith, the use of "rowdies" in elections was declining in the wake of new systems of registration. A decade later one newspaper reported the same, specifically citing the power of Driscoll's Whyos. Some attributed the change to increasing rates of conviction of gang leaders and the lack of "political backing" they formerly enjoyed."[59] A century later the same actions for which Driscoll hanged would never generate a conviction for first-degree murder, much less an execution. Evidence like Beezy Garrity's dying declaration is now inadmissible in courts of law. The failure of the prosecution to recover the murder weapon might be grounds for acquittal.

But no one should wrap a halo around Danny Driscoll's head. He thrived on violent intimidation, a willingness to pick up a gun and kill in retaliation for a simple verbal insult. Much of Driscoll's community support originated from fear, not respect. Driscoll, wrote one, sought "to defy all law, to make war upon society, to play the king in a small sphere and to put the law of force in place of all other laws."[60] His final act of violence —the shooting of Beezy Garrity—exemplified how he was motivated by the need to defend his personal honor rather than any sense of social justice. Like most outlaws Driscoll was not out for equity but for a fast buck. Robin Hood he was not.

Yet Danny Driscoll exemplified how poverty and economic depression in the final decades of the nineteenth century created the conditions for "social bandits" and "noble robbers." Throughout the United States certain outlaws were viewed as modern-day Robin Hoods: Jesse James, Billy the Kid, the Molly Maguires. Rural America and the frontier became an American Sherwood Forest. Banks and railroads represented the greedy clergy and wicked nobility, detectives and bounty hunters the evil sheriffs of Nottingham. The popularity of these images, however, was not restricted to rural or frontier America. Driscoll saw himself and was portrayed in much the same manner: a victim of betrayal, a noble robber abandoned and caught within a web of corruption, an individual defending honor and manhood. The West had Jesse James; the Pennsylvania coalfields, the Molly Maguires; and New York, Danny Driscoll.

# 1 4

# Eastern State Penitentiary

**=**

◄ *I left New York for Philadelphia, and began picking pockets in that city. I was very successful for two months and saved enough money for a bank roll to work a more easy and less risky graft called the flim flam (or more plainly speaking, making people make mistakes in giving change for a large bill).*[1]

*I was successful at this flim flam business until one day, being in need of a ten dollar bill to work with, I entered the jewelry store of Gustav Kunz on 9th Street with the honest intention to obtain a ten dollar bill for ten ones. He did not have the ten bill, and I was about to leave the place when I noticed a little gold locket I fancied and asked him the price of it. He put up the tray before me and handed me the locket to examine. As I looked at it, he said: "I'll let you have that for $7.50."*

*I put the locket back on the tray and said, "That's too dear for me."*

*He suddenly grabbed my hand and said, "You didn't come here to buy, you came here to steal." I told him he was crazy and another man in the store went out and got an officer and I was charged with an attempt at petty larceny.*[2]

*I, of course, was as innocent as the very judge who sentenced me. Therefore, I stood trial and the jury found me guilty without leaving their seats. I was sentenced to one year at solitary confinement in the Eastern Penitentiary or "Cherry Hill" as it is commonly called by crooks. I was entirely innocent even in thought, let alone in action, of any intention to steal from Kunz the jeweler. Before my trial, I lay in the Moyamensing Jail for six weeks before my case was called for trial. With the filth and food and having to sleep on the floor of the cell during all them six weeks, I suffered terribly, both physically and mentally.*[3]

*On my arrival at Eastern Penitentiary, my name, age, height, weight and all marks of description was taken and then I was brought to the bathroom. After the bath, I was given a suit of prison clothes and a pair of slippers. Then the keeper threw a monk's robe with a hood and mask around me, pulled the hood over my head and face, and then led me along the jail hall to the centre and up one flight of stairs and along the cell tier and unlocked the two doors of cell P, North 3rd. He told me to stoop and bend my head and pushed me gently into the cell, where I took off the robe and handed it out to the keeper, who said to me: "Your number is 9082, cell P, North 3rd. You will find the rules and regulations of the place on the wall, read them." He then slammed both doors, locked them, and went away.[4]*

*I then looked around the cell. There was an opening in the ceiling about 18 inches long, four inches wide and tapering down, cone shaped, an apology for a window. The ceiling was ten feet above the floor and nothing but the four bare walls to look at, a canvas cot to sleep on, and a bread-bag hanging on a little book shelf in a corner. I sat down on the cot and said to myself, "This is a tough deal for an innocent man. If I were guilty, I would not mind it so much."*

*Just then the door opened and my block keeper (Mr. Howard by name) said to me: "I'm going to put you to work at toeing stockings tomorrow. Did you ever work at it before?"*

*"No sir, I don't even know what kind of work that is."*

*"Well," said he, "I'll put a good fellow in here as a cell mate who will instruct you in the business tomorrow. How much time have you?" I told him one year. "Oh, that will slip around soon," said he and slammed the door and went away.*

*About ten minutes later, another keeper came to the door, opened the wicket and pushed in to me a soup pan and cup and a spoon, saying, "The dinner will be along soon, so be ready to hand out your pan for soup." He closed the wicket and left. Soon after, I heard the rumbling of [the] grub wagon and stood ready with the pan. The wicket flew open and a large piece of bread was pushed through at me. I handed out the pan which was passed back filled with greasy water and a piece of tough meat that smelled anything but good. Nevertheless, I sat down on the cot and ate enough to satisfy my hunger. As there was nothing to read, I lay down and went to sleep.*

I was awakened by the rumbling noise of the grub wagon. I got up and took my tin cup and stood at the door. The wicket opened and a ration of bread was pushed through and my cup filled with so-called tea sweetened with molasses.

The next morning after breakfast, the keeper came, opened my doors, threw the robe and hood at me, told me to put them on and come with him. I stepped out on the tier and the keeper led me a short distance, stopped and unlocked a cell door and said, "Jack here is a partner for you, show him how to do his work." As I stepped into the cell, I took off the robe and hood and found myself in a cell with two cots, a table and two stools, a book shelf and a canvas bread bag and a cell-mate, who's name was John Northcross, convicted for grand larceny and sentenced for two years. He had only five more weeks to serve out of the two years.[5] He began to instruct me how to toe stockings and in two days I was turning out my task (18 dozen per day). The keeper, Mr. Howard, was greatly pleased and rewarded Jack and me with a paper of chewing tobacco each.

Finally, Jack's time expired and the keeper came one morning,

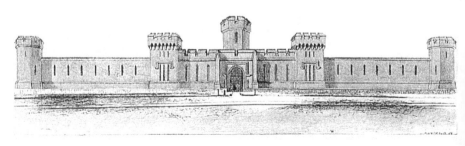

*Eastern State Penitentiary—Appo's home in 1886.*

*threw the robe and hood at Jack and said to him, "Come on! Time expired."*

*Jack, after shaking hands with me, said to the keeper, "That's the last time I'll ever put on this monk's robe," and out he went.*[6]

For a brief time Philadelphia's Eastern State Penitentiary was the world's most famous prison. In contrast to most American prisons, Eastern State isolated each prisoner for his entire term of incarceration. Whereas Sing Sing prisoners were cloistered in individual cells at night and congregated in silence in common workshops during the day, Eastern's inmates were separated day and night, hence the labels of "congregate" and "separate" applied to each respective system. Bathing occurred once a week, while daily activities like eating, working, and sleeping took place in individual cells. Eastern's cells even had separate exercise yards, making them among the largest in the United States. Prisoners were virtually transformed into monks, donning robes with hoods as Appo described to avoid visual and other contact with inmates. Even religious services were administered via a peephole in the cell door. Eastern officials hoped that prohibiting all social intercourse among prisoners would literally strike terror in the hearts of inmates. Appo, however, described the practice as "enough to drive one mad."[7]

By the time of Appo's incarceration, Eastern State Penitentiary was the only separate system prison remaining in the United States. Even though the institution was alone in this regard, authorities remained adamant about the benefits of isolating inmates. Official reports alleged that such methods revealed the character of individual prisoners, the origins of their crimes, and their moral and mental defects.[8]

In contrast to Appo's penitentiary experiences in New York, prison guards in Eastern were given greater responsibility over inmates. Administrators insisted that guards and overseers did not merely supervise inmates but "ministered" to them as well, in the words of the Reverend James Ashton. They allegedly received specialized training, which prepared them to exert a benevolent influence over convicts. Guard positions were not political appointments as in New York, so changing administrations did not produce new corrections personnel. The only cause for dismissal was violation of prison rules.[9]

Eastern officials were openly critical of the convict labor system that

Appo experienced in Sing Sing and Clinton. The congregate system with its factories, lockstep, and harsh discipline was little more than "slavery to the State," charged one Eastern report. Individual prisoners were largely ignored and massed together regardless of age, crime, or personality. Inmates were treated not as humans but rather as "part of the machinery of production," alleged another Eastern report.[10]

Eastern authorities also believed that individual isolation discouraged the formation of criminal classes, a product of "the gross evil of convict association." Eastern reports repeatedly proclaimed that New York's congregate system created a "crime class," specifically professional criminals whose livelihoods derived exclusively from illegal activity. On their release former convicts went to cities and reestablished relationships initially fostered in prison. Crime thus became a vocation, concluded another report.[11]

To battle this subculture of deviance, Eastern State Penitentiary adopted a distinct system of contract labor. Inmates were theoretically taught a trade, although by 1881 officials admitted that this rarely happened. Weaving, shoemaking, and picking oakum or wool were the sole industries in Eastern, tasks famous for their drudgery. Hard work, education, and discouraging idleness by young first offenders would inhibit their criminal descent. "Industry is the surest prevention of crime," argued Eastern officials. Placing their faith in individualism and the work ethic, Eastern authorities adopted "overwork" in 1881, permitting inmates to keep 50 percent of their excess production (or "overwork"). The remaining 50 percent went to the county in which they were convicted. This policy even allowed prisoners the opportunity to support their families while in confinement.[12]

The absence of forced convict labor (like that found in Sing Sing) convinced Eastern's defenders that isolation was more benevolent. While the prison initially employed the dark cell, the shower bath, the straitjacket, and the iron gag as punishments, by the 1880s officials claimed those were tortures of the past. In fact isolation allowed for individual treatment of inmates and limited the need to rely on punishment as a means to influence other inmates. Compared with Sing Sing, argued Warden Edward Townsend, Eastern had no punishments. Inmates who violated rules were simply confined to their individual cell, fed only bread and water, prohibited from reading (except the Bible), and denied contact with anyone except official caretakers.[13]

The isolation system came under attack early in its history. The most notable critique originated from the pen of Charles Dickens. During his highly publicized tour of the United States in 1841, Dickens reportedly told one Eastern official that "The Falls of Niagra and your Penitentiary are the objects I most wish to see in America." He was less impressed with the latter. Dickens described the silent system as a "dreadful punishment" of "torture and agony." He compared the black hood worn by Eastern inmates to a "dark shroud, an emblem of the curtain dropped between him and the living world." The total and complete isolation, the lack of communication with even wives, children, and friends convinced Dickens that the Eastern inmate was "a man buried alive."[14]

By the end of the century, prison reformer Frederick Wines echoed Dickens. Penitentiary reformers experimented with systems of solitude, and others with programs of silence. "The one drove men mad," concluded Wines, while "the other drove them into rebellion." The separate system's emphasis on total silence failed because of the constant need for "force, vigilance and repression."[15]

Appo confirmed the testimony of such critics. By the 1880s the rehabilitative purposes of the separate system were effectively abandoned, best evidenced by overcrowding. Upon opening in 1829, Eastern had 496 cells. In 1866, for the first time, the number of inmates exceeded the number of cells, forcing doubling up in twenty-nine cells. Although the prison constructed three large cellblocks from 1877 to 1879, the inmate population outpaced the construction of new cells. By the year of Appo's admission in 1886, the prison's population fluctuated between 1,064 and 1,170. Warden Michael J. Cassidy's daily logbook frequently mentioned that inmates shared cells. A decade later Frederick Wines and other prison advocates noted that more than one hundred cells had two convicts in them, and some had as many as five prisoners. Appo's experience, sharing his cell with John Northcross and later John Cronin, reflected the abandonment of the isolationist ideal.[16]

By this time, however, even prison administrators were growing disenchanted with isolation. In 1886, for example, Warden Cassidy wrote that "most of the prisoners are cheerful and reconciled to their situation, all reply pleasantly to any questions asked to them and apear [sic] to be pleased to have a visit from the warden or any one." By 1891, however, he was far more pessimistic. "Prisoners want to escape," he conceded; "the strength of the structure will not deter many of the inmates of this and all other prisons."[17]

With the breakdown of isolation, prisoners exerted a new level of independence. Warden Townsend expressed frustration in failing to prevent communication between prisoners in nearby or contiguous cells. Most violations involved some form of talking—through a wall, over a skylight, into pipes connecting cells along a block. Frederick Wines admitted that efforts to hinder communication were either ineffectual or too costly. Overseers cleaning out cells usually found many contraband articles. Indeed, Cassidy was incredulous that numerous inmates made "claims to private property as a right, forgetting that they had forfeited all rights when the sentence of the court was imposed on them."[18]

Officials also acknowledged that the separate system stimulated certain undesirable sexual behaviors. By 1870 prison administrators recognized that with individual isolation, the inmate was "still free to indulge in solitary vice," in other words, masturbation. Such activity, concluded Frederick Wines, "enfeeble[d] both body and mind," and ultimately made discharged convicts unable to resist "the temptations of ordinary life."[19]

Eastern officials blamed insanity and other problems on masturbation. Warden Cassidy believed that one prisoner was going insane because of excessive masturbation. When an inmate admitted that he regularly masturbated, Cassidy concluded that such behavior transformed him into "a mental and physical wreck." In the end, concluded the warden, "He is likely to lose his mind altogether if he is not handled carefully." Similarly, complaints by disgruntled former inmates were dismissed by officials like Cassidy as merely the manifestation of excessive masturbation and other forms of "self abuse."[20]

By 1887 George Appo had encountered an astonishing diversity of incarcerations: a year of juvenile reform on the school ship *Mercury*, three sentences in the workshops of Sing Sing, part of a prison term in the wood and hat shops of Clinton, a year on Blackwell's Island, at least six incarcerations in the Tombs, several weeks in Moyamensing Jail, and a year of isolation in Eastern State Penitentiary. Appo's convict life personified the multiplicity of prison experiences. Frequent and repeated punishment and torture characterized state penitentiaries like Sing Sing. Lax security and easy escape typified county penitentiaries like Blackwell's Island. Boredom distinguished the isolation of Eastern State Penitentiary. And class and wealth determined the treatment of inmates in jails like the Tombs.[21]

If Sing Sing was characterized by hard labor, physical torture, and high rates of disease, insanity, and even death, Eastern State Penitentiary reflected the limited remains of the isolationist regimen. Inmates managed to converse while living in separate cells. Overcrowding compelled administrators to allow inmates to share cells and thereby abandon the near-complete control they enjoyed over inmates. Prisoners were no longer isolated in silence from one another in order to contemplate and reflect on the seriousness of their crime. Now they communicated with one another, sometimes at will.

All prisons required a level of consent from the "governed." How this was accomplished, however, extended over a broad range of possibilities. Even in Sing Sing, Appo's experience from his first to his third incarceration changed dramatically. Whereas he recounted brutal beatings during his initial imprisonment, his final term was characterized by a motivation of self-survival: befriending a keeper, obtaining privileges through the intervention of friends, peacefully cooperating, and avoiding any confrontation with the authorities. Appo indeed modified his behavior as prison authorities hoped, but not in the ways they envisioned.

No prison reformed Appo. "I made up my mind to try again to get honest employment and to reform without fear or favor," he admitted after one incarceration. But he added that he did so "not that I feared the discipline of a prison, nor did I favor it."[22] Eastern State Penitentiary warden Cassidy unwittingly concurred. Reformers believed that prison inmates quietly acknowledged the justice of their conviction. In reality few did so. "The majority of prisoners do not regret the commission of the crime for which they were convicted; in many cases they use all the powers of reasoning they possess to justify it," admitted Cassidy. "Repeated convictions do not deter the inherent criminal."[23]

On his release from Eastern State Penitentiary, Appo returned to New York. Echoing Cassidy, he quickly returned to his underworld milieu.

# 1 5

# Green Goods

=

◆§ *I tried hard to get work but failed, and in the course of about one month, I drifted, through necessity, back to the opium joints and stealing for a living again. I was not so reckless and foolish as in former days because during my last term of imprisonment, I studied hard and thought a great deal to prepare myself in case I had to steal again for a living, to work more safely and keep out of prison. So when I had got hold of a bank roll, I gave up the rough graft of picking pockets and started in what was called at that time "sure thing graft" such as the "flim flam," or more properly speaking, short changing with a ten or twenty dollar bill. I worked this graft for about six months and was very successful.*

*In the meantime, I became acquainted with the men in the green goods business and was employed by one of the "writers," that is a man who sent out thousands of green goods circulars throughout the United States and Canada, as his "steerer" or messenger. My part of the business as steerer was to go and meet the "come on," or victim at the hotel where he was instructed to come and do business. Then I told him that I was the confidential messenger of his friend "The Old Gentleman" and sent to conduct him safely to where he could transact business with impunity and safety.*

*I worked as a steerer for over eight years and was very successful. Everyone I steered to the "turning joint" always made a deal from $300 to $1,000. I received only ten percent of the money, while the writer and the man who put up the bank roll of $20,000 each received 45 percent of the deal. The man who put up the bank roll would have as many as 15 writers on his staff and each of these men would bring on at least one or two victims per day.*

*I was then working for Eddie Parmeley who was the boss and financial backer of the business at that time. I worked for Parmeley* about 18 months and he had his headquarters at the time at the Point View Hotel at 110th Street and Central Park.

One day I was sent to the Ryan House in Elizabeth, New Jersey, to bring a come on from Alabama. When I arrived at the Ryan House, I looked at the register and found two men instead of one. So I went up to their room, knocked on their door and walked in. I gave them the password (All is Well) to show them I was the right man to talk business with. I told them I was simply the confidential messenger of their friend, the Old Gentleman, and was sent to conduct them safely to Mott Haven, where the old gentleman was waiting patiently with the goods for them.

"We expected to meet him and goods right here," they said.

"Well, you understand the nature of the business and you certainly cannot expect the old gent, who is 78 years of age to come here with twenty thousand of the goods and display them in a public hotel to two strangers," said I.

"How far is Mott Haven from here?" they asked.

"Only a short distance, and the place is very handy for you to make your train back home after you do business, whether you do business or not. All your expenses, hotel bills and railroad fare are paid to and from your home," said I.

"All right, we'll go at once."

So I got them to New York and brought them to 110th Street, planted them in the sitting room off the bar and went upstairs and told the salesman, Paddy O'Brien or "Paddy the Pig," that there was two guys together downstairs.

"Where are they from?" asked Paddy.

"Alabama," said I.

"Bring them up in ten minutes and I'll be ready for them."

So I went down and in ten minutes I brought them up and introduced old Bill Vosburg as the Old Gent and Paddy as the son of the Old Gent. Paddy said to them: "Why, there are two of you here."

Then turning to me, he said: "Don't you know that I do business with but one man at a time? Take one of them out. I don't care which one it is."

The biggest one of the two said, "I'll do the business and you wait outside."

So I took his partner down to the barroom, left him there and returned to the turning joint (salesroom) and took a seat at the table beside the "guy." Paddy was displaying the goods to him in ones, twos and fives, all spread out on the table.

After the guy had examined them, he said, "I'll take ten thousand of these goods."

So Paddy put the money in $1,000 packages, put $10,000 in the satchel, locked it, and at the same time cautioning the victim about being careful of giving his confidence to friends. A lot more talk [transpired] when suddenly the guy grabbed the satchel and $10,000, pulled out his gun and covered Paddy. I jumped up and snatched the gun from the guy, covered him with the gun, took the bag of money from him, and threw it out the window into the stable yard where Eddie Parmeley's brother was always on the lookout for just such an event. I then emptied the slugs out of the gun, threw them outdoors, and handed the empty gun back to the guy, saying to him: "Now sit down and do business like a man."

Turning to old Vosburg who was standing at the door, I said to him: "This man is all right and is not connected with the United States detectives. I will be responsible for him, knowing he will make a good and safe agent to handle the goods throughout his section of the country."

Old Vosburg shook his head in a doubtful manner and said to the guy: "I am surprised. I didn't think you would do anything like that. After our long correspondence, I had the utmost confidence in you, but no matter. What are your expenses to and from your home, your railroad fare, hotel bills and everything in general? I promised you your expenses whether you did business or not and you will find me a man of my word."

"Well," said the guy, "let me tell you. I and my partner was talking with a man on the train while coming here and he told us that the last time he was in New York he was swindled out of $200 and warned us to be mighty careful, so when you would not let my partner here with me to do business, I became suspicious that things were not all right. I am on the level in this business and you place the goods in my hand and I'll pay for them and pledge you my work that I'll handle them safe enough."

Old Bill Vosburg turned to Paddy the Pig and ordered him to go down and bring up $10,000 of the goods. Paddy went down for the goods and Vosburg said to the guy: "Remember, I am giving you the state rights. You will be the sole agent throughout your section of the country."

After a lot more encouraging talk, up came Paddy the Pig with the bank roll. He opened the bag and threw out the money carelessly on the table, counted out one package of five dollar notes, containing $1,000 in each package, and saying to the guy: "There is $1,000 in each package." As he picked up each package, he would pull off the end elastic and rip the money package up like one would a deck of cards showing the guy the money was there so as to save time instead of counting it all out. He put the ten thousand dollars in the bag, and locked it up.

After giving the guy instructions and warning about making confidential friends and how to handle the goods, he said to the guy, and pointing to me: "My messenger will see you safe to the depot and see that you get your train and get away all right, so I'll bid you

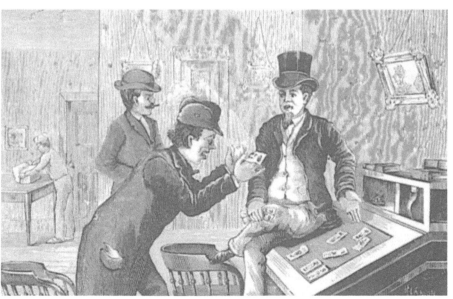

*The green goods game in progress: The "old gentleman" (right) displays the "goods" to the "come on," or "victim," holding the bills.*

*goodbye and, above all, follow my instructions to the letter." Paddy handed me the bag of money and while he was shaking the guy's hand and cautioning him, I was at the door and opened it about 12 inches. In a second, the fellow outside took the money bag from me and handed me a bag of paper. Paddy said he had better let me carry it to the railroad station.*

*"Oh, no, I'll take care of it, never fear." He therefore pulled out a roll of $650 and paid it to Vosburg for the goods.*

*When I got him and his partner near the depot, I advised him to express the goods to his home by the Adams Express Company, telling him that in case of a railroad accident, the goods would be found. By shipping them, they would reach home safely. I merely suggested this, fearing he would open the bag in the depot and discover that he was done and then make trouble. I was glad when he took my advice and expressed the bag of paper to his house. When I left the express office and got them to the depot, I said to them: "I have seen you through safe and this is your train, so good-bye and be careful not to make any confidential acquaintances on the road to your home and follow the old gentleman's instructions to the letter. By doing so, everything will turn prosperous for you." They boarded their train and that was the last I ever saw of them.*[1]

INVITED TO JOIN Eddie Parmeley's gang, Appo entered into the most lucrative confidence game in nineteenth-century America. For the first time he avoided the rough graft of pickpocketing, its many risks, and the threat of frequent incarceration. A better class of thief sought "sure thing graft"—swindling schemes like bunco, dice, short cards, and flimflam. The most profitable was the "green goods game." George Appo was now a con artist, a trickster extraordinaire.[2]

The green goods game worked like this: Operators sent out letters or "circulars" throughout the United States claiming that they possessed stolen or discarded currency engraving plates from the U.S. Treasury. The circular offered genuine-looking counterfeit money, or "green goods," to prospective buyers at cut-rate prices. For one hundred dollars one could purchase twelve hundred dollars in counterfeit notes; six hundred dollars bought ten thousand dollars of the same. For purchasing the maximum, the individual was promised "state rights," or a monopoly on the green goods in his region.

Interested parties—the "guy" or "come on"—were instructed to travel to certain hotels in the New York metropolitan region. There they were met by a "bunco steerer" like Appo who, after an exchange of passwords, "steered" the individual to a "turning joint" in another hotel or office. After meeting the "old gentleman," the buyer examined the alleged counterfeit money, which in fact was authentic legal tender. Usually they elected to make the purchase. During the transaction, when the buyer was not looking, a "ringer" hiding behind a partition or movable wall secretly substituted a moneyless satchel for the one containing the real money. If a victim grew suspicious or discovered the swindle, a "tailer" dressed as a police officer bullied and threatened the individual and told him to leave the city. More often the victim returned home, opened the bag, and discovered worthless sheets of blank paper, a brick, or even sawdust. Bamboozled, humiliated, and empty handed, victims had no legal recourse, for they themselves were guilty of attempting to defraud the federal government.[3]

At first the green goods game did not even have an agreed-upon name. The earliest exposé, Edward Crapsey's *The Nether Side of New York* (1872), identified it as the circular swindle. Some, like the nation's leading detective, Allan Pinkerton, labeled the practice the boodle game, others the panel game. Since perpetrators frequently filled the trick satchel with sawdust, many, like the reformer and founder of the Society for the Suppression of Vice, Anthony Comstock, christened it the sawdust game. Whatever the name, by 1885 the *World* reported that the United States was flooded with circulars.[4]

In the early evolution of the green goods game, small-time writers operated with considerable independence. Some, like letter carrier Frank Webb, started his own green goods swindle while running a gambling and opium den before being shut down by Comstock in 1885. By then, however, smaller entrepreneurs were exceptional. The most successful green goods operations required considerable finance, thoughtful planning, elaborate hierarchies, and police or political protection. Leading financial backers, or "capitalists," supplied bankrolls of three thousand to twenty thousand dollars to display before potential victims, a huge sum of money in an age when unskilled workers earned less than one thousand dollars annually.[5]

By some accounts Barney Maguire was the first major operator, the opium den proprietor and fence who reported Appo to the police in 1882.

Newspaper accounts referred to Maguire as "the pioneer in the green-goods swindle" and "the king of the sawdust men." Some asserted that Maguire then had an estimated fortune of $250,000. According to the writer Louis Beck, Maguire was responsible for recognizing that Appo possessed the qualities necessary for "their peculiar calling." Maguire finally recruited Appo for his gang, first as a folder of circulars and eventually as a steerer.[6]

Potential earnings were enormous. Although no records exist that precisely measure income or profits, some claimed daily green goods revenues ranged between two and eight thousand dollars. The most successful accumulated fortunes in excess of one hundred thousand dollars. Even low-level operatives like Appo maintained they earned thirty to one hundred dollars per day. By 1884 the detective Allan Pinkerton identified this con as the most profitable. A decade later Assistant Postmaster General E. G. Rathbone described the game as "more audacious in its conception, more extensive in its ramifications and more vicious in its results" than any swindling scheme in the country.[7]

"Making a success" in green goods, according to Appo, was the product of deceptive enterprise, patience, and quick thinking. Financial backers like Eddie Parmeley and James "Jimmie" McNally provided the cash up front, but mastery of the con depended on the ability of writers, salesmen, turners, steerers, ringers, and tailers to trick the come on and complete the transaction. As Appo described, suspicious victims could pull out a gun and quickly turn the tables on the swindlers. "Every victim or come on I ever met always carried a gun," Appo believed, "and would use it on the least provocation." Green goods men had to radiate trust and honesty; sometimes their lives literally depended on it.[8] Nor were these tasks for the impatient, temperamental, or careless. Criminal experience and theatricality were virtual prerequisites. Indeed, as sure-thing grafts like the green goods game grew more profitable, men long on criminal activities like George Appo were attracted—indeed recruited—to the business. Appo's conspirators—Paddy the Pig, Bill Vosburg, Adolph Saunders, Harry Hilton—were all seasoned criminals.

By the 1890s Thomas "Paddy" O'Brien—Paddy the Pig to Appo—was a salesman and bunco steerer for Parmeley and McNally. Reputed for his keen observation skills and his forthright hearty manner, O'Brien was so charming, wrote one, that he could "disarm the suspicions of even a suspicious man." He was an ideal green goods operative. After a brief term in the Elmira Reformatory during the 1880s, he entered the trade, and by 1890 he employed as many as thirty to forty green goods men, resulting in profits of two thousand dollars per day. When O'Brien was finally arrested in 1891, police detective Thomas Byrnes believed that O'Brien's gang was responsible for "the biggest series of crimes that New York has known in a long time."[9]

In contrast to Paddy the Pig, William "Old Bill" Vosburg left a longer criminal trail as a bank robber, pickpocket, and green goods turner. By the time he became an accomplice of Appo's, various reporters described him as "a Fagin" and "the father of modern criminals." Details of his criminal career remain murky. Born in Albany in 1826 or 1828, the grandson

*Thomas "Paddy the Pig" O'Brien.*

of a Revolutionary War soldier and the son of a War of 1812 veteran, Vosburg was allegedly orphaned at age seven. He was a member of Dan Noble's gang in the 1860s and 1870s, and later associated with renowned underworld figures Shang Draper and Johnny "the Mick" Walsh, witnessing the latter's murder in 1883. By then he had served lengthy prison sentences in Kentucky, Massachusetts, and New York. Some believed that he was arrested fifteen to twenty times in New York City alone. Vosburg and his associates once reportedly cleared $133,000 in a single week's work. By the time of his death in 1904, Vosburg had stolen an estimated $2 million during his lifetime.[10]

*William "Old Bill" Vosburg.*

Turners like Vosburg and O'Brien and steerers like Appo assumed the physical risks in any green goods operation, evidenced by their confrontation with the two victims from Alabama. Writers, on the other hand, were the brains of the transaction; Appo described the writers who recruited him—Harry Hilton and Dolph Saunders—as well educated. The circulars revealed how astute writers displayed a keen appreciation of the material desires, economic fantasies, and social realities of nineteenth-century American men. Green goods writers understood the psychology of men on the make, always in search of the fast and easy buck.[11]

The language in green goods circulars was vague and oblique. The earliest were elusive: "I am dealing in articles, paper goods—ones, twos, fives, tens and twenties—(do you understand?)," wrote one. "I cannot be plainer until I know your heart is true to me; then I will satisfy you that I can furnish you with a fine, safe and profitable article that can be used in any manner and for all purposes, and no danger." Circulars deliberately avoided references to finance, much less to counterfeiting. One circular even referred to the goods as "a certain brand of cigars."[12]

To reassure customers the swindlers affirmed their integrity. "I swear before the Almighty God in heaven," wrote one, "my purpose is far from harming you either by word, look or action." Writers attested to their individual honesty, that their motives were upstanding: "I claim to be a man of honor, I will never violate a pledge." One circular concluded with an admonition: "Act square; be true and honorable, do me no harm, and you will never regret it."[13]

Circulars frequently capitalized on regional hatred of the federal government. One sent in 1887 discouraged any "conscientious scruples" by potential customers, arguing that "you are injuring no one but a rich government." Residents of the South and West were the most susceptible to such tactics. Resentment of post–Civil War policies of Reconstruction perpetuated by the Republican Party generated enormous hatred of the federal government, particularly in the South. Antigovernment appeals "hit a tender spot," admitted students of the green goods game. Former Confederates were so emotionally embittered and economically indebted that they viewed green goods as "a good way to hurt the government," concluded New York City assistant district attorney Ambrose Purdy. "They became an easy prey of Northern sawdust men."[14]

Writers initially secured lists of individuals who subscribed to lotteries, believing that such people were, according to one reporter, "idiots enough to go into anything." Other swindlers scoured local newspapers for the names of failed or financially embarrassed merchants. A Midwestern bank president complained that green goods operators routinely sent letters to families who were saddled with debt or overdue mortgages.

One circular printed for James McNally bluntly proclaimed, "If you have been unsuccessful in your business, I can supply you with goods with which you can pay off all your debts and start free and clear again."[15]

Over time, operators grew more sophisticated and relied on respected financial reports to identify potential customers. When law enforcement officials arrested Terrence "Poodle" Murphy (a former associate of Danny Driscoll) and "Pretty Frank" Brooks in 1891, for example, police discovered forty-six ledgers with entries for more than sixty thousand names and addresses of businessmen, as well as several issues of the financial publication *Bradstreet's*. Another operative candidly described *Bradstreet's* as "our mainstay and support." Allan Pinkerton was incredulous over the gullibility of businessmen and what he called "the almost universal ignorance which pervades the financial and commercial communities."[16]

The evidence does not provide a clear picture of the many victims of green goods schemes. Undoubtedly a considerable number were dishonest individuals in search of a quick fortune, victims of "the cupidity and dishonesty of mankind," in the words of detective Thomas Byrnes. More disconcerting to observers, however, was the number of respected citizens and civic leaders who fell prey to the con. According to Assistant District Attorney Purdy, victims ranged from clerics to congressmen. On one occasion Appo remembered swindling an African American preacher from Florida who paid one thousand dollars to get ten thousand dollars. Point blank Appo asked how he reconciled his conscience. The minister replied that "he was not doing it for himself, but for the Lord; that his people were trying to build a church, and couldn't raise the money that they wanted." Since this was a "good cause," the minister rationalized that "it was proper enough to take the money."[17]

Some blamed the victims. In one 1895 trial Recorder John Goff severely rebuked a Nebraska farmer for attempting to purchase green goods, declaring buyers of green goods "worse than the seller." Operators simply swindled dishonest men, he argued, while the victim intended "to defraud his honest neighbors with counterfeit money." Police were equally unsympathetic. "Nine out of every ten countrymen who are swindled by rogues in this city," concluded Police Superintendent George Walling, "deserve to lose their money."[18]

In the decades following the Civil War, New York's chief detective, Thomas Byrnes, acknowledged that green goods games operated unmolested from law enforcement authorities. Numerous police officials tolerated green goods activities since New York residents were not victimized. Certain police captains received regular bribes from operatives in return for "protection," sometimes as much as 50 percent of all profits. Dividing the city into specific geographical territories for various backers, captains allowed some operators to work while harassing and arresting others. When victims complained, they were ignored. Other times the police threatened arrest and instructed them to leave New York. Despite receiving approximately fifty circulars daily by the early 1870s, Police Superintendent James Kelso admitted that he threw them in the wastebasket. Byrnes himself may have protected certain green goods operatives. His *Professional Criminals of America*, published in 1886 and revised in 1895, included detailed descriptions and photographs of more than two hundred and six hundred criminals, respectively. Leading green goods operatives like James McNally, Barney McGuire, and Eddie Parmeley were never mentioned.[19]

Even without police protection, green goods perpetrators were difficult to convict. Operators employed scores, if not hundreds, of aliases. Before 1887 green goods complaints were forwarded to Andrew Drummond, chief of the New York District of the U.S. Secret Service, or Anthony Comstock of the Society for the Suppression of Vice. Investigators then required post offices, saloons, or storekeepers providing mail boxes to hold any correspondence and wait for the intended recipient. Since the mail was never claimed, careful surveillance was of little avail. The swindlers simply assumed new names and secured new places for their mail. In 1890, when Comstock arrested operatives Sam Ward and Isaac Rosenthal, he discovered that they employed more than seven hundred aliases.[20]

The most sophisticated green goods operators simply avoided the mail and potential prosecution for illegal use of the postal system. Instead correspondence was handled through private express services. Other operators refused to accept any letters, communicating entirely via telegram with secret passwords, pseudonyms, and aliases. Night telegraph messages were discouraged as they could not be answered promptly. Arrangements were made with telegraph officials to pass on messages sent to fictitious addresses. By the 1890s Anthony Comstock complained about the many telegraph workers in the employ of green goods entrepreneurs.[21]

In 1887 New York tried to address the problem. New state legislation declared that any individual who published or circulated a document offering to sell counterfeit money was guilty of a felony and punishable by from one to five years in prison and a fine of one hundred to one thousand dollars. Police detective Thomas Byrnes then instigated a public campaign to close down various green goods operations, even arresting leading operators like James McNally, Patrick Ryan, and "Little Joe" Little.[22] The new law further inflamed the prosecutorial fire of Anthony Comstock, who arrested more than sixty men in the first seven months of 1888. Others fled New York. Barney Maguire absconded to Canada on hearing of Byrnes's intended raids, while other operators transferred their activities to various hotels in New Jersey, the Bronx, and even Philadelphia. By 1889 the "green-goods men were driven out," proclaimed Police Superintendent William Murray.[23]

A green goods cartoon.

But reports of the con's demise were greatly exaggerated. By the 1890s New York newspapers concluded that green goods games were operating briskly, that the scheme was more profitable than ever and "practically unmolested." In 1894 a New Jersey judge lamented that green goods remained "without doubt one of the most demoralizing swindling schemes ever devised."[24]

⁕ *One day, for some cause or reason unknown to any of the employees (who were old time "crooks," bank burglars, sneaks, pickpockets and sure thing grafters), Eddie Parmeley was forced to close up the business and make room for Jimmie McNally to operate the business with his bankroll. Consequently, most of the crooks who worked for Parmeley had to go back to their rough line of business. Some of them still worked the green goods game under their own system and without giving up protection money to the police. Jim McNally had the police protection, not only in New York, but in New Jersey as well. He took money of the Haymarket pimps (men* who lived off the shame of girls) and made it a business, putting them to work sending out mail of green goods circulars and guaranteeing them protection from arrest.

In a very short time, McNally had the country flooded with his circulars and the victims coming on to do business in droves of fifteen and twenty per day. The ex-pimps would not take a chance as steerers, [so] McNally and his writers or correspondents got some of the steerers who worked for Parmeley and Barney McGuire to go after and bring on their victims to do business and then see them safely on board their train for home.

*James McNally.*

I went to work for two of McNally's correspondents [in 1891]. Their names were Harry Hilton and Dolph Saunders, both former Haymarket pimps and both well educated and confirmed opium habitués. I became acquainted with them in an opium joint owned by McNally on 46th Street and Seventh Avenue. This place was a regular meeting place for all McNally's green goods workers. . . . As they offered me ten percent for my services and give me protection, I went to work for them. . . . I worked for McNally and Saunders for nearly two years and was very successful as a steerer as most every victim I was sent after made a deal.[25]

By 1890 the "king of the green-goods men" was James McNally. Observers acknowledged that McNally, a self-proclaimed sporting man and bookmaker, was handsome, well-dressed, and looked more like a successful broker than a con artist. McNally confirmed detective Thomas Byrnes's description of leading confidence men as industrious, educated, self-assured, ingenious, and "gifted with a good knowledge of human nature." By the 1880s he supplied bankrolls in excess of ten thousand dollars.[26]

McNally was reportedly born in New York in 1864, the son of a liquor dealer, and grew up on the Lower East Side. By his own account McNally left home as a teenager with four hundred dollars. Others claimed that he worked as a pimp and bartender in a Rivington Street saloon described as "a resort for thieves, confidence men and lewd women." There he learned the art of pickpocketing and later became the steerer for Barney Maguire. By the time he was twenty-one, he was head of the McNally Association, an informal political club allied to Tammany Hall. Like Appo, he was an alleged opium addict. Befriended by Alderman Patrick Farley (who ran a hotel, bottling company, and saloon on Grand Street and later the Bowery), McNally parleyed his enterprises into a Tenderloin restaurant. McNally eventually sold the business and used the profits to bankroll his own green goods operation. In 1887 he assumed control of Maguire's business in return for giving a percentage of his profits to Maguire for three years.

In 1890 Anthony Comstock identified McNally and his brother, Walter, as not only the green goods leaders of New York, but for the entire United States. Their activities extended into the suburbs of upstate New York, New Jersey, and Canada. McNally's staff of operatives numbered over thirty-five and employed almost eight hundred different aliases; some were former Tenderloin pimps like Dolph Saunders and Harry Hilton. Together they generated daily revenues between three and eight thousand dollars. McNally so impressed the British reformer and writer William T. Stead that he concluded that McNally elevated "the confidence trick almost to the level of a fine art."[27]

A key to McNally's success was the writers who composed, printed, and sent the circulars, thereby making the initial contacts with victims. Some printed more than two hundred thousand circulars at a time, sending out as many as fifteen thousand daily. By the 1880s McNally promised each writer 50 percent of every successful transaction. McNally structured his operations with various layers of protection against potential prosecution. First, he selected highly respected professional printers so that upon arrest, defense attorneys could emphasize their "good characters." McNally also demanded prompt payments from his writers; otherwise he reported them to the police, which effectively disciplined the gang and avoided bad debts. Finally McNally entrusted writers with the responsibility of paying operatives like George Appo and neighborhood

was only in the room where the circulars were seized; no other evidence linked him to the swindle. Before cases went to trial, the chief witnesses often fled New York; other indictments were simply dismissed. Samuel Ward and Isaac Rosenthal, arrested eight times between 1890 and 1899, for example, were never tried. Comstock claimed that political influence kept such men out of jail.[35]

The best defense, however, was that the green goods game was legal. Since such swindlers displayed genuine currency during their transactions, they were not guilty of fraud, counterfeiting, or any other statutory crime. Secret Service agent Andrew L. Drummond complained that any indictment required an invitation to buy counterfeit money or "bogus bills." A cunning green goods operator used only legal tender, Drummond explained, "which he *pretends* to be counterfeit."[36]

Judges concurred. In 1871 the New York Court of Appeals ruled that the statutory prohibition on obtaining money under false pretenses applied only to those engaged in legal activities. In the precedent-setting case, Henry McCord falsely portrayed himself as a police officer to Charles Miller and claimed he had a warrant for Miller's arrest. Miller immediately gave McCord a gold watch and diamond ring as bail to ensure his appearance in court. The tribunal ruled that McCord was innocent of any fraud or false representation because the law protected only those engaged in "honest" activities. If an individual parted with property for an unlawful purpose, even if he or she was tricked under false pretenses, no grounds for larceny existed. According to the court, the law did not protect "rogues in their dealings with each other." In effect the state only prosecuted certain kinds of fraud.[37]

In 1900 the Appellate Division of the New York Supreme Court reversed the green goods conviction of Henry Livingstone on such grounds. Justice Bartlett Cullen ruled that even though Livingstone defrauded someone of five hundred dollars, the victim believed he was receiving counterfeit money. Such individuals were simply not protected by the law. The court expressed regret at reversing the conviction, and urged the legislature to revise the law and overturn *McCord*. Despite the court's recommendation, however, the decision remained in effect into the 1920s.[38]

The logic supporting these decisions was consistent with Anglo-American jurisprudence. Simply put, fraud never became a significant part of the law until the twentieth century. In the nineteenth century, common law valued economic autonomy, personal independence, and the market over commercial justice. As George Fletcher has argued, a culture organized by market forces did not allow defrauded buyers to second-guess their judgment on learning the "true nature of the goods." In nineteenth-century New York, the task of criminal law was to protect the liberty of the seller and the transaction rather than safeguard commercial justice. Consumer protection simply did not exist. The green goods game was a product of market forces; individual consumers, not the law or the state, were responsible for determining what was or was not a confidence scheme. In effect courts agreed with James McNally: Green goods was founded on the human desire "to get something for nothing."[39] Con men could hardly have asked for anything more.

IN A PROPHETIC but forgotten remark, the prototypical ward boss George Washington Plunkitt of New York's Tammany Hall compared city governance with the swindle. Urban politics, he remarked, "has bigger profits generally than the green-goods business."[40]

What Plunkitt failed to realize was that green goods was bigger than New York. The confidence game represented one of the earliest examples of the nationalization of crime. Other swindles like bunco or the envelope game were local and immediate in their impact. The con was quick and short, a face-to-face encounter involving precious stones, tickets, or comparatively small sums of money. Like street crime it was an episodic, illegal activity spurred by random opportunities. By contrast green goods was a nationwide, market-based crime distributing illegal goods to willing customers. It required an extensive capital investment, high rates of return, a hierarchical and durable structure, the use of violence and corruption to achieve monopoly power, a range of talented operatives (some of whom saw themselves as professionals), and the patience to let the game play itself out over several weeks, if not months. By the 1890s some called it "organized crime."[41]

The green goods game was a new crime, an unintended consequence of the expanding post–Civil War, national market-based economy. In the decades following the Civil War, few issues generated more conflict than did national finance. Debates over paper money, "greenbacks," debt repayment, national banks, and silver remonetization occupied the attention of American leaders in politics and business. These financial contro-

*A youthful George Appo at the height of his criminal career.*

versies ultimately generated new political movements embodied in the Greenback Party and Populism.[42] They also spawned a new urban underworld.

George Appo was hardly alone in abandoning hard graft for the green goods game. In 1878 Jimmy Hope led a dozen men, including Ned Lyons, "Banjo" Pete Emerson, and his son, Johnny Hope, in the single largest bank robbery in nineteenth-century America—$2.76 million in bonds and securities from the Manhattan Savings Bank at Broadway and Bleecker Street. Into the twentieth century, the caper was described as "the greatest bank robbery in the history of the world," Hope as "the Napoleon of bank burglars." But in 1895, after an early release from Sing Sing, the outlaw was living in New York's Tenderloin, working in a West Twenty-ninth Street saloon off Broadway. Approaching his sixtieth birthday, Hope had abandoned bank robbery for an occupation he considered "a strictly legitimate and commendable business." He was a green goods speculator. Green goods men had replaced bank robbers as the aristocrats of crime.[43]

## JERSEY CITY

~§    *One of my experiences for being a good fellow with one of my associates came near causing me the loss of an eye. This man was known by the name of Dick Cronin, and had the reputation of being a fighter. In fact, most everyone who knew him, was afraid of him, and to make matters worse he was so ignorant that he could not read or write. Jim McNally, the financial backer of the green goods business, had Cronin around him as a sort of bodyguard and no one in the business could afford to send him out of town to bring in a victim (come on), because the few he did go after refused to do business after meeting Cronin.[1]*

*It was December 1892 when McNally was forced to move his business over to Jersey City, New Jersey. Therefore, we all had to follow and do our business over there with him. So one cold stormy winter's night, I received a telegram stating: "Come to Green Street, Jersey, at once," signed "Jim." I made all haste and arrived at the meeting place on Green Street, New Jersey, where I met Jim McNally's salesman or turner who said to me. "You will have to go to Elizabeth, New Jersey, tonight. So wait over in the saloon until I get the 'pointers' for you to land the guy (victim) and have him here the first thing in the morning."[2]*

*I then went to the saloon and entered the place by the rear door and was somewhat surprised to see standing at the rear end of the bar an old time crook known as "Old Boston" who had only been out of prison a couple of days after serving a four-and-a-half year term. Naturally, I was pleased to meet him and we drank and talked together on old times. As I knew he was financially broke, I slipped him a five dollar bill and he began to tell me how a fellow by the name of Dick Wolcott was the unintentional cause of his arrest and conviction. Every time he would mention the name of this fellow he would say "Dick." Now there was a screen partition that enclosed the entire rear of the bar room, unknown to me, in the front end of the bar, stood Dick Cronin and another fellow talking and drinking together.*

*Suddenly, Cronin appeared behind the screen where Boston and I were and said to Boston: "What are you talking about me for. I'll*

break your jaw," and at the same time made a swinging blow at
Boston.

I quickly jumped between them, pushed Cronin away, saying:
"Why, Dick, you are mistaken, the man don't know you. He was
talking about another fellow named Dick Wolcott, not you," and in
the meantime I had signaled old man Boston to clear out of the
place.

Cronin said to me: "You lie. What have you got to say about it,"
and at the same time he made a blow at my face with his clinched
fist. I dodged the blow and clinched him and we both fell to the
floor with me on top and grip on his throat. Suddenly I was struck
a violent blow on my left eye with a large-size Wilson's whiskey bottle, cutting me badly and fracturing the bone of the upper eyelid
and rendering me unconscious.

When I came to my senses again, I found myself on the operating
table at the Christ Hospital and the good doctor sewing up the gash
over my eye.[3] When he had finished, a policeman in uniform
brought into the operating room Dick Cronin and asked me: "Is this
the man who struck you?"

I replied: "No, I do not know what hit me." Then the doctor told
the nurse to put me to bed, and as my clothes had already been
removed, I was taken to the ward. When I reached the bed, I said
to the nurse: "I am feeling all right, give me my clothes. I want to
get home as soon as possible."

He replied: "Well, I'll see," and finally came back with my
clothes. I dressed myself and as I missed my necktie I asked the
nurse what had become of it and my diamond stud and $62.

He said: "You had no tie when you were brought here and the
only amount of money you had was $7 and here it is, handing me
an envelope with the $7 inside.

I thanked him and said: "Well, this money will get me home safe,
so I am lucky to be left that amount." I said good-bye to him and left
the hospital with my head all bandaged up, out into the snowstorm.

When I got to the ferry for Cortlandt Street, New York, I met Mr.
Dalton, the railroad detective at the ferry, who asked me what was
the matter and how I got hurt. I told him everything and also about
the diamond stud valued at $250 and the balance of the $62 I lost,
and said to him: "If you can get the diamond back from the person

who stole it from me, I will make you a present of it, and I am quite certain that neither Dick Cronin nor the officer who brought me to the hospital took it."

"Well," said Dalton, "I'll look it up," and sure enough about ten days after, I again met the detective at the Pennsylvania ferry house with the diamond stud in his tie. He told me that the nurse at Christ Hospital had it and told him that after I had left the hospital, he found my tie and diamond on the floor of the clothes room, but did not find my money. So I said nothing more about the loss and soon forgot the misfortune.[4]

Of course, I went looking after the fellow who struck me with the bottle and was told that he was a western crook known only by the name of "Pete" and a stranger in New York, and just happened to be in Dick Cronin's company that night in the bar room. Cronin was jealous of my success in the business and blamed me for his failure. Consequently, [he] tried to make everything disagreeable for me whenever he got the chance. . . . I never heard again or seen Cronin until I learned of his death from consumption on the day of my release from state's prison [on 5 December 1893].[5]

# 1 6

# Poughkeepsie

—

&#x2767; *One day in the month of February, 1893, Jim McNally had some misunderstanding with a police officer named [Michael] Morgan, up in Poughkeepsie, New York, to whom he paid money each week for the protection of his men from arrest, and to allow them to operate without molestation. In fact, during the course of the two years I worked to and from Poughkeepsie, I often met officer Morgan in the bar room of the New York Hotel and talked and drank with him at the bar there. He knew what my business was.*

*One night about 10 p.m., I met Dolph Saunders, the writer for Jim McNally and the man I was steering guys for, by appointment on Sixth Avenue and 28th Street in New York. Saunders said to me: "Now, George, you will have to get up to Poughkeepsie tonight by the next train out, the guy is there now I am sure. Take this letter and pointers and be sure to land him (the victim) because he is a thousand dollar deal and I don't want to lose him."*

*I said, "All right, I'll land him safe enough. Give me the pointers," which were the passwords—"safe and sure one hundred." These passwords were for me to say as an introduction to the victim on meeting him to convince him that he was meeting and talking to the right man. The letter was merely a message stating to the victim that I was merely the confidential messenger of the Old Gentleman who would conduct him safely to where he could transact the business with impunity.*

*I took the next train out and arrived in Poughkeepsie after midnight, February 12, 1893. It was very cold and stormy night. On reaching the New York Hotel, I looked over the hotel register for the name of the guy (Hiram Cassel) to see if he had arrived from North Carolina, but his name was not there on the book. So I asked the bartender, who knew all about the business. He said no guys had* arrived in nearly a week and he wanted to know why they were coming on so slow. I then went to bed and got up at 5 a.m., took a look at the register and not seeing the guy's name, I went to the railroad depot and learned that all the trains were delayed by the snow storm. I then returned to the hotel, where I waited until 8 a.m. As the guy did not arrive yet, I went skating with the hotel proprietor's son on the Hudson River.

At 9:15 a.m., I returned to the hotel and found the names of Hiram Cassel and Ira Hogshead on the hotel register. I went up to the room they were assigned to, knocked on the door and went inside. I found two, big, six-foot men (mountaineers), one sitting on the bed and the other standing by the washstand. As I entered, I said: "Safe and sure, one hundred. I'm glad to meet you." They both put out their hands and gave me a hearty handshake. I then handed them the sealed letter which introduced me as the messenger of this friend, the Old Gentleman, with whom they had been corresponding about the business. I then told them that the Old Gentleman could not understand what had delayed them so long. As he had other very important business that had to be attended to, he told me to wait here for you, and when you arrived, to bring you to Mott Haven, where you could examine the goods and do business with safety.

After a lot more talk with them, they said, "Well, how far is that place from here?"

"Oh," said I, "not far, only a short distance. I will get your tickets and go with you. After you are through business with the Old Gentleman, I will see you safely aboard the train for your home. When we go down to the depot, you and your friend keep together and follow me about ten feet behind and don't talk to and ask questions of anybody, not even me. Remember the nature of the business, and three is a crowd. Don't board the train until you see me get on board. Then take a seat near me. When the train starts, I will hand you your tickets and have a talk with you and give you other instructions. Do you want some lunch?"

"No, we have had plenty," said they.

"Well, our train for Mott Haven leaves in twenty minutes, so if there is anything you need, let me know and I'll get it for you."

"No, there's nothing, but we want to get to business as soon as possible," said they. "So let's go and take the cars and get there."

I then took them downstairs and outside the entrance and walked towards the depot which was only a block away. On reaching there, I bought three tickets for New York. When I got out on the platform of the station, I saw only one of the men standing there. I approached him and asked where his friend was.

He replied: "He stopped to talk with a man up the road."

"Oh," said I, "that will never do. I instructed him not to talk with anybody. You wait here. Don't board this train until I go and see what is detaining him and bring him here."

I left the station and when I reached the end of the street, I saw the guy (Hogshead) standing on the viaduct over the tunnel trying to attract his friend's attention to come back from the depot. On looking further ahead, I saw officer Morgan about 30 feet away, walking with his head turned towards me. I thought nothing of this action at the time, so I approached the guy and said, "What seems to be the trouble? Do you want to lose this train?"

"I don't care to do business. I've changed my mind," said he.

"Well, I'm sorry to hear you talk in such a manner. You go back to the hotel and I'll bring your friend there, and we will talk the matter over. If you are still dissatisfied, I will wire your friend, the Old Gentleman and explain your actions. I am simply the messenger in this matter."

He started with me to the hotel and I left him there and brought his partner from the station and up to the bedroom of the hotel. His partner (Hogshead) stood by the washstand with his small satchel opened on it. Cassel sat down at the foot of the bed and there was space just wide enough between the side of the bed and the wall against which the washstand stood for a person to walk through sideways to get to the door or window. Hogshead opened his satchel and took a large flask of whiskey from it and took a large drink of the liquor and put the flask back again.

I then said, "Well, Mr. Hogshead, what seems to have changed your mind? I know that the Old Gentleman is really in need of an agent throughout your section to handle his goods. I will tell you what I will do to convince you that everything is just as he has represented to you. I will go to Mott Haven and explain to the Old Gentleman that you do not care to go any further and have him to bring the goods here to you in this room where you both can exam-

*ine them. If you find that they are not just as represented, whether
you do business or not, all your expenses to and from your home,
railroad fare, hotel bills and the loss of your time will be cheerfully
paid you both by the Old Gentleman. I am simply his confidential
messenger and I cannot do nothing further in the matter. You
understand me, don't you?"*

*The guy, Mr. Cassel, who was sitting on the bed said, "That's fair
and square, Hiram! What in h—— is the matter with you. Let's
wait and have the goods brought here."*

*"I tell you! I know what I'm doing. I've changed my mind and
that settles it," said Hogshead.*

*"Well, Mr. Hogshead, I'm very sorry to hear you talk in that man-
ner. You are leaving an opportunity of your life go by unheeded, so
I will bid you good-bye," said I, putting out my hand for Hogshead
to shake. But he refused to shake hands. Instead, he again took a
drink of whiskey from the flask.*

*I, in the meantime, turned my back to him in order to shake
hands with Mr. Cassel, who got up, took my hand, and as I was
about to say, "I'm sorry you will not wait here," Hogshead sneakingly
took from his satchel a big Colt's revolver. While I was shaking
hands with Cassel and my back turned to him, he cowardly put the
revolver to the back of my right temple and shot me.*[1]

A PPO LAY UNCONSCIOUS on a bed in room 9. Police and medical attendants quickly rushed to his aid. An attending physician made a hasty
examination, bandaged the wound, and transported him to Vassar Hospital. Several hours later Appo awoke vomiting blood. When Poughkeepsie
recorder Charles Morschauser arrived to take an antemortem statement,
Appo refused to talk. He claimed to remember nothing, insisting that he
was in Poughkeepsie to rendezvous with a skater who had already
departed. At 5:00 p.m. the coroner informed Appo that he was near
death, and a priest administered the last rites.[2]

Newspaper reports quickly revealed that Appo was no stranger to
Poughkeepsie. For three years prior to the shooting, green goods men
openly worked in Poughkeepsie. With a population of approximately
twenty-three thousand in 1893, the small Hudson River town was ideally
situated on the rail route between New York City and Albany; at least
eighteen different trains left Poughkeepsie daily, bound for New York's

Grand Central Station. For a time Appo registered under the name of "Albro" and worked out of the Nelson House, Poughkeepsie's premier hotel. When proprietor Horatio N. Bain discovered Appo's clandestine business, he banned Appo from the establishment.[3]

From the moment Appo landed in Vassar Hospital, James McNally recognized that Appo's recovery and imminent arrest posed a threat to his operation. Less than twenty-four hours after the shooting, his brother, Walter McNally, appeared at Appo's bedside under the alias J. S. Roberts, a self-described Block Island manufacturer. "Keep a close mouth and everything'll be all right," assured McNally. "You ain't goin' to die."[4]

He was right. Within a day Appo's condition stabilized, the hemorrhaging ceased, and he asked for an opium pipe. Three days after the shooting, hospital surgeons removed Appo's right eye and searched unsuccessfully for the bullet. By then physicians expressed no doubt about Appo's recovery.[5]

Appo was not the first green goods operative to encounter a violent response from a potential victim. The green goods game may have been "sure thing graft" to Appo, but as this incident proved, the confidence swindle was riddled with potential violence. Newspapers periodically reported how green goods victims drew revolvers during their transactions and turned the tables on the confidence men by robbing them of their bankroll. In 1891, when John Everett of North Carolina came to New York, he admitted he intended to "beat the 'green goods' game and get some of the 'genuine stuff.'" In 1893 steerer Bob Crumley was shot in the arm by a potential victim. He quickly decided to abandon the business. "I'm going to look for something softer," conceded Crumley, "even if I have to earn an honest living."[6]

Appo recovered. Immediately the wheels of Poughkeepsie justice began turning. On Wednesday, 1 March 1893, the wounded con man was transported to the courthouse and indicted. Appo's damaged appearance, his head wrapped in bandages, "presented a sorry spectacle," claimed one observer. McNally recruited the best legal talent on Appo's behalf. Attorneys Daniel O'Connell and Abram J. Rose were partners in a Broadway law firm in Lower Manhattan, both men having previously served as assistant U.S. attorneys in the prosecution of Samuel Marks in 1889, one of the few successful green goods convictions. Shortly thereafter O'Connell not only left government service, but literally went over to the other side. When James and Walter McNally were indicted in 1891 in federal court, O'Connell successfully quashed the indictment. "It is an open secret," complained one Poughkeepsie newspaper, "that Appo's gang can raise thousands of dollars at any moment, and that they will leave nothing undone to prevent his going to prison." On 1 April 1893 they secured Appo's release on two thousand dollars bail. The bond was furnished by real estate dealer J. W. Morris of New York, alias James W. McNally.[7]

*When I came to, I found myself in the hospital and a nurse at my bedside to whom I asked, "What is the trouble with me?"*

*"Keep quiet, now," and off he went for the doctor.*

*In the meantime I tried to get my senses about me. When the good doctor came, I asked him what was the matter and how long I had been asleep. When I tried to get up I fell back again on the pillow and blood came from my wounded eye. The nurse fixed me alright again, gave me some medicine and I went to sleep. The next morning I awoke and found the sun shining bright and I in full possession of my senses. I then missed my right eye and remembered the two "guys" Cassel and Hogshead and concluded that Hogshead had shot me cowardly from behind. When the doctor came and he asked me how I felt, I said alright, and asked permission to get up, but was told to keep quiet and I would be alright in a day or so.*

*While I was propped up in bed that day, I was surprised by a visit from the policeman Morgan, who came to my bed and asked me, "How are you feeling, George? I did not think that guy would shoot you. Too bad you've lost your eye."*

*I realized at once, remembering seeing Morgan walking with his head turned towards me and Hogshead just before the shooting, that he was the man who spoke and warned Hogshead to have nothing to do with me.*

*I said to Morgan: "That's poor consolation to give me now. If you and my backer (McNally) had any grievance or falling out, why didn't you come to me and say, 'Get out of here! You can't do no business here.' I would have taken heed and left the town."*

*"Well," said he, "it is done and it can't be helped any now, so the less you say about the matter, the better it will be. Keep quiet, and everything may come out all right. I will see you again."*

*On the next day, the doctor gave me permission to get up and sit at the window. On the following day, I was taken from the Vassar*

Hospital to the jail where I was put in a hospital cell and remained there for about ten days when I was released under $1,500 bail.

During the course of those ten days in jail, the keeper came to me one day and asked me if I wanted to see and have a talk with the man who shot me, as he was very anxious to see me. I said to the keeper, "I don't want to see him in particular, but if he wants to see me, and you have no objection, why, all right, I'll see him."

So the keeper unlocked the room door and led me across the tier to another room like the one I was in and unlocked the door and there was the two big guys seated on the cots, looking the most forlorn of all God's creatures, men without a single friend in all the world. I approached Mr. Cassel and, shaking him by the hand, said, "I am sorry to see you locked up here for this shooting, but you need not worry for I will make no complaint. Therefore they will merely hold you as a witness at my trial and then release you."

Cassel said, "I tell you, I'm mighty glad to see you alive and well. I can't understand how that darn fool yonder (pointing at Hogshead) could shoot down a little fellow like you. Why, the whole town's talking mad about him."

I motioned him not to talk and said to him, "It could not be helped. The shooting was an accident, you understand?"

"Do you know," said he, "this darn affair has cost me over three thousand dollars already for lawyers fees and 'fixing things up' as they call it around this section."

I told him not to pay out one cent more and that whoever told them "he was fixing things up" to have him released, [as he] was a fraud and skin [swindler]. I then turned around to his partner, Hogshead, and said in a whisper, "Well, you meant business that time, but accidents will happen and they can't do anything to you for an accident. You understand me? So you need not worry anymore and above all don't pay out another cent of your money to the lawyer."

I then shook hands with them, bid him goodbye and said, "I hope you will get out of this soon and I forgive you."

The keeper then came to the door and I returned with him to my room, and he said to me, "Them two fellows are big husky mountaineers and it's a wonder your head wasn't carried completely off

*your body with the big gun that was found on Hogshead." I left the*
*jail soon after this on $1,500 bonds and in about three weeks after*
*my case was called for trial.*[8]

On 17 April 1893 Appo appeared in the Dutchess County Court House
for his pretrial hearing. Like most well-represented criminal defendants,
Appo was neatly attired in a double-breasted coat and vest, a green patch
covering his injured right eye. "His face, scarred and deformed, presented an eloquent appeal for distinction in itself," wrote one reporter.[9]

The facts of the case were never in dispute. Ephraim Cassel and Ira
Hogshead came to Poughkeepsie to strike it rich. "If I invested three
hundred, I was to get three thousand," declared Cassel. Initially they
described themselves as subsistence farmers from an isolated area in the
western Carolinas. Cassel's gray hair and long beard convinced observers
that he was about seventy years old. He was, in fact, between fifty-six and
fifty-nine. A veteran of the Confederate Army, Cassel claimed that he
had served in the South Carolina calvary without ever seeing battle. After
the war Cassel resided in eastern North Carolina, just north of the South
Carolina border. Hogshead had married Cassel's daughter three years
earlier and lived nearby. The thirty-nine-year-old, six-foot-tall son-in-law
owned and farmed 250 acres of largely uncleared South Carolina moun-

*Ira Hogshead.*

*Ephraim Cassel.*

tain land. Green goods looked like a way to transform their isolated, near-impoverished lives.[10]

Hogshead characterized himself and his father-in-law as victims of a dangerous felon, initially insisting that he feared Appo intended to murder and rob them. After refusing to answer self-incriminating questions regarding the shooting, Hogshead charged that Appo made three requests for them to follow him to New York to view and purchase the green goods. When Hogshead resisted, he testified that Appo called him a coward and that he had them "in his power."[11]

Hogshead, in effect, justified shooting Appo as a righteous assault, a defense of his personal honor. Hogshead portrayed Appo as personally confrontational if not threatening. Appo challenged Hogshead's manhood, generating mixed feelings of anger, indignation, and fear of the unfamiliar surroundings. Hogshead exploded in unpremeditated and impassioned rage. Rather than being victimized by fraud, he directed his fury at the perpetrator of the fraud. Of course all Hogshead and Cassel had to do was walk out the door. He possessed the only firearm in the room. Appo's only weapon was his power of persuasion. Instead Hogshead shot him in the brain.[12]

Cassel and Hogshead were not so hard up in other ways. Census records indicate that by 1870, Cassel and his wife, Catherine, enjoyed some prosperity. He possessed at least two hundred dollars in personal property, and had recently moved from South Carolina with several other family members to a farm valued at fifteen hundred dollars in Transylvania County. By 1893 reports claimed that he had seven children. Similarly, although census records reveal that only thirty acres of Hogshead's property were cleared, he still possessed an unmortgaged title to the land.[13]

Although observers belittled Cassel and Hogshead as simple-minded, ignorant country bumpkins, they were well aware of their intended mission. Only a few months earlier, in December, Cassel received a green goods circular sent to one of his neighbors. Rather than discard it, he and his son-in-law deliberated with their families before electing to respond by telegram, a communication that required them to drive by wagon thirty-five miles to Greenville, South Carolina. Four or five days later Cassel received a response. After a short time a one-dollar sample arrived. This convinced them to head north, traveling by train with more than three hundred dollars and a pistol.[14]

FROM THE BEGINNING Appo's attorneys argued for dismissal of the case on the grounds that the indictment was defective and illegitimate. Daniel O'Connell and Abram Rose employed a strategy used in earlier defenses of green goods operatives. First, Appo's name was misspelled throughout as "Albo" and "Albow," thus creating a defective indictment. Second, the facts described in the indictment failed to constitute a crime. Appo, for example, was indicted as an aider and abettor, which he could not be since no other conspirator was named. Third, the indictment never included the word "counterfeit," the very basis of the indictment. Finally, the indictment mentioned but failed to include any supporting evidence —letters, circulars, or telegrams.[15]

O'Connell's arguments were to no avail. On 25 April 1893, after deliberating for only three minutes, the jurors declared Appo guilty. When the court was called into session and the verdict read, Rose moved for a new trial. Judge Daniel W. Guernsey immediately denied the motion. Rose then issued a plea for mercy, arguing that Appo was now without an eye, his face was paralyzed, and that he suffered excruciating pain. Rose's pleas and threat of appeal went unheeded; Guernsey fined Appo $250 and sentenced him to three years and two months of hard labor.[16]

At that moment, observed one reporter, Appo suddenly shrieked, "I am an innocent man." He sprang from his chair, darted to the long court reporters' table, and grabbed several tumblers. Seized by court officers, Appo shouted, "My character is bad, but I shall not be imposed upon. I am an innocent man." O'Connell and Rose endeavored to calm their client, but to no avail. "Again and again he struggled to get out of the chair," wrote one courtroom observer. Before departing for New York, Appo's attorney declared that his client was insane.[17]

The speedy verdict was no surprise. From the start Appo faced a hostile community. The *Times* described him as "one of the shrewdest green-goods men in the country." Poughkeepsie newspapers complained about how Appo and other green goods swindlers regularly visited the city and robbed numerous "dupes." Appo, in particular, had made Poughkeepsie his headquarters and was well known to police officials and hotel proprietors. The conviction, many believed, would deter others from doing the same.[18]

At the same time, however, Appo had many reasons to shout. First, the deliberations were filled with multiple conflicts of interest. Recorder and prosecutor Charles Morschauser was the sibling of Joseph Morschauser,

Appo's initial counsel. When Daniel O'Connell objected to Charles Morschauser's participation, the presiding judge who rejected O'Connell's objection was Morschauser's former mentor Daniel W. Guernsey. Cassel and Hogshead were represented by Ransom Baker, the law partner of Charles Morschauser. Finally, police officer Michael Morgan's role in the affair was never investigated. Morgan was a thirty-six-year-old officer who had served on the Poughkeepsie force for two years. Active in community organizations like the Knights of Columbus and the Elks, Morgan remained on the police force up to his death in 1921. By then, he was described as one of the leading police officials in the Hudson Valley.[19] His involvement with green goods operators never became public knowledge.

The day after Appo's sentence, Hogshead and Cassel were tried. The prosecution had little evidence against Cassel, so he was quickly discharged. Hogshead's attorneys then introduced witnesses who testified to Appo's bad character. The district attorney, while refusing to grant immunity, had promised Hogshead that if he was truthful, he "would be dealt with mercifully." Yet, on the stand, Hogshead lied, testifying that he went to find a policeman to arrest Appo. Failing to find one, he returned to his room and debated with Appo about going to New York. Appo, Hogshead insisted, put his hand in his pocket. "I was afraid of him and I fired," testified Hogshead. "I didn't mean to kill him."[20]

Despite the perjury, Appo remained a man of his word and refused to implicate Hogshead. On the stand he never mentioned Morgan's role in tolerating green goods operatives, nor did he implicate his employers and associates. Rather Appo lied on their behalf, testifying that he was in Poughkeepsie to learn the location of his father, reportedly in a lunatic asylum "somewhere along the Hudson."[21]

In retrospect Hogshead never needed to cooperate with the district attorney. Judge Guernsey instructed the jury that if Hogshead was threatened and feared bodily harm, he could act in self-defense. The jury, after less than three hours of deliberation, returned a verdict of guilty for second-degree assault. Guernsey then fined Hogshead fifty dollars; upon payment he walked out of the Dutchess County Courthouse a free man.[22]

The disparity in sentences generated a turnaround in public opinion. The *Poughkeepsie Daily Eagle* described the sentence as "the most wretched farce we ever saw in a court of justice." Cassel and Hogshead were not simply innocent victims; rather, both were "morally guilty." The editors compared the circumstances: "One gets his eye shot out, and his life put in serious peril at the hands of the other, and three years in state prison. The other, who does the shooting, goes free on payment of fifty dollars fine. That may be Judge Guernsey's idea of justice. . . . It certainly isn't ours."[23]

THE MOST MYSTERIOUS element surrounding Appo's shooting and trial was the sudden appearance of Appo's common-law wife, Lena Miller. When he regained consciousness on the day of the shooting, Appo requested that someone contact his spouse in New York. Less than twenty-four hours after the shooting, Appo's alleged wife, Lena Miller, appeared at Appo's side, accompanied by her alleged cousin J. S. Roberts. Reporters described their meeting as "affectionate and sorrowful." Miller even soothed Appo's craving for opium. "When she kissed him," noted one observant reporter, "she passed from her lips to his a good sized opium pill."[24]

As his trial commenced, Miller accompanied Appo to trial. Reporters described Miller as "pretty" and attractively dressed with jeweled earrings and cluster diamonds, noting that throughout the proceedings she sat beside the defendant. She was so attentive and affectionate toward Appo that he seemed to ignore much of the proceedings. One reporter claimed that upon his conviction Appo screamed, "I want justice for my wife and child. I'll die before I will be a victim." Before being sent off to prison, Appo kissed Miller good-bye. "You go back to New York, and with your child go to your mother's house, and my body will follow right away, for I shall be dead before tomorrow night," he melodramatically predicted. "I am determined to kill myself, for I have no friend and nothing to live for."[25]

Two days after his sentencing, the *Poughkeepsie Daily Eagle* described the street courtship of Appo and Miller. Appo claimed he met her on an elevated train, while accidentally stepping on her foot. "At that very moment, there was something about her appearance that charmed me," claimed Appo. He then followed her to her residence, where he stopped and invited her to the theater with him the next evening. Not only did she fail to appear, but she moved away. When Appo was leaving her now-former residence, he met a delivery man in the process of moving her belongings. He helped load the truck and then accompanied him to

Miller's new residence. "We had a long chat, and I told her my intentions were honorable," remembered Appo. "After that meetings followed, and we went out together often, and I finally married her." Appo conceded that the events in Poughkeepsie had physically and mentally broken him. He urged Miller to marry another man, but claimed that she ignored his pleas.[26]

Was Lena Miller George Appo's wife? Prior to the events in Poughkeepsie, her name never appeared in any other record regarding Appo. At the time she was always described as "Lena Miller," never as "Lena Appo." Like Walter McNally pretending to be the Block Island "manufacturer" J. S. Roberts, Miller may have simply been an imposter, an actress hired to portray Appo as a loving husband, loyal spouse, and sympathetic defendant. Indeed, Appo never mentioned her name in any later autobiographical accounts. Reporters at the Poughkeepsie trial were suspicious, and when the *Herald* sent reporters to her East Sixty-first Street home, no Lena Miller was found. The address was an empty lot.[27]

Equally suspect was Appo's account of his courtship and marriage. For someone immersed in a social environment of pickpockets, pimps, and prostitutes, who daily frequented dives and opium dens, whose personal associations were filled with duplicity and violence, Appo displayed an uncharacteristically genteel Victorianism in describing his relationship with Miller. Appo's frequent incarcerations, his many travels about the country, and his daily underworld activities would have strained most heterosexual romances, especially one so conventional and domestic as Appo described.

Yet Appo probably did enjoy such a period of domestic bliss. The six years preceding the Poughkeepsie shooting were the most stable and financially successful in Appo's life. Other accounts later confirmed that a woman named Lena Miller considered herself Appo's wife. In 1894 they resided on East Eighteenth Street. "She is a very pretty woman, well formed and wore a tailor-made gown," claimed one reporter. Others concurred, describing her as "handsome and young." Two years later Appo claimed that the relationship had failed for a variety of reasons, that Miller finally abandoned him because "she was afraid of me." He also admitted that the marriage produced two children, a boy born in 1891 and still living with the mother, and another who died in infancy.[28] Perhaps Appo's marriage, seen in context with his earlier homophobic criticism of a Sing Sing keeper, reflected a conventional, domestic sexuality on his part. Appo never revealed if he ever saw them again, quite likely because her abandonment inflicted a deep emotional scar.

But Appo now sat in Clinton prison, a broken man in many ways. His lawyers, however, remained at work on his behalf. On 28 July 1893 a three-member panel of the Supreme Court of New York affirmed Appo's conviction in a two-to-one vote. Despite the setback the dissenting opinion of Judge Calvin E. Pratt gave the defendant hope. Pratt conceded that Appo deserved to be punished under the statute in question but agreed with Appo's attorneys at the same time that the law was poorly worded, and that the indictment contained no concrete proof of fraud.[29]

Pratt's dissent was the crack in the window of opportunity for Appo. Before the New York Court of Appeals in October, O'Connell argued that the indictment was "inconsistent, repugnant and uncertain." Simply to offer paper money for sale did not, by itself, constitute an unlawful act. How could Appo be guilty in a scheme to distribute genuine money? He never explicitly stated that he intended to exchange counterfeit money; indeed, the word "counterfeit" appeared nowhere in the indictment. Giving someone the opportunity to obtain one thousand dollars worth of United States currency for one hundred dollars was certainly generous but hardly criminal. O'Connell added that his argument relied upon *U.S. v. Hess*, a U.S. Supreme Court decision that required all indictments specifically to state all material facts and circumstances relevant to a prosecution. The author of that decision was Chief Justice Stephen Field, none other than the brother of David Dudley Field who defended Appo's father thirty-three years earlier.[30]

O'Connell's logic worked. On 28 November 1893 the New York Court of Appeals overturned Appo's conviction. The defendant "suffered greatly for his crime," observed one Poughkeepsie newspaper, so "he should lead a better life in the future." On 5 December 1893 Appo was discharged from Clinton prison.[31]

The near-fatal assault upon and trial of George Appo generated renewed attention to the green goods game. "The whole town seemed absorbed in the discussion of the case," admitted one observer. The *New York Times* believed that "Nothing has happened here in years which has excited so much interest among all classes." Indeed, New York City

*George Appo shot in Poughkeepsie, as depicted
in the* National Police Gazette.

newspapers recognized the national implications of the incident. Coverage of Appo's trial appeared on the front page of the *Times*. The first public image of Appo appeared in the *National Police Gazette*.[32] The events in Poughkeepsie made George Appo famous. Too famous, as he was about to discover.

## STEALING GUYS

◦§ *One day, unexpectedly, the keeper came to me and said, "Get ready, you are going home."*

*I left everything I had to the convict who worked next to me on the bench and went with the keeper to the state shop, took off the stripes and put on a suit of salt bag citizen's clothes, furnished by the state, by the way. The $40 suit of clothes I brought to prison I never saw again. Anyway, I had $60 in the front office that I brought with me, and as soon as I got to New York, I bought a nice suit of clothes and gave the salt bags to a poor fellow who needed them, and went down to my lawyer's office and thanked him for his untiring efforts in my behalf. Then, of course, I called on my financial backer, Jim McNally. In three days I was again working as steerer for the green goods business for him and continued working for about six weeks, when McNally had to close up.[1]*

*I went to work for Mike Ryan, who had his green goods headquarters down on West and Liberty Streets. He had everything right in that precinct and worked the business without interference or molestation of the police. In fact, Mike Ryan was the political boss of that district and had big influence with police captain Richard O'Connor. When attached to the district attorney's office some years before he became a police captain, O'Connor told Recorder Hackett, before whom I pled guilty to grand larceny, that I was a notorious thief. Consequently, I was sentenced to two years and six months in state prison. When he heard that I was working for Mike Ryan, he told Ryan to keep me away from his precinct. One morning, when I came to work, Ryan took me aside and said, "George, you are the best little fellow I have working and I cannot go into details. In fact, I am forced to tell you not to come down here anymore to work."*

*I replied: "It is not necessary to tell me who gave you that order and you need not fear me intruding on you or him." So I left Ryan, and as there was no other green goods financial backer working under police protection, I hunted up a man named "Dutch Gus" who had a bank roll. I told him I had a scheme to steal all of Ryan's guys if he would take their orders and beat them for the money.*

*Gus said: "You bring the guys and I'll get their coin."*

The next morning, I watched the side entrance of the North River Hotel barroom on West and Barclay Streets. One of Ryan's steerers came along with a guy and entered the sitting room. He sat the guy at a table and told him that he was going to tell the Old Gentleman of his arrival. The steerer left the place and walked down towards Liberty Street to tell Ryan to get the turning joint ready for business.

In the meantime, I entered the sitting room, walked to the guy at the table and said to him, "The regular messenger won't be back and the Old Gentleman is waiting patiently for you with the goods, so follow me."

The guy got up and I took him on a fast walk to Gus. He made a $300 deal, and I then took him to Grand Central Station, saw him safe aboard his train and then returned to Gus and received my share of the deal—$150.

I then went down to Mike Ryan to see how he took the loss of his intended victim. I said to Ryan: "You are the only one now doing business in the city. Everybody is closed up tight. I tried to get a steer from one of the writers but none of them are putting out mail just now. I suppose there's no chance for me down here?"

Ryan said: "You say no one is doing business but me! Don't fool yourself. Why, someone pinched a guy from my steerer this morning, and if I lay hands on him, whoever he is, I'll fix him so he won't do it again."

I told him that I was sorry for his loss, and again asked him if there was any chance for me. He said no, so I left him abruptly and stole two more guys from him at two different times and brought them to Gus who made successful deals with each one separately at $500 apiece. My share was 50 percent of both deals.

I would have continued to steal Ryan's guys every chance that came my way, but one morning an unexpected event happened to me as I left the house where I lived.[2]

# 1 7

# The Lexow Committee

=

> ◆ On reaching the sidewalk, I was approached by two men,
> Arthur Dennett and [Thomas] Carney, who represented themselves
> as officers of the Lexow Committee.
>
> After I demanded their authority, Mr. Dennett handed me a sub-
> poena, saying, "This will explain matters."
>
> I read the paper and as I had no idea what the Lexow Committee
> was or meant, I became suspicious and refused to accompany them.
>
> Then Carney said: "We are sent up here to take you dead or
> alive."
>
> "Well," said I, "if that's the case, I'll go down with you, but I
> assure you there is no information of any importance that I can give
> that would be of any interest or value to you or the Committee. So
> you are only wasting time bothering with me."
>
> "Well, we will see about that," said Mr. Dennett. "All that is wanted
> of you is to tell how you come to get shot up at Poughkeepsie."
>
> When we arrived at Judge [John] Goff's office, I was interviewed
> by him and then taken before the Lexow Committee and put upon
> the witness stand. For three hours I was questioned by the coun-
> selors, Mr. Frank Moss and Hon. Judge Goff. When they got
> through with me, there was nothing else I could say about the sys-
> tematic grafting of the then police. The press then began to write
> me up in all kinds of characters, representing me to the police and
> the underworld associates in anything but a favorable light to them.
> They began to look on me as a dangerous fellow to them.[1]

GEORGE APPO'S LIFE changed forever on 14 June 1894. Testifying
before a special state senate committee investigating the New York City
Police Department, Appo discussed various elements of the green goods
game. The city's newspapers depicted Appo's testimony as revelatory, a

virtual eye peering into a heretofore hidden underworld universe. While Appo was a known figure among law enforcement officials, his testimony transformed him into a small-time celebrity in New York. It was a metamorphosis he lived to regret.

The special senate committee was empowered to investigate corruption in New York City's Police Department, an outgrowth of the antivice and anti–Tammany Hall campaign initiated in 1892 by the Reverend Charles Parkhurst of the Madison Square Presbyterian Church. As Parkhurst compiled more and more evidence of municipal malfeasance, state officials felt ever-increasing pressure to respond. At the end of 1893 the state senate authorized an investigation into Gotham's police department. Democrats immediately charged that the committee was a Republican plot, and Gov. Roswell Flower vetoed the appropriation. New York City's Chamber of Commerce, however, intervened and agreed to subsidize the investigation. Composed of seven state senators, the body was chaired by Republican Clarence Lexow and thus christened the "Lexow Committee."

From inception, the Lexow Committee reflected the hand of Parkhurst. The committee accepted his recommendations for counsel: John W. Goff (who became the commanding figure of the investigation), Frank Moss of the Society for the Prevention of Crime, and the future district attorney of New York City William Travers Jerome. From March to December 1894, the committee called 678 witnesses and produced more than 5,700 pages of testimony and documentary evidence relating to electoral fraud, blackmail, and extortion. The depth of political and police malfeasance extended beyond simple toleration of saloons, brothels, and gambling dens; police officials extorted payments from steamboat operators, produce merchants, sailmakers, bootblacks, pushcart peddlers, and numerous other small merchants. By 1896 even police officials admitted that the police department was "honeycombed with corruption."[2]

Although only ten witnesses discussed the green goods game, they offered some of the most publicized and damaging testimony.[3] The first to take the stand was Appo. He briefly summarized his criminal career, an account that was generally accurate but filled with errors in detail. Then, over the next three hours, Appo presented a virtual lecture on the argot and behavior of the confidence man, describing the purposes of circulars, backers, steerers, writers, ringers, turners, tailers, turning joints, and guys. He explained what circulars contained, how steerers met guys in New Jersey and Hudson River towns, the cooperative role of telegraph operators, the amounts of money stolen. Appo admitted that although police officials often knew his purposes, he "could walk along with impunity."[4]

Appo offered some details about his employers. He identified Walter Haines and James McNally as backers, with the latter being the leading operator in New York. He claimed that McNally had worked with green goods since 1886, possessed more than one hundred thousand dollars in capital, and made as much as eight thousand dollars in a day. Appo himself bragged he once made six hundred dollars in a day. He even offered details regarding McNally's ascent in the underworld: his work as a pimp, his support from ex-alderman Patrick Farley, the location of his headquarters near the Haymarket, and the different addresses from which he operated.[5]

Appo's testimony became an immediate sensation. He was "a half-breed Chinaman," wrote one newspaper, a small, clean-shaven, wiry man with a dark complexion and pompadour-style hair. Most commented on his glass eye and facial scars, all reflecting his many bloody encounters. The *Tribune* described him as "one of the worst criminals in the city." With virtual unanimity Appo's testimony was portrayed as pathbreaking, "a revelation to the entire country," in the words of the writer Louis Beck.[6]

In fact Appo disclosed very little. By the time he sat down in the witness chair, most of what Appo "revealed" was part of the public record. Law enforcement officials were already familiar with McNally and his operatives, like Harry Hilton, whom they arrested in 1891 and 1892. At that time Anthony Comstock was involved in a well-publicized campaign against McNally, detailing how he operated out of Hoboken. In 1893, when Comstock arrested McNally's printer Eugene A. Marvin, he charged that McNally earned nearly $1 million annually. These details were not only known to federal and local law enforcement authorities, they received extensive coverage in the New York media.[7]

More telling was Appo's unwillingness to name names. At various points in his testimony, he refused to admit that Bill Vosburg was employed as "the old gentleman." He feigned ignorance regarding McNally's operatives in the post office. He refused to acknowledge that his one-time associate Michael Ryan or Capt. Richard O'Connor were in the green goods business. In many cases Appo simply repeated others' testimony or public rumors. He conceded that Western Union messengers and postal employees cooperated with green goods operatives, but pleaded ignorance regarding specific individuals. He denied knowing if Eddie Parmeley gave gifts to Capt. William Meakim, adding that Parmeley was retired from the business. He refused to identify *who* paid off the police. In Appo's words he was willing to "give the snap away" but refused to "incriminate a friend."[8]

Appo even lied. He pleaded ignorance regarding the "third degree." He claimed that green goods operatives had no police protection outside New York, despite his glass eye, which was a visible reminder that Poughkeepsie police officer Michael Morgan was in McNally's employ. Appo even said that McNally had never been arrested.[9] Appo's testimony offered few, if any, new details.

Appo was not the only operative to testify against his green goods employer. Three months later, on 10 September 1894, William Applegate, a twenty-two-year-old steerer for McNally, not only disclosed the exact saloons and locations where the gang worked, but identified specific green goods operatives. He named more than a dozen individuals in McNally's employ—writers, police detectives, police captains, police officers, even policemen and detectives in Bridgeport and Jersey City. He gave exact amounts of how much McNally paid them, details on their operations, and even dates when they were in business. He claimed that Capt. William Meakim protected McNally, and that when Meakim was transferred to Harlem, McNally moved his operation uptown. Applegate even described how McNally conspired, one day after Appo's testimony, to avoid testifying before the Lexow Committee. In 1897, when the British writer and reformer William T. Stead published an exposé of Gotham's municipal corruption, he relied on Applegate's revelations, not Appo's.[10]

What was controversial about Appo's testimony was his revelations of police complicity. Appo reminded listeners that he was well known to police. Yet when he passed police with a potential victim, according to Appo, "they [would] bow and look" away. Police critics long suspected that certain police officers tolerated green goods operatives, but Appo offered firsthand confirmation. "This is a new form of protected crime," claimed the *Press*.[11]

At the time the sensational media attention was so focused on municipal corruption that few recognized how the Lexow Committee challenged traditional crime-fighting methods in New York. For half a century, since the creation of the New York City police in 1845, city officials had battled crime through an informal and often corrupt system of negotiation. Justice was not ultimately determined by statute and law but rather by an inconsistent and personalized series of informal settlements among police, judges, and criminals themselves. The police, wrote Lincoln Steffens, were "a dark, mysterious layer of the life of a great city" that resisted penetration.[12] The Lexow Committee not only infiltrated this labyrinth, it generated a national debate regarding law enforcement in American cities.

From their inception urban police departments in the United States were decentralized. Station houses served as command centers, often independent of central headquarters. Unlike Europe, where police departments were frequently attached to a local judiciary, American police were political-patronage instruments of local elected officials. Police officials like George Walling even claimed that local precinct captains were more powerful than upper-level superintendents. The captain, complained Walling, "was an autocrat."[13]

At the lowest level, police officers on the street routinely tolerated certain amounts of crime such as pickpocketing, as long as they received a percentage of the loot, hence the label "percentage copper." On Broadway, streetcars and omnibuses were reportedly "parceled off" among certain pickpockets who enjoyed "privileges" on certain blocks. When well-known pickpockets arrived in New York, claimed one former felon, percentage coppers approached them and demanded money. This system of sidewalk blackmail extended to other illegal activities, particularly prostitution, gambling, and excise violations. Police officers, complained critics, were little more than "criminals in uniform."[14]

Detectives represented another layer of corruption. As early as 1859, one newspaper declared that finding honest detectives in New York was an "impossibility." A state assembly investigation in 1875 concluded that precinct detectives literally managed financial relationships between captains and the "criminal classes" in their precinct. Police captain Max F. Schmittberger admitted that the key to successful detective work was developing close relationships with certain criminals. In effect the detective was a reverse confidence man, someone who employed illegal methods in the name of the law, turning crime fighting into a system of blackmail. Lincoln Steffens dubbed them "crooked crooks."[15]

This system flourished, in part, because it was lucrative. A year prior to Appo's testimony, one newspaper estimated that the police received $7 million to $15 million annually in protection fees from prostitutes, brothel- and saloonkeepers, gambling dens, and green goods swindlers. The police department was "the most perfect machine ever invented in this city," concluded Frank Moss in the Lexow Committee's final report. "It knows every prostitute, it knows every house, and no prostitute, no gambler, can live for a moment in any place in the city without being known." Lincoln Steffens believed that Gotham's police were organized "not to prevent, detect, or arrest crime, but to protect, share with, and direct the criminals." These and other observations simply confirmed Charles Parkhurst's earlier assertions that municipal policing in New York was less interested in fighting crime and more concerned with entrepreneurial opportunity. The police department, argued Parkhurst, not only protected and fostered crime but made "capital out of it."[16]

Such castigation was not simply hyperbolic paranoia by evangelical reformers. Equally harsh criticism of New York's police emanated from labor leaders in New York. George K. Lloyd of the Building Trades Section of the Central Labor Union, for example, considered Gotham's police to be both a menace and a disgrace. Lloyd argued that the problems of policing in New York were not confined to simply a few corrupt officers or captains. Rather, the body of the force was dishonest, violent, and criminal. The police transformed blackmail into a science, charged Lloyd, and thus "maintained a system of terrorism over certain helpless classes of the community."[17]

But numerous citizens at least tolerated, if not preferred, this policing strategy. Victims of crime frequently made the recovery of property their first and sometimes only priority. Consequently thieves of every stripe were invited to return purloined property in return for a reward, no questions asked. Two decades later, when detective Thomas Byrnes revealed that he became rich by obtaining secret information in the stock market, the *Times* objected to calls for his resignation. Such questionable behavior was simply "too ethereal" to condemn.[18]

Gotham's system of negotiated policing transformed the relationship between criminal activity and the law into an informal network of secret, personal relationships. Police officials acted as de facto regulators over New York's underworld economy. Collecting "fees" from proprietors of brothels, gambling dens, dives, and unlicensed saloons, "registering" pickpockets and fences, or "protecting" confidence games like green goods recast the police officer into an arbitrator over various criminal economies. These selective, informal, and negotiated practices transformed law enforcement into "a system of compromise and privilege for crooks and detectives," according to Lincoln Steffens.[19] In this inverted fashion, the agents of criminal justice permitted certain forms of crime to flourish and expand, developing an intertwined, symbiotic relationship with the political economy of the underworld.

Police officer Thomas J. Byrnes personified this system of negotiated policing. Born in Ireland, Byrnes immigrated to New York as an infant and grew up in the Fifth Ward along the Hudson River. Like many teenage males, Byrnes was associated with the local volunteer fire company. After briefly serving in the Civil War, he returned to New York and joined the police force in 1863. He quickly rose through the ranks, becoming chief of detectives in 1880 and superintendent of police in 1892. Known for his charisma and strong personality, Byrnes, wrote one defender, embodied the evolution of the police from an untrained group of watchmen to a disciplined military-like organization.[20]

*Thomas Byrnes.*

Upon his elevation to chief detective in 1880, Byrnes selectively addressed certain high-profile criminal activities without undermining the informal relationships detectives enjoyed with certain underworld elements. For example, Byrnes opened detective offices on both Wall Street and in the New York Stock Exchange Building, hoping to eliminate the thieves and pickpockets in the Wall Street business district, many of whom snatched money from bank messenger boys, depositors, and others cashing checks. By connecting his Stock Exchange office with others in the vicinity, Byrnes's detectives responded to calls for help in less than two minutes. Brynes then established the "dead line"—any known thief or pickpocket found south of Fulton or Liberty Streets was "dead," and the police could arrest him on sight. Aggressive enforcement of the dead line transformed street life in Lower Manhattan, forcing out not only pickpockets but homeless and itinerant workers who slept in the Battery. By 1886 Byrnes bragged that robbery in the business district was "almost extinct," making him a hero among New York businessmen. Byrnes's reputation even persuaded President-elect Grover Cleveland to place him in charge of presidential security during the 1885 inauguration ceremonies in Washington, D.C.[21]

Byrnes built on this success. He created "a system of espionage" in which he infiltrated and monitored Tenderloin haunts on Broadway and Sixth Avenue noted for harboring leading criminals. To assist detectives in identifying suspects, Byrnes expanded and enlarged the rogues' gallery throughout the 1880s. He required professional criminals upon entering the city to come before him at the back door of the Gilsey House, and promise not to engage in any criminal activity while in New York. During the Constitutional Centennial celebration in 1889, Byrnes forced potential suspects to appear at his office daily. On other occasions he did not even bother to wait for the suspects. Before major parades Byrnes's detectives waited in railroad depots and ferry stations in Jersey City, Hoboken, and New York and detained any suspected criminal. Concerns about civil liberties mattered little to Byrnes. He insisted that police officials were entitled to arrest any known thieves whenever they acted suspiciously. To his defenders Byrnes transformed New York's detective force into an unparalleled crime-fighting organization, surpassing Scotland Yard to become the world's best.[22]

Such praise, however, ignored how Byrnes and his detectives tolerated certain criminal activities. Pickpockets banned from Lower Manhattan or required to register on entering the city simply worked in other parts of the city with the compliance of local detectives. Publicized mass detentions of pickpockets masked police toleration of more lucrative criminal activities. In 1884, for example, when District Attorney Peter B. Olney concluded that city detectives protected leading fences, he secretly employed Pinkerton agents to investigate and arrest New York's leading trafficker in stolen goods, Fredericka Mandelbaum. Byrnes later denied any such complicity and accused Assistant District Attorney Henry C. Allen and Pinkerton's detectives of being "enemies of the public good." Furthermore Byrnes indirectly admitted that criminal activities like the green goods game continued as long as such thieves were kept on the East or West Sides of Manhattan, outside the area protected by the dead line.[23]

Byrnes's methods attracted attention in part because he was an astute master of self-promotion. After Allan Pinkerton, Byrnes was the most influential crime writer in the nineteenth-century United States. In 1886 he published *Professional Criminals in America*, a compendium of the leading underworld figures at the time, replete with rogues'-gallery images. In 1891 he joined Helen Campbell and Thomas W. Knox in writing *Darkness and Daylight: Or, Lights and Shadows of New York Life*. Byrnes even became the subject of short stories and melodramas, best exemplified by Julian Hawthorne's five novels allegedly "from the diary of Inspector Byrnes." By 1890 some described Byrnes not only as a detective genius but as "the most celebrated man in the United States."[24]

The dead line illustrated Byrnes's promotional abilities. Summary arrests in a specific area of the city, in retrospect, were more of a public relations ploy than a new law enforcement innovation. American police officers from their creation enjoyed broad personal discretion—considerably more than their counterparts in London. In 1846 New York police regulations explicitly empowered patrolmen "to arrest any person who, from his acts, conduct, situation and character," was "about to commit a felony." Numerous commentators after 1860 remarked on how Gotham's police dispensed summary justice on the street, especially against pickpockets on holidays and before parades. By the 1870s police officers annually arrested more than one thousand suspect persons; by the 1890s, more than two thousand.[25]

Similarly Byrnes's long, harsh interrogation procedure, dubbed "the third degree," was hardly new. As early as the 1850s, the so-called police ring did the same. Police captain John Jourdan of the Eighth Precinct, Police Court justice Joseph Dowling, and members of the district attorney's office reportedly arrested suspects, locked them in the dark cells of the Franklin Street station house, and starved them for weeks, forcing them to confess their crimes and give up their plunder. Some described the method as little more than "a reign of terror."[26]

Violent interrogation methods were routine police procedure. Former police officers admitted that they were trained to beat criminal suspects upon arrest; Cornelius Willemse remembered that policemen were respected and feared because "they dispensed the law with the nightstick." When they arrested suspects, interrogators employed a variety of tactics to generate favorable testimony: punching in the face, hitting with a billy, whipping with a rubber hose, kicking in the abdomen, strangulating with a necktie, and squeezing the testicles. Some methods were designed to leave no visible marks. Appo remembered being locked up in police headquarters for thirty-six hours without food after one arrest. One New York newspaper editor contrasted policing in London and New York: London residents "are generally protected by their police," while "we are generally in need of protection from ours."[27]

Byrnes ached to expand these summary powers. He complained that the law gave professional thieves the same rights as law-abiding citizens. Since police could not legally arrest suspects unless they were caught in a criminal activity, all the advantage was on the side of the criminal. To remedy this Byrnes recommended the Summary Arrest Act. Better known as the "Professional Criminal" Act, and introduced in the state legislature in 1889, the proposed statute empowered police officials to arrest former and suspected criminals on sight when police believed they were congregating in order to commit a crime. The police would then hold them until certain public events were concluded. The legislation passed the senate and received a third reading in the house before Democratic assemblyman Timothy "Dry Dollar" Sullivan successfully tabled the proposal.[28]

Byrnes defended summary arrests and expanding such power with a pessimistic view of human nature. Criminals were never contrite, Byrnes believed. "I do not know of a single case of genuine reformation among professional criminals," he bluntly concluded in 1890. Byrnes claimed that former convicts came to him on their release, acting penitent. He always listened to them and offered assistance but to little avail. "Most of them get back to their old business very soon."[29]

Byrnes, however, never operated with impunity. Summary arrests and arbitrary prosecutions were a source of contention throughout the final decades of the nineteenth century. In 1875, both Mayor William Wickham and a state assembly committee investigating the causes of crime in New York concluded that much of the police force was corrupt. In 1884 an assembly committee chaired by a young Theodore Roosevelt confirmed that police officials promoted certain forms of gambling and prostitution. The Fassett Committee in the state legislature in 1890 documented numerous and specific examples of police corruption, especially in relation to brothels, gambling dens, and illegal saloons. In general, elements in the police force used their power "not to enforce the laws," argued critics, "but to wring from lawbreakers a share of their booty."[30]

These condemnations of policing policy, however, were sporadic, unsustained, and ultimately ineffective. That changed after 1892. On appointment as police superintendent, Byrnes came under attack from the Reverend Charles Parkhurst and various reform groups. Byrnes responded by transferring precinct captains, instituting formal charges of corruption against certain inspectors and captains, and raiding brothels and gambling dens. But these actions did little to placate Parkhurst. By the end of 1892 the minister charged Byrnes with criminal neglect of duty. Over the ensuing two years, Parkhurst and his Society for the Prevention of Crime collected evidence and waged a media campaign against Byrnes and the police.[31]

By the time Byrnes testified before the Lexow Committee in December 1894, he was politically weakened and directly implicated in a wide range of police abuses. By then Byrnes conceded that the police department suffered from corruption, even describing how he personally profited from his position. Relying on the assistance of Jay Gould and Cornelius Vanderbilt, Brynes admitted turning his twelve-thousand-dollar savings into three hundred thousand dollars. The *Mercury* complained that Byrnes was guilty of "prostituting his public office to the service of individual plutocrats." A few months later he resigned.[32]

The immediate result of the Lexow inquiry was the indictments of more than thirty police officials and the ouster of Tammany Hall from political control in New York. In November 1894 William Strong was elected mayor, John Goff recorder, and William Travers Jerome was appointed justice of the Court of Special Sessions, and went on to serve as district attorney. When Strong was sworn in to the mayor's office, he named the Republican reformer Theodore Roosevelt as president of the Board of Police Commissioners. These changes, however, proved short-lived. Tammany Hall rejuvenated itself, continued to maintain control of the police department, and did little to address corruption.[33]

The Lexow Committee hearings proved more influential in challenging old methods of policing. Crime fighting in nineteenth-century New York was organized around the minimal oversight and autonomy of the police captain. The selective, informal, and negotiated methods of law enforcement transformed police detectives and captains into semi-autonomous arbitrators and regulators over certain criminal activities.

The Lexow Committee undermined this strategy of arbitrary compromise and privilege. Beginning with Roosevelt in 1895, the patrolman and detective came under increasing scrutiny. In the ensuing decades, citizens' defense leagues, legal reformers, and police superintendents challenged the intimate relationships police officers enjoyed with criminal elements. A formal, centralized, bureaucratic system replaced the symbiotic, personalized mechanisms of nineteenth-century crime control.[34] The Lexow Committee's revelations represented more than just a new approach to law enforcement: They transformed the relationship between police officials and various underworld economies.

THESE DEVELOPMENTS sent reverberations through George Appo's underworld. On the afternoon of 28 September 1894 Appo was drinking with Michael J. Riordan in the North Park Hotel. Riordan was a onetime candidate for alderman and a former saloon owner. He had recently fallen on hard times and was working as bartender in Sam Pettit's waterfront saloon. More important, Appo knew that Riordan was involved in the green goods business and an ally of the local police captain Richard O'Connor.[35]

Suddenly their conversation grew loud and belligerent. According to witnesses, Appo began to rave "like a madman," allegedly screaming, "I am a liar and a thief, and my life isn't worth two dollars." At that point, he pulled out a penknife, opened the blade, and cried, "I'll cut my throat from ear to ear." Before Riordan could react, Appo stuck the knife in his throat.[36]

Appo, however, had a different version of these events.

> ◄ One morning [28 September 1894] on leaving the office of Judge Goff, I was met on Broadway and Barclay Street by Mike Riordan, who was then the confidential man for police captain Richard O'Connor and Mike Ryan. Riordan stopped me and said: "How are you? Mike Ryan would like to see and have a little talk with you. He is down at the North River Hotel. Come on down with me."
>
> I replied: "All right, what does he want to see me about?"

"I don't know just what it is. But I guess it is about the captain," said he.

So I walked down with him to the North River Hotel, entered the barroom where Riordan met and spoke to the proprietor who went upstairs and returned in a few minutes and said: "Come back here," and led the way to a private sitting room.

"Mike will be here shortly. What will you have to drink?" said he. I ordered a cigar and Riordan said: "Bring me a whiskey. Why don't you drink something, George?"

"No, thank you. I'm just after eating." Instead of the proprietor going to the bar to serve the order, Riordan went out and brought me a cigar and a glass of whiskey for himself. Just then in Ryan [entered,] and we all sat down at a table.

I said: "I will take a little whiskey," knowing that Riordan would drink the same from the same bottle, and the proprietor and Ryan ordered a small bottle of wine. Riordan then went out for the drinks and said to me: "George, I am surprised at you going before that Committee and saying what you did. Did the Committee ask or say anything about Captain O'Connor?"[37]

"No, not that I know of, but they were very much interested about you from the way they questioned me while on the stand. In fact, they know more about your business and yourself than I do. Anything you read in the papers about me and what I said on the stand you must not believe or pay any attention to it. It is all lies and exaggeration. I believe you have some fellow now associated with you, or someone working for you, who is giving information to some reporter who is publishing all that stuff about your doings and making it look as though I was responsible for it," said I.

Just then, Mike Riordan came in with the drinks on a tray. He set the bottle of wine and the wine glasses on the table. I noticed that he was very careful in selecting one of the two glasses containing the whiskey, setting it down in front of me and saying: "Well, drink up George." I took the glass and as I raised it, I noticed an almost imperceptible whitish color floating on the top of the whiskey, but said nothing. I began to talk to Ryan so as to delay drinking it. When Riordan said, "Why don't you drink up?"

I raised the glass and tasted the whiskey. Sure enough, I tasted the drug or the poison that Riordan had put in the whiskey to do me harm. I got up from the table as though to finish the drink, and as I noticed that both doors of the room were closed, I let the glass of whiskey fall from my hand as though by accident. Riordan jumped at me and struck me on the head with a blackjack, but I grasped the wine bottle and smashed him on the nose with it and upset the table so as to give me time to get at the door leading to the bar room. I made a punch at the proprietor with the broken bottle, who was in my way and reached the bar room, when I received another blow on the head, making a bad scalp wound. Before I became unconscious, I smashed the glass on the street door to attract attention. That was all unnecessary because an officer, named O'Connor, who was a relation to the Captain O'Connor, was and had been waiting about the entrance all the time I was in the sitting room with Ryan and the other two.

I was then taken to the Chambers Street Hospital. When I came to, I found myself in bed and my head all bandaged up and Captain O'Connor's relative sitting at my bedside in a uniform. I asked him what hospital I was in. "Shut your mouth up, d—— you!" was his reply to me. I saw the doctor in the ward and called him, and told him I was well enough to get up.

That same afternoon, I was taken to the private room of Captain O'Connor at the Church Street Police Station, who said to me: "What was all the trouble about?" I explained everything just as it happened and my grounds for suspecting their bad intentions to injure me.

"I don't think so, but I'll look into the matter," said the Captain. "By the way, what had you to say about me before that Committee?" asked he.

I replied: "Nothing. I don't remember your name even being mentioned by any person I know of connected with the investigating committee."

He got up from his chair and said to policeman O'Connor: "All right, take him to Court." I was then brought to the Centre Street Court, where Mr. [William] Travers Jerome pleaded my case as counselor and I was released.

About two weeks after this affair, I met a man named Mahoney who was a frequenter of Sam Pettit's saloon on West Street, just south of Liberty Street, where Mike Ryan and his green goods men

used as a meeting place. Mahoney said to me: "You were very lucky.
Ryan and Riordan meant to 'croak' (kill) you and put your body in
a bag. Johns the expressman was to drop it into the river."

"How do you know that?" I asked.

"I overhead it in Sam Pettit's. I advise you to keep away from
around West Street."

I told him, "I have no fear of Ryan or anyone else connected with
him, and you can tell him so when you see him." I had no more
trouble from Ryan.[38]

Appo's appearance before the Lexow Committee made him persona
non grata in Gotham's underworld. Within weeks of his testimony, he
was denied entrance to various opium resorts in the city. Other reports
claimed that Appo was cooperating with Goff to procure evidence against
certain green goods operators, especially police captain Richard O'Connor.[39] The validity of these reports was never corroborated, but some of
Appo's criminal associates feared the possibility of his cooperation with
the committee.

Then on 28 September 1894 Appo reportedly cut his throat in the
North River Hotel. The knife was quickly wrestled away from him, and
police officials arrived on the scene. Appo, wailing in what some
described as "alcoholic mania," was first taken to the nearby police
precinct. A surgeon determined that the wound was not serious, sewed up
the one-inch cut just above the jugular, and removed Appo to the Chambers Street Hospital. He continued to scream uncontrollably, forcing
police officers to put him in a straitjacket. During the night policeman

Michael Riordan's attack on George Appo made the headlines of the New York Tribune.

Thomas Coleman was placed on guard and reported that Appo attempted suicide, for which police officials immediately indicted him.[40]

Lexow Committee investigators quickly determined that this version of the events was fabricated. For the first time committee officials acknowledged that Appo was helping to procure evidence. "He has proven himself truthful, accurate, prompt, and faithful," reported John Goff. The counsel then admitted that this was not the first attempt on Appo's life. Only two nights earlier, after leaving Goff's office, Appo was assaulted outside the General Post Office at Broadway and Park Row. With blood flowing down his face, Appo desperately pursued his assailant. On finding him at an elevated train stop, he asked police officers standing nearby for help. They simply looked at him and smiled.[41]

Investigators quickly pieced together the chain of events. The attending physician testified that Appo's wound was not self-inflicted. Lexow Committee investigators rejected assertions that Appo was drunk at the time, speculating instead that he was drugged as part of a plot to kill him. Appo insisted that he was attacked during the night at the hospital. A male orderly, at the behest of a guarding police officer, punched Appo in the jaw and temple, twisted cords around his left wrist, and attempted to gouge out his remaining eye. In court Appo displayed his left arm, bruised and swollen from hand to elbow, another bruise on his temple, and a swollen jaw. Appo's charges were later bolstered when Thomas Coleman, the policeman assigned to guard Appo, gave an incoherent account of the events in the hospital.[42] Despite the evidence, however, the charges against Riordan were dismissed while Appo's case was postponed, a portent of what lay ahead for him.

In November 1894 Appo came upon Ned Lyons in front of the Brower House, a West Twenty-eighth Street hotel just off Fifth Avenue. Lyons was one of America's most famous criminals. A tough character, he stood five feet eight inches in height and weighed a burly 180 pounds. Lyons was without the top half of his left ear, a "gift" from Jimmy Haggerty, who chewed it off in a Philadelphia street fight in 1869. At least four bullet holes disfigured his body, one of which had left a visible scar on his jaw. Lyons was involved in some of the most lucrative bank robberies in nineteenth-century America, including the $1 million heist of the Ocean Bank in New York City in 1869. In 1872, he successfully escaped from Sing Sing. By 1886, he had abandoned bank robbery for the green goods.

But on 9 October 1894 Lyons's green goods operation in Perth Amboy,

New Jersey, was exposed on the front page of the *New York Sun*. The article claimed that Lyons was having a difficult time, earning only forty dollars weekly. Although the article was full of details only an insider could have provided, no evidence indicated that Appo was a source of information. That, however, mattered little to Lyons; Appo presented a convenient scapegoat. As they passed each other in front of the Brower House, Lyons belted Appo across the face, knocking him into the street.[43]

*Ned Lyons.*

Perhaps Ned Lyons was jealous. George Appo was about to become a celebrity.

# 1 8

# In the Tenderloin

═

❧ *One day [in September 1894] I was standing on Centre Street near Leonard. Suddenly I was tapped on the shoulder and greeted with: "Hello! You are just the fellow I want to see. What are you doing now?" asked the lawyer Edmund E. Price.*

*"Nothing, can you get me something to do?" I replied.*

*"Yes, come with me to my office." I went with him and on entering his office, he said, "Now, George, take a seat." I sat by a centre table and the lawyer said to me: "I have written a play and am about to have it staged. The name of the play will be* In the Tenderloin *and will be under the management of George W. Lederer. Now I would like to have you take a principal part in the green goods scene where Tom Davis gets shot dead by the Texans Holland and Hill, who came on to steal the bank roll from Davis. You remember, George, I had their case in court and had them discharged," said Price.*

*"Yes, I remember both the shooting and the trial of the Texans who shot Davis dead."*

*"Well, George, I want you to take the part of the steerer and be in the turning joint scene when the shooting comes off, and the minor parts in the play. If you are satisfied to do this, I will arrange with Mr. Lederer to pay you $50 per week and expenses while on the road."*

*"All right, I will accept your offer at once," said I. . . .*

*The next morning at 9 a.m., I arrived at the Bijou Theatre and met [the theatrical manager] Dunlevy and all the actors who were to take a part in the play. I was handed my part in writing and we then began to rehearse each [of] our parts. At the end of the rehearsal I was told that I did fine and to always continue to do the same and make no change in my talk or actions in the future. We rehearsed morning and night for one week.*

*The play was produced at the People's Theatre on the Bowery for the first time after much advertising in the daily papers and my picture plastered on the bills of the dead walls of the city. On this first night of my appearance as an actor, I stood behind the scenes with an actor beside me who was told to prompt me so that I would make no mistake. When my turn came to go on the stage, he kept saying, "Watch your cue." All of a sudden he gave me a push between the two other actors, saying: "Introduce Holland & Hill." Now that was all unnecessary for him to do that and he came near causing me to slide in on the stage. Anyway, I controlled myself and as I appeared on the stage with the two Texans (Holland & Hill) I was given a great encore by the audience and the house was packed.*

*After the play was over, Mr. Lederer said to me: "George, you did splendid. I am satisfied." We played at the People's Theatre for one week and then went over to Broadway for another week's stand and played to a full house each night, and at the end of the week the show started on the road.[1]*

T HE LEXOW COMMITTEE was not the only institution offering Appo an alternative to his criminal career. The day after Appo's throat was slashed in the North River Hotel, the entertainment impresario George Lederer

*With his performance in* In the Tenderloin, *Appo's name was plastered on billboards all over the city.*

announced that Appo would appear in the opening of *In the Tenderloin*.[2] Appo's theatrical wizardry in the green goods game was about to move to the stage.

*In the Tenderloin* was a five-part melodrama. Beginning in front of the Hoffman House off Union Square, the production centers on the thief Jack Forsett, played by the well-known actor Frederic Bryton. Relying on slick manners and handsome looks, Forsett infiltrates genteel social circles under the alias Major Primrose and kidnaps the beautiful child of a wealthy businessman. Ensuing scenes depict various Tenderloin locales: John Daly's gambling house, the Thirtieth Street Police Station, and Tom Gould's Sans Souci. One act concludes inside a stage reproduction of Tom Davis's green goods joint, in which Appo appears twice to deliver five or six lines.

In the final act Forsett fails to seduce the country maiden Blanch. As he returns to his garret to kill the child, a fire breaks out, whereupon Carrots "the newsboy" runs in, grabs the child, and leaps out the window to safety on the stage below. The mother appears, presses the child to her breast, and the curtain falls.[3]

*The green goods scene in* In the Tenderloin.

Nineteenth-century melodrama generally avoided moral ambiguity, reducing social and political concerns to simple juxtapositions of good and evil. Invoking hyperbolic language, excessive emotions, and moral polarization, relationships were colored in black-and-white rather than shades of gray. Social problems were reduced to character flaws and stereotypical visions of complete goodness and extreme weakness. Virtue and superiority were equated, and love destroyed all barriers of rank. The hero saved the chaste, refined heroine from the evil villain who sought her seduction.[4]

*In the Tenderloin* superficially adhered to such a formula. Characters like the thief Jack Forsett and Carrots the newsboy embody total evil and complete goodness, respectively. When Forsett tries unsuccessfully to seduce Blanch, she spurns him in true melodramatic fashion: "I know you now, not only as a villain and a thief, but a destroyer of womanly virtue!" Like many melodramas *In the Tenderloin* treated common people seriously, wrestling with conflicts between good and evil while reflecting the hopes and fears of the time. Even critical reviewers like *Life*'s James Seymour Metcalfe described *In the Tenderloin* as "artistic" because "it was largely true" and vice was made "repulsive."[5]

But *In the Tenderloin* digressed from the melodramatic formula in a significant way, marking a controversial departure in New York theatrical history. George Appo, Edmund Price, and George Washington Lederer captured onstage the informal and overlapping relationships shared among the underworld, criminal law, and popular entertainment. *In the Tenderloin* introduced a level of authentic representation never before witnessed on the stage—real live convicts. The *World* described the production as "the finest collection of thugs, crooks and blacklegs ever corralled outside a State prison."[6] For the first time convicted felons were deliberately and openly showcased on stage. The moral nuance found in *In the Tenderloin* fused urban reality with sensational melodrama.[7]

George Washington Lederer was a well-known and controversial figure in 1894. By then he and his partner Thomas Canary managed the Casino, a beautiful twelve-year-old Moorish structure with a popular roof garden, and the Bijou Theater on Broadway. Historians generally identify Lederer as both a theatrical actor and manager, but he is best remembered as Lillian Russell's producer. During his lifetime he was hailed as the originator of the entertainment revue and the father of musical comedy. Like a number of other theatrical promoters, Lederer claimed (falsely) that he invented the word "vaudeville" for variety performances.[8]

Lederer's reputation was also marred by financial scandal. In 1887 while managing a traveling opera company, he secretly withdrew funds from a company account and left the Canadian city where they were playing. When the bank called in the debt, Lederer's partner was jailed. A year later, as the traveling manager for the Rentz-Santley Burlesque Company, Lederer overdrew another account, resulting in the arrest of the company's treasurer. Lederer allegedly "fixed" both cases and was never arrested. In 1893 a theatrical printing firm won a court judgment against Lederer for a $185 debt, which remained outstanding a year later.[9]

More controversial was Lederer's sexual philandering. In fact Lederer and Edmund Price first met in 1889 when Lederer was charged with bigamy and hired Price as his legal counsel. Price managed to have Lederer exonerated, but over the course of the ensuing two decades, Lederer married and divorced at least five different women. His many and varied marital problems and infidelities provided frequent copy for the theatrical press.[10]

Edmund E. Price was the product of a different brand of theater. Born in London in 1832, Price immigrated to the United States and enjoyed a prominent career as a boxer. At his peak the pugilist stood five feet ten inches and weighed between 150 and 165 pounds. On 1 May 1856 Price defeated Joe Coburn in what contemporaries believed was the longest fight up to that point—160 rounds and 200 minutes. After settling in Boston in the 1850s, he developed a reputation for modesty. The fighter made "no pretence whatever for any egotistical display," wrote one admirer. "He is simply 'Ed Price, all the way from London.'"[11]

Sometime after retiring from the ring, Price moved to New York City and became a noted criminal attorney. Working in the police courts during the 1870s, he became identified with an underworld clientele. In addition to representing George Appo in several court cases, Price defended a variety of Bowery saloonkeepers, brothel madams, opium-den proprietors, and concert hall owners; his clients included Billy McGlory and Tom Lee. Some considered Price to be one of the leading criminal attorneys in New York.[12]

While Price's defense of James Holland in 1885 was his most famous case, the attorney liked to portray himself as a defender of the underdog. In 1886 he complained about the injustices associated with the fee system in New York's criminal courts, charging that "unprincipled lawyers made a practice of feeing keepers for exercising their influence in their favor." Yet Price was probably guilty of the same. Several times he was accused of being a "shyster lawyer," and during the 1890s he was allegedly hired by leading brothel madams like Matilda Hermann to act as a go-between with police and Tammany Hall officials in the payments of bribes and protection money.[13]

But Price possessed artistic aspirations beyond the drama of Gotham's police courts. Described as "a good scholar, a facile linguist, and a complete master of the principal modern languages," Price published *The Science of Self Defence: A Treatise on Sparring and Wrestling* in 1867. Then, beginning in 1883, while working as a variety actor, he started writing plays. Over the ensuing decade he authored two comedies and at least five melodramas, two of which showcased the heavyweight boxing champion John L. Sullivan.[14]

With boxers and other celebrities attracting a growing theater patronage and the seating capacity of theaters doubling in the 1890s, presenting convicted felons on stage made economic sense to producers like Price and Lederer. Appo's lack of theatrical experience was hardly a deterrent. The success of Sullivan and other pugilists convinced Price and Lederer that fame (or infamy) was more important than theatrical talent. Appo was hardly Hamlet or Lear, they acknowledged, but his looks and language made him "the incarnation of the green-goods art."[15]

So on Thanksgiving Day 1894, *In the Tenderloin* opened at the Grand Opera House in New Haven. The production "seems to be the sort of play the Yale boys like," satirized the *Herald*. With "a thrill in every scene and murders at judicious intervals," he added that the collegians "went wild with delight." The other controversial performer, Tom Gould, received an enthusiastic greeting from the audience, including a floral horseshoe that was passed over the footlights to him. Appo received less applause, but the *Herald* concluded that "his name appears in the programme in just as black letters as Gould's, and that may be fame enough."[16]

After a two-week run at the Star Theater in Brooklyn, *In the Tenderloin* debuted in New York at Henry C. Miner's People's Theatre on the Bowery. Not only was People's one of the three largest theaters in New York, the playhouse attracted leading writers and actors. At first *In the Tenderloin* generated favorable reviews. One paper proclaimed it "a success, and it has come to stay." Even the amateurs onstage garnered compliments. "Gould did not have much to do, but what he did he did well, and the same may be said of Appo," wrote one critic.[17]

Tepid acceptance, however, quickly gave way to critical outrage. A variety of reviewers described the production as "useless," "a disgrace to the stage," and the "deepest depth of the degradation of drama." The presence of convicted felons onstage generated the most heated criticism. "If genuine dive-keepers, burglars, 'green goods' men and bruisers are to be exhibited on the stage, why not genuine bawds and murderers?" satirized one critic. "Why not have a man killed, say at every hundredth performance, instead of giving away souvenir spoons?" Even though Appo and Gould played themselves on stage, he pronounced them poor actors.[18]

Critics worried that *In the Tenderloin* reflected a new pattern in American popular culture. Several surmised that Lederer and Price were motivated by the need for large audiences and greater profits—to keep "the money-bags jingling," wrote one. Complaints about popular taste in Bowery theaters were commonplace throughout the nineteenth century, but the growing number of theatrical venues and the appearance of new immigrant-based forms of theater after 1890 evoked renewed concern. Not only did audiences vocalize their appreciation, but the cast of characters—anarchists, union organizers, Talmudic scholars, flamboyant actors, pious women with shawls, overworked shopkeepers, garment workers—bore little resemblance to middle-class America. Theatrical promoters increasingly mixed elements of melodrama, variety, and sensationalism. *In the Tenderloin* embodied such a production.[19]

Most important, *In the Tenderloin* represented a new entertainment genre, "freak drama" according to one critic. Like the border dramas and Wild West shows of Buffalo Bill, Texas Jack, and Pawnee Pete, which introduced authentic cowboys and Indians to the stage, theater producers resorted to a new form of profit-driven, sensational realism. Prominent bandits, train robbers, swindlers, and confidence men made stage appearances after 1890. The famed bank robbers Frank James and Cole Younger even sponsored their own traveling show. In 1899 Fayne Moore, an indicted opium-den proprietor, was released on bail from the Tombs in order to star in *King of the Opium Ring*. All this "marked a new era in stage realism," lamented the *World*.[20]

Freak dramas like *In the Tenderloin* transformed and redefined the meaning of "the criminal." Although Price portrayed the production as a melodrama, both the public and critics recognized that it was something different. Few paid any attention to the leading actor, Frederic Bryton. Instead critics and audiences directed their gaze to Appo and Gould. While each assumed the constructed roles of criminals on stage (and in real life, for that matter), they were not treated as melodramatic examples of evil. Now they were ambiguous characters. The sharp boundaries that divided the criminal from the noncriminal, the illegitimate from the legitimate, faded. Audiences now cheered for the villain. No longer a marginalized deviant, the convicted felon represented urbanity and modernity, city life in its paradoxical complexity. The criminal was now a celebrity.

The presence of Appo and Gould onstage introduced a level of moral relativism absent in conventional melodrama. Like twentieth-century portrayals of organized crime figures, the criminal was less a villain and more a hero. As convicts recast as theatrical luminaries, Appo and Gould participated in a new social construction of the criminal. Wittingly or not, they acted as agents in the fabrication of their own images.

*In the Tenderloin* appeared at a moment when interest in Gotham's criminal underworld was attracting increasing theatrical attention. During the 1880s and early 1890s productions like *Shadows of a Great City*, *The Dark Side of the Great City*, and *Sin and Its Shadows* were among the first New York stage performances explicitly to highlight underworld themes. In 1891 *A Trip to Chinatown* at Charles H. Hoyt's Madison Square Theater depicted various stereotypes of New York's Chinese underworld while including popular songs like "On the Bowery" and "Push Dem Clouds Away." The production played for more than three hundred performances, then the longest run in New York theatrical history. By offering a detailed, factual tour of Gotham's underworld milieu, *In the Tenderloin* went one step further. The trend continued into the next century as a variety of "Tenderloin" musical compositions and theatrical productions depicted a New York populated by prostitutes, pimps, gamblers, and other underworld characters.[21]

Price and Lederer recognized that such freak dramas enjoyed an appeal beyond New York. When *In the Tenderloin* traveled to Syracuse, Youngstown, Cincinnati, and Indianapolis, "hinterland" reviewers proved far more tolerant and less condescending than their New York counterparts. Indeed, the objects of outrage from Gotham's critics—the "low" audience of "floaters," the sensationalized realism of urban life, Price's criminal associations, the frank treatment of "vice"—were cited favorably. In Cincinnati newspapers reported that the performers played before standing-room-only crowds. Syracuse audiences gave the performers—especially Appo and Gould—boisterous receptions, allegedly because of the realism depicted onstage.[22]

Hyperbolic praise proved more common. "Nowhere in the history of modern melodrama has such an instantaneous success been achieved as that which greeted Mr. Edmund E. Price's latest realistic success," wrote the reviewer for the *Cincinnati Tribune*. The production's strengths were the reproduction of actual events, presented in genuine locations where they took place, "a facsimile of occurrences in the heart of New York." The characters played by Appo and Gould embodied an element of everyday life in New York. Rather than exalt moral turpitude, *In the Tenderloin* conveyed moral lessons and deserved the public's attention.[23]

The favorable reviews and approving audiences must have pleased Appo. Indeed, now he was famous. By the end of the year Appo was identified among the "People Who Made the History of 1894" in the *World*. He was even the subject of verse:

> George Appo, always getting thumped because he made his squeal;
> Depew, who on the Bowery stumped along with Ollie Teall.[24]

But managers Price and Lederer proved less impressed with Appo's bravura performance.

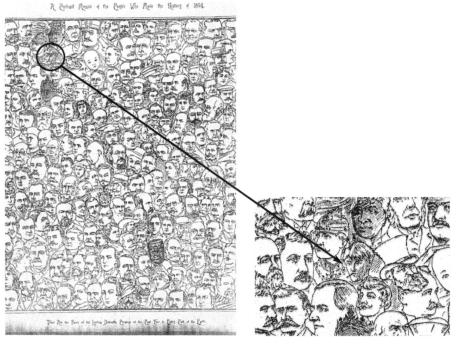

*The* World's *"A Portrait Mosaic of the People Who Made the History of 1894"
included George Appo in the upper left corner.*

◆ *The two first weeks I played at the London and Brooklyn The-
atres, I was paid my salary of $50 per week. But when we started on
the road, I never got one cent of my salary for three weeks, nor did
any of the others of the company get paid. Yet, we were drawing full
houses wherever we played and Lederer was making good sums of
money. When we disbanded at Indianapolis, and after much anxiety
and waiting, our hotel bill and railroad fare was paid and we were
told that our three weeks salary ($150) would be paid when we
arrived in New York City. . . .*

*When I arrived in New York, I went direct to the Bijou Theatre
to get my money and found two of the actors of the company there
ahead of me, waiting to see the treasurer for their money. I asked
them if they had been paid yet. "No! Nor do we expect to be paid a
cent. It seems to me that Lederer intends to do us all," said one of
the actors to me.*

*"Well," said I, "you as a professional actor can make him pay you
what he owes you for your labor by bringing him into court."*

*They both began to laugh at me and said: "Let me tell you some-
thing. There is not an actor in the business who has nerve enough
to make a complaint when he gets beat out of his salary. Every one
of us gets the worse end of it quite often and we dare not complain.
If we did, we would find attached beside our names in the books of
the dramatic agency a big 'K' which denotes 'Kicker.' When a company is being formed, the manager looking for actors to fill parts in
the play, and sees the big 'K' beside the name, that actor will never
get a date."*

*While he was telling me this, in walks the treasurer, bowing and
smiling, and said: "Well, gentlemen, what can I do for you?"*

*I said: "I was sent here by the manager, Mr. Dunlevy of the play*
In the Tenderloin *to be paid three weeks salary now due me
($150.00)."*

*"Oh, yes, you are George Appo. Well, Mr. Lederer is in the city
today and you come here tomorrow and I will let you have five dollars to see you through until then." He handed me five dollars and
a receipt for the same for me to sign. I signed it and went away.*

*As I got to the street, I met another actor of the company who
asked me if the treasurer was inside. I said: "Yes, and he paid me five
dollars."*

"Did you sign a receipt for the five dollars?"

"Yes, of course," said I.

"You were foolish to do so. Now you won't get another cent out of Lederer and no matter how hard you kick. He has the best of you for six years on that receipt," said the actor to me . . .

Such was my experience on the stage in my efforts to earn an honest living. I found that the system of cheating the actors out of their hard earned money was a common practice with such men as George W. Lederer who financially back the shows they take on the road. The poor actor dare not complain for fear of the loss of a future date with some other show. In fact, I tried time and again to see Lederer and obtain at least a portion of the money owed by him, but failed. I even consulted the lawyer, Edmund E. Price, who got me to sign the contract and take the part needed in the play. The only encouragement he gave me was: "I can't do nothing in the matter. Wait until you see Mr. Lederer and I guess he will settle up with you alright then."

So I got tired and disgusted in my efforts to connect with Lederer, and as I was completely without means of support and without a cent, I began to search high and low, so to speak, for employment of some kind, but failed.[25]

# 19

# A Marked Man

—

◦§ *The daily papers kept continually writing articles about me exposing the evil doings of the police and many other exaggerated lies about crooks being allowed by them to ply their crooked business with impunity by paying the police protection money. The consequences of all this newspaper talk made many bad and dangerous enemies for me, especially among my former associates and friendly acquaintances among the political ward heelers in the different parts of the city. The reporters would write and publish articles about me criticizing the high police officials and their administration and a lot of other things I never mentioned, that were lies from beginning to end. In fact, these same reporters I had never seen or met or talked with any person on the articles that were published. I mention this to show why I was assaulted so frequently by the police and others and forced to defend myself after the Ryan affair and the publications of the press.*[1]

*One day [9 April 1895], soon after the first article published about the police with my name signed to it, I was on the northeast corner of Sixth Avenue and 28th Street to meet an actor named Theodore Babcock.*[2] *When he appeared, I invited him to have a drink, and on entering the saloon, I noticed a young fellow whom I knew as a Haymarket "cadet" (pimp) standing in front of the side door of the saloon talking with an officer in uniform. I saw him nudge the policeman and point at me. As Babcock and me had our drinks placed before us, this young cadet came and stood beside Babcock and gave him a push, saying, "What's the matter, do you want the whole bar to yourself?" Of course, Babcock became surprised and indignant and the cadet struck him a violent blow in the face.*

*I immediately smashed the cadet and he clinched me. In a*

*moment, the policeman (Rein by name) rushed in from the side
door and struck me a violent blow on the head, splitting the scalp
open about three inches. I held on to the cadet and grabbed a glass
from the counter and struck him with it, and took all the fight out
of him. In the meantime, the officer kept hitting me on the back
and sides with his club. I managed to get my penknife out and
opened. In order to protect myself from the club, I rushed in on the
policeman and give him all he deserved. He laid on the sidewalk
after he sneaked out of the saloon.*

    *I remained there and two other policemen came and locked me
up after the doctor sewed up the wound on my head. My sides were
bruised and painful from the beating I received. The next morning
I was brought to court and charged with felonious assault and held
for the grand jury under $500 bail. When my case was called to
plead to my indictment, I was forced to plead guilty <u>in self-defense</u>
before Judge [Rufus B.] Cowing who presided at the General Sessions Court. I was sentenced to a term of six months in the Penitentiary, Blackwell's Island.*[3]

Ｇ EORGE APPO SAT in the Jefferson Market Courthouse on 9 April 1895,
waiting for his hearing in the assault of police officer Michael J. Rein. In
walked James McNally. For the first time since Appo began cooperating
with the Lexow Committee, the former green goods associates stood
face-to-face. McNally had just returned from Europe the previous day.
"There you are, you ———," sneered McNally. "I [knew] that's where
you would end up, you ——— ——— squealer you."

    McNally's sudden appearance stunned Appo. But he quickly realized
what was happening. "I know who's at the bottom of this," he bellowed.
"You have put up this job for me, but I'll show this conspiracy up."
Moments later an indolent Appo testified in court that the charges were
fabricated, part of a nefarious plot by McNally and the police "to get me
out of the way." McNally, Appo swore, intended to kill him.[4]

    George Appo was hardly the only cooperative witness before the
Lexow Committee. Police captain Timothy Creeden acknowledged that
he paid fifteen thousand dollars for his promotion to captain, the money
originating from "backers" later reimbursed by extorting various busi-
nesses in the precinct. Police captain Max Schmittberger confessed to
the widespread use of bribery and extortion of brothel keepers and oth-

ers in the underground economy. Concert saloon impresario Harry Hill described how Capt. Michael Murphy demanded an initiation fee of eight hundred dollars and monthly payments of fifty dollars during the 1880s. In 1890, when Murphy upped the ante to one thousand dollars, Hill refused and was forced to close.[5]

Nor was Appo alone in suffering police harassment. Charles Krumm, the proprietor of Krumm's Concert Hall on Christie Street, complained that the police hounded him after he testified. "They have given no rest to me for telling the truth," complained Krumm. That was in 1899, five years after his testimony.[6]

None, however, was punished like Appo. The madam Mathilda Her-mann was intimidated and briefly arrested for allegedly breaking a brothel door in May 1895. Charles Priem, the first brothel owner to testify, was found dead in a furnished room in April 1895, but his passing was never directly connected to his Lexow testimony. Even Schmittberger remained on the police force and was later promoted to chief inspector.[7]

Appo's confrontation with Rein was but one of at least six such assaults on Appo in the ten months following his Lexow testimony. "I was hounded by some of the old-time detectives under Chief Byrnes and [Police Chief] Devery's administration," he charged, "who feared I knew too much about their crooked dealings with the 'sure thing grafters.' " Appo became "a veritable Ishmaelite [sic]," according to the writer Louis Beck, hated by the green goods fraternity and viewed with suspicion by law-abiding citizens. Two days after his testimony, Appo learned from McNally's chief assistant that McNally and Ryan had hired two men to kill him.[8]

Appo appeared to be an easy target. Less than five feet four inches in height, the former convict weighed under 120 pounds, hardly a physically intimidating opponent. When Appo spoke, his soft, high voice was barely louder than a whisper. He was deaf in the left ear, and the hearing in his right was badly impaired. Appo's body displayed visible reminders of his many confrontations. In addition to the loss of his right eye, a bad wound was visible over his right eye. Michael Riordan's attempt to slit Appo's throat left a long scar on his throat and the left side of his neck. Reportedly sixteen other scars marked his body.[9]

Appo's alienation from McNally and his decision to cooperate with the Lexow Committee were motivated in part by revenge. Appo believed that on his recovery from his injuries in Poughkeepsie, his green goods employer blacklisted him from working in the green goods business. "McNally would do me all the injury he could to stop me from getting and living," charged Appo.[10]

A second motivation was Appo's belief that McNally abandoned him. After his successful appeal and release from prison in 1894, Appo wanted help. He called on McNally, believing that after four to five years of loyal service—during which time McNally earned five hundred thousand dollars—he deserved some financial support. Appo met McNally's chief assistant in Bridgeport, Connecticut, and was informed that McNally was out of town. After waiting five days, Appo discovered McNally was hiding. Appo finally cornered McNally, who immediately promised to help him. "I will see you to-morrow in New York at 12 p.m. sharp at Roach's Corner, 38th Street and 7th Avenue, and fix you up alright," promised McNally. He never appeared.[11]

Appo even suspected that McNally set him up. Before the Lexow Committee Appo suggested that Cassel and Hogshead were "dummy come-ons," part of a "put-up job" designed to kill Appo because of an earlier argument with McNally. Remembering that James Holland had been acquitted for a similar crime against green goods dealer Tom Davis in 1885, Appo surmised that McNally thought he had little to lose.[12]

But Appo's resentment was more than just personal. By 1894 he openly disdained green goods backers. Such individuals, he charged, were "not willing to take a chance such as are taken by pickpockets or a burglar." Men like McNally were little more than pimps "who live off the shame of women." Worse, they worked in conjunction with the police, serving as "stool pigeons for the Central Office."[13] Such "capitalists" in Appo's mind failed to adhere to the unwritten code of the good fellow; they, not he, were traitors to their class.

Appo, however, paid a price for his anger—his life was now in danger. The indictment hearing revealed that individuals were actively conspiring to kill Appo. Police officer Michael Rein charged Appo with stabbing him while placing him under arrest for creating a disturbance. Under cross-examination, however, Appo's counsel, Frank Moss, challenged the veracity of Rein's story and the media's coverage of the event. The officer testified that after the confrontation with Appo, he returned to the precinct house, undressed, and slept in the station that evening. Only the next day, he admitted, did he bother to notice the stab wound.[14]

Appo was indeed cooperating with the Lexow Committee. Not only was he represented by Frank Moss, but his five-hundred-dollar bond was furnished by Mary F. Sallade, a prominent figure in moral reform circles in New York and sometimes called "the female Parkhurst." Such encouragement bolstered Appo. He insisted that "no matter what the police tried they could not again drive him into the ranks of crooks." Psychologically and emotionally liberated, Appo defended his Lexow testimony. "I was no longer ashamed to walk the streets and no longer afraid of the police. . . . Beat me, starve me, do as they like, I'm going to be honest." In Appo's words, he felt like "a new man."[15]

Not completely. A week later Appo failed to appear for his trial, thus forfeiting Sallade's bond. Appo later defended his flight as self-defense. On the day of his release, Appo was assaulted by two unknown men on West Seventeenth Street, just off Seventh Avenue. "I was struck in the head and cut with some weapon, but through fear of my life, I did not complain," he later explained. Instead Appo fled to Albany and then Buffalo. Parkhurst believed that Appo was singled out because his testimony was "too truthful to be palatable."[16]

In Buffalo, Appo ran into a green goods operator. Fearing for his life, he absconded to Toronto. Working under the alias George Waring, Appo must have resorted to his connections from his brief acting career, joining a theatrical company called "The Derby Mascot." In Montreal, to Appo's chagrin, the company disbanded. "I was left without a dollar," he later reported. Appo telegraphed Sallade, begging her for money to purchase a train ticket and promising to return to New York. When she refused, Appo somehow made his way to Buffalo, where he met a New York Central Railroad detective from whom he obtained a pass to New York.[17]

On 30 September 1895 Appo appeared before Judge Rufus Cowing and pleaded guilty. Cowing was probably the most sympathetic magistrate Appo could have faced. The fifty-five-year-old Harvard Law graduate was the sole Republican serving on the state bench in New York City and possessed a well-known independent streak. In national and state elections, Cowing had maintained his Republican Party affiliation but remained bipartisan in city politics; from 1879 to 1906 he was a judicial candidate on both the Republican and Democratic tickets. Cowing was also respected by judicial reformers. During the 1890s he repeatedly tried to eliminate pigeonholed indictments by requiring the district attorney to deposit all indictments with the clerk of the Court of General Sessions and opening them to the public.[18]

Standing before Cowing, Appo affirmed his innocence. "I'm here simply because I was a witness before the Lexow Committee and not because I assaulted Policeman Rein," he charged. Two years earlier when green goods operators James McNally and Mike Ryan were in business, "No policeman would have dared to lay a finger on me," insisted Appo. Cowing must have believed him; he sentenced Appo to only six months in the penitentiary.[19]

Judge Rufus Cowing.

    *My time expired [5 April 1896] and I was roaming about the city in search for some honest employment.[20] I accidently met the policeman Rein on Sixth Avenue and 29th Street in citizen's clothes. He greeted me with: "Hello there! When did you come out?"*

*I replied, "About 8 days ago."*

*Then said he: "Do you know, I felt d—— sorry after you got 'settled' (sentenced). If I knew as much then as I do now, that trouble between us never would have happened."*

*I replied: "Well, it's all over now, but you were to blame and you ought not to have paid any attention to that pimp from the Haymarket who pointed me out to you in order to curry favor of you, for himself and his girl."*

*"Let us have a drink. I want to have a talk with you," said he.*

*"No thank you, I'm not drinking anything. I am on some business now and will see you again. Good bye," said I, and walked away and never saw him again.*

*In the meantime, I tried to get some work to do and after about six weeks search, I gave it up and through necessity, I began to drift back to my former crooked life and to associate with some of my former acquaintances, who nevertheless were seemingly afraid to be seen in my company for fear of being put down as a squealer by the police.*

*One morning [10 July 1896], about three months after my release from the Penitentiary, I was on the corner of Mott Street to meet a friend by appointment. Not seeing him around, I entered the saloon on the corner of Mott Street and Chatham Square, thinking he* might be there, but he was not in. After buying a drink and a cigar, I said to the bartender: "Eddie, did you see Frank Tuttle around this morning?" This bartender, Eddie Erwin by name, gave me an ugly, sneering look and with a filthy remark, told me to take a sneak out of the place.

I was surprised at his ugly disposition as we were always on friendly terms. I said: "Why, Eddie! What is the matter? Are you mad at me? Explain why?"

He snatched up a bottle from the back counter and said to me: "If you don't get out, I'll knock your brains out with this."

I laughed at him and said, "You better not try it." I left the saloon by the side door and took a seat on the iron railing just outside to the left of the side entrance of the saloon. I had just seated myself and [was] about to read the paper when the side door opened and Erwin rushed at me and struck me a violent blow on top of my head with a blackjack. I jumped for him as he ran into [the] side entrance, but was stopped and grabbed by the throat by a ward heeler, named [John] Atwood. I took a tight hold of him and got my penknife out and cut him badly in self-defense, but before he let go [of] my throat and fell, I was struck on the head by a policeman named Stephen Loughman.

My scalp was sewed up, [and] I was pushed violently into a cell by the policeman Loughman, who said to me after closing the cell door: "Your hash will be cooked up well this time, d—— you." I remained in the cell without food all that day and night and [was] then taken to police court and held to await the results of Atwood's injury. I was informed that the bartender Erwin had three manufactured witnesses beside himself to swear falsely that I was drunk and cut Atwood for no provocation whatsoever. When my case was called for trial, there was the five men sitting together on the front bench in the courtroom ready to take the witness stand to commit perjury. These men were all friends and associates of Erwin's and were not even in the neighborhood at the time of the assault on me. I was personally acquainted with two of these witnesses, their names were Mike Walsh and [?] Hartigan. Both of them were bartenders by occupation.

At the time I was brought into court, I was still suffering from the two blows I received on the head by Erwin and the policeman goods operatives. Purdy recognized that success as a defense attorney necessitated frequent and sensational publicity. On one occasion a client was accused of drugging and robbing an acquaintance. When the prosecution charged that the vials in question contained chloral hydrate—"knock-out drops" in common parlance—Purdy jumped up. "Nonsense," he thundered. "Please give me that bottle. It wouldn't kill a child." Purdy promptly swallowed the contents. His audacity, however, got the better of him; Purdy fell unconscious in seconds. He remained bedridden for a week after physicians pumped the drug out of him.[27]

Purdy viewed himself as a reformer, allying himself with Charles Parkhurst and the City Vigilance League in 1894. Most likely, he met Appo through this relationship; in 1895 Purdy briefly served as Appo's counsel when he was arrested for assaulting policeman Rein. When Appo was accused of stabbing Atwood in 1896, Purdy again came to his defense.[28]

Purdy's goal was simple—to have the court declare Appo insane. By the 1890s judicial reformers were increasingly critical of the absence of careful mental and physical examinations of convicted felons prior to sentencing. At the same time theories of "hereditary transmission" of insanity and "congenital" criminal behavior were gaining popularity in the medical community. In certain respects Appo fit such psychiatric models: the offspring of interracial marriage, juvenile delinquency, adult criminal conduct, opium addiction, a drunken and dissipated lifestyle, and a life of "moral degradation." Purdy exploited these stereotypes.[29]

Appo presented his version of the events before the Commissioners of Charities and Correction on 6 October 1896. He traced the origins of the assault to his release from the Blackwell's Island Penitentiary in April 1896. At that point Appo approached John Goff, Rufus Cowing, and other Lexow Committee reformers, begging them to help him find employment. They ignored his pleas. At the same time Appo's former underworld associates not only considered him an informer but wanted him dead. Appo, in his words, was "a marked man."[30]

Furthermore, two days prior to the controversial events, on 8 July 1896, two detectives noticed him standing at Bayard and the Bowery. One said, "There's that Appo, the son of a bitch." They crossed the street, entered a saloon, and continued their surveillance of him. A short time later an acquaintance approached Appo, warning that the two detectives "are going to do you." He immediately fled. Appo then recounted a series of meetings, including one with a friend who urged him to avoid Erwin's saloon.

The veracity of Appo's testimony, however, was undermined by his own counsel. As Appo provided a detailed day-by-day account of the events culminating in the assault, Purdy interrupted: "That is all. I am through," he pronounced. "You see, doctor, he is wandering."[31] Appo, Purdy insisted, was insane, and should be transferred to a hospital.

But was George Appo insane? Some of his earlier behavior confirmed such suspicions. In 1877, for example, Appo reportedly attempted suicide during his transfer from Sing Sing to Clinton. Five years later, after being sentenced to three and a half years in Sing Sing, Appo made two more attempts on his life. While being escorted out of the Tombs courtroom, he suddenly pulled a vial of opium from his pocket and emptied the contents into his mouth. When that failed Appo was ushered outside, where he tried to throw himself under the wheels of a passing truck. After reaching his cell, he was strapped into a straitjacket and forced to take an emetic to counter the effects of the opium. The pills soon ran out, and Appo "howled until he had all the officers and inmates of the Tombs nearly as crazy as himself," claimed one reporter.[32]

A decade later, after his conviction in Poughkeepsie, Appo displayed similar suicidal tendencies. Before being sent off to Clinton, he kissed his wife good-bye, urged her to return to New York with their child, and promised that "my body will follow right away. . . . I am determined to kill myself." Other reports charged that he made four unsuccessful suicide attempts after his Poughkeepsie conviction.[33]

Intermittent reports of Appo's insanity appeared after his release. When his throat was slashed by Michael Riordan in 1894, initial press accounts portrayed the event as an attempted suicide. Even when that version was refuted, newspapers described Appo as "raving like a madman." He acknowledged on several occasions that the pressure and fear of assault were unbearable. "This persistent hounding [by police and criminals] has driven me nearly crazy and I have frequently been tempted to do something desperate," he told one reporter. "Life is worth nothing to me." Appo believed that he was without friends or assistance. As his case for assaulting Michael Rein came up, Appo lamented, "I wish to God I had died when I was shot in Poughkeepsie."[34]

Even supporters suspected Appo's psychological health. The superintendent of the Society for the Prevention of Crime speculated that Appo was mentally impaired. "You are probably aware that he has been shot in the head, and the bullet still remains in his brain," he wrote to Judge Cowing in 1895. "In consequence of this I do not think he is quite right in his head."[35]

Numerous law enforcement officials reached similar conclusions. Tombs keepers reported that Appo displayed more characteristics of mental deterioration than during his previous incarcerations. Bellevue physicians and others concurred, concluding that Appo was suffering from multiple ailments: tuberculosis, inflammation of the brain, tubercular meningitis, tubercular enteritis, and consumption of the intestines. The latter disease, one predicted, would be mortal. George Appo, reported the *Sun*, "is dying."[36]

Appo's own words gave these observations, however ill informed, legitimacy. "Look at me," he later testified. "I have twenty scars on me from police clubs for nothing at all. Give me a knife, doctor and I will prove it, just because I exposed these scoundrels who live off the shame of women. I don't care for life and to prove it I am willing to lay right down here and let you cut that bullet out of my head."[37]

Insanity pleas served multiple purposes in late-nineteenth-century New York. For some criminal attorneys they were a last-ditch resort to keep a client out of state prison. In 1890 a former Ward's Island Insane Asylum keeper testified that numerous inmates under his watch were sane. They were declared insane by error or as a punishment by prison authorities at other institutions. On the other hand, state officials acknowledged that insanity pleas were sometimes an effective form of punishment. When Sing Sing inmate Edward Meredith threatened to reveal the corruption among prison officials in 1888, prison physician Hiram Barber declared the inmate insane and had him transferred to Auburn and then Matteawan. In 1893 attorney Linwood Pratt alleged that anyone knowledgeable about prison management practices was likely to be sent to an insane asylum. In 1895 Appo's green goods accomplice William Vosburg tried to be declared insane to avoid a long sentence, a ploy rejected by the judge.[38]

Such abuses were commonplace because no state licensing of psychiatrists existed in New York before 1930. During murder and other high-profile trials, so-called experts testified to advance their theories and "fanciful conclusions," complained one observer. "The public is confused, the juries are misled, and courts become disgusted with the spectacle," concluded one state investigation. Others described such expert testimony as little more than "a burlesque."[39]

Dr. Joseph F. Terriberry, an expert on nervous diseases at the Manhattan Eye and Ear Hospital, provided scientific support that Appo was insane. The physician described Appo as emaciated and concluded that his version of the assault was unsubstantiated. Terriberry doubted that the bullet in Appo's head or his opium addiction was the cause of any mental illness. Rather, Appo's weakened mental state was hereditary, "a form of mental derangement known as Monamania [sic] of the type called persecutive." Terriberry even questioned Appo's testimony that Riordan tried to poison him because Appo provided no physical evidence. Appo was delusional, concluded Terriberry: "He imagines persecutions which do not exist."[40]

But Terriberry's prognosis also revealed the subjectivity of psychological evaluations in the 1890s. Terriberry provided a list of factors he believed confirmed the defendant's mental illness: Appo's willingness to defend picking pockets, his refusal to worship in church, his lack of any formal education, his misunderstanding that the court stenographer was a newspaper reporter, his many years in prison. When asked if he was insane, Appo replied only "when somebody hits me or abuses me." Terriberry concluded that all this proved that Appo was insane.[41]

In reality, Appo was depressed and terrified. His earlier suicide attempts reflected the fear and anxiety associated with incarceration, not mental illness. At one point, Appo regretted his decision to confront his former criminal employers. After being warned to abandon New York, he said, "If I had taken this warning, left the city and gone to some other place under another name, I could have been happy with my wife."[42] Instead she had left him, in part because the many physical assaults posed a threat to her personal safety. The succession of violent encounters following Appo's Lexow testimony more than just humbled and humiliated him; they destroyed his life.

Furthermore the forces that determined a felon's sanity were subject to the corruption and bribery that characterized other parts of New York's criminal justice system. Most likely Ambrose Purdy bribed the Bellevue officials, who were known to engage in questionable practices. Prior to 1901, for example, city examiners at Bellevue charged private fees for evaluating those held for examination. Supreme Court judges customarily signed commitments without any inquiry about the recommendation of two qualified examiners in lunacy. Under such conditions, admitted one public charities commissioner, sane persons were "railroaded" through Bellevue to insane asylums. Even after examination, clinical histories of patients were rarely, if ever, kept. Indeed, no record of Appo's mental health examinations exists today.[43]

In Appo's case the pseudoscience of late-nineteenth-century psychology won the argument. On 23 December 1896 Judge Martin T. McMahon declared Appo legally insane, one of only two arrests in New York City to earn such a distinction that year. Appo thus became one of the first individuals subjected to the principles of Progressive Era criminology, namely a psychological examination before sentencing. The very month of the Atwood incident (July 1896), New York penal institutions were, for the first time, required to have convicts examined by two legally qualified "examiners of lunacy" unaffiliated with a state penal institution.

*George Appo after 1894.*

If the individual was "certifiably insane," judges were empowered to send the indicted but unconvicted individual to the Matteawan State Hospital for the Criminally Insane.[44]

George Appo entered Matteawan on Christmas Eve of 1896. Abandoned by both friend and foe, he now sought sanctuary in an insane asylum. Within a short time one observer claimed that he was "a hopeless wreck."[45]

# 20

# Buried Alive

## =

→ *On my arrival at this institution [Matteawan State Hospital for the Criminally Insane], I was brought into the private office of Superintendent Dr. Henry E. Allison, who began to examine me and try to find out what my insane delusions were. Whatever his conclusions were about my mental condition, I do not know.*

*I was then taken to what is known as the Court Patients Ward. My good clothes were taken from me, [I was] given a bath and then a regulation hospital suit of clothes was handed to me by one of the attendants who stood and watched me very closely as I put them on. He then said: "Now go in the ward and sit down and rest yourself." I then stepped from the bathroom into the ward and took the first vacant chair I saw and sat down. I began to watch the actions of the poor, unfortunate, insane men who were walking up and down the floor, some of them singing hymns and others talking loudly to themselves and gesticulating to imaginary foes.*

*When I had been seated about 20 minutes, one of the patients came and took a seat beside me and said: "I guess you don't remember me, George. I used to work in the stove foundry when you were runner for Paddy Mackin, the 'screw' (keeper) at Sing Sing. That is many years ago. My name is Jimmie Reilly. You know me, don't you?"*

*"Oh, yes, I remember you well. You had a ten year bit (sentence). How long have you been here in this place?" I asked.*

*"About seven years or more, and I guess I'll never get out of this rat hole."*

*"Why, you look well and all right mentally. If your time has expired, I don't see why the doctors hold you here."*

*He suddenly jumped from the seat and began to shout out his insane delusions about the doctors and judges conspiring against him and warning me to look out for all kinds of danger. He then began to walk rapidly up and down the ward floor, laughing to himself and shaking his finger at the attendant who was watching him closely. I mention this incident, as it was my first day's experience in an insane ward with a patient whom I really believed at first was as sane as a judge, so to speak. I never was more surprised to see how mistaken I was. After that, I was always very careful when a patient came to talk with me, to humor him. . . .*

*Every morning the same doctor [Robert B. Lamb] with the supervisor and his attendants would visit the ward and as they stepped into the ward, the same order would be called out, "Seats!" When every patient would be seated, the doctor would make his rounds and view every patient as he passed them. Should a patient attempt to talk or complain to the doctor, the attendant would stop him.*

*When I had been there about three weeks, I was surprised, one afternoon, by my unfortunate father entering the ward and walking over to where I was seated, reading a book. He sat down on the next chair to me and began to talk very sensible and sane for about half an hour. Suddenly, I noticed a change in his actions and talk. He began to spring his insane delusions about his great wealth, and that he was the Commander of the Laws of Nature and was going to blow up all the prisons and with his army exterminate all keepers and doctors in them. I began to humor him, and in a few minutes he became normal and sensible in his talk once more. He then left the ward to attend to his work in the Imbecile Ward, where he acted in the capacity as nurse to poor, helpless patients unable to control themselves or leave their beds or chairs when necessary.[1]*

QUIMBO APPO'S manslaughter conviction for killing Mary Fletcher in 1859 destroyed his life in more ways than one. By some measures he never recovered. In 1869, more than a decade after the traumatic event, Quimbo Appo was released from Sing Sing. The elder Appo's activities over the next two years remain difficult to trace and full of contradictory evidence. Some accounts claimed that Appo moved to a Donovan's Lane tenement with other Chinese immigrants and became intimately involved with Kate Burke, a woman described in press accounts as "notorious" and a "common woman." Shortly thereafter Quimbo assaulted and beat one of Burke's other "lovers" but went unpunished. Another claimed that after his release, Appo lived on Cherry Street, where he quarreled with and accidentally killed a woman named Lizzie Williams. He was incarcerated in the Tombs, but released without trial after a year. By 1871, wrote another, Quimbo Appo's "children were so scattered that he never looked for them, and his only luxury was whiskey, rye, or bourbon."[2]

George Appo, however, had a considerably different memory. The younger Appo remembered that when he was twelve years old, "I first met or knew I had a father living." George believed that his father briefly worked as a tea tester while they resided together in a Park Street rooming house kept by a Mrs. McNamara, the wife of a policeman, just around the corner from Donovan's Lane. Other accounts claimed that the elder Appo was briefly employed as a cigar seller and a candy store proprietor.[3]

In any event Quimbo Appo had another confrontation shortly after. On 9 August 1871 he was arrested for assaulting Joseph Linkonski, a shoemaker working at 14 Baxter Street. Appo reportedly hit Linkonski with a stone, hospitalizing him for nearly two months. Hospital surgeons initially believed that Linkonski's condition was hopeless, so Appo sat in the Tombs for more than four months before finally going to trial. Linkonski, however, recovered, and Appo's trial ended in a hung jury.[4]

The verdict hardly discouraged legal authorities, who immediately reindicted Appo. This time prosecutors lowered the charge from an assault with the intent to kill to assault with a dangerous weapon. Prosecutors were even more vigilant, as one prosecutor described Appo as "a bad, reckless, bloody man." The strategy worked. Not only was Quimbo Appo convicted but Judge Gunning S. Bedford imposed the maximum sentence—five years in prison. On 5 January 1872 Quimbo Appo returned to Sing Sing.[5]

This time Sing Sing literally drove Appo insane. Most likely the harsh conditions simply overwhelmed the fifty-year-old man, and he suffered a mental breakdown. On 24 May 1875 prison officials removed Appo from Sing Sing, transferring him to the insane asylum at Auburn prison. No record exists of Appo's treatment for his two-and-one-half months in Auburn, except that he earned seventeen days of commutation for good behavior. Appo's conduct in prison must have been exemplary—his sentence was reduced by one year and three months before his release from Auburn on 7 August 1875.[6]

Appo quickly fell afoul of the law again, and again and again. Less than two months out of prison, Appo was charged with brutally beating the German-born wife of a Chinese man while she was walking along Baxter Street. For that he was sentenced to six months in the penitentiary. For reasons not evident in existing records, Appo was released early on 1 January 1876. Less than a month later, on 30 January 1876, Quimbo was in a fight with Hyman Bernstein, which resulted in another six-month sentence to Blackwell's Island.[7]

In October 1876 Quimbo committed his final assault. At the time he was allegedly out on bail and charged with defrauding the federal government through the illegal sale of unstamped cigars. While playing checkers in a Chatham Street lodging house, Appo and his opponent, John Kelly, began arguing. The confrontation escalated, and the assailants physically struggled with each other, literally rolling from the third to the first floor. Appo suddenly drew a knife and stabbed Kelly twice. The first blow inflicted only a flesh wound, but the second struck his heart.[8]

Quimbo defended his assault as self-defense. After he beat Kelly and several others at checkers, Appo claimed, Kelly "cursed him outrageously." Indeed, one witness acknowledged that Kelly struck Appo several times, even though Appo retreated and the witness tried to hold Kelly back. Appo pointed to the bruises over his left eye and on his leg as evidence.[9]

By this time, however, it was probably impossible for Appo to receive a fair trial. Numerous reports demonized the Chinese immigrant. Appo was described as "one of the most notorious criminals known to the Police," and "as fit to be at large as the Bengal tiger of a menagerie." Not only did Appo display "an insatiable craving for blood," charged the writer Louis Beck, but he "was a veritable Caliban, dead to all human emotions."[10]

More revealingly, observers fabricated a mythical biography emphasizing Quimbo's "inherent" viciousness. The details of the Fletcher incident in 1859, for example, were literally transformed into fiction. Various reports erroneously described Mary Fletcher as an Englishwoman, Quimbo's wife, and even his mistress. Others believed the incident occurred in 1857, in 1875, and on St. Patrick's Day. Fletcher's death was transformed into four murders in one report; others attributed three murders to Appo between 1863 and 1867. Reporters conveniently ignored the fact that Quimbo Appo was in Sing Sing during these years.[11]

During his trial before Judge Henry A. Gildersleeve, Quimbo was represented by attorney William F. Howe. It did little good; Appo was convicted of second-degree manslaughter and sentenced to seven years in prison. Leaving the courtroom, Appo vented his feelings toward Gildersleeve, the prosecutor, and the jury, swearing revenge and "uttering the most horrible oaths," according to one witness. On 22 December 1876 Quimbo Appo was back in Sing Sing.[12]

But not for long. Within weeks after Quimbo Appo entered Sing Sing, his twenty-year-old son was sentenced to his first term in Sing Sing on 9 January 1877. The judge was none other than Henry A. Gildersleeve. The family reunion in Sing Sing, however, proved short. On 30 January 1877, Quimbo Appo was transferred to Auburn prison. A year later, on 5 January 1878, Auburn medical officials concluded that Appo suffered from a variety of ongoing and seemingly permanent delusions. He was admitted to Auburn Prison State Hospital for the Criminally Insane.[13]

Asylum officials treated Appo in accordance with the new science of criminal anthropology developed by Caesar Lombroso. The founder of a hotly disputed school of criminology, Lombroso believed criminal behavior was hereditary, that criminals could be identified by distinctive physical features: large jaws, high cheekbones, handle-shaped ears, dark skin, low brows, and small heads. Congenital criminality was exhibited by insensitivity to pain, tattooing, excessive idleness, excellent eyesight, and "love of orgies." Grounding his pseudoscience in evolutionary theory, Lombroso posited that the criminal mind was comparatively undeveloped and childlike.[14]

Although Appo entered the Auburn asylum less than two years after the publication of Lombroso's *Criminal Man* (1876), medical evaluations of Appo reflected the rapid spread of Lombrosian criminal theory. At one point a "cephalometrical chart"—used to determine the ratio of the maximum width to the maximum length of the skull—included twenty-four different measurements of Appo's head. He was described as poorly educated, possessing inferior intelligence, and childlike. His short stature, "great bodily vigor," and "Mongolian" characteristics convinced medical experts that Appo was an ideal representation of Lombroso's born criminal.[15]

Appo's delusions were of greater concern for asylum officials. He attributed his violent behavior to various "spirits and 'ciples' (deciples) [*sic*]." Appo's frequent escapes from capital punishment convinced him that no one could kill or seriously injure him. By 1878 his fantasies grew more vague and wider in scope, many of them identifying political parties as the source of his problems: the "doctors' party," "Abe Lincoln's Party," the "Superintendents' Party." Appo described himself as "ready to die at any time," confident that he was going to heaven.[16]

On 14 August 1880 Appo learned of George Appo's arrest for the attempted murder of Jack Collins. Quimbo blamed his son's misfortune on the asylum superintendent. In protest he spit on some apples on a table and encouraged his fellow patients to do the same. Appo was immediately placed in seclusion, whereupon he staged a one-day food strike. When he remained verbally belligerent, officials isolated Appo for another six weeks.[17]

This proved to be a significant event. Before his forced seclusion Appo was described as a model patient and generally good-natured. Thereafter Appo grew ever more disruptive and verbally abusive. On 29 October 1880 "he became very noisy, cursing and swearing in such a manner as to disturb the whole ward," according to one report. After a physical struggle with attendants, Appo was injected with a sedative. Two months later, on Christmas Day, he assaulted another patient. By 1882 officials frequently commented on his violent temper, leading to his strict confinement in the ward.[18]

The use of seclusion as a method of punishment reflected how the Auburn asylum was a hospital in name only. Nineteenth-century insane asylums were noted for "hospitalizing" patients—"the insane were all alike and should all lead the same life," in the words of one critic. Patients resided on a single corridor or an open ward. There all activities took place: sitting, reading, working, exercise, and eating. The result was a deadly, monotonous existence, "such as might well drive a sane man mad," wrote one.[19]

The event that most often precipitated Appo's violent outbursts was a defeat in a game of cards or checkers. At different times, they noted that Appo became "irritable," "abusive," and swore at various political parties whenever he lost. Just as a game of checkers generated his fatal confrontation with John Kelly in 1876, the same activities provoked violent reactions from Appo throughout his asylum incarceration.[20]

More significantly Appo never left the confines of state incarceration. When his term expired in December 1883, he remained in the Auburn asylum. Patients like Appo, "insane and belonging to the criminal class," argued state lunacy commissioners Stephen Smith and Carlos MacDonald, were retained at Auburn as long as they required care. Mentally ill patients were, legally speaking, no longer convicts when their sentences expired, but they nevertheless warranted incarceration. Appo and other asylum patients challenged their detentions but to no avail. By 1900 Matteawan detained nearly three hundred such men with expired terms.[21] Here was a new form of custodial care—those deemed "criminally insane" remained indefinitely detained by the state.

Appo grew ever more delusional over the next several years. Among other things he declared that dead persons passed through his body before going to their final destination, adding that former presidents Grant and Garfield had undergone the experience. At various times he claimed ownership of Madison Square Garden and various hotels in New York. He was, in his words, "the first Chinaman that ever came to America," the emperor of China, and the "King of the World." Combined with his threats of violence and the occasional assaults on attendants and patients, officials were convinced that Quimbo Appo was too dangerous to be released. When Matteawan opened in 1892, Appo was transferred to the new facility.[22]

I F GEORGE APPO had any doubts about his father's mental illness, their early encounters in Matteawan convinced him otherwise. George quickly realized that his father generally talked sensibly, only to claim, suddenly and without warning, that he possessed great wealth, commanded the "laws of nature," and controlled an army that was going to blow up all prisons. Yet Quimbo Appo's delusions displayed a distinctive fatherly pride in his son. In 1898 Quimbo declared that his son was "a very wealthy man and has the *entré* to the most elegant society." In later years Quimbo bragged that George was president of the United States.[23]

Ironically, the two years and six months Quimbo and George Appo resided together in Matteawan represented their longest shared residence since George's very early childhood. Although Quimbo was frequently confined to the infirmary suffering from hip pain and rheumatism, officials allowed him frequent visits to his son in ward number two. Quimbo reportedly believed that George was in Matteawan to ensure that his father received proper care. When George later left the facility, Quimbo grew more quarrelsome and irritable, making it "impossible for him to get along with any of the other patients," according to doctors' reports.[24]

Quimbo Appo's condition was exacerbated by state policies. Under the old law improved or "harmless" patients were discharged into the custody of the various county superintendents of the poor. But after 1895 New York State relieved counties from caring for this part of the mentally ill population. Instead convicts still diagnosed as insane at the expiration of their term were detained until they recovered or were legally discharged. In 1893, 19 percent of Matteawan inmates fell into this category; by 1897, 29 percent of the asylum population had expired terms.[25]

Doctors like Superintendent Henry Allison believed that patients such as Quimbo Appo were predisposed to crime, habitual criminals who were "congenitally or naturally weak-minded." As evidence, Allison pointed out their "physical signs of degeneracy"—abnormalities of cranial development; peculiarities of palate, teeth, and jaws; asymmetry of facial expression, scantiness of beard, and other bodily defects. All these physical features contributed to "an arrested development of the mental faculties."[26] The simultaneous presence of George Appo probably only convinced Allison of the hereditary foundation of criminal life.

    *I was about 14 months confined in the court patient's ward, when one day the head attendant came to me. He told me I was to be transferred to another ward and took me with him to Ward No.2 South, which was known as the Violent Ward. On entering this ward, I noticed many prison acquaintances, some were violently insane, made so by the brutality and abuse inflicted on them during imprisonment under the silent system of Superintendent Louis D. Pilsbury's administration. Whenever I found any one of them in a normal state of mind, I would sit down, talk with them, keep them in good humor and play checkers with any who wanted play. I could not understand why I was transferred to a violent ward. As I could get no satisfactory answer from any of the ward attendants or the visiting doctor Dr. Edgar J. Spratling, I asked permission to see the superintendent. I was told I would have to wait until he made his rounds of the wards, which was about once every three months, unless something special happened for his attention. I had to wait and be patient.*

*One day, about 3 p.m., the order was shouted, "Seats!" In walked the superintendent with his bodyguard. He passed and viewed each patient, some of whom would jump up and curse and call him all sorts of evil names, only to be grasped by the neck and thrown back into his chair again. Finally, the superintendent came to my seat and began to give me a searching look, and said to me "How are you getting on over here?"*

*I replied, "Quite well. I cannot complain, but would be pleased to know why I was transferred from the court patients ward to this ward."*

*"Oh, overcrowded there, I suppose."*

*"By the way, Doctor, I would ask your permission to write a letter to a lawyer and have my case looked after. I've been confined here now over 16 months and during the course of that time, I am sure I have shown no sign of insanity. I have already written several letters to reliable friends outside and have received no response from them. I cannot account for their silence."*

*"All right, let him have writing material," he said to the attendant of the ward. Then the superintendent walked away and left the ward.*

*On the following day I received a sheet of writing paper and a pencil. I wrote to Ambrose H. Purdy, but never got one word in reply. In fact, the letters I had written never left the institution. Such was the red tape and rascality of the officials at Matteawan Asylum.*

*I came to the conclusion that I was buried alive.*[27]

At first glance the Matteawan State Hospital for the Criminally Insane looked nothing like a place to "bury alive" the mentally ill. Located in Fishkill, New York, the institution occupied a bucolic, 250-acre plateau. The stunning scenery convinced state officials and medical experts alike that the isolated environment would generate "peaceful enjoyment and pleasurable emotions," considered an advantage in treating the mentally ill. On opening in 1892, Matteawan was hailed as one of the finest public buildings in the state, its stated mission "to cure, not to punish."[28]

In 1859 New York opened the nation's first asylum for insane criminals. Located at Auburn prison, the institution had as its specific mission to separate insane criminals from both convicted felons in prisons and the mentally ill in insane asylums. Initially the facility served convicts allegedly driven mad while incarcerated. A decade later, however, county courts began committing "unconvicted criminal lunatics"—individuals

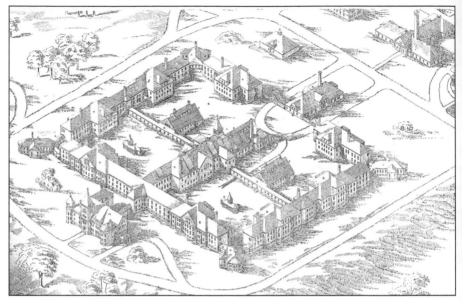

*Matteawan State Hospital for the Criminally Insane.*

charged with a crime but who escaped conviction on the grounds of insanity. Overcrowding quickly became a problem. By 1883 the men's ward was so packed with inmates that patients slept on the corridor floors. Such conditions soon convinced state officials to construct a new institution. Nearly a decade later a new State Lunatic Asylum for the Insane opened in Fishkill; a year later the facility was renamed the Matteawan State Hospital for the Criminally Insane.[29]

The name change was significant. Matteawan embodied how the treatment of mental illness shifted from the insane asylum in the nineteenth century to the hospital in the twentieth. Whereas "alienists" earlier in the century were preoccupied with individuals classified as "sane" and "insane," late-nineteenth-century psychiatrists increasingly measured mental health according to a more complicated scale of normality. Matteawan also reflected the growing popularity of classifying certain forms of insanity. Individuals identified as "criminally insane" or epileptics were separated from the "ordinary insane" and transferred to distinct and segregated institutions of their own.[30]

Mattaewan was a state-of-the-art facility, attracting penologists from around the world. The architect I. G. Perry designed the structure with twenty-inch-thick walls, no external doors, and windows set six feet above the floors, expressly to "assure the safe custody of the most dangerous patients." Matteawan's 250 acres of land included farm and workshop facilities that employed Matteawan patients and included an icehouse, garment factory, laundry, and bakery.[31]

By the time George Appo entered Matteawan, the facility accommodated three types of patients. First were citizens thought to be mentally ill who were charged with violating the law, like Appo. In such cases legal proceedings were indefinitely suspended pending the patient's "recovery." A second category included state prison inmates who became insane during incarceration. Finally, convicts with expired terms like Quimbo Appo remained under detention on the grounds that they were too dangerous for release.[32]

The experience of both Appos, however, revealed how little had changed in Matteawan. Magnificent new physical facilities and a transformation in status from an asylum to a hospital failed to address many of the problems associated with earlier treatment of the mentally ill. Like the Auburn asylum, Matteawan quickly surpassed capacity. Built to house 550 patients, it had at least that many pass through its doors in the first year of operation. In 1895 asylum officials reported that the institution was full. By then Matteawan had admitted nearly as many inmates in its first four years of existence as had been admitted in the previous fourteen years at Auburn. A year later, with 559 residents, officials conceded that the hospital's population exceeded capacity. In the year of Appo's arrival, Matteawan's population was 632, 93 percent of whom were men; on his release the population stood at 719. By then state officials were rapidly constructing a similar facility at Clinton State Prison.[33]

Overcrowding transformed Matteawan almost overnight from a model penal and health facility to a daily nightmare for patients. Officials admitted that many were without beds and thus compelled to sleep on the floor. Chairs were absent in the dining hall and other rooms throughout the complex. Since most patients were poor or committed under aliases and assumed names, court and prison officials knew virtually nothing about them. Treatment under such conditions was little more than guesswork.[34]

The neglect of inmates was compounded by the poor quality of attendants. Various superintendents described Matteawan's staff as part of an "itinerant" or "unstable" class, moving from one hospital to another. Other sources confirm that more than 90 percent of the Matteawan attendants exhibited the social profile of a transient population. The overwhelming majority were male, single, widowed, or divorced; fully 33 percent originated from Ireland. The long hours, low pay, and few promotions attracted employees who viewed the job as only a "temporary makeshift," complained one official. Since Matteawan attendants earned considerably less than state prison guards, annual turnover exceeded 50 percent.[35]

The combination of overcrowding, poor training, and frequent turnover resulted in benign neglect of patients at best. Capable patients assumed tasks like shoemaking, repairing clothes, carpentry, or masonry, but they comprised less than 10 percent of the inmate population. Most refused such work and instead spent the day playing cards, reading, chatting with other patients, or amusing themselves as they pleased. Individuals suffering from various forms of delusion were largely ignored, composing themselves, wrote one, "with great dignity in their chairs and confer[ring] dukedoms and earldoms upon their attendants and their fellow patients." One visitor noted how doctors and attendants were accustomed to such ravings, "but to a stranger who has never heard them before they are infinitely sad." Others simply died. Between 1897 and 1899, according to official Matteawan reports, twenty to twenty-four men died annually, roughly between 3 and 4 percent of the entire male population.[36]

This neglect was illustrated by the "voluntary insanity" of inmates like George Appo. Corrections officials recognized that significant numbers of Matteawan inmates were perfectly healthy. Elmira Reformatory superintendent Zebulon Brockway admitted that every year numerous inmates in that institution faked insanity as a means of escape. Prison officials elsewhere acknowledged that this was common. An inspector at Eastern State Penitentiary in Philadelphia admitted that inmates with "simulated insanity" proved more troublesome than those suffering from genuine mental illnesses. Ironically, state officials unwittingly contributed to these statistics; from 1875 to 1893 more than eighty inmates were declared insane for masturbating.[37]

Cases of phony inmate insanity masked a fundamental reality of Matteawan's population: Long-term incarceration drove many convicts insane. By 1893 convicts serving life sentences in New York numbered 196, 33 (17 percent) of whom were inmates at Matteawan. While some life convicts were insane at the time they committed their crime, wrote one prison official, "many others undoubtedly become so by reason of the situation which confronts them after their life sentence is imposed."[38] Corrections officials elsewhere concurred. In 1886 Eastern State Penitentiary warden Michael Cassidy admitted that one of his inmates was insane but discouraged moving him to a hospital because "there are fifty others here who are as crazy as he is."[39]

&#8766; *I began to use my wits, so to speak, to find a way out of the hole. After I had been there over two years, one day after finishing work up in the dormitory, I approached one of the sane patients named John Murphy[40] whom I knew to be a good and all right fellow, a man who would not tip off or squeal on another were he to see one trying to escape. I needed his assistance in my efforts. I said to him: "Well, Johnny, we are all through work for the day. How long have you been here and what prospects have you of getting out of here? I see an opening to beat it (escape) and if you want to take a chance with me, just say so and I will take all the chances and responsibility in case of a 'tumble' (discovery)."*

*"George, I just got a letter from my mother who is up in Albany now. I will be discharged from here in a week or so, but if I can help you to beat it, you can rely on me to do so. But take my advice, George, and not try it, unless you have got a sure thing of making it. I'll tell you why. Your prospects of getting out on the square are brighter than you think. The fact that the doctors allow you to come up here and do work in the dormitory without even an attendant to watch us is a sure indication that they have confidence in you, as being all right mentally. . . . Now George, take my advice and do nothing foolish. If I can help you out in any way after I get out of here, just let me know and you can bet your life I will keep my word and do all I can for you. But don't make any bad 'breaks' to beat it."*

*Sure enough, on the next week after our talk he told me his mother was coming to take him home in a couple of days and that if I wanted to get a letter out on the quiet, he would mail it for me safe. I then got a sheet of writing paper and wrote a letter to the*

*Hon. Judge Goff and gave it to Murphy. The next day he was taken from the ward and discharged as cured.*

*Two weeks after Murphy's release, I was surprised by an attendant taking me from the ward to the private office of the superintendent, Dr. H. E. Allison, who greeted me in a very pleasant manner. "How are you feeling? How long have you been here now?"*

*I replied: "Very well in general, I thank you, and I have now been here two years, eight months and two weeks."*

*"Well," he said, "you appear in good condition both physically and mentally, and there has been no complaints made against your behavior since you have been here. You are discharged and the attendant here will have you dressed and see you to the station. If you want to see and have a talk with your father before you leave, you can do so."*

*I thanked him and left the office with the attendant who took me to a hallway and told me to wait there and he would bring my father so we could talk together in private. . . . I made sure not to excite him, and said, "How is everything with you? You are looking fine. Is there anything particular that you are in need of? I have just got good news from a friend. In a day or so I will be able to get you anything you need."*

*"I want you to get me a pair of good eyeglasses, No.9, my sight is getting very bad. That is all I need."*

*After talking with him about twenty minutes and trying to get some information I needed concerning two brothers of my mother's, his whole demeanor changed. He began to pour out his insane delusions about his great wealth and his great army of soldiers and all the wonderful things he was going to do to benefit the unfortunate patients and convicts and blow up all the penal institutions, keepers and police with dynamite. Seeing him excited, I began to humor him and when he became somewhat rational, I said: "Well, I will have to go now. So good-bye, and I will do all I possibly can for you and you will have a nice pair of gold eye-glasses in a couple of days, and anything else you need."*

*The attendant came and took me to the clothes room where I put on a suit of clothes. I then was brought to the clerk's office and signed some sort of paper and left the institution a free man once more.*[41]

George Appo bade farewell to more than just a madhouse. That was the final time he saw his father. In 1899 physicians declared Quimbo Appo "hopelessly insane," according to Louis Beck, "and there he lives to this day, seemingly forgotten by all the world." Some newspapers even claimed that he was dead.[42]

In the decade after his son's release, the Matteawan patient notes reveal Quimbo Appo's sad downward spiral. By 1910 he was a tired, withered old man suffering from diarrhea and frequent incontinence. Suddenly, in June 1912, Appo complained that he felt sick, but doctors failed to identify any source for his discomfort. Weary, ill, delusional, and probably heartbroken, Quimbo Appo died on 23 June 1912.[43]

Quimbo Appo was approximately ninety years old at the time of his death. He spent thirty-seven of them—more than one-third of his tragic life—in institutions for the criminally insane. In death he was back in the news. A *World* headline read "DEVIL" APPO'S SON, THOUGHT DEAD, IS ALIVE. News accounts claimed that George Appo, forgotten like his father, learned of his father's death while he was living in Trenton, New Jersey. He immediately sent a telegram to Matteawan officials promising to take charge of the body. But he never appeared. Quimbo Appo's remains were buried in an unmarked grave on the grounds of Matteawan.[44]

*The unmarked gravesite of Quimbo Appo.*

# A Genuine Reformation

—

❧ *On my arrival in New York, I went direct from the Grand Central Depot down to Mott Street. After paying my railroad fare, I had but forty cents left to exist on, so I went to Mott Street to search for a friend from whom I could obtain a loan of a couple of dollars. Not seeing him around, I entered the saloon at 6 Mott Street and was surprised to find Eddie Erwin in attendance behind the bar and the two false witnesses, Walsh and Hartigan, in front of the bar. Both of the latter men looked to be suffering in the last stages of consumption.*

*I was about to leave the place when I heard someone call out: "Hello there, George. When did you get out?" I turned and met Mr. Paddy Mullen the proprietor of the saloon, who with two other young men invited me to have a drink. I accepted and Mr. Mullen said to me: "What do you intend to do?"*

*I replied: "As soon as I can see my friend to borrow enough money to get out of New York, I will leave here for Philadelphia at once. I believed I would find my friend in here. That's why I drifted into the place."*

*"Oh, that's all right, George, how much money do you need?" inquired Mr. Mullen.*

*"Just my car fare, that's all," said I.*

*To my surprise he went down into his pocket and handed me $15, saying: "If you need more, say so."*

*I told him that the $15 was more than I needed, but he forced me to take it and forget all about it. So I took the $15 and thanked him, saying I would return the money with gratitude in a short time.*

*"Forget it, you owe me nothing," said Mr. Mullen.*

*During all the time that Mullen and I was talking there stood the three men, Erwin, Walsh and Hartigan, all of them employed about* the place, with open-eyed wonder, at the kind-hearted generosity of Mr. Mullen to one whom they so cowardly framed up to send to state prison after being assualted by Ed Erwin.

I then left the place and went to Pennsylvania Railroad Station and took a train for Philadelphia. On arriving at Philadelphia, I started right in the crooked business again by working the flim flam, or properly speaking, short changing business people with a ten dollar bill by making them make a mistake in the change to their loss of $4.90. I remained in Philadelphia about three weeks and was quite successful during the course of that time.

One night while laying in an opium joint at 911 Race Street, smoking the drug, I began to think what a fool I was to go back to the opium pipe after being away from it so long a time. As I had formed no habit for the drug as yet, I made up my mind to keep away from it entirely before it was too late. For three days I never went near or touched the drug, and during that time I felt no desire for it. Finally, that set me thinking very deeply and the conclusion of my thoughts were that if I could break away so easily and so often as I had from the opium habit, why not muster up nerve enough to break away from a crooked life? I made up my mind to try again to get honest employment and to reform without fear or favor, not that I feared the discipline of a prison, nor did I favor it. I made up my mind to return to New York and make an effort to do right under all circumstances and conditions. . . .[1]

I was again out of work and remained idle for many months without a steady position, but owning to an occasional job given me by Mrs. Sallade. I managed to just exist through the kindly interest she still had for my welfare and she tried in every way to obtain a steady position for me after the failure of her own business, but was unsuccessful in her efforts for me. She then left New York for Lowell, Massachusetts.

I then began to search for work of some kind but met with no success. I finally made up my mind to hunt up George W. Lederer and try to have him pay me a portion of the money ($145.00) that he still owed me for my salary while on the stage. One day while on Broadway and 42nd Street watching for Lederer to appear, I was met by an old associate and a former burglar named Frank Taylor, alias "Brooklyn Beefer," whom I had not seen for over fifteen years.

After we got over our surprise and hand shaking, he said to me: "What are you doing now?"

I replied: "Nothing, but at present I am looking for a square job at anything outside of graft. At this very moment I am trying to meet a theatrical fellow who owes me $145 and see if I can get some portion of it from him."

"You will never get a cent of it. I heard you were on the stage, but I was out of town at the time and did not see you act. I am now in a business of my own in Philadelphia. Here is my business card and if you want to come to work for me, just say so and I will take you with me tomorrow to Philadelphia and put you right on the job," said Taylor.

"All right," said I, "when and where will I meet you tomorrow?"

"You can come now with me to my flat and I will introduce you to my wife and son. We then can make all arrangements and leave for Philadelphia the first thing in the morning. I have been very busy here in New York for the past ten days. I have tuned up and repaired 32 pianos in that time. I have a man looking after my business at Philadelphia during my absence," said he. . . .

On my arrival there, he brought me to his place of business on 15th and Sansom Streets, where he had the whole house rented. On the ground floor he had six pianos of different makes, all in perfect order. In the rear room he had his shop where he put up a fine wood finish, under the name of "The Bull Dog Wood Finish." In fact, that finish could be applied to a nonstained floor and after two coats were applied, it would be perfectly dry in ten minutes and no smell of paint. The finished floor would look as bright as a polished piano and guaranteed to remain that way for two years.

I asked him who had learned him to tune and repair pianos and to make up the wood finish. He said about ten years previous he was arrested for burglary in the city of Baltimore, and being caught dead right, he pleaded guilty and was sentenced to a term of five years to the Maryland Penitentiary. He was assigned to work in the cabinet shop of the prison as an assistant to a German convict who had a fifteen-year sentence and who was a skilled cabinet and piano maker. This convict took an interest in Taylor and taught him the piano tuning business and gave him the formula to make up the wood finish. When he was released from the Penitentiary, he gave up all crooked business and started right in making up the wood finish, and was very successful with it. He then bought himself a set of tools for the piano tuning and traveled all over the country tuning pianos and selling his wood finish. Finally, he established his business at 15th and Sansom Streets, Philadelphia, where I worked with him for about three months.

During the course of that time he did a good business in the wood finish sales and I used to wonder why he was always in debt and could not pay his bills. But I soon learned that he was gambling his money away on the horses and faro. As a consequence, he had to close up the business on Sansom Street and go out on the road tuning pianos again.

I returned to New York and began a search for employment without any success, and I was having a very hard time of it, being down and out, so to speak, and felt like the most forlorn of all God's creatures—a man without a single friend in all the world. This sense of feeling set me thinking very deeply about former friends who flutter around like butterflies for a season. When in prosperity, they can make use of one; but let misfortune overtake one, they soon forget you are alive. Still, I did not get discouraged and continued my search for employment.[2]

GEORGE APPO LEFT Matteawan a changed man. On 14 June 1899 the Special Supreme Court concluded that Appo had recovered his sanity. Equally important, the district attorney admitted that no one knew if John Atwood, the complaining witness, was even still alive. Conviction being improbable, the prosecutor agreed to Appo's release. Appo donned a stylish new black serge suit, a derby hat, and a black tie; he walked out of the courtroom a free man.[3]

By now Appo's underworld universe no longer existed. Local and national law enforcement campaigns had destroyed most green goods operations. James McNally, Appo's former employer and later enemy, was no longer in business. Five years earlier, in the wake of the Lexow Committee exposés, he proclaimed, "I am broke." After purchasing a country home in Connecticut in 1893 for thirty thousand dollars, McNally was forced to relinquish the property for failing to meet the mortgage payments. In 1895 he moved his operation to Chicago. By then he was too well known, and shortly thereafter he was convicted of postal violations.

Upon release from Joliet Prison in 1899, he discovered that his one hundred thousand dollars savings was gone, stolen by former accomplices. McNally never recovered. In 1905 he was working as a waiter in a Coney Island restaurant. Two years later, homeless and penniless, McNally walked into the Tombs police court and begged to be admitted to the workhouse.[4]

McNally was not alone. After 1895 the green goods game went into decline. Some believed that the Lexow Committee revelations, combined with the replacement of Police Chief Thomas Byrnes and the arrival of Theodore Roosevelt, eliminated police toleration of the game. The new regime, wrote the legal reformer Arthur Brisbane, sought to treat criminals as a farmer treats weeds: "to root them out and prevent them from coming back again." Federal postal authorities moved more aggressively to prosecute green goods operators, the Jimmie McNally case in point. By 1914 a police instruction manual no longer mentioned green goods in identifying the most common confidence games in the city.[5]

Even if Appo wanted to continue as a con man, he could not. By his own account he was still being harassed by the police. Physical confrontations and various forms of harassment were frequent occurrences. "No sooner do I get out of jail than back in jail they put me," complained Appo about Gotham's police. So pronounced were the threats and persecution that Appo briefly fled New York.[6]

Wherever Appo turned for help, he met frustration. He no longer knew where to find Dr. Henry Kane, whom Appo had assisted in his opium research. He continued to pursue without success the $150 George Lederer owed him for his performance in *In the Tenderloin*. While Appo went unpaid, Lederer opened a new theater on Forty-second Street, produced the first American musical to achieve major international success, *The Belle of New York* (1897), and became a manager and producer at the New York Theater. Over the next three decades Lederer staged one production that reportedly earned more money than any other musical comedy in the world. Lederer died in 1938 without ever compensating Appo for his performances.[7]

Appo's decision to, in his words, "break away from a crooked life" really began in 1894. His Lexow testimony did more than pit him against his underworld subculture. Appo's cooperation unwittingly injected him into the world of urban evangelical reform. The most influential figures in his life thereafter—Frank Moss, Alexander M. Hadden, Mary Sallade —were affiliated with this movement. More than twenty years after the event, Appo described his Lexow Committee testimony as "my great fortune," the turning point in his life. Through the intercession of Moss and Sallade, Appo claimed that he obtained his first "honest employment."[8]

Frank Moss was the most prominent example of evangelical influence on Appo. Moss was born in upstate New York in 1860 and moved to the city at the age of eight. A lawyer and member of the Republican Party, Moss was well connected to New York's Protestant elite. He served as a trustee for the Trinity Methodist Episcopal Church, while remaining an active member in the Methodist Social Union, the Good Government Club, and the Harlem Republican Club. Moss also wrote several well-received books, including the three-volume *The American Metropolis* (1897) and *America's Mission to Serve Humanity* (1919).

Moss first gained public notice when the Presbyterian minister Howard Crosby hired him as counsel for the Society for the Prevention of Crime (SPC), a private, anticrime organization founded by Crosby in 1878. On behalf of the SPC and various homeowners, Moss instigated prosecutions of brothel owners in 1887. When the Reverend Charles Parkhurst assumed control of the SPC in 1891, Moss and the SPC began a decade-long campaign against police corruption associated with Tammany Hall. In addition to teaming up with John Goff as a counsel for the Lexow Committee, Moss succeeded Theodore Roosevelt as president of the Board of Police Commissioners in 1897. Two years later he was the lead counsel for the Mazet Committee, another legislative investigation into municipal corruption.[9]

*Frank Moss.*

Moss liked George Appo. "I felt a friendship for the man the moment I saw him," admitted Moss.[10] Several years later, as Appo sat in Matteawan Hospital, Moss concluded that a formal education and better environmental influences could have enabled Appo to become "an intelligent and estimable person." Appo's life was emblematic of hundreds of other children in New York, who slept in alleys and taught one another to steal. Moss repeated Appo's explanation for his life of crime: He "was not brought up" but "kicked up." Although Appo remained irreligious and "a slave" to alcohol and opium, Moss concluded that Appo nevertheless experienced "a genuine reformation."[11]

For both Appo and Moss, reformation was conversion. "After I gave my testimony I had a different feeling," Appo later remembered. "I thought I had left the old life." His epiphany continued when Appo accompanied Moss to Rev. Thomas Dixon's Twenty-third Street Baptist Church after Appo's Lexow appearance. Dixon was about to abandon his ministry and return to his native South to write *The Clansman: An Historical Romance of the Ku Klux Klan* (1905), the inspiration for D. W. Griffith's epic but racist film *The Birth of a Nation* (1915). Sitting in a pew, Appo read a leaflet of songs. "There is a fountain filled with blood," read one verse. "The dying thief rejoiced to see." Appo's eyes welled up with tears; he whispered to the man next to him, "That's me; that's me."

"I don't know whether George Appo is really converted," Moss later recounted, "but I do know that he has awakened to a new life." George Appo—that "half-breed," "hybrid," and "alien" man—was thus "born again" in the temple of a prophet of twentieth-century racism.[12]

But evangelical conversion went only so far. Moss and other evangelical reformers equivocated in their support of Appo. Alexander Hadden, a prominent physician and Calvary Episcopal Church volunteer, employed Appo to address envelopes and polish floors in his residence but nothing permanent. Mary Sallade maintained a correspondence with Appo but never offered financial assistance. Appo briefly offered lectures to merchants on the intricacies of street crime, but no one volunteered to promote him. The writer Louis Beck hired Appo to help research the first book-length account of New York's Chinatown in 1898 and devoted a full chapter to Appo. Yet he concluded that a lawbreaker like Appo was not only "born to crime," but that "such a man is better dead." Even Moss was pessimistic about the sincerity of criminals. "It is," he lamented, "almost impossible for the criminal to reform."[13]

Such suspicions by Appo's friends made going straight easier said than done. In the three-month period between Appo's release from the Blackwell's Island Penitentiary and his arrest for assaulting John Atwood in 1896, Moss arranged a job for Appo at the SPC that paid four dollars a week. He was offered a chance to lecture in Buffalo on the effects of crime, but was denied a permit and then forced to leave town by police officials. His efforts to sweep streets and find other forms of work failed. Appo quickly realized the fundamental difficulty of earning an honest living versus picking pockets: The latter provided a life of comfort, while legal, low-wage labor left him without common necessities. "I don't know where to go or what to do," bemoaned Appo.[14]

Appo's foibles typified the frustrations nineteenth-century felons confronted on release from prison. Convicts were given three dollars and three cents for every mile of travel from the prison to their county of origin, a sum that state prison inspectors acknowledged barely covered transit costs. Before 1878 the only institutional assistance discharged convicts enjoyed originated from the Prison Association, a private reform group that alienated many former inmates with its policy of refusing "to help those who refuse to help themselves." When Appo requested financial support from Prison Association leader Elisha Harris, he was rejected. In 1868 the association spent a meager $1,885 to assist discharged prisoners.[15]

In 1878 New York State officials funded a state agent for discharged convicts. The new official visited each prison monthly, conferring with soon-to-be released inmates within the month and giving them assistance. In some cases the agent provided the discharged with tools; other times he subsidized transit costs and living expenses to procure employment.[16]

In reality, however, state assistance was minimal. In 1880 Superintendent Louis Pilsbury acknowledged that the state agent for discharged prisoners was badly underfunded, and recommended increasing his annual budget to $10,000. In fact agents never spent more than $5,200 in any one year on prisoner assistance. Between 1886 and 1893 only 61 percent of all discharged prisoners in New York received any aid, and on average a mere nine dollars. In 1895 the state abolished the position and the program.[17]

Privately funded reclamation programs usually reflected an evangelical orientation. One example was Michael Dunn's House of Industry for the Reclamation of Convicts at 304 Water Street, which opened in 1879. A fifty-three-year-old ex-convict who reportedly spent thirty-five years in prison, Dunn claimed that he continually returned to prison because he had "no home, no occupation, no refuge" when released.

Dunn's home reflected the link between Protestant evangelism and nineteenth-century urban reform. With support from John D. Rocke-feller and Cornelius Vanderbilt, the home held religious meetings almost nightly, employing moral suasion in encouraging ex-convicts to reform. Applicants were so numerous that the home moved to larger quarters four times between 1881 and 1891 and was renamed the New York Home of Industry and Refuge for Discharged Convicts. That facility included a second-floor workshop for manufacturing brooms and brushes, with two upper floors designed as sleeping quarters for thirty-five men. By 1892, 3,087 men had passed through the home, an average of 237 per year. Of that group, however, home officials admitted that only 43 percent (1,342) found employment.[18] Annual reports remained silent on what happened to those who left without finding work.

Appo followed a similarly depressing pattern of underemployment on his release from Matteawan. He briefly worked as a car cleaner in Grand Central Terminal, and a handyman at Calvary Church, the Sallade dress factory, and Alexander Hadden's residence. Like his previous efforts to go straight—setting up an express business with Tom Lee, applying for work in hat factories, asking Elisha Harris of the Prison Association for assistance, acting in a George Lederer production, traveling with the Derby Mascot theater company in Montreal—Appo's employment proved short-lived and insecure. In each case Appo's return to pocket picking, flimflam, or green goods was a reaction to failing to secure stable work.

Appo's workplace tribulations reflected how changing "criminal" behavior was deeply rooted in the economics of employment opportunity. Appo's accidental meeting with Frank Taylor illustrated the limited prospects available to former felons, and the importance of social networks in finding legal work. Appo had no family connections, craft training, or formal education—the very relationships, experiences, and social structures that offered upward mobility and economic prosperity for middle- and skilled working-class men. Success was predicated on exploiting certain social networks. Appo knew only people like Taylor. The personal connections offering the most prospects to Appo and other former convicts remained those associated with the underworld. For that reason, Appo admitted, "I and the other men always returned to a life of a crook as soon as discharged."[19]

Such a series of lifelong frustrations probably contributed to the contrite image Appo presented in his autobiography. In the entirety of his life experience, the only steady employment ever offered to Appo originated from evangelically motivated reformers like Moss, Hadden, and Sallade. "I really believe were I not fortunate enough to meet good people who took a kindly interest to secure honest employment for me," admitted Appo, "I don't know what would have become of me."[20] Despite the difficulties of reforming, the loss of income and decline in lifestyle, Appo displayed no anger or resentment at those who facilitated the transformation. Indeed he felt indebted to them.

After his employment by Hadden, Appo vanished from the public record. A full decade ensued before any record of Appo reappeared. Then, in June 1912, when Quimbo Appo died, Matteawan officials reportedly located Appo in Trenton, New Jersey. The *World* reported that many were surprised to learn that George Appo was alive. "Dead for thirteen years as far as the world knew, George Appo . . . has been heard from." By then he was described as "decrepit although only fifty-eight years old," weighing only one hundred pounds.[21]

## MEMORY AND AUTOBIOGRAPHY

But Appo was not living in Trenton. Rather he was an undercover agent for the SPC. Beginning in 1911, and continuing at least until 1915, Appo assisted the SPC in its investigation of opium dens and the growing popularity of cocaine. Appo initially received a monthly six-dollar salary, as well as another six dollars for monthly rent. Within a year he was earning a salary of ten dollars per month. His name disappeared from SPC records in 1917.[22]

During his employment with the SPC, Appo wrote an autobiography. He never explained the genesis of this document. Perhaps money was a motivation. Perhaps he wanted to disprove charges of an early death. Perhaps he wanted to refute the multiple, negative images of being a "mongrel," "hybrid," and "half-breed." Perhaps, after the death of his father in 1912, he felt his own mortality and needed to confront his past. Perhaps he wanted to reveal the horrors of the penitentiary.[23] Quite likely officials from the SPC encouraged Appo to write his life story.

Appo enjoyed writing. Illiterate early in life, he became a man of letters in his later years. This was hardly unusual. "Writing is the prisoner's traditional avocation," wrote longtime Sing Sing warden Lewis Lawes in 1932. "Almost every prisoner feels that he has a story to tell, an autobiography that is worth the telling." At different points Appo even wrote poetry that recounted his prison experiences.[24]

Lawes wrote in the early twentieth century, ignorant of how relatively recent this phenomenon was. While fictional narratives and criminal broadsides, usually confessional in tone, are centuries old, urban crime narratives only began appearing in the middle of the nineteenth century. American crime reporting as a distinct genre—what some label "true crime" today—appeared with Edgar Allan Poe and his successors, like George Foster, George Lippard, George Thompson, and George Wilkes, all of whom exploited the public's fascination with the antebellum under-world.[25] These initial forays into the dark side of city life, at once sensational and morbid in tone, emerged out of the penny press. Many authors of criminal lore began their careers as reporters, frequently providing the first crime coverage in American newspapers. In most cases they depicted the city as a dichotomy, divided into areas, both geographic and social, of darkness and daylight, sunshine and shadow, respectability and unrespectability.

Sensational crime narratives remained popular throughout the century, exemplified by authors and titles like Matthew Hale Smith's *Sunshine and Shadow in New York* (1868), Edward Crapsey's *The Nether Side of New York* (1872), and James D. McCabe's *New York by Sunlight and Gaslight* (1882). Criminal attorneys like William Howe and Abraham Hummel exploited similar themes with *In Danger* (1888), warning readers about "the snares and pitfalls of the crime and vice that await the unwary in New York." Even reformers like Charles Loring Brace, Anthony Comstock, and Helen Campbell, and leading law enforcement operatives like Thomas Byrnes and Allan Pinkerton, resorted to similar literary devices in their descriptive accounts. The detective and the professional criminal alike became fixtures in crime literature.[26]

When criminals wrote memoirs they presented their lives as moral adventures. For example George Bidwell, in *Forging His Chains* (1888), insisted that his story was not a simple catalogue of crime, but a warning to American youth to avoid temptation. Even those that explicitly rejected evangelical conclusions nonetheless emphasized the fundamental hardships of a life of crime. Sophie Lyons, for instance, insisted that crime did not benefit even "the really great criminals." Others echoed similar judgments. Men who spent much of their adult lives engaged in criminal activity made little money, believed the ex-con Eddie Guerin.

"Only a man out of his senses, or inherently wicked," he concluded, "could waste his life as I have wasted mine."[27]

Alongside these evangelical jeremiads and epistolatory warnings, however, appeared a new type of criminal memoir. Josiah Flynt's *The World of Graft* (1901), based on actual interviews with underworld figures, and Hutchins Hapgood's *The Autobiography of a Thief* (1903) were devoid of religious or moralistic agendas. Instead these autobiographies presented authentic renderings of criminal life. Both emphasized the environmental roots of crime, the horrors of prison life, the widespread corruption and criminal activity of public officials, and the absence of genuine alternatives for criminals hoping to reform their behavior. Nuanced, subtle, and ultimately more complicated, such accounts were less interested in entertaining readers with adventure tales or providing warnings against turpitude. These interpretations of the criminal world dripped with pessimism.[28] George Appo's autobiography emerged from this genre of literary realism.

Some criminal accounts articulated an openly political and oppositional voice. Alexander Berkman's *Prison Memoirs of an Anarchist* (1912), Julian Hawthorne's *The Subterranean Brotherhood* (1914), and Eugene V. Debs's *Walls and Bars* (1927) treated incarceration as a form of capitalist and class control or a system in need of abolition. As their titles suggest, such accounts concentrated on the prison experience and devoted little attention to the complexity of the criminal subcultures of most inmates.[29]

Appo's autobiography professed no such political sensibility. Rather Appo appeared more indebted to Jim Caulfield, the narrator in Hapgood's *Autobiography of a Thief*. Both shared several themes: the environmental causes of crime, the traumas of prison life, and the desire by longtime criminals to go straight. Hapgood believed that, given his subject's upbringing, the world of graft was a natural recourse and outcome. Caulfield, like Appo, considered prison conditions nothing less than a "systematic crime against humanity." Crime and the subculture surrounding it were a young man's world. Both claimed that they grafted with Daniel Driscoll as youths. Eventually the difficulties of such a life were too much for even the most hardened. Echoing Appo, Caulfield admitted, "that a time comes in the lives of many grafters when they desire to reform."[30]

Appo's memoir, however, departed from Caulfield's and other criminal autobiographies in one significant way. Appo's autobiography was a sporadic and evolutionary product, the result of more than twenty years of musing on the meaning of the underworld. During Appo's 1895 trial for stabbing police officer Michael Rein, attorneys Arthur F. Dennett and Frank Moss urged Appo to write a brief autobiographical account of his criminal experiences. They hoped that he might receive a lenient sentence.

Entitled "The full History of my life," Appo's nine-page handwritten testimony sketched out the broad, general details he later developed in his autobiography: his birth in 1858 (not 1856), his father's conviction for murder, the death of his mother, his lack of schooling, his numerous terms in Sing Sing. This version presented a stark image of Appo's childhood and teenage years. After being discharged from the *Mercury*, he tried to obtain legitimate work but failed because of his illiteracy and small size. So dire were his circumstances, Appo wrote, that "I was compelled to sleep in hallways, [and] had nothing whatever to eat." He resorted to picking pockets simply, he confessed, "to obtain the means to keep me alive."[31]

Appo, in 1895, was desperate. "I earnestly hope that, after my release, some good Samaritan will give me employment and afford me chance to earn an honest living," he told Judge Rufus Cowing. Appo not only proclaimed his innocence but saw himself as a victim of persecution: "All the world seems to think my word of no value, and the Police are ready to swear to anything." Appo admitted that he was without friends and support. "I have pleaded guilty and throw myself at the mercy of the court," he begged.[32]

Appo's strategy worked. Cowing described the document as "the most extraordinary record of persistent crime" he had ever heard in his many years on the bench. The judge admitted that Appo's recidivism justified a long prison term, but he was more impressed by Appo's sincerity. Cowing limited Appo's sentence to six months in the penitentiary.[33]

On Appo's release from Blackwell's Island in 1896, Frank Moss expressed concern about George's destitution. His remedy was to pay Appo to write a brief memoir of his life. "If you had heard Appo tell this story you would have been charmed by his gentle and polite manner and by his soft and flexible voice and pleasing enunciation," Moss later wrote. This version—longer than the one written a year earlier, but shorter than the 1915 autobiography—appeared in Moss's three-volume study *The American Metropolis* in 1897. Moss himself claimed that this account originated from Appo's hand.[34]

By the time Appo began writing a longer and more detailed memoir, he had already thought about key events of his life. His mind and recollections worked in ways familiar to students of the processes of memory. Then fifty-nine to sixty years of age, Appo was probably going through "the final stage of memory," a life review filled with elements of both candor and omission. His memory displayed typical weaknesses: He erred regarding his age; he had trouble with the chronology of events and the passage of time between them; he remembered precise details of seemingly innocuous events while omitting major ones (like being married with children). In general he remembered more details in the second half than at the beginning of his life.[35]

Appo's manuscript departed from other autobiographies in its authenticity. This was an unfinished narrative—a raw text of thirteen paragraphs and ninety-nine typewritten pages. Appo hired no ghostwriter. Unlike Jim Caulfield or even Mother Jones, he did not have Hutchins Hapgood or Mary Field Parton, respectively, to transcribe his thoughts and then fashion those tales into a compelling narrative. He never even enjoyed the benefits of an editor to correct grammar, spelling, and punctuation.[36]

Appo's memoir digressed from traditional autobiographies in another significant way—his emphasis on personal humiliation. Indeed, the way Appo described various physical assaults and embarrassments reflected how he did not consider victimization at someone else's hand as dishonorable, a personal disgrace to expunge from one's memory. Rather the many physical assaults Appo experienced are integral to his autobiography. Whereas other criminal memoirs offer precise details of their authors' criminal successes, Appo devoted far more attention to his failures. Missing were detailed reminiscences of the amounts of money and objects Appo purloined (much less the personal pride he undoubtedly felt), his many nights in dives like Geoghegan's, McGlory's, and the Haymarket, or tricking numerous victims in the green goods game. Instead Appo presented vivid descriptions of his physical suffering, his individual indignities: the two times he was shot, having his teeth knocked out in prison, being assaulted in New Jersey and New York. Character for Appo derived from tolerating these random acts of violence and turning them into honorable rituals of suffering.

Yet Appo was silent regarding his more intimate humiliations. Women and romance are nonexistent. Discussions of gender are muted and entirely masculine. He mentions childhood friends and associates who later became famous (or, more accurately, infamous) without explaining their precise relationships with him. In his personal life Appo displayed little introspection. He avoided looking inward or tracing the development of his mind or personality. He never questioned his psychic processes or emotions. In his own way Appo concentrated on his public, not private, life while emphasizing the ideals of manhood.

But such omissions are not unusual. Historians who have written on obscure but emblematic figures—Natalie Zemon Davis on Martin Guerre, Alfred Young on George Robert Twelves Hewes, Paul Johnson on Mayo Greenleaf Patch, Laurel Thatcher Ulrich on Martha Ballard—have shown that a wide narrative is easy to assemble. Certain episodes and events can be reconstructed in considerable detail. But numerous and important points must rest on inference and outright guesswork. "Scholars who demand certainty should stay away from [such] people," warns Paul Johnson.[37] George Appo was one such person.

Appo's silences might be explained by an unacknowledged desire to depict his life as a metaphor of redemption. Like many early-twentieth-century underworld autobiographies, Appo's argues that by going straight its author overcame a lifelong relationship with the criminal world. Even a "hybrid" member of "the dangerous classes" like Appo was potentially redeemable. Given the desperation found in his earlier autobiographical musings, this probably influenced Appo when he wrote in 1915 and 1916. In Appo's mind rejection of the underworld and pursuit of legitimate labor marked his personal pursuits in the twenty years after his Lexow Committee testimony. This was a battle to avoid what Appo considered the abyss of continual crime. Just as religious conversions sometimes ignore a writer's earlier angers and resentments, Appo's masked his youthful torments and aggressions.[38]

For unknown reasons Appo's memoir was never published. In 1932, in his history of Sing Sing, Warden Lewis Lawes quoted Appo's unpublished description of nineteenth-century Sing Sing. Lawes, however, never revealed the source, location, or origins of the document.[39] The transcript eventually became the possession of the Society for the Prevention of Crime. When that organization disbanded in 1936, its records were donated to Columbia University. There, to this day, lie Appo's forgotten and unpublished words.

# Epilogue

# The Finest Crook

═

> ❧ *In conclusion of this truthful statement of my life up to the present time, I am glad to be able to say that for nearly 18 years I have lived an honorable life and for several of these recent years I have had steady employment through the kindness of the good Christian people connected with the S.P.C. I am extremely grateful to them for their kindly interest and the confidence placed in me. During the course of these years, I worked faithfully and endeavored to have these good people know that the fruits of kindness had not been sown in a barren soil.*[1]

SO ENDED GEORGE APPO'S AUTOBIOGRAPHY, marking one of the final times he appeared in any written record. By 1929 Appo was residing in the Hell's Kitchen neighborhood on Manhattan's West Side. Then, on 10 August 1929, he was admitted to the Manhattan State Hospital on Ward's Island, where he remained for more than eight months. One report described Appo as "a withered little man, almost totally blind and hard of hearing." On 17 May 1930, two months shy of his seventy-fourth birthday, George Appo died of general arteriosclerosis. After more than a dozen physical assaults, including bullets in his stomach and head, George Appo died of

*George Appo
as an elderly man.*

old age. Three days later he was interred in Mount Hope Cemetery in Hastings-on-Hudson, New York.[2]

After his death those who remembered Appo often cast him in a romantic light. One obituary described him as "one of the wiliest of pickpockets, burglars and confidence men up to the time he reformed in the late 90s," while exaggerating his time in prison to twenty-two years. Another described Appo as "the finest crook that ever turned a new leaf."[3]

Matteawan superintendent Henry E. Allison frequently recounted a personal encounter with Appo. Allison once invited the former pickpocket to lunch while he was a patient at the asylum. Appo entered the room, and Allison arose to give him a chair. When Appo took his seat, Allison remarked, "I understand George, that you are a famous pickpocket."

"Well, doctor," replied Appo, "I don't know about being famous but I am a good pickpocket."

"Will you show me just how you would take my pocketbook from the back pocket of my trousers?" asked Allison.

"Doctor," answered Appo, "when you thought I accidentally jostled you I got your poke (pocketbook) and here it is. I was going to take your kettle (thieves argot for watch) too, but did not have the heart to do it."[4]

Appo was "a remarkable man," Allison concluded.

In these accounts Appo was no longer part of a new "class of criminals," to quote Judge Henry Gildersleeve. Forgotten were recommendations like Recorder John Hackett's that pickpockets like Appo deserved to be shot. He was no longer that "bad man" as described by prison officials, or someone "better dead," as writer Louis Beck concluded.[5] In death he was a simple, mischievous, even harmless, petty thief. George Appo was transformed into myth.

*Cartoon of George Appo
after picking
Allison's pocket.*

BUT WHO was George Appo? Like most anyone writing from memory, Appo presented a perplexing self-description. His language was fraught with layers of confusion, contradiction, and ambivalence. He frequently framed his words with limiting phrases like "so to speak"—"I soon learned the knack, so to speak, how to pick a pocket." At other points Appo took pride in being a good fellow, while admitting that such behavior was "foolish" and "a very bad thing to be." In court he defended and justified his pickpocketing, but later described those activities as "crooked" and "evil."[6]

Such vacillation perhaps reflected how Appo mellowed in his old age. "A criminal can be reformed, not through fear of brutal prison discipline, but by a kind and encouraging word and a friendly act," he wrote. But Appo lacked a vernacular to describe his values, to express his resistance, to articulate his anger. Not surprisingly he adopted the pejorative language used to characterize his behavior, without necessarily accepting its censorious meanings. Criminologists believe that such indecision and inconsistency are normal for individuals who have no other means of redress, no easy outlet for self-expression. Criminal acts like pickpocketing may be exceptions to norms as defined by political and ecclesiastical authorities; but in Appo's social milieu they embodied something else.[7]

But does this explain George Appo? Is there a larger lesson to be drawn from his life? Perhaps the questions should be more specific. How many parentless youths like Appo sought their succor on the streets of nineteenth-century New York? How many homeless children and immigrant offspring resorted to their wits to survive, scraping by as newsboys or bootblacks, or perhaps resorting to an occasional "touch" as pickpockets? How many of those unloved children became part of the more than eighty thousand annually arrested in New York during the final quarter of the nineteenth century? Perhaps millions of nineteenth-century Americans themselves were answers to these questions, affected as they were by the very same social forces as Appo. But we will never have precise answers—only stories and autobiographies like Appo's. Most remain nameless and forgotten.

George Appo's life was a mixture of the apocalyptic and the absurd: a street urchin who never attended a single day of school but later wrote an autobiography; the son who met his father in prison and again in the insane asylum; a subject in one of the earliest experiments in juvenile reform on the school ship *Mercury*, only to serve terms in Sing Sing, Eastern State Penitentiary, Blackwell's Island, and the Tombs; an expert pick-pocket by age ten, a successful confidence man as an adult. Involved in a network of criminal activity tolerated and organized by local political and police officials such as Tom Lee and Thomas Byrnes, Appo was directly involved with the first medical research on opium smoking; the first book on New York's Chinatown; and the first significant investigation of corruption in the New York police department. He was one of the first celebrity criminals to appear on the American stage.

By certain measures Appo was a completely alienated man. By age seven he was effectively orphaned. He grew up in the most impoverished urban community of nineteenth-century America. He never learned to read or write until adulthood and behind bars. Forced to survive by wit and deception, he lived by robbing others. Any effort to change his circumstances during the first forty years of his life met with disdain and failure. To the only long-term community he ever had, he was a stool pigeon and pariah.

But as the historian E. P. Thompson once noted, human beings cannot be reduced to abstract categories, no matter how intricate or subtle they are. All individuals create their own personal syntheses out of the events and structures that directly impinge their lives. All humans share a double-sided possibility of either succumbing to the multifarious pressures of society or rebelling and seeking to master them. All are simultaneously active and passive.

The complexity of those social structures was evidenced in how Appo defined himself. He never identified himself as Chinese, Irish, or Roman Catholic, although he was all of those by birth and baptism. Like the polyglot world of Baxter Street where he grew up, Appo never labeled himself by a single ethnic category. Others so classified him. In ways he or his contemporaries little appreciated, Appo functioned in a truly multicultural world. He worked at various points with Chinese criminal entrepreneurs like Tom Lee, Irish ones like Barney Maguire and Jimmie McNally, and native-born associates like Ike Vail and Bill Vosburg. His childhood companions had surnames like Dolan, Lyons, Tobin, and Driscoll.

Rather than being Catholic, Irish, or Chinese, Appo was a "good fellow," someone who displayed courage—"a nervy crook"—while at the same time using wit and guile to make a living and lavishing the proceeds on others—"a money getter and spender." Most important, a good fellow accepted the consequences of his actions, even serving prison time "for some other fellow's evil doings," according to Appo. SPC superintendent Howard Barber described Appo as "loyal to the core," adding that the reformed convict "was one of the most fearless men I have ever known."[8]

Being a good fellow was exclusive of religion, race, ethnicity, or class for George Appo. Even geography mattered little, as revealed when he forgave Ira Hogshead of South Carolina for shooting out his eye. Some, like detective Thomas Byrnes, rejected any notion of loyalty among criminals. Appo not only believed that such a code existed, he identified with it. "Many times I have been assaulted by would be toughs and I have defended myself and never howled for the police for satisfaction in the courts, even while I got the worst of the fight," insisted Appo. Why not seek help from legal authorities? Because, in his words, "that was the way I was taught" growing up in Five Points. Life was about taking risks and suffering the consequences. "Fear was not known among the crooks who were my boyhood associates," bragged Appo. Whenever he was apprehended, Appo insisted, "I was the one who took all the chances and consequences of an arrest and conviction."[9]

Other criminals concurred. Loyalty, camaraderie, and honor, insisted Sophie Lyons, were not simply part of the code of professional criminals, pickpockets, and con men; such traits exemplified the foundation upon which it rested. Criminals like Adam Worth, insisted Lyons, were known and admired in the underworld because of their unwavering loyalty to associates—never squealing and never abandoning friends. Lyons claimed witnessing "innumerable instances where criminals risked their own liberty and even their lives in order to assist a comrade in danger."[10]

Appo lived according to this ethic of loyalty, sharing both his riches and his sufferings. He endured solitary confinement at Clinton prison for refusing to identify the contract foreman who gave him a newspaper. He traveled to Ohio to inform the family of his Eastern State Penitentiary cellmate John Cronin of his whereabouts. He pickpocketed and schemed his way to Canada to bring an ailing Thomas Wilson back to his childhood home. He balked at prosecuting Dick Cronin for assaulting him in Jersey City. He refused to implicate police captain Richard O'Connor as James McNally's green goods "protector" when testifying before the Lexow Committee. And again he forgave Ira Hogshead for blowing out his eye in Poughkeepsie. In many cases Appo played the Good Samaritan, assisting someone in desperate need, or as in the case of Hogshead, just plain desperate.

Equally important, violence was embedded in Appo's concept of being a good fellow, but in antithetical ways. A good fellow's honor, manhood, and masculinity revolved around deception. Brains, not brawn, made a good fellow. Rather than strong-arming opponents or inflicting violence to assert himself—"gorillas," in the argot of the underworld—Appo relished risk and avoided force. More often a good fellow endured violence inflicted by others. "During the course of my unfortunate criminal life, I have received many violent assaults with weapons in the hands of unprincipled men," he wrote. "I still bear the scars on my head, neck and body." Despite their physically intimidating size, such men were cowards. The "only provocation I had given them," insisted Appo, "was for being a 'good fellow.' "[11]

Appo tolerated such violence, in part, because of his own sense of manhood. If one could not inflict pain, one's ability to suffer it was a quintessential virtue. Hardness and toughness meant not only administering violence but enduring physical assault. At times, however, he second-guessed his judgment. All too often, Appo conceded, he "generally got the worst of it" for being a good fellow.[12]

In tolerating physical pain and psychological abuse, a good fellow like Appo never appealed to the police or the law to resolve conflict. To do so was to be a traitor. Despite charges that his testimony before the Lexow Committee was just such a betrayal, Appo maintained that he remained faithful to this underworld code of honor. "During all my unfortunate crooked life in and out of prison, there is not one of my former associates can say I ever wronged them in any manner, shape or form," insisted Appo. "I always tried to do what was considered the right thing by them and took all kinds of chances and risks to be strictly on the level."[13]

Such remarks may reflect Appo's criminal's conceit, a retrospective arrogance, even self-delusion. Yet however self-serving, Appo's glory as a good fellow embodied a rejection of the dominant norms of nineteenth-century America, a resistance to the values of the so-called legitimate world. As a pocket-picking child and a green goods steerer, Appo not only evaded the law, but also the emerging urban bourgeois norms of street behavior, domesticity, and respect for individual property. The *mentalité* of a good fellow implied a shared fellowship and loyalty, an unspoken mutuality with other criminals. A good fellow was dedicated and courageous, audacious and bold. Unwavering in his rejection of legal authority, he refused to give testimony against enemies when assaulted. Appo harbored few grudges.

While some romanticized Appo in death, he was never a "primitive rebel," a noble outlaw, or an urban Jesse James. Appo's poignant saga challenges views depicting the Victorian criminal as part hero or part dreadful moral exemplar. Appo was hardly a "good criminal" intent on righting social wrongs. He never displayed a prerevolutionary or reformist ideology built on a tradition of resistance. Nor was he a "bad criminal," violating the law without qualification or for its own sake. Neither a latter-day Robin Hood nor a Jack the Ripper, Appo was a rather ordinary working-class man compelled to commit certain crimes because of very specific social conditions.[14] Appo's conception of himself as a good fellow was derived from experiences in his "workplace" and recreational spaces. He never displayed anger or class antagonism against the rich. He never articulated a philosophy of opposition—much less revolution—to the social structure of society. A socialist Appo was not.

Despite his bad luck and certain unfortunate experiences, his many arrests and years in prison, and the violence he endured, Appo was not bitter. Reading between the lines, Appo displayed a certain *joie de vivre*, a transcendent exuberance at surviving it all. Class resentment, the few times it appeared, was manifested against others in the underworld. His anger was not directed at the rich or even the legitimate world, but at successful criminals who violated the code of good fellows. Men like James McNally, Mike Riordan, and Mike Ryan were cowards, Appo charged, unwilling "to take a chance such as are taken by pickpockets or a burglar." In this inverted fashion, Appo displayed a level of class consciousness, but grounded in the internal milieu of his distinct subculture. When push came to shove, "capitalists" like McNally sided with corrupt police officers like Richard O'Connor. They were little more than, in Appo's words, "stoolpigeons for the Central Office."[15]

This is not to dispute that many individuals in Appo's world violated the code of good fellows. Appo's own life evidenced such failings and breakdowns. Criminals were human. They lied to one another; they cheated their companions. They assaulted, if not killed, both friend and foe. But human fallibility hardly refutes or denies the existence—indeed the compelling power—of such a worldview or moral universe. Even after his evangelical conversion, Appo defended his earlier principles and beliefs, revealing the tender sympathies of his nature and an unwillingness to inflict violence. Despite witnessing the frequent collapse of such loyalties, Appo remained a good fellow to the end of his life.

But Appo was foolhardy and naive. Not only did he expect others to adhere to his code of honor, he had little understanding of how his compatriots in crime viewed that world, how they defined what constituted a good fellow. Appo's Lexow testimony displayed how out of touch he was. "What was more surprising to me," he later wrote, "was to see many of my former associates who are known as rough grafters (pickpockets and burglars) and called by the underworld 'good fellows' turn on me for giving evidence against a crooked detective who would not hesitate to frame anyone of them up on a false charge and send them to state prison in order to square up his own rascality in those days."[16]

Appo's life was characterized by a nonexistent family structure; poor schooling; an early introduction to crime; an inability to find, obtain, or sustain regular jobs; and little institutional involvement excepting law enforcement. The very structures that shaped most individual behavior in nineteenth-century America—the family, the school, the church, the workplace—were invisible for Appo.[17] Instead Appo became immersed in a subculture organized around interpersonal violence, antisocial hierarchies molded and bolstered by the prison, an argot and underworld language shaped in part by illiteracy. Over time, this subculture was reinforced in his adult years via certain male rituals or rites of passage: the peer culture embodied in child street life, the social networks found in jails and prisons, and a drug culture facilitated by his opium addiction.

In myriad ways Appo's life embodied the changing structure of crime and punishment in nineteenth-century America. First, Appo's many arrests and incarcerations—on the *Mercury*, in the Tombs, on Blackwell's Island, in various penitentiaries—reflected the persistent failure of municipal law enforcement to deter criminal behavior. Second, Appo's horrifying tortures in penitentiaries like Sing Sing and Clinton illustrated the devolution of prison reform into systematic physical abuse and psychological emasculation. Third, Appo's opium addiction coincided with the birth of Gotham's first "bohemia" and a new recreational drug culture.

Finally Appo personified the emergence of the professional criminal connected to a national network of illegal activity. By the 1880s Appo was immersed in an informal but complex system of pickpockets, fences, opium addicts, and, most important, green goods operators. The latter required substantial capital, high investment returns, an ongoing hierarchical organization, the use of violence to achieve monopoly power, and talented or "professional" operatives. Green goods was among the earliest nationwide, market-based crimes distributing illegal goods to willing customers.

Facilitated by new urban technologies like the railroad and telegraph, novel economic instruments like greenbacks and paper money, and changing patterns of leisure in the form of dives and opium dens, Appo's criminal activities were, for the first time, national in their scope and reach. By the twentieth century the same enterprises would be labeled "rackets," shyster lawyers would become "fixers," opium would be replaced by other recreational drugs, and dives would be transformed into cabarets and nightclubs. In ways Appo little understood, his life reflected the advent of the first forms of organized crime, activities linked less to ethnicity and more to the new social and economic structures of the modern metropolis.[18] George Appo—marginalized, ostracized, and criminalized in his time, forgotten in ours—speaks to us a century later in unexpected ways.

We are drawn to tales of underdogs like George Appo. Such criminals have long held liminal positions in Western society, antiheroes if not real

*George Appo's gravestone in Mount Hope Cemetery in Hastings-on-Hudson, New York.*

heroes. Nineteenth-century writers like Charles Dickens and Victor Hugo transformed Oliver Twist and Jean Valjean into modern Davids taking on the Goliaths of the new industrial, urban society. Even in the twentieth century, Mario Puzo's Vito Corleone and Elmore Leonard's Chili Palmer evoke envy, if not outright admiration, because of their pluck and derring-do. Their ability to surmount high obstacles in the face of unrelenting odds engenders at worst reluctant admiration. But these are thin veils of romanticism, the benefit of vivid forms of fiction. In George Appo's world David rarely beat Goliath.

# Acknowledgments

$=$

THIS BOOK took too long to write. For over a decade, I accumulated many debts to many people, most of whom have probably forgotten when and how they helped me. Let me refresh their memories. Colleagues and friends read the initial prospectus and supported this project in early stages: Dana Barron, Anthony Cardoza, Daniel Czitrom, the late Sigmund Diamond, Joseph Gagliano, Susan Hirsch, Kenneth T. Jackson, Cheryl Johnson-Odim, Theodore Karamanski, Michael Khodarkovsky, Harold Platt, Barbara Rosenwein, Thomas J. Sugrue, and Luke Travers, O.S.B. Jo Hays and Robert Bucholz offered helpful assistance, advice, and wisdom regarding the underworlds of nineteenth-century London. Still others offered encouragement at key moments when my self-doubt started to overtake my self-confidence: Randy Bergstrom, Robert Bireley, S.J., Tim Bishop, Patricia Cline Cohen, Robert Devens, Lewis Erenberg, Michael Ebner, David Goldfield, Helen Horowitz, Suzanne Kaufman, Ray Mohl, Bill Sites, and Camilo Vergara. My colleagues in the department of history at Loyola University Chicago remained enthusiastic about this subject, even when my interest waned at times. Hilary Hinzmann of W. W. Norton, in particular, demonstrated far more faith in this project in the early stages than I deserved.

Numerous librarians and archivists helped me navigate the underworld of obscure primary sources. Lorna Newman, Ursula Schultz, and Vicky Waldron always managed to locate obscuria for me through Loyola University Chicago's interlibrary loan system. Elizabeth Cooper in the Loyola Law School library helped me locate nineteenth-century legal cases. Patti Schor, Sherry Anderson, Susan Sink, and Monica Salinas-Liening at the Loyola University Center for Instructional Design reproduced photographs and images on short notice. James D. Folts, William

Gorman, and Richard Andress of the New York State Archives in Albany helped me locate valuable and important documents, and were especially generous with their time, advice, and encouragement. Tricia Barbagallo offered many helpful hints on navigating sources in the New York State Library. Joseph Van Nostrand and Bruce Abrams at the New York County Clerk's Records Office provided a hospitable environment and a big table in making accessible nineteenth-century New York State census manuscripts and court cases.

In their own way, each of the following individuals helped me find little-known materials that I would have ignored without their help: Robin Leckbee in the rare book collection at Lake Forest College; Wayne T. De Cesar at the National Archives in College Park, Maryland; Gregory J. Plunges at the National Archives–Northeast Region; Myra Morales at the Adriance Memorial Library and Eileen Hayden of the Dutchess County Historical Society, both in Poughkeepsie, New York; Margaret Keiser and Steven Greenberg at the History of Medicine Division of the National Library of Medicine, Bethesda, Maryland; Alice Birney at the Library of Congress; Sgt. Griffin Graham at the Fishkill Correctional Facility in Beacon, New York; Andre Varin, Robert Ercole, and Arthur Wolpinsky at Sing Sing Penitentiary; Robert Arminio and N. MacDonald at the Ossining Historical Society Museum; the Reverend Thomas Pike, Nancy Styer, Sally Larson, and Linda Sheehan at Calvary-Saint George Episcopal Church in New York City; Nenetta Sarmiento at Saint James Roman Catholic Church in New York City; Joan Naverro in the New Jersey Room of the Jersey City Public Library; Carol Grieger and Frances Skelton at the New Haven Colony Historical Society in New Haven, Connecticut; Dominick Palermo at the Police Museum of New York City; Norman Brouwer at the Melville Library of the South Street Seaport Museum; Susan Johnson and Larry Cenotto of the Amador County Archives in California; Lorrayne Kennedy of the Calaveras County Archives in California; Peter Blodgett of the Huntington Library; Thomas Bourke in the Map Room of the New York Public Library; Liz Gardner of the Pennsylvania State Archives in Harrisburg; Ward Childs at the Philadelphia City Archives; John Dicrosta at the Philadelphia Records Services Center; and Katherine Hamilton-Smith at the Curt Teich Postcard Archive, Wauconda, Illinois.

Other individuals offered suggestions along the way. Tyler Anbinder generously shared his research on Five Points with me. George Lipsitz and Mary Seematter answered questions I had about St. Louis. Christopher Gray provided advice on one difficult source. Roger Daniels and John Kuo Wei Tchen helped me understand the history of Asian migrations to the United States. Carlo M. DeFerrari, historian of Tuolumne County in California, Sybil Zemitif of the California State Library, and Robert Chandler at Wells Fargo graciously assisted in tracking down details regarding Quimbo Appo's period in California. Claudia Milne, Robert Fitts, and Reginald Pitts at the Five Points Archeological Project helped me located hard-to-find census materials. Mary Snow of Saint Mary's Roman Catholic Church in New Haven, Connecticut, helped me find George Appo's baptism record. Wendy W. Schnur at the Mystic Seaport Museum and Norman Brouwer at the South Street Seaport Museum provided information on the school ship *Mercury*. Jeffrey McIllwain shared his research on Chinese crime. Andrew Cohen and Michael Willrich discussed their ideas on the history of crime with me, often directing me to sources that sharpened or challenged my arguments. David Schuyler's expertise on New York City is sprinkled throughout the book.

My students David Blanke, David Cholewiak, the Reverend William Corcoran, Gregory DiBenedictus, Andrew Eisen, Jerry Foust, Cheryl Lemus, Nona Martin, Catherine Maybrey, Laura Milsk, Jodi Morrison, Timothy Neary, Melinda Schlager, Adam Stewart, Matthew Szromba, Claudette Tolson, and Byron White dutifully helped in my researches. Their ideas, suggestions, and comments are part of the final product. The Loyola University Chicago undergraduates in my honors colloquium in the spring of 1995 raised questions I might otherwise have ignored.

Several institutions gave me time and money. Loyola University of Chicago provided two paid leaves of absence to initiate and complete the project. Fellowship support from the Newberry Library in Chicago, the National Endowment for the Humanities, the National Museum of American History of the Smithsonian Institution, and the John Simon Guggenheim Memorial Foundation was invaluable. The Minow Family Foundation provided funds for another project that gave me time to complete this one.

At the Smithsonian, I benefited from the help and hospitality offered by Lonnie Bunch, Fath Ruffins, Charles McGovern, Ann Kuebler, David Haberstich, Susan Strange, David Shayt, and Robert Leopold. Shelly Foote generously spent the greater part of a day literally showing me pockets in the costume collections of the Smithsonian. While working at the Newberry Library, I profited from the numerous conversations and criticisms generously offered by curators, staff, and fellows, pushing me in directions in which I was reluctant to venture: Tom Bauman, Richard Brown, Jim Cook, Jim Diedrick, Stephen Foster, Elliott J. Gorn, James Grossman, Ruth Hamilton, Sidney Harring, Fred Hoxie, Michael Calvert, Nancy Shoemaker, Timothy Spears, Carol Summerfield, Stephen Wade, Elissa Weaver, and Kathleen Wilson. My debt to Alfred Young is considerable: He not only offered constructive criticism in seminars and personal discussions, but his essay on George Robert Twelves Hewes provided me with a model and an inspiration.

Ben Franklin once said that visitors were like fish—after three days they start to stink. Fortunately, I have many friends and family members with diminished senses of smell who endured my lengthy invasions of their homes: Marian and Michael Harper in Dayton, Ohio; Marilyn and Nino Sferrella in Columbus, Ohio; Sheila and Scott Martin in Delaware, Ohio; Doron and Jo Ben-Atar in New Haven, Connecticut; Charisse and Tom Comer in Stamford, Connecticut; Barbara, Kenneth, and Kevan Jackson, Mark Kaminsky, Michael and Mary Norton, and Myra Sletson in Manhattan; Michael and Jennifer McCarthy in Brooklyn; Joseph Lynch and Chris McNickle in the Bronx; Daniel and Ellen Parker in New Rochelle, New York; Thomas J. Sugrue and Dana Barron in Philadelphia; Thomas Hyde and Mary Curtin in Washington, D.C.; Peter Levy and Diane Kresja in Maryland; and Adele Alexander and Alex Ambruso in Southern California.

This book relies heavily on manuscript collections, many of which remained untouched by human hands for over a century. I would never have been able to locate and examine these sources but for the kindness, selflessness, and dedication of the librarians and staff at the New York City Municipal Archives and Records Center. For more than two decades, Ken Cobb, Leonora Gidlund, and Evelyn Gonzales have shared their unsurpassed knowledge of the hidden sources of New York history. I owe an immeasurable debt to Mr. Cobb in particular for making many hard-to-find materials accessible to me on short notice. Without his help and trust, this book would have been impossible to write. I am similarly grateful to Jean Ashton and Bernard R. Crystal at the Rare Book and Manuscript Library of Columbia University, who generously gave me access to George Appo's manuscripts and allowed me to quote extensively from them.

I presented portions of this project to different audiences that offered both encouragement and positive criticism: the Organization of American Historians annual meeting, the Newberry Library Fellows Seminar, the Researching New York Conference at the State University of New York at Albany, the City Seminar at Columbia University, the Labor History Seminar at the Newberry Library, the Urban History Seminar at the Chicago Historical Society, the Urban Forum of St. Louis, Missouri, Colgate University, and Phi Alpha Theta at Northeastern Illinois University. I am thankful for the suggestions and support Henry Binford, Owen Gutfreund, Richard Hamm, Graham Hodges, Lisa Keller, Carol Krinsky, Russell Lewis, Eileen McMahon, Patricia Mooney-Melvin, Steve Rosswurm, Eric Sandweiss, Carl Smith, Robert Snyder, and Allen Steinberg offered at these presentations.

I owe much to the individuals who read portions of the manuscript: Robert Brazeau, Leon Fink, Helene Greenwald, Regina Kunzel, Susan Levine, Sam Mitrani, Susan Pearson, Jack Salzman, and Craig Wilder. Joseph Bigott, Stuart Blumin, Patricia Bonomi, Daniel Czitrom, Gary Dunbar, Leslie Fishbein, the late Daniel Goodwin, Elliott J. Gorn, Kenneth Jackson, the late Eric Monkkonen, Timothy Shannon, Daniel Richter, and Robert Wesser deserve special praise for reading the entire manuscript in a much longer, tedious form. The sacrificed time and invaluable suggestions represent debts I can never fully repay. I want to thank the editorial board of New York History for recognizing A Pickpocket's Tale with the Dixon Ryan Fox Prize while it was still in manuscript form. I am especially appreciative to Elliott Gorn for listening to my complaints about reconstructing the life of George Appo, and sometimes life itself.

Steve Forman at W. W. Norton has been a model of editorial patience in tolerating my missed deadlines and lengthy drafts of various chapters. My copy editor, Sue Llewellyn, corrected many embarrassing mistakes. My thanks also to Rebecca Arata and Liz Pierson. All have made this a much better book.

My greatest thanks goes to my family. At various points, my brother, Jerry, sister-in-law Linda, and mother-in-law, Adele Alexander, not only gave me support and encouragement but offered what some consider the supreme sacrifice: the use of their cars to drive to various archives. When I needed some time to write, Reyna Cerrato played with and cared for my children as if they were her own. For that I am forever grateful.

My mother and father deserve a special mention. Some parents drive their children crazy; mine literally drove me to my sources. Mom and Dad helped me find George Appo's tombstone in Mount Hope Cemetery, Quimbo Appo's forgotten burial site on the grounds of the Fishkill Correctional Facility (formerly the Matteawan State Hospital for the Criminally Insane), and Danny Driscoll's unmarked grave in Calvary Cemetery in Queens. They waited patiently outside libraries and local historical societies throughout New York while I spent days perusing old manuscripts and local newspapers. They spent two weeks of vacation time in Albany enabling me to complete my research in the New York State Archives. Only a parent can comprehend such devotion. My greatest regret is that neither lived to see the final product of their personal sacrifices.

I began writing this book with two parents and no children. It ends with no parents and two children. Maria and Danielle Gilfoyle have spent their short lives wondering why Daddy has that photograph of a criminal on his desk, next to theirs. More often they wondered why it was taking so long. I am grateful for the many interruptions to play with the computer, fill the pool, and drive to soccer, ballet, swimming, and piano practices. The years of joyful distraction were more fun and far better than finishing the book "on time."

My greatest debt and singular love belong to my wife, Mary Rose Alexander, who suffered through the ups and downs of this project more deeply and longer than anyone. Her patience and devotion are unsurpassed. She is probably happier than I am to see the book's completion. The dedication expresses my profound admiration, eternal appreciation, and heartfelt love.

# Appendixes

===

Number of teenagers ages 14 to 19 in parentheses ( ), followed by percentage of teenagers within inmate population.

| YEAR | AUBURN | CLINTON | SING SING | TOTAL |
|------|--------|---------|-----------|-------|
| 1870 | 941 (126–13) | 456 (71–16) | 1,129 (260–23) | 2,526 (457–18) |
| 1871 | 931 (124–13) | 529 (93–18) | 1,260 (119 9) | 2,720 (336–12) |
| 1872 | 1,119 (128–11) | 549 (89–11) | 1,083 (318*–29) | 2,751 (913–33) |
| 1873 | 1,104 (134 12) | 567 (79–14) | 1,237 (243–20) | 2,908 (456 16) |
| 1874 | 1,202 (159–13) | 552 NA | 1,185 (135–11) | 2,939 NA |
| 1875 | 1,312 (155–12) | 553 NA | 1,487 (234–16) | 3,352 NA |
| 1876 | 1,281 (150–12) | 623 NA | 1,452 (218–15) | 3,356 NA |
| 1877 | 1,388 (156–11) | 566 NA | 1,613 (397–25) | 3,567 NA |
| 1878 | 1,193 (125–10) | 649 NA | 1,646 (474–29) | 3,478 NA |
| 1879 | 1,104 (96–9) | 472 NA | 1,596 (305–19) | 3,171 NA |
| 1880 | 897 (65–7) | 522 NA | 1,518 (256–17) | 2,936 NA |
| 1881 | 903 NA | 530 NA | 1,518 NA | 2,951 NA |
| 1882 | 912 (77–8) | 499 NA | 1,526 (276–18) | 2,937 NA |
| 1883 | 882 (72–8) | 484 NA | 1,462 (225 15) | 2,828 NA |
| 1884 | 765 (60–8) | 572 NA | 1,539 (212–14) | 2,876 NA |
| 1885 | 876 (59–7) | 544 NA | 1,541 (217–14) | 2,961 NA |
| 1886 | 1,084 (82–8) | 539 (13–2) | 1,532 (201–13) | 3,155 (296–9) |
| 1887 | 1,111 (72–6) | 760 (45–6) | 1,425 (201–14) | 3,296 (318–10) |
| 1888 | 1,242 (87–7) | 755 (24–3) | 1,405 (192–14) | 3,402 (303–9) |
| 1889 | 1,227 (86–7) | 867 (88–10) | 1,386 (161–12) | 3,480 (335–10) |
| 1890 | 1,151 (65–6) | 804 (83–10) | 1,533 (140–9) | 3,488 (288–8) |
| 1891 | 1,263 (89–7) | 759 (75–10) | 1,592 (118–7) | 3,614 (282–8) |
| 1892 | 1,273 (92–7) | 953 (105–11) | 1,369 (102–7) | 3,595 (299–8) |
| 1893 | 1,186 (90–8) | 1,031 (110 –11) | 1,275 (104–8) | 3,492 (304–9) |
| 1894 | 1,158 (76–7) | 1,031 (111 –12) | 1,365 (89–7) | 3,554 (276–8) |
| 1895 | 1,126 (53–5) | 1,007 (116–12) | 1,375 (85–6) | 3,508 (254–7) |
| 1896 | 1,014 (57–6) | 886 (93–10) | 1,220 (55–5) | 3,120 (205–7) |
| 1897 | 1,005 (68–7) | 881 (96–11) | 1,243 (55–4) | 3,129 (219–7) |
| 1898 | 969 NA | 947 NA | 1,286 NA | 3,202 NA |
| 1899 | 1,063 NA | 938 NA | 1,349 NA | 3,350 NA |
| 1900 | 1,126 (32–3) | 1,021 (113–11) | 1,229 (49–4) | 3,376 (194–6) |

NA = not available or given that year

* The report for 1872 gave the following for ages when convicted: 1 for age 14, 21 for age 15, 674 for ages 16 to 19, and 296 for ages 20 to 29. It appears that the 674 and 296 figures should be reversed, giving 318 for ages 19 or less. To employ the higher figure would mean that the teenage population would have exceeded 60 percent, an unlikely figure given the data in the preceeding and ensuing years.

SOURCES: Inspectors of State Prisons, *Annual Reports* (Albany, 1871–1877); Superintendent of State Prisons, *Annual Reports* (Albany, 1878–1901).

NOTE: Figures are based on population of each institution on 30 Sept. of the year.

## APPENDIX 2  NEW YORK STATE PRISON EXPENDITURES, 1866–1900

Total prison expenditures in thousands of dollars, followed by average expenditure per inmate in dollars, followed by amount of deficit or surplus in thousands of dollars.

| YEAR | AUBURN | | | CLINTON | | | SING SING | | | NEW YORK TOTAL | | |
|---|---|---|---|---|---|---|---|---|---|---|---|---|
| | TOTAL | AVE. | D/S | TOTAL | AVE. | D/S | TOTAL | AVE. | D/S | TOTAL | AVE. | D/S |
| 1866 | NA | | | NA | | | NA | | | 220 | | −95 |
| 1867 | NA | | | NA | | | NA | | | 255 | | −121 |
| 1868 | NA | | | NA | | | NA | | | 300 | | −129 |
| 1869 | 171 | | −42 | 317 | | −60 | 351 | | −87 | 839 | | −189 |
| 1870 | 166 | 182 | −35 | 306 | 671 | −32 | 362 | 320 | −72 | 834 | 330 | −139 |
| 1871 | 166 | 178 | −29 | 311 | 588 | −86 | 267 | 212 | −122 | 744 | 274 | −237 |
| 1872 | 191 | 171 | −55 | 457 | 832 | −117 | 342 | 316 | −245 | 990 | 360 | −417 |
| 1873 | 185 | 168 | −50 | 322 | 568 | −81 | 319 | 258 | −167 | 826 | 284 | −298 |
| 1874 | 197 | 164 | −102 | 327 | 592 | −181 | 263 | 222 | −179 | 787 | 268 | −462 |
| 1875 | 193 | 147 | ? | 290 | 524 | −98 | 251 | 169 | −168 | 734 | 219 | −266* |
| 1876 | 195 | 152 | −116 | 294 | 472 | −230 | 271 | 187 | −258 | 843 | 251 | −604 |
| 1877 | 180 | 130 | −96 | 230 | 406 | −96 | 216 | 134 | −126 | 626 | 175 | −318 |
| 1878 | 151 | 127 | −34 | 103 | 159 | −77 | 176 | 107 | +43 | 430 | 124 | −68 |
| 1879 | 127 | 115 | +2 | 109 | 231 | −61 | 188 | 118 | +39 | 423 | 133 | −20 |
| 1880 | 130 | 145 | −15 | 91 | 174 | −36 | 184 | 121 | +33 | 405 | 138 | −18 |
| 1881 | 119 | 131 | −5 | 98 | 185 | −36 | 187 | 123 | +42 | 404 | 137 | +1 |
| 1882 | 123 | 135 | −3 | 100 | 200 | −39 | 193 | 126 | +48 | 416 | 142 | +6 |
| 1883 | 120 | 136 | +5 | 95 | 196 | −50 | 183 | 125 | +54 | 398 | 141 | +9 |
| 1884 | 115 | 150 | −0.7 | 99 | 173 | −52 | 176 | 120 | +63 | 391 | 136 | +10 |
| 1885 | 112 | 128 | −35 | 98 | 180 | −34 | 173 | 112 | +73 | 383 | 129 | +3 |
| 1886 | 125 | 115 | | 83 | 154 | | 167 | 109 | +75 | 374 | 119 | +4 |
| 1887 | 136 | 122 | | 94 | 124 | | 163 | 106 | +19 | 393 | 119 | −60 |
| 1888 | 132 | 106 | | 109 | 144 | | 163 | 114 | +6 | 405 | 119 | −154 |
| 1889 | 136 | 111 | | 129 | 149 | | 162 | 117 | −132 | 420 | 121 | −369 |
| 1890 | 136 | 118 | −49 | 129 | 160 | −49 | 169 | 110 | −15 | 434 | 124 | −113 |
| 1891 | 144 | 114 | | 143 | 188 | | 189 | 119 | −116 | 464 | 128 | −201 |
| 1892 | 142 | 112 | | 151 | 158 | | 204 | 149 | −39 | 485 | 135 | −140 |
| 1893 | 153 | 129 | | 161 | 156 | | 190 | 149 | | 504 | 144 | −477 |
| 1894 | 157 | 136 | −129 | 157 | 152 | −142 | 151 | 111 | −95 | 465 | 131 | −366 |
| 1895 | 169 | 150 | | 166 | 165 | | 153 | 111 | | 488 | 139 | −332 |
| 1896 | 159 | 157 | | 162 | 183 | | 168 | 138 | | 489 | 157 | −353 |
| 1897 | 163 | 162 | | 162 | 184 | | 174 | 140 | | 499 | 159 | |
| 1898 | NA | | | NA | | | NA | | | NA | | |
| 1899 | 135 | 127 | | 146 | 156 | | 180 | 133 | | 461 | 138 | |
| 1900 | 150 | 133 | | 143 | 140 | | 167 | 136 | | 460 | 136 | |

Ave. = average expenditure per inmate

D/S = deficit or surplus

*  = includes only Clinton and Sing Sing totals

NA = not available or given that year

SOURCES: Inspectors of State Prisons, *Annual Reports* (Albany, 1871–1877); Superintendent of State Prisons, *Annual Reports* (Albany, 1878–1901); New York State Assembly, *Report of the Assembly Special Committee on Convict Labor in the Penal Institutions of the State*, Assembly Doc. 66 (Albany, 1899), 37.

NOTE: Totals may differ from individual prison inputs because inputs are rounded. Expenditures per inmate are based on population of each institution on 30 Sept. of the year.

## Appendix 3 Sing Sing Death and Insanity Rates, 1870–1900

( ) = number under 40 years of age

| Year | Deaths | Death % <40 | Mortality per 1,000 | Sent to (NYS) Asylum | Insane per 1,000 | Suicides | Death/Insanity Rate per 1,000 |
|------|--------|-------------|---------------------|----------------------|------------------|----------|-------------------------------|
| 1870 | 14 (11) | 71 | 12.4 (15.77) | 4 | 3.5 | o | 15.9 |
| 1871 | 19 (17) | 89 | 15.1 | 6 | 4.8 | o | 19.8 |
| 1872 | 15 (13) | 87 | 13.9 | 14 | 12.9 | o | 26.8 |
| 1873 | 10 (8) | 80 | 8.0 | 8 | 6.5 | o | 14.5 |
| 1874 | 16 (12) | 75 | 13.5 | 2 | 1.7 | 1 | 15.2 |
| 1875 | 11 (10) | 91 | 7.3 | 13 | 8.7 | o | 16.1 |
| 1876 | 19 (16) | 84 | 13.2 | 5 | 3.4 | o | 16.5 |
| 1877 | 16 (11) | 69 | 9.9 | 6 | 3.9 | 1 | 11.8 |
| 1878 | 7 (6) | 86 | 4.3 | 10 | 6.1 | 1 | 10.3 |
| 1879 | 19 (19) | 100 | 11.9 | 8 | 5.0 | o | 16.9 |
| 1880 | 11 (10) | 91 | 7.2 (17.38) | 7 | 4.6 | 1 | 11.9 |
| 1881 | 20 | | 13.2 | 5 | 3.3 | ? | 16.5 |
| 1882 | 14 (11) | 79 | 9.2 | 11 | 7.2 | ? | 16.4 |
| 1883 | 18 (14) | 78 | 12.3 | 8 | 5.5 | o | 17.8 |
| 1884 | 27 (19) | 70 | 17.5 | 13 | 8.4 | o | 26.0 |
| 1885 | 18 (15) | 83 | 11.7 | 7 | 4.5 | o | 16.2 |
| 1886 | 12 (11) | 92 | 7.8 | 7 | 4.6 | 2 | 12.4 |
| 1887 | 16 (11) | 69 | 11.2 | 10 | 7.0 | 1 | 18.2 |
| 1888 | 15 (9) | 56 | 10.7 | 4 | 2.8 | 1 | 13.5 |
| 1889 | 25 (22) | 88 | 18.0 | 13 | 9.4 | o | 27.4 |
| 1890 | 35 (29) | 83 | 22.8 (15.17) | 17 | 11.1 | o | 33.9 |
| 1891 | 53 (41) | 77 | 33.3 | 21 | 13.2 | 1 | 46.5 |
| 1892 | 41 (36) | 88 | 29.9 | 26 | 19.0 | o | 48.9 |
| 1893 | 16 (12) | 75 | 12.5 | 24 | 18.8 | o | 31.4 |
| 1894 | 30 (19) | 63 | 22.0 | 13 | 9.5 | o | 31.5 |
| 1895 | 19 (15) | 79 | 13.8 | 23 | 16.7 | o | 30.5 |
| 1896 | 10 (8) | 80 | 8.2 | 21 | 17.2 | o | 25.4 |
| 1897 | 8 (7) | 88 | 6.4 | 16 | 12.9 | o | 19.3 |
| 1898 | NA | | | NA | | | |
| 1899 | NA | | | NA | | | |
| 1900 | 8 (6) | 75 | 6.5 | 7 | 5.7 | o | 12.2 |
| TOTAL | 542 (418) | 77 | | 326 | | 9 | |

NA = not available or given that year

Sources: Inspectors of State Prisons, *Annual Reports* (Albany, 1871–1877); Superintendent of State Prisons, *Annual Reports* (Albany, 1878–1901); *New York Tribune*, 23 Jan. 1883 (1878–1882); *New York Times*, 17 Nov. 1880.

Note: Mortality and suicide rates are based on the population on 30 Sept. of the year.

APPENDIX 4     AUBURN DEATH AND INSANITY RATES, 1870–1900

( ) = number under 40 years of age

| YEAR | DEATHS | % <40 | MORT. RATE DAILY POP. | MORTALITY PER 1,000 | SENT TO ASYLUM | INSANE PER 1,000 | SUICIDES | DEATH/ INSANITY RATE PER 1,000 |
|------|--------|-------|----------------------|---------------------|----------------|------------------|----------|-------------------------------|
| 1870 | 6 (5)   | 83 | 6.4  | 6.4  | 3  | 3.2  | 0 | 9.6  |
| 1871 | 8 (7)   | 88 | 8.3  | 8.6  | 12 | 12.9 | 2 | 21.5 |
| 1872 | 8 (5)   | 63 | 7.2  | 7.1  | 6  | 5.4  | 0 | 12.5 |
| 1873 | 12 (7)  | 58 | 10.8 | 10.8 | 6  | 5.4  | 0 | 10.9 |
| 1874 | 15 (13) | 87 | 12.5 | 12.5 | 12 | 10.0 | ? | 22.5 |
| 1875 | 19 (14) | 74 | 15.0 | 14.5 | 18 | 13.7 | 2 | 28.2 |
| 1876 | 30 (19) | 63 | 21.7 | 23.4 | 13 | 10.1 | 0 | 33.5 |
| 1877 | 16 (11) | 69 | 11.5 | 11.5 | 17 | 12.2 | 0 | 23.7 |
| 1878 | 13 (9)  | 69 | 9.7  | 10.9 | 17 | 14.2 | 0 | 25.1 |
| 1879 | 18 (11) | 61 | 15.7 | 16.3 | 12 | 11.0 | 2 | 27.3 |
| 1880 | 12 (7)  | 58 | 12.0 | 13.4 | 15 | 16.7 | 0 | 30.1 |
| 1881 | 21 ?    |    | 23.0 | 23.3 |    | ?    |   |      |
| 1882 | 20 (15) | 75 | 21.5 | 21.9 | 9  | 9.9  | 1 | 31.8 |
| 1883 | 12 (11) | 90 | 12.9 | 13.6 | 15 | 17.0 | 0 | 30.6 |
| 1884 | 14 (8)  | 57 |      | 18.3 | 17 | 22.2 | 0 | 40.5 |
| 1885 | 6 (3)   | 50 |      | 6.8  | 8  | 9.1  | 1 | 15.9 |
| 1886 | 25 (18) | 72 |      | 23.0 | 43 | 39.7 | 0 | 62.7 |
| 1887 | 32 (23) | 72 |      | 28.8 | 27 | 24.3 | 2 | 53.1 |
| 1888 | 22 (14) | 64 |      | 17.7 | 18 | 0.8  | 1 | 18.5 |
| 1889 | 25 (18) | 72 | 19.7 | 20.4 | 38 | 31.0 | 0 | 51.4 |
| 1890 | 20 (18) | 62 |      | 25.2 | 19 | 16.5 | 0 | 41.7 |
| 1891 | 52 (37) | 71 | 30.0 | 41.2 | 25 | 19.8 | 1 | 61.0 |
| 1892 | 34 (30) | 77 | 35.0 | 47.9 | 31 | 24.4 | 0 | 72.3 |
| 1893 | 34 (30) | 88 | 26.6 | 28.7 | 28 | 23.6 | 0 | 52.3 |
| 1894 | 43 (33) | 77 |      | 37.1 | 18 | 15.5 | ? | 52.6 |
| 1895 | 22 (16) | 73 | 18.1 | 19.5 | 12 | 10.7 | 0 | 30.2 |
| 1896 | 17 ?    | ?  |      | 16.8 | 9  | 8.9  | ? | 25.7 |
| 1897 | 9 (4)   | 44 | 8.7  | 09.0 | 22 | 21.9 | 1 | 30.9 |
| 1898 | NA      |    |      |      | NA |      |   |      |
| 1899 | NA      |    |      |      | NA |      |   |      |
| 1900 | 18 (12) | 67 | 16.0 | 16.0 | 13 | 11.5 | 2 | 27.5 |
| TOTAL 1870-1900 | 583(398) | 68 |  |  | 483 |  | 15 |  |

NA = not available or given that year

SOURCES: Inspectors of State Prisons, *Annual Reports* (Albany, 1871–1877); Superintendent of State Prisons, *Annual Reports* (Albany, 1878–1901).

NOTE: Mortality and suicide rates are based on the population on 30 Sept. of the year.

## APPENDIX 5    CLINTON DEATH AND INSANITY RATES, 1870–1900

( ) = number under 40 years of age

| YEAR | DEATHS | | % <40 | MORTALITY PER 1,000 | SENT TO ASYLUM | INSANE PER 1,000 | SUICIDES | DEATH/ INSANITY RATE PER 1,000 |
|---|---|---|---|---|---|---|---|---|
| 1870 | 10 | (7) | 70 | 21.9 | 4 | 8.8 | 0 | 30.7 |
| 1871 | 5 | (3) | 60 | 9.5 | 2 | 3.8 | 0 | 13.2 |
| 1872 | 6 | (3) | 50 | 10.9 | 5 | 9.1 | 0 | 20.0 |
| 1873 | 13 | (8) | 62 | 22.9 | 1 | 1.5 | ? | 24.7 |
| 1874 | 8 | (7) | 88 | 14.5 | 4 | 7.2 | 0 | 21.7 |
| 1875 | 4 | (3) | 75 | 7.2 | 3 | 5.4 | 0 | 12.7 |
| 1876 | 30 | | | 48.2 | NA | | 0 | >48.2 |
| 1877 | 16 | | | 28.3 | NA | | | >28.3 |
| 1878 | 12 | (9) | 75 | 18.5 | 5 | 7.7 | 0 | 26.2 |
| 1879 | 4 | (2) | 50 | 8.5 | 10 | | 0 | 29.7 |
| 1880 | 10 | (8) | 80 | 19.2 | 9 | 17.2 | 0 | 36.4 |
| 1881 | 15 | ? | | 28.3 | NA | | ? | >28.3 |
| 1882 | 20 | (11) | 55 | 40.1 | 4 | 8.0 | 0 | 48.1 |
| 1883 | 12 | (6) | 50 | 24.8 | 4 | 8.3 | 0 | 33.1 |
| 1884 | 11 | (7) | 64 | 19.2 | 4 | 7.0 | 1 | 26.2 |
| 1885 | 14 | (10) | 71 | 25.7 | 10 | 18.4 | 1 | 44.1 |
| 1886 | 12 | (11) | 92 | 22.3 | 13 | 22.3 | 0 | 46.4 |
| 1887 | 6 | (6) | 100 | 7.9 | 4 | 5.3 | 0 | 13.2 |
| 1888 | 22 | (17) | 77 | 29.1 | 9 | 11.9 | 0 | 41.1 |
| 1889 | 14 | (8) | 57 | 16.1 | 14 | 16.1 | 2 | 34.3 |
| 1890 | 19 | (16) | 84 | 23.6 | 14 | 17.4 | 0 | 41.0 |
| 1891 | 17 | (15) | 88 | 22.4 | 12 | 15.8 | 0 | 38.2 |
| 1892 | 14 | (9) | 64 | 14.7 | 21 | 22.0 | 0 | 36.7 |
| 1893 | 9 | (6) | 67 | 8.7 | 19 | 18.46 | 0 | 27.2 |
| 1894 | 13 | (8) | 62 | 12.6 | 11 | 10.7 | ? | 23.3 |
| 1895 | 9 | (6) | 67 | 8.9 | 18 | 17.9 | 0 | 26.8 |
| 1896 | 9 | (4) | 44 | 10.2 | 11 | 12.4 | 0 | 22.6 |
| 1897 | 6 | (4) | 67 | 6.8 | 13 | 14.8 | 0 | 21.6 |
| 1898 | NA | | | | NA | | | |
| 1899 | NA | | | | NA | | | |
| 1900 | 9 | (5) | 56 | 8.8 | 5 | 13.7 | 0 | 13.7 |
| TOTAL 1870–1900 | 349 | (199) | 57 | | 229 | | 4 | |

NA = not available or given that year

SOURCES: Inspectors of State Prisons, *Annual Reports* (Albany, 1871–1877); Superintendent of State Prisons, *Annual Reports* (Albany, 1878–1901).

NOTE: Mortality and suicide rates are based on the population on 30 Sept. of the year.

# Notes

=

All newspapers refer to New York City publications unless otherwise indicated. Commonly used abbreviations in the notes are:

| | |
|---|---|
| AD | New York State Assembly Document. |
| *Albow* | *People v. George Albow* (1893), New York Court of Appeals, Cases and Briefs on Appeal (J2002), NYSArc. |
| Appo | Autobiography of George Appo (typewritten manuscript), box 32, Society for the Prevention of Crime Papers, Rare Book and Manuscript Library, Columbia University, New York, N.Y. |
| AR | Annual Report. |
| BR | Billy Rose Theater Collection, Lincoln Center, New York Public Library, New York, N.Y. |
| CAS | Children's Aid Society of New York. |
| CCNYA | County Clerk of New York Archives, 31 Chambers Street, New York, N.Y. |
| CGS | New York City Court of General Sessions, District Attorney Papers, NYCMA. |
| DAP | District Attorney Indictment Papers, New York County, Court of General Sessions, NYCMA. |
| DAS | District Attorney Scrapbooks, New York County, NYCMA. |
| Drummond Papers | Daily Reports of A. L. Drummond, Records of the U.S. Secret Service, Record Group 87, National Archives and Records Administration, College Park, Md. |
| ESP | Eastern State Penitentiary, Population Records, Record Group 15, Records of the Department of Justice, Pennsylvania State Archives, Harrisburg. |
| ESP Inspectors | Inspectors of the State Penitentiary for the Eastern District of Pennsylvania. |
| *Increase of Crime* | New York State Assembly, *Report of the Select Committee Appointed by the Assembly of 1875 to Investigate the Causes of the Increase of Crime in the City of New York*, AD 106 (New York, 1876). |
| *Leslie's* | *Frank Leslie's Illustrated Newspaper*. |
| *Lexow Committee* | New York State Senate, *Investigation of the Police Department of New York City* (Albany, N.Y., 1895), 5 vols. |

| | |
|---|---|
| *Mazet Committee* | New York State Assembly, *Special Committee Appointed to Investigate Public Officers and Departments of the City of New York* (Albany, 1900), 5 vols. |
| MGS | Minutes of the New York County Court of General Sessions, NYCMA. |
| MP | Mayors' Papers, NYCMA. |
| *NPG* | *National Police Gazette.* |
| NYC | New York City. |
| NYCMA | New York City Municipal Archives and Records Center, 31 Chambers Street, New York, N.Y. |
| NYHS | New-York Historical Society, 170 Central Park West, New York, N.Y. |
| NYPL | New York Public Library, Fifth Avenue and 42nd Street, New York, N.Y. |
| NYS | New York State. |
| NYSA | New York State Assembly. |
| NYSArc | New York State Archives, Albany, N.Y. |
| NYSCC | New York State Crime Commission. |
| NYSL | New York State Legislature. |
| NYSPC | New York State Prison Commission. |
| NYSS | New York State Senate. |
| NYSSP | New York Superintendent of State Prisons. |
| PANY | Prison Association of New York. |
| PCA | Philadelphia City Archives, 9th Floor, 401 N. Broad Street, Philadelphia, Pa. |
| PCC | New York City Department of Public Charities and Correction. |
| PCDB | Police Court Docket Books or Magistrates (Police) Court Docket Books, NYCMA. |
| PRSC | City of Philadelphia Records Storage Center, Room 220, 401 N. Broad Street, Philadelphia, Pa. |
| *Quimbo Appo* | *People v. Quimbo Appo,* 20 NY 531 (1860), New York Court of Appeals, Cases and Briefs on Appeal (J2002), NYSArc. |
| QA Case File | Quimbo Appo Case File, #456, box 7, Matteawan State Hospital Inmate Case Files, 1880–1960 (A1500), NYSArc. |
| RG 21 | Record Group 21, U.S. District Court Records, National Archives–Northeast Region, 201 Varick Street, New York, N.Y. |
| SCC | New York Supreme Court Cases, unprocessed collection, New York County District Attorney Indictment Papers, NYCMA. |
| SD | New York State Senate Document. |
| SPC | Society for the Prevention of Crime. |
| SPC Papers | Society for the Prevention of Crime Papers, Rare Book and Manuscript Room, Butler Library, Columbia University, New York, N.Y. |
| SPCC | Society for the Prevention of Cruelty to Children. |
| SSAR | Sing Sing Inmate Admission Registers, NYSArc. |
| WC | Warshaw Collection of Business Americana, Archives Center, National Museum of American History, Smithsonian Institution, Washington, D.C. |

## PREFACE

1. James D. Horan, *The Pinkerton Story* (New York, 1951), 314 (evillest); *Times*, 4 May 1866 (extraordinary robberies); *NPG*, 24 Aug. 1867 (Carnival of Crime); *Tribune*, 19 July 1883, 2 Feb. 1896 (Carnival of Crime); 13 June 1897 (Murderers' Alley); *Herald* clipping, 8 Jan. 1887 (rampant), vol. 30, DAS; Edward Dana Durand, *The Finances of New York City* (New York, 1898), 288, 376–77 (police expenditures); Kenneth T. Jackson, ed., *The Encyclopedia of New York City* (New Haven, Conn., 1995), 166 (budget), 297–98 (murder rates), 911,923 (population). On high rates of larceny before 1900, see chap. 5, esp. note 2. Examples of the growing fear of crime in New York after 1860 are abundant. See *Increase of Crime*; statement of grand jury foreman James M. Dunbar in Mayor William Wickham to Police Commissioners, 7 Oct. 1875, copy in folder 261, box 1264; unmarked clipping, 14 July 1875, folder 157, box 1237, both in MP; Charles Sutton, *The New York Tombs: Its Secrets and Its Mysteries* (New York, 1874), 2–3; Frank Moss, *The American Metropolis* (New York, 1897), III: 220–23; and numerous clippings, 1889–1896, in DAS.

2. *Star* clipping, 4 June 1884 (class of criminals), vol. 8, DAS; Thomas Byrnes, *Professional Criminals of America* (New York, 1886 and 1895).

3. 396, entry for George Dixon, vol. 11; 173, entry for George Wilson, vol. 14; 269, entry for George Appo, container, 6, vol. 20; 140, entry for George Albow, container 10, vol. 28, all in SSAR; *Newark* [Ohio] *Daily Advocate*, 15 June 1896. I was unable to learn the meaning of Appo's tattoos.

4. Appo, 20, 29 ($600); *NPG*, 4 May 1895 (gilt-edged swindlers); Byrnes, *Professional Criminals* (1895 ed.), 205 (gilt-edged); Allan Pinkerton, *Thirty Years a Detective* (Chicago, 1884), 71 (most remunerative); *Tribune*, 11 Sept. 1894; Moss, *American Metropolis*, III:136–38 ($50,000 to $200,000 fortunes).

5. Appo, 81. Appo employed the term "good fellow" ten times in his autobiography and spelled it with a space between the words. I have retained that spelling throughout this book. See Appo, 15, 25, 81, 84, 95, 96. The earliest use of the term I found was in Hutchins Hapgood, ed., *The Autobiography of a Thief* (New York, 1903), 58–59, 103, 111, 119, 191, 196, 229, 242, 314. He gives no description or definition, and includes cooperative prison keepers in his definition. Joseph Matthew Sullivan, "Criminal Slang," *American Law Review* 52 (1918), 891, defined a good fellow as "a thief, man or woman who pay their bills," the earliest approximation to Appo's use of the term. More general and less precise usages appear in Josiah Flynt, *Notes of an Itinerant Policeman* (Boston, 1900), 18; William B. Moreau, *Swindling Exposed: From the Diary of William B. Moreau, King of the Fakirs* (Syracuse, N.Y., 1907), 189; and John O'Connor, *Broadway Racketeers* (New York, 1928), 15. None includes the associations provided by Appo. Significantly it did not appear in O'Connor's glossary of underworld terms (249–55). Later dictionaries defined "good head" as "a trustworthy and faithful person," "old time criminals who have proved their reliability," "criminals worthy of trust from fellow criminals," and "a kind-hearted person, one charitably disposed to tramps," all of which are closer approximations to Appo's use of the term "good fellow." See Noel Ersine, *Underworld and Prison Slang* (Upland, Ind., 1933), 40; Eric Partridge, ed., *A Dictionary of the Underworld* (New York, 1949), 299; Godfrey Irwin, *American Tramp and Underworld Slang* (New York, 1931), 88; Elisha K. Kane, "The Jargon of the Under-

world," *Dialect Notes* 5 (1927), 448; Hyman E. Goldin, ed., *Dictionary of American Underworld Lingo* (New York, 1950), 84.

6. Nicholas Pileggi, *Wiseguy: Life in a Mafia Family* (New York, 1985). "Criminal classes" and "dangerous classes" were commonly used terms in nineteenth-century America. See Charles Loring Brace, *The Dangerous Classes of New York and Twenty Years' Work Among Them* (New York, 1872); *Increase of Crime*, 26, 39, 61; *Tribune*, 19 July 1883; Eric H. Monkkonen, *The Dangerous Class: Crime and Poverty in Columbus, Ohio, 1860–1885* (Cambridge, Mass., 1975). For a more detailed discussion, see Timothy J. Gilfoyle, "Introduction to Special Issue on New Perspectives on Crime and the American City," *Journal of Urban History* 29 (2003), 519–24. Throughout this book I use "culture" as employed in the social sciences and reflecting certain normative ways of life, in contrast to Matthew Arnold's definition of culture as "the best that has been thought and said." See Clifford Geertz, "Ritual and Social Change," *American Anthropologist* 59 (1957); Claude S. Fischer, *To Dwell Among Friends: Personal Networks in Town and City* (Chicago, 1982), 6–15; "Toward a Subcultural Theory of Urbanism," *American Journal of Sociology* 80 (1975), 1319–41. Terms like "informal," "illicit," and "underground" economies are problematic, relational, and discursive categories, but the lack of a suitable alternative vocabulary forces me reluctantly to employ them. See Viktor E. Todman, "The Informal Sector in Latin America: From Underground to Legality," in *Beyond Regulation: The Informal Economy in Latin America*, ed. Viktor Todman (Boulder, Colo., 1992); and Philip Harding and Richard Jenkins, *The Myth of the Hidden Economy: Towards a New Understanding of Informal Economic Activity* (Philadelphia, 1989).

7. Appo.

8. James D. McCabe, Jr., *The Secrets of the Great City* (Philadelphia, 1868), 15; *Pall Mall Gazette*, 6 July 1885.

## 1. THE TRIALS OF QUIMBO APPO

1. Appo, 1. George Appo spelled his father's birthplace "Ning Poo." Appo erroneously believed that he was born on 4 July 1858 at 2 George Street. New Haven birth and baptismal records indicate that he was born on 4 July 1856 on George Street. See New Haven Births, vol. 11, 23, Registrar of Vital Statistics, 200 Orange Street, New Haven, Conn.

2. Census and newspaper accounts gave conflicting dates regarding Quimbo Appo's birth and immigration dates. Court records and census schedules indicate that he was never naturalized and erroneously claim that he never learned to read or write. See People v. Quimbo Appo, 14 Mar. 1859; 15 Nov. 1876, both in DAP; People v. the Court of Oyer and Terminer of New York and Quimbo Appo in the Return of Quimbo Appo, New York Supreme Court, Index #WR-D 977, 7 and 22 Nov. 1859, CCNYA (hereafter "Return"); entries for Quimbo Appo, 308, 6 Jan. 1872, unnumbered vol.; 161, 22 Dec. 1876, vol. 14, both in SSAR; Twelfth Federal Census Population Schedules, Fishkill Township, Dutchess County, N.Y., 1900, vol. 32, Enumeration District 155, sheet 2A, line 6, National Archives Reel 1022 (born Jan. 1822, 1844 immigration); Thirteenth Federal Census Population Schedules, Fishkill Township, Dutchess County, N.Y.,

1910, Enumeration District 50, sheet 2A, line 35, National Archives Reel 0936 (born 1821 or 1822, 1837 immigration); typed transcript of California State Census, 1852, County of Tuolumne (Genealogical Records Committee, Daughters of the American Revolution of California, 1935), 205 (born 1824), California State Archives, California State Library, Sacramento, Calif. (hereafter Calif. Census of 1852).

3. Roger Lotchin, *San Francisco, 1846–1856: From Hamlet to City* (New York, 1974), 7–8; Frank Marryat, *Mountains and Molehills; or Recollections of a Burnt Journal* (London, 1855), 338–40; Sucheng Chan, "Chinese Livelihood in Rural California: The Impact of Economic Change, 1860–1880," *Pacific Historical Review* 53 (1984), 278–79; Chan, *Asian Californians* (San Francisco, 1991), 5, 28; Ronald Takaki, *Strangers from a Different Shore: A History of Asian Americans* (New York, 1989), 32–36, 80–81; Stanford M. Lyman, *The Asian in the West* (Las Vegas, 1970), 11; Gunther Barth, *Bitter Strength: A History of the Chinese in the United States, 1850–1870* (Cambridge, Mass., 1964), 1–2, 20–31, 78–84; Kil Young Zo, *Chinese Emigration into the United States* (New York, 1978), 4–5, 54–63, 83–84; Eve Armentrout-Ma, "Urban Chinese at the Sinitic Frontier: Social Organizations in United States' Chinatowns, 1849–1898," *Modern Asian Studies* 17 (1983), 109 (90 percent from Kwangtung); Otis Gibson, *The Chinese in America* (Cincinnati, 1877), 162–63 (different dialect in Ningbo); Susan Lee Johnson, *Roaring Camp: The Social World of the California Gold Rush* (New York, 2000), 58 (few from north China).

4. Chan, "Chinese Livelihood," 281–82; Takaki, *Strangers*, 79–83 (24,000 miners); Rodman Paul, *California Gold: The Beginning of Mining in the Far West* (Lincoln, Neb., 1947), 43 (20,000 miners), 130, 243; Peter J. Blodgett, *Land of Golden Dreams: California in the Gold Rush Decade, 1848–1858* (San Marino, Calif., 1999), 106–9; Johnson, *Roaring Camp*, 243–46.

5. 205, William E. Cutrell, enumerator, California Census of 1852. Appo was living with a male companion named Chan Ching. I am indebted to Carlo M. DeFerrari for explaining how Chinese miners and immigrants in Tuolumne County were rarely identified by name and more often grouped together anonymously by census enumerators. Conversation with DeFerrari, Feb. 2000.

6. Ibid.; I. J. Benjamin, *Three Years in America, 1859–1862* (Philadelphia, 1862; reprint, 1956), II:70–71; Paul, *California Gold*, 321; Blodgett, *Land of Golden Dreams*, 106–7; Dolores Yescas Nicolini, Richard Yescas, and Roberta M. McDow, "Chinese Camp," *Pacific Historian* 10 (1972), 47–51.

7. Thomas Robertson Stoddart, *Annals of Tuolumne County*, Carlo M. DeFerrari, ed., (Fresno, Calif., 1977), 54–55, 67 (Chinese), 101–5 (5,000 pop.), 159, 173 (Chinese camp); Hinton R. Helper, *Land of Gold: Reality versus Fiction* (Baltimore, 1855), 175–76 (description of Sonora); Thomas H. Pitt, "A Sojourn in the Diggings," *Chispa: The Quarterly of the Tuolumne County Historical Society* 14 (1974), 471 (Babel); Benjamin, *Three Years*, II:74–77; Alley, *History of Tuolumne County*, 2–5 (Chinese restaurant); Dale L. Morgan and James R. Scobie, eds., *William Perkins' Journal of Life at Sonora, 1849–1852* (Berkeley, Calif., 1964), 1, 27 (mixed population); Marryat, *Mountains*, 272 (13,000); Paul, *California Gold*, 111 (international center).

8. Stoddart, *Annals* 69 (murder), 85, 87, 132–33, 139 (crimes), 147 (daily murders); Marryat, *Mountains*, 275; Morgan and Scobie, *Perkins' Journal*, 159–60, 167 (so common), 328–29, 197–211, 225–26, 293; Ottley, "Early Sonora," 10 (Bancroft); Alley, *History of*

*Tuolumne County*, 55–150 (over 20 murders; Vigilante Committee); *Sonora Herald*, 27 July 1850, 1 Feb. 1851, 5 July 1851; Benjamin, *Three Years*, II:76; Helper, *Land of Gold*, 29 (4,200 murders), 253 (1,200 murders, one conviction).

9. Stoddart, *Annals*, 85, 87, 138; *San Francisco Daily Evening News and Picayune*, 4 Mar. 1854; *William Perkins'*, 326–28; Benjamin, *Three Years*, II:76; J. S. Holliday, *Rush for Riches* (Berkeley, Calif., 1999), 172–73 (tax).

10. Appo, 1; *Stockton San Joaquin Republican*, 15 Jan. 1853. I was unable to find any evidence of Quimbo Appo's claim, based on phone conversations with Lorrayne Kennedy of the Calaveras County Archives (13 Dec. 2001) and Larry Cenotto of the Amador County Archives (17 Dec. 2001). On gold in the Sonora area, see *San Francisco Daily Evening News and Picayune*, 9 Feb. 1854, 3, 4, 15 Mar. 1854; *Perkins' Journal*, 118, 213; Gudde, *California Mining Camps*, 328 ($11 million); *Sonora Herald*, 25 Jan. 1851.

11. Dr. Joseph Pownall to Dr. O. C. Powell, May 1850, n.p., Dr. Joseph Pownall Papers, Journal and Letterbook, 1849–1880, Huntington Library.

12. Appo, 1.

13. *Stockton San Joaquin Republican, San Francisco Daily Alta California*, 26 Jan. 1853.

14. Barron, "Celestial Empire," 454. For examples of interethnic violence between Mexicans and Chinese, see *San Francisco Daily Evening News and Picayune*, 9 Feb. 1854; *San Francisco Daily Alta California*, 1, 16, 20, 24, 29 Dec. 1851; 31 Jan. 1853; *Stockton San Joaquin Republican*, 29 Jan. 1853 (Mexicans driven out); 2, 19, 23 Feb. 1853; Chan, *Asian Californians*, 42–46. Historian Carlo M. DeFerrari was unable to locate any court record in which a Chinese killed two Mexicans while they attempted to rob him. See DeFerrari to Gilfoyle, 10 Sept. 1996, letter in author's possession. Historians remain divided on whether Joaquin Murieta really existed or if he was a composite figure based on different individuals named Joaquin.

15. Holliday, *Rush for Riches*, 103–6.

16. *World, Times* (walking advertisement), *Sun* (Robertson), 22 Oct. 1876; *Tribune*, 23 Oct. 1876 (*Vandalia*); John Kuo Wei Tchen, *New York Before Chinatown: Orientalism and the Shaping of American Culture* (Baltimore, 1999), 91. No Robertson & Sons appears in Boston city directories after 1860.

17. Quimbo Appo was identified as "Crimpo Appo" in both New York City and New Haven directories in 1855. See *Benham's New Haven Directory and Annual Advertiser, 1855–56* (New Haven, Conn., 1855), xii; ibid. (New Haven, 1856), 16; *Trow's New York City Directory* (New York, 1855), 36; ibid. (1857), 36.

18. *World*, 22 Oct. 1876 (good looking, rather free); *Sun*, 9 Mar. 1859 (Dublin, 28 years); *Brother Jonathan*, 19 Mar. 1859 (Dublin, 28 years). At least 92 individuals named Catherine Fitzpatrick (spelled a variety of ways) immigrated through New York City from 1847 to 1851, half of whom were between fifteen and twenty-five years of age. See Ira Glazier and Michael Tepper, *The Famine Immigrants: Lists of Irish Immigrants Arriving at the Port of New York, 1846–1851* (Baltimore, 1983–85), vols. I–II; Brian Mitchell, *Irish Passenger Lists, 1847–1871: Lists of Passengers Sailing from Londonderry to America on Ships of the J. & J. Cooke Line and the McCorkle Line* (Baltimore, 1988). Census records reveal that in 1850, one Catherine Fitzpatrick, a single, twenty-year-old Irish immigrant, resided just north of New Haven in Woodstock, Connecticut, where she worked as a servant on a farm. See Seventh Federal Census Population

Schedules, State of Connecticut, 1850, Windham County, 264, National Archives Microfilm, roll 51.

19. *Times*, 26 Dec. 1856; *Herald*, 12 Apr. 1859. The New Haven Marriage Index, 1750–1860, vols. 1–10, has no record of this marriage under the names of Appo, Chang, Crimpo, Ah, Lee, or Bow. Similarly Appo (under any of these names) does not appear in Ronald Vern Jackson and Gary Ronald Teeples, *Connecticut 1850 Census Index* (Bountiful, Utah, 1978). Various newspaper accounts gave the date of the Appo marriage as 1851 (*Tribune*, 9 Mar. 1859), 1852 (*Times*, 10 Mar. 1859), and approximately May 1854 (*Times*, 26 Dec. 1856). The 1856 article on Appo was accurate on other details (George Appo's birthdate, Spring Street business).

20. *Times*, 26 Dec. 1856.

21. Appo, 1. Appo incorrectly gave the address as 45 Oliver Street. He misspelled his father's employer as "Christainson and Wells." City directories reveal that Edward T. Christianson owned the New York and China Tea Company from 1845 to 1852, when the firm was redesignated Christianson and Company. Quimbo Appo probably had some connection to the firm in either the late 1850s or after 1869.

22. "Return," 17 (owns tea store); *World*, 22 Oct. 1876 (advertising medium; Leiber & Henry); *Sun*, 23 Oct. 1876 (Vose & Joyce); *Times*, 26 Dec. 1856 (comfortably settled); *Leslie's*, 19 Mar. 1859.

23. *Times*, 26 Dec. 1856; 10 Mar. 1859.

24. *Times*, 26 Dec. 1856. This is the first reference to Appo being named after George Washington. In fact he was christened as *Georgium Josephum* (in Latin), or "George Joseph" on 20 July 1856. See 344, Baptisms, St. Mary's Roman Catholic Church. Later references to Appo as "George Washington" include Bruce Edward Hall, *Tea That Burns: A Family Memoir of Chinatown* (New York, 1998), 38–39, 122. As an adult Appo sometimes signed his name with a middle initial, W., and claimed that his middle name was "Washington." See People v. George Appo, 19 Apr. 1895, New York Supreme Court, box 10100, location 106231 (unprocessed collection), DAP; People v. George Appo, 24 July 1896, New York District Attorney Records, Cases #9126 (9—Washington) and #9127, box B-2, location 12817, Supreme Court Cases, all in NYCMA; George W. Appo to Frank Moss, 13 Dec. 1894, box 2, SPC Papers.

25. Appo, 1–2. Appo erred in describing the specific results of his father's trial.

26. *Tribune, Herald, Sun*, all for 9 Mar. 1859; *Brother Jonathan*, 19 Mar. 1859; handwritten testimony of Catherine Appo, dated 9 Mar. 1859, in People v. Quimbo Appo, 14 Mar. 1859, DAP; *Quimbo Appo*, 31.

27. *Tribune, Herald*, 9 Mar. 1859 (I killed her); handwritten testimony of James Youngs, dated 9 Mar. 1859, in DAP; *Sun*, 9 Mar. 1859; *Brother Jonathan*, 19 Mar. 1859.

28. *Brother Jonathan*, 19 Mar. 1859 (wails); *Sun*, 9 Mar. 1859; *Herald*, 9 Mar. 1859 (struck Fletcher).

29. *Herald* (desirous of killing), *Sun, Tribune* (raved like a madman), all 9 Mar. 1859.

30. *Times, Herald, Sun*, 10 Mar. 1859.

31. People v. Quimbo Appo, 14 Mar. 1859, DAP; *Sun*, 9 (I must die), 10 Mar. 1859 ("You see"); *Times*, 10, 15 Mar. 1859; *Herald*, 10 Mar. 1859; *Leslie's* and *Brother Jonathan*, 19 Mar. 1859 (too much society).

32. "Return," 3–4; *Herald*, 12 Apr. 1859; *People v. Appo*, 20 N.Y. 531, 19, 21, 25–29. The

police officers Appo requested to testify on his behalf included Jeremiah Brooks, James Twaddle, and Charles Williams. On Stuart, see *Leslie's*, 7 Oct. 1871.

33. *Herald*, 30 Mar. 1859 (appalling), 1 Apr. 1859 (appalling); 31 Dec. 1859 (40–59 murders); 24 Feb. 1860; Edward Crapsey, *The Nether Side of New York* (New York, 1872), 174.

34. *Tribune*, 2 Nov. 1859 (dispatch); Allen S. Williams, *The Demon of the Orient* (New York, 1883), 70 (first Asian).

35. *Brooklyn Eagle*, 7 May 1859; *Leslie's*, 23 Apr. 1859; *Herald*, 28 Apr. 1859; Court of Oyer and Terminer, Minute Book, 7 May 1859, 1–2, NYCCA; NYSS, *Report of the Governor on Pardons, Commutations and Reprieves Granted During 1859*, SD 23 (Albany, 1860), 4; *Tribune*, 9 May 1859 (Davies quotes); *Sun*, 9 May 1859; *Brother Jonathan*, 14 May 1859 (Appo wept); "Return" in *Quimbo Appo*, 3.

36. *Brooklyn Eagle*, 9 May 1859; Court of Oyer and Terminer, Minute Book, 7 May 1859, 1–2, NYCCA; *Herald*, 8 May 1859; *Sun, Tribune*, 9 May 1859; *Brother Jonathan*, 14 May 1859; Eric Monkkonen, *Murder in New York City* (Berkeley, Calif., 2001); Monkkonen, "Racial Factors in New York City Homicides, 1800–1874," in Darnell F. Hawkins, ed. *Ethnicity, Race, and Crime: Perspectives Across Time and Space* (Albany, N.Y., 1995), 113.

37. *Sun*, 9 Mar. 1859 (dilapidated); *Leslie's*, 19 Mar. 1859 (dilapidated); *Quimbo Appo*, 10, 14. Occupants in 43 and 45 Oliver Street suffered from typhus in 1864. See Citizens' Association of New York, *Report of the Council of Hygiene and Public Health of the Citizens' Association of New York upon the Sanitary Condition of the City* (New York, 1866), II:43; E. R. Pulling, M. D. and F. J. Randell, *Sanitary and Social Chart of the Fourth Ward of the City of New York to Accompany the Report of the Fourth Sanitary Inspection District . . . Hygiene Council to the Citizens Association* (New York, 1864), in NYPL.

38. Elizabeth Blackmar, *Manhattan for Rent, 1785–1850* (New York, 1989); *People v. Appo*, 20 N.Y. 531, 16; *Herald*, 9 Mar. 1860, 4 Jan. 1860. Both Fletchers were thirty-nine-year-old illiterate Irish immigrants, with four children ranging in age from two to thirteen, all of whom were born in New York. See 213, Ward 4, New York City, Seventh Federal Census Population Schedules, State of New York, 1850; 892, Ward 4, Election District 2, New York City, Eighth Federal Census Population Schedules, State of New York, 1860, National Archives Microfilm, roll 789.

39. Election District 2, Ward 4, New York State Manuscript Census, 1855, CCNYA; Tchen, "Quimbo Appo's Fear of Fenians: Chinese-Irish-Anglo Relations in New York City"; and Graham Hodges, " 'Desirable Companions and Lovers': Irish and African Americans in the Sixth Ward, 1830–1870," both in Ronald H. Bayor and Timothy J. Meagher, eds., *The New York Irish* (Baltimore, 1996), 130–31, 107–24. On the paucity of Chinese residents, see entry #285, 14, Election District 2; and 9, Election District 5, both in Ward 4, New York State Manuscript Census, 1855; entries #217, 242, 260, 267, 270, 26–32, Election District 5, Ward 6, New York State Manuscript Census, 1870, all in CCNYA.

40. *Herald*, 9 Mar. 1859 (regular fights); *World*, 22 Oct. 1876 (astray); "Return," 9, 18 (Williams).

41. Moses Yale Beach, *The Wealth and Biography of the Wealthy Citizens of the City of New York* (New York, 1855), 30; James Grafton Rogers, *American Bar Leaders* (Chicago, 1932), 50–55; Henry M. Field, *The Life of David Dudley Field* (New York, 1898), vii, 38,

86–96, 121–61; David Dudley Field, *Speeches, Arguments, and Miscellaneous Papers of David Dudley Field* (New York, 1884), I:339; Steven Hutchins, *Civil List and Constitutional History of the Colony and State of New York* (Albany, 1880), 445; *Herald*, 30 Oct. 1856; *Sun*, 28 Jan. 1877.

42. *Herald*, 18 Oct. 1859; *Quimbo Appo*, 33. On Assistant District Attorney John G. Doyle prosecuting the case, see *Sun*, 12 Apr. 1859, 18 Oct. 1859 (irregularities); *Herald*, 18 Oct. 1859 (tamper); *World*, 22 Oct. 1876 (hiring Field). On the respites, see note 53 below.

43. "Return," 13–15, 23–24; *Quimbo Appo*, 18–20; *Herald*, 8 May 1859 ("China nigger"); *Brother Jonathan*, 14 May 1859 (China nigger); *Sun*, 18 Oct. 1859.

44. "Return," 16–17, 24–26; *Quimbo Appo*, 30–31.

45. *Quimbo Appo*, 11, 13, 16, 20, 28, 31–32; handwritten testimony of Catherine Appo, dated 9 Mar. 1859, in People v. Quimbo Appo, 14 Mar. 1859, DAP; "Return," 11, 24.

46. "Return," 18.

47. Ibid., 17; *Trow's New York City Directory* (New York, 1859), 427 (Irish). Mention of the letters appears on 25, vol. 2, Executive Clemency and Pardon Application Ledgers and Correspondence (AO629), NYSArc.

48. "Return," 18–21, 24; *Quimbo Appo*, 25–27.

49. "Return," 28–30; *Herald*, 28 Apr. 1859, 18 Oct. 1859; *Quimbo Appo*, 34; *Sun*, 12 Apr. 1859 (jurors).

50. Monkkonen, "Racial Factors in New York City Homicides, 1800-1874," 111–13; Iver Bernstein, *The New York City Draft Riots: Their Significance for American Society and Politics in the Age of the Civil War* (New York, 1990), 34, 226–27, 299.

51. The biography of James J. Roosevelt is confusing because he was and is frequently referred to as James I. Roosevelt, in part because he occasionally signed his name this way. The most reliable sources identify the judge as James J. Roosevelt. See Henry Hall, *America's Successful Men of Affairs* (New York, 1895–96), I:553 (stainless, unimpeachable); Allan Nevins, ed., *The Diary of Philip Hone, 1828–1851* (New York, 1927), 470, 474; Charles Barney Whittelsey, compiler, *The Roosevelt Genealogy, 1649–1902* (Hartford, Conn., 1903?), 51, 79–80; Hutchins, *Civil List*, 220, 442; Allen Churchill, *The Roosevelts: American Aristocrats* (New York, 1965), 106–9; *Appleton's Cyclopaedia of American Biography* (New York, 1888), V:319; Nathan Miller, *The Roosevelt Chronicles* (New York, 1979), 122–27.

52. *Herald*, 25 Oct. 1859. The full text of Roosevelt's decision appears in *Quimbo Appo*, 36–40 (dated 24 Oct. 1859). On Roosevelt's support of Field's codes, see Field, *Life of David Dudley Field*, 48.

53. *Times*, 16 Apr. 1860. On the respites, see Executive Orders of Gov. Edwin Morgan, 21 June 1859 and 10 Oct. 1859, box 6, vol. 6, New York Department of State, Executive Orders for Commutations, Pardons, Restorations, and Respites (BO049); 464, 482, vol. for 1859 (respite until 21 Feb. 1860), Executive Journals of Governors' Actions and Decisions (AO607), both in NYSArc; NYSS, *Report of the Governor on Pardons, Commutations and Reprieves Granted During 1859*, SD 23 (Albany, 1860), 4; *Herald*, 1, 8 Nov. 1859, 14, 31 Dec. 1859; 20 Jan. 1860; *Brother Jonathan*, 2 July 1859 (respite to 14 Oct.), 19 Nov. 1859 (respite to 25 Feb.), 3 Mar. 1860 (respite to 1 June); *Brooklyn Eagle*, 1, 11 Nov. 1859, 23 Feb. 1860 (writ of prohibition and respites); *Leslie's*, 19 Nov. 1859

(respite until 21 Feb. 1860). The full text of the district attorney's argument, written by Assistant District Attorney John G. Doyle, appears at the end of *Quimbo Appo*, 1–5.

54. *Brother Jonathan*, 19 May 1860 (public will approve). On Quimbo Appo's admission to Sing Sing, see entry for Tues., 8 May 1860, 349, vol. for 1860, Executive Journals of Governors' Actions and Decisions (AO607); 25, vol. 2; vols. 17–18, all in Executive Clemency and Pardon Application Ledgers and Correspondence (AO629); vols. 7–8, Department of State, Executive Clemency and Pardon Records, Executive Pardons (BO042); entry for 8 May 1860, vol. 3, Sing Sing admissions, 1842–1874 (n.p.), Executive Register of Commitments to Prisons; entry for Quimbo Appo, 29 Mar. 1869, Executive Reports of Deduction of Sentences by Prison Agents, 1863–1883 (AO601), vol. 1, all in NYSArc.

55. *Sun*, 9 Mar. 1859; *Leslie's*, 19 Mar. 1859 (exact same quote). George Appo was, in fact, two years and nine months of age at the time of the homicide.

## 2. URCHINS, ARABS, AND GUTTER-SNIPES

1. Appo, 1–2. Appo spelled the location "Donavan's Lane."

2. Lydia Maria Child, *Letters from New-York* (New York, 1842), 14; Charles Dickens, *American Notes* (1842; reprint, Oxford, Eng., 1987), quoted in Ladies of the Mission, *The Old Brewery, and the New Mission House at the Five Points* (New York, 1854), 20. *Times*, 22 Feb. 1860; George W. Bromley, *Atlas of the City of New York, Manhattan Island* (New York, 1891), plate 5; NYC Board of Commissioners of Taxes and Assessment, *Maps of the Sixth Ward* (1838); ibid. (1871), both in Record of Assessment, maps, Wards 1–8, microfilm roll #1, NYCMA. The best history of Five Points is Tyler Anbinder, *Five Points* (New York, 2001). The four streets were Park (originally Cross), Worth (originally Anthony), Baxter (originally Orange), and Little Water. They were renamed in 1854.

3. Citizens' Association of New York, *Report of the Council of Hygiene and Public Health of the Citizens' Association of New York Upon the Sanitary Condition of the City* (New York, 1866), II:74–77, 84; Graham Hodges, " 'Desirable Companions and Lovers': Irish and African Americans in the Sixth Ward, 1830–1870," in Ronald H. Bayor and Timothy J. Meagher, eds., *The New York Irish* (Baltimore, 1996); John Duffy, *A History of Public Health in New York City, 1625–1866* (New York, 1966), 535–38 (death rates); Samuel Osgood, *A Discourse Delivered Before the New York Historical Society* (New York, 1867), 84 (69 murders from 1 Nov. 1864 to 31 Oct. 1865).

4. *Daily Graphic*, 18 Mar. 1873 (Arcadia); Citizens' Association, *Report*, II:76–77, 80; *Tribune*, 2 Aug. 1862.

5. André Chavanne, "The Burning of the Golden Gate in July 1862," *California Historical Society Quarterly* 19 (1940), 29–42; *Daily Alta California*, 7, 8 Aug. 1862; San Francisco *Evening Bulletin*, 7, 9 Aug. 1862; *Harper's Weekly*, 23 Aug. 1862. Lists of passengers were inconsistent and incomplete. See *Tribune*, 8, 9, 12, 18 Aug. 1862; *Times*, 10, 12 Aug. 1862; *Daily Alta California* and *Evening Bulletin*, 7, 18 Aug. 1862. I looked for other possible shipwrecks that Appo might have confused with the *Golden Gate*, but found no evidence of the Appos.

6. Later historians believed that Appo never left New York, but stayed in Donovan's Lane

while his mother and sister traveled to California. See Arthur Bonner, *Alas! What Brought Thee Hither? The Chinese in New York, 1800–1950* (Madison, N.J., 1997), 15; John Kuo Wei Tchen, *New York Before Chinatown: Orientalism and the Shaping of American Culture, 1776–1882* (Baltimore, 1999), 285.

7. Entry for 15 Apr. 1874, container 3, vol. 11, 396, SSAR ("sister" Mary Ann Allen). A number of Allens appear in the federal manuscript censuses. Mary Allen, a thirty-year-old washerwoman at 102 Bayard Street, appears on 31, Ward 6, Election District 4, Federal Census Population Schedules, City of New York, 1860. An eleven-year-old Mary Ann Allen appears in entry #1056, 54, Ward 4, Election District 2, New York State Manuscript Census, 1855, CCNYA. On Irish widows in 1850s New York, see Carol Groneman Pernicone, "The 'Bloody Ould Sixth:' A Social Analysis of a New York City Working-Class Community in the Mid-Nineteenth Century" (Ph.D. thesis, University of Rochester, 1973), 128. On working-class family strategies, see Bruce Bellingham, "Waifs and Strays: Child Abandonment, Foster Care, and Families in Mid-Nineteenth-Century New York" in Peter Mandler, ed., *The Uses of Charity: The Poor on Relief in the Nineteenth-Century Metropolis* (Philadelphia, 1990), 123–60.

8. NPG, 21 Feb. 1880 (Donovan's Lane); *Leslie's*, 16 Mar. 1872 (illustration); *Daily Graphic*, 18 Mar. 1873 (entrance on Baxter). This was block #160. Some records indicate that the main entrance lay between 474 and 476 Pearl Street. A street directory located Donovan's Lane's entrance from Pearl Street. Donovan's Lane disappeared from fire insurance maps by 1884. See *New York City Directory for 1851–1852* (New York, 1851), appendix, 70 (spelled "Donavan's Lane"); William Perris, *Map of the City of New York* (New York, 1867); ibid. (New York, 1875); ibid. (New York, 1884), all in NYHS; NYC Board of Commissioners of Taxes and Assessment, *Maps of the Sixth Ward* (1838); ibid. (1871), both in Record of Assessment, maps, wards 1–8, microfilm roll #1, NYCMA; entry #1049, 49–51, Election District 5, Ward 6, New York State Manuscript Census, 1855; and 88–93, Election District 5, Ward 6, New York State Manuscript Census, 1870, both in CCNYA; Bromley, *Atlas* (1891), plate 5; *Times*, 22 Feb. 1860.

9. 6, Ward 6, Election District 3, Federal Manuscript Census Population Schedules, City of New York, Second Enumeration, 1870, reel 1017 (Chinese residents); Citizens' Association, *Report*, II:77–78; *Times*, 11 Mar. 1860; *Brother Jonathan*, 24 Mar. 1866; *Herald*, 26 Dec. 1869 (Celestial Habitations); *Times*, 26 Dec. 1873 (Chinese); *Leslie's*, 5 July 1873 (opium and Chinese tenement); *Harper's Weekly*, 7 Mar. 1874; NPG, 21 Feb. 1880 (opium smoking); Tchen, "New York Chinese," 168–70, 174–75. On the interracial population of Five Points, see NPG, 24 Aug. 1867; *New York Evening Day Book*, 11 May 1858, cited in John Kuo Wei Tchen, "Quimbo Appo's Fear of Fenians: Chinese-Irish-Anglo Relations in New York City," in Bayor and Meagher, *New York Irish*, 125–52; Anbinder, *Five Points*, 42–50, 344–46; 367–423; Hodges, "Desirable Companions," 107–24.

10. On Jacob Cohen, see entry for 20 Apr. 1876, vol. 13, SSAR. On the more than fifty Baxter Street residents and workers with the surname "Cohn" or "Cohen," see *Trow's New York City Directory* (New York, 1859–64); William Riordan, *Plunkitt of Tammany Hall*, introduction by Terrence McDonald (1905; reprint, New York, 1992), 101. On Baxter Street's identification with the large number of German Jews, unlicensed street peddlers, junk shops, and used clothing stores, see Citizens' Association, *Report*, II:77;

Pernicone, "The 'Bloody Ould Sixth,' " 35, 38, 96, 122; George Foster, *New York in Slices; By an Experienced Carver* (New York, 1849), 13.

11. Appo, 3. Elsewhere Appo claimed that he began picking pockets at age seven. See Appo's statement on 6 Oct. 1896, p. 21, in People v. George Appo, 24 July 1896, New York District Attorney Records, case #9126, box B-2, location 12817, Supreme Court Cases, NYCMA.

12. *Harper's Weekly*, 19 Sept. 1868. On the growing fear of street children, see Timothy J. Gilfoyle, "Street-Rats and Gutter-Snipes: Child Pickpockets and Street Culture in New York City, 1850–1900," *Journal of Social History* 37 (2004), 853–82.

13. Detailed documentation on orphaned and school-age children appears in Gilfoyle, "Street-Rats and Gutter-Snipes," notes 2, 3, 4, 7, and 9. Only in 1881 did the state begin prohibiting children from "begging, gathering or picking or sorting rags, from collecting cigar stumps, or bones or refuse from markets." See *Harper's Weekly*, 30 July 1881.

14. Foster, *New York in Slices*, 103 (modern civilization); Edward Spann, *The New Metropolis*, 23–44, 71 (Greeley), 137. On the bootblack as a "modern innovation," see *Harper's Weekly*, 19 Sept. 1868. On various crises in the nineteenth-century U.S. economy and the decline of artisanal trade, see David M. Gordon, Richard Edwards, and Michael Reich, *Segmented Work, Divided Workers: The Historical Transformation of Labor in the United States* (New York, 1982); Alexander Keyssar, *Out of Work: The First Century of Unemployment in Massachusetts* (New York, 1986), 1–4, 340–44; Sean Wilentz, *Chants Democratic: New York City and the Rise of the American Working Class, 1789–1850* (New York, 1982), 107–44, 299–361; Elizabeth Blackmar, *Manhattan for Rent, 1785–1850* (New York, 1989).

15. Charles Loring Brace, *The Dangerous Classes of New York, and Twenty Years' Work Among Them* (New York, 1872), ii, 26–27, 344; CAS, *Nineteenth AR* (New York, 1871), 5.

16. For more on the subculture of street children, including statistics on the overall rate of child commitments and incarceration, see Gilfoyle, "Street-Rats and Gutter-Snipes," 855–58, esp. notes 15 and 50.

17. Hutchins Hapgood, ed., *The Autobiography of a Thief* (New York, 1903), 35; CAS, *First AR* (New York, 1854), 3; CAS, *Eighteenth AR* (New York, 1870), 51 (boy's crime); *Nineteenth AR*, 8; CAS, *Sixteenth AR* (New York, 1868), 6 (too quick); *Times*, 6 Apr. 1875; Josiah Flynt, *The World of Graft* (New York, 1901), 26 (teenage pickpockets); Josiah Flynt, *Notes of an Itinerant Policeman* (Boston, 1900), 34–35 (slum origins), 55–56 (newsboys); John J. O'Connor, *Broadway Racketeers* (New York, 1928), 31 (slum origins); Edwin H. Sutherland, *The Professional Thief: By a Professional Thief* (Chicago, 1932), 21, 23 (slum origins).

18. Gilfoyle, "Street-Rats and Gutter-Snipes," note 17.

19. CAS, *Seventeenth AR*, 48 (City Hall Park); William F. Howe and Abraham H. Hummel, *In Danger; or, Life in New York. A True History of a Great City's Wiles and Temptations* (New York, 1888), 20; unmarked clipping, 2 Feb. 1884, DAS ("paradise").

20. I examined grand and petty larceny cases that involved removing personal property from a person, the charge under which most pickpockets were prosecuted by the New York district attorney in the Court of General Sessions. The database totaled 1,176 individuals in the years 1859, 1864, 1869, 1871, 1872, 1874, and 1876 (which included

166 children). See Gilfoyle, "Street-Rats and Gutter-Snipes," notes 19 and 20, for a more detailed description.

21. For occupational breakdown, see Gilfoyle, "Street-Rats and Gutter-Snipes," note 22.

22. On the "education" of pickpockets, see Gilfoyle, "Street-Rats and Gutter-Snipes," notes 23, 26, and 27. On the absence of formal schooling, see George Appo's statement on 6 Oct. 1896, pp. 18, 22 (never went to school), People v. George Appo, 24 July 1896, case #9126; NYSL, *AR of the Board of Commissioners of the Metropolitan Police* (Albany, 1864), 9; *NPG*, 18 Feb. 1880; Jacob Riis, *The Battle with the Slum* (New York, 1902), 231 (dead law).

23. Gilfoyle, "Street-Rats and Gutter-Snipes," 865 and notes 31, 32, and 33.

24. Ibid., note 34.

25. Campbell, *Darkness*, 124 (quote), 151–54. On the high rate of native-born child pickpocket prosecutions and incarcerations, see Gilfoyle, "Street-Rats and Gutter-Snipes," note 35. On the lack of discussion of ethnicity or immigration as a factor in criminal or "underworld" identity, see ibid., note 36.

26. George Appo statement to the Commissioners of Public Charities and Corrections, 6 Oct. 1896, 17–18, in People v. George Appo, 24 July 1896, case #9126. On the differences between alternative and oppositional subcultures and their relationship to a dominant culture, see Raymond Williams, *Problems in Materialism and Culture: Selected Essays* (London, 1980), 40–42.

27. Appo, 3; Gilfoyle, "Street-Rats and Gutter-Snipes," 867–70, notes 37 and 38.


## 3. A House of Refuge at Sea

1. Appo, 3–4. On Judge Joseph Dowling, see *National Cyclopedia of American Biography* (New York, 1909), 3:391; Matthew Breen, *Thirty Years of New York Politics Up to Date* (New York, 1899), 516–24; Matthew Hale Smith, *Sunshine and Shadow in New York* (Hartford, Conn., 1868), 167–71; Tyler Anbinder, *Five Points* (New York 2001), 169–70, 293, 310–11, 320–21, 328, 334.

2. Henry Adams, *The Education of Henry Adams* (New York: Houghton Mifflin, 1918; reprint, 1974), 8; Rev. J. F. Richmond, *New York and Its Institutions, 1609–1871* (New York, 1871), 299–314, 321–59 (5,700), 572 (quote); Charles Loring Brace, *The Dangerous Classes of New York and Twenty Years' Work Among Them* (New York, 1872).

3. *Times*, 23 Jan. 1860 (House of Refuge), 31 Jan. 1860, 17 Aug. 1865 (death by whipping); Richmond, *Institutions*, 568–71; NYC, *Manual of the Corporation of the City of New York* (New York, 1869), 397–404; PANY, *Twenty-fourth AR for 1868*, SD 10 (Albany, 1869), 195–97. On the early history, see Charles Sutton, *The New York Tombs: Its Secrets and Its Mysteries* (New York, 1874), 33–34; Hastings H. Hart, *Preventive Treatment of Neglected Children* (New York, 1910), 11; Robert S. Pickett, *House of Refuge: Origins of Juvenile Reform in New York State, 1815–1857* (Syracuse, 1969).

4. Appo, 6.

5. PCC, *Cruise of School-Ship "Mercury" in Tropical Atlantic Ocean, 1870–71* (New York, 1871), 3; *Times*, 9 Dec. 1871 ("wild"). On Massachusetts introducing the first nautical school in 1860, see PANY, *Twenty-fourth AR*, 34, 184; Wines and Dwight, *Report*, 355–56. On the history of the *Mercury*, see PCC, *Tenth AR for 1869* (New York, 1870), 359;

PANY, *Twenty-fifth AR for 1869*, SD 21 (Albany, 1870), 262–64; William Armstrong Fairburn, *Merchant Sail* (Center Lovell, Me., 1945–55), II:1201, 1271; Norman Brouwer, "The Hart's Island Schoolship Mercury," *South Street Reporter* 11 (Fall 1977), 20–21.

6. *Times*, 3 Nov. 1867; *Sailors' Magazine and Seamen's Friend* 40 (1868), 101–2; PANY, *Twenty-fourth AR*, 35, 33; B. K. Pierce, *A Half Century with Juvenile Delinquents; or, the New York House of Refuge and Its Times* (New York, 1869), 71–72, 310–12; Charles J. Jones, "The Moral Power of the Sea," *Sailors' Magazine and Seamen's Friend* 37 (1865), 41 (teacher); William McNally, *Evils and Abuses in the Naval and Merchant Service Exposed* (Boston, 1839), 53–62; Richmond, *Institutions*, 573; Sutton, *Tombs*, 32; *Sailors' Magazine and Seamen's Friend* 48 (1876), 195; ibid. 45 (1873), 260. On advocating a native-born merchant marine, see *Tribune*, 12 Mar. 1860; *Times*, 11 Mar. 1860, 14 Apr. 1867, 22 Mar. 1867 (Chamber of Commerce).

7. *Times*, 9 Dec. 1871; *World*, 14 Apr. 1879; PCC, *Tenth AR*, 359 (parents pay stipend); PCC, *Twelfth AR for 1871* (New York, 1872), 237–38; Charles E. Thompson to Mayor William Wickham, 22 Jan. 1875 (parents pay), folder 206, box 1259, MP.

8. Enrollment figures for 1869 and 1870 were 504 and 972 boys, respectively. See Richmond, *Institutions*, 526, 572–73; PCC, *Ninth AR for 1868* (New York, 1869), 27–29; PCC, *Eleventh AR for 1870* (New York, 1871), 298 (584 boys); *World*, 16 Aug. 1885 (pauper graves). On boxing on Hart, see Elliott J. Gorn, *The Manly Art: Bare-Knuckle Prize Fighting in America* (Ithaca, N.Y., 1986), 71.

9. *Times*, 5 Apr. 1873 (knots); Richmond, *Institutions*, 573–76; PANY, *Twenty-fifth AR*, 264–66; *Harper's Weekly*, 27 Nov. 1869; PCC, *Tenth AR*, 363–68, 371–82 (rules), 376–78 (knots and riggings).

10. Richmond, *Institutions*, 575.

11. PCC, *Tenth AR*, 363–68, 371–82 (erect carriage); PCC, *Twelfth AR*, 238; PCC, *Cruise of School-Ship*, 4, 8 (erring boys); *Times*, 9 Dec. 1871; Brouwer, "Schoolship Mercury," 21; Richmond, *Institutions*, 573–77; PANY, *Twenty-fifth AR*, 264–66; *Harper's Weekly*, 27 Nov. 1869.

12. *Times*, 1 Jan. 1873; PCC, *Twelfth AR*, 242; PCC, *Sixteenth AR for 1875* (New York, 1876), 264; Richmond, *Institutions*, 577.

13. On Giraud, see PCC, *Eleventh AR*, 299.

14. Appo, 4–5. Appo misspelled Giraud as "Gerard." Tropical calms and the doldrums were common in the equatorial Atlantic. See Maria Graham, *Journal of a Voyage to Brazil* (London, 1824), 95–96.

15. Richmond, *Institutions*, 572–77. The first winter cruise began on 20 Dec. 1870. See PCC, *Eleventh AR*, 300. For other trips and conditions, see PCC, *Tenth AR*, 362; ibid. (J. W. S. Arnold), *Report to the Commissioners of Public Charities and Correction, on the Scientific Portion of the Cruise of the "Nautical School-Ship Mercury" During the Winter of 1871–72* (New York, 1872); *Increase of Crime*, 117; *Times*, 5 Apr. 1873, 24 Jan. 1875, 14, 20 Mar. 1875.

16. *Times*, 1 Jan. 1873; 24 Feb. 1873; PCC, *Twelfth AR*, 238; PCC, *Cruise of School-Ship*, map. For sailor and traveler memoirs commenting on the beauty of Madeira, see B. R. Burg, *An American Seafarer in the Age of Sail: The Erotic Diaries of Philip C. Van Buskirk 1851–1870* (New Haven, Conn.,1994), 19–20, 176, note 25; Graham, *Journal*, 82.

17. PCC, *Eleventh AR*, 299; PCC, *Twelfth AR*, 238 (Giraud); *Times*, 5 Apr. 1873. Similarly

positive reports appeared in PANY, *Twenty-fifth AR*, 263–64; *Times*, 9 Dec. 1871; 1 Jan. 1873; 24 Feb. 1873; *Sailors' Magazine and Seamen's Friend* 44 (1872), 364; *World*, 22 May 1875.

18. Appo, 5.
19. NYSS, *Proceedings Before the Special Committee of the New York State Senate* (Albany, 1876), 48.
20. PCC, *Twelfth AR*, 242 (number of pupils); PCC, *Sixteenth AR*, 261–66 (aversion); PCC, *Eleventh AR*, 299, 303–04 (instruction suspended); NYSS, *Proceedings Before the Special Committee*, 49; *Times*, 5 Apr. 1873.
21. PCC, *Eleventh AR*, 299, 238; PCC, *Sixteenth AR*, 262–64; PCC, *Twelfth AR*, 239 (deaths); *Times*, 5 Apr. 1873 (deaths). After two voyages only 130 boys had entered the navy, while 200 joined the merchant marine. See *Times*, 1 Jan. 1873. Of the 259 boys who made the initial cruise, 100 were subsequently recommended to serve in the merchant marine or navy. See PCC, *Cruise of School-Ship*, 4, 8. On numerous youths contracting typhus in 1875, resulting in at least four deaths, see PCC, *Sixteenth AR*, 266; *World*, 22 May 1875; *Times*, 14 Mar. 1875.
22. PCC, *Sixteenth AR*, 263; "Licentiousness of the Navy," *Advocate of Peace*, Aug. 1844 (floating Sodoms).
23. Burg, *American Seafarer*, 26, 74–79 (chickenship), 81. For an allusion that similar behaviors were common in the House of Refuge, see Hutchins Hapgood, ed., *The Autobiography of a Thief* (New York, 1903), 71.
24. *Times*, 23 Jan. 1860; NYSA, *Report of the State Commission on Prison Labor* (Albany, 1871), 33–34; Burg, *American Seafarer*, 26, 75–78 (chaw), 113 (onanists)
25. *World*, 25 May 1875 (great number, mutiny), 14 Apr. 1879 (magistrates' orders); PCC, *Eleventh AR*, 299 (discharge); PCC, *Sixteenth AR*, 261, 264 (Johnson). During the first four months of operation, from 1 Sept. to 31 Dec. 1869, 18 (of 242) boys deserted. See PCC, *Tenth AR*, 361. In 1875 only three desertions were reported. See PCC, *Sixteenth AR*, 268.
26. On the *Mercury's* budget, see PCC, *Sixteenth AR*, 266 (Johnson), 268–70; *Times*, 19 Nov. 1875; *Increase of Crime*, 66.
27. PCC, *Tenth AR*, 380–81; NYSS, *Twenty-fifth AR*, 266; Myra C. Glenn, *Campaigns Against Corporal Punishment: Prisoners, Sailors, Women, and Children in Antebellum America* (Albany, 1984), chaps. 2 and 5.
28. Official rules prohibited corporal punishment, the most severe penalty being confinement on bread and water for three days and privation of "customary amusements." See PCC, *Twelfth AR*, 237–38.
29. Appo, 5–6.

VIOLENCE

1. Appo, 93–94. The 1870 and 1880 manuscript censuses did not have any "Maher" listed at 300 Pearl Street. Catherine Meyer, a thirty-two-year-old housekeeper, was listed at 543 Pearl in 1870. See Population Schedules of the Ninth Census of the United States, 1870, New York County, Second Enumeration (lists addresses), reel 1014, Ward 2, Election District 1, 3, 20. On St. Luke's Hospital, then located at Fifth Avenue and

Fifty-fourth Street, see Rev. J. F. Richmond, *New York and Its Institutions, 1609–1871* (New York, 1871), 367–70.

## 4. FACTORIES FOR TURNING OUT CRIMINALS

1. Appo, 25–26. Appo's first term in Sing Sing extended from 15 Apr. 1874 to 2 Apr. 1876. He erroneously believed he was sixteen years old at this time. In fact he was nearly eighteen. Appo also confused two different arrests in this part of his autobiography. This description of Hackett occurs later and out of sequence in the manuscript auto-biography. Appo attempted to pickpocket John Bannon on 20 Mar. 1874, an arrest he discussed earlier in the autobiography (6). Giving the alias of "George Dixon," this was Appo's second known arrest and first sentence to Sing Sing. His arrest and prison records can be found in entry for 20 Mar. 1874, pp. 475–76, First District, PCDB (age sixteen); entry for "George Dixon," 15 Apr. 1874, 396, vol. 11, SSAR; entry for 13 Apr. 1874, vol. 3, Sing Sing admissions, 1842–1874 (n.p.), Executive Register of Commitments to Prisons, NYSArc.

2. In an earlier version Appo claimed that this experience occurred during his second sentence in Sing Sing in 1878. See Frank Moss, *The American Metropolis* (New York, 1897), III:126–28.

3. Appo, 6–8.

4. Ibid., 9.

5. Lewis E. Lawes, *Twenty Thousand Years in Sing Sing* (New York, 1932), 68–69 (Sint Sinks and Ossine Ossine); Charles Sutton, *The New York Tombs* (New York, 1874), 583, 587; *Leslie's*, 16 Feb. 1878 (32 miles north); *NPG*, 30 Aug. 1879 (Grace Church); NYSPC, *Investigation of the State Prisons and Report Thereon, 1876* (Albany, 1877) (hereafter *Investigation 1876*), 18 (lime); Amos O. Squire, *Sing Sing Doctor* (Garden City, N.Y., 1937), 5–7. The literature on nineteenth-century prisons is extensive and diverse in emphases, but most of it focuses on administrative goals and penal ideology. For brief summaries of this literature, see Timothy J. Gilfoyle, "New Perspectives on Crime and Punishment in the American City," *Journal of Urban History* 29 (2003), esp. note 6; and Larry Goldsmith, "History from the Inside Out: Prison Life in Nineteenth-Century Massachusetts," *Journal of Social History* 31 (1997), 121–22.

6. Lewis E. Lawes, *Life and Death in Sing Sing* (Garden City, N.Y., 1928), 29; *Leslie's*, 16 Feb. 1878 (grim); Sutton, *Tombs*, 585; *NPG*, 29 Dec. 1866, 30 Aug. 1870, 30 Aug. 1879; *Sun* clipping, 26 Nov. 1886, vol. 28, DAS; NYSPC, *Thirteenth AR for the Year 1907* (Albany, 1908), 30–31.

7. See note 6 above; *Times*, 2 Nov. 1874; unmarked clipping, 1 July 1885, vol. 22 (slop buckets), DAS.

8. Appo, 31; PANY, *Thirty-fifth AR for 1879*, SD 34 (Albany, 1880), 14–15 (no bathing); NYSPC, *Investigation 1876*, 634 (pond); NYSA, *Report of the Committee on State Prisons Upon the Charges of the New York Star Against the Management of the Prisons of this State*, AD 121 (Albany, 1883), 4 (no baths); NYSA, *Testimony Taken Before the Assembly Committee on State Prisons in the Investigation of Sing Sing Prison*, AD 131 (Albany, 1882) (hereafter *Investigation 1881*), 39–40 (no baths), 50 (shop basins), 113; ibid., *Report of the Superintendent of State Prisons in Response to the Resolution of January 11, 1883*, AD 29 (Albany, 1883), 15 (no toilets).

9. Appendix 1; NYSCP, *Thirteenth AR*, 31 (refrigerator); NYSPC, *Investigation 1876*, 93 (dampness of lower tiers), 142 (bedbugs), 241 (stench), 301 (stench), 397–98, 654 (brick up); New York Superintendent of State Prisons, *AR for 1887* (Albany, 1888), 54 (unwholesome), 106 (buckets); *Press* clipping, 28 June 1891, vol. 87, DAS (fatal illnesses); PANY, *Thirty-fifth AR*, 13 (offensive); *Times*, 3 July 1865 (bedbugs); NYSA, *Report Upon the Charges of the Star*, 3 (cells with vermin, unfit to breathe); NYSS, *Twenty-fifth AR of the Inspectors of State Prisons [for 1872]*, SD 30 (Albany, 1873), 6 (1,191 cells); Sutton, *Tombs*, 583, 589 (unfit); Lawes, *Life and Death*, 57–58, 193 (unfit).

10. *Leslie's*, 16 Feb. 1878 (emporium); Frederick Howard Wines, *Punishment and Reformation: A Study of the Penitentiary System* (New York, 1895 and 1919), 199 (manuf. establishment); ESP Inspectors, *51st AR for the Year 1880* (Philadelphia, 1881), 38–39 (large manufacturing establishment). On Sing Sing's industrial shops comprising the largest factory in the world, see Glen A. Gildemeister, *Prison Labor and Convict Competition with Free Workers in Industrializing America, 1840–1890* (New York, 1987), 182; Roger Panetta, "Up the River: A History of Sing Sing Prison in the Nineteenth Century" (Ph.D. thesis, City University of New York, 1999), 293.

11. *Leslie's*, 16 Mar. 1878 (160 in laundry; 1,500 boots; 200 stoves daily); NYSS, *Twenty-second AR of the Inspectors of State Prisons [for 1869]*, SD 71 (Albany, 1870), map; *Times*, 16 Mar. 1882, 31 May 1885 (130 in laundry); NYSA, *Testimony Taken Before the Assembly Committee*, 13 (laundry severest), 22; *Sun* clipping, 7 Feb. 1887 (laundry unattractive), vol. 30, DAS. By 1878 the various shops were consolidated into five: foundry, laundry, clothes depot, hat factory, and shoe factory.

12. NYSS, *Twenty-second AR of the Inspectors of State Prisons*, map; NYSS, *Twenty-third AR of the Inspectors of State Prisons [for 1870]*, SD 21 (Albany, 1871), 10 (inexhaustible, 225 convicts); NYSA, *Sixteenth AR of the Inspectors of State Prisons [for 1863]*, AD 11 (Albany, 1864), 18; NYSPC, *Investigation of the State Prisons and Report Thereon, 1876* (Albany, 1877)(hereafter *Investigation 1876*), 139 (hogs), 238–39.

13. Nationally, 756 cotton establishments employed 172,544 workers; in New York State, 36 factories employed 9,227. In iron and steel 140,978 workers were employed in 1,005 establishments. Nationwide, thirty-six Bessemer mills employed 10,835 workers. See U.S. Census Office, *Report on the Manufactures of the United States at the Tenth Census, 1880* (Washington, D.C., 1883), II:10–11 (cotton mills), II:738 (iron and steel), II:756. Employee totals in 1880 for Cambria Iron Co. (4,200), Lackawanna Iron and Steel (3,000), Bethlehem Iron Co. (2,900), Pennsylvania Steel (1,600), and Carnegie's Edgar Thompson works (1,500) sometimes included more than one plant and other employees such as miners. See Daniel Nelson, *Managers and Workers: Origins of the New Factory System in the United States, 1880–1920* (Madison, Wis., 1975), 4–6.

14. Appo, 92 (factories); Peter Kolchin, *American Slavery, 1619–1877* (New York, 1993), 101; Roger L. Ransom and Richard Sutch, *One Kind of Freedom: The Economic Consequences of Emancipation* (New York, 1977), 73–78 (50 slaves); Robert William Fogel, *Without Consent or Contract: The Rise and Fall of American Slavery* (New York, 1989), 50–52 (50 slaves); Robert William Fogel and Stanley Engerman, *Time on the Cross: The Economics of American Negro Slavery* (New York, 1974), 22 (Caribbean), 200 (over 200 in Mississippi). On Sing Sing's population over time, see appendix 1.

15. NYSPC, *Investigation 1876*, 2, 636. On the highways and railroad, see NYSS, *Twenty-second AR of the Inspectors of State Prisons*, Sing Sing illustration (77 acres); NYSS,

*Proceedings Before the Special Committee of the NYSS* (Albany, 1876), 1093–94; NYSS, *Twenty-sixth AR of the Inspectors of State Prisons [for 1873]*, SD 5 (Albany, 1874), 22; *Times*, 3 July 1874; *World*, 25 Apr. 1874.

16. NYSA, *Sixteenth AR of the Inspectors of State Prisons*, 18 (wholly unprotected); NYSS, *Twenty-second AR of the Inspectors of State Prisons*, Sing Sing illustration; NYSS, *Twenty-sixth AR of the Inspectors of State Prisons*, 22 (no wall); *Times*, 2 Nov. 1874 (Tappan Zee), 3 July 1874, 10 June 1876 (Tousey); PANY, *Thirty-fifth AR*, 15; NYSPC, *Investigation 1876*, 269 (escapes); NYSS, *Proceedings Before the Special Committee of the NYSS*, 1093–94 (Tousey); NYSA, *Report of the Committee on State Prisons, of Their Investigations into the Causes of the Late Outbreaks in the Sing Sing Prison*, AD 187 (Albany, 1869), 4–5.

17. NYSPC, *Investigation 1876*, 2, 81, 111 (lewd women), 110 (contraband), 113 (peddlers), 191 (disreputable women), 265 (grocers), 626 (gunpowder), 635–36 (wharves, grocers).

18. *Leslie's*, 16 Feb. 1878 (hopeless); *Times*, 23 Feb. 1877, 15 Sept. 1877; *World*, 16 May 1920 (wall); *Tribune*, 14 Jan. 1880 (iron fence); NYSPC, *Investigation 1876*, 25; NYSA, *First AR of the Superintendent of State Prisons [for 1877]*, AD 10 (Albany, 1878), 7; NYSA, *Second AR of the Superintendent of State Prisons [for 1878]*, AD 10 (Albany, 1879), 6, 18; NYSA, *[Third] AR of the Superintendent of State Prisons [for 1879]*, AD 21 (Albany, 1880), 5; Lawes, *Twenty Thousand Years*, 77–78, 89.

19. *Tribune*, 13 Apr. 1875 (self-supporting); *Leslie's*, 16 Mar. 1878; NYSA, *Second AR of the Superintendent of State Prisons*, 6 (idleness).

20. Wines, *Punishment and Reformation*, 166, 199; NYS, *Report of the State Commission on Prison Labor* (Albany, 1871), xii (spread of contract labor); PANY, *Twenty-fourth AR for 1868*, SD 10 (Albany, 1869), 515; David W. Lewis, *From Newgate to Dannemora: The Rise of the Penitentiary in New York, 1796–1848* (Ithaca, N.Y., 1965), 179–200; Brian Greenberg, *Worker and Community: Response to Industrialization in a Nineteenth-Century American City, Albany, New York, 1850–1884* (Albany, N.Y., 1985), 146–47; Jonathan Grossman, "The Molders' Struggle Against Contract Prison Labor," *New York History* 23 (1942), 449–57.

21. Appendix 2; *World*, 26 May 1874; NYSS, *Twenty-fifth AR of the Inspectors of State Prisons*, 10; NYSAA, *Supplementary Report of the Majority of the Prison Committee*, AD 86 (Albany, 1876). On the unprofitability of contract labor before 1877, see NYSS, *Twenty-fourth AR of the Inspectors of State Prisons [for 1871]*, SD 22 (Albany, 1872), 9 (machinery); NYSS, *Twenty-fifth AR of the Inspectors of State Prisons*, 10 (3 factors); NYS, *Report on Prison Labor*, xiii. On expenditures over time, see appendix 2.

22. PANY, *Twenty-fourth AR*, 517 (favoritism), 521, 522; *Tribune*, 3 Oct. 1876 (loosely conducted); NYSPC, *Investigation 1876*, 19–20 (swindled); NYS, *Report on Prison Labor*, xxi (75 percent). Between 1847 and 1874 Sing Sing operated with an annual deficit. See appendix 2; table 9 in NYSA, *Twenty-seventh AR of the Inspectors of State Prisons [for 1874]*, AD 18 (Albany, 1875), 28–29. On Alfred Walker, see NYSS, *Twenty-sixth AR of the Inspectors of State Prisons*, 27; NYSA, *Twenty-seventh AR*, 31, 116; NYSA, *Twenty-eighth AR of the Inspectors of State Prisons [for 1875]*, AD 11 (Albany, 1876), 10; PANY, *Twenty-fourth AR*, 522–24; PANY, *Twenty-fifth AR for 1869*, SD 21 (Albany, 1870), 38; NYSPC, *Investigation 1876*, 47, 85, 118, 426, 488–508; *Sun*, 17 Jan. 1877.

23. PANY, *Twenty-fourth AR*, 532; PANY, *Twenty-sixth AR*, 119 (Hubbell), 155–56; NYS, *Report on Prison Labor*, xxvi, xxxii (eliminate politics); *Times*, 23 Apr. 1871; *Tribune*, 13

Apr. 1875; NYSA, *Report of Thomas Kirkpatrick, Inspector of State Prisons*, AD 93 (Albany, 1875), 1–13.

24. Augustine E. Costello, *Our Police Protectors: History of the New York Police* (New York, 1885), 139 (Amos Pilsbury); Matthew Hale Smith, *Sunshine and Shadow in New York* (Hartford, Conn., 1868), 177–79; *Leslie's*, 27 Aug. 1859; *Times*, 11 Apr. 1860, 3, 5 Mar. 1860; *Herald*, 12 Dec. 1859.

25. Appo, 9–10.

26. Ibid.; NYSA, *First AR of the Superintendent of State Prisons*, 6–7, 13; NYSPC, *Investigation 1876*, 11–12, 24–25; *Leslie's*, 16, 23 Feb. 1878; Lawes, *Life and Death*, 62; Lawes, *Twenty Thousand Years*, 15; PANY, *Twenty-fourth AR*, 61–64; Lewis, *From Newgate to Dannemora*, 52–80.

27. *Leslie's*, 16, 23 Feb. 1878 (quotes); *Herald* clipping, 2 Mar. 1887, vol. 32, DAS; Eddie Guerin, *I Was a Bandit* (New York, 1929), 21; NYSPC, *Investigation 1876* (Albany, 1877). On the abolition of the lockstep, see "Stripes and the Lockstep," *Charities Review* 10 (Mar. 1900), 15; "Abolishment of the Lockstep," *Charities Review* 10 (Aug. 1900), 281.

28. Appo, 9–10; NYSS, *Twenty-fifth AR of the Inspectors of State Prisons*, 10; NYSA, *First AR of the Superintendent of State Prisons*, 6–7, 13; NYSA, *[Third] AR of the Superintendent of State Prisons*, 11; *Times*, 12 Jan. 1881. At the end of 1877, 1,409 of the 1,616 convicts (87 percent) in Sing Sing were employed in contract work. See *Tribune*, 31 May 1878 (earnings), 16 May 1878 (self-supporting); NYSA, *Twenty-ninth AR of the Inspectors of State Prisons*, 6–7; *Times*, 2, 5 Feb. 1876, 11 June 1876, 15 Aug. 1876. Also see *Tribune*, 30 Dec. 1876, 17 Feb. 1877, 26 Mar. 1877, 16, 31 May 1878, 26 Mar. 1877, 31 Dec. 1877; *Times*, 26 Mar. 1880; Greenberg, *Worker and Community*, 106, 148–49, 195, 205–6.

29. Sutton, *Tombs*, 591 (wound up); *Leslie's*, 2 Mar. 1878 ("as the machinery"); ESP Inspectors, *51st AR*, 38–39 (leading principle).

30. PANY, *Twenty-fourth AR*, 526 (placed in shops); Lawes, *Twenty Thousand Years*, 97, 161 (health); NYS, *Report on Prison Labor*, 6–8 (jealousy); NYSPC, *Investigation 1876*, 317 (terrorism), 321; *Sun* clipping, 26 Nov. 1886 (cell assignments), vol. 28, DAS; ESP Inspectors, *51st AR*, 7, 38–39; NYSA, *Report Upon the Charges of the Star*, 8–9; *Times*, 29 Jan. 1880 (overwork).

31. NYS, *Report on Prison Labor*, xviii (contrary), 6–8 (alcohol), 96–101; PANY, *Twenty-fourth AR*, 521–22 (favors), 525 (contraband articles); *Times*, 1 Jan. 1880 (citizen employees). For examples of bribery and corruption relating to overwork see *Tribune*, 26 June 1878 (hatmaking contract); NYSPC, *Investigation 1876*, 11 (overwork), 22 (wood contract), 109 (barter), 136 (newspapers), 345 (whiskey), 700 (barter).

32. *Times*, 15 Sept. 1877 (honest work), 9 Apr. 1871; *Tribune*, 1 June 1875 (senseless notion); ESP Inspectors, *59th AR for the Year 1888* (Philadelphia, 1889), 115–16; NYSA, *[Third] AR of the Superintendent of State Prisons*, 11 (thorough discipline).

33. Lawes, *Twenty Thousand Years*, 36 (last words); Lawes, *Life and Death*, 99–100 (third-degree), 101 (no weapons), 103–4 (hard-boiled); NYSPC, *Investigation 1876*, 574 (guards and revolvers).

34. PANY, *Twenty-fourth AR*, 74 (crucifix), 540–41 (the buck; shower bath), 657; Enoch Cobb Wines and Theodore W. Dwight, *Report on the Prisons and Reformatories of the United States and Canada* (Albany, 1867), 165 (shower bath, ball and chain, iron cap, buck, yoke, or crucifix); *Times*, 3 July 1865 (yoke); *World*, 16 May 1920 (crucifixion). A

slightly different version of the yoke was employed at Auburn. See NYSPC, *Investigation 1876*, 804. Also see *NPG*, 30 Aug. 1879; *Leslie's*, 16 Feb. 1878, 16 Mar. 1878. On the severity of punishment before 1860, see Panetta, "Up the River," 171–82, 229–34. On the elimination of whipping in 1847, see Lewis, *From Newgate to Dannemora*, 146–56, 254–55. On the shower bath, see *NPG*, 5 Jan. 1867, 30 Aug. 1879 (high tide); Lewis, *Newgate to Dannemora*, 269–72 (160 times); *Times*, 3 July 1865; *Harper's Weekly*, 17 Apr. 1869. The "cap" or "bishop's mitre" was an open iron frame, hinged on the back and fastened on the front with a padlock. Once it was placed over an inmate's head, he wore the eight- to ten-pound device day and night. See NYSPC, *Investigation 1876*, 110 (8–10 lbs.); *NPG*, 5 Jan. 1867, 30 Aug. 1879; *Leslie's*, 16 Feb. 1878, 16 Mar. 1878.

35. NYSS, *Twenty-third AR of the Inspectors of State Prisons [for 1870]*, SD 21 (Albany, 1871), 10; NYSA, *Investigation 1881*, 111, 118, 126, 148, 191; *Tribune*, 17 Jan. 1877; NYSPC, *Investigation 1876*, 9, 66, 69, 90; PANY, *Thirty-fifth AR*, 13; *Times*, 3 July 1865. On the "dark cell" remaining in effect until 1913, see *World*, 16 May 1920.

36. PANY, *Twenty-fifth Annual Report for 1869* (Albany, 1870), 74–75 (ban on corporal punishment), 223–24; *Times*, 6 Jan. 1870 (ban on corporal punishment), 9 Sept. 1880, 16 Mar. 1882, 2 Apr. 1882, 27 Jan. 1883 (administered by p.k., deputy warden, guards); Lawes, *Twenty Thousand Years*, 36 (last words); Lawes, *Life and Death*, 99–100, 103–4; *NPG*, 30 Aug. 1879, 1 Apr. 1882; NYSA, *Investigation 1881*, 105 (150–60 blows), 102 (300 blows); *Times*, 27 Jan. 1883. Numerous reports of the shower bath, crucifix, yoke, lash, cat-o'-nine-tails, and other "cruel punishments" continuing beyond 1870 and until at least 1888 appear in: Sutton, *Tombs*, 592–93; *NPG*, 30 Aug. 1879; *Press* clipping, 10 July 1892, vol. 100; unmarked clipping, 27 Oct. 1892, 3 Nov. 1892; *Recorder* clippings, 28, 29 Oct. 1892, vol. 103, all in DAS. On the use of the cap and paddle, see *Leslie's*, 16 Feb. 1878, 16 Mar. 1878; *Tribune*, 26 July 1879, 23 Feb. 1883; *Times*, 2 Apr. 1882. On the prevalence of paddling, spanking, whipping, and hanging by the wrists in other state prisons in the 1890s, see New York State Board of Charities, *Report and Recommendations on the Investigation of the Elmira State Reformatory* (Albany, 1894), later reprinted by the *World*, copy in Prisons Box, WC; *Times*, 11 Dec. 1892; NYSPC, *Investigation 1876*, 107, 675; *World*, 5 Oct. 1894.

37. NYSA, *Investigation 1881*, 85–86 (Catholics), 88 (suicide), 101 (suicide), 105 (raw liver), 186–92 (Killoran); Appo, 32–33 (inmates unable to stand). On punishments referred to as "torture," and the various implements as "instruments of torture," see *Times*, 1 May 1868, 3 Apr. 1869.

38. NYSPC, *Investigation 1876*, 66–68, 91, 94, 97, 116, 131, 133, 137–38 (haste), 144, 230 (verbal orders), 673 (no rule); *Press* clipping, 10 July 1892, vol. 100; unmarked clippings, 27 Oct. 1892, 3 Nov. 1892; *Recorder* clippings, 28, 29 Oct. 1892, vol. 103, all in DAS. On guards allowed to hit inmates, see NYS, *Investigation of the State Prisons and Report* (Albany, 1876), 94.

39. Sing Sing reports inconsistently reported punishment rates before 1877, when reportage ceased.

| Year | Total | Capped | Dark Cell | Pullied |
|------|-------|--------|-----------|---------|
| 1863 | 1,213 | | | |
| 1864 | 1,403 | | | |
| 1870 | 372 | 72 | 92 | 208 |
| 1871 | | NA | | |

| YEAR | TOTAL | CAPPED | DARK CELL | PULLIED |
|------|-------|--------|-----------|---------|
| 1872 |       | NA     |           |         |
| 1873 | 364   | 94     | 198       | 72      |
| 1874 | 682   | 292    | 390       |         |
| 1875 | 1,353 | 303    | 1,050     |         |
| 1876 | 1,433 | 391    | 1,042     |         |

See Lawes, *Twenty Thousand Years*, 86 (1863 and 1864 statistics), 89 (claims corporal punishment banned in 1870); NYSS, *Twenty-third AR of the Inspectors of State Prisons [for 1870]*, SD 21 (Albany, 1871), 72, 168, 213; NYSS, *Twenty-fourth AR of the Inspectors of State Prisons*, 9, 259 (insubordinate); NYSS, *Twenty-sixth AR of the Inspectors of State Prisons*, 86; NYSA, *Twenty-seventh AR*, 127; NYSA, *Twenty-eighth AR*, 144; NYSA, *Twenty-ninth AR of the Inspectors of State Prisons*, 106; NYC, *Manual of the Corporation of the City of New York* (New York, 1869), 452 (limits punishment to warden).

40. NYS, *Investigation of the State Prisons and Report*, 94 (private contractors), 217; NYSA, *Investigation 1881*, 191 (butchered); *World* clipping, 9 Oct. 1886, vol. 26, DAS; NYS, *Report on Prison Labor*, xi–xii (50 percent); NYSS, *[Fifth] AR of the Superintendent of State Prisons [for 1881]*, SD 15 (Albany, 1882), 5 (without cruel punishments); *Harper's Weekly*, 17 Apr. 1869, p. 254 (verge of death); *Tribune, Times*, 28 Mar. 1882; *Tribune*, 23 Feb. 1883 (60 percent), 17 July 1886 (Ward); PANY, *Thirty-fifth AR*, 13 (saddles). For charges of inmates being overworked and punished for failing to meet work quotas, and denials by prison officials, see NYSA, *Investigation 1881*, 110–40, 203–22; NYSA, *Report Upon the Charges of the Star*, 2–4; *Times*, 25 Feb. 1882, 11, 12 Mar. 1882.

41. Lawes, *Life and Death*, 76–77; NYSPC, *Investigation 1876*, 3 (far from secure); *Tribune* clipping, 11 Jan. 1886 (frequent), vol. 17; *Sun* clipping, 12 June 1887 (taking to the river), vol. 36, all in DAS; *World*, 3 Oct. 1869 (hiding in the bucket shop). Official reports show an average of 7.7 escapes annually between 1870 and 1879. Between 1870 and 1876 the average was 10.4 escapes.

42. NYSS, *Report of Inspectors of State Prisons Relative to Escapes of Convicts*, SD 91 (Albany, 1874); *Times*, 4, 7 Apr. 1874; *World*, 4 Apr. 1874.

43. *Times*, 22 Oct. 1876 (Lyons); *Times* (?) and unmarked clippings, 4 Dec. 1886, vol. 28; *Morning Journal* clipping, 25 Oct. 1889, vol. 66, all in DAS; undated clipping for John Quigley, entry for 20 Mar. 1884, 462, vol. 21, SSAR; Allan Pinkerton, *Criminal Reminiscences and Detective Sketches* (New York, 1878), 208–10.

44. *Times*, 12 Apr. 1874 (Black Jim); *Tribune*, 21, 22, 23 Feb. 1883. For a rare example of a failed prison revolt on 18 Mar. 1869 that resulted in the death of one keeper, see *Harper's Weekly*, 3 Apr. 1869.

45. PANY, *Twenty-fourth AR*, 151 (minors, demoralized); Sutton, *Tombs*, 658.

46. These statistics are based on my tabulation of entries between 15 Apr. 1874 and 2 Apr. 1876 (dates of Appo's first Sing Sing incarceration), vols. 11 (15 Apr. 1874–29 Oct. 1874), 12 (30 Oct. 1874–19 July 1875), 13 (20 July 1875–2 Apr. 1876), SSAR.

47. Byrnes, *Professional Criminals*, 182–83, 211–13, 233, 236–37, 260, 264–65, 274–75.

48. Appo, 9–10 (brutes). On prisoners being allowed visitors once every two months, see *Leslie's*, 16 Feb. 1878; *Times*, 31 May 1885. On prisoners being legal "slaves of the state," see *Ruffin v. Commonwealth*, 62 Va. (21 Gratt.) 790 (1871), quoted in Friedman, *Crime and Punishment*, 529.

49. On the rise of gangs and "supergangs" in prisons after 1960, see James B. Jacobs, *Stateville: The Penitentiary in Mass Society* (Chicago, 1977), 138–74, esp. 152–53; and David M. Oshinsky, *"Worse Than Slavery": Parchman Farm and the Ordeal of Jim Crow Justice* (New York, 1996), 249–51.

50. Appo, 8.

## 5. The "Guns" of Gotham

1. Appo, 8–9.

2. Allan Pinkerton, *Thirty Years a Detective* (Chicago, 1884), 36; Hutchins Hapgood, ed., *The Autobiography of a Thief* (New York, 1903), 13–49 (pervasive pickpocketing), 35 (halcyon days); Josiah Flynt, *Notes of an Itinerant Policeman* (Boston, 1900), 67–68; Flynt, *The World of Graft* (New York, 1901), 2–15; Lawrence M. Friedman, *Crime and Punishment in American History* (New York, 1993), 108–10. Nearly half (48 percent) of all crime in 1866–67 was some type of larceny, and never dropped below 36 percent until after 1887. In 1927 robbery (25 percent) surpassed larceny (24 percent) for the first time. See NYSS, *Proceedings Before the Special Committee of the New York State Senate* (Albany, 1876), 1192a (statistics before 1876); and table no. 1 in NYSCC, *Report to the Commission of the Sub-Commission on Penal Institutions—1928* (Albany, 1928), 33. "Gun" was reportedly an abbreviated form of the Yiddish word for "thief," or *gonnif*. See Edwin H. Sutherland, *The Professional Thief: By a Professional Thief* (Chicago, 1932), 44.

3. George F. Fletcher, *Rethinking Criminal Law* (Boston, 1978), 3–5 (primordial), 30–42, 90, 100–12.

4. Appo, 29.

5. Appo, 81, 84, 94–96; James D. McCabe, Jr., *The Secrets of the Great City* (Philadelphia, 1868), 359–60; Allan Pinkerton, *Professional Thieves and the Detective* (New York, 1880), 69; *NPG*, 29 Apr. 1882 (artist).

6. Hapgood, *Autobiography*, 51–53 (special part); Pinkerton, *Thirty Years*, 33–39, 48–50; Herman Melville, *Pierre, or The Ambiguities* (New York, 1852; reprint, 1984), 281; McCabe, *Secrets*, 358 ("foreign tongue"), 359 ("bugger"), 369 ("beats"); A. E. Costello, *Our Police Protectors: History of the New York Police* (New York, 1885), 417; *Tribune*, 2 July 1883, 25 Dec. 1887. For lists of underworld slang, see Timothy J. Gilfoyle, "Street-Rats and Gutter-Snipes: Child Pickpockets and Street Culture in New York City, 1850–1900," *Journal of Social History* 37 (2004), note 28. For examples of street gang or group organization of pickpockets, see People v. Charles Cassel, 9 July 1869; People v. Witt and Malloy, 8 Aug. 1876, both in DAP; unmarked clipping, 8 July 1889, vol. 62, DAS; Thomas Byrnes, *Professional Criminals of America* (New York, 1886), 36–37; Phil Farley, *Criminals of America* (New York, 1876), 202–3. For examples of married and heterosexual couples working as pickpockets, see People v. John Williams and Bella Williams, 16 Sept. 1864; People v. Bridget McGuire, 19 Dec. 1859; People v. Ellen Wilson, 5 Sept. 1872, all in DAP; *World* clipping, 2 Aug. 1885, vol. 13, DAS.

7. Flynt, *Graft*, 40; Pinkerton, *Thirty Years*, 33–39; *Sun*, 4 Mar. 1861; Jonathan Slick, *Snares of New York; or, Tricks and Traps of the Great Metropolis* (New York, 1879), 37–38; Byrnes, *Professional Criminals*, 36–37; *Star* clipping, 8 Oct. 1883, DAS; *Tribune*, 2 July 1883, 25 Dec. 1887.

8. Hapgood, *Autobiography*, 53 (jumps out), 78–82; Munro, *New York Tombs*, 172; Flynt, *Graft*, 39 (jump out); Pinkerton, *Thirty Years*, 31–37; Benjamin P. Eldridge and William B. Watts, *Our Rival, the Rascal* (Boston, 1897), 16; McCabe, *Secrets*, 366–70; *NPG*, 27 May 1882; *Tribune*, 25 Dec. 1887. On preventive arrests, see *Tribune*, 7 Aug. 1885; *World*, 8 Aug. 1885; unmarked clipping, 22 Apr. 1889, vol. 60, DAS; Byrnes, *Professional Criminals*, 34–35; Helen Campbell, Thomas W. Knox, and Thomas Byrnes, *Darkness and Daylight: or, Lights and Shadows of New York Life* (Hartford, Conn., 1891), 704 (rovers). On preventive arrests of Appo, see *World*, 6, 7 Aug. 1885; *Brooklyn Eagle*, 2 May 1889.

9. Hapgood, *Autobiography*, 51; People v. Charles Cassell, 8 July 1869; People v. John Riley, 21 Nov. 1864; People v. John Brown, 13 Dec. 1864. For pickpockets in churches, see People v. Maria Anderson, 2 June 1874; People v. Henry Maler, 8 June 1876; People v. John Danaker, 17 Feb. 1869; People v. James Watson, 8 Apr. 1869; People v. Maria Brown, 19 Apr. 1869, all in DAP. Arrest and prosecution statistics in this chapter are based on the sampling of 1,176 individuals arrested for pickpocketing from 1859 to 1876 and described in chapter 2, note 20; and Gilfoyle, "Street-Rats and Gutter-Snipes," notes 19 and 20. Of 1,176 individuals prosecuted, trial and other testimony revealed that at least 279 (24 percent) worked with one or more accomplices, 51 percent worked on the street, 14 percent in a concert saloon or restaurant, and 13 percent on a streetcar or other form of public transit.

10. People v. Henry Gibson, 6 Dec. 1871; People v. John McClane, 9 July 1872; People v. James Carson, 5 Dec. 1876, all in DAP; *Harper's Weekly*, 20 May 1871 (in league); *Increase of Crime*, 24 (hustle passengers); McCabe, *Secrets*, 367 (Beware); Sutherland, *Professional Thief*, 44 (warning signs). On crowded streetcars, see *Herald*, editorial, 2 Oct. 1864; *Tribune*, editorial, 2 Feb. 1866.

11. *Star* clipping, 8 Oct. 1883 (delicately); unmarked clipping, 8 Aug. 1895, vol. 144; *Times* clipping, 7 July 1890 (knockdown pickpockets), vol. 75, all in DAS; Hapgood, *Autobiography*, 39–40; George W. Walling, *Recollections of a New York Chief of Police* (New York, 1887), 330; *NPG*, 27 May 1882; Byrnes, *Professional Criminals*, 34; *Tribune*, 25 Dec. 1887; Farley, *Criminals of America*, 202. Only 11 percent (114 in number) of those arrested in the sample were "knockdown pickpockets."

12. Of 1,176 individuals prosecuted for pickpocketing, 940 were male (80 percent) and 236 female (20 percent). The breakdown by age was:

| AGES | TOTAL | PERCENTAGE OF TOTAL | PERCENTAGE OF ADULTS |
|---|---|---|---|
| 10–14 | 57 | 5 | — |
| 15–17 | 109 | 9 | — |
| 18–19 | 179 | 15 | 18 |
| 20–24 | 372 | 32 | 37 |
| 25–29 | 203 | 17 | 20 |
| 30–34 | 110 | 9 | 11 |
| 35–39 | 57 | 5 | 6 |
| 40–44 | 22 | 2 | 2 |
| 45–49 | 11 | 1 | 1 |
| 50 AND ABOVE | 5 | .4 | .5 |
| UNKNOWN | 51 | 4 | 5 |

For examples of pickpockets identifying themselves as "gentlemen" and "entrepreneurs," see People v. Charles Gibbons, 7 Apr. 1876; People v. James O'Brien, 17 Jan. 1876, both in DAP. To categorize the occupations given by prosecuted pickpockets, I relied on the classification scheme devised by Michael B. Katz in *The People of Hamilton, Canada West: Family and Class in a Mid-Nineteenth-Century City* (Cambridge, Mass., 1975), 343–48; and "Occupational Classification in History," *Journal of Interdisciplinary History* 3 (1972), 63–88. With roman numeral I identifying occupations with high socioeconomic ranking to roman numeral V for those with low socioeconomic ranking, pickpockets fell into the following categories:

| TOTAL IN CATEGORY | I | II | III | IV | V | VI | UNKNOWN |
|---|---|---|---|---|---|---|---|
| 1,176 | 14 | 90 | 406 | 249 | 265 | 69 | 69 |
| | (13M/1F) | (85M/5F) | (390M/16F) | (228M/21F) | (142M/123F) | (13M/56F) | |
| TOTAL % (OF 1,107) | 1.3 | 7.6 | 37 | 23 | 24 | 6 | 1 |
| MALE % (OF 871) | 1.5 | 9.7 | 49 | 26 | 16 | 1.5 | |
| FEMALE % (OF 222) | — | 2.3 | 7 | 9 | 55 | 25 | |

Roman numeral VI includes "unclassified occupations." Newsboys and bootblacks were not included in Katz's classification, and I recategorized servants and laundresses from "unclassifiable occupations" to category V.

13. Campbell, *Darkness*, 705–6 (Byrnes); Pinkerton, *Thirty Years*, 37 (female thieves); Byrnes, *Professional Criminals*, 35–36; Farley, *Criminals of America*, 206–7. On female mobs, see People v. Ellen Daley and Mary Ann Williams, 5 Aug. 1859, DAP; unmarked clipping, 30 June 1885, vol. 13; unmarked clipping, 11 Aug. 1895, vol. 144, both in DAS. Among the 241 females prosecuted for larceny or grand larceny, 43 percent were arrested in a panel house (a house of prostitution where male clients were systematically robbed), brothel, saloon, or concert saloon. Another 22 percent were arrested in the street.

14. People v. Catharine Smith, 25 Nov. 1864; People v. Catherine Columbus, 16 Nov. 1864; People v. Josephine Thompson, 9 Mar. 1869, all in DAP.

15. *Star* clipping, 8 Oct. 1883 (big city), DAS; *Tribune*, 12 Aug. 1876; Slick, *Snares of New York*, 39; *Tribune*, 12 Aug. 1876.

16. R. I. Davis, *Men's Garments, 1830–1900: A Guide to Pattern Cutting* (London, 1989), 54, 60 (decline of frocks); H. Matheson, *H. Matheson's Scientific and Practical Guide for the Tailor's Cutting Department* (New York, 1871), 14 (popular garment); Frederick T. Croonberg, *The Blue Book of Men's Tailoring* (1907; reprint, New York, 1977), 14–15 (Every man; plenty of pockets); R. L. Shep, "Introduction" in Louis Devere, *The Handbook of Practical Cutting on the Centre Point System* (London, 1866, 1868; reprint, Lopez Island, Wash., 1986).

17. *World* clipping, 14 Oct. 1885, vol. 14, DAS; Pinkerton, *Thirty Years*, 42–44; Appo, 25. On the lack of attention to men's pockets, see Matheson, *Scientific and Practical Guide*, 16, 46–48, 50; Augustus Koch, *The Cutters' Centennial Guide; A New System in the Art and Science of Garment Cutting* (Poughkeepsie, N.Y., 1876), 21–23.

18. Hapgood, *Autobiography*, 34; *Sun*, 4 Mar. 1861; Munro, *New York Tombs*, 41.

19. Steffens, *Autobiography*, 222–26, 288.

20. Hapgood, *Autobiography*, 77–78, 225.

21. Flynt, *Graft*, 39, 46–47, 56; *Brother Jonathan*, 28 Jan., 24 Mar. 1860 (police familiarity); *Lexow Committee*, II:1801–2 (Vosburg and Noble); unmarked clipping, 11 Nov. 1886, vol. 27; unmarked clipping, 22 Apr. 1889, vol. 60, both in DAS; NYSCC, *Report—1929* (New York, 1929), 107 (habeas corpus).

22. Hapgood, *Autobiography*, 35; *World* clipping, 14 Oct. 1885 (careless), vol. 14, DAS; Allan Pinkerton, *Criminal Reminiscences and Detective Sketches* (New York, 1878), 96–97 (judge); Walling, *Recollections*, 497–500, 531–32 (messenger; Higgins); *Times*, 31 Dec. 1894 (Wall Street), 14 Apr. 1892.

23. Appo, 29 ($600), 18, 20 ($600–800). The total number of victims was smaller in number than the pickpocket total because nearly one-quarter of all victims were victimized by more than one pickpocket. Of 1,010 victims 740 (73 percent) were male, 264 (26 percent) were female, and 6 (0.6 percent) were of unknown gender. In 1,010 incidents the breakdown of objects stolen was:

        538  (53 percent) money or pocketbook with money
        408  (40 percent) watch and/or chain
        32   (3 percent) watch and money
        25   (2 percent) jewelry
        7    (0.7 percent) unknown

  For individual cases, see People v. Charles King and Charles May, 5 Feb. 1864; People v. Patrick Riley, 21 May 1869 (McKenna); People v. Frank Linton, 10 July 1871; People v. Peter McGee, 18 June 1872 (Nevins); People v. William Devlin, 9 Mar. 1874 (Boyden); People v. Charles Gibbons, 7 Apr. 1876, all in DAP. On pickpockets earning $1,500 per week, see Andrew Bruce and John Landesco, "The Criminal Underworld of Chicago in the '80's and '90's: How the Life of Eddie Jackson, the Immune Pickpocket, Was Secured," *Journal of Criminal Law and Criminology* 25 (Sept. 1934), 345.

24. *Star* clipping, 8 Oct. 1883, DAS; *NPG*, 27 Dec. 1845, 3 Jan. 1846, 10 Jan. 1846, 4 Apr. 1846; George Thompson, *Adventures of a Pickpocket; or Life at a Fashionable Watering Place* (New York, 1849); George G. Foster, *New York by Gas-Light* (New York, 1850), 85; Campbell, *Darkness*, 704.

25. *Times* clipping, 7 July 1890 (worst criminals), vol. 75; *Truth*, 4 June 1883 (no mercy); *World* clipping, 30 Mar. 1890 (Byrnes), vol. 72, all in DAS.

26. On the sample from the DAP and related methodology, see note 9 above; People v. Joseph Brunner, 17 Nov. 1876; People v. John McGrath, 17 Nov. 1876; People v. Hoy, 17 June 1879; People v. Ellen Wilson, 5 Sept. 1872, all in DAP. For cases involving unemployed men pleading for mercy, see People v. James Delany, 6 July 1876 (2.5 years); People v. Joseph Carroll, 29 June 1876 (4.5 years), both in DAP. On judges issuing severe penalties against "knockdown pickpockets" to deter others, see *Times* clipping, 7 July 1890, vol. 75, DAS.

27. People v. Henry Ducketts (14 years old), 24 June 1879; People v. John Kelly (19 years old), 16 Mar. 1871; People v. John Golden (17 years old), 14 Jan. 1874; People v. Alfred Johnson (19 years old), 3 June 1874; People v. Lawrence Dixon (19 years old), 6 Feb. 1874, all in DAP. For an earlier charge against Ducketts when he was nine, see People v. Henry Ducketts, 21 Apr. 1874, DAP.

28. For statutes defining pickpocketing and various forms of larceny, see Laws of 1860, chapter 508, sections 33, 34; revised in Laws of 1862, chapter 374, sections 2, 3 (assault with intent to steal); revised in Laws of 1882, chapter 410, sections 3 (attempted larceny), 63 (grand larceny), 531 (larceny in the second degree), 686 (punishment for unsuccessful attempt), 1447. Grand larceny was the felonious taking and carrying away of another's personal property valued in excess of twenty-five dollars. Larceny in the second degree included unlawful appropriation of property of any value from a person. Courts upheld convictions of attempted larceny even if nothing was in the victim's pocket or the perpetrator gained control of no property. See *Commonwealth of Massachusetts v. McDonald*, 5 Cush. 365; *People v. Jones*, 46 Mich. 441; *State of Connecticut v. Wilson*, 30 Conn. 500; 1862 LEXIS 24; *Rogers v. Commonwealth of Pennsylvania*, 5 Serge. & Rawle 463; *People v. Bush*, 4 Hill 133. For examples and a good summary of the above statutes and cases, see *People of the State of New York v. Thomas Moran*, 123 N.Y. 254; 25 N.E. 412; 20 Am.St.Rep. 732; 1890 N.Y. LEXIS 1730; Fletcher, *Rethinking Criminal Law*, 4–5.

29. Unmarked clipping, 10 June 1883, DAS; Board of Police Justices of the City of New York, *Second Annual Report for the Year 1875* (New York, 1876), 9; *NPG*, 31 Dec. 1881.

30. Arthur Train, *The Prisoner at the Bar: Sidelights on the Administration of Criminal Justice* (New York, 1923), 8, 11–12, 24–25, 33–38.

31. William Francis Kuntz II, *Criminal Sentencing in Three Nineteenth-Century Cities* (New York, 1988), 358–59, 370; Monkkonen, *Murder in New York City*, esp. 167; Monkkonen, "Racial Factors in New York City Homicides," 113 (2 percent); Monkkonen, "The American State from the Bottom Up," 521–31.

32. The data and information below are based on the sample in DAP, 1859–74, described in chapter 2, note 20. In 1871, 1872, and 1874, 101 individuals were convicted of larceny, 54 of whom were sentenced to three or more years in prison. Court of General Sessions indictments in 1859 and 1864 frequently did not include the final punishment on convicted defendants. Only twenty-one indictments and convictions involving individuals who stole $100 or more in valuables provided a final sentence.

PERCENTAGE BREAKDOWN OF PRISON SENTENCES

| YEAR | TOTAL CASES | TOTAL SENTENCED | <1 YEAR | 1–1.9 | 2–2.9 | 3+ | SUSPEND. | H. OF REF. |
|---|---|---|---|---|---|---|---|---|
| 1859 | 54 | 26 | 35 | 8 | 31 | 27 | 0 | 0 |
| 1864 | 118 | 40 | 35 | 8 | 28 | 3 | | 0 |
| 1869 | 91 | 47 | 9 | 15 | 30 | 38 | 0 | 9 |
| 1871 | 144 | 84 | 12 | 7 | 14 | 52 | 11 | 4 |
| 1872 | 144 | 74 | 9 | 16 | 38 | 31 | 9 | 5 |
| 1874 | 316 | 245 | 14 | 12 | 42 | 20 | 1 | 11 |
| 1876 | 301 | 219 | 10 | 20 | 33 | 27 | 0 | 11 |
| TOTAL | 1,168 | | | | | | | |

33. *Truth*, 4 June 1883, DAS (shot); Matthew Hale Smith, *Sunshine and Shadow in New York* (Hartford, Conn., 1868), 569; People v. John Smith, 25 Nov. 1872, DAP. For other examples of long sentences, see People v. John Jackson, 17 Nov. 1876; People v. Henry Lee, 15 June 1876, all in DAP.

34. Entry for 20 Mar. 1874, 475–76, First District, PCDB (Appo); entry for "George Dixon,"

15 Apr. 1874, 396, vol. 11, SSAR; entry for 13 Apr. 1874, vol. 3, Sing Sing admissions, 1842–1874 (n.p.), Executive Register of Commitments to Prisons, NYSArc; People v. John Williams, 15 Sept. 1871 (5 years for a $60 watch); People v. Emma Wilson and Catherine Love, 16 Oct. 1874 (3 years for a $6 watch); People v. Jane Crane, 20 Oct. 1874 (3 years for $2.30); People v. Jane Loughlin, May 1876, all in DAP; *Morning Journal* clipping, 20 Dec. 1886 (25 years), vol. 29, DAS. For other examples of lengthy Hackett sentences to teenagers, see entry for George Smith, age nineteen (2.5 years), 11 Sept. 1875, 56; entry for John McCauly, age eighteen (2 years), 17 Sept. 1875, 80, both in vol. 13, SSAR. Near the end of his career, Hackett allegedly became insane and issued even heavier sentences.

35. *National Cyclopedia of American Biography* (New York, 1909), 11:572; Francis L. Wellman, *Gentlemen of the Jury: Reminiscences of Thirty Years at the Bar* (New York, 1924), 250–55 (Gildy, rifle team).

36. People v. Timothy Leary, 30 June 1876, DAP; *Star* clipping, 4 June 1884 (class of criminals), vol. 8, DAS. For other examples of harsh sentences given by Gildersleeve, see People v. John Delehanty, 7 Dec. 1876, DAP; entry for John Downey (nineteen years old, two years for petty larceny), 8 Mar. 1876, 310, vol. 13, SSAR; *Sun*, 16 Jan. 1877 (five years for pickpocketing $1), 19 Jan. 1877 (fifteen years for highway robbery), 23 Jan. 1877 (six months for gambling); 26 Jan. 1877 (fifteen and twenty years for assault and robbery).

37. Appo, 8–9. Appo confused the names of the judge and victim in this part of the autobiography. He mistakenly believed that he pickpocketed John A. Bannon and that he was tried before "Judge Cowen," the latter a reference to Rufus Billings Cowing, who judged Appo in a later trial in 1895. I replaced Cowing's name with Gildersleeve's. See entry for "George Wilson," 11 Jan. 1877, 173, vol. 14, SSAR; entry for George Wilson, 12 Dec. 1878 (deduction date), vol. 2, Reports of Deductions of Sentences by Prison Agents, Wardens and Superintendents (AO601), NYSArc.

## 6. DRAFTED

1. Appo, 9. Sing Sing admission records indicate that Appo could read and write *before* his second sentence to Sing Sing. See entry for 15 Apr. 1874 (George Dixon), 396, vol. 11; entry for 11 Jan. 1877 (George Wilson), 173, vol. 14, both in SSAR.

2. NYSA, *First AR of the Superintendent of State Prisons [for 1877]*, AD 10 (Albany, 1878), 30, 47, 61, 171; NYSA, *Second AR of the Superintendent of State Prisons [for 1878]*, AD 10 (Albany, 1879), 24, 31, 35, 43, 56, 67; appendix 2; entries for 20 July 1877, 13 Oct. 1877 (Appo draft), Diary of the Principal Keeper of Clinton Prison, NYSArc.

3. NYSA, *Supplementary Report of Majority of the Prison Committee*, AD 86 (Albany, 1876), 2–4; *Times*, 3 July 1874; Lewis E. Lawes, *Twenty Thousand Years in Sing Sing* (New York, 1932), 14 (Siberia); NYSPC, *Investigation of the State Prisons and Report Thereon, 1876* (Albany, 1877) (hereafter *Investigation 1876*), 563; NYSA, *Resolutions Relative to the Removal of the State Prison at Clinton to Ward's Island*, AD 128 (Albany, 1877); NYSA, *Twenty-ninth AR of the Inspectors of State Prisons [for 1876]*, AD 14 (Albany, 1877), 266 (isolation); NYSA, *Second AR of the Superintendent of State Prisons*, 9–10; NYSA, *Third AR of the Superintendent of State Prisons [for 1879]*, AD 21 (Albany, 1880), 6–7; David W. Lewis, *From Newgate to Dannemora: The Rise of the*

Penitentiary in New York, 1796–1848 (Ithaca, N.Y., 1965), 260–62. No Clinton prison admission records covering the years Appo was there have survived.

4. Times, 3 July 1874; NYSPC, Investigation 1876, 577–78, 583, 598; NYSA, Twenty-ninth AR of the Inspectors of State Prisons, 8 (unprofitability).

5. NYSPC, Investigation 1876, 137, 150, 238 (hardest men).

6. NYSA, Second AR of the Superintendent of State Prisons, 8; NYSA, First AR of the Superintendent of State Prisons, 10–12.

7. NYSSP, AR for 1888 (Albany, 1889), 34; NYSSP, AR for 1887 (Albany, 1888), 14–15; NYSS, Twenty-fifth AR of the Inspectors of State Prisons [for 1872], SD 30 (Albany, 1873), 167 (Parkhurst); NYSA, First AR of the Superintendent of State Prisons, 160.

8. Tribune, 26 June 1878; NYSPC, Investigation 1876, 22. Clinton's contract labor population during Appo's term was:

| YEAR | TOTAL POP. | HATS | STATE WORK | SICK OR UNEMPLOYED |
|---|---|---|---|---|
| 1878 | 649 | 243 (37%) | 245 (38%) | 96 (15%) |
| 1879 | 472 | 290 (61%) | 148 (31%) | 34 (7%) |
| 1880 | 521 | 341 (65%) | 152 (29%) | 28 (5%) |

See NYSA, Second AR of the Superintendent of State Prisons, 70; NYSA, Third AR of the Superintendent of State Prisons, 76; NYSA, Fourth AR of the Superintendent of State Prisons [for 1880], AD 13 (Albany, 1881).

9. NYSA, First AR of the Superintendent of State Prisons, 9 (meals in cells); Times, 3 July 1874; NYSS, Twenty-fifth AR of the Inspectors of State Prisons, 6 (544 cells).

10. NYSPC, Investigation 1876, 529 (bathing), 594 (shanties).

11. PANY, Twenty-fourth Report, 525 (contractors); Sun clipping, 20 Dec. 1886 (tobacco), vol. 29; Herald clipping, 9 Nov. 1894 (whiskey), vol. 134, both in DAS.

12. NYSPC, Investigation 1876, 595 (chickens), 596 (inmate guards), 607 (steak); Tribune, 25 Jan. 1896 (errands); Eddie Guerin, I Was a Bandit (New York, 1929), 26.

13. Appo spelled the keeper's name as "Hagerty." Civil service reports spelled his surname as "Haggerty." Appo believed that the incidents involving Haggerty took place in 1879. Most likely he meant 1878, since he was released on 8 January 1879. I have changed the date from 1879 to 1878. See Appo, 10–11, 52.

14. E. D. Ferguson was the Clinton physician from 1876 to 1 June 1878. Appo misspelled his name as "Furgeson." See NYSA, Twenty-ninth AR of the Inspectors of State Prisons, 358; NYSA, First AR of the Superintendent of State Prisons, 246; NYSA, Second AR of the Superintendent of State Prisons, 73.

15. Appo, 51–52. Appo was slightly confused about the year. He was in Clinton prison between 13 Oct. 1877 and 8 Jan. 1879. See entries for "George Wilson," 20 July 1877, 13 Oct. 1877, 8 Jan. 1879, Diary of the Principal Keeper of Clinton Prison, NYSArc. Clinton prison admission records do not cover Appo's years. Consequently it was not possible to corroborate the existence of Mike Hicks.

16. Entry for 17 Apr. 1878, 468–69 (escape); 15 Mar. 1878, 18 Mar. 1878, 14, 19 Aug. 1878; 28 Aug. 1877 (guards suspended); 24, 29 Apr. 1877, 1, 4, 6, 20, 22 May 1877 (escapes); 5 June 1877 (guard attack), all in Diary of the Principal Keeper of Clinton Prison, NYSArc; Times, 21 Oct. 1877 (guards assaulted).

17. Entries for 3 Sept. 1878, 20, 21 Nov. 1878, Diary of the Principal Keeper of Clinton

Prison, NYSArc. Published accounts offered no discussion of this event. See NYSA, *Second AR of the Superintendent of State Prisons*, 59–76.

18. *Times*, 3 Aug. 1891 (Haggerty's Christmas Tree), 12 Feb. 1892, 20 Feb. 1893; *Tribune*, 17 Feb. 1892 (reckless keepers).

19. Appo, 10–11; Frank Moss, *The American Metropolis*, III:127–28. These parts of the autobiography were written as if these events occurred in Sing Sing, but the details Appo provides indicate that he was in Clinton. Records reveal that it was a day earlier and that his sentence was reduced. See entry for George Wilson, 12 Dec. 1878 (deduction date), vol. 2, Reports of Deduction of Sentences by Prison Agents, Wardens and Superintendents (AO601), NYSArc; entry for George A. Wilson, 8 Jan. 1879, Diary of the Principal Keeper of Clinton Prison, both in NYSArc. I found no mention of Appo's charges in the *World* from 30 Dec. 1878 to 28 Apr. 1879; *Herald*, Jan. 1879; and *Sun*, Jan. 1879. Newspaper exposés of cruelty and brutality in New York prisons were common after 1870.

20. Appo, 10–12. Appo referred to the hat company as "Gardner & Co., 182 Greene St." I have changed the name in the text to Garden & Co., which was identified as a package hat house at 458 Broome Street from 1870 to 1872, and then a hat manufacturer at either 80 or 82 Greene Street from 1875 to 1880. See *Trow's New York City Directory* (New York, 1870–80).

## 7. Opium Dens and Bohemia

1. Appo, 12–13. "Graft" was a general, generic slang term used by criminals for all kinds of theft and illegal practices. See Josiah Flynt, *The World of Graft* (New York, 1901), 4. On "sure thing graft," see Frank Moss, *The American Metropolis* (New York, 1897), III:132. "Hand shakers" were confidence men known for outwardly friendly methods. They were sometimes called "bunco steerers."

2. Appo, 8–9.

3. Ibid. (crooks), 12–13 (different systems); Allen S. Williams, *The Demon of the Orient, and His Satellite Fiends of the Joints: Our Opium Smokers as They are in Tartar Hells and American Paradises* (New York, 1883), 72–75 (addict by 1875); Moss, *American Metropolis*, III:132.

4. Williams, *Demon*, 7, 88; Martin Booth, *Opium: A History* (New York, 1996), 63 (opium use greater than tobacco use). In 1881 China and the United States signed a treaty prohibiting "natives of either country" from selling opium in the other. Designed to prevent conflicts related to the Opium Wars from occurring, it unintentionally discriminated against Chinese den operators. See *Tribune*, 18 Apr. 1882, 23 July 1883; *Morning Journal* clipping, 26 Dec. 1886, vol. 29; *Recorder* clipping, 10 Nov. 1891, vol. 91, both in DAS; Charles E. Terry and Mildred Pellens, *The Opium Problem* (New York, 1928), 745. Numerous localities classified opium as a "poison," allowing only medical professionals to sell or distribute it. See *Herald* clipping, 20 Aug. 1882, DAS; William Rosser Cobbe, *Doctor Judas: A Portrayal of the Opium Habit* (Chicago, 1895), 198. By 1898 at least twenty "pharmacies" in Chinatown sold opium in twenty-five- to fifty-cent portions. See Louis J. Beck, *New York's Chinatown: An Historical Representation of Its People and Places* (New York, 1898), 144. On opium as a cure for alco-

holism, see Williams, *Demon*, 89. The best studies of nineteenth-century opium use are David T. Courtwright, *Dark Paradise: Opiate Addiction in America before 1940* (Cambridge, Mass., 1982), 1–36, 54–56, 79–83; David F. Musto, *The American Disease: Origins of Narcotic Control* (New York, 1987 edition), 1–70; Jill Jonnes, *Hep-Cats, Narcs, and Pipe Dreams: A History of America's Romance with Illegal Drugs* (Baltimore, 1996); Joseph Spillane, "The Making of an Underground Market: Drug Selling in Chicago, 1900–1940," *Journal of Social History* 32 (1998), 28; Diana L. Ahmad, "Opium Smoking, Anti-Chinese Attitudes, and the American Medical Community, 1850–90," *American Nineteenth-Century History* 1 (2000), 53–68.

5. E. W. Syle, "A Chinese Mission in New-York," *Spirit of the Missions* (July 1854), 285; unidentified clipping, 12 May 1883, DAS; unmarked clipping, 12 May 1883, DAS; Horace B. Day, *The Opium Habit, with Suggestions as to the Remedy* (New York, 1868), 8; Cobbe, *Doctor Judas*, 126. On the widespread belief that most, if not all, Chinese men smoked opium, see George W. Walling, *Recollections of a New York Chief of Police* (New York, 1887), 419–20; Jacob Riis, *How the Other Half Lives* (New York, 1890), 94–95; Helen Campbell, Thomas W. Knox, and Thomas Byrnes, *Darkness and Daylight: or, Lights and Shadows of New York Life* (Hartford, Conn., 1891), 552; Mary Roberts Coolidge, *Chinese Immigration* (New York, 1909), 9. These critics conveniently forgot that opium smoking was introduced to China by Europeans. See Peter Ward Fay, *The Opium War, 1840–1842* (Chapel Hill, N.C., 1975); Jonathan D. Spence, *The Search for Modern China* (New York, 1990), 120–32, 143–64; Frederic Wakeman, Jr., *Strangers at the Gate: Social Disorder in South China, 1839–1861* (Berkeley, Calif., 1966); Jonnes, *Hep-Cats*, 43.

6. James L. Ford, *Forty-Odd Years in the Literary Shop* (New York, 1921), 202–3 (origins of "joint" and "dope").

7. Augustine E. Costello, *Our Police Protectors: History of the New York Police* (New York, 1885), 517–23; Thomas Byrnes, *Professional Criminals of America* (New York, 1886), 13–17; Virginia Berridge and Griffith Edwards, *Opium and the People: Opiate Use in Nineteenth-Century England* (New York, 1981), 202–4; Bingham Dai, *Opium Addiction in Chicago* (1937; reprint, Montclair, N.J., 1970) 17–19; Jonnes, *Hep-Cats*, 29–30 (dope).

8. *Tribune*, 21 July 1876, 10 July 1877, 12 July 1882; Beck, *New York's Chinatown*, 253–54; Williams, *Demon*, 10–11; *Times*, 26 Dec. 1873 (miserable alley), 22 Mar. 1880 (400–500 Chinese); *Harper's Weekly*, 7 Mar. 1874, (Homer), 222; Alonzo Calkins, *Opium and the Opium-Appetite* (Philadelphia, 1871), 53; Walling, *Recollections*, 432 (6,000–7,000 Chinese); *Harper's Weekly*, 22 Nov. 1890.

9. Williams, *Demon*, 12 (vicious, depraved, criminal); Beck, *New York's Chinatown*, 156 (imported vice); Walling, *Recollections*, 419–20.

10. *Star* clippings, 26 Dec. 1888, 8 Feb. 1884 (4 Mott), vol. 7, DAS; Beck, *New York's Chinatown*, 113 (17 Mott), 118 (17 Mott); correspondence attached to Police Inspector Moses D. Cortwright to Peter Conlin, Chief of Police, 1 Oct. 1896, box 90-SWL-45, MP; Williams, *Demon*, 59–61 (poor town), 67 (Poppy); H. H. Kane, "American Opium-Smokers," *Harper's Weekly* 25 (8 Oct. 1881), 646; H. H. Kane, *Opium-Smoking in America and China* (New York, 1882), 2, 8; *Star* clipping, 8 Feb. 1884, vol. 7, DAS. On the location of Chinatown opium dens below or behind laundries, boarding-houses, groceries, and gambling dens, see Williams, *Demon*, 12–17, 75 (17 Mott

Street); Campbell, *Darkness and Daylight*, 550. On the growth of Chinese laundries and their links to opium, see Williams, *Demon*, 59–61; unmarked clipping, 9 Nov. 1891, vol. 91; *Herald* clipping, 17 Mar. 1892, vol. 96; unmarked clipping, 30 Mar. 1896 (202 E. 104th Street), vol. 153; *Herald* clipping, 11 Dec. 1898, vol. 175, all in DAS; Clifton R. Wooldridge, *Hands Up! In the World of Crime; or Twelve Years a Detective* (Chicago, 1906), 218–19, 221–22; People v. Ah Wing et al., 27 May 1887; People v. Ah Gong and Ah Wing, 24 June 1887, both in box 9963, location 106094, SCC.

11. *Sun*, 12 Feb. 1882; "Closure of the Opium 'Joints' in New York," *American Journal of Stimulants and Narcotics* 1 (1882), 26 (4 Mott St.); *Star* clippings, 26 Dec. 1888, 8 Feb. 1884 (4 Mott), vol. 7, DAS; *Evening Post*, 21 Aug. 1882, quoted in John Liggins, *Opium: England's Coercive Opium Policy and Its Disastrous Results in China and India; The Spread of Opium-Smoking in America* (New York, 1883), 6. The *Evening Post* reporter misspelled "Poppy" as "Pape." Allen Williams claimed that "Old Pop" on Mott Street was Quong War. See Williams, *Demon*, 60, 63, 67.

12. *Leslie's*, 12 May 1883 (other half); Ford, *Forty-Odd Years*, 202–3; Albert Parry, *Garrets and Pretenders: A History of Bohemianism in America* (New York, 1933), ix (intellectual proletariat); Charles Warrington Earle, "Opium-Smoking in Chicago," *Chicago Medical Journal and Examiner* 52 (1886), 105. For brief descriptions of New York's "Bohemia," see *NPG*, 31 Dec. 1881; Ford, *The Literary Shop and Other Tales* (New York, 1894); Ford, *Bohemia Invaded* (New York, 1895). The den was located at 10 Pell Street. See Beck, *New York's Chinatown*, 154.

13. Parry, *Garrets and Pretenders*, xiii, 1–5, 8–10, 14–21, 26–37, 55–61; Maxwell F. Marcuse, *This Was New York* (New York, 1969), 82–85; Ford, *Forty-Odd Years*, 61–62 (Clemenceau). On Fitz-James O'Brien's description of opium creativity, see Williams, *Demon*, 91–103. On Clapp, see *National Cyclopaedia of American Biography* (New York, 1907), IX:121; Henry Clapp, Jr., "Prison Sonnets" in Charles Spear, ed., *Voices from Prison; A Selection of Poetry Written Within the Cell* (Boston, 1848), 122–23. Pfaff's was located at 653 Broadway, the Free Love League at 555 Broadway. On "free love," see Helen Lefkowitz Horowitz, *Rereading Sex: Battles over Sexual Knowledge and Suppression in Nineteenth-Century America* (New York, 2002), 268–71, 288–96, 295.

14. *Tribune*, 16 Oct. 1881 (sporting men); *NPG*, 13 Sept. 1879; Timothy J. Gilfoyle, *City of Eros: New York City, Prostitution, and the Commercialization of Sex, 1790–1920* (New York, 1992), 92–116.

15. Fitz-Hugh Ludlow, *The Hasheesh Eater: Being Passages from the Life of a Pythagorean* (New York, 1857); Ludlow, "What Shall They Do To Be Saved? [Opium Eating and Opium Eaters]," *Harper's New Monthly Magazine* 35 (1867), 377–85. On Ludlow, see *National Cyclopaedia of American Biography* (Brooklyn, 1906), 13:463; Dumas Malone, ed., *Dictionary of American Biography* (New York, 1933), 11:491; William Dean Howells, *Literary Friends and Acquaintance: A Personal Retrospect of American Authorship* (New York, 1901), 70; "Once Bohemia," *Leslie's*, 4 Apr. 1874, 55; *Harper's Bazar* [sic] 3 (12 Nov. 1870), 723, 736 (obituary and cartoon); Parry, *Garrets and Pretenders*, 8–9. On Poe's opium use or addicted characters, see Booth, *Opium*, 49; Alethea Hayter, *Opium and the Romantic Imagination* (London, 1968), 132–50.

16. Ford, *Forty-Odd Years*, 202–3; *Evening Post*, 21 Aug. 1882, quoted in Liggins, *Opium*, 6.

17. Beck, *New York's Chinatown*, 139, 150–51; Byrnes, *Professional Criminals*, 383, 387 (paradise); *Evening Post*, 21 Aug. 1882, quoted in Liggins, *Opium*, 6; Kane, "American Opium-Smokers," 683; Kane, *Opium-Smoking*, 43; *Tribune*, 16 Oct. 1881; *Commercial Advertiser* clipping, 28 Sept. 1891, vol. 90; *Herald* clipping, 17 Mar. 1892, vol. 17, both in DAS; Stephen Crane, "Opium's Varied Dreams" (1896), in Fredson Bowers, ed., *The Works of Stephen Crane: Tales, Sketches and Reports* (Charlottesville, Va., 1973), VIII:365–70; Courtwright, *Dark Paradise*, 68–84. For others describing opium smoking as a private act, see Costello, *Our Police Protectors*, 523; Byrnes, *Professional Criminals*, 385; Campbell, *Darkness and Daylight*, 550–58, 573.

18. See note 17.

19. *Leslie's*, 12 May 1883.

20. Beck, *New York's Chinatown*, 143, 154, 158, 164; Kane, *Opium-Smoking*, 8, 131–32; Cobbe, *Doctor Judas*, 125–30 (lusts); Dai, *Opium Addiction in Chicago*, 135–38; Ahmad, "Opium Smoking, Anti-Chinese Attitudes, and the American Medical Community, 1850–90," (2000), 53–68.

21. For complaints of prostitution on Mott, Pell, and Doyers Streets, see Businessmen and Property Owners to Mayor Abram Hewitt, 11 Sept. 1888, box 87-HAS-33; Testimony of Mary Ann Flynn, 1887, box 87-HAS-26, both in MP; People v. Ah Chung, 18 Aug. 1882, box 9892; People v. Ah Chung, 15 May 1883, box 9903; People v. Ah Lee, 13 Jan. 1885, box 9925; People v. Charles Lee, 19 Mar. 1890, box 10,008, all in SCC; unmarked clipping, 28 May 1888, vol. 49; unmarked clipping, 21 Oct. 1890, vol. 77; *Sun* clipping, 13 Apr. 1891, vol. 84; *Commercial Advertiser* clipping, 16 Sept. 1891, vol. 90; *Sun* clipping, 17 Sept. 1891, vol. 90, all in DAS.

22. Byrnes, *Professional Criminals*, 385; Ford, *Forty-Odd Years*, 202–3; Costello, *Our Police Protectors*, 524; Calkins, *Opium*, 53.

23. *Tribune*, 16 Oct. 1881, 30 Jan. 1882 (actors and actresses); Ford, *Forty-Odd Years*, 202–6; Williams, *Demon*, 20, 77 (aristocracy), 85–86 (Bessinger's at 148 E. 14th Street); Costello, *Our Police Protectors*, 524; Norr, *Stories of Chinatown*, 47 (actors). On the close relationships among the theatrical, criminal, and "sporting" worlds, see Ernest Booth, *Stealing Through Life* (New York, 1927), 107–13, 129–31; "Yellow Kid" Weil, *The Con Game and "Yellow Kid" Weil* (New York, 1948), 129, 154.

24. Wong Chin Foo, "Chinese in New York," 311 (indolent and rich; keep straight); *Evening Post*, 21 Aug. 1882 (respectable), quoted in Liggins, *Opium*, 6, 21; Wooldridge, *Hands Up!*, 211 ("beggar"), 216 ("sexes"), 218; *Leslie's*, 12 May 1883 (richly dressed ladies); Beck, *New York's Chinatown*, 254; *Tribune*, 16 Oct. 1881 (society women); unmarked clipping, 12 May 1883; *Sun* clipping, 23 Dec. 1884, vol. 10; unmarked clipping, 23 Oct. 1891 (best class of customers), vol. 91, all in DAS.

25. Unmarked clipping, 25 July 1891 (Union League), vol. 88; unmarked clippings, 8, 9 Dec. 1884 (richly dressed, police raid), vol. 9; *Tribune* clipping, 1 June 1883 (police raid); *Herald* and other unmarked clippings, 22 Dec. 1884 (police raid), vol. 10; *World* clipping, 14 Apr. 1899, vol. 180, all in DAS; Campbell, *Darkness and Daylight*, 551.

26. Beck, *New York's Chinatown*, 163; *World* clipping, 14 Apr. 1899, vol. 180; *Herald* clipping, 25 Dec. 1884, vol. 10; unmarked clipping, 4 Mar. 1890, vol. 17, all in DAS; "Closure of Opium Joints in New York," *American Journal of Stimulants and Narcotics* 1

(1882), 26; Williams, *Demon*, 64; Terry and Pellens, *The Opium Problem*, 808. Copies of the Koch Law appear in Costello, *Our Police Protectors*, 517; Williams, *Demon*, 130.

27. On the Greenwich Village bohemia, see Christine Stansell, *American Moderns: Bohemian New York and the Creation of a New Century* (New York, 2000); Judith Schwarz, Kathy Peiss, and Christina Simmons, " 'We Were a Little Band of Willful Women': The Heterodoxy Club of Greenwich Village," in Peiss and Simmons, eds., *Passion and Power: Sexuality in History* (Philadelpia, 1989), 118–37.

28. Appo, 22. In an earlier version of Appo's encounter with Lee, Appo admitted that Lee bought an express wagon and horse for Appo's use, but he was unable to work because "detectives hounded him for every larceny they fancied he might have committed." See Williams, *Demon*, 71.

29. *Lexow Committee* II:2242 (mayor of Chinatown); Campbell, *Darkness and Daylight*, 551 (mayor); *Tribune*, 21 June 1885 (restaurant at 4 Mott); *Star* clipping, 8 Feb. 1884 (Tom Lee cigar store and gambling den at 4 Mott), vol. 7, DAS; *Herald*, 25 Apr. 1883; Williams, *Demon*, 12, 32, 71 (Appo related).

30. *Star* clipping, 9 June 1884, vol. 8, DAS (Celestial). On Lee's origins from Sing Ching, see *Times*, 24 Apr. 1883. On conflicting dates of his birth, see obituaries in *Times*, 11 Jan. 1918 (1842); *Tribune*, 11 Jan. 1918 (1841); *Herald*, 11 Jan. 1918 (1828–39); Baptist); *Sun*, 11 Jan. 1918. Biographical details appear in *Times*, 2 Apr. 1882 (Philadelphia), 17 Aug. 1904 (St. Louis); Arthur Bonner, *Alas! What Brought Thee Hither? The Chinese in New York, 1800–1950* (Madison, N.J., 1997), 42–46, 57, 61–62, 71, 85–86, 136–53. On his allegedly illegal naturalization in 1876, see *Tribune*, 28 Sept. 1904. On Lee's connections to Tammany Hall, see *Times*, 15, 16 Sept. 1881; *Tribune*, 16 Sept. 1881; *Herald*, 5 Mar. 1879; *Sun*, 11 Jan. 1918. On Lee's marriage, see *Morning Journal* clipping, 9 June 1885, vol. 12, DAS; *Harper's Weekly*, 27 Aug. 1910, p. 10. Also see Tyler Anbinder, *Five Points* (New York, 2003), 411–15.

31. Eve Armentrout-Ma, "Urban Chinese at the Sinitic Frontier: Social Organizations in United States' Chinatowns, 1849–1898," *Modern Asian Studies* 17 (1983), 120–21 (*huikuan*); Peter Kwong, *Chinatown, New York: Labor and Politics, 1930–1950* (New York, 1979), 39–41 (*kung saw, hui-kuan, fong*).

32. *Times*, 28 Apr. 1880; *World*, 28 Feb. 1880; *Times*, 11 Jan. 1918; *Tribune*, 18 Oct. 1885; *Sun*, 31 Jan. 1881; Beck, *New York's Chinatown*, 14–19, 135; Anbinder, *Five Points*, 412, 504. *On Leong* meant "Protective of Good People Society." See Van Norden, *Who's Who*, 91–93.

33. Van Norden, *Who's Who*, 83, 87; Beck, *New York's Chinatown*, 269 (traveling salesman, collector, and bookkeeper); *Trow's New York City Directory* (New York, 1891), 1491 (supplier); *Times*, 1 Aug. 1883 (Wongs).

34. In 1881, Lee reportedly opened a fan-tan shop at 34 Mott Street, although considerable evidence indicates he was involved in such activities earlier. See *Tribune*, 21 June 1885; *Star* clipping, 8 Feb. 1884, vol. 7, DAS; *Herald*, 25 Apr. 1883; Williams, *Demon*, 12, 32; *Trow's New York City Directory* (New York, 1884–96); *Harper's Weekly*, 27 Aug. 1910, p. 10.

35. *Times*, 13, 17, 19 May 1883 (Ah Toy quote); unmarked clipping, 21 Mar. 1887, vol. 33 (41 Bowery); *Star* clipping, 8 Feb. 1884, vol. 7; *Times* clipping, 5 Jan. 1885, vol. 10, all in DAS; People v. Ah Lee, 13 Jan. 1885, box 9925, SCC. In 1873, 13 Mott Street was described as one of three or four "boarding-houses kept by Chinamen and fitted up

for the accommodation of the Chinese." See *Times*, 26 Dec. 1873. On raids of 13 Mott Street, see *Times*, 27 Mar. 1879; *World*, 27 Mar. 1879. On Ah Sing's 17 Mott Street den, see "Closure of Opium Joints in New York," 26; Kane, "American Opium-Smokers," 647; Kane, *Opium-Smoking*, vii; Norr, *Stories of Chinatown*, 47–48. On gambling at 17 Mott Street, see People v. Tom Lee, et al., 1 May 1883, box 9903, SCC; unmarked clipping, 21 Dec. 1886, vol. 29; *Mail and Express* clipping, 9 Dec. 1891, vol. 92, all in DAS. On prostitution at 17 Mott Street, see Beck, *New York's Chinatown*, 112–13, 118.

36. For detailed descriptions of gambling dens and weekly payments to Lee, see testimony in People v. Tom Lee, et al., 1 May 1883, box 9903, SCC. On opium dens, see People v. Ah Chung, 15 May 1883, both in box 103, folders 1098, 1101, CGS; *Times*, 25 Apr. 1883, 26 Apr. 1883, 3 May 1883; *Daily Graphic*, 28 Mar. 1879 (18 Mott). On protection money and bail, see unmarked clipping, 2 Apr. 1882; *Star*, 12 May 1883, 16 May 1883, all in DAS; *Times*, 17 May 1883. On Lee control of various Mott Street properties, see block 162, lot 3 (4 Mott St.); block 162, lot 10 (18 Mott St.); block 162, lot 9 (16 Mott St.), in Block and Lot Folders, NYCMA; 467, liber 2031, 20 May 1887; 162, liber 2178, 5 Nov. 1888; 170, 216, liber 2291; 276, liber [record number] 40, 22 Mar. 1897; 328, 336, liber 1732, 30 Apr. 1883; 380, liber 1757, 8 Dec. 1883; 306, liber 39, 13 Jan. 1897; 115, 120, liber 1729, 27 Apr. 1883; 380, liber 1757, 8 Dec. 1883; 357, liber 2133, 16 June 1888; 162, liber 2178, 5 Nov. 1888, all in Pre-1917 Conveyance Records, New York City Hall of Records.

37. People v. Tom Lee, Tuck Hop, and Lee Sing, 1 May 1883, box 9903, SCC (home at 4 Mott St.; deputy sheriff since 1879); *Times*, 7 Apr. 1883 (Lee purchase of 18 Mott Street), 24 Apr. 1883 (rebellion), 25 Apr. 1883 (Price), 3 May 1883, 17 May 1883 (Price); 13 May 1883 (bribery); *Morning Journal* clipping, 2 June 1883, DAS; *Star* and *Times* clippings, 26 Apr. 1883, vol. 4; *Star* clipping, 8 Feb. 1884 (4 Mott St.), vol. 7; *Star* clippings, 1 June 1884, 9 June 1884, all in vol. 8; *Journal* clipping (deputy sheriff), 11 Oct. 1884; *World* clipping (laundries), 20 Oct. 1884, both in vol. 9, all in DAS. On Lee owning or controlling sixteen dens from 2 to 19 Mott Street, see *Star* clippings, 1 June 1883; 9 June 1884, vol. 8, both in DAS; Chinese of New York and Brooklyn to Mayor Abram Hewitt, 15 July 1887, box 87-HAS-31, MP; *Mail and Express* clipping, 9 Dec. 1891, vol. 92, DAS.

38. *Star* clipping, 9 June 1884, vol. 8, DAS; *Times*, 12 Apr. 1883; *Times*, 24 Apr. 1883; *Leslie's*, 12 May 1883.

39. Beck, *New York's Chinatown*, 96, 110–13 (prostitution), 124–26, 133–35, 263–69 (Moy), 286 (Lee family—3,000); Van Norden, *Who's Who*, 91 (On Leong—400); Bonner, *Alas!*, 138–39; *Times*, 11 Jan. 1918; *Herald*, 11 Jan. 1918 (4 attempts); *Tribune*, 8 Apr. 1883 (evict), 11 Jan. 1918 ($5,000 bounty); *Times*, 17 May 1883 (Ah Toy); *Mail and Express* clipping, 9 Dec. 1891 (Lee gang; 700), vol. 92, DAS; *World*, 5 July 1891 (Lee clan; 500).

40. *Harper's Weekly*, 27 Aug. 1910; unmarked clipping, 22 July 1894, vol. 129, DAS; Campbell, *Darkness and Daylight*, 551; Bonner, *Alas!*, 136, 138–44.

41. Appo is probably referring to the "Seven Corners" district along the west bank of the Mississippi River where Washington, Cedar, and Wine (later Fifteenth Avenue South) Streets converged.

42. On Elm Street and the surrounding area as a neighborhood populated with prostitutes and pickpockets, see Joseph A. Dacus and James W. Buel, *A Tour of St. Louis: or, The*

*Inside Look of a Great City* (St. Louis, 1878), 407, 450–56, 462–66. On street geography, see Richard J. Compton, *Pictorial St. Louis: The Great Metropolis of the Mississippi Valley, A Topographical Survey* (St. Louis, 1875), plates 1, 4, 24; David B. Gould, *Gould's St. Louis Directory for 1881* (St. Louis, 1881), 53; *Campbell's Revised Guide Map of St. Louis* (St. Louis, 1882), all available at Missouri Historical Society, St. Louis, Mo.

43. Appo, 22–24.

## 8. THE OLD HOMESTEAD

1. Appo, 13. Appo confused several memories here. The "dead line" was not established until 1880 by Chief Detective Thomas J. Byrnes.
2. *World*, 10 Feb. 1879; *World*, 14 Apr. 1879; Charles Sutton, *The New York Tombs: Its Secrets and Its Mysteries*, 628 (decaying bodies); *NPG*, 31 Jan. 1880 (ulcer); David Dudley Field, "Municipal Officers (1879)," in A. P. Sprague, ed., *Speeches, Arguments, and Miscellaneous Papers of David Dudley Field* (New York, 1884), II:178 (municipality of misery).
3. Lydia Maria Child, *Letters from New-York* (New York, 1842), 188; *Times*, 20 Sept. 1886; Louis Berg, *Revelations of a Prison Doctor* (New York, 1934), 31–32. Child's observations also appeared in "The Prison at Blackwell's Island," *Liberator*, 28 Oct. 1842. For details on various Blackwell's Island institutions, see J. F. Richmond, *New York and Its Institutions, 1609–1871* (New York, 1871), 524, 530–542, 542; John Duffy, *A History of Public Health in New York City, 1625–1866* (New York, 1968), 483–501; Robert A. M. Stern, Thomas Mellins, and David Fishman, *New York 1880: Architecture and Urbanism in the Gilded Age* (New York, 1999), 266–70.
4. Governors of the Almshouse, *AR for 1850* (New York, 1851), 2; Commissioners of Public Charities and Correction, *Second AR for 1861* (New York, 1862), 8 (ornamental); Duffy, *Public Health*, 483; Presentment of the Grand Jury, February Term, 1894, pp. 4–5, box 89-GTF-2, MP; *Harper's Weekly*, 6 Feb. 1869; Index of Almshouse/Department of Welfare Collection, NYCMA; Richmond, *Institutions*, 524, 528 (largest), 540; Stern et al., *New York 1880*, 266–70.
5. Richmond, *Institutions*, 531, 542–43; Joel Ross, *What I Saw in New York* (Auburn, N.Y., 1852), 115; NYSS, *Proceedings Before the Special Committee of the New York State Senate* (Albany, 1876), 7–9, 27; NYSPC, *Thirteenth AR*, (Albany, 1908), 54; Sutton, *Tombs*, 613. In order to avoid sending them to state prison, judges sometimes sentenced juveniles and other convicts to long terms in the Blackwell's Island Penitentiary. See Warden John M. Fox to Joshua Phillips, 28 Jan. 1875, folder 18, box 1241, MP.
6. Governors of the Almshouse, *AR for 1850*, 8–9 (wicked), 127–28 (lazar house); Governors of the Almshouse, *Fourth AR for 1852* (New York, 1853), 115 (general receptacle); Presentment of the Grand Jury, February Term, 1894, 3–5 (large percentage), box 89-GTF-2, MP; Richmond, *Institutions*, 542; *Times*, 20 Sept. 1886; unmarked clipping, 1 Feb. 1900, vol. 188, DAS; NYSA, *Report of the Special Committee on Convict Labor in the Penal Institutions of the State*, AD 66 (Albany, 1899), 50. On inmates in both the workhouse and penitentiary working together, see Governors of the Almshouse, *AR for 1850*, 121–24; Charles

Dickens, *American Notes* (1842; reprint, Oxford, Eng., 1987), 94. By 1893, 70 percent of Almshouse inmates were over fifty years of age, 56 percent over sixty; the death rate was 17 percent (656 deaths out of 3,400 admissions). See Presentment of the Grand Jury above. Before passage of the Children's Act of 1876 in New York, the almshouse and workhouse were filled with children. See Resolution of Commissioners of Department of Public Charities and Correction, 10 Nov. 1875, box 83-CE-3, MP; Michael Katz, *In the Shadow of the Poorhouse: A Social History of Welfare in America* (New York, 1986), 104–6.

7. *Increase of Crime*, 65 (intermingling), 111 (innocent youth), 114–16; Governors, *AR for 1850*, 126; *World*, 14 Apr. 1879; Richmond, *Institutions*, 533–34 (one-half under twenty-five). In 1876, 331 of just less than 1,000 penitentiary inmates were teenagers. See PANY, *Thirty-second AR for 1876*, SD 41 (Albany, 1877), 20–21. The annual commitments to Blackwell's Island were:

| YEAR | TOTAL CITY COMMITMENTS | < 16 | 16–20 YRS. | PERCENTAGE UNDER 16 | PENIT. | WORKHOUSE |
|------|------------------------|------|-----------|---------------------|--------|-----------|
| 1862 | 41,299 | 1,424 | 3,156 | 3.44 | | |
| 1863 | 32,592 | 1,641 | 3,357 | 5.03 | | |
| 1864 | 31,251 | 2,260 | 4,202 | 7.23 | | |
| 1865 | 39,616 | 2,209 | 4,423 | 5.57 | | |
| 1866 | 42,621 | 2,280 | 5,510 | 5.34 | | |
| 1867 | 47,313 | 1,993 | 5,943 | 4.21 | 2,311 | |
| 1868 | 46,476 | 2,197 | 5,247 | 4.72 | | |
| 1869 | 42,209 | 1,906 | 4,617 | 4.51 | | |
| 1870 | 49,423 | 1,229 | 5,017 | 2.48 | | |
| 1871 | 51,466 | 1,630 | 5,746 | 3.16 | | |
| 1872 | 48,956 | 1,977 | 4,963 | 4.03 | | |
| 1873 | 52,324 | 1,561 | 6,028 | 2.98 | | |
| 1874 | 49,251 | 1,726 | 4,622 | 3.50 | 2,236 | 28,999 |
| 1875 | 54,655 | 1,872 | 5,745 | 3.42 | | |
| 1876 | 57,084 | 2,641 | 6,594 | 4.62 | 2,203 | 22,845 |

See PANY, *Annual Reports* (Albany, 1862–80); *Harper's Weekly*, 6 Feb. 1869; *Tribune*, 21 Feb. 1879.

8. Grand Jury Presentment on Blackwell's Island, Sept. 1890, box 88-GHJ-5, MP; *Times*, 3 Feb. 1889, 13 Sept. 1890; Richmond, *Institutions*, 531; PANY, *Thirty-second AR for 1876*, SD 41 (Albany, 1877), 5, 7 (778 cells); *Times*, 20 Sept. 1886; *Herald* clipping, 3 Nov. 1886, vol. 26, DAS (1,100 daily pop.); Governors, *AR for 1850*, 6 (905 daily average); Ross, *What I Saw*, 115.

9. Table in Department of Charities and Corrections folder #1, box 87-HAS-2, MP; Richmond, *Institutions*, 543 (15,000–20,000); John Josiah Munro, *The New York Tombs, Inside and Out!* (Brooklyn, 1909), 284 (no less than 20,000 from Manhattan); unmarked clipping, 1 Feb. 1900, vol. 188, DAS; Sutton, *Tombs*, 628 (7,000); NYSS, *Proceedings Special Committee*, 6 (5,300–6,000); Richmond, *Institutions*, 524 (8,000); *Tribune*, 21 Feb. 1879 (workhouse pop. 954 men and 846 women).

10. *Increase of Crime*, 63, 112; *Herald* clipping, 3 Nov. 1886, vol. 26, DAS (1,100); NYSS, *Proceedings Special Committee*, 11 (almshouse 10,000–15,000), 26; *Times*, 8 June 1887; *Herald* and other clipping, 8 June 1887, vol. 36; *Morning Advertiser* clipping, 21 Dec. 1895, vol. 149, all in DAS.

11. See appendix 1.

12. Johann Most, "Behind Bolt and Bar," (1886), quoted in *Herald* clipping, 28 Nov. 1886, vol. 28; Most, "The Horrors of Blackwell's Island," (1887), quoted in *Sun* clipping, 2 May 1887, vol. 34; both in DAS; NYSS, *Proceedings Special Committee*, 197 (no heat).

13. NYSS, *Proceedings Special Committee*, 197 (sinkholes); *Journal* clipping, 17 Oct. 1886 (washing, soap), vol. 26, DAS. On the charity hospital, see Report of the Committee of the Grand Jury: Selected to Investigate Institutions on Blackwells [sic] Island, 12 Sept. 1890, box 88-GHJ-5, MP; *Press* and *Herald* clippings, 13 Sept. 1890, vol. 76, DAS.

14. *Journal* clipping, 6 June 1886 (workhouse scurvy), vol. 20; Most, "The Horrors of Blackwell's Island," quoted in *Sun* clipping, 2 May 1887 (certificate of death), vol. 34, both in DAS; *Tribune*, 7 Mar. 1894; *Times*, 4 Sept. 1890 (penitentiary scurvy).

15. *World*, 14 Apr. 1879 (worst governed); Berg, *Revelations*, 33 (dunghill); *Tribune*, 3 Mar. 1860; *World*, 24 Feb. 1879; PANY, *Thirtieth AR for 1874*, SD 78 (Albany, 1875), 60; NYSS, *Proceedings Special Committee*, 20–26 (18 guards at night), 1093 (political influence); *Journal* clipping, 6 June 1886 (political appointments), vol. 20; *Journal* clipping, 3 Oct. 1886, vol. 26, both in DAS. On salaries, see *Increase of Crime*, 64; *Sun*, 18 Jan. 1877. Ratios were even larger in the workhouse and almshouse. In 1869, only 15 officers and employees were responsible for the 531 workhouse inmates (average), a ratio greater than 35 to 1. In the penitentiary 31 employees guarded 620 inmates, a ratio of 20 to 1. See NYSA, *Report of the State Commission on Prison Labor* (Albany, 1871), 134, 138.

16. NYSS, *Proceedings Special Committee*, 10, 1093–94 (cruelty of keepers), 44 (damnedest scoundrels); *Journal* clippings, 3 Oct. 1886 (sexual impropriety), 17 Oct. 1886 (Osborn), vol. 26; Most, "The Horrors of Blackwell's Island," quoted in *Sun* clipping, 2 May 1887 (dark cell), vol. 34, both in DAS. For reports of guards killing penitentiary inmates and keeper brutality, see *Tribune*, 8 Sept. 1875; *Times*, 18 Aug. 1887.

17. *Journal* clipping, 3 Oct. 1886 (boat), vol. 26; *Journal* clipping, 13 Aug. 1887 (raping), vol. 39, both in DAS; NYSS, *Proceedings Special Committee*, 372–73 (fraternization), 1093–94; *Times*, 13 Jan. 1876; *Tribune*, 3 Mar. 1860 (rumshop, prostitutes); Frederick Howard Wines, *Punishment and Reformation: A Study of the Penitentiary System* (New York, 1895 and 1919), 220–21 (locked up).

18. *Journal* clipping, 6 June 1886, vol. 20, DAS; Governors, *AR for 1850*, 124–25; Governors, *Fourth AR for 1852* (New York, 1853), 87–88 (convicts as asylum keepers). On convicts dispensing drugs and medicine, see Report of the Committee of the Grand Jury: Selected to Investigate Institutions on Blackwells [sic] Island, 12 Sept. 1890, box 88-GHJ-5, MP; *Press* and *Herald* clippings, 13 Sept. 1890, vol. 76, DAS.

19. Compare "View of Penitentiary" (1853), WC, with similar images in Richardson, *Institutions*, 531; photographs in NYC Department of Public Charities, *AR* (New York, 1908?); and NYSPC, *Fourteenth AR* (Albany, 1909).

20. NYSA, *Report on Prison Labor*, 135–36 (repeater); Presentment of the Grand Jury, February Term, 1894, 3, box 89-GTF-2, MP. Daniel O'Connell was committed to the workhouse twenty-five times between February 1885 and December 1888, Minnie Wren twenty-eight times from August 1886 to October 1888, and John Lyons seventeen times from February 1886 to February 1889 and forty times prior to 1886. See Report to the Sub-Committee on Legislation of the Committee of Seventy, 1–2, January 1895, box 90-SWL-7, MP.

21. Munro, *Tombs*, 285; *Increase of Crime*, 65, 114–16; NYSS, *Proceedings Special Committee*, 10; PANY, *Thirtieth AR*, 18; Board of Police Justices of the City of New York, *Second AR for the Year 1875* (New York, 1876), 18 (over 100 times); *Tribune*, 18 Dec. 1876; *Times*, 18 Aug. 1887 (winter increase); Wines, *Punishment and Reformation*, 220–21; John J. McCook, "Some New Phases of the Tramp Problem," *Charities Review* 1 (June 1892), 355.

22. Governors, *AR for 1850*, 126 (Keen); Governors, *Fourth AR*, 115; Ross, *What I Saw*, 116 (Keen); PANY, *Thirty-first AR for 1875*, SD 54 (Albany, 1876), 79; Frederick Howard Wines, *The County Jail System: An Argument and Appeal for Its Abolition* (Springfield, Ill., 1877), 16 (revolvers, Old Homestead); *Times*, 13 May 1890 (rounders); *Tribune*, 16 Aug. 1891 (Old Homestead).

23. Governors, *AR for 1850*, 9, 124–25 (habeas corpus); Governors, *Fourth AR*, 120–21 (venereal hospital); Wilkes, *Mysteries*, 13–14 (writs); *Harper's Weekly*, 6 Feb. 1869 (venereal disease); *Mail & Express* clipping, 9 Sept. 1884 (unsupervised females), vol. 9, DAS.

24. *Tribune*, 24, 27 Sept. 1842 (Matsell); *Times*, 13 May 1890, 20 Sept. 1886 (political influence).

25. *Times*, 28 Oct. 1878 (5,000 of 20,000); Sutton, *Tombs*, 617 (20–40 times); table in Department of Charities and Corrections folder #1 (11 percent), box 87-HAS-2, MP; NYSA, *Report on Prison Labor*, 140 (50 percent).

26. On Vail's long criminal record, see A. E. Costello, *History of the Police Department of Jersey City* (Jersey City, N.J., 1891), 417; *Times*, 13 Apr. 1882; Thomas Byrnes, *Professional Criminals of America* (New York, 1886), 64a, 66; Frank Moss, *The American Metropolis* (New York 1897), III:24, 145–46; James L. Ford, *Forty-Odd Years in the Literary Shop* (New York, 1921), 103; *World* clipping, 22 Nov. 1885, vol. 15; *Morning Journal* clipping, 11 Mar. 1895, vol. 138; unmarked clipping, 30 July 1895, vol. 144, all in DAS; Deductions of 21 Mar. 1864, vol. 1, Reports of Deduction of Sentences by Prison Agents, Wardens and Superintendents (AO601); Commitments to New York Penitentiary, Blackwell's Island, Aug. 1895 (n.p.), vol. 20, Executive Register of Commitments to Prisons (AO603), all in NYSArc; Minutes of the New York County Court of General Sessions, vol. 134, 45, 11 June 1879; vol. 140, 501, 514, 10, 12 Apr. 1882; People v. John Eastman et al., 11 June 1879, DAP; People v. Isaac S. Vail, 20 Feb. 1880, box 9872, location 106002; People v. Isaac S. Vail, 10 Apr. 1882, box 9890, location 106020, both in SCC; Almshouse Collection, vol. 226, 427, Mar. 1892, all in NYCMA.

27. *Increase of Crime*, 65, 116 (eloped); Hutchins Hapgood, ed., *The Autobiography of a Thief* (New York, 1903), 117–20 (1880s); *Times*, 3 May 1881, 28 Nov. 1882 (runners); NYSS, *Proceedings Special Committee*, 28–29, 1093; NPG, 31 Jan. 1880.

28. NPG, 31 Jan. 1880 (more loaded); NYSS, *Proceedings Special Committee*, 29 (coxswain drunk); *Times*, 1 Sept. 1879 (coffins); *Tribune*, 16 Aug. 1891, 18 Feb. 1879, 5 Aug. 1883 (coffins); PANY, *Thirtieth AR*, 59–60 (least governed); *Herald* and other clippings, 4 Aug. 1888 (forged discharges), vol. 52, DAS; *Times*, 13 Aug. 1879 (drunken guards), 4, 9 Aug. 1888. Examples of escapes from Blackwell's Island institutions were plentiful. See *Tribune*, 7 Apr. 1860; *World*, 19 Apr. 1874, 9 Nov. 1876; *Times*, 7 Apr. 1860, 8 Oct. 1872, 5 Jan. 1873, 23 June 1876, 1 Dec. 1876, 15 Oct. 1877, 17 Nov. 1877, 11 Jan. 1878, 18 Feb. 1879, 2 May 1879, 13, 15 Aug. 1879, 28 Nov. 1882, 22 July 1892. Vagrants were

to be discharged only with the signed authorization of the committing magistrate. See NYSS, *Proceedings Special Committee*, 18–19.

29. *Times*, 7 Aug. 1874. For similar examples, see *Times*, 4 Aug. 1888, 9 June 1874.

30. Pilsbury to Brennan, 8 Aug. 1888, box 87-HAS-2, MP; *Herald* clipping, 3 Nov. 1886, vol. 26, DAS; *Tribune*, 16 Aug. 1891, 7 May 1892, 8 Mar. 1898.

31. *Journal* clipping, 17 Oct. 1886 (Yes sir); *Herald* clipping, 3 Nov. 1886 (visitors), both in vol. 26; Most, "Behind Bolt and Bar," quoted in *Herald* clipping, 28 Nov. 1886 (lockstep), vol. 28, all in DAS; *Tribune*, 16 Aug. 1891 (escapes).

32. *Times*, 20 Sept. 1886 (Riker's Island purchased); G. F. Britton to Josephine Shaw Lowell, Jan. 1886, MP; *Herald* clipping (Pilsbury recommendation), 3 Nov. 1886, vol. 26, DAS; *Sun* and other clippings, 1 June 1893 (grand jury criticism), vol. 113, DAS; *Times*, 11 Dec. 1890; Berg, *Reflections*, 32.

33. Child, *Letters from New-York*, 190–92; NYSS, *Proceedings Special Committee*, 1090. On the persistence of overcrowding, disease, and poor conditions on Blackwell's Island into the twentieth century, see Joseph F. Fishman, *Crucibles of Crime: The Shocking Story of American Jails* (Montclair, N.J., 1969, orig. 1923), 34–35.

34. Appo, 13–14.


## 9. THE DIVES

1. Appo, 24–25. Appo spelled Geoghegan's as it sounded—"Oney Gaghen's."

2. Appo, 81. On patrons spending as much as five hundred dollars nightly in dives and other "gay spots," see "Yellow Kid" Weil, *The Con Game and "Yellow Kid" Weil* (New York, 1948), 154.

3. Irving Lewis Allen, *The City in Slang* (New York, 1993), 146–48; George Ellington, *The Women of New York* (New York, 1869), 163; Edward Crapsey, *The Nether Side of New York* (New York, 1872), 159; *Lexow Committee*, V:5324–25, 5591–92, 5727 (Byrnes's definition); *NPG*, 8 Dec. 1866 (free and easies), 18 Sept. 1879; unmarked clipping, 25 Jan. 1885 (definition), vol. 10, DAS; George Washington Walling, *Recollections of a New York Chief of Police* (New York, 1887), 479 (dance halls). On the common usage of "dives" and the difficulty of defining the term, see James T. Brown to Abram Hewitt, 30 Mar. 1887, folder 246, box 1366, Hewitt Papers, MP; Jonathan Slick, *Snares of New York; or, Tricks and Traps of the Great Metropolis* (New York, 1879), 78–81; Henry Collins Brown, *Valentine's Manual of Old New York, 1927* (New York, 1926), 192.

4. *Lexow Committee*, V:5325 (open all night; criminal classes), 5331; Walling, *Recollections*, 479; Franklin Matthews, "Wide-Open New York," *Harper's Weekly*, 22 Oct. 1898; *World*, 12 Jan. 1877; *Times*, 16 June 1893 (Crumley); *NPG*, 15 May 1880; Hutchins Hapgood, ed., *The Autobiography of a Thief* (New York, 1903), 50, 74. On the failure of the concert saloon statute, see "Annual Report of the Board of the Metropolitan Police Commissioners for the Year 1865" in *Times*, 5 Jan. 1866.

5. Cornelius W. Willemse, *Behind the Green Lights* (New York, 1931), 69. The best historical account of licensing is Daniel Czitrom, "The Politics of Performance: From Theater Licensing to Movie Censorship in Turn-of-the-Century New York," *American Quarterly* 44 (1992), 525–32. On the 1862 statute, see *Times*, 20 Jan. 1876. For municipal reports, see New York Metropolitan Police, *Annual Report* (New York, 1866), 19–

20 (223 saloons); "List of Theaters, Halls, Concert Rooms, etc." undated (1875–76), folder 262, box 1264, Wickham Papers, MP. For the concert saloon's influence, see Robert W. Snyder, *Voice of the City: Vaudeville and Popular Culture in New York* (New York, 1989), 3–25; Gunther Barth, *City People: The Rise of Modern City Culture in Nineteenth-Century America* (New York, 1980), 194–214; Brooks McNamara, *The New York Concert Saloon* (New York, 2002); Timothy J. Gilfoyle, *City of Eros: New York City, Prostitution, and the Commercialization of Sex, 1790–1920* (New York, 1992), 224–32.

6. *NPG*, 10 Jan. 1880; *Times*, 21 Oct. 1884 (rough atmosphere).

7. Sam Austin, "The Gay and Festive Boxing Resorts," *Ring Magazine*, June 1946. Biographical information on Geoghegan appears in *NPG*, 14 Aug. 1880; George T. Pardy, "Gang Wars and Politics of the Prize Ring," *Ring Magazine*, June–December 1937; Internment record of John Geoghegan, section 8, range 40, plot Y, graves 11/12 (1841 birth), Calvary Cemetery, Woodside, N.Y.; *Times*, 2 June 1878.

8. People v. Owen Geoghegan, 29 Apr. 1875 (stealing dogs); People v. Owen Geoghegan and James McManus, 29 Feb. 1876 (assault); People v. Owen Geoghegan, 20 May 1878 (Rose); People v. Owen Geoghegan and William Hennessy, 9 May 1872, all in DAP; Minutes of the New York County Court of General Sessions, vol. 114, 9 May 1872, 445; 29 May 1872, 515; vol. 115, 5 June 1872, 24 (acquittal); *NPG*, 1 June 1878, 15 May 1880 (Rose); Elliott J. Gorn, *The Manly Art: Bare-Knuckle Prize Fighting in America* (Ithaca, N.Y., 1986), 174.

9. People v. Owen Geoghegan et al., 28 Feb. 1865 (first Irving incident); People v. Owen Geoghegan, 22 Jan. 1867 (second Irving assault); People v. Owen Geoghegan and James McManus, 29 Feb. 1876, all in DAP; entries for 21 Feb. 1887, 809; 28 Feb. 1887, 847, all in vol. 37, Drummond Papers (Irving incidents); *Times, Tribune*, 6 Dec. 1866. On Geoghegan's political career, see *Times*, 5 Dec. 1866; 8, 9, 10, 11 Nov. 1871; Alexander B. Callow, Jr., *The Tweed Ring* (New York, 1965), 282, 245. On colonizing, see unmarked clipping, 1 Nov. 1884, vol. 9; *Star* clipping, 2 May 1889, vol. 60, all in DAS; Charles Sutton, *The New York Tombs: Its Secrets and Its Mysteries* (New York, 1874), 496. On "colonizing" elsewhere in New York, see unmarked clipping, 24 Oct. 1888, vol. 54; *World, Morning Journal, Tribune*, and other clippings, 1 Nov. 1888, vol. 55, all in DAS; *Lexow Committee*, IV:3579–80, 3612–14; James L. Davenport, *The Election Frauds of New York City and Their Prevention* (New York, 1881).

10. Austin, "The Gay and Festive Boxing Resorts." Herbert Asbury claimed that murders were frequent in Geogheghan's. See Asbury, *The Gangs of New York* (New York, 1927), 191–92. I have found no evidence of this.

11. *NPG*, 10 July 1880 (obscene songs), 14 Aug. 1880 (Bastille); J. W. Buel, *Metropolitan Life Unveiled; or the Mysteries and Miseries of America's Great Cities* (St. Louis, 1882), 49; *Times* (fight) and other clippings, 21 Jan. 1885, DAS; People v. Owen Geoghegan, 29 May 1882 and 1 June 1882 (excise violation), CGS; James L. Ford, *Forty-Odd Years in the Literary Shop* (New York, 1921), 200; "Character of Various Places of Amusement Furnished by SPCC," Apr. 1882, in box 84-GWR-14, MP; Michael T. Isenberg, *John L. Sullivan and His America* (Urbana, Ill., 1988), 84–85, 89, 96, 108, 120. On ex-convicts in Geoghegan's, see *Sun* clipping, 15 Sept. 1884, vol. 9; unmarked clipping, 13 Dec. 1885, vol. 16, DAS; *NPG*, 30 Jan. 1880, 10 Jan. 1880; *Sun*, 12 Jan. 1877; *Lexow Committee*, V:5235–38. Locations of Geoghegan's establishments are identified in People v. Owen Geoghegan, 9 May 1872, DAP (First Ave. and Twenty-second St.); *Times*,

25 June 1877, 8 Oct. 1877 (103 Bowery); SPC, *Report* (New York, 1879), 15 (105 Bowery); SPCC, *Ninth Annual Report* (New York, 1884), 9 (103 Bowery); unmarked clippings, 14 Apr. 1883 (105 Bowery); 1 Nov. 1884 (103 Bowery), all in vol. 9, all in DAS; Harlow, *Old Bowery Days*, 397–400 (105 Bowery).

12. Unmarked clippings, 29 May 1883 (excise violations); 14 Apr. 1883; 1 Nov. 1884; *Sun* clipping, 18 June 1883, all in vol. 9, DAS; *Times* and other clippings, 21 Jan. 1885, DAS; Harlow, *Old Bowery Days*, 397–400.

13. *Bridgeport Daily Standard*, 30 Apr. 1883; *Herald*, 25 Apr. 1883. On Geoghegan's funeral, see Ford, *Forty-Odd Years*, 200; *Times*, 25 Jan. 1885, 26 Jan. 1885; *World*, 17 July 1885. Geoghegan is buried in an unmarked grave in Calvary Cemetery, Queens. The grave contains ten bodies, including Owen Geoghegan's Irish-born parents, Mary (buried 18 June 1869, age 60) and John (buried 11 Dec. 1881, age 73). See interment record of John Geoghegan, section 8, range 40, plot Y, graves 11 and 12, Calvary Cemetery, Woodside, N.Y.

14. *Times* clipping, 21 Jan. 1885, vol. 10, DAS.

15. *World*, 6 Feb. 1884 (Bowery boy); *Star* clipping, 14 Feb. 1884 (height and weight); *Herald* clipping, 27 Jan. 1882, both in DAS.; *Times*, 13 Aug. 1884 (Thompson); *World*, 16 Aug. 1885 (college). On "McGrory" as McGlory's original surname, *World*, 6 Feb. 1884; unmarked clipping, 11 Dec 1891, vol. 92, DAS. McGlory was also nicknamed "the Prince" and "the Grand Duke of Hester Street." See *Sun*, 29 Jan. 1888 ("Napoleon"); *Morning Advertiser* clippings, 30 Dec. 1891, vol. 92; *World* clipping, 29 May 1891, vol. 86 (wickedest); 9 Jan. 1892 clipping, vol. 93 (priest); 13 May 1893 clipping, vol. 112; unmarked clipping, 1 Feb. 1884 ("Duke"); *Star* clipping, 14 Feb. 1884 ("Prince"), all in DAS. On the country home in Baldwin, Long Island, see *World* clipping, 10 July 1891, vol. 87; unmarked clippings, 17 July 1891, vol. 88, all in DAS.

16. Armory Hall was located at 156–58 Hester Street. Windsor Palace (sometimes called Alhambra Hall and "Burnt Rag No. 2") was identified at the same address as Geoghegan's—103 and 105 Bowery. See unmarked clipping, 28 Nov. 1886, vol. 28, DAS. Examples of McGlory's frequent excise and assault violations are in People v. McGlory, 26 June 1883, box 106, folder 1131, CGS; unmarked clipping, 29 May 1883; *Journal* clipping, 27 Jan. 1884; *Star* and other clippings, 28 Jan. 1884; *Star* and *World* clippings, 30 Jan. 1884; 1, 2 Feb. 1884 clippings; 21–23 Oct. 1885 clippings, vol. 14; *Tribune* clipping, 21 Feb. 1886, all in DAS.

17. Police Report to Mayor W. R. Grace, 10 Jan. 1886, box 86-GWR-26; John Voorhis to Mayor Abram Hewitt, 31 Mar. 1887 (former armory), box 87-HAS-37, both in MP; *Star* clipping, 29 Jan. 1882 (orchestra); *Times* clipping, 21 Jan. 1885, vol. 10; *World* clipping, 1 May 1887, vol. 34 (Corinthian); unmarked clipping, 14 Mar. 1883; *Press* clipping, 23 Sept. 1888, vol. 53, all in DAS; *Sun*, 29 Jan. 1888.

18. Charles Rillings Report, in People v. McGlory, 26 June 1883, box 106, folder 1131 (dancing) (hereafter Rillings Report), CGS; *Star* clipping, 29 Jan. 1882; *Press* clipping, 23 Sept. 1888, vol. 53 (prostitutes); unmarked clipping, 8 Feb. 1884, vol. 7; *Star* clipping, 28 Jan. 1884; *World* clipping, 12 May 1886, vol. 20 (Pompeiian dances); *World* clipping, 1 May 1887, vol. 34; *Morning Journal* clipping, 6 Dec. 1891 (fights), vol. 92, all in DAS; *World*, 16 Aug. 1885 (suckers); Hapgood, *Autobiography*, 77, 223; Asbury, *Gangs*, 187. For examples of controversy concerning McGlory at other balls, see unmarked clipping, 24 Jan. 1889, vol. 57; unmarked clipping, 10 Mar. 1889, vol. 59, DAS. For com-

plaints against McGlory, see the letters to Mayor Abram Hewitt in box 87-HAS-38, all in MP.

19. Walling, *Recollections*, 489; *World* clipping, 12 May 1886, vol. 20; *World* clipping, 6 Dec. 1891 (names of criminals), vol. 92; *Recorder* clipping, 29 Apr. 1895 (opium smokers), vol. 140, both in DAS; Rillings Report. On the ten-year prison terms of McGlory's employees, see Subpoenas, 26 Jan. 1883, in People v. William McGlory, 2 Dec. 1891 and 22 Dec. 1891, box 461, folders 4234 and 4235, CGS. For stories of barroom brawls and robberies in McGlory's, see *Sun*, 11, 25 Jan. 1879; *World*, 25 Jan. 1879.

20. *World*, 7, 9 Jan. 1879; *Sun* clipping, 18 June 1883 (teetotaler); unmarked clippings, 14, 21 May 1883 (McAuley revival), DAS; *Times*, 13 Aug. 1884 (Republican); Harlow, *Old Bowery Days*, 400.

21. People v. William McGlory, 17 Dec. 1883, box 122, folder 1289; People v. McGlory, 31 Jan. 1884, box 126, folder 1321 (bedfellows), both in CGS; *Herald*, 25 Apr. 1883; *Tribune* clipping, 7 Feb. 1884; unmarked clippings, 7 Feb. 1884, all in DAS. Newspapers gave McGlory's trial and prison stay extensive coverage. See *Star* and other clippings, 4, 5 Feb. 1884, DAS; *Tribune*, 31 Jan. 1884, 5 Feb. 1884. A copy of the appeal as well as several other McGlory cases can be found in People v. William McGlory, 22 Dec. 1891, box 461, folder 4235, CGS. McGlory frequently listed his property in his wife Annie McGlory's name. See unmarked clipping, 5 Feb. 1891, vol. 79; unmarked clippings, 29, 30 Dec. 1891, vol. 93, all in DAS.

22. *Times*, 13 Aug. 1884 (release); unmarked clipping, 7 Feb. 1884 (Gibbsey); *Star* clipping, 14 Feb. 1884 (large crowd); *Truth* clipping, 11 Aug. 1884 (hurrah), vol. 8; unmarked clipping, 21 Dec. 1891 (defiance); *Morning Advertiser* clipping, 9 Jan. 1892 (awestruck), both in vol. 93, all in DAS.

23. *World* clipping, 6 Dec. 1891 (Peter Patience), vol. 92; unmarked clipping, 14 Mar. 1883 (performers); *Press* clipping, 23 Sept. 1888 (women in silk), vol. 53, all in DAS; *Sun*, 29 Jan. 1888.

24. *Press* clippings, 23, 25 Sept. 1888, vol. 53; unmarked clipping, 10 Mar. 1889 (phony license), vol. 59; *Star* clipping, 26 Jan. 1889; *Journal* clipping, 13 Apr. 1890 (police blackmail), vol. 72; unmarked clipping, 17 July 1891 ($87,000), vol. 88, all in DAS; *World*, 23 Mar. 1887; NYC Department of Police, *Report* (New York, 1888), 37; "Arrests for Violations of Theatrical Law," Oct. 1886, in box 86-GWR-26, MP.

25. *Times*, 5 Feb. 1893; unmarked clipping, 22 June 1891, vol. 86; *World* clipping, 16 Sept. 1891, vol. 90; *Morning Journal* clipping, 6 Dec. 1981, vol. 92; *Herald* clipping, 4 Dec. 1891, vol. 92, all in DAS; People v. William McGlory, 22 Dec. 1891, box 461, folder 4235, CGS. On Corey's relationship with McGlory, see *Morning Journal* clipping, 6 Dec. 1891, vol. 92 (stepfather and uncle); *Morning Telegraph* clipping, 5 June 1900, vol. 191; unmarked clipping, 20 May 1899, vol. 181, all in DAS.

26. People v. William McGlory, 2 Dec. 1891 and 22 Dec. 1891, box 461, folders 4234 and 4235, CGS; unmarked clippings, 14 Dec. 1891, vol. 92; *Commercial Advertiser* and other clippings, 21 Dec. 1891; *Morning Advertiser* and other clippings, 9 Jan. 1892 (Smyth); unmarked clippings, 30 Dec. 1891; *Herald* clipping, 30 Dec. 1891 (Fellows); *Recorder* clipping, 9 Jan. 1892, all in vol. 93, DAS.

27. *Tribune*, 5 Feb. 1893, 2 July 1893, 17 Aug. 1893; *Times*, 5, 14 Feb. 1893, 2 July 1893; unmarked clipping, 13 May 1893, vol. 112; *Journal* clipping, 3 Jan. 1900; *Tribune, Herald*, and other clippings, 12, 13, 14, 16 Jan. 1900, all in vol. 187; 1 Feb. 1900 clipping,

vol. 188; unmarked clipping, 21 Mar. 1900, vol. 189; unmarked clipping, 31 Dec. 1900, vol. 196, all in DAS.

28. Walling, *Recollections*, 480–82; Willemse, *Behind the Green Lights*, 69–70 (marketplace); *NPG*, 31 Jan. 1880; 8 Feb. 1879 (Argyle Rooms), 29 Nov. 1879 (Argyle Rooms); *World* clipping, 21 Dec. 1885, vol. 16, DAS; Gilfoyle, *City of Eros*, 227–28, 395.

29. Stephen Crane, "The 'Tenderloin' As It Really Is" (1896); and "Sixth Avenue," both in Fredson Bowers, ed., *The Works of Stephen Crane* (Charlottesville, Va., 1973), VIII:392, X:109; *Mazet Committee*, I:44–46; II, 1590, 2027 (1890s); unmarked clipping, 22 Jan. 1900, vol. 187, DAS. On Seventh Avenue as "more rough, than the Bowery," see *Morning Advertiser* clipping, 25 Nov. 1892, vol. 104, DAS. For similar descriptions of the Tenderloin, see *Press* clipping, 28 Oct. 1898, vol. 174; *World* clipping, 13 Oct. 1885, vol. 14, both in DAS.

30. *NPG*, 31 Jan. 1880 (pimps); unmarked clipping, 20 May 1899, vol. 181, *Morning Telegraph* clipping, 14 Nov. 1898, vol. 175, all in DAS. On other names, see *Herald* clipping, 19 Oct. 1898, vol. 173, DAS. The Artistic Club was located at 56 West Thirtieth Street.

31. Willemse, *Behind the Green Lights*, 70; *Morning Journal* clipping, 6 Dec. 1891, vol. 92; unmarked clipping, 20 May 1899, vol. 181; unmarked clippings, 13 Mar. 1900, vol. 189; *Morning Telegraph* clippings, 5 June 1900, 12 June 1900, both in vol. 191, all in DAS; *Mazet Committee*, II:1382–83, 1390 (degenerates), 1590, 2397–98 (women robbing); Richard O'Connor, *O. Henry: The Legendary Life of William Sidney Porter* (Garden City, N.Y., 1970), 143–44. Reports listing closed concert halls (including the Haymarket) are in Supt. William Murray to Mayor Abram Hewitt, 11 Mar. 1887, Licensing of Theaters Folder, Police Department, box 87-HAS-37, MP. During the 1880s William McMahon was the Haymarket's proprietor.

32. *Mazet Committee*, I:44–46; II:1384–91, 1591, 2025–27 (Cairo); unmarked clipping, 28 Feb. 1887 (Chelsea), vol. 32; *Herald* clipping, 24 Jan. 1900, both in vol. 187, all in DAS; *World* clipping, 19 Dec. 1885, box 108, scrapbook 9, William R. Grace Papers, Columbia University.

33. *Cincinnati Times-Star*, 19 Jan. 1895 (most noted); Walling, *Recollections*, 484 (good-looking); *Times*, 20 Feb. 1900 (handsome); *Herald* clipping, 18 Feb. 1887, vol. 32; unmarked clipping, 29 Apr. 1887; *Morning Journal* clipping, 30 Apr. 1887 (15 lives), both in vol. 34; *Sun* clipping, 13 Aug. 1888, vol. 52 (Congress); unmarked clippings, 21 Dec. 1892, vol. 105 (clerk), all in DAS.

34. On the "Burnt Rag," see *Recorder* clipping, 27 Dec. 1891, vol. 93; *World* clipping, 1 May 1887, vol. 34, both in DAS. By 1875 Gould's saloon was at 1187 Broadway, and he resided at 74 West Thirty-sixth Street. The "official" owner of Gould's was Thomas F. Parker of New Haven, Gould's brother-in-law. For arrests and excise violations, see People v. Thomas Gould, 13 Oct. 1886, CGS; 9 July 1886 clipping, vol. 22; *Sun* clipping, 5 Sept. 1886, vol. 25; *World* clipping, 18 Feb. 1887, vol. 32, all in DAS. On fronts, see *Herald* clipping, 6 Jan. 1887, vol. 30, DAS.

35. Walling, *Recollections*, 484; People v. Thomas Gould, 22 June 1881 (Keller testimony); People v. Thomas E. Gould, 8 Feb. 1887, box 256, folder 2476, both in CGS; Elbridge Gerry to Mayor Franklin Edson, 17 Apr. 1884, box 85-EF-13, MP. Gould's license was sometimes in someone else's name (William Munn in 1881, brother-in-law Thomas F. Parker in 1886). See Inspector Thomas Thorne to Supt. George W. Walling, 8 Mar.

1881, box 83-CE-26; Report on Tom Gould's, 1885, box 85-EF-13; Capt. Alexander Williams to Inspector Henry V. Steers, 24 Nov. 1886, box 86-GWR-26; Murray to Board of Police, 8 Nov. 1886; Steers to Murray, 26 Nov. 1886, both in folder 98, box 1334, Grace Papers, all in MP; *World* clipping, 19 Dec. 1885, box 108, scrapbook 9, in Grace Papers; People v. Gould, 13 Oct. 1886, CGS.

36. People v. Thomas E. Gould, 8 Feb. 1887, box 256, folder 2476, CGS; *Herald, Star,* and *Sun* clippings, 17, 18 Feb. 1887; unmarked clipping, 6 Mar. 1887 (Canada), all in vol. 32, DAS; *Times,* 18, 19 Feb. 1887.

37. The restaurant was at 372 Sixth Avenue, on the southeast corner of West Twenty-third Street. See *Times,* 27 Jan. 1892 (picture); *Herald* clipping, 22 June 1891 (brisk business), vol. 86; *Herald* clipping, 27 Dec. 1891 (bouncers); *Recorder* clipping, 29 Dec. 1891 (rogues' gallery); *Recorder* clipping, 27 Dec. 1891, all in vol. 93, DAS. Most papers claimed that Gould and Wogan were cousins. See unmarked clipping, 16 Feb. 1888; *Star* clipping, 18 Feb. 1888, both in vol. 45; *Sun* clipping, 13 Aug. 1888, vol. 52; unmarked clipping, 21 Dec. 1889, vol. 68; *Herald, World,* and other clippings, 26 Dec. 1891; 13 Feb. 1890, vol. 70; *Morning Journal* and other clippings, 28 Oct. 1890 (Gould quote), vol. 77, all in DAS. Others said they were brothers-in-law. See *Herald* clipping, 26 Dec. 1891, vol. 93, DAS.

38. People v. Thomas Gould, 12 Feb. 1880, CGS (Freeman); *Sun* and other clippings, 28 Sept. 1891 (waiter), vol. 90; *Tribune, Times, Journal, Herald,* and other clippings, 20–22 Oct. 1890, vol. 77, all in DAS; *Times,* 28 Oct. 1890. On Wogan, see unmarked clippings, 26–30 Dec. 1891, vol. 93, DAS. Gould was indicted for keeping a house of ill fame, but the case was never prosecuted and was discharged in 1898. See People v. Thomas E. Gould, 12 Jan. 1892, CGS. Coverage of the trial can be found in unmarked clippings, 21–23 Dec. 1892, vol. 105, DAS.

39. Unmarked clipping, 26 Sept. 1890 (People's Municipal League), vol. 77; *Press* clipping, 22 Oct. 1891 (Liquor Dealers), vol. 91, both in DAS.

40. *Times, Tribune,* 20 Feb. 1900. Gould worked as the superintendent at Iron Pier on Coney Island, and died at his home at 712 Ninth Avenue. No records for Owen Geoghegan, William or Billy McGlory, Harry Hill, or Tom Gould appear in the Index to Wills, Administrations, Transfer Tax, or Decrees on Accounting, New York City, Room 405, Surrogate's Court Record Room, 31 Chambers Street, New York, N.Y.

41. *Lexow Committee,* V:4919–30; *Nation,* 4 Nov. 1875, p. 288, quoted in Callow, *Tweed Ring,* 193; *Tribune,* 4 Dec. 1866; *World,* 11 July 1891; *Herald* clipping, 11 July 1891, vol. 87; unmarked clipping, 18 Mar. 1892, vol. 96, DAS; *Times,* 11 July 1891. On McGlory, see *Times,* 13 Aug. 1884.

42. SPC, *Report* (New York, 1879), 17; City Club of New York, *The Police Department of the City of New York: A Statement of Facts* (New York, 1903), 386, copy in Police Box, WC. Police officer Patrick McGinley was Geoghegan's brother-in-law. See *Times,* 25, 26 Jan. 1885; *World,* 17 July 1885. On Corey's relationship with McGlory, see note 25 above. On police officers drinking in McGlory's, see Rillings Report.

43. *Sun* clipping, 5 Sept. 1886, vol. 25; *Herald* clipping, 6 Jan. 1887 (Gould's and others), vol. 30, DAS. On Allen's many arrests, see *Morning Advertiser* clipping, 10 Sept. 1895 (pigeonholed indictment), vol. 145; unmarked clipping, 29 Jan. 1898, vol. 166; *Journal* clipping, 23 Apr. 1898, vol. 169 (33 arrests), all in DAS.

44. *Sun* clipping, 5 Sept. 1886 (Gould; unlicensed places), vol. 25, DAS. On complaints about the double standard regarding upscale hotels, see *World* clipping, 10 Oct. 1885,

vol. 13, DAS. On McGlory claiming to be a teetotaler, see *Sun* clipping, 18 June 1883; unmarked clippings, 14, 21 May 1883 (McAuley revival), all in DAS.

45. Eugene O'Neill, "The Haymarket," *New London Telegraph*, 21 Nov. 1912, quoted in Louis Sheaffer, *O'Neill: Playwright and Son* (Boston, 1968), 137. For the Tenderloin's influence on the literature of O'Neill, Crane, and Porter, see Crane, "Opium's Varied Dreams" (1896); "In the Tenderloin: A Duel Between an Alarm Clock and a Suicidal Purpose" (1896); "In the Tenderloin" (1896); all in Bowers, *Crane*, VIII:365–70, 384–96; Arthur and Barbara Gelb, *O'Neill* (New York, 1962), 124–26; O'Connor, *O. Henry*, 92–94, 143–45; R. W. Stallman, *Stephen Crane: A Biography* (New York, 1968), 102–5.

46. Appo, 24–25; Hapgood, *Autobiography*, 27 (celebrities of the saloon).

47. On Theodore "The" Allen described in these various ways, see *Herald, World, Times*, 11 July 1891; unmarked clippings, 11, 12 July 1891, vol. 87; unmarked clipping, 17 July 1891, vol. 88; *World* clipping, 16 Apr. 1898, vol. 169, all in DAS.

## JACK COLLINS

1. Appo probably confused religious orders here. St. Vincent's Hospital was a Roman Catholic institution founded by the Sisters of Charity of Saint Vincent DePaul in 1849. Some Sisters of Mercy may have served as nurses in St. Vincent's Hospital. See Rev. J. F. Richmond, *New York and Its Institutions, 1609–1871* (New York, 1871), 344–46, 375–78; Hasia R. Diner, *Erin's Daughters in America: Irish Immigrant Women in the Nineteenth Century* (Baltimore, 1983), 134–35.

2. Appo, 21–23. I reversed the order of the final two sentences of this passage. Newspaper accounts confirm most of the details Appo described in this incident. See *Times, Tribune*, 4 Sept. 1880; *Times*, 6, 7, 8 Aug. 1880; *Tribune*, 7 Aug. 1880; *Brooklyn Eagle*, 7 Aug. 1880; PCDB, First District, vol. 17, 32, microfilm roll 21, negative 10167, 6 Aug. 1880.

## 10. TOMBS JUSTICE

1. John Josiah Munro, *The New York Tombs, Inside and Out!* (Brooklyn, 1909), 17 (criminal barracks); Alfred Trumble [Richard K. Fox], *The New York Tombs: Its History and Its Mysteries* (New York, 1881), 5 (most famous); Augustine E. Costello, *Our Police Protectors: History of the New York Police* (New York, 1885), 507; PANY, *Thirtieth AR for 1874*, SD 78 (Albany, 1875), 68. While he never discussed the Tombs in detail, Appo mentioned the Tombs three times. See Appo, 3, 25, 64. Appo's name or alias appears in the First District Police Court Docket Books six times. Appo was arrested and incarcerated during Byrnes's crackdown on pickpockets just prior to the funeral services of Ulysses S. Grant. See *World*, 6, 7 Aug. 1885. Prior to his sentence to Blackwell's Island, Appo was in the Tombs from 8 August to 4 October 1895. See unmarked clipping, 9 Aug. 1895, DAS; *Times*, 1 Oct. 1895.

2. Elizabeth Oakes Smith, *The Newsboy* (New York, 1854), 90–92 (death); Charles Dickens, *American Notes* (1842), 83–86; George Foster, *New York in Slices; By an Experienced Carver* (New York, 1849), 5, 19–22 (lazar house); Herman Melville, "Bartleby, The Scrivener. A Story of Wall Street," *Putnam's Monthly Magazine*, Nov. and Dec. 1853, 546–57, 609–15, reprinted in Howard P. Vincent, ed., *Bartleby the Scrivener*

(Kent, Ohio, 1966); Herman Melville, *Pierre, or, The Ambiguities* (London, 1923), 502–5. Other accounts of the Tombs are identified in Timothy J. Gilfoyle, " 'America's Greatest Criminal Barracks': The Tombs and the Experience of Criminal Justice in New York City, 1838–1897," *Journal of Urban History* 29 (2003), 545–46, note 2.

3. *New York Evening Post*, 1 Apr. 1837 (Egyptian); *New-York As It Is* (New York, 1839), 24 (Haviland); *New York Evening Post*, 1 Apr. 1837 (Egyptian); Charles Sutton, *The New York Tombs: Its Secrets and Its Mysteries* (New York, 1874), 48; Richard G. Carrott, *The Egyptian Revival: Its Sources, Monuments and Meaning, 1808–1858* (Berkeley, Calif., 1978), 146–92; Gilfoyle, "Criminal Barracks," 526, 546, note 4.

4. A more detailed discussion of the inconsistent reportings on the numbers of cells in the Tombs appears in Gilfoyle, "Criminal Barracks," 526–28, 547. On the evolution of the inferior court judicial apparatus, see Michael Willrich, *City of Courts: Socializing Justice in Progressive Era Chicago* (New York, 2003), 3–58; Allen Steinberg, *The Transformation of Criminal Justice: Philadelphia, 1800–1880* (Chapel Hill, N.C., 1989); Michael Hindus, *Crime, Justice, and Authority in Massachusetts and South Carolina, 1767–1878* (Chapel Hill, N.C., 1980).

5. Gilfoyle, "Criminal Barracks," 547, note 6.

6. Ibid., note 7.

7. Ibid., 547–48, notes 8 and 9.

8. Ibid., 548, note 10.

9. *Increase of Crime*, 58–59; J. F. Richmond, *New York and Its Institutions, 1609–1871* (New York, 1871), 516–17; Gilfoyle, "Criminal Barracks," 548, note 12.

10. Mary Roberts Smith, "The Social Aspect of New York Police Courts," *American Journal of Sociology*, 5 (1899), 152 (95 percent). On post–Civil War vagrancy statutes, summary justice, and arrest figures, see Amy Dru Stanley, "Beggars Can't Be Choosers: Compulsion and Contract in Postbellum America," *Journal of American History* 78 (1992), 1265–93; John H. Warren, Jr., *Thirty Years' Battle With Crime* (Poughkeepsie, NY, 1897), 174–87, 195–256; Gilfoyle, "Criminal Barracks," 530–31, table 1. In "Criminal Barracks," I neglected to include the word "adult" in concluding that the total number of men arrested every five years roughly equaled New York City's entire adult male population.

11. Frank Moss, *The American Metropolis* (New York 1897), III:69, 71; unmarked clipping, 9 Feb. 1891, vol. 82; *World* clipping, 20 Dec. 1896, vol. 160, both in DAS; *Increase of Crime*, 52 (injustice); NYSS, *Twenty-fifth AR of the Inspectors of State Prisons [for 1872]*, SD 30 (Albany, 1873), 236. Appo's bail in some cases was $1,000, an exorbitant sum. See People v. George Appo, 24 July 1896, New York District Attorney Records, cases #9126 and #9127, box B-2, location 12817, Supreme Court Cases, NYCMA.

12. *Tribune*, 6 Aug. 1877; George Wilkes, *The Mysteries of the Tombs* (New York, 1844), 13–14; *Lexow Committee*, III:3310–12; *World* clippings, 26, 29 June 1886, vol. 22; Charles Gardner, "The Tombs Mint," *Morning Journal*, 12 Aug. 1894, vol. 130; *World* clipping, 20 Dec. 1896, vol. 160; unmarked clipping, 16 July 1899, vol. 182 (steerers), all in DAS; PANY, *Twenty-fourth AR for 1868*, SD 10 (Albany, 1869), 3; Gilfoyle, "Criminal Barracks," 549, notes 15–18.

13. *Tribune*, 6 Aug. 1877 (gentleman); *Times*, 17 July 1880 (list of privileges); Matthew Hale Smith, *Sunshine and Shadow in New York* (Hartford, Conn., 1868), 166 (in style); Munro, *New York Tombs*, 20 (sexual favors); *Increase of Crime*, 105 (empty cells; extorting); James D. McCabe, Jr., *The Secrets of the Great City* (Philadelphia, 1868), *Secrets*, 99 (wealthier class).

14. *Times*, 22 Dec. 1872 (fancy), 17 July 1880 (privileges); *World* clippings, 24 Mar. 1886 (Jaehne), 3 Oct. 1896 (stars), vol. 159, both in DAS; *Sun*, 14 Oct. 1882 (stars); Sutton, *Tombs*, 94–96, 332–33 (Stokes), 491; *Tribune*, 6 Aug. 1877 (meals furnished); George W. Walling, *Recollections of a New York Chief of Police* (New York, 1887), 397; J. H. Green, *Twelve Days in the Tombs; or, A Sketch of the Last Eight Years of the Reformed Gambler's Life* (New York, 1850), 70–80.

15. On the considerable legal income from fees for sheriffs, tax collectors, excise officers, customs officials, and county clerks, see *Morning Advertiser* (?) clipping, 4 Apr. 1890, vol. 72, DAS; *Tribune*, 6 Aug. 1877; New York State Laws and Statutes, *Draft of the Political Code of the State of New York* (Albany, 1859), 312–33; Gilfoyle, "Criminal Barracks," 533, 549, note 19.

16. *Times*, 7 Jan. 1887; *Tribune*, 29 May 1887; *Leslie's*, 1 Feb. 1873; Costello, *Police Protectors*, 509; *Tribune* (?) clipping, 29 May 1887, vol. 35, DAS; *Tribune*, 15 Dec. 1879; Munro, *New York Tombs*, 21, 232; Gilfoyle, "Criminal Barracks," 550, note 22.

17. *Leslie's*, 29 Mar. 1873; *Increase of Crime*, 59; *Tribune*, 29 June 1895; *Morning Advertiser*, 21 Dec. 1895, vol. 149; 1 July 1895 clipping (kitchen), vol. 143, both in DAS; *Mazet Committee*, 31 May 1899, 1311–12, 1318; Gilfoyle, "Criminal Barracks," 550, note 23.

18. G. F. Britton to Abram Hewitt, 11 Jan. 1888, Charities and Correction folder, box 87-HAS-2, MP (whiskey); unmarked clipping, 22 May 1896 (keepers), vol. 154; unmarked clipping, 26 Jan. 1895 (liquor), vol. 137, DAS; Gilfoyle, "Criminal Barracks," 534, 550, notes 24 and 25.

19. *Tribune* and *World* clippings (Walsh), 21, 22 Jan. 1888, vol. 44, DAS; *Tribune*, 3 June 1899. On Appo, see Allen S. Williams, *The Demon of the Orient, and His Satellite Fiends of the Joints: Our Opium Smokers as They are in Tartar Hells and American Paradises* (New York, 1883), 71–73.

20. Trumble, *New York Tombs*, 49. On pickpockets, see *Times*, 31 Jan. 1873. On escapes, see *Tribune*, 14 June 1893.

21. Sutton, *Tombs*, 83–84, 333; *Times*, 13, 14 Aug. 1879; *Tribune*, 29 May 1887; Trumble, *New York Tombs*, 9 (ten-day prisoners). For more on voluntary inmates, see Gilfoyle, "Criminal Barracks," 537, 551, notes 28–30.

22. Governors of the Almshouse, *Second AR for 1850* (New York, 1851), 47–49; Governors of the Almshouse, *Fourth AR for 1852* (New York, 1853), 44; PANY, *Twenty-fourth AR for 1868*, 2; PANY, *Thirtieth AR for 1874*, 69; *Increase of Crime*, 59; Gilfoyle, "Criminal Barracks," 551, note 31.

23. Hutchins Hapgood, ed., *The Autobiography of a Thief* (New York, 1903), 45–46 (bang a super), 48, 61; *Sun* clipping, 8 Sept. 1884 (de mob), vol. 9; *Morning Advertiser* clippings, 27 July 1895 (school of crime), vol. 144, all in DAS; *Harper's Weekly*, 29 Mar. 1873 (seminaries of crime); Charles Loring Brace, *The Dangerous Classes of New York and Twenty Years' Working Among Them* (New York, 1872), 399; Munro, *New York Tombs*, 12–13, 120–25 (schools of crime), 241; Governors, *Second AR for 1850*, 47–49; *Tribune*, 29 May 1887; PANY, *Thirtieth AR for 1874*, 57–58; PANY, *Thirty-first AR for 1875*, SD 54 (Albany, 1876), 24–25. On the "large number of short-term convicts" in the Tombs, see PANY, *Thirtieth AR for 1874*, 24–25. For other reports of teenage male incarceration, see *Times*, 9 Jan. 1882; *Herald*, 13 Jan. 1882, both in DAS; *World*, 13, 27 Jan. 1879; CAS, *Eighteenth AR*, 51–52; CAS, *Nineteenth AR*, 8.

24. Hapgood, *Autobiography*, 61; *Herald* clipping, 29 July 1887 (mark of distinction), vol. 38; *World* clipping, 19 Mar. 1888 (done his bit), vol. 46, DAS.

25. Levi L. Barbour, "Jails: A Paper Read at the Convention of the County Agents of the State Board of Corrections and Charities of Michigan," (1885), 4–5, in Prisons Box, WC (common sense, enlightenment); *Increase of Crime*, 62 (qualification); *Tribune*, 16 June 1895 (patronage).

26. *Times*, 20 Mar. 1881. For similar observations, see *World* clipping, 10 May 1885, vol. 12, both in DAS; *Times*, 4 Jan. 1861, 28 Nov. 1866; Smith, "New York Police Courts," 153; *NPG*, 22 Mar. 1879; Wilkes, *Mysteries of the Tombs*, 10–11.

27. Smith, "New York Police Courts," 150–51; Moss, *American Metropolis*, III:72–73; "Police Court Sketches," *Daily Graphic*, 2 May 1872. On the performative aspects of nineteenth-century trials, see Patricia Cline Cohen, *The Murder of Helen Jewett: The Life and Death of a Prostitute in Nineteenth-Century New York* (New York, 1998), 310–11; Katherine Fischer Taylor, *In the Theater of Criminal Justice: The Palais de Justice in Second Empire Paris* (Princeton, N.J., 1993).

28. Smith, "New York Police Courts," 150; Reginald Heber Smith, *Justice and the Poor* (New York, 1924), 10; A. G. Warner, "Politics and Crime," *American Journal of Sociology* 1 (1895), 290–91; "To Reform Courts of Inferior Jurisdiction," *Survey* 24 (30 April 1910), 177–78; Kate Holladay Claghorn, *The Immigrant's Day in Court* (New York, 1923), 220.

29. McCabe, *Secrets*, 101 (Dowling); unmarked clippings, 25 July 1887 (rush), vol. 38; 26 June 1899 (Brann), vol. 182; *World* clipping, 29 May 1887 (Duffy), vol. 35; unmarked clipping, 25 Aug. 1894, vol. 131, all in DAS; *World*, 29 May 1887; Arthur Train, *The Prisoner at the Bar: Sidelights on the Administration of Criminal Justice* (New York, 1923), 58–59; Smith, "New York Police Courts," 150–51; Sutton, *Tombs*, 328 (drunk reporter); *Times*, 12 May 1860, 20 Mar. 1881 (Gatling gun); *World*, 17 May 1875; Gilfoyle, "Criminal Barracks," 551–52, note 36.

30. Smith, "New York Police Courts," 149–51 (Hewitt, 79 percent); Smith, *Justice and the Poor*, 10 ("Poor Man's Court"); *Increase of Crime*, 38–47; *Times*, 23 Oct. 1909; Train, *Prisoner at the Bar*, 61, 57–59; Munro, *New York Tombs*, 206. For more on these points, see Gilfoyle, "Criminal Barracks," 552, notes 38 and 39.

31. *Times*, 25 Dec. 1886 (Power); *Increase of Crime*, 39. Judges of higher courts were constitutionally prohibited from reviewing their own decisions. Yet this frequently happened. See *Increase of Crime*, 45.

32. On bail as "grantable as of course" in nearly all misdemeanors, see Seymour D. Thompson, "Bail in Criminal Cases," *Criminal Law Magazine* 6 (Jan. 1885), 6–7; Sean McConville, "Local Justice: The Jail," in Norval Morris and David J. Rothman, eds., *The Oxford History of the Prison* (New York, 1997), 311–13.

33. *Increase of Crime*, 51; *NPG*, 26 July 1879; *Sun*, 30 Aug. 1885; PANY, *Twenty-fifth AR for 1869*, SD 21 (Albany, 1870), 41 (sham); Warner, "Politics and Crime," 291–93; *Tribune*, 29 June 1895. On the extensiveness of judicial discretion, see Thompson, "Bail in Criminal Cases," 10–37. On the networks of straw bondsmen, see Gilfoyle, "Criminal Barracks," 541–42, 552, notes 43–44.

34. Gilfoyle, "Criminal Barracks," 553, note 48.

35. NYSS, *Report of the Justices of the Special Sessions of New York City*, SD 26 (Albany, 1867), 2–3; *Herald* clipping, 6 Jan. 1887 (out on bail), vol. 30, DAS.

36. *Increase of Crime*, 43; NYSS, *Proceedings Before the Special Committee of the New York State Senate* (Albany, 1876), 1034; Gilfoyle, "Criminal Barracks," 553, note 51.

37. NPG, 19 July 1879; Wilkes, *Mysteries*, 13–14; Campbell, *Darkness*, 341–42; Foster, *New York in Slices*, 20; unmarked clipping, 10 Sept. 1887, vol. 39; *Herald* clipping, 16 Jan. 1887 (Walsh), vol. 30, all in DAS; Richard H. Rovere, *Howe & Hummel: Their True and Scandalous History* (New York, 1947), 10–11. For similar stories, see unmarked clipping, 25 Aug. 1894, vol. 131, DAS. On the origins and folklore regarding the term "shyster lawyer," see Gilfoyle, "Criminal Barracks," 550–51, note 26.

38. *Mail & Express* clipping, 9 Sept. 1884, vol. 9, DAS; see Gilfoyle, "Criminal Barracks," 551, note 27.

39. *Morning Journal*, 24 July 1884, vol. 8 (Mandelbaum); *World* clipping, 26 Dec. 1887, vol. 43, both in DAS.

40. Gilfoyle, "Criminal Barracks," 553, note 52.

41. *Subterranean*, 7 June 1845 (Walsh), in People v. Michael Walsh, 18 June 1845, DAP; Board of Police Justices of the City of New York, *Second AR for the Year 1875* (New York, 1876), 10–11 (perjury); Train, *Prisoner at the Bar*, 289 (25–75 percent); *Tribune* clipping, 5 June 1882 (jury fixing; bogus bonds), in DAS; O. F. Lewis, "The Administration of Justice in the United States," *Survey* 24 (16 Apr. 1910), 114–16 (perjury); *Herald* clipping, 16 Sept. 1891 (jury fixing), vol. 90, DAS.

42. *Times* (?) clipping, 13 May 1883; *Daily Register* clipping, 16 Jan. 1886; unmarked clipping, 24 Feb. 1886, both in vol. 17, all in DAS; Governors, *Second AR for 1850*, 4 (cruel and unjust); Moss, *American Metropolis*, III:68–69.

43. PANY, *Thirty-first AR for 1875*, 78–79; *Sun*, 30 Aug. 1885; *Sun* clipping, 2 Sept. 1885 (no index), vol. 13; *World* clipping, 20 Dec. 1896, vol. 160; unmarked clipping, 22 Jan. 1900, vol. 187, all in DAS; Gilfoyle, "Criminal Barracks," 553, note 53.

44. Smith, "New York Police Courts," 145 (dockets closed); *World*, 22 Oct. 1894 (unable to verify); *Herald* clipping, 8 Jan. 1887 (lumping cases), vol. 30, DAS; *Times*, 9, 12 Aug. 1909.

45. *Sun*, 30 Aug. 1885 (panic); *World*, 23 Oct. 1894; *World* clipping, 9 June 1895, vol. 142, DAS. For later examples of defense attorneys bribing court officers to change court records on behalf of their clients, see *Times*, 20 Mar. 1909. On Hochstim, Nelson, Blumenthal, and prominent officials linked to the bail bonding business, see Gilfoyle, "Criminal Barracks," 553–54, notes 46 and 58.

46. Garry Wills, *Certain Trumpets: The Call of Leaders* (New York, 1994), 226 (Augustine); Warner, "Politics and Crime," 290–91.

GOOD FELLOWS

1. One member of Barney Maguire's gang was Tommy Wilson. It is unclear if this was the same individual. On the membership of Maguire's gang, see William Norr, *Stories of Chinatown: Sketches from Life in the Chinese Colony* (New York, 1892), 47; *Lexow Committee*, II:1653 (Frank Maguire cousin); "Closure of the Opium 'Joints' in New York," *American Journal of Stimulants and Narcotics* 1 (1882), 26.

2. A grip was a small amount of luggage wrapped in a sack or covering and held together by a strap or grip.

3. Wilson was probably suffering from tuberculosis.

4. Appo probably took the Grand Trunk Railway from Toronto to Port Hope (sixty-three

miles to the east), and then the Midland Railway north to Lindsay (approximately forty miles). See *John Lovell's Canadian Dominion Directory for 1871* (Montreal, 1871), 106, 472, 2453–55; M. G. Bixby, ed., *Industries of Canada: Historical and Commercial Sketches: Peterboro, Lindsay, . . . Its Prominent Places and People* (Toronto, 1887), 61–70.

5. The only directory from this period listed three males with the surname "Woods" in Lindsay: Edward Woods, tinsmith of E. Woods and Son, Kent Street; Henry Woods, engineer, Queen Street; and William Woods, tinsmith of E. Woods and Son. See *John Lovell's Canadian Dominion Directory for 1871* (Montreal, 1871), 475; Noel Montgomery Elliot, ed., *The Central Canadians, 1600–1900: An Alphabetized Directory of the People, Places, and Vital Dates* (Toronto, 1994), III:3142–44.

6. Appo, 26–30. Appo referred to Maguire's as a "swell opium joint" on 23–24. Appo spelled Maguire's surname as "McGuire." Since this differs from nearly every other reference to him, I have used the more common spelling of "Maguire."

## 11. FENCES

1. Appo, 30–31. For the arrest and trial, see 222, vol. 20, 1 Apr. 1882, First District, Manhattan, microfilm roll 24, PCDB; *Times*, 31 Mar. 1882, 27 Apr. 1882; People v. George Appo, 18 Apr. 1882, box 9889, location 106019, SCC; *Times, Tribune*, 27 Apr. 1882. Pedro F. del Valle was not an ambassador but a twenty-one–year-old member of the Mexican legation, and described in newspapers as "a Mexican gentleman."

2. Allen S. Williams, *The Demon of the Orient* (New York, 1883), 27–28; Richard H. Rovere, *Howe & Hummel: Their True and Scandalous History* (New York, 1947); Arthur Train, *True Stories of Crime* (New York, 1908), 315–38; Hutchins Hapgood, ed., *The Autobiography of a Thief* (New York, 1903), 38 (fall money).

3. On the lawsuit filed by N. B. Foster, see entry for 13 July 1885, 473–76, vol. 33, Drummond Papers. By 1885 Maguire was working out of 64 Bowery. On Maguire's role in the prosecution of counterfeiter William Cluff, see *Times*, 24 Oct. 1879; entries for 29 Sept. 1879, 181; 30 Sept. 1879, 197; 3 Oct. 1879, 257; 14 Oct. 1879, 333; 23 Oct. 1879, 396–97; 27 Oct. 1879, 406, all in vol. 16; 3 Jan. 1880, 2, vol. 17; 2 Apr. 1880, 12, vol. 18; 31 May 1881, 387; 3 June 1881, 439 (Maguire arrest), both in vol. 22; 20 Mar. 1884, 91–93; 22 Mar. 1884, 109–10; 26 Mar. 1884, 131; 31 Mar. 1884, 136; 9 July 1884, 793–94, all in vol. 30, all in Drummond Papers. On counterfeit stamps, see entry for 28 Feb. 1880, 469–70; 28 Feb. 1880, 484, all in vol. 17. On Maguire's role in prosecuting counterfeiter George B. Butler, see entry for 9 Nov. 1882, 239, vol. 27, all in Drummond Papers.

4. "Closure of the Opium 'Joints' in New York," *American Journal of Stimulants and Narcotics* 1 (1882), 26; Williams, *Demon*, 27–28 (Prince); *Lexow Committee*, II:1661 (Matt Grace); Louis J. Beck, *New York's Chinatown: An Historical Representation of Its People and Places* (New York, 1898), 256 (king); unmarked clipping, 11 Aug. 1899 (swell joints), vol. 183, DAS.

5. Sophie Lyons, *Why Crime Does Not Pay* (New York, 1913), 186–87; Edward Crapsey, *The Nether Side of New York* (New York, 1870), 85–90 (specializing), 91 (leading industries); unmarked clipping, 26 Nov. 1892 (specializing), vol. 104, DAS; Helen Campbell

et al., *Darkness and Daylight: or, Lights and Shadows of New York Life* (Hartford, Conn., 1891), 686–88 (fencing).

6. *Times*, 24 Feb. 1876, 23 Apr. 1876; *World* (?) clipping, 10 Apr. 1888, vol. 47, DAS; *NPG*, 27 May 1882; A. G. Warner, "Politics and Crime," *American Journal of Sociology* 1 (1895), 291; *Lexow Committee*, III:2488, 2498–99. On pawnbrokers, see unmarked clipping, 11 Dec. 1887, vol. 43, DAS; *World*, 5 Apr. 1874; George Foster, *New York in Slices; By an Experienced Carver* (New York, 1849), 30–36. On the importance of pawnbrokers and fences to pickpockets, see *Times*, 5 Jan. 1865; Crapsey, *Nether Side*, 83–91; *World* clipping, 14 Oct. 1885, vol. 14; unmarked clipping, 22 Sept. 1889, vol. 65, both in DAS; *Tribune*, 25 Dec. 1887.

7. *Harper's Weekly*, 7 Sept. 1867; Lyons, *Why Crime Does Not Pay*, 207; NYSCC, *Report—1927* (Albany, 1927), 46–47.

8. *Tribune*, 15 Sept. 1894; Crapsey, *Nether Side*, 91; *Times*, 24 Feb. 1876, 23 Apr. 1876; George W. Walling, *Recollections of a New York Chief of Police* (New York, 1887), 280; James D. McCabe, Jr., *The Secrets of the Great City* (Philadelphia, 1868), 363–64. On denying uncorroborated evidence by a pickpocket in prosecuting receivers of stolen goods, see *People v. William Kupperschmidt*, 237 N.Y. 463, 143 N.E. 256, 1924 N.Y. LEXIS, 32 A.L.R. 447 (1924); NYSL, *Annual Report of the Board of Commissioners of the Metropolitan Police* (Albany, 1865), 5–7; NYSCC, *Report—1927*, 46–47, 48 (diligent inquiry); NYSCC, *Report—1929* (New York, 1929), 97 (reasonable inquiry); NYSCC, *Report to the Commission of the Sub Commission on Courts* (Albany, 1929), 7 (reasonable inquiry). On treating crimes of larceny and receiving stolen goods as separate, distinct offenses, see *People v. Zimmer*, 174 App. Div. 471, 473; 220 N.Y. 597; 1917 N.Y. LEXIS 1047. On twentieth-century courts recognizing subjective criminal behavior, see George P. Fletcher, *Rethinking Criminal Law* (Boston, 1978), 154. Section 550 of the New York Penal Code stated that the receiver of stolen goods had to *know* that the items were stolen. See *People v. Jaffe*, 78 N.E. 169, 185 N.Y. 497, 21 June 1906 (New York Court of Appeals).

9. J. F. Richmond, *The Institutions of New York* (New York, 1871), 183; Hapgood, *Autobiography*, 96; Frank Morn, *"The Eye That Never Sleeps": A History of the Pinkerton National Detective Agency* (Bloomington, Ind., 1982), 114–15, 119.

10. Matthew Hale Smith, *Sunshine and Shadow in New York* (Hartford, Conn., 1868), 150; Crapsey, *Nether Side*, 91; *Lexow Committee*, I:40; *Times*, 29 Nov. 1866; *Times, Tribune*, 11 Sept. 1894; *World* (?) clipping, 10 Apr. 1888, vol. 47, DAS.

11. *Times*, 27 Feb. 1894 (most notorious); Lyons, *Why Crime Does Not Pay*, 187; Crapsey, *Nether Side*, 87–88; *Times*, 24 July 1884; Frank Moss, *The American Metropolis* (New York, 1897), III:26; Benjamin P. Eldridge and William B. Watts, *Our Rival, the Rascal* (Boston, 1897), 294–96. Nicknames for Mandelbaum appear in *Times*, 24 July 1884; *Morning Journal* clipping, 24 July 1884; *World* clipping, 31 July 1884, both in vol. 8, DAS. For historical coverage, see Rovere, *Howe & Hummel*, 6; James D. Horan, *The Pinkerton Story* (New York, 1951), 314 (greatest receiver); Moss, *American Metropolis*, III: 209–10; James L. Ford, *Forty-Odd Years in the Literary Shop* (New York, 1921), 48–52; Luc Sante, *Low Life: Lures and Snares of Old New York* (New York, 1991), 210–11; Ben Macintyre, *The Napoleon of Crime: The Life and Times of Adam Worth, Master Thief* (New York, 1997), 29–36, 31, (most influential), 205–6.

12. Lyons, *Why Crime Does Not Pay*, 190; *Times*, 27 Feb. 1894; Rovere, *Howe & Hummel*, 79; *Tribune*, 16 Apr. 1860 (pickpockets' ball); *Times* and *World* ($1 million) clippings,

24 July 1884; *World* clipping, 31 July 1884, all in vol. 8, DAS; *Times*, 27 Feb. 1894 (born in 1829). Mandelbaum's real estate holdings are outlined in *Herald* clipping, 5 Dec. 1884, vol. 9, DAS; *Times*, 26 July 1884. Wolfe Mandelbaum appears in: *New York City Directory, 1861–1862* (New York, 1861), 565 (cigar salesman); *Trow's New York City Directory for 1864* (New York, 1863), 572 (peddler); *Trow's New York City Directory for 1867* (New York, 1866), 669 (dry-goods salesman); *Trow's New York City Directory for 1870* (New York, 1869), 733. On Mandelbaum's children, see *Morning Journal* clipping, 24 July 1884, vol. 8, DAS; Lyons, *Why Crime Does Not Pay*, 196; *Times*, 26 July 1884.

13. Lyons, *Why Crime Does Not Pay*, 191, 195–96 (clearing house); Walling, *Recollections*, 241–44, 261–68, 278, 281, 283; *World* clipping, 19 Oct. 1883, DAS; *Times*, 24, 26 July 1884; Rovere, *Howe & Hummel*, 6, 18, 29–30, 79; Hapgood, *Autobiography*, 38 (fall money). Newspapers reported that Mandelbaum owned 77 and 79 Clinton Street, but no record of Mandelbaum or 79 Clinton Street appears in real estate records. See Clinton Street entries, Record of Assessment, Seventeenth and Thirteenth Wards, 1879–1883, NYCMA.

14. When silk and other forms of cloth were stolen, fences removed any identifying mark. See *Times*, 24, 26 July 1884, 27 Feb. 1894 (credit).

15. *World* clippings, 24, 27 July 1884, vol. 8; 25 Mar. 1886 (Jaehne), DAS; Lyons, *Why Crime Does Not Pay*, 191, 193.

16. People v. Fredericka Mandelbaum, Herman Stoude and Julius Mandelbaum, 14 Aug. 1884, CGS; Walling, *Recollections*, 287; *Times*, 23 July 1884; *Times* clipping, 24 July 1884, vol. 8, DAS; *Tribune*, 29 July 1884.

17. NYSA, *Pardons and Commutations During 1885*, AD 48 (Albany, 1886), 3–4; Thomas Byrnes, *Professional Criminals of America* (New York, 1886), 194a, 195–96. Pinkerton critics later charged that Mandelbaum's arrest was a result of revenge because Byrnes's Wall Street office ended much of the Pinkerton business on Wall Street. See *Lexow Committee*, V:5671–72.

18. Walling, *Recollections*, 281; *Times*, 23, 24, 26, 31 July 1884; 16, 20 Sept. 1884; 20 Nov. 1884; 3–7, 9, 10, 11, 13 Dec. 1884; 27 Feb. 1894; *Tribune*, 6, 9 Dec. 1884; *Herald* clipping, 5 Dec. 1884, vol. 9; *World* clipping, 24 Mar. 1886, DAS.

19. On the mixture of Irish and Italian youths, as well as bootblacks on Mott Street, see *Star* clipping, 8 Feb. 1884, vol. 7, DAS. On non-Chinese proprietors, see John Ryan to W. R. Grace, 14 Aug. 1882; Sgt. William Thompson to Supt. Thomas Thorne, 18 Aug. 1882, both in folder 2, box 84-GWR-14, MP. Maguire was forced to close his Crosby Street joint in late 1882, although he allegedly operated several dens nearby. See "Closure of Opium 'Joints' in New York," 26; *World* clipping, 4 Oct. 1885, vol. 13, DAS.

20. J. Frank "Flotty" Kernan, *Reminiscences of the Old Fire Laddies* (New York, 1885), 204 (garden); *Tribune*, 19 Sept. 1876 (spectacle); Niblo's obituary in *Tribune*, 22 Aug. 1878; Floyd Stovall, ed., *The Collected Writings of Walt Whitman* (New York, 1963), I:24 (nightlife); Richard Moody, *Edwin Forrest: First Star of the American Stage* (New York, 1960), 341 (largest theater with 3,500 capacity); George C. D. Odell, *Annals of the New York Stage* (New York, 1949), XIII:35–37 (Crook), 252–53 (1833), 453–55 (dog shows); XIV:48–51, 283–86 (Bowery), 562–64 (corpse); XV:53–55. For pictures of Niblo's in 1828 and later, see Theater Box, WC; "Diagram of Niblo's Theater," 5 May 1887, Police Department, folder 87, Licensing of Theaters, box 87-HAS-37, MP.

21. *Tribune*, 5 Mar. 1890, 13 Apr. 1890; *Sun*, 12 Feb. 1882; *Leslie's*, 12 May 1883; Jacob Riis,

*How the Other Half Lives* (New York, 1890), 94–95; Beck, *New York's Chinatown*, 139–41, 167 (Chinese exclusion); H. H. Kane, "Some Medico-Legal Aspects of Morphia-Taking," *Alienist and Neurologist* 3 (1882), 422–23 (Chinese exclusion); *Mazet Committee*, 2525 (features); Stephen Crane, "Opium's Varied Dreams" (1896), in Fredson Bowers, ed., *The Works of Stephen Crane: Tales, Sketches and Reports* (Charlottesville, Va., 1973), VIII:365–70; Williams, *Demon*, 30, 60, 63. For the emphasis on secrecy and privacy, see unmarked clippings, 25 July 1891, vol. 88; 11 Aug. 1899, vol. 183, both in DAS; Anonymous, *Secrets of New York* (Boston, 1896), 4, 9–11, located in Front Envelope, box 3, New York Series, WC. Chinatown dens offered a shell of opium, a pipe, and bunk for one dollar. Uptown dens charged as much as five dollars for the same. See *World* clipping, 4 Oct. 1885, vol. 13, DAS.

22. Unmarked clippings, 24, 25 July 1891 (West Thirty-ninth St.), vol. 88; *Herald* clipping, 2 July 1899 (Soubrette Row), vol. 182, both in DAS; Williams, *Demon*, 46–48 (pioneer), 60, 63; Byrnes, *Professional Criminals*, 385; Sworn Testimony of George A. McDermott, 24 Feb. 1882 (Cremorne), box 84-GWR-14, MP; *Sun*, 12 Feb. 1882 (Cremorne). On the erotic atmosphere, see unmarked clipping, 4 Oct. 1899, vol. 184, DAS; *Mazet Committee*, 2524; *Lexow Committee*, II:1577. On Chinese in the uptown opium trade, see unmarked clippings, 9, 14 Mar. 1883, vol. 9; unmarked clippings, 22 Dec. 1884, vol. 10; *Journal* clipping, 23 Jan. 1887, vol. 30, all in DAS; Williams, *Demon*, 135–37; Byrnes, *Professional Criminals*, 385; Capt. James Kealy to Inspector William Murray, 25 Nov. 1883, folder 89, Dept. of Police, box 85-EF-12, MP; People v. Tom Lee, Lee Sing et al., 1 May 1883, box 9903, SCC.

23. *Journal* and other unmarked clippings, 12 June 1890; unmarked clipping, 15 June 1890, both in vol. 74; unmarked clipping, 25 July 1891 (dainty women), vol. 88, all in DAS. On West Thirty-third Street (as well as West Twenty-eighth and Fifty-seventh Streets) having the "best-known joints" by the 1890s, see *Appleton's Dictionary of New York and Vicinity* (New York, 1898), 205; *World* and other unmarked clippings, 15 June 1890, vol. 74; unmarked clipping, 25 July 1891, vol. 88; *Commercial Advertiser* clipping, 28 Sept. 1891, vol. 90, all in DAS. On Hess's (alias Sam Hayes) arrests, see unmarked clipping, 4 Mar. 1887; *World* clippping, 5 Mar. 1887, vol. 32; *World* clipping, 3 Dec. 1887; *Star* and other clippings, 4 Dec. 1887; *Journal* clipping, 6 Dec. 1887; unmarked clipping, 8 Dec. 1887, all in vol. 42; unmarked clipping, 25 Dec. 1887, vol. 43, all in DAS; People v. Sidney Heyman, 14 Dec. 1887, folder 2746, box 288; People v. George B. Oliver and Charles A. Forth, 15 Dec. 1887, folder 2756, box 289, both in CGS.

24. Cornelius W. Willemse, *Behind the Green Lights* (New York, 1931), 159–60.

25. Appo, 36–38; Kane, "American Opium-Smokers," *Harper's Weekly*, 25 (24 Sept. 1881), 646; Kane, *Drugs That Enslave: The Opium, Morphine, Chloral and Hashisch Habits* (Philadelphia, 1881); and *Opium-Smoking in America and China* (New York, 1882); Williams, *Demon*, 50–51, 127.

26. Williams, *Demon*, 51, 127, 129, 132; Kane, "Chloral Hydrate: Chloral Delirium—Contra-Indications," *Philadelphia Medical Times* 11 (1881), 227; Kane, *Drugs That Enslave*, 18. On Kane's treatment program and his exaggerated claims of success, Kane, *The DeQuincey Home Method by Means of Which any Individual Can Cure Himself Promptly, Painlessly and Permanently of the Opium, Morphine or Chloral Habit and Alcoholic Inebriety* (New York, 1883).

27. Odell, *Annals*, 14:644, 15:158, 177, 725, 737; *NPG*, 24 Nov. 1894; unmarked clipping, 25

July 1891 (morphine use), vol. 88, DAS; Charles E. Terry and Mildred Pellens, *The Opium Problem* (New York, 1928), 74. On morphine and heroin replacing opium as the drug of choice in the underworld after 1890, see David T. Courtwright, *Dark Paradise: Opiate Addiction in America before 1940* (Cambridge, Mass., 1982), 2–3.

28. Beck, *New York's Chinatown*, 168–75. James McNally reportedly financed the Forty-sixth Street opium den run by Samuel "Sammy" Goldstein and Harry A. Hamberger. Hamberger previously ran another opulent opium den under the alias of Robert Howe (whose aliases included Ralph Howell, Harry Hamberg, and Harry DeFord) on West Thirty-ninth Street. See 24, 25 July 1891 clippings, vol. 88, DAS. Appo believed that the McNally-Hamberger opium den was on West Forty-second Street, so I inserted the correct address. See *Lexow Committee*, II:1659.

29. Appo, 30–31. Appo confused judges and arrests in this portion of his autobiography. He erroneously believed that he was sentenced by Recorder John J. Hackett, who served in that position from 1866 to 1878. In fact Hackett sentenced Appo to Sing Sing in 1874. Details of that case appear in chapter 4, note 1. In this arrest, Appo pleaded guilty and was sentenced to three and one half years in Sing Sing by Judge Solon B. Smyth on 25 Apr. 1882. See People v. Appo, 18 Apr. 1882, SCC. I have replaced Hackett's name with Smyth's.

## 12. "That Galling Yoke of Servitude"

1. Official reports denied that Sing Sing was plagued by epidemics between 1875 and 1884.

2. Appo, 33–34. Appo confused his second and third incarcerations in this part of his autobiography. Biglin was principal keeper of Sing Sing from 18 June 1876 to 1 April 1880, which coincided with Appo's second incarceration from 11 January 1877 to 13 October 1877 in Sing Sing and 14 October to 8 January 1879 in Clinton. See entry for George Wilson, 11 Jan. 1877, SSAR; entries for George A. Wilson on 13 Oct. 1877, 8 Jan. 1879, Diary of the Principal Keeper of Clinton Prison, NYSArc. Appo's third Sing Sing term extended from 26 April 1882 to 26 December 1884. See entry for 26 Apr. 1882, SSAR; 47, vol. 1, Executive Register of Discharges of Convicts by Commutation of Sentences (AO604), NYSArc; Frank Moss, *The American Metropolis* (New York, 1897), III: 128. On Biglin, see NYSPC, *Investigation of the State Prisons and Report Thereon, 1876* (Albany, 1877), 131; *Times*, 2 Apr. 1880. Appo misspelled Patrick Mackin's surname as "Macken." I have included the correct spelling hereafter. On Mackin's reputation for cruelty, see NYSA, *Testimony Taken Before the Assembly Committee on State Prisons in the Investigation of Sing Sing Prison*, AD 131 (Albany, 1882), 15, 103, 172–80 (hereafter *Investigation 1881*). On Martin Moran, see entry for 29 May 1877, 137, vol. 15, SSAR; Sing Sing admissions, 1877, vol. 6 (n.p.), Executive Register of Commitments to Prisons (AO603), NYSArc. I found no record of Greenfield.

3. *Times*, 2 Feb. 1871, 10 May 1881. For good conduct in prison, state law allowed inmate sentences to be shortened one month on each of the first two years, two months on third to fifth years, and four months on each remaining year over five. Good conduct in a seven-year sentence generated two years' and three months' commutation. See

PANY, *Twenty-fourth AR for 1868*, SD 10 (Albany, 1869), 153, 159, 163; *World* clipping, 16 Jan. 1887, vol. 30, DAS.

4. NYSPC, *Investigation of the State Prisons and Report Thereon, 1876* (Albany, 1877) (hereafter *Investigation 1876*), 2, 318–19, 637 (shanties), 654 (gambling); *World*, 25 Apr. 1874; *Times*, 2 Nov. 1874; *World*, 19 Jan. 1877; *Tribune*, 28 Mar. 1882 (hospital jobs); PANY, *Twenty-fourth AR*, 530 (hospital jobs), 656 (bookkeepers); NYSA, *Twenty-ninth AR of the Inspectors of State Prisons [for 1876]*, AD 14, 15–16; NYS, *Report of the State Commission on Prison Labor* (Albany, 1871), 6 (pamphlets); *Morning Journal* clippings, 3 Nov. 1889 (put up), vol. 67; 31 May 1891, vol. 86; 18 Jan. 1889, vol. 57; *Herald* clipping, 8 Nov. 1894, vol. 134, all in DAS. On opium and other drug smuggling in prison, see *Tribune*, 14 Dec. 1897; William Rosser Cobbe, *Doctor Judas: A Portrayal of the Opium Habit* (Chicago, 1895), 157–58. For specific privileges, "privileged convicts" and the inmate "aristocracy," see *Times*, 7 Sept. 1871; *Tribune*, 17 Jan. 1877; NYSPC, *Investigation 1876*, 12–15, 112–13, 197, 208, 211, 217, 244.

5. PANY, *Twenty-fourth AR*, 529, 656; NYSS, *Twentieth AR of the Inspectors of State Prisons [for 1867]*, SD 30 (Albany, 1868), 98 (pardon).

6. Rothman argues that a consensus of historians of the penitentiary subscribe to this interpretation. See David Rothman, *The Discovery of the Asylum: Social Order and Disorder in the New Republic* (Boston, 1971; rev. 1990), xxix.

7. PANY, *Twenty-fourth AR*, 627; NYSPC, *Investigation 1876*, 96, 143 (poor instruction), 605 (drinking); *Times*, 3 July 1865 (unfit guards), 9 May 1892 (no training); *Herald*, 9 Oct. 1871; NYSA, *Third AR of the Civil Service Commission of the State of New York*, AD 49 (Albany, 1886), 62.

8. NYSPC, *Investigation 1876*, 2–3 (unfit), 14–15, 96 (Smith), 105 (few instructions), 113, 114, 145 (uniforms), 654 (unfit); NYSSP, *AR for 1900* (Albany, 1901), 21; PANY, *Thirty-fifth AR for 1879* (Albany, 1880), 25 (salary); Lewis E. Lawes, *Twenty Thousand Years in Sing Sing* (New York, 1932), 18.

9. PANY, *Twenty-fourth AR*, 21, 527; NYSS, *Twenty-sixth AR of the Inspectors of State Prisons [for 1873]*, SD 5 (Albany, 1874), 16 (Hubbell, no experience); NYSPC, *Investigation 1876*, 6 (fitness), 109 (appointed by inspectors), 254 (85 percent); *Harper's Weekly*, 17 Apr. 1869; *Tribune*, 17 Jan. 1877; *Times*, 2 Feb. 1871, 9 Apr. 1871, 23 Apr. 1871; Frederick H. Wines, *Punishment and Reformation: A Study of the Penitentiary System* (New York, 1895 and 1919), 199; Rebecca Mary McLennan, "Citizens and Criminals: The Rise of the American Carceral State, 1890–1935" (Ph.D. diss., Columbia University, 1999), 76–79.

10. PANY, *Twenty-sixth AR for 1870*, SD 5 (Albany, 1871), 119 (Hubbell); NYSS, *Twenty-sixth AR of the Inspectors of State Prisons*, 16–17; NYSS, *Twenty-second AR of the Inspectors of State Prisons [for 1869]*, SD 71 (Albany, 1870), 17 (guard turnover); Lawes, *Twenty Thousand Years*, 18, 27 (stool pigeons, spies), 96 (Hubbell); *Tribune*, 13 Apr. 1875, 3 Oct. 1876 (dishonesty); *Times*, 7 Sept. 1871 (rotten), 9 Apr. 1871; NYSPC, *Investigation 1876*, 6–7 (politics), 135, 361 (Hubbell), 699–700; NYSA, *Report of Thomas Kirkpatrick, Inspector of State Prisons*, AD 93 (Albany, 1875), 1–13.

11. *Times*, 10 June 1876 (state law, 42 guards), 31 May 1885 (45 guards); *Harper's Weekly*, 3 Apr. 1869 (state law). Annual prison reports inconsistently gave the specific numbers of keepers and guards in New York's prisons. The ratios between the guard and keeper populations in Sing Sing were:

| | GUARDS | KEEPERS | TOTAL | RATIO | MALE INMATE POP. |
|---|---|---|---|---|---|
| 1868 | 42 | 53 | 95 | 1:12 | 1,100 |
| 1869 | 30 | 30 | 60 | | 1,338 |
| 1873 | 31 | | | | 1,237 |
| 1876 | 41 | 32 | 73 | 1:20 | 1,452 |
| 1877 | 42 | | | | 1,613 |
| 1878 | 24 | | | | 1,646 |
| 1885 | 45 | | | | 1,541 |
| 1887 | 25 | 43 | 68 | 1:21 | 1,425 |
| 1889 | 23 | 38 | 61 | 1:23 | 1,385 |
| 1893 | 36 | 41 | 77 | 1:17 | 1,275 |

Whenever possible these figures include principal keepers, hall keepers, yard keepers, kitchen keepers, and storekeepers. See NYSA, *Report of the Committee on State Prisons, of Their Investigations into the Causes of the Late Outbreaks in the Sing Sing Prison, AD 187* (Albany, 1869), 4; NYSS, *AR of the Inspectors of State Prisons* (Albany, 1869–76); NYSPC, *Investigation 1876*, 113, 153, 231, 269; NYSA, *AR of the Superintendent of State Prisons* (Albany, 1877–1893); NYSA, *AR of the Civil Service Commission* (Albany, 1887–1893); *Harper's Weekly*, 3 Apr. 1869; *Leslie's*, 16 Feb. 1878; *Tribune*, 14 Jan. 1880.

12. Appo, 9, 35, 89. Appo misspelled Biglin as "Bigbin."

13. NYSA, *Twenty-ninth AR of the Inspectors of State Prisons [for 1876]*, AD 14 (Albany, 1877), 16; NYSA, *First AR of the Superintendent of State Prisons [for 1877]*, AD 10 (Albany, 1878), 19; NYSA, *Second AR of the Superintendent of State Prisons [for 1878]*, AD 10 (Albany, 1879), 16–17, 30; *Leslie's*, 16 Feb. 1878. On Biglin, see entry for 22 Feb. 1869, Diary of the Principal Keeper, Clinton Prison (BO115), NYSArc (first Biglin appointment); *Times*, 11 June 1876; NYSPC, *Investigation 1876* (Albany, 1877), 103, 131, 673; *Times*, 2 Apr. 1880.

14. Appo, 89 (immorality); PANY, *Twenty-fourth AR*, 530 (immoral keepers); Havelock Ellis, *Studies in the Psychology of Sex* (Philadelphia, 1901, 1930), II:25–26; Clyde B. Vedder and Patricia G. King, *Problems of Homosexuality in Corrections* (Springfield, Ill., 1967), v (pariah topic); Joseph F. Fishman, *Sex in Prison: Revealing Sex Conditions in American Prisons* (New York, 1934), 57–75. Twentieth-century studies of prison homosexuality are highly inconsistent, with estimates ranging from 6 to 90 percent of all inmates. For a summary of the early literature, see Alice M. Propper, *Prison Homosexuality: Myth and Reality* (Lexington, Mass., 1981), 9–11.

15. *Times*, 7 Sept. 1871 (great abuses); NYSPC, *Investigation 1876* (Albany, 1877), 6 (degrading practices); NYSA, *Investigation 1881*, 22 (species), 114, 143 (immoral practices), 230. On the lockstep encouraging homosexual "play," see Fishman, *Sex in Prison*, 90; Propper, *Prison Homosexuality*, 9; Vedder and King, *Problems of Homosexuality*, 14.

16. Thomas Mott Osborne, *Society and Prisons: Some Suggestions for a New Penology* (New York, 1916), 141; Lawes, *Twenty Thousand Years*, 246–47; Louis Berg, *Revelations of a Prison Doctor* (New York, 1934), 140–43; Amos O. Squires, *Sing Sing Doctor* (Garden City, N.Y., 1937), 6.

17. NYSA, *Investigation 1881*, 114 (Morgan), 219 (social beings).

18. NYS, *Report on Prison Labor*, 6; NYSA, *Investigation 1881*, 213 (Henry, Makinson). On the perceived "dangers" of masturbation in twentieth-century prisons, see Fishman, *Sex in Prison*, 115–17. On the history of masturbation, see Jean Stengers, *Masturbation:*

*The History of a Great Terror* (New York, 2001); Thomas Laqueur, *Solitary Sex: A Cultural History of Masturbation* (New York, 2003).

19. Berg, *Revelations*, 138–51 (quote 147). For descriptions of teenagers five feet or less in height and under eighty pounds in weight, see entry for James Lyons, 28 May 1875, 278; entry for John Reilly, 19 Apr. 1876, 374, both in vol. 12, SSAR. On high rates of sexual assault in twentieth-century prisons, see A. J. Davis, "Sexual Assaults in the Philadelphia Prison System and Sheriff's Vans," *Trans-Action* 6 (1968), 3, quoted in Daniel Lockwood, *Prison Sexual Violence* (New York, 1980), 7.

20. ESP Inspectors, *57th AR for the Year 1886* (Philadelphia, 1887), 7–8; ESP Inspectors, *58th AR for the Year 1887* (Philadelphia, 1888), 139; ESP Inspectors, *59th AR for the Year 1888* (Philadelphia, 1889), 122. No similar information appeared in reports from 1889 to 1892.

21. My argument here builds on ideas developed in Richard C. Trexler, *Sex and Conquest: Gendered Violence, Political Order, and the European Conquest of the Americas* (Ithaca, N.Y., 1995).

22. On the Sing Sing stove and wire contract for Perry & Co., see NYSA, *[Fourth] AR of the Superintendent of State Prisons [for 1880]*, AD 13 (Albany, 1881), 19; *Times*, 10 Apr. 1878; NYSA, *Report of the Superintendent of State Prisons in Response to the Resolution of January 11, 1883*, AD 29 (Albany, 1883), 9; NYSA, *Report of the Committee on State Prisons Upon the Charges of the New York* Star *Against the Management of the Prisons of this State*, AD 121 (Albany, 1883), 11–12; NYSS, *Report of the Superintendent of State Prisons in Response to a Resolution of the Senate, Relative to Prison Labor*, SD 63 (Albany, 1882), 1–2; New York Superintendent of State Prisons, *AR for 1887* (Albany, 1888), 13. On Meredith, see unmarked clipping, 10 Aug. 1893, vol. 116; *Herald* clipping, 8 Nov. 1894, vol. 134; unmarked clipping, 15 Sept. 1891, vol. 90, all in DAS; *Herald*, 10 June 1891; *Times*, 11 June 1891; 16 Sept. 1891; 10, 11, 12, 15, 16, 17, 18 (quote), 19 Aug. 1893.

23. *Tribune*, 17 Jan. 1877; NYSPC, *Investigation 1876*, 13; NYSCC, *Special Report on Penal Institutions* (Albany, 1930), 8–9.

24. NYSPC, *Investigation 1876*, 137 (locksmiths), 155 (Gill, convicts as guards), 179 (marble and lime works), 180 (apothecaries), 240 (account books), 514 (gates), 619–20, 627 (account books).

25. *Sun* clipping, 26 Nov. 1886, vol. 28; *Sun* clipping, 20 Dec. 1886, vol. 29; *Morning Journal* clipping, 3 Nov. 1889, vol. 67; *Herald* clipping, 9 Nov. 1894 (run of the prison), vol. 134; *Star* clipping, 3 Feb. 1887, vol. 30, all in DAS; *People of the State of New York v. Henry J. Jaehne* (1886) 103 N.Y. 182; 8 N.E. 374; 1886 N.Y. LEXIS 1049. On Ward, see *Times*, 6 Oct. 1889, 10 Aug. 1893; unmarked clipping, 10 Aug. 1893, vol. 116, DAS.

26. *Morning Journal* clipping, 3 Nov. 1889 (easy position), vol. 67, DAS; *Times*, 13 Mar. 1882. On Hope, see *Investigation 1881*, 12–14; *Star* (?) clipping, 24 Jan. 1887, vol. 30; *Morning Journal* clipping, 3 Nov. 1889, vol. 67, all in DAS; Thomas Byrnes, *Professional Criminals of America* (New York, 1886), 80–82. For ongoing charges of corruption and privileges in Sing Sing, see *Times*, 25 Apr. 1893; unmarked clipping, 10 Sept. 1895, vol. 145; unmarked clipping, 14 July 1886, vol. 23; *Herald* clipping, 16 July 1886, vol. 23; *Morning Journal* clipping, 29 Oct. 1886, vol. 29; 10, 24, 29 Jan. 1887 clippings, vol. 30; *Morning Journal* clipping, 18 Jan. 1889, vol. 57; *Herald* clipping, 9 Nov. 1894, vol. 134; 10 Sept. 1895, vol. 145, all in DAS.

27. *NPG*, 1 Apr. 1882; *Tribune*, 28 Mar. 1882 (loaf); *Sun* clipping, 26 Nov. 1886, vol. 28; *Sun* clipping, 20 Dec. 1886, vol. 29; *Morning Journal* clipping, 3 Nov. 1889, vol. 67; unmarked clipping, 10 Aug. 1893, vol. 116; *Herald* clipping, 9 Nov. 1894, vol. 134; *Star* clipping, 3 Feb. 1887, vol. 30, all in DAS; *Times*, 13 Mar. 1882, 6 Oct. 1889, 10 Aug. 1893.

28. NYSPC, *Investigation 1876*, 8, 107; PANY, *Thirty-fifth AR*, 14; unmarked clipping, 16 July 1886, vol. 23; *Press* clipping, 10 July 1892 (butchers), vol. 100, both in DAS; *Times*, 31 May 1885. Some evidence indicates that Sing Sing officials employed a version of the weighing machine as early as 1873. See *Times*, 21 Aug. 1873; *Tribune*, 17 Jan. 1877; NYSS, *Twenty-sixth AR of the Inspectors of State Prisons [for 1873]*, SD 5 (Albany, 1874), 86. On paddling inmates while they were in the weighing machine, see PANY, *Thirty-fifth AR*, 14; *Herald* clipping, 16 July 1886, vol. 23; 14 Mar. 1887, vol. 33; *Morning Journal* clipping, 11 Aug. 1886, vol. 24; *Morning Journal* clipping, 18 Jan. 1889, vol. 57, all in DAS; *Tribune*, 17 July 1886.

29. NYSA, *Response to the Resolution of January 11, 1883*, 15; NYSPC, *Investigation 1876*, 8; *Herald* clipping, 16 July 1886, vol. 23; 14 Mar. 1887, vol. 33 (Cleveland); *Morning Journal* clipping, 18 Jan. 1889, vol. 57, all in DAS; *World*, 16 May 1920.

30. *Press* clipping, 10 July 1892, vol. 100; unmarked clippings, 27 Oct. 1892, 3 Nov. 1892; *Recorder* clippings, 28, 29 Oct. 1892, vol. 103, all in DAS. Connaughton was principal keeper from 4 Apr. 1883 to 1893. On his frequent use of the machine, see *Star* (?) clippings, 10 Jan. 1887, 24 Jan. 1887, all in vol. 30; *Press* clipping, 10 July 1892, vol. 100; unmarked clipping, 27 Oct. 1892, vol. 103; *Herald* clipping, 9 Nov. 1894, vol. 134; unmarked clipping, 10 Sept. 1895, vol. 145, all in DAS; *Tribune*, 17 July 1886.

31. *Morning Journal* clipping, 29 Oct. 1886, vol. 29, DAS.

32. *Investigation 1881*, 135; *Tribune*, 17 July 1886 (Ward), 29 Dec. 1881 (Brush; self-maiming); *Star* (?) clippings, 24, 29 Jan. 1887; *Sun* clipping, 7 Feb. 1887, all in vol. 30; unmarked clipping, 1 July 1886 (cut off fingers; iron on feet), vol. 22, all in DAS.

33. Appo may be referring to M. J. Tiernan, who was appointed keeper on 1 May 1878 and was still identified as a keeper as late as 1887. See NYSA, *Fourth Report of the Civil Service Commission* (Albany, 1887), 154.

34. "Ginger" Thompson could have been a number of people admitted to Sing Sing from New York during any of Appo's sentences. From 1874 to 1882, at least 43 inmates answered to the name of Thompson or Thomson. See vols. 6, 20, 21, Sing Sing Admissions, Executive Register of Commitments to Prisons (AO603), NYSArc.

35. Appo, 33–35.

36. Ibid., 9–11, 51–52, 65–68, 80–81, 88–89, 91–93; PANY, *AR for 1868*, 541; NYSS, *AR of the Inspectors of State Prisons [for 1871]*, 145–46.

37. *Investigation 1881*, 88, 101 (attempted suicides), 131 (Smith), 206–8; NYSA, *Report Upon the Charges of the New York* Star, 2. A highly critical view of Sing Sing's management appears in NYSA, *Minority Report of the Committee on State Prisons Upon the Charges of the New York* Star *Against the Management of the Prisons of this State*, AD 122 (Albany, 1883). The Treadway letter was later suppressed during the inquest. See *Morning Journal* clipping, 3 Nov. 1889, vol. 67, DAS. On reports of suicides, see *Morning Journal* clipping, 13 July 1886; unmarked clipping, 16 July 1886, both in vol. 23; unmarked clipping, 1 July 1886, vol. 22; *Star* (?) clipping, 24 Jan. 1887; *Sun* clipping, 7 Feb. 1887, both in vol. 30, all in DAS. On Sing Sing punishments and work making

inmates suicidal or insane, see *Investigation 1881*, 95–96, 128–31, 222–29; *Herald*, 23 Feb. 1882; unmarked clipping, 1 July 1886, vol. 22; *World* clipping, 9 Oct. 1886, vol. 26; *Herald* clipping, 14 Mar. 1887, vol. 33, all in DAS; *Times*, 3 Aug. 1891; entry for 23 Feb. 1886; entries between 1 Jan. 1886 and 8 Mar. 1887, vol. 5, Warden's Daily Journals, Prison Administration Records, ESP; Report of the Prison Labor Reform Commission quoted in *Times*, 5 Mar. 1887, vol. 32, DAS.

38. *Investigation 1881*, 211 (beats), 218 (beats); *Times*, 16 Aug. 1891 (brutal ruffians), 9 Sept. 1880 (under punishment).

39. Appo, 92 (the Butcher); *Investigation 1881*, 204 (Barber); NYSA, *Response to the Resolution of January 11, 1883*, 14 (Brush). During those same years (except for 1890), the inmate mortality rate in all New York prisons was usually lower than the statewide rate. The mortality rates of New York State and the three male prisons in census years were:

| Year | Inmate Deaths | Inmate Population | Inmate Deaths Per 1,000 | NYS Deaths Per 1,000 |
|---|---|---|---|---|
| 1870 | 30 | 2,526 | 11.88 | 15.77 |
| 1880 | 33 | 2,936 | 11.24 | 17.38 |
| 1890 | 74 | 3,488 | 21.22 | 15.17 |
| 1900 | 35 | 3,376 | 10.37 | |

See U.S. Census Office, *Population of the United States in 1860* (Washington, D.C., 1864), I:327; U.S. Census Office, *Statistics of the United States in 1860* (Washington, D.C., 1866), IV:xviii, xx, 3; U.S. Census Office, *Ninth Census of the U.S.: Vital Statistics* (Washington, D.C., 1872), II:3 (N.Y.S., 1850–70); U.S. Census Office, *Report on the Mortality and Vital Statistics of the U.S., as Returned at the Tenth Census, 1880* (Washington, D.C., 1885), XI:xx–xxi, 3; U.S. Census Office, *Tenth Census of the U.S.: Report on the Social Statistics of Cities* (Washington, D.C., 1886), I:533; U.S. Census Office, *Statistics of the Population of the United States at the Tenth Census* (Washington, D.C., 1883), I:3; U.S. Census Office, *Report on the Population of the United States at the Eleventh Census: 1890* (Washington, D.C., 1895), I:370–71, 395, 398, 471; U.S. Census Office, *Compendium of the Eleventh Census: 1890* (Washington, D.C., 1894), II:10; U.S. Census Office, *Twelfth Census of the United States Taken in the Year 1900* (Washington, D.C., 1901), I:lxxxii, 31.

40. The New York State mortality statistics in 1880 were:

| | Total | Male | Female | M.< 10 | F.<10 | NYS Pop. (male) |
|---|---|---|---|---|---|---|
| NYS | 88,332 | 45,952 | 42,380 | 20,215 | 17,215 | 5,082,871 (2,505,322) |

Nationwide, 67 percent (260,628) of all male deaths were boys five years old or less. See U.S. Bureau of the Census, *Report on the Mortality and Vital Statistics of the U.S., as Returned at the Tenth Census, 1880* (Washington, D.C., 1885), XI:xxvii, 10. In New York City from 1850 to 1865, more than 50 percent of all children died before the age of five. See Metropolitan Board of Health, *Annual Report* (New York, 1866), 10; John Duffy, *A History of Public Health in New York City, 1625–1866* (New York, 1968), 578–79.

41. The precise figures on insanity were:

| Year | Hospitalized Insane in US | Insane per Thousand | Hospitalized Insane in NY | Insane per Thousand |
|------|------|------|------|------|
| 1880 | 91,959 | 1.83 | 14,055 | 2.76 |
| 1890 | 106,485 | 1.70 | 17,846 | 2.97 |
| 1903 | 150,151 | 1.86 | 26,176 | 3.39 |

See U.S. Bureau of the Census, *Insane and Feeble-Minded in Hospitals and Institutions, 1904* (Washington, D.C., 1906), 9.

42. See appendixes 3–5.

43. NYSA, *Twenty-seventh AR of the Inspectors*, 94 (Smith); *Morning Journal* clipping, 3 Nov. 1889 (poor record keeping), vol. 67, DAS; NYSSP, *AR for 1887* (Albany, 1888), 105 (Hoxsie); NYSSP, *AR for 1893* (Albany, 1894), 181 (Ransom).

44. New York Superintendent of State Prisons, *AR for 1888* (Albany, 1889), 49 (Tombs); NYSSP, *AR for 1889* (Albany, 1890), 12, 43–44; *Times*, 4 Feb. 1889 (doubling up); *Tribune*, 12 Aug. 1894 (doubling up).

45. NYSA, *Second AR of the Superintendent of State Prisons*, 23–25; NYSA, *[Third] AR of the Superintendent of State Prisons*, 24. The figures are representative of other years. See NYSA, *First AR of the Superintendent of State Prisons*, 31–32; NYSA, *Twenty-ninth AR of the Inspectors of State Prisons [for 1876]*, AD 14 (Albany, 1877), 112. On the unhealthy conditions in the stove factory, see *Investigation 1881*, 18. In the workshops inmates working in the slate shop accounted for the largest number of applicants (6,935 of 20,617) and represented 34 percent of all applicants. Laundry workers like Appo accounted for 27 percent (5,504 of 20, 617), followed by the buckle (3,403) and shoe (2,900) shop workers. See NYSA, *Twenty-eighth AR of the Inspectors of State Prisons [for 1875]*, AD 11 (Albany, 1876), 109–10; NYSPC, *Investigation 1876*, 177, 180.

46. *Tribune*, 12 Aug. 1894; Wines, *Punishment and Reformation*, 394.

47. This literature is enormous. The most recent overview is Norval Morris and David J. Rothman, eds., *The Oxford History of the Prison* (New York, 1995). Other important studies are identified in Timothy J. Gilfoyle, " 'America's Greatest Criminal Barracks': The Tombs and the Experience of Criminal Justice in New York City, 1838–1897," *Journal of Urban History* 29 (2003), 555, note 59.

48. On the decline of torture as a public spectacle, see Michel Foucault, *Discipline and Punish: The Birth of the Prison*, Alan Sheridan, trans. (New York, 1977), 7–11.

49. Ibid., 55.

50. Lewis E. Lawes, *Life and Death in Sing Sing* (Garden City, N.Y., 1928), 59 (WWI vet); Orlando Figes, "Reconstructing Hell," *New York Review of Books*, 12 June 2003 (gulag).

51. Appo, 91.

52. Appo, 35, 91–92. Chaplain Silas W. Edgerton's name was spelled "Edgerton" and "Edgarton" in official reports.

53. Appo, 35, 91–92; *Tribune*, 23 Feb. 1883 (drunk, profane); *Morning Journal* clipping, 3 Nov. 1889 (hurried), vol. 67, DAS.

54. George Appo, "A Convict's Grave," undated, box 32, SPC Papers.

55. Appo, 35 (twenty-fifth gallery); *Press* clipping, 28 June 1891 (twenty-fifth gallery), vol. 87, DAS; NYSPC, *Investigation 1876*, 641–42 (no funerals).

56. Appo, 89–90 (many scenes, degenerates), 93 (galling yoke). Appo spelled McCormick "McCormack."

## 13. DANNY DRISCOLL AND THE WHYOS

1. Appo, 93. I found several individuals named "Thomas Tobin" in police, court, and newspaper records, but was unable to determine which was Appo's acquaintance. Driscoll and Lyons are briefly mentioned in Frank Moss, *The American Metropolis* (New York, 1897), III: 108, 118, 141; Herbert Asbury, *The Gangs of New York* (New York, 1927), 228–29. On the confusion of Daniel Lyons (1857–87), a pickpocket, member of the Whyo gang, and associate of Driscoll, with a different Daniel Lyons, who shot and killed the athlete Joseph Quinn in 1887, see Timothy J. Gilfoyle, "Scorsese's *Gangs of New York*: Why Myth Matters," *Journal of Urban History* 29 (2003), note 23.

2. Unmarked clipping, 27 June 1886, vol. 22; *Herald* (?) clipping, 21 July 1887, vol. 38, both in DAS.

3. Unmarked clippings, 29 Sept. 1886, 1 Oct. 1886 (swagger), all in vol. 26; unmarked clipping, 27 June 1886, vol. 22; unmarked clipping, 21 July 1887 (every evil), vol. 38, all in DAS.

4. On Driscoll's birth in England in 1858, see interment list for Bridget Waters, sec. 8, range 50, plot CC, grave 15, Calvary Cemetery, Woodside, N.Y.; *Sun*, 25 Jan. 1888 (born 1856); People v. Driscoll and William Harris, 26 June 1883 (born 1863), box 105, folder 1124, CGS. On "Apple Mary," see unmarked clipping, 27 June 1886 (11 Pell St.), vol. 22; unmarked clipping, 24 Sept. 1891, vol. 90, both in DAS.

5. People v. Wallace, 9 May 1874; People v. Wallace, 15 Nov. 1876 (three years in Sing Sing), both in DAP; *World*, 24 Jan. 1888 (1870 and 1873 convictions; 18-month sentence for watch); entry on 8 Mar. 1875, 157 (excise violation), vol. 122, MGS; People v. Daniel Driscoll, 5 Mar. 1875 (excise violation), DAP. In a later indictment when Driscoll was past his twentieth birthday, he listed his occupation as "newsdealer," possibly indicating earlier work as a newsboy. See People v. Driscoll, 10, 11 Aug. 1881, box 44, folder 517, CGS. On Driscoll and his gang associated with pickpocketing, see the arrests of 1884 in *Sun* clipping, 6 Oct. 1884, vol. 9; unmarked clipping, 24 Sept. 1888, vol. 53, all in DAS.

6. Unmarked clippings, 29 Sept. 1886 (scars), vol. 26; unmarked clipping, 27 June 1886 (40 or 50 affrays), vol. 22; unmarked clipping, 21 July 1887, vol. 38; *Tribune* and *World* clippings, 21, 23 Jan. 1888 (five to seven bullets), vol. 44, all in DAS; Hutchins Hapgood, ed., *The Autobiography of a Thief* (New York, 1903), 280 (no anesthesia).

7. On the 1881 incident, see entries for 18 July 1881, 93, vol. 139; for 10 Aug. 1881, 154; for 11 Aug. 1881, 166; for 17 Aug. 1881, 194, all in MGS; People v. Driscoll, 10, 11 Aug. 1881, box 44, folder 517, CGS; *World*, 24 Jan. 1888. On the 1883 incident, see entries for 26 June 1883 and 3 July 1883, 76, 123, vol. 144, roll 44, MGS; People v. Daniel J. Driscoll and William Harris, 26 June 1883, box 9904, location 106034, SCC; People v. Driscoll and William Harris, 26 June 1883, box 105, folder 1124, CGS; unmarked clipping, 23 Jan. 1888, vol. 44, DAS.

8. On Green, see 27, 28 June, 1, 2 July 1886, vol. 22; 23, 24 Jan. 1888, vol. 44, all in DAS. On Ohm, see *Sun* clipping, 6 Oct. 1884, vol. 9, DAS; Police Dept. Memo, 27 Sept.

1884, in People v. Daniel J. Driscoll, 8 July 1886, box 225, folder 2209, CGS (hereafter People v. Driscoll, 1886). This case, when I examined it, was unprocessed and found in box 9948, location 106079, New York Supreme Court, DAP. On Driscoll's support from local politicians, see unmarked clipping, 27 June 1886, vol. 22, DAS.

9. *Sun* clipping, 6 Oct. 1884, vol. 9, DAS (27 arrests, 12 in 1884); unmarked clipping, 27 June 1886 (San Antonio), vol. 22; unmarked clipping, 30 Sept. 1886 (6 arrests, 4 prison terms), vol. 26, all in DAS; entry for 18 Jan. 1885, p. 98, vol. 32, Drummond Papers; Hapgood, *Autobiography*, 280–81 (San Antonio). Many of these arrests and incidents are recounted in unmarked clippings, 27, 28 June, 1, 2 July 1886, vol. 22; 23, 24 Jan. 1888, vol. 44, all in DAS. On Driscoll's family and personal life, see unmarked clipping, 27 June 1886, vol. 22, DAS; Deposition of Mary Driscoll, 3 Jan. 1888, in People v. Driscoll, 1886.

10. On the scattered residences of Whyo gang members, see *Sun* clipping, 15 Sept. 1884 (Oh! Why!), vol. 9; *Herald*, 29 July 1884; unmarked clippings, 27, 28 June, 1, 2 July 1886, vol. 22; unmarked clippings, 15 Aug. 1887, vol. 39; unmarked clippings, 23, 24 Jan. 1888 (Oh! Why!), both in vol. 44; *Herald* clipping, 29 July 1884, vol. 38; unmarked clipping (pickpockets), 24 Sept. 1888, vol. 53, all in DAS.

11. On the racially mixed Baxter Street area, see unmarked clipping, 1 July 1886, vol. 22; *World* clipping, 19 Mar. 1888, vol. 46; *Star* clippings, 25 Dec. 1888 (color line; Simmons), 26 Dec. 1888 (mongrel population); *Morning Journal* clipping, 24 Dec. 1888 (Simmons), all in vol. 56, all in DAS; *Tribune*, 26 Dec. 1877 (Irish girls); Helen Campbell, Thomas Knox, and Thomas Byrnes, *Darkness and Daylight: or, Lights and Shadows of New York Life* (Hartford, Conn., 1891), 471–72 (Simmons's saloon at 47 Baxter Street). On racial and ethnic integration in twentieth-century gangs and the nineteenth-century criminal underworld, see Roger Lane, *Roots of Violence in Black Philadelphia, 1860–1900* (Cambridge, Mass., 1986), 28–32; Eric Schneider, *Vampires, Dragons and Egyptian Kings: Youth Gangs in Postwar New York* (Princeton, N.J., 1999) 83–105.

12. Unmarked clippings, 27 June 1886, vol. 22, DAS. On McCarty's boardinghouse at 163 Hester Street as a house of prostitution, see Recorder's Charge, 13; Testimony of Carrie Wilson before Coroner, 1 July 1886; Judgment of C. J. Ruger, N.Y. Court of Appeals, 29 Nov. 1887, p. 2, all in People v. Driscoll, 1886. Newspaper and other accounts spelled McCarty's name as "McCarthy." He signed his name as "McCarty," and I have used that here. See Deposition of John McCarthy [*sic*], 27 June 1886, in People v. Driscoll, 1886.

13. Deposition of John Mulholland, 27 June 1886, in People v. Driscoll, 1886. On McCarty's criminal record, see entry for 23 June 1887, 532–34 (counterfeiting); entries for 25 and 29 June 1887, 550, all in vol. 38, Drummond Papers; unmarked clipping, 3 Dec. 1887, vol. 42; *World* clipping, 19 Mar. 1888; unmarked clipping, 30 Sept. 1886, all in DAS.

14. John Mulholland Deposition and Peter Monahan Deposition, both 26 June 1886; testimony of Emanuel Devos and Peter Monahan, both in Coroner's Report, 1 July 1886, all in People v. Driscoll, 1886; unmarked clippings, 2 July 1886, vol. 22; unmarked clippings, 29 Sept. 1886, vol. 26, all in DAS.

15. Unmarked clippings, 30 Sept. 1886, vol. 26, DAS; *Sun, World*, 24 Jan. 1888.

16. People v. Driscoll, 1886; entry for 25 June 1887, 550 (Garrity a prostitute), vol. 38,

Drummond Papers; *World*, 24 Jan. 1888 (worshipper); unmarked clippings, 27 June 1886 (Garrity respectable; latest love), vol. 22, DAS.

17. Unmarked clipping, 29, 30 Sept. 1886, vol. 26, DAS; Richard H. Rovere, *Howe & Hummel: Their True and Scandalous History* (New York, 1947), 6, 25, 47.

18. Unmarked clippings, 29 Sept. 1886, vol. 26, DAS.

19. Testimony of Margaret Sullivan, undated, in People v. Driscoll, 1886; unmarked clippings, 30 Sept. 1886 (quote), vol. 26, DAS; *Sun, World*, 24 Jan. 1888.

20. Driscoll's testimony is in unmarked clippings, 30 Sept. 1886, vol. 26, DAS.

21. Ibid.

22. Unmarked clipping, 1 Oct. 1886 (wildfire, bated breath); unmarked clippings, 9 Oct. 1886, all in vol. 26, DAS.

23. Asbury, *Gangs*, xvi–xviii (natural destiny), 244 (terrorists), 246 (criminal); Jacob Riis, *How the Other Half Lives: Studies Among the Tenements of New York* (1890), David Leviatin, ed. (New York, 1996), 210–11; Jacob Riis, *A Ten Years' War* (New York, 1900), 139–68; Jacob Riis, *The Battle with the Slum* (New York, 1902), 226–55.

24. Asbury, *Gangs*, 63, 225; Riis, *How the Other Half Lives*, 209–10 (worst depravity). On the Whyos in Bottle Alley, see Riis, *A Ten Years' War*, 202; Riis, *Battle with the Slum*, 307–09.

25. *Truth* clipping, 24 Aug. 1884; *World* clipping, 25 Aug. 1884, both in vol. 8; *Sun* clipping, 8, 15, 20 Sept. 1884 (nearly every street), vol. 9, all in DAS. The literature on gangs and juvenile delinquency, and their relation to more organized forms of crime, is voluminous but concentrated on the twentieth century. See Frederic M. Thrasher, *The Gang: A Study of 1,313 Gangs in Chicago* (Chicago, 1927); William Foote Whyte, *Street Corner Society: The Social Structure of an Italian Slum* (Chicago, 1943); Albert K. Cohen, *Delinquent Boys: The Culture of the Gang* (Glencoe, Ill., 1955); Lewis Yablonsky, *The Violent Gang* (New York, 1966); Richard A. Cloward and Lloyd B. Ohlin, *Delinquency and Opportunity: A Theory of Delinquent Gangs* (New York, 1960); Terry Williams, *The Cocaine Kids: The Inside Story of a Teenage Drug Ring* (Reading, Mass., 1989); Martin Sanchez Jankowski, *Islands in the Street: Gangs and American Urban Society* (Berkeley, Calif., 1991); Schneider, *Vampires, Dragons and Egyptian Kings*.

26. NYSL, *Annual Report of the Board of Commissioners of the Metropolitan Police* (Albany, 1864), 9; NPG, 18 Feb. 1880; Riis, *Battle with the Slum*, 231.

27. Edwin G. Burrows and Mike Wallace, *Gotham: A History of New York City to 1898* (New York, 1999), 409–15, 601–45, 1020–32, 1023 (25 percent), 1185–91.

28. *Sun* clippings, 8, 15 Sept. 1884, vol. 9, DAS; Moss, *American Metropolis*, III:275. On municipal police officers and expenditures, see the table in Timothy J. Gilfoyle, "Street-Rats and Gutter-Snipes: Child Pickpockets and Street Culture in New York City, 1850–1900," *Journal of Social History* 37 (2004), note 46.

29. These various names appeared in *Mail & Express*, 9 Sept. 1884; *Sun* clipping, 8, 15, 20 Sept. 1884, all in vol. 9; *Herald* clipping, 29 July 1887, vol. 38; *World* clipping, 19 Mar. 1888, vol. 46; unmarked clipping, 19 Aug. 1895, vol. 144, all in DAS.

30. Unmarked clipping, 19 Aug. 1895, vol. 144; *Herald* clipping, 29 July 1887 (curse), vol. 38; *World* clipping, 19 July 1888 (lushes), vol. 51; unmarked clipping, 26 Oct. 1898, vol. 173, all in DAS; Cornelius F. Cahalane, *Police Practice and Procedure* (New York, 1914), 20–21 (lush workers).

31. *Sun* clippings, 15 Sept. 1884; 8 Sept. 1884 (unfavorably situated; few gangs in Tender-

loin), vol. 9; *Herald* clipping, 29 July 1887 (no gangs), vol. 38, all in DAS; Walling, *Recollections*, 138–43. On river thieves, see *NPG*, 1 July 1882; *NPG*, 9 Mar. 1879, 1 July 1882; Charles Sutton, *The New York Tombs: Its Secrets and Its Mysteries* (New York, 1874), 471–73; *Sun* clippings, 15 Sept. 1884, 14 Sept. 1884, 8 Sept. 1884, vol. 9; *Herald* clipping, 29 July 1887, vol. 38, all in DAS. On slaughterhouse gangs, see *Truth* clipping, 24 Aug. 1884, vol. 8; *Recorder* clipping, 26 Aug. 1893, vol. 118, DAS; Moss, *American Metropolis*, III:104–5. On adult males in waterfront gangs, see *World* clipping, 19 Mar. 1888, vol. 46, DAS; *Tribune*, 19 July 1887.

32. Undated Report of Capt. E. O. Smith [1890?], box 90-SWL-48, MP; *Sun* clippings, 8 and 20 Sept. 1884, vol. 9; *Sun* (?) clipping, 13 May 1888, vol. 49; *Press* clipping, 16 Apr. 1893 (cotton theft more than $50,000), vol. 110, all in DAS; *Leslie's*, 23 Feb. 1878.

33. *Sun* clipping, 20 Sept. 1884, vol. 9, DAS.

34. See note 32 above.

35. *Sun* clipping, 6 Oct. 1884 (pothouse); *Mail & Express* clipping, 9 Sept. 1884, both in vol. 9; *Truth* clipping, 24 Aug. 1884, vol. 8; *World* clipping, 19 Mar. 1888, vol. 46; *Star* clipping, 2 May 1889, vol. 60, all in DAS; Riis, *How the Other Half Lives*, 211. On the tension between judges and police, see *Times*, 26 June 1895; *Herald*, 29 July 1884, in vol. 38, DAS; Walling, *Recollections*, 600; William McAdoo, *Guarding a Great City* (New York, 1906), 326, 269–72.

36. *Sun* clipping, 6, 11 Oct. 1884 (secured release), vol. 9; *World* clipping, 21 Jan. 1888, vol. 44; *World* clipping, 5 Feb. 1888, vol. 45; *Star* clipping, 2 May 1889 (Whyo's pull), vol. 60, all in DAS; *World*, 24 Jan. 1888. On colonizing, see chapter 9, note 9. The best study of Walsh is Tyler Anbinder, *Five Points* (New York, 2001), 269–73, 280, 328, 335–36.

37. Unmarked clippings, 28 Sept. 1886, 30 Sept. 1886, 1 Oct. 1886 (Fellows), all in vol. 26; unmarked clipping, 3 Dec. 1887, vol. 42, all in DAS.

38. Unmarked clippings, 24, 23 Jan. 1888, vol. 44; *World* clipping, 19 Mar. 1888 (rejoiced), vol. 46, all in DAS.

39. *Sun* clipping, 8 Sept. 1884 (hero), vol. 9; unmarked clipping, 24 Jan. 1888 (successful thief), vol. 44, all in DAS; Campbell, *Darkness*, 492; *World*, 24 Jan. 1888; McAdoo, *Guarding a Great City*, 129.

40. *Truth* clipping, 24 Aug. 1884 (bricks), vol. 8; unmarked clippings, 23, 24 Jan. 1888 (bricks), vol. 44; *Sun* clipping, 15 Sept. 1884, vol. 9, all in DAS; Cornelius W. Willemse, *Behind the Green Lights* (New York, 1931), 39–40 (bricks); Moss, *American Metropolis*, III:103; Arthur Pember, *The Mysteries and Miseries of the Great Metropolis* (New York, 1874), 1–29.

41. Unmarked clipping, 23 Jan. 1888 (policeman's head), vol. 44, DAS. A large literature exists linking violence in northern cities with evolving conceptions of male honor. See especially Elliott J. Gorn, *The Manly Art: Bare-Knuckle Prize Fighting in America* (Ithaca, N.Y., 1986); Monkkonen, *Murder in New York*.

42. Unmarked clipping, 19 July 1887 (terrorism), vol. 38; *Morning Journal* (?) clipping, 7 Aug. 1892 (terrorized by gangs), vol. 101, both in DAS; note 6 above (Driscoll's scars and bullets). For accounts that the United States specifically and Western society in general became less violent from 1750 to 1900, see Norbert Elias, *The Civilising Process* (1939; reprint, Oxford, England, 1982); Louis P. Masur, *Rites of Execution:*

*Capital Punishment and the Transformation of American Culture, 1776–1865* (New York, 1989).

43. *Herald* clipping, 29 July 1884, vol. 38; *Sun* clipping, 8 Sept. 1884, vol. 9, both in DAS; Walling, *Recollections*, 600. For similar comments, see *Sun* clipping, 15 Sept. 1884, vol. 9, DAS; *Sun*, 8 Jan. 1888. On police brutality, see *Times* clipping, 4 Apr. 1890, vol. 72; *Press* clipping, 30 May 1892, vol. 99, both in DAS; *Lexow Committee*, III:2826; IV:3598; Lincoln Steffens, *The Autobiography of Lincoln Steffens* (New York, 1931), I:207; *Leslie's*, 7 Aug. 1876.

44. *Truth* clipping, 24 Aug. 1884, vol. 8, DAS.

45. See note 10 above (on geographical origins); unmarked clippings, 1 July 1886, vol. 22; 24 Sept. 1888, vol. 53, DAS. On the diversity and high degree of organization of the Whyos, see *Sun* clipping, 15 Sept. 1884, vol. 9, DAS. On the Whyos' association with prostitution and pimping, see *Herald*, 29 July 1884, vol. 38; unmarked clippings, 23 Jan. 1888, vol. 44, all in DAS; *Sun*, 29 Jan. 1888. On Driscoll counterfeiting, see entry for 18 Jan. 1885, 98, vol. 32, Drummond Papers. On running a saloon in San Antonio, see unmarked clipping, 27 June 1886, vol. 22, DAS. On Danny Driscoll; his wife, Mary; and Owen Bruen denying either the existence of or membership in the Whyos, see Deposition of Daniel Driscoll, 4 Jan. 1888; Deposition of Mary Driscoll, 3 Jan. 1888, all in People v. Driscoll, 1886; *Morning Journal* (?), 10 July 1887, vol. 37; unmarked clippings, 24 Jan. 1888 (Mary Driscoll), vol. 44; unmarked clipping, 30 Sept. 1886 (Bruen), vol. 26; unmarked clippings, 24 Jan. 1888 (Bruen), vol. 44; unmarked clipping, 25 Feb. 1888 (Bruen), vol. 45, all in DAS. During Driscoll's trial, under intense questioning by Fellows, Bruen admitted attending meetings of the Whyos. See unmarked clipping, 30 Sept. 1886, vol. 26, DAS.

46. *World*, 24 Jan. 1888; unmarked clippings, 15 Aug. 1887 (Brooklyn, Tenth Ave.), vol. 39; unmarked clippings, 27, 28 June, 1, 2 July 1886, vol. 22; 23, 24 Jan. 1888, vol. 44, all in DAS. On pickpockets and "cannon mobs" referring to their criminal activities as "rackets" prior to 1930, see John O'Connor, *Broadway Racketeers* (New York, 1928), 31, 50; Edwin Hardin Sutherland, *The Professional Thief: By a Professional Thief* (Chicago, 1937). On the beginnings of organized or "syndicate" crime with Paul Kelly's Five Points gang or Monk Eastman's Lower East Side gang in the 1890s, or with Italian "criminal" associations like the "Black Hand," the Mafia, or the Cosa Nostra, see Nelli, *Business of Crime*, 106–8; Craig Thompson and Allen Raymond, *Gang Rule in New York: The Story of a Lawless Era* (New York, 1940), 354–63; Donald R. Cressey, *Theft of the Nation: The Structure of Crime in America* (New York, 1969); Nicholas Gage, ed., *Mafia, U.S.A.* (Chicago, 1972); Stephen Fox, *Blood and Power: Organized Crime in Twentieth-Century America* (New York, 1989). Good critiques of this literature are Alan A. Block, *Space, Time and Organized Crime* (New Brunswick, N.J., 1994); Anton Blok, *The Mafia of a Sicilian Village, 1860–1960: A Study of Violent Peasant Entrepreneurs* (New York, 1974); R. T. Naylor, *Wages of Crime: Black Markets, Illegal Finance, and the Underworld Economy* (Ithaca, N.Y., 2002).

47. *Sun*, 11 Feb. 1887, in vol. 30, DAS.

48. Deposition of Daniel Driscoll, 4 Jan. 1888; Deposition of Mary Driscoll, 3 Jan. 1888, and corroboration by Patrick Foster, 30 Dec. 1887; Carrie Wilson Testimony, 11 Jan. 1888, all in People v. Driscoll, 1886; *Morning Journal* (?), 10 July 1887, vol. 37; *Star* clippings, 14 and 17 Jan. 1888, vol. 44, all in DAS.

49. *Tribune* and *World* clippings, 21, 22 Jan. 1888, vol. 44, DAS; *World*, 24 Jan. 1888.
50. Judgment of C. J. Ruger, N.Y. Court of Appeals, 29 Nov. 1887, p. 11, in People v. Driscoll, 1886; unmarked clippings, 30 Nov. 1887, vol. 42, DAS.
51. *World*, 24 Jan. 1888 (sacrificed); *Sun*, 29 Jan. 1888 (150 men); unmarked clippings, 19, 21 Jan. 1888; *Sun, Morning Journal* clippings, 25 Jan. 1888 (death threats to Walsh), all in vol. 44, DAS; *NPG*, 24 Jan. 1881 (strange passion).
52. Unmarked clippings, 17–24 Jan. 1888, vol. 44, DAS.
53. *World*, 24 Jan. 1888 (Good-bye Owen; Walsh); unmarked clipping, 23 Jan. 1888 (scapular), vol. 44, DAS.
54. *Sun*, 24 Jan. 1888 (desperate); *World*, 24 Jan. 1888 (poem, assassin); *Herald* (?) clipping, 24 Jan. 1888 (stunted), vol. 44, DAS.
55. *World*, 24 Jan. 1888; *Herald* (?) clipping, 24 Jan. 1888, vol. 44, DAS.
56. *Sun, Morning Journal* clippings, 25 Jan. 1888, vol. 44; unmarked clipping, 17 Aug. 1887, vol. 39, all in DAS. On Driscoll's burial in an unmarked grave, see interment list for Bridget Waters, sec. 8, range 50, plot CC, grave 15, Calvary Cemetery, Woodside, N.Y.
57. *Morning Journal* clipping, 10 Oct. 1886 (bandit chieftain), in vol. 26, DAS. The literature on social bandits is extensive. Especially see Eric Hobsbawm, *Bandits* (New York, 1981); Eric Hobsbawm, *Primitive Rebels: Studies in Archaic Forms of Social Movement in the Nineteenth and Twentieth Centuries* (New York, 1959); Blok, *Mafia of a Sicilian Village,* Blok, "The Peasant and the Brigand: Social Banditry Reconsidered," *Comparative Studies in History and Society* 14 (1972), 494–505; Richard White, "Outlaw Gangs of the Middle Border: American Social Bandits," *Western Historical Quarterly* 12 (1981), 387–408; Paul Kooistra, *Criminals as Heroes: Structure, Power and Identity* (Bowling Green, Ohio, 1989); T. J. Stiles, *Jesse James: The Last Rebel of the Civil War* (New York, 2002), 381–95.
58. *Herald* clipping, 2 Oct. 1886, in vol. 26, DAS.
59. *Mail & Express* clipping, 9 Sept. 1884 (Solon Smith), vol. 9, DAS. On the decline of gang influence on elections, see unmarked clipping, 19 Aug. 1895, vol. 144; unmarked clipping, 26 Oct. 1898, vol. 173, DAS; Norman Thomas and Paul Blanshard, *What's the Matter with New York?* (New York, 1932), 79–91; Anbinder, *Five Points,* 333; Michael Kaplan, "The World of the B'hoys: Urban Violence and the Political Culture of Antebellum New York City, 1825–1860" (Ph.D. thesis, New York University, 1996), 93.
60. *Morning Journal* clipping, 10 Oct. 1886, in vol. 26, DAS.

## 14. EASTERN STATE PENITENTIARY

1. Flimflam was a confidence scheme that relied on confusing cashiers and inducing them to make mistakes in giving change for a large bill.
2. Appo erroneously believed that the jeweler's name was "Augustus Kunze," and that his store was located on North Tenth Street. I have corrected both in the text here. Gustav Kunz was listed as a watchmaker or jeweler in the firm of Breitinger and Kunz in city directories from 1879 to 1891. The business was located at 107 North Ninth Street in 1880. By 1883 the firm had moved to 37 North Ninth Street, probably the address Appo visited. See James Gopsill, *Gopsill's Philadelphia City Directory for 1879* (Philadelphia, 1879–91).

3. Eastern State Penitentiary was called "Cherry Hill" by local Philadelphians because it was located on the site of a former cherry orchard. See Negley K. Teeters and John D. Shearer, *The Prison at Philadelphia, Cherry Hill: The Separate System of Penal Discipline: 1829–1913* (New York, 1957), 3. Appo referred to Moyamensing Jail as "May——." Appo, alias George Leon, was in the jail for five, not six, weeks, as he claimed. See Prisoner for Trial Docket, vol. KKK, 370, entry 75, record group 38.38, PCA.

4. Appo was no. 3178. See Descriptive Registers, volume for 1884–95, 8 Apr. 1886, 54–55, microfilm roll 401; Convict Reception Registers, volume for 1869–86, entry no. A3178, microfilm roll 395; and Admission and Discharge Book, volume for 1875–88, entries for Apr. 1886 and Mar. 1887, microfilm roll 393, all in ESP; ESP Inspectors, *Fifty-seventh AR for 1886* (Philadelphia, 1887), 55, 72.

5. Appo did not provide enough information to identify Northcross (which was most likely an alias) precisely in published and unpublished prison records.

6. Appo, 13–16. Appo believed that he was incarcerated from Apr. 1880 to 9 Mar. 1881. Also see Frank Moss, *The American Metropolis* (New York, 1897), III:128. No such case, however, appears in the indictments from the Philadelphia Court of Quarter Sessions from 1879 to 1881. Appo was arrested and sentenced under the alias "George Leon." See Commonwealth of Pennsylvania v. George Leon, 5 Mar. 1886, Court of Quarter Sessions Indictments, box 263–27444 (center row), PRSC. The indictment listed the value of the watch at $3.50. On Appo employing "George Leon" as an alias, see *Brooklyn Eagle*, 2 May 1889; Mary Havens to George Leon, 27 Oct. 1917, box 2, SPC Papers.

7. Appo, 16; Max Grunhut, "Introduction," in Teeters and Shearer, *Prison at Philadelphia*, viii (famous), 69; PANY, *Twenty-fourth AR for 1868*, SD 10 (Albany, 1869), 62; David J. Rothman, *The Discovery of the Asylum: Social Order and Disorder in the New Republic* (Boston, 1971), 79–83; Richard G. Carrott, *The Egyptian Revival: Its Sources, Monuments and Meaning, 1808–1858* (Berkeley, Calif., 1978).

8. ESP Inspectors, *AR for the Year 1884*, 11–12, 94. Eastern State Penitentiary was the only penitentiary with the isolation system as early as 1864. See Frederick Howard Wines, *Punishment and Reformation: A Study of the Penitentiary System* (New York, 1895 and 1919), 160–62.

9. ESP Inspectors, *51st AR for the Year 1880* (Philadelphia, 1881), 43; ESP Inspectors, *59th AR for the Year 1888* (Philadelphia, 1889), 93 (dismissal), 136–37 (ministered); Teeters and Shearer, *Prison at Philadelphia*, 137–41.

10. ESP Inspectors, *55th AR for the Year 1884* (Philadelphia, 1885), 10–11.

11. ESP Inspectors, *AR for the Year 1880*, 6–7 (gross evil, criminal classes); ESP Inspectors, *59th AR*, 99 (crime class), 114 (crime class), 136–37 (Ashton); ESP Inspectors, *52nd AR for the Year 1881* (Philadelphia, 1882), 79–80; ESP Inspectors, *57th AR for the Year 1886* (Philadelphia, 1887), 23–24.

12. ESP Inspectors, *AR for the Year 1881*, 40–41 (rarely happened), 78 (overwork); ESP Inspectors, *59th AR*, 95 (industry), 114; ESP Inspectors, *55th AR*, 95; Teeters and Shearer, *Prison at Philadelphia*, 147.

13. ESP Inspectors, *59th AR*, 113; ESP Inspectors, *AR for the Year 1880*, 45; Teeters and Shearer, *Prison at Philadelphia*, 100–4, 168–73.

14. Charles Dickens, *American Notes* (1842; reprint, Oxford, Eng., 1987), 99–10; Teeters and Shearer, *Prison at Philadelphia*, 27–28, 113–32 (Niagara), 206–12.

15. Frederick Howard Wines, "The Problem of Crime," *Charities Review* 7 (Oct. 1897), 652–53.

16. Teeters and Shearer, *Prison at Philadelphia*, 68, 110, 201–23, 242; entry for 3 May 1886, vol. 5, Warden's Daily Journals, Prison Administration Records, ESP (Cassidy); PANY, *AR for 1868*, 61–63.

17. Entry for 17 Jan. 1886, vol. 5, Warden's Daily Journals, Prison Administration Records, ESP (cheerful); ESP Inspectors, *61st AR for the Year 1890* (Philadelphia, 1891), 114, 116.

18. Entry for Feb. 1880, box 4, Handwritten Warden's Reports to the Visiting Inspectors, Prison Administration Records; entry for 14 May 1886 (private property), vol. 5, Warden's Daily Journals, Prison Administration Records, both in ESP; Wines, *Punishment*, 165–66.

19. Wines, *Punishment*, 165–66.

20. Entries for 14 May 1886; 27 June 1886; 6, 23 Sept. 1886, all in vol. 5, Warden's Daily Journals, Prison Administration Records, ESP. For other accounts linking masturbation and insanity, see Teeters and Shearer, *Prison at Philadelphia*, 173–77; NYS, *Nineteenth AR of the Medical Superintendent of the State Asylum for Insane Criminals, Auburn, New York* (Albany, 1879), 12.

21. On the diversity of prisons and prison experiences in the second half of the twentieth century, see Norval Morris, "The Contemporary Prison, 1865-Present," in Morris and David J. Rothman, eds., *The Oxford History of the Prison* (New York, 1995), 228.

22. Appo, 72.

23. ESP Inspectors, *AR for the Year 1890*, 114, 116.


## 15. GREEN GOODS

1. Appo, 38–42. Vosburg's surname was frequently spelled "Vosburgh" in newspapers. Appo and Thomas Byrnes, *Professional Criminals of America* (New York, 1886), 60–61, used "Vosburg," and I have employed that spelling. Appo was also inconsistent regarding the amount of time in which he worked for Parmeley, eighteen months on 39 and fifteen months on 43.

2. On the origins of the term "confidence man," based on its application to William Thompson in 1849, see Johannes Dietrich Bergmann, "The Original Confidence Man," *American Quarterly* 21 (1969), 560–77; Lawrence M. Friedman, *Crime and Punishment in American History* (New York, 1993), 195. Appo defined "sure thing graft" as bunco, dice, short cards, flimflam, fake jewelry, and green goods. See Frank Moss, *The American Metropolis* (New York, 1897), III:132.

3. Descriptions of the green goods game appear in Edward Crapsey, *The Nether Side of New York* (New York, 1872), 63–73; Jonathan Slick, *Snares of New York; or, Tricks and Traps of the Great Metropolis* (New York, 1879), 131–36; Anthony Comstock, *Frauds Exposed; or, How the People are Deceived and Robbed, and Youth Corrupted* (New York, 1880), 196–201; Allan Pinkerton, *Thirty Years a Detective* (Chicago, 1884), 71–81; Byrnes, *Professional Criminals*, 47–49; Byrnes, 2nd ed. (New York, 1895), 32–34; George W. Walling, *Recollections of a New York Chief of Police* (New York, 1887), 126–27; Augustine E. Costello, *History of the Police Department of Jersey City* (Jersey City, N.J., 1891), 189–99; *Lexow Committee*, III:2575–76; Benjamin P. Eldridge and William

B. Watts, *Our Rival, the Rascal* (Boston, 1897; reprint, 1973), 197–203; William T. Stead, *Satan's Invisible World Displayed, or Despairing Democracy: A Study of Greater New York* (New York, 1897; London, 1898), 108–9; William B. Moreau, *Swindling Exposed: From the Diary of William B. Moreau, King of the Fakirs* (Syracuse, N.Y., 1907), 185–90. On other swindles, see Walling, *Recollections*, 127–37; Matthew Hale Smith, *Sunshine and Shadow in New York* (Hartford, Conn., 1868), 694–705. The earliest printed circular I found dated from 1875 and is in folder 218, box 1260, MP.

4. Crapsey, *Nether Side*, 63–73 (circular swindle); Pinkerton, *Thirty Years*, 71 (boodle game); *World* clipping, 24 Jan. 1885 (flooded), vol. 10, DAS. For use of the term "sawdust," see Comstock, *Frauds Exposed*, 196–201; Walling, *Recollections*, 126–27; *Tribune*, 3 June 1883; *World* clipping, 24 Jan. 1885, vol. 10, DAS.

5. *Tribune*, 11 Sept. 1894; *World* clipping, 15 Oct. 1885, vol. 14, DAS; People v. Frank Webb, 27 Feb. 1880, box 7, folder 95; People v. Frank Webb, 27 Feb. 1881, box 32, folder 389, both in CGS; case #1158, RG 21.

6. Louis J. Beck, *New York's Chinatown: An Historical Representation of Its People and Places* (New York, 1898), 256; Costello, *Jersey City*, 192–94; *Sun* and unmarked clipping, 4 Dec. 1887 (king), vol. 42; *World* clipping, 1 Apr. 1888 (pioneer), vol. 47; unmarked clipping, 6 Jan. 1887, vol. 30, all in DAS.

7. *Morning Advertiser* clipping, 17 June 1894 (Rathbone), vol. 128, DAS; Stead, *Satan's Invisible World*, 108–9; *NPG*, 4 May 1895 (gilt-edged swindlers); Byrnes, *Professional Criminals* (1895), 205 (gilt-edged swindlers); Pinkerton, *Thirty Years*, 71; *Tribune*, 11 Sept. 1894. Appo claimed that James McNally earned an average of $8,000 per day and possessed wealth of $100,000. Other Lexow Committee testimony claimed that the largest sum ever swindled on a single day was $3,500. See *Lexow Committee*, II:1639, 1647, 1812. On fortunes of $50,000 to $200,000, see Moss, *American Metropolis*, III:136–38.

8. Appo, 42.

9. Since he worked out of the Point View Hotel, O'Brien was probably working with McNally by this time. None of these arrests resulted in a conviction. See unmarked clipping, 3 Oct. 1891, vol. 90, DAS. On O'Brien's arrests and biography (aliases of John Allen, David Harman, "Big Tom," and Patrick O'Brien), see entry for 7 Jan. 1885, 16, vol. 148, MGS; *Press*, *Morning Journal*, and other clippings, 9 Jan. 1891, vol. 79; unmarked clipping, 21 Aug. 1891 (30–40 men; $2,000/day); *Press* clipping, 22 Aug. 1891, all in vol. 89; unmarked clipping, 5 Feb. 1892, vol. 94; 24, 26 Mar. 1892 clippings, vol. 96; *Herald* clipping, 19 Feb. 1893, vol. 108, all in DAS; *Times*, 6, 7, 9 Oct. 1890, 18 Dec. 1891; 9 Jan. 1891, 26 Aug. 1891; *Tribune*, 9 Jan. 1891; Byrnes, *Professional Criminals* (1895), 204–9, #326.

10. *Times*, 28 Oct. 1891 (father of modern criminals), 1 May 1904. Vosburg also had aliases of William Pond, William Watson, Tom Green, and John Lee. For arrests and biographical details, see *NPG*, 19 Aug. 1882; *World* clipping, 19 Oct. 1883; unmarked clipping, 17 Oct. 1883; unmarked clipping, 13 Dec. 1885, vol. 16; unmarked clipping, 28 Apr. 1888, vol. 48; unmarked clipping, 2 Dec. 1895; *Press* clipping, 28 Nov. 1895, both in vol. 148; unmarked clippings, 12 Dec. 1895, *Times*, *Morning Advertiser,* and *Journal* clippings, 25 Dec. 1895, all in vol. 149, all in DAS; entry for 14 June 1877 (grand larceny), vol. 129, 56, 120, MGS; Reports of Deduction of Sentences by Prison Agents, Wardens and Superintendents (AO601), vol. 2, entry for 16 Dec. 1878, NYSArc;

Byrnes, *Professional Criminals*, 60–61; Slick, *Snares of New York*, 177; *Lexow Committee*, II:1632, 1799–1801; Moss, *American Metropolis*, III:22–23.

11. On Hilton's green goods arrest with George Wilson (who may be George Appo), see unmarked clipping, 10 Feb. 1891, vol. 87, DAS; entry for 10 Feb. 1891, Second District, PCDB. Other descriptions and arrests of Hilton appear in *Times*, 5, 11 Mar. 1887; unmarked clipping, 4 Mar. 1887; *World* clippping, 5 Mar. 1887, vol. 32; *World* (manhood); *Herald, Sun, Times* (suave), and other clippings, all for 25 May 1892, vol. 98, DAS; *Lexow Committee*, III:2637.

12. William Hayes circular, in *World* clipping, 24 Jan. 1885, vol. 10 (profitable article); unnamed clipping, 2 Dec. 1885, vol. 15 (cigars), both in DAS; L. L. Ward circular, 11 July 1889; handwritten circular signed "I remain yours in confidence," [1889?]; William Hunter to John L. Andrews, 28 July 1885; F. B. Ostrander to "Dear Friend," undated, all in box 87-HAS-36; J. D. Baldwin to Dear Sir, 16 June 1890; Baldwin to George Stork, 30 June 1890, both in box 88-GHJ-41, all in MP.

13. William Hayes circular, in *World* clipping, 24 Jan. 1885, vol. 10, DAS (Almighty God); Crapsey, *Nether Side*, 64 (man of honor); "Strictly Confidential" circular of "Yours Very Truly in Honor and Confidence," undated [1887], box 87-HAS-36, MP (never regret it).

14. *Herald* clipping, 3 Sept. 1885, vol. 13, DAS (Purdy); *Poughkeepsie Courier*, 19 Mar. 1893 (tender spot); *World* clipping, 24 Jan. 1885, vol. 10, DAS; confidential circular of "Faithfully Your Friend," undated [1887], box 87-HAS-36, MP (rich government); circular in People v. Frank Brooks, 16 Dec. 1891, folder 4222, box 460, CGS (hereafter Frank Brooks case); "Dear Sir" letter from W. B. Andrews in U.S. v. James McNally and others, June 1891, U.S. District Court, New Jersey District, criminal case #570, June 1891, reel 233, RG 21 (powerful government) (hereafter v. James McNally Criminal Case #570); People v. George Mink, 9 Feb. 1893, folder 4672, box 513, CGS (Republican) (hereafter George Mink case). On victims from the South and West, see *Tribune*, 26 Jan. 1887, 25 Jan. 1888, 20 Mar. 1892; *Times*, 1 Apr. 1887, 25 Jan. 1888, 15 Aug. 1890 (Russell B. Harrison, son of President Harrison), 9 Oct. 1890, 15 Jan. 1892; unmarked clipping, 6 Jan. 1887, vol. 30, all in DAS. On the success of these tactics, see *World* clipping, 3 Dec. 1887, vol. 42, DAS; Joseph Meyer, *Protection: The Sealed Book*, 3rd ed. (Milwaukee, 1911), 93.

15. Unmarked clipping, 4 Dec. 1887, vol. 42 (idiots); *World* clipping, 24 Jan. 1885, vol. 10, DAS (financially embarrassed); F. W. Boeltcher, president of the German Bank of Eureka, S.D., to Mayor William Strong, 26 Dec. 1894, box 87-HAS-36, MP; "Strictly Confidential" circular of "Yours Very Truly in Honor and Confidence," undated [1887], box 87-HAS-36, MP.

16. Unmarked clipping, 4 Dec. 1887, vol. 42, DAS; Campbell, *Darkness and Daylight*, 736–37; *Herald* clipping, 7 Dec. 1887, vol. 42, DAS (mainstay); Pinkerton, *Thirty Years*, 20. On Murphy and Brooks, see *New York Recorder* and *Morning Journal* clippings, 26 Oct. 1891; unmarked clipping, 29 Oct. 1891, vol. 91, DAS; Frank Brooks case; People v. Terrence Murphy, 23 Nov. 1891, folder 4207, box 458, both in CGS (hereafter Murphy case). On Murphy as an accomplice of Daniel Driscoll, see entry for 18 Jan. 1885, p. 98, vol. 32, Drummond Papers.

17. Meyer, *Protection*, 93; Campbell, *Darkness and Daylight*, 737 (cupidity); Moss, *American Metropolis*, III:141 (Appo); John H. Warren, Jr., *Thirty Years' Battle With Crime*

(Poughkeepsie, N.Y., 1875), 327–30; *Herald* clipping, 3 Sept. 1885, vol. 13; *Journal* clipping, 6 Dec. 1887, vol. 42, both in DAS (minister).

18. *Herald* clipping, 3 Dec. 1895, vol. 148, DAS (Goff); *Tribune*, 3 June 1883 (Walling); Crapsey, *Nether Side*, 66, 68.

19. *Times*, 2 Mar. 1889; Byrnes, *Professional Criminals*, 49; A. G. Warner, "Politics and Crime," *American Journal of Sociology* 1 (1895), 293; *Lexow Committee*, II:1806–10; III:3240 (territories); *Tribune*, 30 June 1894 (Kelso); Thomas Byrnes to Mayor Franklin Edson, 5 June 1884, box 85-EF-12, MP; Josiah Flynt, *The World of Graft* (New York, 1901), 94.

20. Sgt. John Dunn to Supt. William Murray, 15 Aug. 1887; Capt. John Gallagher to Inspector Alexander Williams, 30 Oct. 1894, both in box 87-HAS-36, MP; *World* clipping, 24 Jan. 1885, vol. 10; *Herald* clipping, 3 Sept. 1885, vol. 13; *Journal* clipping, 6 Dec. 1887, vol. 42; *Tribune* clipping, 3 Sept. 1885, vol. 13; *Journal* (?) and other clippings, 2 Dec. 1885, vol. 15, all in DAS; People v. David Smythe, case #1159, RG 21; *Times*, 19 Oct. 1890 (700–800 aliases); *Lexow Committee*, II:1806–10; Warren, *Thirty Years'*, 327–30. On the difficulty of prosecuting counterfeiters, see Drummond's court testimony in *Times*, 15 Jan. 1881, 12 Mar. 1881. On the difficulty of prosecuting green goods operatives, see *Times*, 26 Jan. 1888, 15 Aug. 1890.

21. Crapsey, *Nether Side*, 65; confidential circular of "Faithfully Your Friend," undated [1887]; undated telegram to Andrew Kent, both in box 87-HAS-36, MP; *Times* clippings, 29 and 30 July 1892, 2 Aug. 1892, vol. 101, DAS; *Tribune*, 4, 10 May 1894. On Comstock's complaints, see unmarked clippings, 21 Jan. 1898, vol. 166; 2 Feb. 1900, vol. 188, DAS.

22. *Times*, 2 Dec. 1887; *Herald* and *World* clippings, 3 Dec. 1887; *Sun* and unmarked clipping, 4 Dec. 1887, all in vol. 42, DAS. For other arrests, see *Star* and other clippings, 4 Dec. 1887; unmarked clipping, 8 Dec. 1887, all in vol. 42, all in DAS. The specific legislation is in chapter 687, section 527, of the penal code, passed on 24 June 1887. See unmarked clipping, 26 Nov. 1887, vol. 41; *Times* clippings, 2 Dec. 1887, vol. 42, all in DAS.

23. NYC, *Report of the Police Department for 1887* (New York, 1888), 81; *World* clipping, 23 Sept. 1889 (Murray), vol. 65; *World* clipping, 2 Aug. 1888, vol. 52; *World* clipping, 24 Jan. 1885, vol. 10; *Sun* clipping, 26 July 1889; unmarked clipping, 25 July 1889; *Morning Journal* clipping, 28 July 1889; *Star* clipping, 1 Aug 1889, all in vol. 63, all in DAS; *Times*, 25 July 1889; U.S. v. William Burns, 1889, #1445; U.S. v. Samuel Marks, Bill of Exceptions filed in U.S. Circuit Court, Southern District of New York, 17 Dec. 1889, #1447, both in RG 21; People v. Samuel Marks, 13 Aug. 1889, box 363, folder 3411, CGS. Several prominent operators, notably William C. Byrnes (aliases Burns and Boyle) and Samuel Marks, received eighteen-month sentences. See People v. William C. Byrnes, 13 Aug. 1889, box 9999, location 106129, Supreme Court Cases, DAP.

24. *Press* clipping, 11 Mar. 1890 (briskly), vol. 71; *Sun* clipping, 19 Oct. 1890, vol. 77; *Times* clipping, 30 July 1892 (unmolested), vol. 101, all in DAS; *World*, 1 Oct. 1894.

25. Appo, 42–43. Appo earlier claimed he worked for McNally for five years. See Moss, *American Metropolis*, III:133. Appo erroneously identified the address of McNally's den as the northwest corner of Forty-third Street and Seventh Avenue, where Seventh Avenue merges with and briefly becomes Broadway at Forty-third Street. According to Louis Beck, the joint operation of Samuel "Sammy" Goldstein, Harry A. Hamberger,

and McNally was at Forty-sixth Street, which I have used here. See Beck, *New York's Chinatown*, 168–75.

26. Byrnes, *Professional Criminals*, 41; *Tribune*, 11 Sept. 1894 (king); Beck, *New York's Chinatown*, 168–75, 258 (king); *Times*, 1 July 1894 (king); *Herald* clipping, 11 Sept. 1894 (king), vol. 131, DAS; Stead, *Satan's Invisible World*, 107–16; 108–9; *Lexow Committee*, II:1812.

27. See note 26; *Bridgeport Evening Post*, 12, 13 Sept. 1894 (millionaire); *Times*, 1, 15 July 1894; *Lexow Committee*, II: 1638–47 (pimps; Farley), 1812, III:2493–94, 2513–17; *Sun* clipping, 19 Oct. 1890, vol. 77, vol. 131, DAS. These and other sources indicate that McNally was born around 1861. On McNally's arrests in New York, see *Times* clipping, 2 Dec. 1887; *Herald* and *World* clippings, 3 Dec. 1887; *Sun* and unmarked clipping, 4 Dec. 1887, all in vol. 42, DAS; *Tribune*, 11 Sept. 1894. For arrests in New Jersey, see James McNally Criminal Case #570; unmarked clippings, 13, 14 Dec. 1891, vol. 92, DAS. On Samuel Ward and Isaac Rosenthal, who worked for McNally, see the extensive coverage in *Times*, 19, 20, 21 Oct. 1890; People v. Samuel Ward and Isaac Rosenthal, 30 Oct. 1890, folder 3839, box 415, CGS (dismissed in 1899).

28. *Bridgeport Evening Post*, 12 Sept. 1894 (15,000); Stead, *Satan's Invisible World*, 110–13; *Lexow Committee*, III:2587–89, II:1645, 1658 (writers earn 50 percent); *Tribune*, 15 June 1894; *World* clipping, 1 Apr. 1888, vol. 47; unmarked clipping, 24 May 1889, vol. 61, both in DAS; Costello, *Jersey City*, 194.

29. Marvin was involved in printing circulars for at least fifteen years. See People v. Eugene Marvin, 14 Feb. 1893, box 513, CGS; *People v. Eugene A. Marvin*, 29 N.Y.S. 381 (15 June 1894); 39 N.E. 494 (11 Dec. 1894); *Century Edition of American Digest: Cases Before 1896* (St. Paul, Minn., 1899), XIII:1160; U.S. v. Samuel Marks, Bill of Exceptions filed in U.S. Circuit Court, Southern District of New York, 17 Dec. 1889, B1447, RG 21; *Times*, 17 Dec. 1892, 15 June 1893 (500,000), 17 June 1893; George Mink case; People v. George Frosh, 9 Feb. 1893, folder 4664, box 512, both in CGS; unmarked clippings, 17 Dec. 1892, vol. 104; *Morning Advertiser* clippings, 20 and 23 Dec. 1892, vol. 105; 30 Apr. 1893, vol. 111; *Morning Journal* clipping, 18 May 1893, vol. 113; *Morning Advertiser* clippings, 16, 17, 23 June 1893, vol. 114; *Morning Advertiser* clipping, 17 June 1894, vol. 128, all in DAS.

30. *Tribune*, 12 Sept. 1894 (chased out); note 29 above.

31. *Recorder*, 13 Sept. 1894, repeated in *Bridgeport Evening Post*, 13 Sept. 1894.

32. *Lexow Committee*, III:2584–2609, 2632–33 (Hanley); V:5631–32 (Meakim); Stead, *Satan's Invisible World*, 107–16; *Times*, 7 (paradise), 9 May 1893, 7 July 1893 (investigation), 4 May 1894; *Tribune*, 11, 12 Sept. 1894; *Herald* and other clippings, 11 Sept. 1894; *World* clipping, 14 Sept. 1894, vol. 131, DAS. For examples of Meakim's correspondence with his superiors in which he claims that various proprietors denied knowledge of the green goods business, see boxes 87-HAS-36 and 88-GHJ-41, MP. On the Point View Hotel serving as a rendezvous for the green goods business, see *Times*, 26 Aug. 1891, 28 Oct. 1891; unmarked clippings, 19 Aug. 1891, vol. 89; *Telegram* and other clippings, 27 Oct. 1891, vol. 91, all in DAS. On charges of police corruption in Jersey City, see note 4 on William Dalton in "Jersey City" below. For reports of green goods operations in New Jersey, see *Times*, 21 Mar. 1892; *Tribune*, 14 May 1893; U.S. v. Samuel Marks, Bill of Exceptions, Dec. 1889, #1447, p. 36, RG 21. Steerers met potential victims as far away as Bethlehem, Pennsylvania. See *Tribune*, 7 Mar. 1894, 29 Nov. 1894.

33. Entry for 29 Apr. 1881, 197–98, vol. 22, Drummond Papers. On Maguire's role in the prosecution of counterfeiters, see chapter 11, note 3. On Carroll's cooperation with the Secret Service, see entries for 8 May 1880, 295–96; 15 June 1880, 612, all in vol. 18; 5 Jan. 1881, 20; 29 Jan. 1881, 253; 1 Feb. 1881, 272; 2 Feb. 1881, 294, all in vol. 21, all in Drummond Papers. On police knowing the identity of operatives, see *Tribune*, 20 June 1894.

34. *World* (?) clipping, 23 Dec. 1887, vol. 43, DAS; People v. Anthony Nelson, 14 Dec. 1887, folder 2755, box 289, CGS. Court records indicate Nelson was tried and acquitted and that the circulars *did* include dollar signs.

35. People v. Samuel Ward and Isaac Rosenthal, 30 Oct. 1890, folder 3839, box 415, CGS; *Times*, 7 Aug. 1892. On the difficulty of prosecution, see People v. Sidney Heyman, 14 Dec. 1887, folder 2746, box 288; Terrence Murphy case; Frank Brooks case; People v. Cornelius Wynkoop, 10 Dec. 1890, folder 3897 (suspended), box 421; People v. James H. Day and George L. Hopma, 22 Dec. 1892, folder 4599, box 505; People v. Odell Walters and Sam Little, 23 Nov. 1891, folder 4219, box 459; People v. James Miller, 23 Feb. 1892, folder 4297, box 469; People v. George B. Oliver, 15 Dec. 1887, folder 1756 (dismissed in 1892), box 289, all in CGS; *Times*, 27 Sept. 1890.

36 Unmarked clipping, 6 Jan. 1887, vol. 30, DAS (Drummond; emphasis added).

37. *Henry McCord v. The People*, 46 New York 470 (*New York Reports [Court of Appeals]*, vol. 46, 470–77, 20 Nov. 1871); Arthur Train, "The Last of the Wire-tappers," *American Magazine* 62 (June 1906), 150; Arthur Train, *True Stories of Crime* (New York, 1908), 112–21.

38. *People v. Livingstone*, 47 App. Div. 283; and 62 N.Y.S. 9 (*New York Supplement*, 9 Jan. 1900, vol. 62, 9–11). Livingstone was acquitted of larceny on false and fraudulent representation and simple larceny. For discussions of the case, see entries for Henry Livingstone, 128, 757, vol. 20, Drummond Papers. Other swindles were unsuccessful in such appeals. For a case involving "faro," see *People v. Dean*, 12 N.Y.S. 749 (*New York Supplement*, 29 Dec. 1890, vol. 12, 749–51). Only in 1901 did New York courts distinguish between larceny and obtaining money by false pretenses. Larceny occurred when one gained possession of property by artifice or trick and the title of the owner remained unchanged. False pretense occurred if the owner was deceived into surrendering title and possession of their property by means of fraudulent representation. An overview of the case law appears in *People v. Miller*, 64 App. Div. 450; and 72 N.Y.S. 253 (*New York Supplement*, 11 Oct. 1901, vol. 72, 253–70). On the persistence of this legal interpretation, see Arthur Train, *The Prisoner at the Bar: Sidelights on the Administration of Criminal Justice* (New York, 1923), 17–21; Edwin H. Sutherland, *The Professional Thief* (Chicago, 1937), 177.

39. *Recorder*, 13 Sept. 1894, repeated in *Bridgeport Evening Post*, 13 Sept. 1894 (something for nothing); George P. Fletcher, *Rethinking Criminal Law* (Boston, 1978), 54; Jerome Hall, *Theft, Law and Society* (Indianapolis, 1952), 58–62.

40. William Riordan, *Plunkitt of Tammany Hall*, introduction by Terrence McDonald (1905; reprint, New York, 1992), 81.

41. Crapsey, *Nether Side*, 63. On the small scale of other confidence schemes, see *Times*, 9 July 1871. On green goods as one of several examples of "organized crime," see *Evening World* (?) editorial, 1 June 1895, vol. 141, DAS. On the Mafia and "Italian syndicates" involved with counterfeiting at this time, see *Times*, 17 Jan. 1896. Another

early use of the term "organized crime" was employed by Charles Parkhurst in reference to Tammany Hall. See Society for the Prevention of Crime, *Report* (New York, 1896), 6–7. On the definition of "organized crime," see R. T. Naylor, *Wages of Crime: Black Markets, Illegal Finance, and the Underworld Economy* (Ithaca, N.Y. 2002), 14–16. For other important works on organized crime, see chapter 13, note 46.

42. Irwin Unger, *The Greenback Era: A Social and Political History of American Finance, 1865–1879* (Princeton, N.J., 1964), 3; David R. Johnson, *Illegal Tender: Counterfeiting and the Secret Service in Nineteenth-Century America* (Washington, D.C., 1995); Friedman, *Crime*, 111, 195–97, 436–37.

43. Cleveland Moffett, "The Enemies of Society—How They Operate," *Illustrated American* 18 (20 July 1895), 70; Byrnes, *Professional Criminals*, 80–83 (largest robbery), 135, 139–40; Byrnes, *Professional Criminals* (1895 edition), 53 (retired), 74–75; Sophie Lyons, *Why Crime Does Not Pay* (New York, 1913), 146–72, 149 ("Napoleon"); James D. Horan, *The Pinkerton Story* (New York, 1951), 311. On bank robbers as the aristocrats of crime, see Roger Lane, "Introduction," in Eldridge and Watts, *Our Rival*, ix. On Hope's underworld reputation, see Hutchins Hapgood, ed., *The Autobiography of a Thief* (New York, 1903), 175–77.

JERSEY CITY

1. In the early 1880s, Dick Cronin was associated with Barney Maguire's gang. See William Norr, *Stories of Chinatown: Sketches from Life in the Chinese Colony* (New York, 1892), 47.

2. Appo erroneously believed this event took place in December 1891. See Appo, 81. Other sources indicate that Appo was shot in the abdomen in Jersey City on 24 Dec. 1892. See *Poughkeepsie Daily Eagle*, 14 Feb. 1893.

3. Christ Hospital was an Episcopal Church institution founded in 1873, incorporated in 1874, and given that name in 1880. In 1888 it moved to 176 Palisade Avenue, Jersey City, N.J., where it remains today.

4. William H. "Billy" Dalton (1846–?) was a police detective in Jersey City. See Augustine E. Costello, *History of the Police Department of Jersey City* (Jersey City, N.J., 1891), 274–76; *Gopsill's Jersey City, Hoboken, Union Hill, West Hoboken, and Weehawken Directory* (Washington, D.C., 1880–95), all in the New Jersey Room, Jersey City Public Library (after 1888, he is listed as "detective"); *Jersey City Evening Journal*, 20, 28 Jan. 1892; 1, 16, 17 Feb. 1892. On Dalton receiving protection money to allow McNally to operate in Jersey City, see *Lexow Committee*, III:2605; *Tribune*, 12 Sept. 1894. On other charges of police corruption in Jersey City at this time, see *Jersey City Evening Journal*, 1, 16 Dec. 1892, *Times*, 17 Jan. 1896.

5. Appo, 81–84.

16. POUGHKEEPSIE

1. Appo, 44–48. At different points, Appo erroneously believed that these Poughkeepsie events occurred in 1894, that he was shot on 11 January 1893, and that he awoke on 22 January. See Appo, 44–45. I have inserted the correct dates in Appo's narrative. Appo

referred to Cassel as "Castle" in his autobiography. I have employed "Cassel" because it was the most frequently used. Hogshead's name was also spelled "Hogshed" and "Hogsed."

2. *Albow*, 9–24; *Poughkeepsie Daily Eagle*, 13 Feb. 1893; 26 Apr. 1893; *Herald*, 13 Feb. 1893; *Poughkeepsie News-Press*, 13 Feb. 1893; *Poughkeepsie News-Telegraph*, 18 Feb. 1893; *Tribune*, 13 Feb. 1893; *NPG*, 4 Mar. 1893; *Poughkeepsie Sunday Courier*, 19 Feb. 1893; *Tribune*, 13 Feb. 1893; *Times*, 13 Feb. 1893 (Appo will die). No records of Vassar Hospital have survived from this era.

3. *Poughkeepsie Courier*, 12 Feb. 1893 (railroad timetables), 19 Feb. 1893; *Times*, 20 Mar. 1893; *Tribune*, 13 Feb. 1893. On the Nelson House, see Frank Hasbrouck, ed., *The History of Dutchess County, New York* (Poughkeepsie, 1909), 752; undated image and description, Nelson House advertisement, 1899; and "Hospitality Plus" advertising brochure on Nelson House, all in box 11, Hotel Series, WC.

4. *Poughkeepsie Daily Eagle*, 14 Feb. 1893; *Herald*, 14 Feb. 1893; *Poughkeepsie Sunday Courier*, 19 Feb. 1893. According to Louis Beck, J. S. Roberts was Walter McNally, brother and accomplice of James McNally. Block Island never had any manufacturing establishments. See Louis J. Beck, *New York's Chinatown: An Historical Representation of Its People and Places* (New York, 1898), 258; Robert Downie, *Block Island—The Sea* (Block Island, R.I., 1998). I am indebted to Robert Downie of the Block Island Historical Society for this information.

5. *Poughkeepsie Daily Eagle*, 14 Feb. 1893 (opium pipe); *Poughkeepsie News-Telegraph*, 18 Feb. 1893 (opium pill); *Poughkeepsie Sunday Courier*, 19 Feb. 1893.

6. *Herald* clipping, 26 Oct. 1891 (Everett), vol. 91, DAS, *Times*, 11, 16 June 1893 (Crumley); *Tribune*, 14, 15, 16, 17, 24 May 1893. For other examples of potential victims robbing the bankroll, see *Times*, 6, 7, 9 Oct. 1890, 9 Jan. 1891, *Tribune*, 9 Jan. 1891.

7. *Poughkeepsie Daily Eagle*, 2 Mar. 1893 (spectacle); *Poughkeepsie Courier*, 2 Apr. 1893; *Times*, 26 Jan. 1890 (Marks); 29 Mar. 1893; *Poughkeepsie Courier*, 19 Feb. 1893 (open secret), 12 Mar. 1893 (spectacle); *Poughkeepsie News-Press*, 21 Apr. 1893 (former U.S. attorney). McNally gave his name as J. W. Morris of New York, a real estate dealer. O'Connell represented James McNally and his associates in U.S. v. James McNally and others, June 1891, U.S. District Court, New Jersey District, criminal case #570, June 1891, reel 233, RG 21. O'Connell and Rose prosecuted and convicted Samuel Marks in U.S. v. Samuel Marks, Bill of Exceptions, Dec. 1889, #1447, 24, reel 233, RG 21; *Albow*, 4–5, 8.

8. *Appo*, 48–50.

9. *Poughkeepsie Daily Eagle*, 18 Apr. 1893 (Appo's eye); *Poughkeepsie News-Press*, 21 Apr. 1893 (scarred and deformed).

10. Details on Hogshead and Cassel are in *Albow*, 10–29; *Poughkeepsie Daily Eagle*, 15 Feb. 1893, 25 Apr. 1893; *Poughkeepsie News-Telegraph*, 18 Feb. 1893; *Poughkeepsie News-Press*, 13 Feb. 1893.

11. *Albow*, 19–20, 25–26, 29–31 (coward); *Poughkeepsie News-Press*, 25 Apr. 1893; *Poughkeepsie News-Telegraph*, 29 Apr. 1893; *NPG*, 4 Mar. 1893 (murder and rob).

12. *Albow*, 25–26, 29–31. On "righteous assault," see Jack Katz, *Seductions of Crime* (New York, 1988), 12–51.

13. Hogshead also rented a house on his property to Edward Cassel (probably Ephraim Cassel's son), six years Hogshead's junior, and his wife. Vol. 21, 422, 423, Eastatoey (?)

Twp., Transylvania Co., State of North Carolina, 1870, Ninth Federal Census Population Schedules, National Archives Microfilm, roll 1161; Stuart W. Bradley, ed., *North Carolina 1870 Census Index* (Bountiful, Utah, 1989), I:455. By 1893 conflicting reports claimed Cassel had children numbering from two to seven. *Albow*, 10–24 (3 children); *Poughkeepsie Daily Eagle*, 15 Feb. 1893 (no means, 2 children); *Poughkeepsie News-Telegraph*, 18 Feb. 1893 (7 children). Census records indicate that Hogshead's children were two and three years old in 1893. See lines 11–24, sheet 9, E.D. 22, vol. 16, Cleveland Twp., Greenville County, State of South Carolina, 1900, Twelfth Federal Census Population Schedules.

14. *Albow*, 9–24; *Poughkeepsie News-Press*, 13 Feb. 1893; *Poughkeepsie News-Telegraph*, 18 Feb. 1893; *Poughkeepsie Daily Eagle*, 25 Apr. 1893.

15. *Albow*, 2–7, 35–42; *Poughkeepsie News-Press*, 21 Apr. 1893; *Poughkeepsie Daily Eagle*, 21 Apr. 1893, 26 Apr. 1893; *Poughkeepsie News-Telegraph*, 22 Apr. 1893; *Tribune*, 18 Apr. 1893. Appo was tried as "George Albow" on 24–25 Apr. 1893 in the Court of Oyer and Terminer in Poughkeepsie's "Old Court House" for violating Section 527 of the penal code.

16. *Poughkeepsie Daily Eagle*, 26 Apr. 1893; *Albow*, 44–45. Appo erroneously believed that the members of the jury did not even leave their seats. See Appo, 50.

17. *Poughkeepsie Daily Eagle*, *Poughkeepsie News-Press*, *Times*, 26 Apr. 1893.

18. *Poughkeepsie Sunday Courier*, 19 Feb. 1893; *Times*, 20 Mar. 1893; *Poughkeepsie Daily Eagle*, *Poughkeepsie News-Press*, 13 Feb. 1893.

19. *Poughkeepsie Daily Eagle*, 2 Mar. 1893, 25 Apr. 1893; *Poughkeepsie Courier*, 12 Mar. 1893. Charles Morschauser (1858–30 Dec. 1926) was recorder from 1890 to 1893. In 1885 Ransom Baker was defeated by Joseph Morschauser in the election for justice of the peace. On their relationship, see *Poughkeepsie New Yorker*, 3 Nov. 1947. Details on Michael Morgan (1856–26 Aug. 1921) are in R. V. LeRay, *Poughkeepsie City Directory* (Poughkeepsie, 1889–1897); *Poughkeepsie Eagle-News*, 26 Aug. 1921 (Hudson Valley), 27 Aug. 1921, 30 Aug. 1921 (K of C, Elks); *Poughkeepsie Sunday Courier*, 28 Aug. 1921.

20. *Poughkeepsie Daily Eagle*, *Poughkeepsie News-Press*, 27, 28 Apr. 1893; *Poughkeepsie Courier*, 30 Apr. 1893.

21. Ibid.

22. Ibid.; *Times*, 27 Apr. 1893.

23. *Poughkeepsie Daily Eagle*, 27 Apr. 1893.

24. Ibid., 14 Feb. 1893; *Poughkeepsie News-Telegraph*, 18 Feb. 1893 (opium pill); *Poughkeepsie Sunday Courier*, 19 Feb. 1893; *Herald*, 14 Feb. 1893; Beck, *New York's Chinatown*, 258 (common-law wife).

25. *Poughkeepsie News-Press*, 21 Apr. 1893, 25 Apr. 1893; *Poughkeepsie Daily Eagle*, 18, 21 Apr. 1893; *Poughkeepsie News-Telegraph*, 22 Apr. 1893; *Poughkeepsie Courier*, 12 Mar. 1893 (attentive). The same quotes on Appo's suicide threat appear in *Poughkeepsie Daily Eagle*, 26 Apr. 1893; *Times*, 26 Apr. 1893.

26. *Poughkeepsie Daily Eagle*, 27 Apr. 1893.

27. *Herald*, 13 Feb. 1893; *Times*, 13 Feb. 1893 (111 East Sixty-first Street); Beck, *New York's Chinatown*, 258. Other references to Miller as Appo's wife appear in *Poughkeepsie Daily Eagle*, 13 Mar. 1893, 25 Apr. 1893; *Poughkeepsie News-Press*, 26 Apr. 1893. The only other example of a romantic, heterosexual relationship in Appo's life was with an opium-addicted actress named Ida with whom Appo smoked at 17 Mott Street in the

early 1880s. See William Norr, *Stories of Chinatown: Sketches from Life in the Chinese Colony* (New York, 1892), 48–50.

28. Appo's statement on 6 Oct. 1896, 8–11, People v. George Appo, 24 July 1896, New York District Attorney Records, case #9126, box B-2, location 12817, SCC (two children); *Times*, 30 Sept. 1894; *Tribune*, 30 Sept. 1894; *Journal* clipping, 30 Sept. 1894, vol. 132, DAS. Appo's residential address appears in entry for George W. Appo, 9 Apr. 1895, PCDB, Second District, roll #70, neg. 10369, NYCMA. A later record indicates Appo moved to 221 West Eighteenth Street at the end of March 1895. See People v. George Appo, 19 Apr. 1895, New York Supreme Court, box 10100, location 106231 (unprocessed collection), DAP. This latter indictment indicated that Appo was *not* married. In 1893 Appo claimed to be living at 409 West Thirtieth Street with his wife "Lana Albon" and J. W. Delaro. See entry for 26 Apr. 1893, SSAR.

29. *People v. Albow*, 71 Hun, 123; 24 NY 519 (*New York Supplement*, St. Paul, Minn., 1893), XXIV:519–21 (28 July 1893); *Albow*, 56–62; *Poughkeepsie Courier*, 30 July 1893.

30. *Albow*, 3–4 (*Hess*), 7–12, 16–28, 31–35, 42.

31. *Albow*, 42; *Poughkeepsie News Telegraph*, 2 Dec. 1893 (better life); book #10, entry for 7 Oct. 1893, Minutes of Causes, N.Y. Court of Appeals (J2006), NYSArc. On Appo's release from Clinton, see Appo, 50; entry for "George Albo," #2242, April 1893 (5 Dec. 1893), Clinton Prison Chaplain's Office Statistical Register (BO105), NYSArc.

32. *Times*, 20 Mar. 1893 (excited); *NPG*, 4 Mar. 1893; *Poughkeepsie News-Press*, 21 Apr. 1893 (whole town); *Poughkeepsie News-Telegraph*, 22 Apr. 1893 (whole town).

STEALING GUYS

1. This version of events after his release departs considerably from Appo's earlier contention that he unsuccessfully confronted McNally in Bridgeport. See Moss, *American Metropolis*, III:133–34. Also see Beck, *New York's Chinatown*, 259, which describes a similar confrontation between McNally and Appo.

2. Appo, 56–57.

## 17. THE LEXOW COMMITTEE

1. Appo, 56–57.

2. NYC, *Report of the Police Department for 1896* (New York, 1897), 13 (honeycombed). Accounts of the Lexow Committee appear in Charles Parkhurst, *Our Fight with Tammany* (New York, 1895), 8–25, 240–45; Lincoln Steffens, *The Autobiography of Lincoln Steffens* (New York, 1931), I:199, 250–54; Lloyd Morris, *Incredible New York: High Life and Low Life of the Last Hundred Years* (New York, 1951), 220; M. R. Werner, *It Happened in New York* (New York, 1957), 36–116 (commanding figure, 65); Maxwell F. Marcuse, *This Was New York!* (New York, 1969), 51, 53, 276–83; Isabelle K. Savell, *Politics in the Gilded Age in New York State and Rockland County: A Biography of Senator Clarence Lexow* (New City, N.Y., 1984), 9–56, 226–27; Jay Stuart Berman, *Police Administration and Progressive Reform: Theodore Roosevelt as Police Commissioner of New York* (Westport, Conn., 1987); Marilynn S. Johnson, *Street Justice: A History of Police Violence in New York City* (Boston, 2003), 50–56.

3. See the following pages in *Lexow Committee* for testimony regarding green goods: George Appo, II:1622–58; Frank Clark, II:1799–1831; Charles Hanley, III:2483–2517; Rose Hanley, III:2520–24; Alonzo Sloane, III:2526–39; William Applegate, III:2539–45, 2563–67, 2569–71, 2573–2641, 2645–47; Joseph M. Reinschreiber, III:2545–63; Edward Schrader, III:2567–69; Frederick P. Forester, III:2571–73; Samuel J. Young, V:4678–79.

4. *Lexow Committee*, II:1622–24, 1645 (impunity), 1658 (impunity); *Tribune*, 15 June 1894.

5. *Lexow Committee*, II:1638–47.

6. *Tribune, Times*, 15 June 1894; Louis J. Beck, *New York's Chinatown: An Historical Representation of Its People and Places* (New York, 1898), 259. For similar reactions to Appo's testimony, see *Morning Advertiser* clipping, 15 June 1894; *Press* clipping, 15 June 1894, all in vol. 128, DAS.

7. On Hilton's green goods arrest, see unmarked clipping, 10 Feb. 1891, vol. 87, DAS; entry for 10 Feb. 1891, Second District, PCDB. Also see *World, Herald, Sun, Times,* and other clippings, 25 May 1892, vol. 98, DAS. On McNally's many arrests (including that by Thomas Byrnes), prosecution of his operatives, and the extensive newspaper coverage of his green goods activities before 1894, see chapter 15, notes 26, 27, 31, and 32.

8. *Lexow Committee*, II: 1631–40, 1642–44, 1660–61; *Times*, 15 June 1894 (incriminate), 9 Sept. 1894 (snap). More damaging testimony against O'Connor came from later witnesses. See *Lexow Committee*, II:2013–15. On Appo refusing to give names before the committee, see *Morning Advertiser* clipping, 15 June 1894, vol. 128, DAS.

9. *Lexow Committee*, II, 1649–50. Appo claimed that after he was shot in Poughkeepsie, Judge Charles Morschauser attempted to blackmail him. Morschauser denied the accusation. See *Lexow Committee*, II:1656; *Tribune*, 15 June 1894; *Times*, 16 June 1894.

10. *Lexow Committee*, III:2527–2641 (Applegate testimony); *Tribune*, 11, 12 Sept. 1894; George W. Appo, "The full History of my life" (handwritten), undated; and Appo deposition, 3 Oct. 1895, both in People v. George Appo, 19 Apr. 1895, New York Supreme Court, box 10100, location 106231 (unprocessed collection), DAP; *Herald* and other clippings, 11 Sept. 1894, vol. 131, DAS; William T. Stead, *Satan's Invisible World Displayed, or Despairing Democracy: A Study of Greater New York* (New York, 1897; London, 1898), 112–13. For Meakim's correspondence denying knowledge of the green goods business, see boxes 87-HAS-36 and 88-GHJ-41, MP.

11. *Press* clipping, 15 June 1894 (new form), vol. 128, DAS; *Lexow Committee*, II:1634–35, 1646, 1657.

12. Steffens, *Autobiography*, I:198.

13. Edward Crapsey, *The Nether Side of New York* (New York, 1872), 12; George W. Walling, *Recollections of a New York Chief of Police* (New York, 1887), 126–27, 380, 577; Berman, *Police Administration and Progressive Reform*, 62. On the history of policing in the United States, see David R. Johnson, *Policing the Urban Underworld: The Impact of Crime on the Development of the American Police, 1800–1887* (Philadelphia, 1979); Eric Monkkonen, *Police in Urban America, 1860–1920* (New York, 1981); Wilbur R. Miller, *Cops and Bobbies: Police Authority in New York and London, 1830–1870* (Chicago, 1977); Sidney Harring, *Policing a Class Society: The Experience of American Cities, 1865–1891* (New Brunswick, N.J., 1983). On police independence from the judiciary, see Allan Steinberg, *The Transformation of Criminal Justice: Philadelphia, 1800–1880* (Chapel Hill, N.C., 1989).

14. Hutchins Hapgood, ed., *The Autobiography of a Thief* (New York, 1903), 79–80, 86, 116; Josiah Flynt, *The World of Graft* (New York, 1901), 94, 96, 116 (percentage copper); unmarked clipping, 7 Jan. 1894 (criminals in uniform), vol. 123, DAS; *Lexow Committee*, V:5193 (parceled out); *Times*, 30 Dec. 1894 (sidewalk blackmail); *Tribune*, 10 July 1875.

15. *Increase of Crime*, 26 (precinct detectives); *Leslie's*, 19 Mar. 1859 (impossibility); Steffens, *Autobiography*, I:270–71, 288, 379 (crooked crooks); NYC, *Report of the Police Department for 1896*, 13 (blackmail); George McWatters, *Knots Untied, or Ways and By-Ways in the Hidden Life of American Detectives* (Hartford, Conn., 1873), 648–50; Lawrence Friedman, *Crime and Punishment in American History* (New York, 1993), 204–7 (reverse con man); unmarked clipping, 14 July 1875, William Wickham Papers, folder 157, box 1237, MP.

16. Parkhurst, *Our Fight*, 5; unmarked clipping, 16 June 1894 ($7 million); *Morning Advertiser* clipping, 17 June 1894 ($7 million); *Recorder* clipping, 2 June 1894, vol. 128 (blackmail), all in vol. 128, DAS; *Lexow*, IV:4496 (Moss); Steffens, *Autobiography*, I:376; City Club of New York, *The Police Department of the City of New York: A Statement of Facts* (New York, 1903), 356 ($7 million), copy in Police Box, WC.

17. *Times* clipping, 4 Apr. 1890, vol. 72, DAS. On working-class criticisms of nineteenth-century police brutality, see Johnson, *Street Justice*, 30–32.

18. Crapsey, *Nether Side*, 57–58; *Times* clipping, 31 Dec. 1895, vol. 136, DAS.

19. Steffens, *Autobiography*, I:261.

20. *Times* clipping, 10 Dec. 1893, vol. 122; unmarked clipping, 25 July 1895, vol. 144, both in DAS (military body). Conflicting lists of precincts Byrnes captained appeared in *Times*, 30 Dec. 1894; *Herald* clipping, 28 May 1895, vol. 141, DAS. For biographical details, see *Leslie's*, 22 May 1880; *Times*, 14 Apr. 1892; *Tribune*, 13 Apr. 1892, 28 May 1895; unmarked clipping, 19 Mar. 1895, vol. 139; *Times* clipping, 10 Dec. 1893, vol. 122; *Morning Advertiser* clipping, 25 Aug. 1893, vol. 117; unmarked clipping, 19 Mar. 1895 (promotion to Detective Bureau), vol. 139; *Herald*, 19 July 1895, vol. 143, all in DAS. For Byrnes's denials of party affiliation, see *Times* clipping, 10 Dec. 1893, vol. 122, DAS. On conflicts with Tammany Hall, see *Tribune*, 8 Nov. 1892. Some reports claimed that Byrnes was born in New York City. See *Tribune*, 28 May 1895. His date of birth was 15 June 1842. On Byrnes as "the preventive police force of New York," see *Morning Journal* clipping, 27 Oct. 1889, vol. 66, DAS.

21. *Tribune* clipping, 10 Jan. 1892, vol. 93; unmarked clipping, 13 June 1890, vol. 74; unmarked clipping, 22 Dec. 1892 (Cleveland inauguration), vol. 105; *Herald* clipping, 19 Feb. 1893 (Wall Street), vol. 108; unmarked clipping, 17 June 1894 (popular with businessmen), vol. 128; unmarked clipping, 3 Oct. 1886; *Herald* clipping, 28 May 1895, vol. 141, all in DAS; *Times*, 31 Dec. 1894, 14 Apr. 1892; *Tribune*, 13 Apr. 1892, 28 May 1895 (17 Wall Street); Helen Campbell, Thomas W. Knox, and Thomas Byrnes, *Darkness and Daylight: or, Lights and Shadows of New York Life* (Hartford, Conn., 1891), 520–21; James F. Richardson, *The New York Police: Colonial Times to 1901* (New York, 1970), 210. Byrnes was often identified as the originator of the "dead line" and the "third degree" interrogation. See Ric Burns and James Sanders, *New York: An Illustrated History* (New York, 1999), 198; Johnson, *Street Justice*, 123–24. For a favorable view of Byrnes's interrogation methods, see *Sun* clipping, 15 May 1887, vol. 35, DAS. On the third degree, see Zechariah Chafee, Jr., Walter H. Pollak, and Carl S. Stern,

*The Third Degree* (New York, 1931), 83–101; Emanuel H. Lavine, *The Third Degree: A Detailed and Appalling Expose of Police Brutality* (Garden City, N.Y., 1930); Johnson, *Street Justice*, 3, 124–48. The specific boundaries of the "dead line" were Fulton Street on the north, Greenwich Street on the west, the Battery on the south, and the East River.

22. Unmarked clipping, 14 July 1875, folder 157, box 1237, MP; *Tribune*, 5 Jan. 1890, 28 May 1895 (Scotland Yard); unmarked clippings, 3 Oct. 1886, 27 Oct. 1886, both in vol. 26; *Herald* clipping, 4 Jan. 1888 (best in world), vol. 43; *Press* clipping, 17 Apr. 1889 (centennial; arrest well-known thieves), vol. 60; *Tribune* clipping, 10 Jan. 1892, vol. 93; *Times* clipping, 10 Dec. 1893, vol. 122; *Herald* clipping, 28 May 1895 (Scotland Yard), vol. 141; *Herald*, 19 July 1895, vol. 143; all in DAS; Campbell, *Darkness*, 520–21; Steffens, *Autobiography*, I:201, 226–27; Flynt, *Graft*, 95 (criminals report); Richardson, *New York Police*, 210. On the acceptance of police corruption by criminals, see A. G. Warner, "Politics and Crime," *American Journal of Sociology* 1 (1895), 294. George W. Walling claimed that he was the first to arrest suspected pickpockets on holidays and during parades. See Walling, *Recollections*, 196, 219.

23. *Tribune*, 26 July 1884 (Mandelbaum); unmarked clipping, 13 June 1890 (expert thieves), vol. 74; unmarked clipping, 17 June 1894 (crime on East and West Sides), vol. 128, both in DAS. On the Byrnes report, see *Truth* and other clippings, 3 Aug. 1884, DAS.

24. Byrnes, *Professional Criminals*; Campbell, *Darkness*; New York *Dramatic Mirror*, 8 Dec. 1894 (story papers, melodramas). The five novels authored by Julian Hawthorne with the subtitle "From the Diary of Inspector Byrnes" include *An American Penman* (New York, 1887), *The Great Bank Robbery* (New York 1887), *A Tragic Mystery* (1887), *Another's Crime* (New York, 1888), and *Section 558* (New York, 1888). Praise of Byrnes appears in *World* clipping, 26 Dec. 1887 (wonderful man), vol. 43; unmarked clipping, 13 June 1890 (unexcelled detective genius), vol. 74; *Tribune* clipping, 10 Jan. 1892 (first policeman), vol. 93; *Times* clipping, 31 Dec. 1895 (most intelligent), vol. 136, all in DAS.

25. Walling, *Recollections*, 194, 216–19, 387 (London); Smith, *Sunshine*, 180–84 (summary arrests); *NPG*, 29 Nov. 1845; *Times*, 12 Sept. 1854 (summary arrests); *Herald*, 18 Oct. 1859; unmarked clipping, 1 Nov. 1896 (mass arrests), vol. 159, DAS. On police invoking the dead line to harass citizens, see *New York Mercury* clipping, 25 July 1895, vol. 144, DAS; against agents of the SPC, see *Press* clipping, 26 July 1895, vol. 144, DAS; Board of Police Justices for the City of New York, *Third Annual Report* (New York, 1877), 4 (1,074 suspicious persons); NYC Board of City Magistrates, *Twenty-Second Annual Report for 1895* (New York, 1896), 16–17; NYC Board of City Magistrates, *Twenty-Third Annual Report for 1896* (New York, 1897), 16. On the wide discretionary power of the police, see Miller, *Cops and Bobbies*, 20–21, 57; Amy Dru Stanley, "Beggars Can't Be Choosers: Compulsion and Contract in Postbellum America," *Journal of American History* 78 (1992), 1265–93.

26. *Times*, 14 May 1876.

27. Cornelius W. Willemse, *Behind the Green Lights* (New York, 1931), 20, 31, 35, 37; unmarked clipping, 14 Aug. 1895 (London police), vol. 144, DAS; Appo, 30–31; Allen S. Williams, *The Demon of the Orient* (New York, 1883), 71–72 (36 hours). Appo gave two different versions of these events. In 1883 he reported that he tried to escape dur-

ing this arrest. He later claimed that he went with the detectives and was brought before the police court the next day, never mentioning that he was without food for thirty-six hours.

28. *Press* clipping, 17 Apr. 1889, vol. 60; *World* clipping, 30 Mar. 1890 (Professional Criminal), vol. 72, both in DAS. On police officials supporting similar legislation in the early twentieth century, see Frank Marshall White, "New York's Ten Thousand Thieves," *Harper's Weekly* 50 (29 Dec. 1906), 1892–93.

29. *World* clipping, 30 Mar. 1890 (no single case), vol. 72; *Sun* clipping, 16 Feb. 1890, vol. 71, both in DAS; *Sun*, 12 Feb. 1888.

30. *World* clipping, 15 June 1894 (booty), vol. 126, DAS. On police corruption in the 1870s, see Mayor William Wickham to Police Commissioners, 7 Oct. 1875, copy in folder 261, box 1264; Fifteenth Ward Citizens Protective Association and Taxpayers League to William H. Wickham, 17 Jan. 1876, folder 225, box 1261, both in MP; *Increase of Crime*, 7 (demoralized). On the Roosevelt investigation, see the transcript of the Report of the Investigation of the Police Department of New York City in unmarked clipping, 16 May 1884, DAS; NYSA, *Report of the Special Committee Appointed to Investigate the Local Government of the City and County of New York*, AD 153 and 172 (Albany, 1884). On the Fassett Committee, see *World* clipping, 12 Apr. 1890; *Journal* and *Press* clippings, 13 Apr. 1890, all in vol. 72, DAS.

31. *Times*, 31 Dec. 1894 (unable to control captains); *Tribune*, 24 Feb. 1894 (raids); *World* and other clippings, 13 Jan. 1893 (charges), vol. 106; unmarked clipping, 20 Apr. 1892 (transfers), vol. 97; *Recorder* clipping, 8 Dec. 1892, vol. 104; *Morning Advertiser* clipping, 25 Aug. 1893, vol. 117; numerous clippings for 21 Sept. 1894, vol. 132; *Herald*, *Recorder*, and other clippings, 14 Mar. 1895, vol. 138; *Sunday Advertiser*, 26 May 1895, vol. 141, all in DAS.

32. *Lexow Committee*, V:5030–38, 5709–58 (Byrnes testimony); *Times*, 30 Dec. 1894; unmarked clipping, 19 Mar. 1895, vol. 139; *Mercury*, *Times*, *Herald* clippings, 28 May 1895, all in vol. 141, DAS. On Byrnes's toleration of green goods, see *Lexow Committee*, III:2632, 3119–23. On Byrnes permitting William McLaughlin's assault on Augustin Costello, see *Lexow Committee*, IV:4518–31, V:4654–78, 5154–56, 5701–5. On Byrnes's real estate activity, see *Tribune*, 14 Jan. 1893; on his wealth and resignation, see *Times*, 30, 31 Dec. 1894.

33. Most indictments were either dismissed, acquitted, or overturned on appeal. Capt. William Devery was acquitted and later named Chief of Police. Only Capt. John T. Stephenson was convicted and punished for crimes exposed by the Lexow Committee. See unmarked clipping, 25 June 1898, vol. 176; *World* clipping, 13 Dec. 1894 (Stephenson conviction), vol. 135, DAS. On the limited impact of the Lexow Committee, see Richardson, *New York Police*, 240–45, 262–63; Johnson, *Street Justice*, 54–56.

34. On the growing centralization of the police department after 1901, see Richardson, *New York Police*; Johnson, *Street Justice*, 57–113; Berman, *Police Administration*.

35. *Sun*, *Times*, 29, 30 Sept. 1894. Pettit's saloon was at 87 West Street. Since Richard O'Connor was police captain in the Fourth Precinct along the East River for a year, it is possible that O'Connor joined forces with Riordan. On O'Connor, see *World* clipping, 29 Oct. 1891, vol. 91, DAS. On Michael Riordan, see "List of Registered Voters" in "Officers and Subordinates in the Departments of the City and County Government," *City Record* (1 Nov. 1893), supplement (registered at 160 Greenwich Street).

On Samuel "Sam" Pettit, see *Sun* clipping, 15 Sept. 1884, vol. 9, DAS; *Trow's New York City Directory* (New York, 1884–96); "List of Registered Voters" in "Officers and Subordinates in the Departments of the City and County Government," *City Record* (1 Nov. 1890), Assembly District 1, Election District 11.

36. *Sun, Tribune, Times*, 29 Sept. 1894. The hotel was located at West and Barclay Streets.

37. New York newspapers had printed stories several weeks earlier that Appo was going to appear before the Lexow Committee and betray his associates in the green goods business. See *Times*, 9 Sept. 1894.

38. Appo, 57–61. Appo misspelled Riordan's name as "Readon" and "Reardon" in several places in this passage.

39. Unmarked clipping, 3 Aug. 1894 (opium dens), vol. 130, DAS; *Tribune*, 29 Sept. 1894 (cooperating with Goff), 12 Sept. 1894; *Sun*, 29 Sept. 1894; *Times*, 2 Oct. 1894 (cooperating), 9 Sept. 1894.

40. Entry for 29 Sept. 1894, PCDB, First District, roll 62, neg. 10408, NYCMA; *Sun*, 29 Sept. 1894; *Times*, 29 Sept. 1894 (alcoholic mania), 3 Oct. 1894 (Coleman); *Times, Tribune*, 30 Sept. 1894; unmarked clipping, 29 Sept. 1894; *World* clipping, 30 Sept. 1894 (O'Connor), both in vol. 132, DAS.

41. *Tribune*, 29 Sept. 1894; unmarked clipping, 27 Sept. 1894 (Post Office), vol. 132, DAS; *Times*, 2 Oct. 1894 (Post Office). Prior to this assault, Appo was beaten with another process server at Second Avenue and First Street. See *Times*, 2 Oct. 1894; *Sun*, 29 Sept. 1894.

42. *Sun*, 30 Sept. 1894; *Tribune*, 30 Sept. 1894; *Brooklyn Eagle*, 29 Sept. 1894; *World, Journal, Recorder*, and unmarked clippings, 30 Sept. 1894, vol. 132, DAS; *Times*, 3 Oct. 1894 (Coleman); *Lexow Committee*, II:2836–61 (Coleman).

43. *World*, 9 Nov. 1894; *Sun*, 9 Oct. 1894. The Brower House was at 22 West Twenty-eighth Street. See *Goulding's New York City Directory* (New York, 1876), 162. On Lyons, see chapter 15, note 43. For other reports of police captains and others issuing orders to attack witnesses before and after they came before the committee, see *Times*, 1 Oct. 1894, 8 Aug. 1895; *Sun*, 9 Oct. 1894; *World*, 11 Oct. 1894; *Lexow Committee*, II:1980–84, III:2740–43; unmarked clipping, 3 Aug. 1894, vol. 130; *Morning Journal* clipping, 9 Oct. 1894, vol. 133; unmarked clippings, 3 May 1895, vol. 140, all in DAS; *Tribune*, 12 Sept. 1894.

## 18. IN THE TENDERLOIN

1. Appo, 72–74. Appo was confused about the precise chronology of these events. In his autobiography he erroneously placed his encounter with Price after his release from Matteawan in 1899. He also believed that *In the Tenderloin* opened at the London Theater on the Bowery. The earliest production was in fact at the Grand Opera House in New Haven, Connecticut, on 29 Nov. 1894. In early December 1894, the production moved to the Star Theater in Brooklyn, and then opened in New York on 17 Dec. 1894 at Henry C. Miner's People's Theater, 201 Bowery. See *Illustrated American*, 5 Jan. 1895; *Herald*, 30 Nov. 1894; *Dramatic Mirror*, 15 Dec. 1894 (Star Theater); *In the Tenderloin* playbill, People's Theater, 17 Dec. 1894, BR; George C. D. Odell, *Annals of the*

New York Stage (New York, 1949), XIV:63. I changed the name of the theater in this passage.
2. *Sun*, 29 Sept. 1894.
3. No published or copyrighted version of *In the Tenderloin* exists. This description was compiled from *In the Tenderloin* playbill, People's Theater, 17 Dec. 1894; *World*, 21 Oct. 1894, in clipping file, both in BR; *Herald*, 30 Nov. 1894; *Cincinnati Tribune*, 20 Jan. 1895; *Cincinnati Times-Star*, 19 Jan. 1895; *Indianapolis News*, 29 Jan. 1895; Timothy J. Gilfoyle, "Staging the Criminal: *In the Tenderloin*, Freak Drama, and the Criminal Celebrity," *Prospects: An Annual of American Cultural Studies* 30 (2005), notes 6 and 18.
4. Peter Brooks, *The Melodramatic Imagination: Balzac, Henry James, Melodrama, and the Mode of Excess* (New York, 1976 and 1985), 13-16, 30-31; Robert W. Snyder, *The Voice of the City: Vaudeville and Popular Culture in New York* (New York, 1989), 1-7; David Grimsted, *Melodrama Unveiled: American Theater and Culture, 1800-1850* (Chicago, 1968), 175-248; Gilfoyle, "Staging the Criminal," esp. note 7.
5. *Indianapolis News*, 29 Jan. 1895 (destroyer); *Life*, 27 Dec. 1894.
6. *World*, 21 Oct. 1894, in clipping file, BR.
7. On criminals and gangsters as "celebrities," see Lawrence M. Friedman, *Crime and Punishment in American History* (New York, 1993), 446-47; David E. Ruth, *Inventing the Public Enemy: The Gangster in American Culture, 1918-1934* (Chicago, 1996); David R. Papke, *Framing the Criminal: Crime, Cultural Work, and the Loss of Critical Perspective, 1830-1900* (Hamden, Conn., 1987); Gilfoyle, "Staging the Criminal," note 10.
8. *Times*, 9 Oct. 1938; Michael MacDonald Mooney, *Evelyn Nesbit and Stanford White: Love and Death in the Gilded Age* (New York, 1976), 60. The word "vaudeville" preceded Lederer's birth. See Gunther Barth, *City People: The Rise of Modern City Culture in Nineteenth-Century America* (New York, 1980), 196-200; Snyder, *Voice of the City*, 11-25.
9. *Herald* clipping, 25 Oct. 1889, vol. 66, DAS; *World*, 13 Nov. 1894.
10. For biographical information on Lederer and coverage of his bigamy case, see Gilfoyle, "Staging the Criminal," notes 12-14.
11. *The American Fistiana: Showing the Progress of Pugilism in the United States from 1816 to 1860* (New York, 1860), 26-27, 72-74 (quote); Elliott J. Gorn, *The Manly Art: Bare-Knuckle Prize Fighting in America* (Ithaca, N.Y., 1986), 105-7, 168, 274.
12. *World* clipping, 29 May 1891, vol. 86; unmarked clipping, 9 Jan. 1892, vol. 93, both in DAS. On Price's legal career, see Gilfoyle, "Staging the Criminal." Price defended Appo in his assault case involving James Collins. See Appo, 21-23.
13. *Tribune*, 26 June 1886, 8 July 1886; *Lexow Committee*, IV:4168-70; *World*, 3 Nov. 1894.
14. Ed Price, *The Science of Self Defence: A Treatise on Sparring and Wrestling* (New York, 1867), copy in the Newberry Library; *American Fistiana*, 26-27, 72-74 (linguist); Odell, *Annals*, XIII:509, XV:240-41; *World*, 21 Oct. 1894 (Sullivan), in clipping file, BR. On Price's dramatic production, see Gilfoyle, "Staging the Criminal."
15. *World*, 21 Oct. 1894, in clipping file, BR.
16. *Herald*, 30 Nov. 1894.
17. Unmarked clipping, 17 Dec. 1894, clipping file, BR (quotes); *In the Tenderloin* playbill, People's Theater, 17 Dec. 1894; *Dramatic Mirror*, 15 Dec. 1894 (Star); *Spirit of the*

*Times*, 15, 22 Dec. 1894 (People's); Capt. Anthony Allaire to Supt. William Murray (leading actors), 27 Apr. 1887, folder 246, box 1366, Hewitt Papers, MP.

18. *Dramatic Mirror*, 22 Dec. 1894 (useless); *Spirit of the Times*, 22 Dec. 1894 (disgrace); *Life*, 27 Dec. 1894; *Illustrated American*, 5 Jan. 1895 (shameless, poor actors). On the critical reaction to *In the Tenderloin* and nineteenth-century cultural conflict, see Gilfoyle, "Staging the Criminal."

19. *Illustrated American*, 5 Jan. 1895 (money-bags); *Life*, 27 Dec. 1894 (more profit); *Dramatic Mirror*, 15 Dec. 1894, 22 Dec. 1894 (sensational melodrama); *Cincinnati Enquirer*, 23 Jan. 1895 (sensational); *Indianapolis News*, 29 Jan. 1895.

20. *World*, 11 Nov. 1894; *Journal* and other clippings, 29, 30 Jan. 1899 (Moore), vol. 177, DAS; T. J. Stiles, *Jesse James: Last Rebel of the Civil War* (New York, 2002), 395.

21. For dates and theaters with productions in the 1880s, see Odell, *Annals*, 14:64, 163, 194, 300, 303–4, 473, 583, 621, 644, 760, 765; 15:114–15, 158, 177, 247, 398, 657–58, 725, 737, 821–22.

22. *Cincinnati Tribune*, 21 Jan. 1895; *Cincinnati Enquirer*, 21 Jan. 1895; 23, 24 Jan. 1895; *Syracuse Standard*, quoted in *Youngstown Daily Vindicator*, 16 Jan. 1895; Gilfoyle, "Staging the Criminal."

23. *Cincinnati Tribune*, 20 Jan. 1895.

24. *World*, 30 Dec. 1894. For national coverage, see Gilfoyle, "Staging the Criminal," note 46.

25. Appo, 74–76. Appo indicated that he wrote this portion of his autobiography on 17 July 1915. An earlier examination of *In the Tenderloin* erroneously claimed that Appo disappeared before the production was closed, generating theories that he was murdered or was on an "opium spree." See M. R. Werner, *It Happened in New York* (New York, 1957), 76.

### 19. A MARKED MAN

1. Newspaper accounts claimed that Appo worked as a subpoena server and informant for the Lexow Committee after his testimony. See *Times*, 30 Sept. 1894, 2 Oct. 1894; *Sun*, 29 Sept. 1894.

2. Coverage of Theodore Babcock's career appears in *Herald*, 8 Nov. 1892; George C. D. Odell, *Annals of the New York Stage* (New York, 1949), XV:305, 603, 604, 637, 796; *Dramatic Mirror*, 5 Mar. 1894.

3. Appo, 60–62. Appo erroneously thought that his bond was $1,500. Other reports indicate that it was $500. Appo also believed that he received a one-year sentence, when in fact he was sent to the Blackwell's Island Penitentiary for six months. See *Tribune*, 11 Apr. 1895; Blackwell's Island Register, Oct. 1895, vol. 20, Executive Register of Commitments to Prisons, NYSA; unmarked clipping, 5 Oct. 1895, DAS. I have changed the original text in these two instances.

4. *Tribune*, *World*, 10 Apr. 1895; *Sun*, *Morning Advertiser* clippings, 10 Apr. 1895, vol. 140, DAS; entry for George W. Appo, 9 Apr. 1895, PCDB, Second District, roll #70, neg. 10369, NYCMA; George W. Appo, "The full History of my life" (handwritten), undated; and Appo deposition, 3 Oct. 1895, both in People v. George Appo, 19 Apr. 1895 (two men to kill me), New York Supreme Court, box 10100, location 106231

(unprocessed collection), DAP (hereafter Appo, "The full History of my life," and Appo deposition, respectively).

5. *Lexow Committee*, II:1926–50 (Hill); V:4919–31, 4966–82 (Creeden); V:5311–85 (Schmittberger); V:4950–60, 4982–5024, 5047–65 (saloonkeeper John Reppenhagen); Lincoln Steffens, *The Autobiography of Lincoln Steffens* (New York, 1931), I:254, 266–84 (Schmittberger). I am indebted to Daniel Czitrom for distinguishing among the various Murphys on the New York police force.

6. Unmarked clipping, 12 May 1899, vol. 180, DAS.

7. Unmarked clippings, 3 May 1895 (Matilda Hermann), vol. 140, DAS; M. R. Werner, *It Happened in New York* (New York, 1957), 114 (Priem, Schmittberger), 101 (Herman).

8. Appo, 95; *Recorder* clipping, 5 Oct. 1895, vol. 146, DAS; Louis J. Beck, *New York's Chinatown: An Historical Representation of Its People and Places* (New York, 1898), 200. At least five assaults on Appo can be corroborated in court and newspaper accounts: 26 Sept. 1894 (outside Post Office), 28 Sept. 1894 (by Ryan and Riordan), 8 Nov. 1894 (by Ned Lyons), 19 Dec. 1894 (in Brooklyn and 117th Street and Eighth Avenue), and 10 Apr. 1895 (after bail release). See Appo, "The full History of my life," and Appo deposition; unmarked clipping, 20 Dec. 1894, vol. 136, DAS.

9. *Newark* [Ohio] *Daily Advocate*, 15 June 1896 (from *Buffalo Express*). Appo's height and weight appear in 396, entry for George Dixon, vol. 11; 173, entry for George Wilson, vol. 14; 269, entry for George Appo, container 6, vol. 20; 140, entry for George Albow, container 10, vol. 28, all in SSAR.

10. *Lexow Committee*, II:1631, 1633, 1641–47, 1654. On Ryan telling Appo that McNally blackballed him, see Appo, "The full History of my life," and Appo deposition.

11. *Recorder* clipping, 5 Oct. 1895 ($500,000), vol. 146, DAS; Frank Moss, *The American Metropolis* (New York, 1897), III:133–34; *Tribune*, 15 June 1894 (felt betrayed); *Lexow Committee*, III:2610–11 (Roach's).

12. *Sun*, 29 Sept. 1894; Beck, *New York's Chinatown*, 259 (put-up job). Most evidence refutes this, including Appo's autobiography, in which he maintains that he never betrayed McNally, even in his Lexow testimony.

13. *Tribune*, 16 June 1899; Appo testimony, 6 Oct. 1896, p. 16 (shame of women), in People v. George Appo, 24 July 1896, New York District Attorney Records, Cases #9126 and #9127, box B-2, location 12817, SCC.

14. *Tribune*, 11 Apr. 1895; *Times*, 8 Oct. 1894. *Press* clipping, 13 Apr. 1895, vol. 140, DAS. On Michael J. Rein, see "Officers and Subordinates in the Departments of the City and County Government," *City Record* (31 Jan. 1887), 230; "Officers and Subordinates" (31 Jan. 1896), 290; (31 Jan. 1901), supplement; *Lexow Committee*, III:2906–7. Newspapers referred to Rein as "Ryan" and "Reiman."

15. Unmarked clipping, 3 Aug. 1895, vol. 144 ("female Parkhurst"); *Sunday Advertiser* clipping, 28 Apr. 1895, vol. 140, both in DAS; *Times*, 8 Oct. 1894; *NPG*, 25 Aug. 1894.

16. *Tribune*, 11 Apr. 1895 (release); *Sunday Advertiser* clipping, 28 Apr. 1895 (Parkhurst), vol. 140, Appo, "The full History of my life," and Appo deposition (fear for life); *Times*, *Tribune*, *World*, 17 Apr. 1895 (bond forfeiture); *Newark Daily Advocate*, 15 June 1896.

17. *Brooklyn Eagle*, 30 Sept. 1895. Other accounts claimed Appo was arrested in Buffalo on 7 August 1895, and arrived in New York a day later. See Appo, "The full History of my life"; *Times*, 8 Aug. 1895. Another claimed that he assaulted a waiter in a Montreal saloon. See *Times*, 22 May 1895.

18. *Times*, 8 May 1920; *Tribune*, 12 Mar. 1879; unmarked clipping, 14 Feb. 1895, vol. 138; unmarked clippings, 31 Mar. 1895, vol. 139, all in DAS; *World*, 26 Oct. 1894 (pigeon-holed indictments); Moss, *American Metropolis*, III:124–25.

19. *Times*, 1 Oct. 1895; *Tribune*, *Times*, 4 Oct. 1895; *Morning Advertiser*, *Herald*, and other clippings, 4 Oct. 1895; *Recorder* clipping, 5 Oct. 1895 (Appo quote), all in vol. 146, DAS.

20. *Tribune*, 11 Apr. 1895; Blackwell's Island Register, Oct. 1895, vol. 20, Executive Register of Commitments to Prisons, NYSA.

21. Appo, 63–64. Appo identified the arresting police officer as Michael Rein from his earlier confrontation. Court and newspaper records indicate that Stephen Loughman was the officer, whose name was spelled "Lockman," "Lochman," "Loughran," and "Laughlin." I use "Loughman," which was the spelling in PCDB, First District, 11 July 1896, 172, microfilm roll 68, negative 10414; People v. George Appo, 24 July 1896, DAP, cases #9126 and #9127, box 10131, location 106262, SCC; George Appo testimony, 6 Oct. 1896, 8–11, in People v. George Appo, 24 July 1896, case #9126, box B-2, SCC. Although these documents concern the same case, the manuscript indictments contain different notations on each.

22. *Times*, 11 July 1896 (I've been drinking), 12 July 1896; *Tribune*, 11 July 1896; *Sun*, *Herald*, and other unmarked clippings, 11, 12 July 1896, vol. 157, DAS. Appo was first charged with carrying a dangerous weapon and later with first-degree assault.

23. Ibid. Atwood later admitted that he was from out of town and staying at a Bowery hotel. See Statement of John W. Atwood, 1, in People v. George Appo, 24 July 1896, case #9126, box B-2, SCC.

24. *Sun* clipping, 11 Oct. 1896 (Goff disgusted), vol. 159, DAS; *Tribune*, 9, 12 Aug. 1895. Goff assigned Purdy to Appo's case.

25. PCDB, First District, 11 July 1896, p. 172, microfilm roll 68, negative 10414, NYCMA; *Advertiser* clipping, 28 July 1896, vol. 157, DAS. O'Reilly was a lawyer and judge (1884–91). See *Trow's New York City Directory* (New York, 1884–95).

26. *Times*, 24 Dec. 1887; Augustine E. Costello, *Our Police Protectors* (New York, 1885), 506; *Times*, 13 Aug. 1919; *Tribune*, 8 Mar. 1886 (Cowing). On Purdy's defense of more than a dozen counterfeiters, see vols. 17, 27–29; indexes of vols. 30–38, under "Purdy," all in Drummond Papers. On Purdy's role in the prosecution of Danny Driscoll, see unmarked clippings, 27, 28 Sept. 1886, vol. 25, DAS.

27. *Herald* clipping, 9 Jan. 1892 (McGlory), vol. 93; unmarked clipping, 21 Oct. 1890 (defending green goods men), vol. 77; *Telegram* clipping, 11 Mar. 1891, in vol. 82; unmarked clipping, 6 Apr. 1891, vol. 84; *Commercial Advertiser* clipping, 24 Apr. 1893, in vol. 111; *Evening World* clipping, 12 Oct. 1893, vol. 119 (Ellison); unmarked clipping, 1 Nov. 1895, vol. 147; *World* clipping, 1 Jan. 1897 (boodle), vol. 161, all in DAS; *Tribune*, 26 Nov. 1893 (Ellison); U.S. v. Samuel Marks, Bill of Exceptions filed in U.S. Circuit Court, Southern District of New York, 17 Dec. 1889, #1447, RG 21. On Ward and Rosenthal, see *Herald*, *Sun*, and other clippings, 19–21 Oct. 1890, vol. 77, DAS. On the knockout-drop case, see unmarked clippings, 27 Oct. 1893, vol. 120; *World* clipping, 1 Jan. 1897, vol. 161, all in DAS; *Tribune*, 27 Oct. 1893. On Purdy as a "shyster lawyer," see *Tribune*, 1, 9 Jan. 1897.

28. *Morning Advertiser*, 27 Apr. 1894 (CVL supporter), vol. 127, DAS; People v. George Appo, 19 Apr. 1895, box 10100, location 106231, SCC.

29. Herbert S. Brown, "The Insane," *Charities Review*, 9 (Nov. 1899), 371; "Dr. J. B. Thomson on the Congenital Imbecility of Criminals," *American Journal of Insanity* 18 (Oct. 1861), 191 (moral degradation); Martin W. Barr, "Some Studies of Heredity," *Journal of Nervous and Mental Disease* 24 (1897), 155–62.

30. *Times*, 17 June 1896; George Appo testimony, 6 Oct. 1896 (typewritten), 7–8, in People v. George Appo, 24 July 1896, New York District Attorney Records, case #9126, box B-2, SSC. The handwritten version is in People v. George Appo, 24 July 1896, case #9126, box 10131, SCC. These statements included many details later described in his autobiography.

31. Ibid. Appo gave the bartender's name as "Eddie Irving." This indictment and People v. George Appo, 24 July 1896, cases #9126 and #9127, box 10131, SCC, listed Appo's address as 48 East Fourth Street. Appo claimed that he was "on business for Louis Beck."

32. *Tribune, Times*, 27 Apr. 1882; Allen S. Williams, *The Demon of the Orient* (New York, 1883), 71–74; Beck, *New York's Chinatown*, 255; unmarked clipping, "The Rogues' Gallery," 23 Apr. 1883 (attempted suicide), DAS. Appo's consumption of opium or laudanum may simply have been a fit related to his opiate addiction. The *Tribune*, however, reported that Appo said "he wanted to die."

33. *Sun*, 30 Sept. 1894 (four suicide attempts); *Poughkeepsie News-Press*, 21 Apr. 1893, 25 Apr. 1893; *Poughkeepsie Daily Eagle*, 18, 21 Apr. 1893; *Poughkeepsie News-Telegraph*, 22 Apr. 1893; *Poughkeepsie Courier*, 12 Mar. 1893; Beck, *New York's Chinatown*, 258. The same quotes on Appo's suicide threat appear in *Poughkeepsie Daily Eagle*, 26 Apr. 1893; *Times*, 26 Apr. 1893.

34. *Sun, Tribune, Times*, 29 Sept. 1894 (raving like a madman); *Recorder* clipping, 5 Oct. 1895, vol. 146, DAS.

35. Arthur Dennett (SPC Superintendent) to Cowing, 2 Oct. 1895, in People v. George Appo, 19 Apr. 1895.

36. *Sun* and unmarked clipping, 11 Oct. 1896, both in vol. 159, DAS; *Brooklyn Eagle*, 11 Oct. 1896.

37. Appo testimony, 6 Oct. 1896, 16, People v. George Appo, 24 July 1896, case #9126, SCC.

38. Unmarked clipping, 15 July 1890, vol. 75, DAS; *Times*, 12 Aug. 1893. On Meredith, see chapter 12, note 22. On Vosburg, see *Press* and other clippings, 8, 9, 12, 16 Nov. 1895, vol. 147; *Sun, Tribune, Recorder*, and other clippings, 11, 12 Dec. 1895, vol. 149, all in DAS. For examples of convicts feigning insanity to be transferred out of prison, see *Times*, 14 Feb. 1893.

39. NYSCC, *Special Report on Psychiatric and Expert Testimony in Criminal Cases* (Albany, 1930), 6–7; NYSCC, *Report—1929* (Albany, 1929), 179; NYSCC, *Special Report on Psychiatric and Expert Testimony in Criminal Cases* (Albany, 1929), 5. Legislation requiring certification of psychiatric witness was not proposed until the 1920s. On the process of determining insanity at Bellevue and elsewhere during the nineteenth century, see Matthew D. Field, "Detention Hospitals for the Insane," *Journal of Nervous and Mental Disease* 20 (1893), 599–60; C. Eugene Riggs, "The Care and Handling of the Insane," *Journal of Nervous and Mental Disease* 20 (1893), 627–28.

40. Statement of Dr. Joseph Terriberry, 9 Oct. 1896, 26–28, 32–33, in People v. George Appo, 24 July 1896, case #9126, SCC.

41. Appo testimony, 6 Oct. 1896, 10–20, 22 (quote), People v. George Appo, 24 July 1896, case #9126, SCC.
42. *Recorder* clipping, 5 Oct. 1895, vol. 146, DAS.
43. *Times* clipping, 19 Oct. 1895, vol. 146; *Tribune* and *Herald* clippings, 27 Dec. 1900 (railroaded), vol. 196, all in DAS. On the unsystematic procedures in state examinations for insanity, see "A New Lunacy Law," *Journal of Nervous and Mental Disease* 23 (1896), 334–35. City examiners charged fees of $20 to $30 per case. On the failure of Bellevue physicians to maintain clinical histories of patients before 1915, see NYC Board of Estimate and Apportionment [Henry C. Wright], *Report of the Committee on Inquiry into the Departments of Health, Charities, and Bellevue and Allied Hospitals* (New York, 1913), 35–36. On corruption in Bellevue, see *Herald* clipping, 27 Dec. 1900; *World* clipping, 29 Dec. 1900; unmarked clipping, 1 Jan. 1901; *Press* clipping, 9 Jan. 1901; unmarked clippings, 10 and 12 Jan. 1901, all in vol. 196; unmarked clipping, 16 Feb. 1901, vol. 197, all in DAS.
44. "The Commitment of Patients and the New Insanity Law," *Journal of Nervous and Mental Disease* 24 (1897), 107–9; New York County District Attorney, Record of Cases, July 1896, vol. ?, 19, microfilm roll 1, cases #9126 and #9127, NYCMA; NYC, *Report of the Police Department for 1896* (New York, 1897), 66 (only two to Matteawan); *Times*, 24 Dec. 1896 (McMahon); NYSA, *Thirty-Seventh Annual Report of the Medical Superintendent of the State Asylum for Insane Criminals, for Year Ending Sept. 30, 1896*, AD 67 (Albany, 1897), 280–81.
45. W. C. Johnston to Albert Stangler, 20 Jan. 1971, in QA Case File; Beck, *New York's Chinatown*, 200 (wreck).

## 20. BURIED ALIVE

1. Appo, 66–67.
2. *World*, *Times*, 22 Oct. 1876 (Kate Burke); *Sun*, 22 Oct. 1876 (Cherry Street, children scattered; Lizzie Williams); entry for Quimbo Appo, 217, 5 Apr. 1869, for Deductions of Sentences, Executive Journals of Governors' Actions and Decisions, 1859–1916 (AO607); Entry for Quimbo Appo, 29 Mar. 1869, vol. 1, 1863–75, Executive Reports of Deduction of Sentences by Prison Agents, (AO601), both in NYSArc. Quimbo Appo never received a pardon; his sentences were commuted. See entry for 8 May 1860, 349, vol. for 1860, Executive Journals of Governors' Actions and Decisions (AO607); 25, vol. 2; vols. 17 (index), 18 (index), all in Executive Clemency and Pardon Application Ledgers and Correspondence (AO629); vols. 7–8 (indexes from 1853 to 1918), Department of State, Executive Clemency and Pardon Records, Executive Pardons (BO042); entry for 8 May 1860, vol. 3, Sing Sing admissions, 1842–74 (n.p.), Executive Register of Commitments to Prisons, all in NYSArc. I am indebted to James Folts for locating these and other relevant sources related to Quimbo Appo. Evidence of Quimbo Appo residing in Five Points appears in *Herald*, 5 Jan. 1872 (14 Baxter); People v. Quimbo Appo, 13 Dec. 1871, DAP; *Trow's New York City Directory* (New York, 1872); p. 6, Ward 6, Election District 3, Federal Manuscript Census Population Schedules, City of New York, Second Enumeration, 1870, reel 1017 (hereafter Second Enumeration, 1870).

3. Appo, 2–3; *Trow's New York City Directory* (New York, 1872); *Times*, 26 Dec. 1856.

4. *Herald*, 10 Aug. 1871 (hopeless); Quimbo Appo (plaintiff in error) v. People of N.Y., 30 Mar. 1872 (writ of appeal), New York Supreme Court, VR-P #543, CCNYA (hereafter Quimbo Appo writ of appeal); People v. Appo, 13 Dec. 1871, DAP (9 Aug.); *Times*, 30 Sept. 1871, 13, 14, 15, 16, 19 Dec. 1871; *Tribune*, 30 Sept. 1871; *Herald*, 5 Jan. 1872 (Linkonski), 6 Jan. 1872, 22 Oct. 1876 (stone); *World*, 21 Oct. 1876, 21 Dec. 1876. Details of the assault later appeared in *World, Times*, 22 Oct. 1876.

5. *Herald*, 6 Jan. 1872 (bloody man); *Brooklyn Eagle*, 6 Jan. 1872. The writs of error were filed on 9 Jan. and 30 Mar. 1872. See People v. Appo, 13 Dec. 1871, DAP; *Herald*, 6 Jan. 1872; Quimbo Appo entry, 6 Jan. 1872, p. 308, vol. 10, SSAR; entry for 5 Jan. 1872, vol. 3, Sing Sing admissions, 1842–74 (n.p.), Executive Register of Commitments to Prisons (AO603); vol. 2, Reports on Deduction of Sentences by Prison Agents, Wardens and Superintendents (AO601), all in NYSArc; Quimbo Appo writ of appeal; *World, Times*, 22 Oct. 1876; NYSA, *Twenty-eighth AR of the Inspectors of State Prisons [for 1875]*, AD 11 (Albany, 1876), 111, 148 (conviction as "assault to harm").

6. Unpaginated typed report, QA Case File (dates in Auburn); vol. 1, Reports on Deduction of Sentences by Prison Agents, Wardens and Superintendents (AO601), NYSArc (17 days, commutation); *World, Times, Sun*, 22 Oct. 1876.

7. Different accounts identified the victim as Mrs. Yah Maung, Eliza Nahering, and Elizabeth Nomoen. See entry for "Crimpo Appo," 20 Sept. 1875, p. 144, First District, vol. 5, roll 9, negative 10155, PCDB; *World*, 23 Sept. 1875, 22 Oct. 1876; *Times*, 22 Oct. 1876. On the Bernstein incident, see 31 Jan. 1876, 150, 1st Dist., vol. 6, roll 10, neg. 10156, PCDB; *Tribune*, 23 Oct. 1876; *Sun*, 22 Oct. 1876 (released 1 Jan. 1876).

8. *World*, 21 Oct. 1876, 21 Dec. 1876; *Times*, 21 Oct. 1876; p. 135, 21 Oct. 1876, 1st District, vol. 8, roll 12, neg. 10158, PCDB.

9. *World*, 21, 22 Oct. 1876; *Times*, 22 Oct. 1876.

10. *Times*, 21 Oct. 1876 (notorious), 22 Oct. 1876; *Tribune*, 23 Oct. 1876; *Brooklyn Eagle*, 28 Oct. 1876; Louis J. Beck, *New York's Chinatown: An Historical Representation of Its People and Places* (New York, 1898), 9.

11. *World*, 21 Oct. 1876, 21 Dec. 1876 (Englishwoman, 1857); *Sun*, 22 Oct. 1876 (St. Pat's Day); *Tribune*, 23 Oct. 1876 (St. Pat's Day), 30 Sept. 1871 (killed wife), 7 Aug. 1880 (killed wife); *World*, 22 Oct. 1876 (killed wife); *Herald*, 22 Oct. 1876 (killed wife); Williams, *Demon of the Orient*, 74 (mistress); Beck, *New York's Chinatown*, 9–10 (1875 date). On Quimbo Appo committing multiple murders or murders while in Sing Sing, see *World*, 7 Aug. 1880; *Tribune*, 21, 23 Oct. 1876, 22 Dec. 1876; *Sun*, 22 Oct. 1876; Beck, *New York's Chinatown*, 9–10; *World*, 21 Oct. 1876, 21 Dec. 1876. For accounts claiming that Quimbo was pardoned by Gov. John Hoffman in 1863, even though Edwin Morgan was governor from 1859 to 1863, see *Times*, 21 Oct. 1876 (Hoffman), 22 Oct. 1876; *World*, 21, 22 Oct. 1876, 21 Dec. 1876; *Sun*, 22 Oct. 1876; *Tribune*, 23 Oct. 1876; Beck, *New York's Chinatown*, 9–10; Tchen, "Quimbo Appo's Fear of Fenians," 148.

12. Entry for 21 Dec. 1876, vol. 6, Sing Sing Admissions, 1875–82 (n.p.), Executive Register of Commitments of Prisons (AO603); QA Case File (second-degree manslaughter); entry for Quimbo Appo, 161, 22 Dec. 1876, vol. 14, SSAR, all in NYSArc; entry for 21 Oct. 1876, 135, vol. 8, 1st District, PCDB; People v. Quimbo Appo, 15 Nov. 1876,

DAP; NYSA, *First AR of the Superintendent of State Prisons [for 1877]*, AD 10 (Albany, 1878), 67 (seven-year sentence); *World*, 21, 22 Dec. 1876; *Times*, 21, 22 Dec. 1876.

13. 1, Physicians Report, and "Certificate of Insanity," 5 Jan. 1878, QA Case File.

14. "Dr. J. B. Thomson on the Congenital Imbecility of Criminals," *American Journal of Insanity* 18 (Oct. 1861), 191–92 (mental imbecility); Stephen Jay Gould, *The Mismeasure of Man* (New York, 1981, 1996), 152–75. On Lombroso's impact, see Stephan Hurwitz and Karol O. Christiansen, *Criminology* (Rutherford, N.J., 1983), 23–27; Lombroso, *Crime: Its Causes and Remedies*, trans. Henry P. Horton (Boston, 1911).

15. 1–2, typed report, QA Case File; Caesar Lombroso, *Criminal Man* (New York, 1911), 10, 241 (cephalic index).

16. 1, typed report, QA Case File.

17. Entries from 14 Aug. 1880 to 1 Oct. 1880, 2, typed report, QA Case File. On George Appo's trial, see Appo, 21–23, *Times*, 6, 7, 8 Aug. 1880; *Tribune*, 7 Aug. 1880; entry for 6 Aug. 1880, 32, First District, vol. 17, roll 21, neg. 10167, PCDB.

18. Entries for 1 Apr. 1878, 30 June 1878 (good-natured), 30 Oct. 1880, 25 Dec. 1880, 1 July 1882, 8 Oct. 1883, 3, typed report, QA Case File.

19. C. Eugene Riggs, "The Care and Handling of the Insane," *Journal of Nervous and Mental Disease* 20 (1893), 624.

20. Entries for 30 June 1878, 27 Dec. 1879, 2 July 1880, 1 July 1881, 2 Apr. 1884, 1–4, typed report, QA Case File.

21. 1; entries for 15 Apr. 1881, 1 Sept. 1884, 3–4 (Appo challenged), all in typed report, QA Case File; NYSA, *Thirty-Seventh AR of the Medical Superintendent of the State Asylum for Insane Criminals*, AD 67 (Albany, 1897), 277–78; NYSA, *Better Provision for Insane Criminals*, 8 (Smith, MacDonald, criminal class); H. E. Allison, "Recent Additional Provision for the Criminal Insane in the State of New York," *American Journal of Insanity* 56 (Apr. 1900), 740; NYSA, *[Eighth] AR of the Superintendent of State Prisons [for 1884]*, AD 11 (Albany, 1885), 158 (Smith). On asylum patients challenging their ongoing detention, see NYSA, *Better Provision for Insane Criminals*, 9. Retention of Appo was legal under legislation passed in 1869 and revised in 1874 providing for "the safe custody and care of insane criminals" upon expiration of their sentences. See *American Journal of Insanity* 28 (July 1871), 121–22; John P. Gray, "An Abstract of the Laws of the State of New York in Regard to the Commitment of Insane to Asylums," *American Journal of Insanity* 35 (Jan. 1879), 359–74.

22. Entries from 29 Dec. 1884 to 26 Feb. 1890, 30 Apr. 1895, 4 Jan. 1899, 4–7, typed report, QA Case File. Assaults or threats of assault are documented on 30 Oct. 1880, 1 Nov. 1880, 25 Dec. 1880, 1 Jan. 1882, 8 Oct. 1883, 10 Apr. 1899.

23. Appo, 66; entries for 14 Aug. 1880, 12 Feb. 1893, 29 July 1893, 10 July 1898, 20 Apr. 1902, 7 Jan. 1903, 5 Oct. 1903, 1 Dec. 1904, 8 June 1905, 3, 6–9, typed report, QA Case File; *Sun* clipping, 6 May 1894 (delusions), vol. 127, DAS. Evidence that George and Quimbo Appo maintained a relationship prior to George's admittance to Matteawan is revealed in entries for 1 Dec. 1892, 12 Feb. 1893, 17 July 1896, 10 July 1899, 30 Apr. 1902, 7 Jan. 1903, 22 Dec. 1903, 8 June 1905, 5–9, QA Case File.

24. Entry for 10 July 1899, 7, typed report, QA Case File.

25. Ibid. (properly cared); NYSA, *Thirty-Fourth AR of the Medical Superintendent of the State Asylum for Insane Criminals*, AD 66 (Albany, 1894), 222 (19 percent); NYSA, *Thirty-Sixth AR of the Medical Superintendent of the State Asylum for Insane Criminals*,

AD 58 (Albany, 1896), 238, 247 (State Care Act); NYSA, *Thirty-Eighth AR of the Medical Superintendent of the Matteawan State Hospital* (n.p., 1898?), 9–10; NYSA, *Thirty-
Seventh AR for Insane Criminals*, 277–78.

26. NYSA, *Thirty-Fifth AR of the Medical Superintendent of the State Asylum for Insane
Criminals*, AD 78 (Albany, 1895), 221 (Allison).

27. Appo, 64–68. George Appo's medical record from Matteawan is missing from the Matteawan State Hospital Inmate Case Files, NYSArc. Appo misspelled Spratling as "Dr.
Spradley."

28. *Sun* clipping, 6 May 1894 (to cure), vol. 127, DAS; Beacon, N.Y., Golden Jubilee, "Souvenir Program," 1–8 June 1963 (peaceful), Dutchess County Historical Society, Poughkeepsie, N.Y.

29. "N.Y. Asylum for Criminal Insane," *American Journal of Insanity* 15 (Apr. 1859), 446;
"Statistics for 1862," ibid., 21 (Apr. 1864), 528a; "Asylums for Insane Criminals," ibid.,
37 (Apr. 1881), 473–76 (separation); Richard Dewey, "Provision for Insane Criminals,"
*Journal of Nervous and Mental Disease* 5 (1878), 664–89 (Auburn first); *Times*, 3 Nov.
1892; NYSA, *Report of the Commission on Better Provision for Insane Criminals*, AD 62
(Albany, 1887), 1–7; NYSA, *[Seventh] AR of the Superintendent of State Prisons [for
1883]*, AD 11 (Albany, 1884), 95 (doubling; corridor), James J. Walsh, *History of Medicine in New York: Three Centuries of Medical Progress* (New York, 1919), III.711.

30. Riggs, "Care and Handling of the Insane," 625, 627 (ordinary insane); Elizabeth Lun-
beck, *The Psychiatric Persuasion: Knowledge, Gender, and Power in Modern America*
(Princeton, N.J., 1994); John Chynoweth Burnham, "The New Psychology: From Nar-
cissism to Social Control," in *Change and Continuity in Twentieth-Century America:
The 1920's*, ed. John Braeman, Robert H. Bremner, and David Brody (Columbus,
Ohio, 1968), 383–84.

31. NYSA, *Twenty-Third [sic] AR for Insane Criminals*, 218–19; NYSA, *Report of the Commission on New Asylum for Insane Criminals of the State of New York*, AD 73 (Albany,
1890), 10–14 (20-inch walls). On recommendations to employ asylum patients in farm-
ing, see NYSA, *[Seventh] AR of the Superintendent of State Prisons [for 1883]*, AD 11
(Albany, 1884), 92, 96; NYSA, *Report of the Commission on Better Provision for Insane
Criminal*, AD 62 (Albany, 1887), 3–5.

32. NYSA, *Thirty-Seventh AR for Insane Criminals*, 277–78 (suspension of legal proceedings), 296 (three classes).

33. H. E. Allison, "Recent Additional Provision for the Criminal Insane in the State of
New York," *American Journal of Insanity* 56 (Apr. 1900), 738–40; NYSL, *Thirty-Eighth
AR of Matteawan*, 5 (632); NYSL, *Fortieth AR of the Medical Superintendent of the
Matteawan State Hospital* (n.p., 1900?), 7 (719 in 1899). The average daily population
in 1895 was 387. See NYSA, *Thirty-Seventh AR for Insane Criminals*, 277–78 (built for
550 patients); NYSA, *Thirty-Fourth AR for Insane Criminals*, 237 (550 for year, 387 daily
population); NYSA, *Thirty-Sixth AR for Insane Criminals*, 231, 239, 248. By June 1900,
the population was 722. See Twelfth Federal Census Population Schedules, Fishkill
Township, Dutchess County, New York, 1900, vol. 32, Enumeration District 155, sheets
2A–9A, reel 1022, National Archives Microfilm (hereafter Twelfth Census). By 1909,
the institution held approximately 750 inmates. See Frank Hasbrouck, ed., *The History
of Dutchess County, New York* (Poughkeepsie, N.Y., 1909), 588–89.

34. NYSA, *Thirty-Seventh AR for Insane Criminals*, 277–78; NYSL, *Thirty-Eighth AR of*

*Matteawan*, 9. Only in 1912 did the state legislature finally pass legislation requiring courts to provide a record of all proceedings in cases involving the mentally ill. See NYSL, *Fifty-third AR of the Medical Superintendent of the Matteawan State Hospital* (n.p., 1913?), 18.

35. NYSL, *Fifty-Third AR of Matteawan*, 28–29 (unstable class); NYSA, *[Seventh] AR of State Prisons* 100; NYSA, *Twelfth Report of the New York Civil Service Commission*, AD 51 (Albany, 1895), 70, 243–44 ($300–384 salary); NYSA, *Eleventh Report of the New York Civil Service Commission*, AD 74 (Albany, 1894), 252–54; Twelfth Census; Thirteenth Federal Census Population Schedules, Fishkill Township, Dutchess County, New York, 1910, Enumeration District 50, sheet 2A, reel 0936, both in National Archives Microfilm (hereafter Thirteenth Census).

36. NYSL, *Fifty-First AR of the Medical Superintendent of the Matteawan State Hospital* (n.p., 1911?), 15. On death rates, see NYSL, *Thirty-Eighth AR of Matteawan*, 5–10; NYSL, *Thirty-Ninth AR of the Medical Superintendent of the Matteawan State Hospital* (n.p., 1899?), 5–8, 12; NYSL, *Fortieth AR of the Matteawan*, 7–10; NYSL, *Fifty-Third AR of Matteawan*, 14; *Sun* clipping, 6 May 1894, vol. 127, DAS; Thirteenth Census, sheets 2A–10A.

37. Herbert S. Brown, "The Insane," *Charities Review* 9 (Nov. 1899), 372; ESP Inspectors, *61st AR for the Year 1890* (Philadelphia, 1891), 118 (simulated insanity); NYSA, *Thirty-Sixth AR for Insane Criminals*, 250; NYSA, *Thirty-Eighth AR of Matteawan*, 7; NYSA, *Thirty-Fourth AR for Insane Criminals*, 238–39.

38. NYSA, *Thirty-Fourth AR for Insane Criminals*, 222.

39. Entry for 20 Jan. 1886, vol. 5, Warden's Daily Journals, Prison Administration Records, ESP.

40. Appo may have been confused about Murphy. No record exists for John Murphy in the Inmate Case Files, Matteawan State Hospital (A1500), NYSArc. No John Murphy appears in the manuscript census or annual Matteawan reports. An attendant by the name of John Murphy appears in the 1900 federal census, then a twenty-nine-year-old (born 1870) Irish immigrant. Several patients with the surname "Murphy" do appear in Twelfth Census, sheets 3B, 5B, 6A, 6B.

41. Appo, 68–71. Appo later attributed his discharge to the letter he sent out with Murphy. I have edited this passage by deleting several repetitive sentences and some extraneous information. Appo was discharged on 14 June 1899. See Johnston to Stangler, 20 Jan. 1971, in QA Case File; *Times*, 15 June 1899.

42. Beck, *New York's Chinatown*, 9–10; *Press* and other unmarked clipping, 11 July 1896, vol. 157, DAS.

43. Entries for 2 Jan. 1909, 30 Apr. 1910, 23 Nov. 1910, 3 Feb. 1911, 18 and 23 June 1912, typed report, QA Case File; *Times*, 16 May 1901. Appo's autopsy attributed his death to chronic interstitial nephritis.

44. Entry for 23 June 1912, and p. 1, typed report; handwritten notes, Autopsy Report; and *World* clipping, 29 June 1912, all in QA Case File.

## 21. A Genuine Reformation

1. Appo, 71–74.
2. Appo, 76–80. Appo erroneously referred to Mary F. Sallade as "Mrs. Salrade." By this time she was married to Harrison Eugene Havens, a former Missouri congressman, attorney, railroad executive, and newspaper editor.
3. People v. George Appo, 24 July 1896, New York District Attorney Records, case #9126, box B-2, location 12817, SCC; handwritten comments from Assistant District Attorney Unger, in People v. George Appo, 24 July 1896, DAP, case #9127, box 10131, location 106262, New York Supreme Court (unprocessed collection), NYCMA; Tribune, 15, 16, 17 (improbable) June 1899; Tribune, Herald clipping, and unmarked clipping, 15 June 1899, all in vol. 181, DAS.
4. World, 6 Oct. 1894; Tribune, 12 Oct. 1894 (broke), 7 Feb. 1895 (Connecticut house); Lincoln (Neb.) State Journal, 23 Dec. 1898 (convicted 1895); Sandusky (Ohio) Star, 11 Feb. 1899 (Joliet); Louis J. Beck, New York's Chinatown: An Historical Representation of Its People and Places (New York, 1898), 173, 258; Washington Post, 11 Mar. 1907 (poverty); Times, 11 Mar. 1907 (workhouse), 17 Mar. 1907; William B. Moreau, Swindling Exposed: From the Diary of William B. Moreau, King of the Fakirs (Syracuse, N.Y., 1907), 189–90.
5. Washington Post, 24 June 1906; NYC, Report of the Police Department for 1896 (New York, 1897), 65; unmarked clippings, 25 and 30 July 1895 (Brisbane), vol. 144, DAS; Franklin Matthews, "'Wide-Open' New York," Harper's Weekly, 22 Oct. 1898; Cornelius F. Cahalane, Police Practice and Procedure (New York, 1914), 163–66; NPG, 25 Apr. 1903.
6. World, 29 June 1912, in QA Case File.
7. Appo, 75–76; Times, 9 Oct. 1938.
8. Appo, 95–97. Appo wrote this passage in 1916, and used the terms "honest employment," "honest endeavors," "honest life," or "honest living" eight times in the final third of his autobiography. See Appo, 62, 72, 76, 88, 95, 96, 97.
9. Appo, 80, 96. On Moss, see Tribune, 23 Apr. 1897; David McAdam et al., History of the Bench and Bar of New York (New York, 1897), 287.
10. Sun, Tribune, 8 Oct. 1894.
11. Frank Moss, The American Metropolis (New York, 1897), III:118–21 (estimable); Sun, Tribune, 8 Oct. 1894.
12. Sun (old life), Tribune, 8 Oct. 1894; James L. Ford, The Literary Shop and Other Tales (New York, 1894), 130–31 (half-breed, hybrid); Beck, New York's Chinatown, 250–61, 252 (hybrid brood). On the Rev. Thomas Dixon, Jr., in New York City, see Trow's New York City Directory and City Register (New York, 1889–1901); Joel Williamson, The Crucible of Race: Black-White Relations in the American South Since Emancipation (New York, 1984), 152–58.
13. Beck, New York's Chinatown, 250–60; Moss, American Metropolis, III:118, 143; Newark (N.J.) Daily Advocate, 15 June 1896. On Hadden and his work at Calvary, see Robert Graham, "The Coffee-House as a Counteraction of the Liquor Saloon," Charities Review 1 (Mar. 1892), 215–18; Calvary Evangel (Feb. 1889), I:29; Commercial Advertiser clipping, 26 Mar. 1896, 145, Calvary Church Scrapbook; Calvary Parish (Church) Yearbook (New York, 1888–1900); Calvary Evangel (Dec. 1888), I:19; (Nov. 1889), II:7–8; (Feb. 1901), XIII:60, all in Calvary–St. George's Parish House, 209 East Sixteenth

Street, New York, N.Y. Appo was described as a sexton at Calvary in an obituary in *World*, 21 May 1930, box 32, SPC Papers, but church records offer no mention of George Appo, Frank Moss, Mary Sallade, or Mary Havens.

14. *Times*, 17 June 1896.

15. *World*, 23 Jan. 1877; NYSS, *Twenty-third AR of the Inspectors of State Prisons [for 1870]*, SD 21 (Albany, 1871), 11–12 ($3); ESP Inspectors, *51st AR for the Year 1880* (Philadelphia, 1881), 39–40; PANY, *Thirtieth AR for 1874*, SD 78 (New York, 1875), 17; PANY, *Twenty-fourth AR for 1868*, SD 10 (Albany, 1869), 39 ($1,885), 58–59.

16. NYSSP, *AR for 1895* (Albany, 1896), 20; *World*, 23 Jan. 1877.

17. NYSA, *[Fourth] AR of the Superintendent of State Prisons [for 1880]*, AD 13 (Albany, 1881), 7 (Pilsbury); NYSSP, *AR for 1895* (Albany, 1896), 20. Annual reports only provided data on assisted convicts from 1886 to 1894.

|      | NUM. OF CONVICTS | NUMBER ASSISTED | EXPENDED (DOLLARS) | AVERAGE SPENT PER PRISONER ASSISTED |
|------|------|------|------|------|
| 1886 | 914 | 751 | 5,003 | $6.66 |
| 1887 | 921 | 675 | 5,119 | $7.58 |
| 1888 | 1,034 | 512 | 5,113 | $9.99 |
| 1889 | 338 | 133 | 3,519 | $26.46 |
| 1890 | | NOT AVAILABLE | | |
| 1891 | 1,016 | 585 | 4,385 | $7.50 |
| 1892 | 1,070 | 606 | 4,402 | $7.26 |
| 1893 | 1,008 | 590 | 5,056 | $8.57 |

See NYSSP, *Annual Reports* (Albany, 1887–94).

18. *New York Evening Telegram*, 28 Apr. 1882; *Leslie's*, 12 Apr. 1879; *Times*, 20 Jan. 1890; New York Home of Industry and Refuge for Discharged Convicts, *First Public Report* (New York, 1884); New York Home, *AR* (New York, 1887); New York Home, *AR* (New York, 1888); New York Home, *Report* (New York, 1892), 5; *New York Evening Telegram*, 28 Apr. 1882; *World*, 10 July 1891; *Journal* clipping, 19 Apr. 1884, DAS.

19. Appo, 95.

20. Appo, 79–80, 95. Appo's correspondence with Mary Havens from 1915–17 is in box 2, SPC papers.

21. *World*, 29 June 1912, in QA Case File. Appo was living in New York in 1912. See box 32, SPC Papers.

22. Minutes of the SPC Board of Directors, 16 Nov. 1911–7 Apr. 1913, 4 Dec. 1916, box 13, SPC Papers.

23. Ford, *The Literary Shop and Other Tales*, 130–31 (half-breed, hybrid); Beck, *New York's Chinatown*, 250–61, 252 (hybrid brood). Appo indicated that he was writing the manuscript on 17 July 1915 and into 1916. See Appo, 76, 96.

24. Lewis E. Lawes, *Twenty Thousand Years in Sing Sing* (New York, 1932), 243. See poems entitled "A Convict's Grave," "Good-Bye Old Cell," and "There's A Brighter Day A Coming"; Appo to Moss, 13 Dec. 1894, all in box 2, SPC Papers.

25. This literature is voluminous, but some of the most representative works are Edgar Allan Poe, "The Mystery of Marie Roget," "The Murder in the Rue Morgue," and "The Purloined Letter" in *The Complete Tales and Poems of Edgar Allan Poe* (New York, 1938); George Foster, *Celio: or, New York Above-Ground and Under-Ground* (New York, 1850); George Lippard, *The Empire City; or, New York by Day and Night* (New York,

1850); *The Quaker City* (Philadelphia, 1845); George Thompson, *City Crimes; or, Life in New York and Boston* (Boston, 1849); George Wilkes, *The Lives of Helen Jewett and Richard Robinson* (New York, 1849).

26. William F. Howe and Abraham H. Hummel, *In Danger; or, Life in New York, a True History of a Great City's Wiles and Temptations* (New York, 1888), v; Charles Loring Brace, *The Dangerous Classes of New York, and Twenty Years' Work Among Them* (New York, 1872); Anthony Comstock, *Frauds Exposed* (New York, 1880); Helen Campbell, *Darkness and Daylight; or, Lights and Shadows of New York Life* (New York, 1893); Thomas Byrnes, *Professional Criminals of America* (New York, 1886).

27. Sophie Lyons, *Why Crime Does Not Pay* (New York, 1913), 9; Eddie Guerin, *I Was a Bandit* (New York, 1929)1, 74; George Bidwell, *Forging His Chains: The Autobiography of George Bidwell* (Chicago, 1888); Langdon W. Moore, *His Own Story of His Eventful Life* (Boston, 1893).

28. Josiah Flynt, *The World of Graft* (New York, 1901); Hutchins Hapgood, ed., *The Autobiography of a Thief* (New York, 1903). For an overview, see Larry K. Hartsfield, *The American Response to Professional Crime, 1870–1917* (Westport, Conn., 1985).

29. Alexander Berkman, *Prison Memoirs of an Anarchist* (New York, 1912); Jack Black, *You Can't Win* (New York, 1926); Eugene Victor Debs, *Walls and Bars* (Chicago, 1927); Julian Hawthorne, *The Subterranean Brotherhood* (New York, 1914); H. Bruce Franklin, *Prison Literature in America: The Victim as Criminal and Artist*, expanded edition (New York, 1989), 146–50.

30. Hapgood, *Autobiography*, 9–10, 344.

31. George W. Appo, "The full History of my life" (handwritten), undated; and Appo deposition, 3 Oct. 1895, both in People v. George Appo, 19 Apr. 1895, New York Supreme Court, box 10100, location 106231 (unprocessed collection), DAP.

32. Appo, "The full History of my life."

33. *Times*, 4 Oct. 1895; People v. George Appo, 19 Apr. 1895, box 10100, location 106231, SCC; unmarked clippings, 4–5 Oct. 1895, vol. 146, DAS. In *Lexow*, II:1623, and *Times*, 15 June 1894.

34. Moss, *American Metropolis*, III:121, 119.

35. My interpretation of Appo's memory is influenced by Alfred F. Young, "George Robert Twelves Hewes (1742–1840): A Boston Shoemaker and the Memory of the American Revolution," *William and Mary Quarterly* 38 (1981), 561–623, esp. 568–69; Alfred F. Young, *The Shoemaker and the Tea Party* (Beacon, 1999); Ian M. L. Hunter, *Memory* (London, 1957), chapter 6.

36. Elliott J. Gorn, *Mother Jones: The Most Dangerous Woman in America* (New York, 2001), 280–81.

37. Paul Johnson, "The Modernization of Mayo Greenleaf Patch: Land, Family, and Marginality in New England, 1766–1818," *New England Quarterly* 55 (1982), 490; Natalie Zemon Davis, *The Return of Martin Guerre* (Cambridge, Mass., 1983); Laurel Thatcher Ulrich, *A Midwife's Tale: The Life of Martha Ballard, Based on Her Diary, 1785–1812* (New York, 1990); Young, "George Robert Twelves Hewes," 561–623; and Young, *Shoemaker*.

38. For an example of how religious conversion affects later memory, see Young, "George Robert Twelves Hewes," 561–623; Young, *Shoemaker*.

39. Lawes, *Twenty Thousand Years*, 90–93.

EPILOGUE

1. Appo, 98.
2. George Appo Death Certificate, NYCMA; Report of Dr. I. J. Furman to Howard Barber, 17 May 1930; *Bronx Home News* clipping, 15 June 1930; Mount Hope Cemetery, Hastings-on-Hudson, New York, Single Grave Certificate for Section 88, Lot 100, Grave 123, 20 May 1930, all in box 32, SPC Papers (withered).
3. *Evening Journal* clipping, 21 May 1930 (new leaf); *Bronx Home News* clipping, 15 June 1930 (wiliest), both in box 32, SPC Papers.
4. *New York News* clipping, 1934, in QA Case File. Similar stories involving Allison and Appo appeared in *Newark* [Ohio] *Daily Advocate*, 15 June 1896; *Middletown* [N.Y.] *Argus*, 3 Mar. 1898.
5. *Truth* clipping, 4 June 1883 (Hackett); *Star* clipping, 4 June 1884 (Gildersleeve), vol. 8, both in DAS; Appo, 6, 32 (bad man); Louis J. Beck, *New York's Chinatown: An Historical Representation of Its People and Places* (New York, 1898), 250–60.
6. Appo, 3, 36, 76, 79, 81, 84, 93, 96. For Appo's defense of pickpocketing, see Appo statement to the Commissioners of Public Charities and Corrections, 6 Oct. 1896, 17–18, in People v. George Appo, 24 July 1896, New York District Attorney Records, case #9126, box B-2, location 12817, Supreme Court Cases, all in NYCMA.
7. Appo, 96. On historical applications of resistance and neutralization, see Lawrence Levine, *Black Culture and Black Consciousness* (New York, 1977); Edward L. Ayers, *Vengeance and Justice: Crime and Punishment in the 19th-Century American South* (New York, 1984); Terry Williams, *The Cocaine Kids: The Inside Story of a Teenage Drug Ring* (Reading, Mass., 1989); Alex Lichtenstein, "'That Disposition to Theft, With Which They Have Been Branded': Moral Economy, Slave Management, and the Law," *Journal of Social History* 21 (1988), 413–40.
8. Appo, 81; *Bronx Home News* clipping, 15 June 1930, box 32, SPC Papers.
9. Appo, 98.
10. Sophie Lyons, *Why Crime Does Not Pay* (New York, 1913), 47 (Adam Worth), 257–61.
11. Appo, 81, 84; Joseph Matthew Sullivan, "Criminal Slang," *American Law Review* 52 (1918), 891 (gorillas).
12. Appo, 81, 84, 96.
13. Appo, 96.
14. Eric J. Hobsbawm, *Primitive Rebels: Studies in Archaic Forms of Social Movement in the Nineteenth and Twentieth Centuries* (New York, 1959), esp. 23; Hobsbawm, *Bandits* (New York, 1981), esp. 18.
15. *Tribune*, 16 June 1899; *Times*, 16 June 1899 (stool pigeons).
16. Appo, 95.
17. For a similar description of the poor or "underclass" in the late twentieth century, see Jacqueline Jones, "Southern Diaspora: Origins of the Northern 'Underclass'"; and Joe William Trotter, Jr., "Blacks in the Urban North: The 'Underclass Question' in Historical Perspective," both in Michael B. Katz, ed., *The "Underclass" Debate: Views from History* (Princeton, N.J., 1993), 30–59.
18. On pickpocketing, confidence games, and other criminal activity described as "a

racket," and the similarity of "fixers" with shyster lawyers, see Edwin H. Sutherland, *The Professional Thief* (Chicago, 1937), 43–99; Hutchins Hapgood, ed., *The Autobiography of a Thief* (New York, 1903), 38–42, 243. On the definition and origin of the term "racketeer," see John Gunther and James W. Mulroy, "The High Cost of Hoodlums," *Harper's*, 159 (Oct. 1929), 529–40.

# Illustration Credits

━━

*Page* 106 "Recent Escape of Blackwell's Island Convicts." "Four more convicts escaped from a Blackwell's Island patrol-boat yesterday. The affair has caused the greatest surprise to the authorities, as the guards are all muscular men, are well armed, and have heretofore been considered trustworthy." *Frank Leslie's Illustrated Newspaper*, 30 Aug. 1879.

*Page* 113 *National Police Gazette*, 14 Aug. 1880.

*Page* 114 *National Police Gazette*, 19 Jan. 1884.

*Page* 118 Courtesy Brooklyn Museum.

*Page* 120 Unmarked clipping, 18 Feb. 1888, vol. 45, District Attorney Scrapbooks, courtesy New York City Municipal Archives and Records Center.

*Page* 128 *The Tombs* (1850), by W. Heine. Personal collection of Timothy Gilfoyle.

*Page* 132 George Washington Walling, *Recollections of a New York Chief of Police* (New York, 1887).

*Page* 136 J. W. Buel, *Metropolitan Life Unveiled; or the Mysteries and Miseries of America's Great Cities* (St. Louis, 1882).

*Page* 145 William H. Wallace, *Niblo's Garden Theater, rear on Crosby Street*, 1870, etching, Eno Collection #394, Miriam and Ira D. Wallach Division of Art, Prints and Photographs, The New York Public Library, Astor, Lenox and Tilden Foundations.

*Page* 150 Sophie Lyons, *Why Crime Does Not Pay* (New York, 1913).

*Page* 166 *National Police Gazette*, 1 Apr. 1882.

*Page* 176 Undated nineteenth-century postcard, folder 12, box 69b, Sing Sing Prison Pictures, Ossining Historical Society Museum.

*Page* 179 Jacob Riis Collection, courtesy Museum of the City of New York.

*Page* 198 Eastern State Penitentiary, *Annual Report for 1880* (Philadelphia, 1881).

*Page* 207 Allan Pinkerton, *Thirty Years as a Detective* (Chicago, 1884), 76a.

*Page* 211 *Herald*, 19 Feb. 1893.

*Page* 211 Thomas Byrnes, *Professional Criminals of America* (New York, 1886), 56.

*Page* 215 "Two Worthy Rascals," unidentified clipping, 21 Jan. 1888, vol. 44, District Attorney Scrapbooks, courtesy New York City Municipal Archives and Records Center.

*Page* 216 William B. Moreau, *Swindling Exposed: From the Diary of William B. Moreau, King of the Fakirs* (Syracuse, N.Y., 1907).

*Page* 222 Louis Beck, *New York's Chinatown* (New York, 1898).

*Page* 233 *Poughkeepsie Sunday Courier*, 19 Feb. 1893.

*Page* 233 *Poughkeepsie Sunday Courier*, 19 Feb. 1893.

*Page* 240 *National Police Gazette*, 4 Mar. 1893.

*Page* 249 Warshaw Collection of Business Americana—Police, Archives Center, National Museum of American History, Behring Center, Smithsonian Institution.

*Page* 257 *Tribune*, 29 Sept. 1894.

*Page* 259 *Sun*, 9 Oct. 1894.

*Page* 261 *World Sunday Art Supplement*, 11 Nov. 1894, District Attorney Scrapbooks, courtesy New York City Municipal Archives and Records Center.

*Page* 262 *Illustrated American*, 5 Jan. 1895.

*Page* 268 *World*, 30 Dec. 1894.

*Page* 276 *Daily Graphic*, 1886.

*Page* 279  *Frank Leslie's Illustrated Newspaper*, 23 Nov. 1878.

*Page* 284  Louis Beck, *New York's Chinatown* (New York, 1898), 251.

*Page* 294  New York State Assembly, *Report of the Commission of the New Asylum for Insane Criminals*, Assembly Documents, vol. 12, no. 63 (Albany, 1891).

*Page* 299  Personal collection of Timothy Gilfoyle.

*Page* 305  Frank Moss, *The American Metropolis* (New York, 1897), vol. 1.

*Page* 315  Society for the Prevention of Crime Papers, Rare Book and Manuscript Library, Columbia University, New York, N.Y.

*Page* 316  *New York News* clipping, 1934, in Quimbo Appo Case File, #456, box 7, Matteawan State Hospital Inmate Case Files, 1880–1960 (A1500), NYSArc.

*Page* 323  Personal collection of Timothy Gilfoyle.

# Index

=

# Index